Social Work
Treatment

SOCIAL WORK TREATMENT

Interlocking Theoretical Approaches

THIRD EDITION

Edited by

Francis J. Turner

With a Foreword by

Katherine A. Kendall

FP

THE FREE PRESS

New York   London   Toronto   Sydney   Tokyo   Singapore

The Free Press
A Division of Simon & Schuster Inc.
1230 Avenue of the Americas
New York, N.Y. 10020

Printed in the United States of America

printing number

10

NOTE TO READERS OF *SOCIAL WORK TREATMENT*

A chart that compares twenty-one social work practice
theories along a spectrum of thirty-three variables,
measuring thirty-six by forty inches, constitutes an efficient
resource for teachers, students, and practitioners. It is a
useful supplement to the book and can be ordered from:

DR. Francis J. Turner
186 Claremont Ave.
Kitchener Ontario
Canada N2M 2P8

Price including postage $35.00

Library of Congress Cataloging-in-Publication Data

Main entry under title:

Social work treatment.

Includes index.
1. Social service—Addresses, essays, lectures.
I. Turner, Francis Joseph.
HV37.S579   1986   361   85–24717
ISBN 0–02–933100–5

Copyright Acknowledgments

To Joanne

Contents

Foreword

A collection of twenty-two articles on theories underlying social work practice attracts attention not only in the United States but all around the world. To a number of its friends and critics in other countries, North American social work is equated with psychoanalytically oriented case work focused on the inner life of the individual with scant regard for the many outside forces that produce social problems. Does this cornucopia of established and emerging theories project a different image? The answer is definitely in the affirmative with, however, some reservations readily acknowledged by Dr. Turner in his review of the range of theories and systems of thought presented in this volume. The reservations are important, but what must come first in any consideration of the utility of this collection is the realization that social work practice in the United States and Canada now rests on a pluralistic conceptual base. This is a welcome message to all who work toward the recognition and strengthening of social work as an international discipline, capable of making common cause with diversity and applicable in widely different contexts.

Social work everywhere is becoming more complex. The profession is being asked to deal with many aspects of the human condition in increasingly difficult situations—environmental, social, and emotional. The emergence of new thought systems and the broadening of well-established theories reflects a commitment on the part of North American social work scholars to search for theories that will better explain these many differing contexts and realities. The broader range of theories clearly expands the applicability of social work practice in different cultures and with different groups, thus enriching the effectiveness of the profession wherever it is found. Dr. Turner notes the increasing comfort with diversity apparent in the current collection as compared with the two previous editions. This, in turn, has produced two important consequences (1) a better understanding on the part of practitioners of the "pitfalls in a practice that is either devoid of theory or overdependent upon a single theory," and (2) a stronger commitment to "the importance of tested theory."

The pitfalls of overdependence upon a single theory are sadly demonstrated in the continuing excoriation of North American social work by some of our colleagues in the Third World, and even in a number of Western countries, as insatiably dependent upon psychoanalytic theory. This perception is the product of the shadowy remains of historical events that have long since faded into oblivion. Following World War II, American casework emerged as a catalytic agent in the transformation of European social work from a somewhat paternalistic and manipulative practice to a more democratic, nonjudgmental, and scientifically based approach to people and their problems. The scientific base was indeed weighted with psychoanalytic theory, which many Europeans initially viewed with misgivings but accepted when they found it opened the way to a better understanding of themselves in relation to their clients as well as the interplay of objective and subjective factors in working with people, thus leading to a completely new conception of social work practice.

In the developing world, newly established schools of social work, in many instances organized or guided by American consultants, borrowed heavily from the West because that was the source of experience and expertise. What impressed them most was American casework with its well-developed methodology. As the profession matured, social work educators in the Third World saw and to some extent acted upon the need to refashion their programs of social work education and practice to place their major emphasis on massive social problems such as poverty, and on community, social, and economic development rather than on the well-being of the individual.

Meanwhile, American casework has moved on from its heavily weighted psychoanalytic underpinnings of the 1940s and 1950s to a more balanced view of the responsibility of the profession to foster both individual and societal change. Unfortunately, its critics have remained fixed on the presumed lack of concern in North American social work with societal forces as a significant cause of human and social problems. Does this new edition of *Social Work Treatment* break the stereotype?

The answer is yes and no. This volume, after all, has to do with theories of clinical practice, albeit in Turner's view a practice that covers a broad spectrum of work with individuals, families, groups, and communities. The theories range widely from those that offer an orientation to the broader society such as systems theory and Marxist theory, to those that have to do with a philosophy of life and man's place in the universe, such as existential theory and meditation, and those that delve into the conscious and unconscious components of human behavior and personality, such as ego psychology and psychoanalytic theory. With so many prophets, it is obvious that there is no one true gospel directing social work practice in the United States and Canada.

On the other hand, there has been less progress than Dr. Turner, in earlier editions, had anticipated toward broadening the scope of practice to include more explicit and extensive work on environmental factors. While expressing reservations about the continuing overemphasis on one-to-one treatment, he is convinced that there is a true consensus that "social work practice must continue to be what it always has been, a commitment to person-in-situation." He believes that continuing conceptualization will increasingly affirm the importance of work with the situation as well as the person.

Questions must inevitably arise as theories multiply. At what point does diversity become anarchy? From Turner, one can deduce that anarchy is avoided when there is recognition of a common core of knowledge, skills, and values together with comfort in tapping the resources of the various systems to find interconnections and interlocking concepts. In the current presentations, he has found what he calls "a diminution of intensity of some of our holy wars" because of the growing awareness that "each system need not stand alone but can be enriched by seeking and permitting areas of connection with other systems." In other words, social workers are coming to terms with a pluralistic conceptual base. Turner puts it well when he states:

> Even the most declared unitheory practitioners appear to be multitheory influenced. Over the past decade we have all become more behaviorally oriented, more cognitive in our practice, more existential in our perceptions, more systems conscious, more role oriented, more family sensitive, more task focused, more evaluative oriented. Our practice is very much in the here and now, it probably always was, yet few have put aside completely psychodynamic theory and a developmentally based approach to treatment.

Does this mean that a general practice theory may emerge from the interlocking perspectives of these many systems of thought? It is noted in the preface to the second edition that we have not yet reached the point where we can anticipate the emergence of a general practice theory. In that edition, too, Turner notes a continuing emphasis on "one man, one method," instead of any movement toward a multimethod-based practice, which, parenthetically, would be the choice of many colleagues in other parts of the world, but adds that he does not advocate a unitary method. Nor does he think, as he makes clear in the third edition, that there is or ever should be a single theory of social work practice. The image that Turner projects of social work is that of a profession facing increasingly complex tasks in an increasingly complicated world. In advocating a pluralistic theory base, he sees a rich cluster of knowledge, skills, fields of interest, areas of concern, strategies of intervention, and value orientations from which practitioners can draw whatever their particular functions and tasks require to better serve individuals, groups, families, neighborhoods, communities, and whole societies. A volume such as this presents a range of choices, but at the same time helps to legitimize a pluralistic theory base. It also reflects the enrichment that comes when social work scholars continue to search for explanations of our professional activities that can be tested, transferred, scrutinized, and evaluated. While questions can certainly be raised about the validity as theories of some of the systems of thought presented here, there is no question about the value of this effort to recognize and respect the serious work that is being done to enlarge the view and practice of social work in the United States and Canada. What is needed now is a similar volume drawing upon authors from different countries engaged in scholarly work on these same or different theories to increase our knowledge and understanding of cross-national and cross-cultural perspectives on the practice of social work as an international discipline.

Katherine A. Kendall
Honorary President
International Association of Schools of Social Work

Foreword to the First Edition

To many social work educators and practitioners the development of a usable, expanding and internally consistent theory of social work practice is both urgent and long delayed. To others it is an exercise in beating our breasts which fills a good deal of paper but is remote from the daily demands of practice. Is it then an exercise primarily engaged in by academics in their struggle to keep up with other academic Joneses? Or is it so crucial for the improvement of practice that we are rightly to be taken to task for elevating assumptions into theories or concentrating on practice without analyzing the common factors that could be discerned in that practice or testing the fruitful application of theory to it?

Probably the only useful way to resolve this debate is to ask what is the use of theory. The first point is that it must be a good theory, based not only on observation but also on hypothesis in which alternative possible explanations have been ruled out. For instance, an observer in the early nineteenth century noted that men who wore top hats did not die of starvation, and a society to provide free top hats was about to be launched, so it is said, before further observation ruled out the hypothesis. Similarly, in social work the enormous complexity of the scene with which social workers engage, the "big, buzzing confusion," to quote William James, may well have a good deal to do with our failure to develop theories of the right size, i.e., neither so comprehensive that they are of little use for every day purposes or so one-track that they leave most of the real world out of account. To produce usable theories of the right size over a sufficient range of commonly encountered persons in their major life experience is a formidable task. But once again "what is the point of it?" The first thing to be said is that theory is not an end in itself but a means to an end. That end is the objectives or goals of social work; however these may be expressed at any given time they are essentially concerned with enabling people to make a better go of it with themselves and others and to achieve or have provided for them more elbow room in their social circumstances. The hallmark of a good theory is, of course, its capacity to predict the outcome of any given action. It also provides a guide to what is the same and what is different in a range of similar situations, and it should thus be a springboard for the development of further theory that sheds light on fresh interconnections. The point of a good theory is thus that it works in practice and in the very working generates more comprehensive, more powerful theory. The other overwhelming advantage of theory applied and tested in practice is that it is transmissible to other practitioners and is testable by them in a way that does not hold for wisdom acquired through practice or for assumptions.

The present study is significant, indeed a landmark, because it contributes to and springs from the new impetus to pioneer for social work the application of theory in practice without which it cannot advance as a profession—or, what is more important, in its capacity to deliver the goods—at this point in its development. The two-pronged attempt to elucidate theory and to study rigorously what actually happens in practice is now going forward, even if spasmodically, in several different countries. This is important, because we need to discover not only what theories reliably predict outcome within a given culture and circumstances but what in these is directly relayed to universals in human nature and is thus applicable, even by different modes of operation, in different cultures or in cultures within certain similar traditions. All the authors have illustrated from practice the theories they each discuss. This adds greatly to the values of the study from an international point of view. Other countries and continents where the practice of social work, and education for it, has spread rapidly in the last quarter century are greatly in need of studies like those which Dr. Turner and his collaborators have brought together here. It is to be hoped that this book will be widely read, not to be slavishly learned and regurgitated, but for use as a further stimulus to the well-planned study which must go ahead in other situations where social work is practiced. This is essential for the much needed cross-fertilization of well recorded and tested theories. In short, we must develop the attitude of mind that inspired this book, not only for the improvement of practice, but also for the vastly better education of social work students which is so urgently needed in the world as a whole.

Eileen L. Younghusband
Former Honorary President
International Association of Schools of Social Work

Preface

The fact that a third edition of *Social Work Treatment* is necessary augers well for the strength of social work's theory base. It is evident that the quest for an expansion and an enrichment of thought systems that underlie practice continues. What is particularly gratifying is that this quest is not limited to the halls of academe but is very much an active concern of practitioners, committed to make their practice more efficient, more effective, more sensitive to client need, and more accountable.

In the process of preparing this edition, several characteristics of the ongoing developmental process in the profession were noted and are reflected in the various chapters. First, we seem to be much more comfortable with building on our historic knowledge bases and adding to them, rather than an earlier noted trend to reject all that was traditional and replace it with the "new." This renewed comfort with the past does not imply a blind allegiance that eschews change and criticism but a comfort in continuing to test traditional knowledge for its contemporary relevance, reject what is no longer valid, and strengthen what is yet useful. This attitude of open searching is seen in several ways.

The individual authors are less defensive in presenting their various systems and much more ready to accept the possibility and, indeed, the necessity of a plural theory base to practice. With less "turf protecting" there is a marked interest and comfort in seeking for interconnections, for interlocking perspectives. Exciting as this is for the profession, it creates difficulties for an editor as the lines between some systems become less clear. Increasingly, a commitment to a strenthening of the research base of each system can be observed. This is reflected in the expanded bibliographies as well as in the chapters' contents.

Although we are more comfortable with our traditional knowledge bases, we are prudently still open to new ideas and thus continue to expand the repertoire of sources on which to build our practice base. In the second edition five new chapters were added. In this edition there are three additional ones: feminist theory, neurolinguistics, and Marxist theory. Each represents a body of thought that in my estimation is having a recognized significant impact on current clinical practice. Each of these bodies of thought has moved to a point where these theoretical constructs can influence the assessment, intervention, and service delivery components of direct practice in a responsible way. As before, some systems, or declared systems or emerging systems, were not included. In each instance the decision was made that the theory had not as yet made a significant impact on practice or had not been sufficiently developed to present it in the format required for this book. Obviously, there will not be full agreement within the profession as to what should or should not be included. Yet I would certainly think that in a further edition we will want to include a chapter on empowerment theory and perhaps a chapter on deviance theory.

Although there are only a few new chapters there are more new authors; eleven in fact. This change in authorship reflects several factors. First, it reminds us of the reality that our profession matures. Thus, several of the original group of authors have retired from practice, and one has died, Dr. Gordon Hearne, who's original work on systems theory represents a major contribution to the profession's theory base. Second, some authors have moved into other areas of interest, leaving further development of particular theories to their colleagues. I am grateful to the writers who appeared in the earlier editions and equally grateful to the participants new to this edition. The addition of new names is also a reflection of our development; we see well-known colleagues continuing to reflect on the current relevance of earlier thinking as well as the entrance of new colleagues active in the theory-building endeavor.

As with the first two editions, the order of presentation was again a challenge. This problem arose in earlier editions, but only tangentially addressed. As I continue to struggle with this phenomenon of a diversity of theories, I have considered a variety of conceptual bases from which to order them. This is discussed in the first chapter and my current thinking is reflected in the ordering of the following chapters. What is of particular interest to me is that as my ideas clarified about a basis for classification, and in subsequent discussions with colleagues, my logic lead me to identify at least two gaps in the present collection. If the basis for ordering is the range of perspectives of the human condition with which we deal in practice, then there should also be included a chapter on small group theory as well as one on masculine theory. Two of my colleagues here at Hunter College suggested that this latter chapter should be called M.C.P. theory. But putting this suggestion aside, it is evident that if a practitioner needs to understand feminine issues they must also understand related masculine factors, and we should begin to develop theory in this area as well.

On the matter of group theory, since the book addresses all modalities of clinical practice—individuals, dyads, groups, and families—it should, of course, include a chapter on general group theory just as there is one on family theory. These realizations of gaps came only at the end of the editing and reconceptualizing process, and will be addressed in the fourth edition.

Not only does the profession change but so do styles of writing. I was astounded, when reviewing the second edition, which is only six years old, to see how frequently the authors then used only masculine pronouns. This has changed dramatically in the writing and reflects a beginning shift in society and the profession to a growing awareness of some of our societal defects.

One other change of style needs to be noted. In most of the chapters the authors have included in the list of references, or in the annotated items, references that are not directly alluded to or mentioned in the body of the chapter. This is done to provide the reader with an enriched resource of significant readings on the topic. In an earlier format some chapters would have separate sections for reference notes and supplementary materials; with the more recent format of writing these two functions are included in the more general heading "References."

I am most appreciative of the reception this book has received and the support my colleagues have given in enhancing it for this edition. I am particularly pleased because this response reflects our continuing odyssey aimed at ensuring that those individuals, groups, families, and communities who turn to us for help are provided with the best possible interlocking array of skills, resources, and knowledge available to us.

F.J.T.
Hunter College, New York
May 1985

Preface to the Second Edition

The decision to issue a second edition of *Social Work Treatment* was based on two factors. First was the growing awareness that the phenomenon of the rapid emergence of new thought systems marking the last twenty-five years seemed to be waning. Certainly in the past five years some new systems have begun to appear in the literature and to be talked about by practitioners. But, on the whole, these have not been as numerous as before. What is happening, rather, is that new developments are emerging from the established theories and thought systems. New interpretations of traditional thought systems are being made, enriching their utility for practice. At the same time, expanded applications of some of the newer systems, originally seen as having only narrow application, are also occurring. This search for the expansion of theories rather than the creation of new ones is of particular importance to the practice world. It reflects a healthy search for richer applications of available concepts, a process essential to the ongoing development, testing, reformulation, and enrichment of practice.

It was the awareness that this type of enrichment was indeed taking place that led me to decide to give the original authors an opportunity to revise their chapters. All but two did indeed find it necessary to make revisions, and in several instances these revisions were extensive. Most added new items to their bibliographies, making resources even more useful than they were in the first edition.

The other reason for the decision to issue a second edition stemmed from the need to include some additional topics. These had been omitted from the first edition pending further development of their applicability in social work. The inclusion of five new chapters, each devoted to a new treatment approach, speaks to this concern.

Each of these new chapters is viewed as being of significance to current practice and as having become an integral part of the social work tradition. Certainly Transactional Analysis and Gestalt have become widely known in all the helping professions and are increasingly becoming a part—in some cases the principal component—of many therapists' practice base. Task-centered practice is very much a product of social work, of particular relevance to practitioners seeking to make their practice more concrete, organized, and predictable. Meditation as an approach to practice has long been viewed with some discomfort. There has been a lingering fear that it is not really a professionally based practice theory but, rather, a philosophical-religious worldview. This concern has been largely dispelled by increasing awareness that it is possible to demonstrate measurable physical changes in persons in the meditative state. This empirically based understanding of meditation in only part of the emphasis now being given to the need for a closer understanding of the interconnection of biological and psychological man. The use of biofeedback mechanisms as a component of psychotherapy reflects this growing interest, and, undoubtedly in a further revision of his book, a chapter will be necessary on biopsychotherapy as a basis for social work practice.

The ecological or life-model approach to practice is the newest thought system in the book. It is based on the conviction that man cannot be considered apart from the environment in which he functions. In an interesting way, ecological concepts help to strengthen the utility of systems theory and the growing interest in biological man in theory.

I have been most pleased by the reception accorded the first edition. Originally it was thought that it would be useful to the practitioner as a ready reference to the various thought systems available as resources to clients. This goal has been achieved, and for this I am grateful. But the first edition has also been useful to scholars at all levels: undergraduate, graduate, and postgraduate. This trend reflects the continuing search for a stronger theory base for practice. I would caution, however, that a volume such as this one should not be used as the single authoritative source of information on a particular system. It is in an attempt to avoid this problem that particular stress has been put on the bibliographies, and readers are urged to see them as essential to the book and its use. Clearly, each thought system requires a full-scale exposition in its own right. This book is intended, then, as ready reference, not as a substitute for in-depth study.

It is evident that we are not yet at a point in practice where we can anticipate the emergence of a general practice theory. We are, however, certainly at a point where there is commitment to tap the rich resources of all systems and to continue to search for interlocking concepts. It is hoped that this second edition of *Social Work Treatment* will contribute to this needed trend.

F.J.T.
Waterloo, Ontario
June 1978

Preface to the First Edition

The primary goal of this book is to expand and strenthen the theoretical base of social work clinicians. Implicit in this goal is the conviction that an expanded and strengthened theoretical base will contribute positively to the quality and effectiveness of therapy. The method by which this goal is achieved is to bring together in a readily accessible form the spectrum of conceptual viewpoints presently influencing current social work practice.

The rationale for assembling this range of conceptual viewpoints under one cover stems from a conviction that our profession has not been markedly effective in widely sharing with each other the diversity of ideas considered to have rich potential for practice. All of the approaches discussed in this volume have appeared somewhere in our professional literature. But this appearance has been in an uneven manner, so that the potential influence of each body of thought is greatly restricted. I do not suggest that each approach discussed in the book is of equal importance; I do suggest that each should be available to practitioners in a manner and style that will facilitate its examination and assessment for its usefulness.

In recent years the cry has been frequently raised that social work practice does not have an adequate theoretical base. Clearly, like all other professions practicing in the area of human adjustment, we do lack a sufficiently comprehensive and integrated body of theory necessary to understand and explain the myriad of situations we are called upon to assess. But no longer can we say we lack theories. At this point in our history our problem is a superfluity of conceptual frameworks rather than a dearth.

Indeed, it is this abundance of systems that makes current social work practice both exciting and frustrating. Exciting because unlike any other time in our history we do have a range of orientations on which to draw in our endless search for a structure by which we can order that almost infinite complexity of "person in situation." Frustrating because each new approach challenges us to reorder our thinking as we attempt to examine, assess, modify, and, when appropriate, introduce such ideas into our conceptual armamentarium.

This diversity also challenges individual social workers to come to terms with a pluralistic conceptual base. Thus, must one become a free-floating eclectic? Or is it better to pick a framework that appears most appealing and ignore the others? Or, rather, does one attempt to synthesize all of them into some form of general all-encompassing theory?

We are probably not yet ready to answer these questions. Clearly, though, there is a suggested answer underlying the format of this book. It is my conviction that each of the conceptual systems addressed here has something of significance for practicing social workers. This conviction thus implies support for some form of synthesis that is neither eclecticism nor an all-encompassing grand theory. The task for each practitioner from my viewpoint is to develop a theoretical approach to practice with which one is comfortable and to build onto it or modify it as one becomes more knowledgeable about, experienced in, and convinced of the importance and significance of other approaches. The task of further syntheses is not that of individual practitioners but the responsibility of our theoreticians.

However, for practitioners to make full use of available thought systems, the material must be readily available in a form that presents both differential approaches and perceived implications for practice. Thus, each author was asked to write against a common framework to facilitate comparison between chapters. Within this outline each author brought together available thinking about the body of thought he was addressing, his own views about it, and, in particular, the perceived implications for individual, family, group, and community practice.

The principal aim of this volume is to serve as an aid to practitioners. It is this segment of colleagues who most need a quick and ready access to a range of viewpoints to aid them in practice. It is hoped also that it will be of use to students, both those beginning their professional training and those at more senior levels where greater emphasis is put on critical examination and comparison of various stances. It is further hoped it will aid future scholarly studies that seek similarities and differences, gaps and trends, strengths and weaknesses in our theoretical base.

Since the primary target is to develop a useful resource for practitioners, there are some goals to which this volume does not aspire. Thus, in no way does it attempt to be an exhaustive analysis of the various thought systems; instead, it is a scholarly operational approach to them. Each author has instead a selected bibliography for the reader who wishes to pursue more assiduously one or more of the topics. Each author has also included indicators of the direction in which further research might be pursued that could increase the understanding and utility of the conceptual viewpoint.

Other colleagues have identified the need for books such as the present one at this point in our professional history. Since the original idea for this book began to take shape, two related volumes have been published: *Theories of Social Casework* by Robert Roberts and Robert Nee and *Social Casework: Theories in Action* by Dr. Herbert Strean, one of the contributors to this volume. Further, the recently published *Encyclopedia of Social Work* also includes individual articles on some of the topics discussed in this book.

In selecting the topics for consideration, no preference was given to thought systems that originated within our profession as opposed to those we have borrowed from without. Frequently, the criticism has been made by colleagues, students, and interested outsiders that we have relied too heavily on ideas borrowed from outside rather than developing our own distinct body of knowledge. Although this viewpoint is usually presented as a criticism, it may soon be viewed as one of the strengths of our profession. This latter view is clearly my own conviction. With the current shift from closed thought systems to more open ones taking place in other disciplines, this quality of our knowledge base may well be one of our major hallmarks of respectability.

Whatever the outcome of opinion about borrowing, we clearly have borrowed, both frequently and consistently, both bodies of knowledge and interventive methods from other fields. But this borrowing has not been random, reckless, or total. I think we can clearly demonstrate that when we borrow, as we will continue to do, we do so in a judicious manner, always trying to adapt the borrowed concepts and techniques to fit our available state of knowledge to achieve better the goals to which we are working.

This selective borrowing concept applies to the way we adapted psychoanalytic thinking to our practice without aspiring to become analysts, in spite of the popular straw man to the contrary. It is also true, more currently, in the way we are beginning to make use of the thinking techniques and skills of the behavioral school without claiming or aspiring to become behaviorists in any general way.

But borrow as we do, we must never forget that we do more than this. It seems we frequently underestimate the amount and extent of original contribution we have made to the fund of human knowledge about human behavior in interaction with significant environments. Several of the topics considered in the following chapters substantiate this.

Fourteen bodies of thought are included in this book. At the point of beginning this project, these were judged to be those most influencing practice. Throughout recent literature other thought systems have been mentioned and discussed, some of which are experiential, Gestalt, Transactional, organizational, informational, and games theory. Some of these were not included because they were not thought of as having had as yet significant impact on social work practice, others from a lack of adequate knowledge about them, and still others for semantic or conceptual reasons where a different title is used to describe a topic already included.

One of the difficulties experienced in developing the book's outline was the question of distinguishing between different schools of thought. As one examines the topics chosen, it can be seen that they range from headings that encompass the work of many people, such as psychodynamic theory or ego psychology, to those that represent the thinking of a single person, such as the client-centered system of Rogers. It is also expected that some will seriously question the separations that have been made for some of the chapters. For example, distinguishing psychosocial treatment from psychodynamic theory could be seen as artificial and indeed inappropriate. In the same way, separating ego psychology from psychodynamic thinking might be viewed as a presumptuous and distorted division.

In planning the book, choices for chapters to be included were based on usage in our professional literature rather than one conceptual differences; that is, the topics selected were the schools of thought that have been identified in professional circles as representing a particular approach to practice by identifiable segments of the profession, even though they may not in fact represent real differences. Thus, without doubt, psychosocial theory is clearly a psychodynamic approach to practice, but so is problem-solving theory. And we know there are practitioners who would identify themselves as ego psychologists and distinguish themselves from both a psychosocial orientation as well as a problem-solving one. It is because of these differences in usage that each contributor was asked to write against a common framework. This was done to help identify areas of difference, both overt and covert, as well as areas of commonality.

Certainly, in beginning this project, one of the primary motivations was to attempt to establish how much of a common base there is to our practice and also to identify the differences; that is, are we a multitheoretical profession, or is there emerging a general theoretical orientation that permits a variety of specialized applications of this theory for specific situations, as for example crisis theory? Whether this book has helped in resolving this question must be left to the judgment of the reviewers and readers. Certainly it has helped the various authors who have participated and shared their thinking with each other.

In the beginning the title for the book was *The Theoretical Bases of Social Work Practice*. It was this title that was originally presented to the publisher and in the letters of invitation to the contributors. But it soon became clear that our profession has tended to be quite imprecise in the use of the word *theory*. Clearly, many of the topics selected, although frequently designated as theories, do not fulfill all the requirements of the concept of theory. This point is discussed more fully in the first chapter.

If this book helps practitioners and students to expand their conceptual horizons and assists them in being more effective with their clients, the efforts of those involved will be justified. If it also encourages scholars in the continuing pursuit of stronger and better-knit theoretical bases for practice, our task will be fully rewarded.

F.J.T
Kitchener, Ontario
1973

Acknowledgments

One of the distinct privileges of membership in the academic world is the tradition of sabbatical leave. In this instance, my sabbatical coincided with the planned revision of this book, thus permitting me to give the project my full attention. In addition, the timing of this leave also allowed me to accept an invitation from Hunter College's School of Social Work to be the Moses Visiting Distinguished Professor for the year. Being at Hunter provided me with the opportunity to work with a highly stimulating group of colleagues who, along with members of Columbia's faculty, were of considerable assistance in identifying gaps in the content and to conceptualize a basis for classification.

Susan Matloff, a second-year graduate student at Hunter, was of much assistance in organizing and reviewing the materials as was Hilda Holober in typing and retyping various sections.

The authors of the various chapters are to be commended for their enthusiasm, wisdom, and cooperation. Again, although many were distant in miles during the process they seemed close to me. All have influenced me through their writing and support.

My family was also distant throughout much of the process and hence not so directly involved as in earlier editions. I am most thankful for their sufferance of a peregrinating husband and father. Joanne's important support and understanding during this process were indispensable. For once she was freed of the rigors of editing my writing. Francis, Sarah, and Anne-Marie, all scholars now, appreciate well the challenge of writing and editing; their interest and encouragement remain constant. Lady McDuff remained aloof from the project, hoping only that it would not interfere with accustomed household routines.

My deep appreciation to all.

About the Contributors

Michael Blugerman, M.S.W., is a graduate and Fellow of the Gestalt Institute of Toronto. He has taught part-time in the graduate program at the Faculty of Social Work at Wilfrid Laurier University and the Department of Social Work at York University.

Steve Burghardt, M.S.W., Ph.D., is an associate professor of urban policy and practice at Hunter College School of Social Work in New York. A long-time activist in various forms of political organizing since the 1960s, he is the author of *The Other Side of Organizing: Resolving the Personal Dilemmas and Political Demands of Daily Practice*, *Organizing for Community Action*, and numerous articles on policy and practice.

Denise Capps Coburn, M.S.W., is an associate professor at the School of Social Work of Michigan State University. She has extensive training, practice, and teaching experience in Transactional Analysis, and is clinically certified by the International Transactional Analysis Association.

Liane Vida Davis, M.S.W., Ph.D., is assistant professor at the School of Social Welfare, Nelson A. Rockefeller College of Public Affairs and Policy, State University of New York at Albany.

Carel B. Germain, D.S.W., is a professor at the University of Connecticut School of Social Work. Previously, she was professor of social work at the Columbia University School of Social Work.

Alex Gitterman, D.S.W., is a professor of social work practice at the Columbia University School of Social Work, and co-author with Carel Germain of the *Life Model of Social Work Practice.*

Naomi Golan, Ph.D., is currently the John Milner Professor of Child and Family Welfare at the School of Social Work, University of Southern California, and Professor Emerita at the University of Haifa, Israel. She is the author of *Treatment in Crisis and Passing Through Transitions.*

Eda Goldstein, D.S.W., is associate professor at the New York University School of Social Work, where she is chairperson of the practice area. She consults to several New York–area hospitals and social agencies, maintains a private practice, and is a consulting editor to the *Clinical Social Work Journal.* She is also the author of *Ego Psychology and Social Work Practice.*

Thomas Keefe, M.S.W., is a professor at the Department of Social Work, University of Northern Iowa.

Donald F. Krill, M.S.W., is a professor at the University of Denver Graduate School of Social Work where he also directs the postgraduate Family Therapy Training Center. He is in private practice in Denver. Krill is the author of *Existential Social Work.*

Mary MacLean, M.S.W, is assistant professor at the Carleton University School of Social Work in Ottawa, where she coordinates Direct Intervention Field Practice Instruction and has an active private practice in social work.

Judith C. Nelsen, D.S.W., is professor at the Jane Addams College of Social Work, University of Illinois at Chicago, where she teaches social work treatment and research. Her writings include two books: *Communication Theory and Social Work Practice* and *Family Treatment: An Integrative Approach.*

Helen Harris Perlman, M.S.W., D.Litt., is Samuel Deutsch Distinguished Service Professor, Emerita, University of Chicago. She has published six books, the most recent of which is *Relationship: The Heart of Helping People.*

William J. Reid, D.S.W., is a professor at the School of Social Welfare, Nelson A. Rockefeller College of Public Affairs and Policy, State University of New York at Albany. His latest book is *Family Problem Solving.*

Sonya L. Rhodes, D.S.W., is a consultant at the Jewish Board of Family and Children's Service. Formerly on the faculty of Hunter College School of

Social Work and Columbia University, she is the co-author of *Surviving Family Life* with Josleen Wilson.

Margaret R. Rodway, Ph.D., is an associate professor in the Faculty of Social Welfare at the University of Calgary and a consultant to and part-time staff member of the Calgary Family Service Bureau.

William Rowe, D.S.W., is an associate professor in the Department of Social Work at King's College, University of Western Ontario. He maintains a private practice where he provides direct service and consultation to individuals and agencies.

Herbert S. Strean, D.S.W., is Distinguished Professor at the Graduate School of Social Work, Rutgers University. His most recent book is *Resolving Resistances in Psychotherapy*.

Ray J. Thomlison, Ph.D., is professor and dean of the Faculty of Social Welfare, University of Calgary. He has recently published a book entitled, *Perspectives on Industrial Social Work Practice*.

Francis J. Turner, D.S.W., is presently the Moses Distinguished Visiting Professor at Hunter College School of Social Work for the year 1984–85. Formerly executive vice president of Laurentian University, Sudbury, Ontario, Canada. He is the author of *Differential Diagnosis and Treatment in Social Work, Psychosocial Therapy, and Adult Psychopathology*.

Mary Valentich, Ph.D., is an associate professor and assistant dean in the Graduate Program, Faculty of Social Welfare, University of Calgary. She is certified as a sex educator, sex counselor, and sex therapist by the American Association of Sex Educators, Counselors and Therapists.

Harold D. Werner, M.S.W., is executive director of the League for Family Service, Bloomfield, N.J., and edits the journal of Psychiatric Outpatient Centers of the Americas.

Shankar A. Yelaja, D.S.W., is a professor and dean of the Faculty of Social Work, Wilfrid Laurier University. He is the author of several publications, including four books: *Authority and Social Work, Canadian Social Policy, Ethical Issues in Social Work*, and *An Introduction to Social Work Practice in Canada*.

CHAPTER 1

Theory in Social Work Practice

Francis J. Turner

Two principal themes are dominant in this book. The first is an assumption that the nature and style of social work practice should be directly related to the theoretical basis of the profession. The second is a continuing curiosity about the existence, importance, and impact of the broad spectrum of thought systems and theories that are currently influencing clinical social work practice.

Few would disagree with the assumption about the expected relationship between theory and practice. Most would consider this statement to be self-evident and basic to any profession. Fortunately, the debate as to whether clinical practice is an art or a science is now over. We must build our practice on a solid foundation of theoretical knowledge. Although apparently obvious, it is difficult to demonstrate that, in fact, theory and practice are closely related. Some literature firmly concludes that, in some areas at least, practitioners do not appear to be strongly influenced by theory, e.g., R. Carew and J. Hawkins (3, 12). Yet other literature claims there is growing evidence that when practitioners do base their intervention strategies on particular clinical bases, positive results occur (5, 6, 31, 45). Clearly, what is done in practice is varied; however, there is no compromising as to the necessity for this interconnection. Rather, there is a concern as to how to accomplish this goal and how to demonstrate where and when it is operative and with what effect.

The second theme—the interest in the wide range of theories, models, and systems of practice with various levels of interinfluence and interconnection—is an important and underattended reality in contemporary practice. For a long time the profession suffered from a dearth of theory; this was replaced by an almost complete dependence on psychoanalytic thinking, now being replaced by a broad based commitment to the wide range of systems discussed in this book. Whether the current move to a commitment to strengthening the knowledge base of practice has been enhanced by this rich range, or whether it confuses and disillusions our colleagues is still an open matter. It is my view that, in fact, this diversity has strengthened our understanding of the importance of tested theory and demonstrated the pitfalls in a practice that is either devoid of theory or overdependent on a single theory. As a first step in understanding their differential use, the field must know something about each system. Only from this basis can we begin to identify more clearly the relative and differential use of each, and also assess how this type of intersystem comparison contributes to or takes away from ongoing progress to strenthen the knowledge base of practice.

It is evident that many theories exist, that more continue to emerge, and then they increasingly influence practice directly. There is a strong connection between what we know and what we do. While we recognize that we have much to learn, we realize also that considerable progress is being made. The absence of a demonstrable connection between theory and practice does not mean that practitioners function irresponsibly or ineffectively—the history of our day-to-day practice dramatically disproves this. Rather, the situation is that as yet we have not been able to, are not compelled to, or are not equipped to develop a more rigorous conceptual base from the wealth of accumulated practice knowledge.

In the remainder of the chapter we will examine five questions: What is theory? What have we said about theory? What have we done about theory? What can theory do for us? What harm can theory do?

What Is Theory?

Those of us who have been away from formal courses in research concepts and methods for a long time might not be able to give a precise textbook definition of theory or an accurate description of its component parts. Still, most of us know, that theory builds a series of propositions about reality; that is, it provides us with models of reality and helps us to understand what is possible and how we can attain it.

There are four terms usually identified as being essential to theory: *concepts, facts, hypotheses,* and *principles.*

Concepts are symbols developed by a discipline to describe the phenomena with which it is dealing. They are thus abstractions and represent only descriptions of reality. Concepts are the labels by which we communicate with each other; that is, they are agreed-upon terms that describe the world in which we live. Within a body of theory and the practice of a discipline, concepts are presumed to have accuracy and precision and therefore provide a means for clear and effective communication between colleagues. This being the case, responsible theoreticians and practitioners are strongly committed to constantly sharpening and specifying the precision of the concepts used. A concept is not a phenomenon; it is a formulation about a phenomenon that is derived by logical abstraction from our experiences. As we all know, the frequent error of the practitioner and researcher is to treat the abstractions as concrete realities. Examples of concepts in social work practice are relationship, personality strengths, mental mechanisms, homeostasis, and self-identity.

Facts, on the other hand, can be empirically verified; that is, they are observations made about the concepts with which we deal. Clearly, the question of what constitutes adequate empirical verification is an involved and challenging one, and the history of our search for knowledge provides many examples of facts that were once considered proven being replaced by other facts more recently proven.

Theory emerges through the process of ordering facts in a meaningful way; that is, the relationship between facts is posited through observation, speculation, inspiration, and experience, and as these relationships are observed and verified, theory is developed.

New relationships between facts that are formally predicted in emerging theories are called hypotheses. When a hypothesis is developed and found through disciplined observation to be supported, then the theory has been further developed and tested.

As hypotheses are tested and theory develops, principles emerge that are dependable, predictive statements about some aspect of reality. Such principles lead in turn to the development of dependable technical procedures and methods of acting, or of doing things to bring about a desired outcome. In time, such techniques become virtually automatic, so the connection of such techniques to an underlying theoretical stance is often forgotten or lost. When this happens, a person is said to be practicing without theory, carrying out a series of activities without an awareness of the underlying conceptual base. The responsible practitioner needs to remain aware of the connection between technique and theory to assure that the process of theory development is ongoing and thus ever improving the precision, effectiveness, and efficiency of the practitioner's intervention.

One of the difficulties about theory building is that the terms and process can be defined and described in a clear and precise manner, and such descriptions can readily give the false impression that the process of theory building takes place in a clear, highly structured manner. The error in such an impression is that it fails to recognize that the process of developing new systematized knowledge is a complex and intricate human activity involving the whole spectrum of our intellectual and emotional potential—a fact well-known by anyone who has tried to develop even a single testable hypothesis.

What Have We Said About Theory?

In examining material for this chapter, many references to the concept of theory were observed in the writings of colleagues in social work and related disciplines. These references indicated a high degree of consistent understanding of the essence of theory as summarized above. Thus, Gordon Hearn regards theory as "an internally consistent body of verified hypotheses" (13, p. 8). For Herbert Strean (42, p. 5), theory is described as "a more or less verified explanation of observed facts or phenomena." William Goode and Paul Hatt sees theory as the relationship between facts, or the process of ordering facts in some meaningful way (10, p. 9). Alfred Baldwin refers to theory as the explanation of some class of events (1, p. 45). Robert Merton states that theory is the logical interrelatonship between propositions (23, p. 89). Harold Lewis says, "theory in social work is intended to provide explanations for the phenomena of practice" (19, p. 16). Lotte Marcus sees theory as "a systematized and comprehensive set of assumptions" (22). Joel Fischer says that theory is "a more or less formalized explanatory conceptualizaton of the relationship of variables" (5, p. 41). For Carl Rogers, theory is a "fallible changing attempt to construct a network of gossamer threads which will contain the solid facts" (36, p. 9). Talcott Parsons describes theory as: "a theoretical system in the present sense is a body of logically interdependent generalized concepts of empirical reference" (27, p. 212).

When the practitioner looks at theory, the goal is to develop and refine an intellectual structure by which the complex array of facts encountered in practice can be understood, so that the nature of intervention can be deduced and the effects of such intervention predicted. The clinician's principal interest is the utility of theory: What can it tell me about this situation that will permit me to act effectively? It is, therefore, not knowledge for its own sake, but knowledge for use.

Although it is not difficult to demonstrate that in our professional literature we have manifested an understanding of the nature of theory, this attitude is by no means a universal one within our profession (17, 41, 47). The literature of social work practice, especially that of the last decade, has been replete with a dual emphasis: first, a loud decrying of the lack of a strong theoretical base, and, second, a plea for the strengthening of this component of practice (15). Such exhortations underline the earlier observation that we have not put into practice what we already know about the dimensions of, need for, and utility of theory. It may be that this is a phenomenon common to segments of other related disciplines. Be that as it may, we clearly have not been consistent in our application of the concept of theory in general.

Thus, for some clinicians, theory seems to be almost antithetical to fact. An attitude summed up in statements like: "I am a practitioner, not a theoretician." The implication here seems to be that theory inhibits practice and somehow takes away from our commitment to individualization.

For others, the term "theory" seems to be synonymous with value statements about human dignity, the desirability of participation in one's destiny, or the seeking of the public good as a desirable goal.

And for still others, theory seems to describe a form of speculation or a post-factum explanation. Thus, a colleague might say, "I have a theory as to why this happened," or ask, "What's your theory about this situation?" In another vein, theory sometimes seems to be used in the sense of basic axioms or postulates from which a particular logical structure is developed.

When a group or discipline is vague about the concept of theory, it is easy to understand why it would also be divided on the way it applies available theory. Thus it is still said that the lack of available theory seems to be holding us back. However, this does not appear to be the case. Our weakness is not that we suffer from a shortage of theories, but that we have not made full use of what we already have. For example, I believe that the currently strong criticism of clinical social work's heavy reliance on psychoanalytic theory is misguided. A more accurate criticism would be that this theory is not understood and frequently incorrectly applied. Many social workers identified with psychoanalysis only use a portion of the rich body of psychoanalytic theory and are not acquainted with the various subsystems and persons related to this theoretical approach. Thus, much of the criticism of it, and of other theories important to social work, should actually be a criticism of the lack of understanding. The criticism should be leveled against practioners who operate predominantly from an impressionistic ad hoc type of base rather than from one solidly built on available theory.

Strean speculates on some of the reasons for this apparent weakness in our practice. (42). Among the ideas he puts forth is the tradition of human service being used as an explanation for the failure to make full use of available theory; that is, too extensive use of theory is thought to undervalue the nobility of unique human nature.

Undoubtedly, our origins of service and traditions of individual human worth have influenced us and must partially account for our less than full enthusiasm for theory, especially if theory is thought to be antihuman and mechanistic. But I suggest that using our concern for individuals, groups, and communities as a rationale for a disinterest in theory is in reality a denial of the problem. This stance also seems to have an indefensible presumptuousness about it, for it also seems to be saying that those who are interested in theory building, whether within our profession or without, are seen as being without human concern, and only those committed to ignore theory are truly concerned about people and their needs. Neither can we rule out the fact that it is only in the last fifteen years that society has put heavy demands on us to account for what we are doing. Without this pressure, it was easier for us to trust our impressions that what we were doing was good rather than attempt to conceptualize and thus explain our activities.

An additional factor that appears to hinder a more extensive reliance on theory is the very richness of what is available, as is evidenced in the chapters in this book. Because of the broad range of variables on which we draw for understanding, because of the spectrum of disciplines from which our knowledge is drawn, and because of the various numbers of thought systems that have developed within our own discipline, it is easy to become overwhelmed by the mass of available information.

But surely we have frequently and perhaps continuously talked about theory and its needs. Several of the major books in casework included theory in their titles, such as Gordon Hamilton's classic, *Theory and Practice of Social Casework* (11), Ruth Smalley's *Theory for Social Work Practice* (39), and *Theories of Social Casework* by Robert Roberts and Robert Nee (35). A survey of social work journals published over the past fifteen years turned up over sixty articles with the word *theory* in their titles.

Although we have long been interested in theory, we have often used the word imprecisely. Instead of applying the concept in a specific sense proper to a scholarly discipline, we have tended to use it more loosely. Thus we frequently use the word *theory* to describe such things as basic tenets of practice, systematic formulation of ideas, approaches to theory, schools of thought or systems of thought, accumulated practice wisdom, and post factum explanations of basic values rather than the rigorous, correct definition of theory. Bernice K. Simon comments on this in a chapter of *Theories of Social Casework* (35), and questions whether any of the systems discussed in the book are actually theories. An excellent discussion about the nature of theory, the types of theory, and the place of theory in practice is found in Max Siporin's *Introduction to Social Work Practice* (38).

What Have We Done About Theory?

The current strong interest in the need for an expanded and enriched theoretical base is not new to the profession. As has been said, we have been consistent and enduring in this quest. What has varied is the differential approaches we have taken to this necessary task (7). In our literature, fourteen different approaches to theory can be identified.

The first of these is best referred to as pretheory. Included under this heading are the first formal attempts by our early colleagues to conceptualize definitions of practice, components of practice, and classifications of treatment procedures and methods. Examples of these are Mary Richmond's *Social Diagnosis* (33), and Gordon Hamilton's classic *Theory and Practice of Social Casework* (11). In spite of the title, Dr. Hamilton uses the word *theory* only a few times in the book and even less frequently refers to the process of theory building through research. Rather than discuss concepts and verified hypotheses, she talks about "basic assumptions which cannot be proved" (11, p. 3), axioms, values, attitudes, and exhortations. She speaks comfortably and authoritatively from her knowledge of practice but not explicitly from a formal theoretical base. Thus her book is more prescriptive than theory-based. These early writings were, of course, essential first steps at bringing together in a scholarly experience-based manner the practice wisdom of the profession.

The second type of approach to theory is that cluster of writings based on a framework accepted as a theory. I refer specifically to that rich range of writings, so essential to the early development of clinical practice, that were based on the various psychodynamic schools of thought. The authors of these writings accepted one or several schools of psychodynamic theory and then speculated on their implications for social work practice. A long list of articles, monographs, and books can be identified under this heading. Looking at the last fifteen years, two good examples of this type of writing would be Howard Parad's two books, *Ego Psychology and Dynamic Casework* (25) and *Ego-Oriented Casework*, co-authored with Roger Miller (26). Here the authors are not trying to develop a particular theoretical stance but are using an accepted existing one to further develop its applications for clinical practice.

The third approach to theory building in clinical practice in social work can be observed in the work of those authors who have drawn on their practice experience and present a particular stance or conceptual approach that represents their own thinking. Admittedly, such authors draw heavily and explicitly, but not exclusively, on other bodies of thought; that is, they have selected a set of concepts and added their own from which emerges a unique approach to practice. In the casework field, Florence Hollis's "psychosocial system" (14) and Helen Perlman's "problem solving approach" (28) are well-known examples of this. In the group work field, the writings of Gisela Konopka (18) also represents this approach. Both Hollis and Konopka present statements about the theoretical orientations on which their work is based, and Perlman gives a series of axioms or statements of principle as the substructure for her approach to practice. Although clearly these works are based on carefully thought-out and well-organized thought systems, they would not meet the precise parameters of a theory. They represent a system of propositions from which hypotheses could be developed and a theory built.

The fourth identifiable characteristic of our efforts at theory building in clinical practice in social work has been the division of practice into discrete segments; that is, we have long operated from a conceptual framework that separated out various forms of treatment as distinct methodologies with different conceptual underpinnings. Thus our principal writings in clinical practice have developed from either a casework, group work, or family therapy stance (8, 14, 18). Clearly there are historical reasons for this trend that are related to the way in which the various methodologies emerged. Nevertheless, this tradition fostered an assumption that our sought after theoretical base needed a pluralistic foundation related to the various treatment modalities, and until recently gave little attention to the commonalities of different models or the possibility of multimethod practitioners.

Although the majority of our clinical writings have been based on some form of psychodynamic and small group theory, in the past decade we have seen emerging a trend in theory building that introduces new thought systems into practice. Hence, in the late 1950s and the 1960s we began to see a series of important writings stemming from a range of theoretical bases—the fifth identifiable approach. Thus we find Perlman writing a book from a role theory base (29), Parad editing two books from an ego psychology base (24, 25), and later, with Miller, one on crisis theory (26), Harold Werner publishing on cognitive theory (48), Derek Jehu (16) and Edwin Thomas (44) producing major writings from a learning theory approach, and similarly Werner Lutz (21) and Hearn (13) from a systems theory base. Consequently, we begin to see an interest in broadening our conceptual base. Sometimes this was done in a scholarly, searching way and at other times in an earnest, exhortative way, implying that the goal of our long search had been finally reached.

As would be expected, once our clinical field began to move into a more diverse conceptual base, we began to wonder how these theories did or did not fit together and to begin to make comparisons between theories. This seeking for interconnectedness is the sixth characteristic of our theoretical thinking. As before, we still tend to make such comparisons along methodological lines; so Joan Stein (41) and her associates compare the various theories related to family theory, Roberts and Nee (35), and later Strean (42), look at diverse theories in social casework. Hollis's second edition of *Casework, a Psychosocial Therapy* (14) gave us an example of how her own thinking has begun to incorporate several of these newer approaches into her psychosocial framework. In the group field, we find William Schwartz and Serapio Zalba (37) doing a study of the theoretical bases of this modality of practice.

Once it became acceptable, and indeed desirable, to move away from our traditional roots and to look further afield for new ideas, a trend emerged that is reflected in this volume. Instead of remaining limited and interconnected, the base expanded rapidly. We moved from the six systems reported in Roberts and Nees to the more than twenty described in this book. Thus colleagues began to look at new systems, such as Gestalt and Transactional Analysis, to consider bolder thinking and its implications for practice, as in Existentialism and Meditation, and to develop some systems of our own, as in Task-Centered (32) and Life Model (9). Some decried this trend as a confounding example of faddism, while others welcomed it as the responsible and commendable search of a profession to improve and expand its conceptual base.

Accompanying this development, another, less predominant yet highly significant group of writings aimed at improving our theory can be identified —the eighth characteristic. These do not look at particular theories but at the more basic concept of the nature of theory and theory building. They move away from our traditional approaches to theory building and urge us to look at the process in the abstract. Usually, the abstractions are then related to current professional reallity with recommendations to shift our approach. This strategy was considered most carefully by Lutz (21) and Hearn (13), both of whom, interestingly, then moved into the specific applications of theory concepts in a systems orientation. I think these two writings have made significant contributions to our growing understanding of the nature, purpose, and need for theory in our practice, and have been the inspiration for a renewed and more explicit approach to theory formulation in social work.

A ninth strategy in theory building that can be identified in our literature is based on research activities, a stance still greatly neglected by our field. In this mode, various concepts related to our field are operationally defined and tested through the formulation of hypotheses and the examination of resultant data. Lillian Ripple's studies (34) using the concepts of motivation, capacity, and opportunity, are an excellent example of this, as is William Reid and Ann Shyne's (32) work on short-term treatment and Hollis's work on a testing of her paradigm of treatment methods devised from experience-based observations (14) and Fischer's examination of cognitive and behavioral principles (6). Many more projects of this type are needed and can be expected in the next few years.

Another approach to theory building is represented in the present work. Here we are bringing together the range of thought systems related to social work, but unlike other collections also asking the authors to apply their particular orientation to various treatment modalities used in clinical practice, including work with communities. It is hoped that this type of two-way analysis of theory and methods will serve to forge a new strategy of comparison and integration. Clearly, we need more work that seeks both areas of similarity and difference between theories and methods of treatment.

A somewhat different approach to theory building through the search for integration and interconnections between systems as described above, is a commitment to eclecticism. In this approach, the eleventh, selected concepts are adopted from various theories and used as the base of practice. There are two forms of eclecticism observable in current practice. In one, the practitioner selects what appeals to him or her, such choices probably being based on value perspectives and a sense of what appears to fit practice. The second type of eclecticism is that best explicated and demonstrated by Dr. Joel Fischer (6). In this type, responsible practice demands that we only use those elements of theory that have been demonstrated to be effective. Thus, one should build a knowledge base for practice from a research base rather than from preference. This approach is clearly one that ensures the selective and incremental development and testing of theoretical concepts.

Since the first edition of this book, another trend has appeared in the literature, a trend that has positive and important implications for practice. This is the increasing number of articles dealing with highly specific components of discrete theories; that is, rather than attempting to discuss total systems, authors are doing one of two things: they are either looking at a specific application of a thought system, such as the use of crisis theory in a schoolroom context, or they are discussing the application of a discrete concept from a thought system to practice, such as the specific application of the concept of homeostasis in work with married couples (47). Both of these trends indicate a healthy awareness that further progress in theory building will probably be made only on a slow, step-by-step basis.

As interest in and commitment to theory building increases, the long-existing dichotomy between academic and clinical, or theory and practice, is narrowing. Clinicians are beginning to see that practice can be enhanced and more accurately evaluated by the targeted use of theoretical concepts. The process of hypothesis formulating and testing is being seen as closely akin to the process of diagnostic formulation and treatment. Dr. Harold Lewis describes this process well: "Every practitioner should know that her observations are not simply casual scannings; they involve a conceptually ordered search for evidence. Her eyes and ears are trained to help her select evidence relative to some framework that will permit inferences to be drawn, order revealed, meanings surmised, and an exploratory guide for action planned. The organizing frameworks are theories" (19, p. 6). As the close relationship of the process of theory development and treatment become better understood and accepted, there should result a dramatic change in both the teaching and practice of clinical social work.

A number of clinical social workers, however, view theory as antithetical to treatment. They hold the opinion that theory is unimportant and indeed counterproductive to good practice, that effective treatment consists simply of a warm, understanding, respectful reaching out of one human being perceived in all respects to be the equal of the person to whom he or she is reaching. Quantifying, analyzing, testing, and experimenting—the regular scholarly endeavors of an academic approach to theory—are disregarded or looked on with suspicion. Since the second edition of the book, this attitude, although still observable, is diminishing. It is hoped that in subsequent editions it will be possible to report that it is no longer a relevant factor in theory development in clinical practice.

The preceding discussion shows that we have used a wide range of approaches in our search for better integrated and tested thought systems from which we can develop and test theory. Although it is fashionable to engage in rhetorical contests of mutual recrimination of our lack of theory-building efforts, our field has demonstrated that a significant and consistent tradition of commitment to this task has always existed whether through the development of our own theories or in incorporating or modifying theories from other disciplines. Clearly, we are beginning to succeed; more progress will be made if we direct our efforts more to the task of theory building and less into the commitment to criticize each other.

We should not despair, however, because considerable progress is being and has been made. We are certainly conscious of the need for better thought systems and better coordination and utilization of the immense store of practice widsom acquired by our field. The purpose of this volume is both to bring more of this thinking to our colleagues as well as to contribute to the search for a better integration.

What Can Theory Do for Us?

If we are still far from either a theoretical base or even a base of several theories, two questions must be examined: first, what can we hope for in aspiring to such a goal and, second, is theory really related to practice? The latter question could be put another way, "Is a strong theoretical base a necessary component of effective therapy?" Are good therapists also good theoreticians and poor therapists poor theoreticians?

Let's first examine what theory should do for practice. For the clinician seeking to offer responsible, effective intervention, the most essential and important contribution of theory is its ability to predict outcomes, or, in other words, its ability to explain. Theory helps us to recognize patterns and relationships that aid in bringing order to the reality with which we are confronted to "compare, evaluate and relate data" (38). The practitioner who consciously formulates a treatment plan based on an assessment of a situation is involved in either a theory-building or theory-testing activity; that is, a treatment plan aimed at achieving a particular goal presumes a situation is understood to the extent that specific alterations of the situation can be made with predictable outcomes. Without the confidence in predicting outcomes based on a presumed understanding of situations and persons, practice remains for the most part in the area of guesswork and impressionistic responses. This is not to imply that the day is near when we will be certain about the outcome of each of our cases, only that we can anticipate being surer about more of our cases than we are at present.

Theory also aids the practitioner in anticipating future outcomes of some situations and speculating on unanticipated relationships between variables; that is, theory should help us to recognize, understand, and explain new situations. If we understand sufficiently the phenomena with which we are dealing and their interrelationships, we should have the conceptual tools to deal with any unexpected or unanticipated observations in the behavior we meet. To the extent that our theory is sound, we should experience fewer surprises in our practice and be better able to solve problems.

Theory, of course, also helps us carry knowledge from one situation to the next, in aiding us to recognize what is similar and what is different in our ongoing practice experience. This in no way detracts from the concept of individuality or self-determination; in fact, it can enhance these concepts by helping us see not only how the client or situation resembles other clients and situations, but how each is unique.

Theory helps us to expand our horizons as we follow the implications of some observation we have made or some fact that does not appar to fit what we know or have experienced before.

A sound and logically consistent theoretical structure permits us to explain our activity to others; to transfer our knowledge and skills in a testable, demonstrable way; and to permit our activities to be scrutinized and evaluated by others—that is, if we have sound theories, then others can profit by our experience in applying those theories.

Theory further helps us to recognize when we have encountered new situations that indicate gaps in our knowledge. Thus, when the application of a theoretical concept does not result in the expected outcome, we are made aware that we have misunderstood, or that what we have is not sufficient to deal with, the situation at hand. Frequently, practitioners, in meeting a difficult or new practice situation, blame themselves, thinking that if they had been more aware they could have coped more effectively, when, in fact, there may have been no available theoretical construct to explain the presenting phenomena. Hence, it is as important to know what we don't know, as it is to know what is known.

Theory also gives assurance to the worker. We all know the awesome responsibility of the practitioner. We have all experienced the haunting loneliness caused by the weight of this responsiblity. Theory will never completely dispel this feeling, but a firm theoretical orientation helps give us a base on which to order what we do know. We must have a set of anchoring concepts from which to work to avoid the aimless, albeit benevolent, wandering with the client that comes from lack of knowledge. Theory helps us to bring some order to our practice by providing a filter, screen, or framework with which to put into perspective that mass of kmowledge, facts, impressions, and suppositions we develop in the process of therapeutic contact with an individual, family, group, or community. Somewhat cynically, one might suggest that theory, whether it be sound theory or not, gives a sense of security to the therapist, thus increasing authority and, in turn, increasing effectiveness, even if what is done is not related to the theory espoused. If this were true, it would give a new meaning to the saying attributed to Kurt Lewin, "Nothing works better than a good theory."

Reliance on a theory, in addition, permits us to assess other theories; that is, if we are clear about which of our concepts are empirically verifiable and empirically connected, then we are in a much better position to compare what we know with other emerging ideas. In our field especially, there can frequently be several theoretical explanations for a single phenomenon. Determining which is most useful and most effective, requires constant testing. Theoretical explanations different from our own frequently help us better understand and indeed modify our own theoretical stance.

What Harm Can Theory Do?

As we argue the advantages and necessity for a strong theoretical base, we must also examine the opposing arguments of which Noel Timms speaks.

For example, some suggest that too much stress on theory could contradict our commitment to a humanistic basis of practice. Theory would tend to make us mechanistic, to deemphasize the individuality of our clients and to stress classification and labeling. Others suggest that theoreticians are too cerebral and thus cease to be as empathetic to clients as they should, and even that the search for a theory of human behavior diminishes commitment to human freedom and autonomy.

Another concern is that theory tends to become self-fulfilling; that is, we tend to see the world only through a particular theoretical perspective and translate all phenomena into an acceptable fit for our thinking. By doing this we fail to take into account alternative explanations to practice situations.

Finally, it has been suggested that theory and theory building can become ends in themselves, so that the ability to predict, and hence control, becomes the goal while we forget that our quest is toward the facilitating of growth and the optimizing of potential.

Such objections are not to be dismissed lightly. There is an aspect of validity in each. But such objections focus on the way theory and the quest for theory can be misused, not on inherent characteristics of the process. Certainly, we can all fall into these traps, but our efforts must be to avoid this, rather than using fear of these risks to avoid the greater challenge and responsibility to ensure our practice is based on tested knowledge.

Other critics argue that our search for a theory that would fully explain the "person in situation" is one conducted in vain. They say the target of our concern is so complex, individualized, and rapidly changing, that it can be neither understood nor manipulated in a predictable way. Whether this is so or not, and I choose to believe it is not, I think it is abundantly clear that we will always continue our search for the key to the explanation of ourselves, our fellow earth travelers, and the societies and systems in which we function or fail to function.

A more telling and troubling question is how much theory is needed. Although not a respectable question in a profession that seeks increased recognition in the company of scholars, it is not to be discounted. Might it be that the compleat therapist is not the theoretician but is, instead, the artist whose theory is intuition and whose skill is a natural endowment?

In another writing I suggested that one had to conclude that many social workers were in fact skilled diagnosticians, otherwise how could one expain the myriad of highly successfully treated cases? I was strongly taken to task for this suggestion (30), as it was pointed out that it didn't follow that a successfully treated case meant the worker knew what she was doing and why it was being done at all. This question has similarly been raised in discussions concerning curriculum models for teaching social workers. Should one teach theory and practice together or separately? Or, put another way, can one teach techniques of interventions that have been found to be effective without presuming such techniques can be directly related to a body of theory?

Perhaps the state of our practice is such that the artistic component is still stronger than the knowledge base, and for the present, we should leave the two separate. Although it is not something I believe or can be comfortable with, I think that in our search for a better understanding of the therapeutic process, for the how and why of intervention and the assessment of its outcome, we should at least consider the possibliity that a person's practice is not related to the theoretical concepts that are held. If so, we might learn more about practice and its base by studying what, in fact, practitioners do, not their explanations for managing cases in particular ways. Many of the discussions that take place among practitioners revolve around alleged theoretical differences, yet more than one research project has indicated that even when we fly different theoretical flags, we tend to act similarly when we are with clients who are alike in personality, need, and life situation. Thus practitioners who would claim to be diametrically opposed theoretically are frequently observed to do similar things in actual treatment. If it can be established that our practice does not reflect our stated theory base, perhaps one could develop a theory of intervention that is different from the theories of personality, learning, and behavior with which we are familiar and which are the topics of subsequent chapters in this book. What I am suggesting is that at times we may be misled by the idea that our practice directly reflects the theory we hold. In fact, I think one could identify components of our various practice activities that contradict what we say we know about how people learn and behave and about how behavior is modified.

One final item that needs to be discussed in relation to this spectrum of thought systems is the matter of order. This raises questions much more complex than the desire for a comprehensible and logical table of contents. Rather, it challenges us to address a primary theme of this book, the relationship of these systems to each other. This search for an order that was more conceptual than an alphabetical or chronological listing became an interesting and challenging problem. Discussions with colleagues quickly made it evident that others had addressed this question. Several approaches were suggested. For example, one could attempt to range the chapters along various continua such as most abstract to most concrete, most particular to most general, most intrapsyche to most externally oriented, etc. Others suggested that rather than continua we think of clusters—for example, theories could be divided into foundation theories or practice theoris; that is, theories that gave a general orientation about persons and society and those that gave specific orientations to practice. Siporin suggests that theories could also be divided between assessment theories and intervention theories. Golan talks in her chapter about transitional theories that help bind practice to new developments as they emerge as a third category. Each of these divisions is useful as a way of helping us continue to examine and assess the development and utility of theory for practice.

As we considered the needs of the practitioner in this matter and the information that began to emerge as the various systems were compared along common variables, we began to see that one other way in which the systems differed was the aspect of the human condition that was emphasized. Since an underlying thesis of this book is that these systems are differentially effective, then this emphasis on the specific aspect of psychosocial reality by each thought system may help clarify their different utility.

Using this thinking the following table emerged and became the basis on which the table of contents was established.

It is evident that this approach does not automatically give an order to the chapters but does give a basis from which to develop an order. In this instance, we moved from an intrapersonality cognitive basis to our relationship with total nature. This thinking also helped to identify two gaps, the one mentioned earlier, on group theory, and a companion chapter to feminist theory looking at masculine theory. One of the risks of a classification scheme

TABLE 1-1   Classification of Selected Social Work Practice Related Thought Systems from the Perspective of the Principal Human Activity on Which the System Focuses

Distinguishing Area of Focus	Relevant Thought System
Person as a psychological being	Psychoanalytic Functional Gestalt
Person as thinker	Cognitive
Person as learner	Behavior Modification
Person as contemplator	Meditation Existentialism
Person as communicator	Communications
Person as doer	Problem-solving Task-Centered Crisis
Person as a biological entity	Neurolinguistics
Person as individual	Ego-Psychology Client-Centered
Person as family member	Family Transactional Analysis
Person as group member	Group
Person in relation to society	Psychosocial Systems Role Feminism Marxism
Person in relation to the universe	Ecological

Each system deals essentially with the same issues. The differences between and among systems relate to the emphasis given by each system to particular aspects of the psychosocial conditon.

First discussed at Columbia University School of Social Work, February 25, 1985.

such as this is that it will be seen as a definitive classification of the various systems that will overstress differences and minimize similarities. It must be remembered that each system has to look at similar variables, what the table does is to highlight the identified basis from which the system begins.

In summary, this chapter ponts out that our field has long been cognizant of the nature of theory, although it has tended to be free in the use of the term "theory" and even more free in stating what our theories are and showing that we use them in our practice activities.

In subsequent chapters, each of the various thought systems identified as being part of our theoretical base will be presented, with comments on its present place in social work practice, its known implication for practice, and the research challenges that it offers.

In the final chapter, we will discuss some interconnections between these various approaches and speculate on some of the implications for further developments in theory building in social work that might be expected in the coming years.

References

1. Baldwin, Alfred L. *Theories of Child Development.* New York: Wiley, 1968.
2. Bloom, M., and J. Fischer. *Evaluating practice: Guidelines for the Accountable Professional.* Englewood Cliffs, N.J.: Prentice-Hall, 1982.
3. Carew, R. "The Place of Knowledge in Social Work Activity," *British Journal of Social Work*, Vol. 9 (1979), pp. 349–364.
4. Eron, Leonard D., and Robert Callahan. *The Relation of Theory to Practice in Psychotherapy.* Chicago: Aldine, 1969.
5. Fischer, Joel. "A Framework for the Analysis and Comparison of Clinical Theories of Induced Changes," *Social Service Review*, December 1971, pp. 440–454.
6. ———. *Effective Casework Practice: An Eclectic Approach.* New York: McGraw-Hill, 1978.
7. Ford, Donald H., and Hugh B. Urban. *Systems of Psychotherapy.* New York: Wiley, 1964.
8. Freed, A. O. "Building Theory for Family Practice," *Social Casework*, Vol. 63 No. 8 (1982), pp. 472–481.
9. Germain, Carol B., and Alex Gitterman. *The Life Model of Social Work Practice.* New York: Columbia University Press, 1980.
10. Goode, William J., and Paul K. Hatt. *Methods in Social Research.* New York: McGraw-Hill 1952.
11. Hamilton, Gordon. *Theory and Practice of Social Casework*, rev. ed. New York: Columbia University Press, 1951.
12. Hawkins, J. D., and M. W. Fraser. "Theory and Practice in Delinquency Prevention," *Social Work Research and Abstracts*, Vol. 17, No. 4 (1981), pp. 3–13.
13. Hearn, Gordon. *Theory Building in Social Work.* Toronto: University of Toronto Press, 1958.

14. Hollis, Florence. *Casework, a Psychosocial Therapy*, 3rd edition. New York: Random House, 1981.

15. Imre-Wells, Roberta. "The Nature of Knowledge in Social Work," *Social Work*, Vol. 29, No. 1 (January-February 1984), pp. 51–56.

16. Jehu, Derek. *Learning Theory and Social Work*. London: Routledge, 1967.

17. Kadushin, Alfred. "The Knowledge Base of Social Work," in Alfred Kahn (ed.), *Issues in American Social Work*. New York: Columbia University Press, 1959.

18. Konopka, Gisela. *Social Group Work: A Helping Process*. Englewood Cliffs, N.J.: Prentice-Hall, 1963.

19. Lewis, Harold. "Practice, Science and Professional Education: Developing a Curriculum, Responsive to New Knowledge and Values." Paper read at General Session of Symposium on the Effectiveness of Social Work Intervention: Implications for Curriculum Change. New York: Fordham University, 1971.

20. ———. *The Intellectual Base of Social Work Practice*. New York: Haworth, 1982.

21. Lutz, Werner. *Concepts and Principles Underlying Casework Practice*. Washington, D.C.: National Association of Social Workers, 1956.

22. Marcus, Lotte. Personal communication to the Editor, January 1972.

23. Merton, Robert K. *Social Theory and Social Structure*. Glencoe, Ill.: Free Press, 1957, Chapters 1–3.

24. Parad, Howard J. (ed.). *Crisis Intervention: Selected Readings*. New York: Family Service Association of America, 1958.

25. ———. *Ego Psychology and Dynamic Casework*. New York: Family Service Association of America, 1958.

26. ———, and Roger Miller (eds.). *Ego-Oriented Casework: Problems and Perspectives*. New York: Family Service Association of America, 1963.

27. Parsons, Talcott. "The Present Position and Prospects of Systematic Theory in Sociology," *Essays in Sociological Theory*, rev. ed. Glencoe, Ill.: Free Press, 1954, pp. 212–213.

28. Perlman, Helen H. *Social Casework: A Problem-Solving Process*. Chicago: University of Chicago Press, 1957.

29. ———. *Persona: Social Role and Responsibility*. Chicago: University of Chicago Press, 1968.

30. ———. "Diagnosis Anyone." Book review of F. J. Turner (ed.), *Differential Diagnosis and Treatment*, in *Psychiatry and Social Science Review*, Vol. 3, No. 8 (1969–1970), pp. 12–17.

31. Reid, William J., and P. Hanrahan. "Recent evaluations of Social Work: Grounds for Optimism," *Social Work*, Vol. 27, No. 4 (1982), pp. 328–340.

32. Reid, William J., and Ann W. Shyne. *Brief and Extended Casework*. New York: Columbia University Press, 1969.

33. Richmond, Mary. *Social Diagnosis*. New York: Russell Sage Foundation, 1917.

34. Ripple, Lillian, Ernestina Alexander, and Bernice Polemis. *Motivation Capacity and Opportunity: Social Service Monographs*. Chicago: University of Chicago Press, 1964.

35. Roberts, Robert W., and Robert H. Nee. *Theories of Social Casework*. Chicago: University of Chicago Press, 1970.

36. Rogers, Carl. "A Theory for Therapy Personality and Interpersonal Relationships as Developed in the Client-Centered Framework," in S. Koch (ed.), *Psychology: A Study of a Science, Vol. 2, General Systematic Formulations, Learning and Special Processes.* New York: McGraw-Hill, 1949.

37. Schwartz, William, and Serapio R. Zalba (eds.). *The Practice of Group Work.* New York: Columbia University Press, 1971.

38. Siporin, Max. *Introduction to Social Work Practice.* New York: Macmillan, 1975, Chapters 4 and 5.

39. Smalley, Ruth E. *Theory for Social Work Practice.* New York: Columbia University Press, 1967.

40. Smid, G., and R. Van Krieken. "Notes on Theory and Practice of Social Work: A Comparative View," *British Journal of Social Work*, Vol. 14, No. 1 (1984), pp. 11–22.

41. Stein, Joan W. *The Family as a Unit of Study and Treatment.* Seattle: Regional Rehabilitation Research Institute, University of Washington, School of Social Work, 1969.

42. Strean, Herbert F. (ed.). *Social Casework: Theories in Action.* Metuchen, N.J.: Scarecrow Press, 1971.

43. Studt, Eliot. "Social Work Theory and Implications for the Practice of Methods." *Social Work Education Reporter*, Vol. 6 (1968), pp. 22–46.

44. Thomas, Edwin J. *Behavioral Science for Social Workers.* New York: Free Press, 1967.

45. Thomlison, Ray J. "Something Works: Evidence from Practive Effectiveness Study," *Social Work*, Vol. 29, No. 1 (January-February 1984), pp. 51–56.

46. Timms, Noel. *Social Work.* London: Routledge, 1970, pp. 56–57.

47. Turner, Francis J. (ed.). *Differential Diagnosis and Treatment in Social Work.* New York: Free Press, 3rd. edition, 1983.

48. Werner, Harold D. *A Rational Approach to Social Casework.* New York: Association Press, 1965.

CHAPTER 2

Psychoanalytic Theory

Herbert S. Strean

Psychoanalysis is both a theory of personality and a form of psychotherapy. In this chapter we present those concepts and constructs from psychoanalysis that appear to be most pertinent to social work clinicians as they attempt to assess their clients diagnostically, plan treatment for them, and implement treatment plans. First, we will discuss psychoanalysis as a theory of personality. This will be followed by a discussion of psychoanalysis as a therapy. We will then conclude our presentation with a brief discussion of some of the research findings on psychoanalysis.

While there have been many departures from classical Freudian psychoanalysis, this chapter focuses exclusively on Freud and his contribution to social work practice.

Psychoanalysis: A Theory of Personality

In contrast to other theories of the personality that explain only fragments of the human being, psychoanalytic theory postulates the principle of *psychic determinism*. This principle holds that in mental fuctioning, nothing happens by chance. Everything a person feels, thinks, fantasizes, dreams, and does has a psychological motive. How individuals earn a living, whom they choose

19

to marry, what kind of love they give and receive, how they interact with their children, and how much pleasure they extract from work and love are all motivated by inner *unconscious* forces (11, 18).

While external factors are always impinging on the human being, the notions of psychic determinism and the unconscious help the social worker recognize that the behaviors of individuals, dyads, groups, and organizations are not only reactions to situational variables such as family, friends, and neighborhood, but are also shaped by unconscious wishes, unconscious fantasies, unconscious defenses, and unconscious ethical imperatives.

The notion of the unconscious is of enormous aid to social workers in helping them better understand the client's presenting problem. Psychoanalytic practitioners and theorists have been able to demonstrate, for example, that every chronic marital complaint is an unconscious wish of the complainer. The husband who constantly complains that his wife is cold and unresponsive unconsciously wants such a wife—a warm and responsive wife would scare him—and that is why he stays married to the woman about whom he constantly complains. Similarly, parents who consistently complain that their children are too aggressive, or oversexed, or too tomboyish or too effeminate, unconsciously provoke and sustain such behavior in their children. Close examination of parent-child interaction inevitably demonstrates that parents subtly reward their children for the very behavior they consciously repudiate (28, 48).

As social workers utilize the notion of the unconscious in their assessments and treatment plans, they begin to consider with the client who constantly feels rejected by her employer just why this client unconsciously wants to be demeaned by her employer and humiliated by one she experiences as a parental figure. They see the value of exploring with the student who constantly fails, the possible gratifications and protections the student derives from failing. They eventually realize that clients who are very depressed about their single or marital status may unconsciously desire that status. And to help a sexually impotent man they may ask themselves "What unconscious protection and unconscious gratification does this client get from having a flaccid penis?"

When social workers utilize the concept of the unconscious in their work, they begin to recognize that the tempestuous battles of a married couple, the alienation and divisiveness in a family or group, and the dissension in an organization or community all have unconscious meaning that must be understood before therapeutic assistance can be given.

Freud saw the human personality from several distinct but intermeshing points of view: structural, topographic, genetic, dynamic, economic, interpersonal, and cultural. These points of view, when combined, are called the metapsychological approach, and all of them are needed to fully comprehend the functioning of the human personality.

The metapsychological approach utilized by psychoanalysis is the most complete system of psychology available. It considers both the inner experiences and the outer behavior of individuals, both their presents and their pasts, their individual situations and their social circumstances. The completeness of the psychoanalytic approach is often obscured by a variety of misrepresentations that are to be found in both professional and popular literature (2, 9, 13).

Many writers agree that psychoanalysis represents, in the social sciences, the greatest revolution of the twentieth century. It has given mankind a new research tool through the concept of the unconscious and allied factors; it has clarified the possibilities of happiness that exist in philosophies that have been prevalent in previous centuries; and it has provided a solid basis for the investigation of human beings in all of their psychological and social functioning (2, 3, 13, 27, 31, 40, 42).

The Structural Point of View

One of the most helpful orientations that psychoanalytic theory can provide for the social worker is the structural point of view. This perspective points out that there are many aspects of the human psyche that interact and are interdependent. The id, the most primitive part of the mind and totally unconscious, is the repository of the person's drives and is concerned with gratification. The ego, which develops out of experience and reason, is the executive of the personality; it mediates between the inner world of id drives and of superego commands and the demands of the external world. Some of the functions of the ego are judgment, reality testing, frustration tolerance, and relating to others; the ego also erects defenses against anxiety. By assessing a client's ego strenths and weaknesses, the social worker can determine how well she is adapting, because the more severe the client's disturbances, the less operative are the ego functions and vice versa.

The superego is the judge or censor of the mind and is essentially the product of interpersonal experiences. It is divided into two parts, the conscience and the ego ideal. The conscience is that part of the superego which forbids and admonishes—"Thou shalt not!"—while the ego ideal is the storehouse of values, ethical imperatives, and morals. It commands the person in the form of "Thou shalt."

Social workers sometimes overlook the fact that a client with a punitive and exacting superego usually has strong id wishes, usually of a murderous nature, that cause great anxiety. Rather than constantly live with unbearable anxiety, the individual with unacceptable id wishes arranges for the superego to constantly admonish—for example, "Thou shalt not enjoy pleasure!" By staying away from potentially pleasureful situtations, the individual does not have to face the murderous and sadistic fantasies that are in conflict with the superego's commands. To appreciate a human phenomenon, the social work clinician must note how the mind and body are transacting and become aware of what drives, what defenses, and what ethical imperatives are opposing each other and which are working together. This interaction of id, ego, and superego is particularly helpful in understanding and assisting clients with what is one of the most neglected areas in social work practice, namely, our clients' sexual lives and their sexual fantasies.

This can be so stated because in social work practice there is hardly a social work text that carefully examines the sexual dimension of our clients' lives and includes a discussion of the inevitable sexual transference and sexual countertransference issues in client-clinician interaction. To this day, it appears to be much easier for the model social worker to say to the client "You seem to feel angry at me" than it is to say "You seem to want to have sex with me" (47).

The structural point of view leads to the fact that what is at the root of our clients' sexual inhibitions and sexual conflicts is the anxiety that emanates from their unacceptable childish id wishes. If the worker can allow herself to be a benign superego in the treatment situation and encourage the client to explore and verbalize id wishes to devour, to soil, to oedipally complete or homosexually seduce, anxiety is reduced and the ego becomes stronger— strong enough to enjoy a more mature sexual relationship with someone of the opposite sex.

The structual point of view that regards the human being as a complex organism is, of course, not the perspective that most sex therapists utilize. Many of them erroneously contend that sex is essentially a bodily experience and forget that to make love successfully and enjoyably, hate must be reduced, infantile wishes must be mastered, the superego must become less oppressive, and self-esteem must become reasonably sufficient.

Anybody working with human beings on a therapeutic basis should understand how id, ego, and superego function. For example, the person seeking help who consistently fails at work or in love relationships usually has unresolved infantile id wishes for which he has been busily punishing himself. These id wishes have to be discussed in treatment so that clients can see for themselves, in the company of a nonpunitive helper, just how and why they are arranging to fail. Problems that individuals bring to social work clinicians—such as parent-child conflicts, marital disturbances, family pathology, crime, drug addiction, and even poverty—should be appraised in terms of their unique id wishes, superego mandates, and ego functions in addition to the significant environmental factors.

The Ego and Defenses

As psychoanalytically oriented clinicians observed their clients with greater precision, they began to conceptualize the ego not only as a mediator but as a psychic structure that has autonomy and power of its own (5, 17, 30). Further psychoanalytic research has revealed that the ego's power arises primarily from the development of "secondary processes": locomotion, cognition, memory, perception, and rational thought and action.

Once the ego was considered to be more than a mediator, psychoanalytically oriented clinicians became much more interested in their clients' strengths as well as in their neurotic difficulties. In their diagnostic assessments, they now try to determine what gives the client mature pleasure, what parts of the psyche are *not* involved in conflict, and which dimensions of the personality do *not* need to be modified. The psychoanalytically oriented social worker asks, for example, "Have the ego's defenses been overdeveloped?" "Is the client's social situation such that these defenses are necessary adaptations to the environment—for example, a decrepit ghetto?" (48)?

One of the most important ego functions to which the analytically oriented clinician gives much attention is how the client defends against anxiety. When an impulse such as a sexual wish or an aggressive desire is activated, and the person feels that further acknowledgment of the impulse will conflict with ethical mandates or other superego commands, he erects defenses against experiencing the impulses.

Whenever the ego senses that acting on an impulse or even just feeling it will create danger, the ego produces anxiety. The anxiety serves as a *signal* of the impending danger and offers opposition to the emergence of unacceptable impulses. Such opposition is referred to as *defense* (1).

Some of the defenses utilized by the ego are *repression, reaction formation, isolation, projection, turning against the self, regression,* and *undoing* (17). Repression bars from consciousness the id impulse that creates anxiety so that in the individual's conscious life the forbidden wish does not exist. Reaction formation is a mechanism whereby one of a pair of ambivalent attitudes is rendered unconscious by overemphasis on the other—e.g., an individual may find himself feeling uncomfortable with certain hateful feelings; therefore, he overemphasizes his love. Isolation is a defense used to protect the individual against the danger he would feel if he experienced certain emotions in association with certain thoughts—e.g., in order not to feel the full impact of anger, a person might experience the angry thoughts consciously but not permit herself to feel the intensity of her rage, or she might feel the physiological accompaniments of rage, such as rapid heartbeat, but not have any angry ideas at her conscious disposal.

In projection, the individual attributes unacceptable wishes to some other person—e.g., "You have homosexual fantasies toward me, not I toward you." When the individual feels certain emotions toward another person but finds these emotions taboo, he may use the defense mechanism of turning against the self. For example, rather than feeling rage toward another person, particularly one who is valued, loved, or feared, the individual abuses and demeans himself instead.

If adaptation is difficult or reality presents a danger, one may use the defense mechanism of regression—i.e., the return to a less mature form of psychological functioning. For example, a child of three of four who has difficulty coping with anger about the arrival of a baby sister may regress by soiling and urinating in bed, even though he has been toilet-trained for some time. Undoing is an action whose purpose is to disprove the harm the individual unconsciously imagines may be caused if he were consciously to feel certain sexual or aggressive wishes.

In all defense mechanisms there is always an attempt to repudiate an impulse (17). To the id's "yes" the ego defends itself by saying "no," thus avoiding the danger of the forbidden impulse coming to consciousness. The ego can and does use as a defense anything available to it that will lessen the danger arising from the demands of an unwanted instinctual drive (4).

Every good psychosocial assessment should involve a description of the client's major defense mechanisms, other ego functions and dysfunctions, major superego mandates, and frightening id wishes; it is particularly important that it be noted how these various parts of the psychic apparatus interact.

The Topographic Point of View

The topographical approach refers to the *conscious, preconscious,* and *unconscious* states of mind. The conscious is that part of our mental activities of which we are fully aware at any time; the preconscious refers to thoughts and feelings that can be brought into consciousness quite easily; the unconscious refers to thoughts, feelings, and desires of which we are not aware but which powerfully influence all of our behavior. The unconscious not only consists of drives, defenses, and superego mandates but it also contains memories of events and attitudes that have been repressed (18, 19). It is only when unconscious wishes are discharged in fantasies, dreams, or neurotic symptoms that the unconscious becomes known. Otherwise it acts silently and completely beyond the awareness of the observer.

One of the chief characteristics of the unconscious is the *primary process,* a type of mental functioning radically different from rational thinking. The primary process is best observed in dreams, which are frequently illogical or primitive, and do not adhere to the laws of reality. Contrasted to the primary process is the *secondary process,* which governs conscious thinking. It is rational, logical, and obeys all the rules of reality.

As has been indicated earlier in this chapter, one of the basic tenets of psychoanalysis is that the unconscious is always operative in all behavior, adaptive and maladaptive. It accounts for how hostile or loving a person is. Unconscious wishes, unconscious defenses, and unconscious superego mandates play a major role in sexual choices, sexual inhibitions, or sexual abstinence. They determine, in many ways, how fulfilled or unfulfilled the person is on the job. The topographic point of view states that to understand and help a client, whether it be an individual or a group, the unconscious meaning of the client's behavior should be well understood. The psychoanalytically oriented practitioner always wants to know the unconscious purpose of painful symptomology. For example, the practitioner asks himself questions like: What unconscious protection and unconscious gratification does this client get from his ulcers or migraine headaches? What unconscious protection and gratification does this spouse derive from her mate's constant criticisms?

Because unconscious wishes, defenses, and memories strongly influence interpersonal behavior as well as the individual client's self-image and self-esteem, the unconscious appears to be an indispensable concept in diagnosis and treatment.

The Genetic Point of View

Another perspective from psychoanalytic theory that can be useful to the clinician is the genetic or developmental point of view. According to this perspective, all human beings are recapitulating their pasts in the present. The man who hates his boss is frequently fighting an old battle with his father. The woman who is uncomfortable with her husband may be seeking revenge on one or both of her parents. Parents who cannot cope with their children's dependency, sexuality, or aggressiveness have probably not come to terms with their own childish wishes.

In assessing maladaptive behavior, an understanding of the client's psychosexual development seems crucial for treatment planning. For example, Mr. Jones's alcoholism may be a manifestation of acute problems on the trust-mistrust or oral level and he may prefer to suck on a whiskey bottle than depend on the love of another person whom he despises and distrusts. On the other hand, alcoholic Mr. Smith may have all kinds of sexual anxieties and therefore his alcoholism may be interpreted as a type of behavior that is safer for him than sex is. Treatment for the two men will have to be different. In Mr. Jone's case, he will probably need a therapeutic experience that will enable him to express his oral sadism and mistrust of maternal figures, including the therapist. However, if Mr. Smith's alcoholism is a regression that serves to protect him against sexual anxiety at an oedipal level, the therapeutic task, in all probability, will be to help him feel more comfortable with his unacceptable incestuous wishes and frightening phallic sadism.

During the first five or six years of life, a child experiences a series of dynamically differentiated stages that are of extreme importance for the formation of personality. In the oral stage (from birth to about age eighteen months) the mouth is the principal focus of dynamic activity, in the anal phase (from approximately eighteen months to three years) the child turns her interests to elimination functions, in the phallic stage (age three to six) she forms the rudiments of sexual identity, in latency (ages seven to eleven) erotic and libidinal interests are quiescent, and at puberty there is a recrudescence of biological drives, particularly of the oedipal interests that emerged during the phallic phase. Ambivalence toward parents and other authority figures is also characteristic of puberty and adolescence (16, 18).

According to Freudian theory, children are *polymorphously perverse*; that is, they can derive pleasure from bodily activity. From the ages of three to five, the child engages in extensive sexual exploration and tries to find out where babies come from. Frequently she believes that babies are conceived by eating and are born through the rectum; often, a child regards sexual intercourse as an act of sadism. Sex never remains a subject of indifference for any child and even if she is uninformed about sexual matters, there will be fantasies about them.

A phase of development that is a central complex in psychoanalytic theory and occurs in the phallic period is the Oedipal complex. The familial arrangements that a child experiences in most societies creates in him a wish to replace the parent of the same sex and to have bodily contact with the parent of the opposite sex. One of the consequences of the oedipal conflict is castration anxiety in the male and penis envy in the female. The boy anticipates castration as a retaliation for his murderous thoughts about his father and the girl envies the penis because it appears to be a valuable piece of property. The penis is valuable to the girl because it is a part of the father whom she treasures and also because all children want to own everything they see that is not theirs.

Although Freud contended that penis envy is a biological fact of life, most contemporary authors believe that it is a cultural phenomenon in that girls are frequently educated to idealize boys and men. The abundance of clinical data from the play of girls in play-therapy and the associations from the dreams and fantasies of women in intensive psychotherapy strongly suggest that penis envy derives from interpersonal experiences with family members.

Responding to the strong denial that many individuals demonstrate regarding penis envy, Reuben Fine has stated: "It should be emphasized that penis envy is essentially a clinical observation about what women feel, not a derogation of women. Psychoanalysis believes very strongly in the liberation of women, and should be looked upon as one of the major movements in that direction" (13, p. 13).

What is sometimes overlooked in the history of the psychoanalytic movement is that Freud worked very hard to bring women into the profession. Many of his outstanding colleagues, such as Helene Deutsch, Marie Bonaparte, Lou Andreas-Salome, Hilda Doolittle, Ruth Mack Brunswick, and Joan Riviere, have described how psychoanalysis, more than many other profession, helped women achieve and fulfill themselves professionally (15).

Erik Erikson greatly expanded Freud's theory of genetic stages of instinctual development by placing development into a social and cultural matrix (5). He emphasized the tasks of ego mastery presented by each stage of maturation. His eight nuclear conflicts or developmental crises—trust vs. mistrust, autonomy vs. shame and doubt, initiative vs. guilt, industry vs.

inferiority, identity vs. role diffusion, intimacy vs. isolation, generativity vs. stagnation, and integrity vs. despair—correspond to Freud's stages of orality, anality, genitality, latency, puberty, etc.

According to Erikson, the human being not only unfolds according to predetermined biological phases, but human maturation cannot be viewed apart from the social context in which it transpires. For example, an infant's functioning during the oral phase cannot be assessed without taking into consideration transactions with the mother. If the infant and mother mutually gratify each other in many basic ways—e.g., during feeding, playing, etc.— the child will learn to "trust" rather than "distrust" his environment. Similarly, if the child is helped to forego certain pleasures and take on some frustration during toilet training (anal phase) he will develop a sense of "autonomy" rather than feel "shame and doubt." If parents help their child feel comfortable with his sexual interests and impulses, the child will be more apt to participate creatively and constructively in interpersonal relationships, and be "industrious" rather than feel "inferior."

Another important concept in Freudian theory is that of fixation. The term "fixation" is used to describe certain individuals who have never matured beyond a certain point of psychosocial development and are unable, in many ways, to mature further. Individuals may be fixated at any level of development—oral, anal, phallic-oedipal, etc. As part of the diagnostic assessment, the therapist has to determine where the client is fixated. Has she ever learned to trust? Or has she ever established sufficient autonomy? Or, perhaps she has never mastered the maturational task of learning how to relate intimately with another human being?

It is not always easy to determine whether a particular symptom or interpersonal difficulty is a manifestation of regression or fixation. In order to be sure, the therapist has to take into consideration the many dimensions of the client's current functioning, history, and transference reactions to the therapist.

The therapist is not only eager to establish what stage of development the client's conflict is at, but perhaps of more importance, he wants to know how significant others have responded to the patient's needs at a particular stage of development. A client suffering from alcoholism and one suffering from drug addiction may both be trying to cope with anxieties emanating from the oral period. However, in one case the client may have been underfed and in the other instance, she may have been overfed and indulged. If the client has been overfed she will need an experience in therapy where she can learn to take on some frustration, develop controls, and defer gratification—that is, be weaned. If, on the other hand, she was insufficiently nourished, the therapist will attempt to create an atmosphere in which aggressive desires and oral hunger can be expressed and eventually be considered more acceptable to the patient.

As has already been implied, knowledge of the patient's maturational deficits not only helps the clinician understand the client's maladaptive behavior with more certainty, but appreciation of the client's maturational con-flicts provide guides for treatment. Is the homosexual patient defending against an oedipal conflict? Or, is he identifying with an oral mother so that by feeding his sexual partner, he is vicariously ministering to his own oral hunger? Is the gambler storing up "gold" in his fantasies, which would signify an anal problem, or is he omnipotently striving to be an emperor, a conflict that evolves from the early oral phase when the baby wants to be a narcis-sistic king? Is the addict pricking herself in a phallic manner or is she feeding herself in an oral manner? These are crucial questions that the psychoanal-ytically oriented clinician will ask because he is very dedicated to the notion that each client's past participates and shapes current functioning.

The Dynamic Point of View

The dynamic point of view refers to Freud's instinct theory, which is con-cerned with libidinal and aggressive drives. Recognizing the interaction of nature and nurture in the development of the human being, the drives or instincts represent the "nature" factor (43). An instinct has four character-istics: source, aim, object, and impetus. The source is a bodily condition or need—e.g., hunger, sex, or aggression. The aim is always to achieve grati-fication. The object includes both that on which the need is focused—e.g., food—and all the activities necessary to secure it—going to the refrigerator, ingesting, masticating, etc. The impetus of an instinct is its strength, which is determined by the forces or intensity of the underlying need—e.g., hunger, sexual need, aggressive wish—and these needs vary in quantity in different individuals or in the same individual at different times.

In making a diagnostic evaluation, the clinician first wants to ascertain if his client's instincts are being gratified. Is he getting enough food and en-joying it? If not, why? Is he realistically being deprived and/or is he arrang-ing to feel deprived? Does gratifying the hunger instinct create anxiety for the client and is that why he does not want to eat too much? Similar questions may be asked of the client regarding his sexual life and elimination habits. The answers to these questions help the therapist pinpoint conflict, plan in-tervention, gauge the patient's motivation and determine his capacity for a working relationship with the therapist.

The Economic Point of View

The economic point of view stresses the quantitative factor in mental func-tioning. According to this principle, all behavior is regulated by the need to dispose of psychological energy. Energy is discharged by forming "cathexes"; that is, investing a person or an object with psychological energy. Something or somebody is cathected if the object or person is emotionally significant to the person.

Freud felt that energy is needed to fuel the psychic structure and he saw this energy coming from the sexual drives. Later, Heinz Hartmann concluded that the ego works with "deaggressivized" and "desexualized" energy, which he called "neutral" energy (29). It should be stated that the energy concept is among the most controversial in the field and many theoreticians contend that it can be dispensed with entirely (13).

Interpersonal Relationships, Culture, and Values

According to psychoanalytic theory, how an individual relates to others is essentially based on how she experienced herself vis-à-vis family members. The vicissitudes of interpersonal relationships depend very heavily on transferences from the individual's family structure. Although the concept of transference is largely used in connection with psychotherapy, it is a universal characteristic of human beings. The kinds of experiences that offer gratification in the family tend to be pursued while those that frustrate the individual tend to be avoided. Moat relationships in adult life reflect the kinds of gratifications and frustrations that the person experienced in her own nuclear family.

Freud suggested that the child proceeds from a narcissistic stage, in which she is concerned only with herself, to an anaclitic stage, in which she is dependent upon somebody else, and eventually to a stage of object love (20). In object love, there is a mutuality between the person and another human being and this love involves a synthesis of tender and erotic feelings toward the opposite sex. Hartmann has proposed a movement in relationships from those that are "need-gratifying" to those where there is mutuality and "constancy" in the relationship (29). Fine has suggested that relationships start off as "attachment" in infancy and move to "admiration," (of the parents), "sexuality," then to "intimacy," and finally to "devotion" (12). All love relationships, according to Fine, have these phases of interpersonal maturation as components.

In his early work, especially in *Totem and Taboo* (23), Freud claimed that the same psychological mechanisms were to be found in all cultures. While the same libidinal and aggressive drives exist in all human beings and all cultures, they are molded in different ways by different societies.

One of the most notable attempts to unify psychoanalysis and the study of culture was made by Kardiner (34, 35). He coined the term "basic personality structure" to designate a group of character traits in the modal individual of a particular culture. This concept was a refinement of the older term "national character." An example of an American character trait is "ambitiousness."

The question of whether there are any values inherent in psychoanalysis has been much debated. Freud did not speak of values too much but did take the position that the mature person is one who can love and work. Fine has attempted to extend Freud's image of love and work and has argued that psychotherapy is the first scientific attempt to make people happy (10). His "analytic ideal" involves the pursuit of pleasure, the release of positive emotions, elimination of hatred and other negative emotions, enjoying sex, acquiring a meaningful role in the family and a sense of identity in a larger society, enagaging in some satisfying form of work, pursuing some form of creative activity, and being able to communicate with other people.

A Psychoanalytic View of Psychopathology

According to psychoanalytic theory, whenever an individual is suffering from a neurotic symptom, such as an obsession, phobia, or psychosomatic disease, psychic conflict is always present. The individual's defenses—e.g., projection, denial—which have been used to protect him against ideas, thoughts, or memories that are unbearable and cause anxiety, have broken down. As mentioned earlier in this chapter, anxiety is a warning to the person that some unacceptable thought or action will reach consciousness (21). If the drive is too strong or the defense too weak, anxiety erupts and the person forms a neurotic symptom. The symptom expresses concomitantly the individual's impulse and his dread of the impulse. In a phobia—e.g., fear of going out on the streets—two variables are at work: the very situation that the individual fears— the street—and also the fact that the street excites him. The stimulation that is induced causes anxiety because the excitement emanates from sexual fantasies that are unacceptable. A symptom is often referred to as a "compromise formation" because it is a composite expression of the patient's wishes, anxiety, defenses, and fears.

> Bob, an eighteen-year-old college freshman, reported to his social worker that he was plagued by obsessive thoughts and compulsions. The obsessive thoughts took the form of constantly wanting to blurt out in class, "Drop dead, drop dead!" The thoughts created anxiety and interfered with his concentration. In addition, when Bob left his dormitory room he was compelled to make sure that the door was locked. Even after he checked it several times, he had to go back to make sure it was closed.
>
> As the social worker and Bob reviewed the client's history it became quite clear that Bob was very angry about being away from home for the first time in his life. At home and in his community, Bob was loved by all and felt very important; at college, he was one of many and not particularly well known. This situation punctured his narcissism and activated a great deal of anger toward his college peers and toward college authorities. However, the anger that Bob felt about missing home

and being in college was unacceptable to him. He repudiated his dependency feelings (denial), and repressed his anger. Nonetheless, his drives were intense and his defenses were not strong enough to negate them. Consequently, his anger erupted in the obsession, "Drop dead, drop dead!"

Unconsciously, Bob wished that his parents and friends would perhaps surprise him by visiting him on campus. Unconsciously, he wished to leave his door open so they could walk in and be there when he returned from classes.

As Bob was able to share with his social worker his fantasies of kissing and hugging his parents and being a young boy again, his symptoms diminished. As he could acknowledge his anger and his dependency and particularly his wishes to be bathed and fed by mother and cuddled by father, he did not need to use as much energy to defend himself and his functioning improved.

Freud never abandoned the idea that the roots of a psychoneurosis lie in a disturbance of the libidinal life of childhood. However, he soon recognized that the stories his patients told him of having been sexually seduced in childhood were, in fact, fantasies rather than real memories, even though the patients themselves believed them to be true. Although this discovery was at first a blow to Freud, he made a step forward by recognizing that, far from being limited in childhood, such exceptional, traumatic events as seductions, sexual interests, and activities are a normal part of human psychic life from earliest infancy on (4).

In his research on the psychoneurotic symptom, Freud compared a symptom to a dream in that both are compromise formations between one or more repressed impulses and those forces of the personality that oppose the entrance of forbidden impulses into conscious thoughts and behavior. Freud was able to demonstrate that neurotic symptoms, like the elements of a dream, had meaning. Symptoms, like dreams, can be shown to be the disguised and distorted expressions of unconscious fantasies.

By permitting a partial and disguised emergence of an id wish via the psychoneurotic symptom—e.g., Bob's obsession, "Drop dead!"—the ego is able to avoid some of the anxiety it would otherwise develop. By permitting an impulse, a fantasized gratification (like in a dream) that is disguised and distorted, the ego can avoid the displeasure of experiencing extreme anxiety. By coping with his unacceptable thoughts through an obsession, Bob was able to ward off his murderous wishes, his anxiety, and his guilt. This is what is known as the *primary gain* of a neurosis; that is, warding off a dangerous impulse from consciousness and diminishing anxiety and guilt.

Secondary gain refers to the efforts of the ego to exploit the gratifying possibilities of a neurotic symptom. For example, a child may enjoy the overprotection and solicitude he receives when he brings to his parents' attention his school phobia. Similarly, an adult with a psychosomatic problem such as an ulcer may be able to get tender love and care when he complains of acute stomachaches.

It is important to recognize that the differences between the functioning of a "normal" individual and that of a neurotic is one of degree. All individuals have id impulses and most people experience in themselves sadistic, masochistic, incestuous, or murderous wishes that are not acceptable to them. When defenses, which all individuals use, are not strong enough to cope with id wishes, anxiety erupts and symptoms appear.

Fine has stated:

> From the beginning, therapy and theory in psychoanalysis have developed together. The significance of this simultaneous development is that the hypotheses of psychoanalysis have been subject to empirical tests at every step of the way. At an early point in the history of the science, it became apparent that the difference between the "patient" and the "nonpatient" or the difference between the "neurotic" and the "normal" is only one of degree. Furthermore, the method that psychoanalysis developed was one which relies very intensively on a deep and profound study of each individual. As a result, the kind of therapy that was practiced and is practiced now is also a type of research. (13, pp. 6–7)

Psychoanalysis: A Form of Therapy

The psychoanalytic theory of therapeutic intervention parallels its metapsychological orientation to personality functioning. Just as the psychoanalytic theory of human behavior contends that the individual's adaptation to life cannot be fully understood unless the meaning of id wishes, ego defenses, superego admonitions, and history are exposed, a similar perspective is needed in therapy. Clients cannot be substantially helped, psychoanalysis alleges, unless they become aware of certain id wishes, face persistent superego admonitions, and recognize how they are distorting the present and perceiving it as if it were part of their childhood. If neurotic and other dysfunctional behavior are to be significantly altered, clients must become sensitized to how they are unconsciously arranging a good part of their own misery.

Free Association and the Fundamental Rule

To help clients become aware of how they are unconsciously arranging to distort their love and work relationships and not achieving the happiness they consciously desire, they are asked by the therapist to observe "the fundamental rule" (25). This rule prescribes that the client should say *everything* that comes to mind—feelings, thoughts, memories, dreams, and fantasies. While clients in psychoanalysis usually "free associate" on a couch and are seen several times a week, the "free association" rule has much pertinence to social work practice. Many social work clinicians fail to appreciate that one of the most helpful experiences they can offer their clients is to quietly listen to them without interrupting with questions, supportive remarks, or interpretations. Social workers frequently feel that "to earn their keep" they must talk. Often, their talking is to quell their own anxiety (38) and does not really help their clients grow (46).

As the client tells an unintrusive and empathetic listener what she feels and thinks, the client begins to see for herself how she is writing her own script and arranging for her own successes and failures. If she talks uninterruptedly, she will hear herself verbalize fantasies to battle, wishes to provoke, desires to seduce, fears of interacting, and urges to be mistreated.

If the social worker assumes a neutral position and does not side with or oppose the client as he talks about his conflicted marriage, upsetting relationship with employer or family members, the client's self-esteem usually rises. The client begins to feel very much like a child who has confessed a misdeed to an understanding and empathetic parent who does not censure him for what he has reported. Usually, this experience reduces anxiety and heightens self-confidence inasmuch as the therapist is experienced as a benign superego.

As the client is helped to talk without being questioned, advised, or supported, he begins to recall memories that influence his functioning in the present. He begins to see how his battle with a colleague is part of an unresolved problem with a sibling or that his oversensitivity to his wife's demands may be due to his wish to keep her as the punitive mother of his past.

As the client is not judged, censured, or criticized for her productions, she becomes less hateful and more loving. Rather than demean others when they do not agree with her, she tries to recapitulate what her therapist has done with her—understand and empathize. As she is less judgmental with relatives, friends, and colleagues, they appreciate her more.

Resistance

Although more clients welcome the idea of saying everything that is on their minds and usually feel better during the early stages of the therapeutic encounter, eventually the therapy becomes painful and creates anxiety. As clients discover parts of themselves that have been repressed, confront sexual and aggressive impulses, and recover embarrassing memories, they begin to feel guilt and shame. Then they may become silent, evasive, or want to quit the therapy altogether. Or, clients may discuss certain incidents from their pasts or current circumstances and then become angry at the therapist for not reassuring, praising, or admonishing them.

When clients stop producing material and cease to examine themselves, we refer to this kind of behavior as *resistance*. Resistance is any action or attitude of the client's that impedes the course of therapeutic work. Inasmuch as every client, to some extent, wants unconsciously to preserve the status quo, all therapy must be carried on in the face of some resistance (46).

What is referred to as a defense in the client's daily life—e.g., projection, denial, repression, etc.—are resistances in the therapy. If, for example, a client has a tendency to project his anger onto his spouse and other individuals, in the therapy he will try to avoid examining his own angry thoughts and feelings and will instead report how his wife, friends, and relatives are hostile to him. From time to time he will also accuse the therapist of being contemptuous toward him.

Resistance is not created by the therapy. The therapeutic situation activates anxiety and the client then uses habitual mechanisms to oppose the therapist and the therapy (26). To a greater or lesser degree resistances are present from the beginning to the end of treatment (24).

Psychoanalytic therapy is characterized by a thorough and systematic examination of resistances. The therapist attempts to uncover how the client resists, what she is resisting, and why she is doing so. Usually the purpose of resistance is to avoid such painful emotion as guilt or shame, and frequently the guilt or shame has been aroused by an unacceptable id impulse (17, 26).

In contrast to other forms of therapy that evade resistance or attempt to overcome them by suggestion, praise, punishment, drugs, shock, or persuasion, a psychoanalytically oriented therapy seeks to uncover the cause, purpose, mode, and history of the resistances (26, 36).

Resistance takes many forms. To ward off anxiety, a client can resist treatment by coming late to sessions, absenting himself altogether, becoming very silent, refusing to pay fees, or a variety of other direct and indirect ways. The psychoanalytically oriented therapist takes the position that behavior in and of itself does not tell us very much. A resistance like lateness to appointments can have different meanings for different clients. For one client, it is a way of warding off the anxiety that is connected with feelings of intimacy. For another client, it can be a way of expressing contempt toward the therapist, and for still another client, it may be a way of trying to see if the therapist is sufficiently concerned about him, and if the therapist will ask questions about the lateness.

It is extremely important to hear the client's associations about his resistive behavior. Frequently, it takes a good deal of time before the therapist can be absolutely certain just what the resistive behavior is all about. Furthermore, as Langs has pointed out, one must always consider the therapist's possible contribution to the formation of the client's resistive behavior (39). Is the therapist behaving in such a way that the client wants to come late, not cooperate, or quit the treatment?

A resistance that is often overlooked in social work practice is when the client utilizes his situation as a resistance. People often seek out a social worker because they have some situational problem—a poor marriage, a conflicted parent-child relationship, an unsatisfactory job, etc. While a client's spouse, parent, employer, or teacher may not always be mature individuals responsive to the client's needs, it is very important to recognize that when clients continually focus on the problems that significant others impose on them, this is usually a sign of resistance. Most individuals would rather believe that their unhappy marriages, unsatisfactory jobs, or unstimulating interpersonal relationships are caused by forces outside themselves. Frequently, clients hope, and sometimes demand, that the social worker manipulate their environments and change the spouse, boss, or teacher. However, what is of most help to these individuals is to see the many ways they are determining their own fates and writing their own scripts. Usually, when the social worker ascribes all of the client's difficulties to the latter's situation, he is overidentified with the client and does not want to see the client's contributions to the situational difficulties.

In sum, when an individual enters into a therapeutic relationship, part of the person unconsciously works against progress. All clients, no matter how much they consciously want their lives to be different and no matter how much they are suffering, still fear change. Resistances are facts of therapeutic life, and the unconscious reasons for their unique expression must be understood by both client and therapist. Clients resist therapy for many reasons. They worry that they will be punished for their aggression, entrapped for their sexual wishes, demeaned for their dependency, and scoffed at for their childishness. It takes much patient work on the client's and therapist's part to resolve resistances (46).

Transference

Perhaps the most valuable contribution of psychoanalytic theory is the concept of "transference." Anyone who is engaged in helping others make changes in their lives recognizes that in the face of all logic and reason, the client may often behave in an obstinate manner. Therapeutic progress is always hindered by the client's major resistance, the transferance—feelings, wishes, fears, and defenses that influence the client's perceptions of the therapist. Transferential reactions are unconscious attempts by the client to recapitulate with the therapist types of interpersonal interactions similar to those she experienced with significant persons in the past. Every client experiences the therapist not only in terms of how she objectively is, but in terms of how she wishes the therapist to be and fears the therapist might be (24).

If therapists do not understand how they are being experienced by their clients, they cannot be very helpful to them. Each client responds to questions, clarifications, interpretations, directions, or environmental manipulation in terms of her transference to the therapist. If Ms. Brown loves her therapist, she will be inclined to accept and constructively utilize his therapeutic interventions; if she hates the therapist, even the most neutral question, "How do you feel?" for example, will be suspect. Finally, if she has mixed feelings toward the therapist, she will respond to virtually all interventions with ambivalence.

One of the major tasks of the analytically oriented clinician is to help the client see how and why she experiences the therapist as she does. Why does the client act like a compliant child and accept everything the therapist says? Or, why does she argue with the therapist every time the latter says something? Why is the therapist's silence experienced by one client as rejection and by another as love?

Helping clients experience and understand their transference reactions is far from just a didactic exercise. As clients see that their perceptions of and responses to the therapist are similar to their perceptions and responses to significant others, they begin to get some conviction and some understanding of their own role and their own contribution to their interpersonal difficulties.

While transference reactions are always traceable to childhood, there is not a simple one-to-one correspondence between the past and the present, although sometimes there is a direct repetition, such as when the client is quite convinced that the therapist is almost identical to his father, mother, or siblings. On other occasions, there can be a compensatory fantasy to make up for what was lacking in childhood (9).

When the therapist recognizes that transference exists every time a client meets with a clinician, the therapist can look at her therapeutic results more objectively. If the client wants her to be an omnipotent parent to whom he can cling, then he will fight interventions aimed to help him become more autonomous. If the client wants the therapist to be a sibling rival, then he will use the therapist's interventions to continue his sibling fight. Because the client views all of the therapist's interventions through the lens of his transference, the therapist should explore with the client why he wants to perceive the therapist the way he does.

Transference exists in all human relationships. We transfer onto others, parental and sibling introjects, unacceptable id wishes, superego mandates, ego-ideals, and many other unconscious elements. There is no such thing as a client who has "no transference" or in whom transference fails to develop. As clinician and client accept transference as another fact of therapeutic life and constantly study the client's transference responses, they gain an appreciation of the nature of the client's conflicts and aspects of his history that are contributing to his dysfunctional behavior (41, 44).

Countertransference

Countertransference is the same dynamic phenomenon as transference, except that it refers to those unconscious wishes and defenses of the therapist that interfere with his objective perception and mature treatment of the client. Frequently, the client represents for the therapist an object of the past onto whom past feelings and wishes are projected.

Insufficient attention is paid to countertransference reactions in social work schools and social agencies; yet it is probably one of the most important variables in client drop-out. If, for example, the social worker has unresolved problems connected with his own aggression, he may need to placate or be ingratiating with his client. The client, therefore, cannot improve because it is not safe to express aggression toward the therapist and she may have to act out unverbalized hatred by quitting treatment. Similarly, if a therapist is threatened by his own unconscious homosexual feelings, he may be unable to detect homosexual implications in a client's material or may perceive them where they do not exist. Not feeling understood, the client may leave the treatment situation in frustration.

Therapy usually proceeds well when the clinician likes the client. If the clinician does not really care for the person she treats, this will be reflected in her interventions and the client will sense it. While a positive countertransference is a desirable attitude, like a positive transference, it must be studied carefully (9).

A temptation for many social workers is to love their clients too much. When this occurs, the client is not perceived accurately or treated objectively. In their overidentification, social workers often support clients against their real or fantasized opponents rather than helping them understand their own interpersonal conflicts. Overidentification frequently takes place in working on parent-child and marital conflicts where the social worker forms a love and beloved relationship with one spouse or member of a parent-child dyad and covertly or overtly supports the client in his attacks on other family members.

Therapists are human beings and are more like their clients than unlike them (30). Because therapists have wishes, defenses, and anxieties, it is inevitable that their vulnerabilities will be activated in the therapeutic situation and that they will feel hostility toward some of those whom they want to help. It is often difficult for social workers to acknowledge their hostility toward their clients because in our profession angry feelings are considered a liability. Frequently, hostile feelings are denied and repressed, and so they manifest themselves in disguised and subtle forms. Two common expressions of disguised hostility are the use of diagnostic labels and alterations of therapeutic plans (9).

When clients are distrustful, isolate themselves from the clinician, miss appointments, and are unrevealing, it is quite understandable that the therapist gets discouraged, questions her own skills, and feels quite angry at the client, who does not show any progress. In anger, the therapist can give the client a diagnostic label that usually implies deep pathology and poor prognosis. For example, it is infrequent that the label "borderline" is used benignly. Rarely are social work categories such as psychopath, sociopath, hard-to-reach, poorly motivated, ambulatory schizophrenic, pseudoneurotic schizophrenia, acting-out-character disorder, or narcissistic character disorder used empathetically and with warmth and concern. In the days of Mary Richmond, the social worker would honestly and simply say, "Client uncooperative, case closed!" Today, a closing summary might read: "The client's motivation was poor, the quality of his object relations was shallow, his ego was fragmented, his superego had many lacunae, and his transference was negative. Repeated attempts to help him mature were highly resisted. Case closed."

Not only do pejorative diagnostic labels usually denote a negative countertransference, but the constant changing of therapeutic modalities can also be an expression of hostility toward the client. Many a client has been placed in a group so that the therapist could subtly encourage the group members to attack the client. Family therapy has been abused in this manner, too. Occasionally, short-term treatment can be prescribed in order to reject the client. Often drugs, shock therapy, and backward isolation are utilized in the service of an unrecognized negative countertransference. Like transference, positive and negative countertransference are ubiquitous and should always be understood.

Technical Procedures in Psychoanalytic Psychotherapy

As the client talks about what is on his mind, he will run into resistances and transference reactions that evolve from his own unique psychodynamics. Much of the analytically oriented therapist's efforts are devoted to helping the client understand his unique transference reactions and his unique resistances. What are the specific activities of the therapist that will help the client resolve his conflicts?

One of the major tasks of the analytically oriented therapist is to *listen*. As the client produces material, themes emerge and the therapist *asks questions* so that persistent themes receive further elaboration. As certain resistances and other maladaptive behavior become clear to the therapist, she *confronts* the client with it; that is, she draws the client's attention to a particular phenomenon—e.g., persistent lateness to appointments—and tries to help him recognize what he has been avoiding and will have to be further understood. *Clarification*, which involves bringing the psychological phenomena with which the client has been confronted (and which he is now more willing to consider) into sharp focus usually follows confrontation. It involves the "digging out" of significant details from the past that contribute toward the etiology of the phenomenon (26, 44). *Interpretation* of the psychodynamic meaning of the patient's thoughts, feelings, and fantasies, especially in terms of their psychogenetic origin, is the hallmark of psychoanalytic therapy. Its goal is *insight*; that is, the client achieves more self-understanding. *Working through* is the integration of understanding by repeating, deepening, and extending the understanding of resistances and transference. Finally, the client *synthesizes* the insights by working out an adequate way of living in which anxieties are kept to a minimum and pleasure is derived from living.

As we have already suggested, effective *listening* by the clinician inevitably reduces anxiety and guilt, raises self-esteem, and unleashes energy for more constructive problem-solving. An attentive listener must demonstrate that he has grasped the essential points of his client's story. This is frequently done by asking pertinent questions that truly engage the client, clarify ambiguities, and complete a picture of the client's external pressures and internal stresses (33).

In order to help the client become aware of the unconscious forces that are contributing to his problems, the therapist has to *confront* him with certain behavior of which he is unaware, such as absences from interviews after expressing warm feelings toward the therapist. It is extremely important, when confronting a client, that the therapist has enough evidence available to support the confrontation and some assurance that the confrontation will be meaningful to the client (26). Usually a confrontation is most meaningful to the client when the latter has some conviction, himself, about the issues being presented by the therapist.

It is not enough for the client to become aware of an impulse, wish, or idea that has been unconscious; it is equally important that he understand why he is seeking the gratification of the impulse or wish, and what effect it has on his life.

After Mr. Sidney recognized that he was late for interviews with the therapist because he felt hostile toward him, he needed help in clarifying some of the dynamics of his hostility. By studying his transference reactions to the therapist he slowly realized that he was afraid of "falling in love with older men." The therapist, after Mr. Sidney spoke of several memories of his father and how he yearned for him as a boy, could clarify for Mr. Sidney that he was avoiding looking at how much he missed a father, and how much he secretly craved to hug, kiss, and fondle his father.

Currently, the term "interpretation" is being used in the psychoanalytic literature to mean a variety of activities (44):

1. The therapist's inferences and conclusions regarding the unconscious meaning and significance of the client's communications and behavior
2. The communication by the therapist of his inferences and conclusions to the client
3. All comments made by the therapist—confrontations, clarifications, questions, etc.

4. Verbal interventions which are specifically aimed at bringing about dynamic change through the medium of insight.

In order to differentiate interpretation from other therapeutic activities such as confrontation and clarification, interpretation may be considered that activity which makes conscious the unconscious meaning, source, history, mode, or cause of a given psychic event (26). Interpretations are of three main types: *uncovering*, *connective*, and *integrative* (9). The uncovering interpretation is one in which some concealed wish is brought to consciousness. Sometimes the wish is expressed in the client's associations and sometimes it is inferred from the material. The inference cannot be too removed from the client's associations, otherwise it will have little significance to the client.

In the connective interpretation, the present is tied up with the past so that the client can see how he is distorting the present by waging old battles and is still seeking childish gratifications.

The integrative interpretation involves pulling together material from a variety of different sources. It is offered so that the client's problems and life situation are seen in a more adequate perspective than the way he is looking at them. Like all interpretations, integrative interpretations have to be repeated a number of times until the client is able to formulate a perspective in his own terms. With the therapist's help, as the client associates to his past and present, examines fantasies, dreams, defenses, and interpersonal relationships, the client achieves *insight*.

Insight is a dimension of psychotherapy that has been very much misunderstood. Many books, movies, and plays seem to imply that one insight will heal a neurosis. This *never* takes place. An insight has to be "worked through"—that is, elaborated, reviewed, and reconsidered—before it can have a real effect on the client's functioning.

To be effective and alter functioning, insight requires the lifting of repressions, the recovery of lost memories, the feeling of affects that were suppressed, and involves a new grasp of the significance and interrelations of events (45). Recollections take on a meaning that the client had not realized heretofore. It is in the latter connection that he will say, as Freud pointed out, "As a matter of fact I've always known it; only I never thought of it" (22).

Insight, to be effective, *always* must be accompanied with genuine affects and a real sense in the client of how she has distorted her perceptions. Usually a client verbalizes insights and there is no change in her functioning, she is defending against the recall of a memory, repressing a fantasy or an idea, or refusing to experience certain feelings.

Once the client comes to an insight—e.g., understands that her job failure is part of her battle with father—the same interpretation usually has to be reviewed several times by patient and therapist before the conflict ceases to be a problem. This is what is meant by "working through." Greenson has described working through as "referring in the main to the repetitive, progressive, and elaborate explorations of the resistances which prevent insight from leading to change . . . a variety of circular processes are set in motion by working through in which insight, memory, and behavior change influence each other" (26, p. 42).

If insights are worked through, then there will be sustained change. Symptoms and maladaptive defenses will be given up. However, "working through" is like any learning process; it takes time to integrate new ways of looking at attitudes, thoughts, and interpersonal behavior. The client characteristically moves ahead two steps and falls back one. The same issues, fears, decisions must often be "worked through" over and over before the patient can assimilate them and make them her own. When the client has worked out an adequate way of living in which anxieties can be kept to a minimum and pleasure from realistic ventures is at a maximum, *psychosynthesis* has taken place and the client is ready to enjoy work and love.

Psychoanalysis and Research

Psychoanalytically oriented psychotherapy has been subjected to evaluation on numerous occasions. The classical studies in the literature report that between fifty to seventy percent of the clients studied terminated treatment as markedly improved. The first study was published by Fenichel who reviewed the work of the Berlin Psychoanalytic Institute from 1920 to 1930 (7). In 1936, Jones reported on work done at the London Psychoanalytic Institute and, similar to Fenichel's conclusions, found that of the hundreds of patients who were involved in psychoanalytically oriented therapy, about sixty percent gave up their symptoms permanently and improved their ego functioning and interpersonal relationships substantially (32).

In 1937, Alexander reviewed the work of the Chicago Institute for Psychoanalysis from 1932 and 1937; he found that about sixty-five percent of patients treated psychoanalytically improved in their functioning and gave up maladaptive character traits and neurotic symptomology (1).

Since the 1940s, studies by Knight (37), Ferenczi (8), Feldman (6), and Strupp (49) have demonstrated that a psychoanalytically oriented therapy can enhance functioning, diminish anxiety, increase self-esteem, and improve interpersonal functioning.

It has been an old claim that psychoanalysis is untestable scientifically, but those who make the claim ignore the evidence. In their book, *The Scientific Credibility of Freud's Theories and Therapy* (14), Fisher and Greenberg tried to describe every reported experiment relevant to psychoanalysis. They concluded that it is "clearly verified" that Freud's ideas can be reduced to testable ideas and not only are the ideas testable, but they have been tested. They show that the quantity of experimental research data on Freudian ideas "greatly exceeds" that available for most other personality theories. Fisher and Greenberg reported that the existence of unconscious motivation is supported by so much scientific research that little doubt remains. In general, they were impressed with how often the results have borne out Freud's expectations.

The difficulty with much research on human beings is that it must take full account of introspective data. If one human being asks another a question, the answer is a variable one. It depends on the question and the relationship between the questioner and the questionee. Few theories, with the exception of psychoanalytic theory, allow for internal motives in doing research on human beings. Few recognize that what a subject tells the experimenter depends on many transference and countertransference factors, resistances and counterresistances, and a host of other unconscious variables.

While psychoanalysis, like all theories of personality and theories of treatment, is not perfect, and some studies have demonstrated positive outcomes, it is already clear that, psychoanalytically, psychotherapy is effective in many situations. Despite the fact that most people come to a therapist only when they have become desperate, there is evidence that individuals who undergo psychoanalytic therapy move toward what Fine has called the "analytic ideal" (10): they can love more genuinely; seek pleasure; have sexual gratification; have a feeling for life, yet one that is guided by reason; have a role in the family; have a sense of identity; be creative; work; have a role in the social order; be able to communicate; and be free of symptoms.

References

1. Alexander, F. *Five-Year Report of the Chicago Institute for Psychoanalysis*. Chicago: Chicago Institute for Psychoanalysis, 1937.
2. Allan, E. "Psychoanalytic Theory," in Francis J. Turner (ed.), *Social Work Treatment*. New York: Free Press, 1974.
3. Auden, W. *The Age of Anxiety*. New York: Random House, 1947.
4. Brenner, C. *An Elementary Textbook of Psychoanalysis*. New York: International Universities Press, 1955.
5. Erikson, Erik. *Childhood and Society*. New York: Norton, 1950.
6. Feldman, F. "Results of Psychoanalysis in Clinic Case Assignments," *Journal of the American Psychoanalytic Association*, Vol. 16 (1968).
7. Fenichel, O. *Zehn Jahre Berliner Psychoanalytisches Institute*. Berlin: Berlin Psychoanalytic Institute, 1930.
8. Ferenczi, S. "The Problem of the Termination of the Analysis," in *Final Contributions to the Problems and Methods of Psychoanalysis*. New York: Basic Books, 1955.
9. Fine, Reuben. *The Healing of the Mind*, 2nd edition. New York: Free Press, 1982.
10. ———. *The Psychoanalytic Vision*. New York: Free Press, 1981.

11. ———. *The History of Psychoanalysis.* New York: Columbia University Press, 1979.

12. ———. *Psychoanalytic Psychology.* New York: Jason Aronson, 1975.

13. ———. "Psychoanalysis," in R. Corsini (ed.), *Current Psychotherapies.* Itasca, Ill.: F. E. Peacock, Publishers, 1973.

14. Fisher, S., and R. Greenberg. *The Scientific Credibility of Freud's Theories and Therapy.* New York: Basic Books, 1977.

15. Freeman, L., and Herbert Strean. *Freud and Women.* New York: Ungar, 1981.

16. Freud, Anna. "Observations of Child Development," *The Psychoanalytic Study of the Child*, Vol. 6. New York: International Universities Press, 1951.

17. ———. *The Ego and the Mechanisms of Defense.* New York: International Universities Press, 1946.

18. Freud, Sigmund. *An Outline of Psychoanalysis*, Vol. 23, *Standard Edition.* London: Hogarth, 1939.

19. ———. *The Basic Writings of Sigmund Freud.* New York: Random House (Modern Library), 1938.

20. ———. *New Introductory Lectures on Psychoanalysis*, Vol. 22, *Standard Edition.* London: Hogarth, 1933.

21. ———. *The Ego and the Id*, Vol. 19, *Standard Edition.* London: Hogarth, 1923.

22. ———. "Introduction to Narcissism," Vol. 12, *Standard Edition.* London: Hogarth, 1914.

23. ———. "Totem and Taboo," Vol. 12, *Standard Edition.* London: Hogarth, 1913.

24. ———. "The Dynamics of Transference," Vol. 12, *Standard Edition.* London: Hogarth, 1912.

25. ———. "Freud's Psychoanalytic Procedure." Vol. 7, *Standard Edition.* London: Hogarth, 1904.

26. Greenson, R. *The Technique and Practice of Psychoanalysis.* New York: International Universities Press, 1967.

27. Hale, N. *Freud and the Americans.* New York: Oxford University Press, 1971.

28. Hamilton, G. "A Theory of Personality. Freud's Contribution to Social Work," Howard J. Parad (ed.), *Ego Psychology and Dynamic Casework.* New York: Family Service Association of America, 1958.

29. Hartmann, Heinz. *Essays on Ego Psychology.* New York: International Universities Press, 1964.

30. ———. *Ego Psychology and the Problem of Adaptation.* New York: International Universities Press, 1951.

31. Jones, E. *The Life and Work of Sigmund Freud*, Vol. 1. New York: Basic Books, 1953.

32. ———. *Decennial Report of the London Clinic of Psychoanalysis.* London: London Clinic of Psychoanalysis, 1936.

33. Kadushin, A. *The Social Work Interview.* New York: Columbia University Press, 1972.

34. Kardiner, A. *The Psychological Frontiers of Society.* New York: Columbia University Press, 1945.

35. ———. *The Individual and His Society*. New York: Columbia University Press, 1939.

36. Knight, R. "An Evaluation of Psychotherapeutic Techniques." In R. Knight and C. Friedman (eds.), *Psychoanalytic Psychiatry and Psychology*. New York: International Universities Press, 1952.

37. ———. "A Critique of the Present Status of the Psychotherapies," *Bulletin of the New York Academy of Medicine*, Vol. 25 (1949), pp. 100–114.

38. Langs, R. *Resistances and Interventions*. New York: Jason Aronson, 1981.

39. ———. *The Bipersonal Field*. New York: Jason Aronson, 1976.

40. Meltzoff, J., and M. Kornreich. *Research in Psychotherapy*. New York: Atherton Press, 1970.

41. Menninger, K. *Theory of Psychoanalytic Technique*. New York: Basic Books, 1958.

42. Parsons, Talcott. *The Social System*. Glencoe, Ill.: Free Press, 1951.

43. Rapaport, D. *The Oranization and Pathology of Thought*. New York: Columbia University Press, 1951.

44. Sandler, J. *The Patient and the Analyst*. New York: International Universities Press, 1973.

45. Schafer, R. "The Interpretation of Transference and the Conditions for Loving," *Journal of the American Psychoanalytic Association*, Vol. 25, No. 2 (1977), pp. 335–362.

46. Strean, Herbert F. *Resolving Resistances in Psychotherapy*. New York: Wiley, 1983.

47. ———. *The Sexual Dimension*. New York: Free Press, 1983.

48. ———. *Psychoanalytic Theory and Social Work Practice*. New York: Free Press, 1979.

49. Strupp, H. "Ferment in Psychoanalysis and Psychotherapy," in B. Wolman (ed.), *Success and Failure in Psychoanalysis and Psychotherapy*. New York: Macmillan, 1972.

50. Sullivan, H. *The Interpersonal Theory of Psychiatry*. New York: Norton, 1953.

Annotated Listing of Key References

FINE, REUBEN. *The Healing of the Mind*, 2nd edition. New York: Free Press, 1982.
A clear, concise description of the psychoanalytic treatment process. With case illustrations, describes the honeymoon phase of treatment, the first treatment crisis, resolving resistances, and coping with transference problems.

FREUD, ANNA. *The Ego and the Mechanisms of Defense*. London: Hogarth, 1937.
An important basic work in understanding psychoanalytic theory and its relevance for social work practice. Shows how the ego copes with anxiety and examines the various defense mechanisms in detail.

FREUD, SIGMUND. *Collected Papers*. London: Hogarth, 1950
These twenty-four volumes, edited by James Strachey, bring all of Sigmund Freud's notions together. Here we have expositions on psychosexual development, transference, resistance, group psychology, the unconscious, and much more.

HAMILTON, GORDON. "A Theory of Personality: Freud's Contribution to Social Work." in Howard J. Parad (ed.), *Ego Psychology and Dynamic Casework*. New York: Family Service Association of America, 1958.
Focuses on the transference components of the caseworker-client relationship and shows the pertinence of psychosexual development to social work practice. Also traces the impact of Freudian thinking on social work, its contributions and its problems.

STREAN, HERBERT F. *Psychoanalytic Theory and Social Work Practice*. New York: Free Press, 1979.
Examines the history of the relationship between social work and psychoanalysis. Reviews the major concepts of psychoanalysis as a personality theory and as a treatment. Demonstrates through case examples how to apply psychoanalytic theory to social work assessment, social work treatment, and social work research.

STREAN, HERBERT F. *Resolving Resistances in Psychotherapy*. New York: Wiley, 1985.
Written primarily for social workers and other helping professionals, this book attempts to help the clinician understand the inevitability of client resistance from the first phone call through termination. Using case illustrations, Strean attempts to demonstrate how to resolve resistances.

CHAPTER 3

Functional Theory for Social Work Practice

Shankar A. Yelaja

Introduction

The origin and development of functional theory for social work is attributed to the School of Social Work at the University of Pennsylvania. The two pioneers of this theory, Jessie Taft and Virginia Robinson, both taught at the Pennsylvania School of Social Work. Influenced by the philosophy and teachings of Herbert Mead and John Dewey, and later by Otto Rank, they laid the foundations of what became known in social work literature as a "functional school of thought." The pioneering work of Taft and Robinson was sustained by Kenneth Pray and later by Ruth Smalley whose book, *Theory for Social Work Practice*, was a milestone in the history of functional social work. The old but imposing gothic building still standing at 2410 Pine Street in Philadelphia (the school's home until 1966) ws the place where it all began.

The period from 1930 to 1955 in social work history was enlivened by controversy and debate over a legitimate theory for practice. The two major schools of thought—diagnostic, as it came to be called, and functional—differed from each other in several important respects, including underlying assumptions about human growth and development; the nature of the worker-client relationship; the purpose of social work; and, consequently, the theoretical base for practice. It was a conflict that stimulated lively and meaningful debate compelling all social workers, especially caseworkers, to examine their practice. Social workers in the 1980s have developed an appreciation of the similarities and differences among many theories that have had an impact on social work practice (66).

Contemporary social work practice is influenced by a wide range of theories; even within the single domain of personality theory, the influence of psychoanalytic, behavioral, and humanistic theories is strongly felt—not to mention, of course, a large segment of social theories (37, 38). Social work practitioners and educators are confronted with the formidable task of developing a systematic theory for practice that is testable and usable. Theory-building efforts are at a crossroads: whether to test existing theories against practice situations, or whether to test practice against the rigor of theory (5). Divergent approaches to theory building are suggested. Thus social workers of the future, in looking back upon that debate, might very well wonder and ask, "What was the fuss all about?"

In this chapter, I shall neither analyze nor defend the past controversy. Rather, my intention is to restate and recapitulate functional theory as it has evolved, then to consider its relevance for the many challenges that will confront the social work profession in the future. In the context of this chapter I have used the word *theory* not in the strict scientific sense of a closely drawn hypothesis that can be tested and proven or disproven, but more loosely, in the dictionary sense of a "plan for action" or scheme for practice based on a set of identified principles that are interrelated and derive from a common basis in relevant knowledge.

Historical Origins of Functional Theory

In order to understand functional theory for social work, it is important to be aware of its historical origins, the fomentation of thought around the time of its inception, and the landmarks contributing to its development and refinement.

Influenced and paralleled by a revolution in the pure sciences against the mechanistic Cartesian stance of traditional science, the functional approach developed out of a growing negative reaction to the mainstream of social work, which was totally caught up in the sweep of psychoanalytic thought. Gaining momentum in the 1920s and early 1930s, this psychoanalytic movement came, as opposition grew and the rift widened, to be known as the diagnostic school of social work.

Heavily influenced by Freudian concepts of personality development and psychoanalytic treatment, the diagnostic school, to which the great mass of social workers, including some of the future founders of the functional school, claimed allegiance, had adopted wholesale both concepts and methods and were attempting, regardless of setting, to perform a function barely distinguishable from Freudian psychotherapy.

Social work had progressed from its philanthropic beginnings through its first systematized, sociologically oriented phase under Mary Richmond to a psychologically oriented stage that was to dominate the field wholly during the 1920s and 1930s and continues to influence it, to varying degrees, at the present time. Not least among those carried to new and exciting heights of hope and enthusiasm for the helping potential in the Freudian approach were two individuals who, more than any others, can be credited with founding the functional school of social work, Jessie Taft and Virginia Robinson. In a paper discussing the influence of psychiatry on the field of mental health, Jessie Taft recalls the thrill of her first encounter with the "modern psychiatric viewpoint," the seemingly boundless prospect it introduced of bringing mental disease "into the realm of the knowable" (44, p. 60), and the promise heralded by the birth of the psychiatric social worker. In time, however, and under the decisive influence of Otto Rank, a disciple of Freud who had parted ways with the master, Robinson also turned aside from the main path of social work thinking, adapting and developing a psychological position that was later identified as the functional school of social work.

Psychoanalytic or diagnostic social work in its earliest form, unmodified by the influences of the more optimistic neo-Freudians such as Anna Freud and Heinz Hartmann, was based on the principle of scientific determinism; the assumption that individuals are products of their past and that only through understanding and acceptance of the influences that have molded them can they be led to psychological salvation. This emphasis on the past and on the efficacy of probing the unconscious mind to bring to light and so overcome blocks to normal, healthy functioning and fulfillment cast both therapist (social worker) and patient (client) into particular roles. The client was assumed to be psychologically ill, in need of treatment in preparation for which the client would be diagnosed and tentatively categorized, and of which the client would be the passive recipient. The immediate presenting problem was regarded as merely a symptom of a deeper, all-pervading psychological condition, the proper domain of the caseworker-therapist. The therapist assessed and treated over an indefinite stretch of time, assuming sole responsibility for the goal and direction of treatment, operating paradoxically not in dynamic interaction with the client but, rather, from a stance of dynamic passivity. While reflecting and encouraging the client to dredge up from the dim reaches of the unconscious mind origins of fears and anxieties, while receiving, interpreting, and deflecting revived hostilities, the therapist always remained a neutral, basically uninvolved figure. The effect of past influences was regarded as irreversible, so that what was sought in treatment was not change but adjustment. The Freudian view of human change potential was essentially pessimistic in its early days. It was only in the 1950s that the Freudian analytic group, through its emphasis on ego psychology, reflected a more optimistic view of the human race that conceived of individuals to be the creators of themselves as well as the created.

It is this view, first developed for psychotherapy by Rank and later corroborated and developed elsewhere by a considerable body of writers and scientists in a variety of disciplines, that contributed to the thinking of the functional school from its beginning.

This describes, then, in brief outline, precisely what functional casework as it evolved was not. Before presenting, in equally broad delineation, what it, by contrast, did constitute, it would be well to examine some of the influences that directly and indirectly bore upon the thinking of Jessie Taft and Virginia Robinson and their close associates in the Pennsylvania School of Social Work.

As dramatically as the impact of Freud's identification of the unconscious revolutionized the field of psychiatry and, by adoption, the field of social work, the winds of change were sweeping in quite another direction over the entire arena of scientific thought in the early decades of this century. There was, as Peter Drucker records, "a philosophical shift from the Cartesian universe of mechanical cause to the new universe of pattern, purpose and process" (9, p. xi). The static, deterministic view of the physical world was giving way to a new concept of bodies in motion; the stance of predictive certitude to one of probability. In the face of the old, predictable, and rigidly irreversible cause-and-effect order, leaders in the sciences were experiencing a Copernican turnabout and recognizing with increasing clarity that the only thing truly predictable in the universe was unpredictability itself, that change is the essence of all matter and all living organisms. The concept of "being" as a process, but a process with a universally recognizable purpose, was being elaborated by scientists in every field. If change was the one constant, it was also recognized that its polar counterpart, purposive pattern, was an equally universal phenomenon. It was seen that every living cell, every organism, and, by wider application, every person demonstrated a "recurrent patterning of a sequence of changes over time and in a particular direction" (15, p. 15) as opposed to random, chance changes with no interrelationship. Scientists like embryologist George W. Corner (6) and biologist Edmund Sinnott (46) were emphasizing a concept of human growth that expressed purpose and constituted a process. Dr. Corner's description of embryonic life in his classic work, *Ourselves Unborn* (6), laid a base for understanding (1) the nature of human growth in its purposiveness and orderly progression; (2) respective roles of the environment and endowment in their interaction on the course of growth; and (3) the origin and nature of difference between man and other species, and between man and man. Sinnott's writings on human biology opened relatively new vistas for understanding the process of human growth and development. Sinnott considered living things as seekers and creators striving for goals as the essence of all life. He referred to the organizing, goal-seeking quality of life and each human being as "an organized and organizing center, a vortex pulling in the matter and energy and knitting them into precise patterns never known before" (46, p. iii). Sinnott also recognized the influence of environment on the life of the organism. Thinkers in such diverse fields as physics (F. C. S. Northrup) and business administration (Peter Drucker) were calling for the abandonment of the concept of fixed causality and promoting concepts of relativity, energy, particularity, emergence, and potential, relating them to the nature of process and the essence of being. These ideas were also being developed by Banesh Hoffman (14), Julian Huxley, Hans Selye (45), John W. Gardner (12), and Floyd W. Matson, whom Saul Hofstein (15) credited with the best analysis he had encountered of the development of modern concepts of process.

Recognition by these thinkers, and a growing number of others of their persuasion, that the goal-directed whole of any organism transcends the sum of its parts, that each being is unique despite common patterns, that the observer affects the observed despite rigorous striving for scientific objectivity and impersonality, and that will and freedom do exist and play a significant role in the unfolding of a human being, had vital implications for theorists in the field of human services (28). Psychologists—such as Prescott Lecky, with his theory of the unity and consistency of the self—were similarly discovering the error of mechanistic psychological explanations based on the assumption that man was simply "a machine moved by forces" and were calling for a new view of man as "a unit in himself, a system which operates as a whole. His behavior must then be interpreted in terms of action rather than reaction, that is, in terms of purpose" (31, p. 88). Gordon Allport contrasted the outdated Lockean philosophy, which saw man as a purely passive reactive tabula rasa, with the Leibnitzian view, which recognized the person as the activist, the source of acts, not merely the reactor. Human activity, he contended, was not simply the result of pushes by internal and external forces, but was purposive: "To understand what a person is, it is necessary always to refer to what he may be in the future, for every state of the person is pointed in the direction of future possibilities" (2, p. 12). Thus the development of human personality was seen as a process of becoming, a continuous striving toward the realization of all its capacities, toward individuation that means the formation of certain structures—moral conscience, self-conception, hierarchy of interests—unique to each person. Other psychologists and personality theorists—Abraham Maslow, Karen Horney, Andras Angyal, Clark Moustakas (31)—were expanding upon the same theme, the human capacity for positive growth and change, the uniqueness and variation of human nature, the individual self, not static and preshaped by early forces but by being and becoming. It was a new view of man as "order-maker, working consistently through the anticipation, control and direction of change" (9, p. 23). Helen Merrell Lynd (24), exponent of a psychology of potential abundance in reaction to the psychology of scarcity or theory of compensation that had been dominating the scientific scene; Marie Jahoda, with her view of human maturation through a proscribed sequence of capacities to be, each developing through the use of different life opportunities; and Erik Erikson, with his concept of the unfolding process of the life cycle in distinct phases, each offering its peculiar crises, tasks, and opportunities—all these theorists were known to Jessie Taft and Virginia Robinson and other early functionalists, and all contributed to the birth and evolution of a new theory of social work practice (39, 40).

It was the catalytic influence of Otto Rank, who served on the faculty of the Pennsylvania School of Social Work, however, and his dynamic influence in the lives of Taft, Robinson, and the community of social workers in Philadelphia, that shaped the basic ideas of the functional school (with the exception of the use of the social agency function, a pivotal concept, which was the contribution of Jessie Taft alone; it will be discussed at greater length later in this chapter) (55, 56). As Rank reassessed and rejected many of the Freudian tenets and built in their place his own philosophy and therapeutic method, so did the functionalists turn decisively and diametrically away from Freudian-dominated social work theory and practice (17, 34).

Virginia Robinson, who, in close collaboration with her lifelong friend and colleague, Jessie Taft, was among the first social work writers to recognize the significance of the Rankian direction in psychological thought, notes in her milestone work, *A Changing Psychology in Social Casework*, that the "concept of fixed causality in mental and social phenomena has yielded to a conception of a functional correlation between the factors studied" (39, p. 121). No longer could the nucleus of thinkers associated with the Pennsylvania school accept the scientific determinism base of diagnostic social work. The view of the individual as the hapless product of interacting external and internal forces had given way to a positive, hopeful view: people fashioning their own fate, capable of creatively using inner and outer experiences to shape their own lives. A psychology of illness was rejected and in its place a psychology of positive human potential and capacity for change gave impulse and direction to a new method in social work. Turning its back decisively on the diagnostic preoccupation with the past, functionalism placed new and creative emphasis on the present experience and its power to release growth potential. The concept of treatment was replaced by the concept of service, of a helping process in which the use of the relationship, the dynamic interaction of the social worker as helper and the client as determinant of the process, was paramount. The center of change was no longer seen to be in the worker-therapist, but in the client. It was a positive acceptance and adoption of "Rank's concept of the analytic situation as a dynamic situation in which the patient works out his own 'will,' his conscious desires and his unconscious and unaccepted striving against the attitude of the analyst" (39, p. 122). The attitude of the caseworker, as the concept was adapted to social work, was in contrast to the diagnostically conceived role that assigned to the worker complete responsibility for both setting and carrying out treatment goals. An attitude of complete acceptance of the client as she presented herself and problem, a recognition of the client's difference and uniqueness and of the meaning to the client of accepting help, and of the client's ability to use the helping relationship, to release an innate capacity to organize experiences and so resolve the immediate problem, were the most essential principles of functional social work (13, 21). In contrast to the diagnostic approach with its global problem parameters, concentration was directed toward only a phase or fragment of the client's total problem—the presenting problem defined within the limits of the service offered. The assumption being that change in any one hurting area of life could work a salutary effect on total psychological equilibrium. As Kenneth Pray points out: "In helping to relieve pressure of conflict at this point (i.e., the point of the immediate problem), the worker may be releasing energies and opening insights that reach far beyond this moment or this episode" (33, p. 185). In the second assumption, that one of the main sources of human problems was the destructive use of relationships, the client took a fundamental step toward basic positive change through the experience afforded by the caseworker relationship of a new and constructive way of using the self in therapy.

The importance of time as a dynamic element in the helping process marked another departure from the diagnostic approach. The premise was offered that time symbolizes the whole problem of living in that it represents simultaneously both the need to accept limitation and the difficulty in doing so. "It is upon this universal reality of the meaning of time to the individual human being that functional casework bases its use of time in the helping process, with its emphasis upon the present moment and the present relationship, and its dynamic use of the ending of that relationship" (18, p. 26).

Before turning to the core concept of function in the functionalist approach to social work practice, it is vital to consider the rejection of diagnosis as it was understood and employed by the diagnostic school. In Freudian practice, a thorough, although not necessarily definitive, diagnosis based on an extensive collection of facts—particularly from the client's past—was the prime prerequisite for the treatment plan developed by the worker in accordance with the goals set for the client. The functional social worker no longer regarded diagnosis as a disparate step in the treatment process, but as inextricably woven throughout the process with the client's participation actively enlisted and an open sharing along the way. Diagnosis was now seen as "a developing process, worked out by the client himself, as he uses the agency service made available by the worker and as he tests his own capacities and needs in accepting or contesting the conditions and responsibilities he faces in using that service and so in dealing with his own problems" (33, p. 185).

The worker bore responsibility for neither the diagnosis nor the outcome of the service relationship, but for the self-disciplined fostering of "the process that goes into it—the process by which the recipient of help is enabled to face freely and steadily the alternatives open to him" (33, p. 14). This in no way minimizes the importance of a thorough understanding, on the part of the worker, of the factors affecting human development and behavior in general and in the specific application to each individual client, nor does it imply a rejection or devaluation of hard-won psychological insights. Without this knowledge base a worker could not hope to be in command of the helping process. The difference lay essentially in the rejection of helping from a stance of superior wisdom assuming the source of understanding and, therefore, of solutions, to reside solely in the worker. Certainly, diagnostic observations can and should be made and shared, but this is neither the basis nor the substance of the helping or of the social work process that is defined as "the use of a special method by the worker in a relationship with 'others' which leads to a characteristic process marked by engagement in movement towards a mutually affirmed purpose as that purpose finds expression in a specific program or service" (50, p. 16).

Generic Principles for Social Work Practice

One of the significant contributions to conceptualizations of social work practice appears in the writings of Ruth Smalley (47, 48, 51). In *Theory for Social Work Practice* (50), Smalley lists five generic principles for social work practice and emphasizes that these principles can be applied to the various forms of specialized practice (casework, groupwork, and community organization) rather than to combinations and mergers in practice.

Smalley's principles may be paraphrased as follows:

1. Diagnosis should be related to the use of services, should be developed as services are given, should be changed as the phenomenon changes, and should be shared with the client.
2. Time phases in the social work process (beginnings, middles, and endings) should be fully exploited for the use of the client.
3. The use of agency function gives focus, content, and direction to social work processes, assures accountability to society, and engages the client in the process characterized by partialization, concreteness, and differentiation.
4. Conscious use of structure, related to function and process, introduces form into the relationship between client and worker.
5. All social work processes involve a relationship in which choices or decisions are made by the person being helped, and the relationship must be of such a character as to further the making of purposive choices and decisions.

The Function in Functional Social Work Practice

If one had to single out the most distinguishing characteristic, or fundamental dynamic of the functionalist approach, it would be the place and use of agency function in the helping process.

It was Jessie Taft who first recognized the philosophical and psychological implications of the creative, positive acceptance of social agency parameters. Taft introduced agency function as the unifying, direction-giving concept in social work practice. Although Otto Rank exercised the greatest direct influence on all the other significant concepts of functional social work, the early functionalists, and Jessie Taft herself, were careful to exclude Rank from involvement in or influence on the development of this pivotal principle. Rank may have been unable to appreciate the concept, never having worked in an instututional setting himself.

While social work may be regarded, by and large, as an institutionalized profession, there are two widely divergent ways of regarding the institution or social agency through which the services of the profession are delivered. Those claiming allegiance to the diagnostic school tend to identify only in a secondary way with the purpose of the agency; their primary focus being on individual therapy, the treatment of the totality of client need regardless, as already noted, of practice setting. For the functionalists, who do not accept agency service limitations as a necessary evil, the function defined by the social agency provides reality boundaries within which the client can test and discover abilities to work out problems and make a satisfying adjustment or readjustment to the wider realities.

The social agency is seen as "the place where the interests of society and the interests of the individual are joined" (25, 44). Both the need to be served and the form of service deemed most effective to meet that need have been identified by society, which delegates responsibility for service delivery to the agency. The worker, as the representative of both agency and society, operates with a clear understanding of the role and the delineation of the service provided. "The worker sets up the conditions as found in his agency function and procedure; the client . . . tries to accept, to reject, to attempt to control, or to modify that function until he finally comes to terms with it enough to define or discover what he wants, if anything, from this situation" (55, p. 8). Far from being restrictive or repressive, the secure, stable parameters of agency function offer a creative basis, functionalists would argue, for truly effective social work practice, which makes active use of limits on the philosophical and psychological premise that conscious, positive acceptance is the keystone of therapy. It is clear that the purpose and form of service, once defined, cannot remain static, but require continuous review, and that complete identification with agency function on the part of the worker both assumes the timeliness and appropriateness of goals and places upon him partial responsibility for ongoing assessment. Kenneth Pray points out that, although social workers cannot carry responsibility for knowing everything that goes into the formulation and implementation of sound social programs, they are in a very special position to bear witness to their effects.

And we have a corresponding obligation not only to make these specific contributions from our experience, when occasion presents itself, but also to use our influence to its last limit, to see that the legislative and administrative processes

involved in the formulation and execution of policy shall allow full consideration and use of these basic human interests and relationships. (30, p. 16)

The concept of agency function, as agency service or role responsibility within
the organization (it means both), is the substitute for the transference phenomenon within the worker-client relationship. It was conceived of as the
professional control factor. The stress on agency function kept the relationship professional and objective, and helped maintain the clear differentiation
between worker and client (64).

The economic depression of the 1930s had a profound impact on social
services (19). Social agencies were called upon to reassess their services—including their purposes, goals, and delivery—to meet the rapidly growing demand for service as a result of social and economic crises created by the
depression. To what extent the introduction of the social agency as a base for
functional practice was influenced by the economic events of the 1930s is still
far from clear. But it is interesting that Taft in her paper, "Function as the
Basis of Development in Social Work Processes," delivered at the American
Association of Social Workers National Conference in June 1939, made a
statement that gives us a clue to the basis for her thinking. She stated:

> Although some agencies under extraordinary leadership had begun to differ-
> entiate individual helping from the responsible and skillful exercise of a specific
> function, it was not until public relief and assistance forced social workers into
> clarification through actual numbers and pressures of work to be done for tax-
> payers as well as clients, that we came, at least in Philadelphia, to a realization
> of the relation of function to social work practice that seemed little short of
> revelation. (44)

The Functional View of Man and Societal Relationships

George Herbert Mead, whose writings deeply influenced the foundations of
thought of the Pennsylvania school through and beyond Jessie Taft, noted
that "a self can arise only where there is a social process within which the
self has had its initiation. It arises in that process" (29, p. 384). The important
distinction the functionalists make in their view of that process, however, is
in emphasizing the active as opposed to the merely reactive role of the individual in the development of his own unique self.

We have considered emerging concepts of people—purposeful, change-
oriented, potential masters of their own fate—as these were understood by
the early functionalists increasingly dissatisfied with the restrictive, fundamentally pessimistic Freudian view of people as the products of biological
and environmental forces. Although the influence of these forces is by no
means minimized in Rankian thought, it is his revolutionary concept of will
and self-determination that provides the point of departure and gives direction to the new therapeutic approach upon which functional social work is

built. The rationale for this approach, as it identifies and seeks to mobilize the self-helping capacity of the human will, is expressed by Smalley as follows:

> In short, the psychological base for functional social casework practice is a view that the push toward life, health and fulfillment is primary in human nature, and that a person is capable throughout his life of modifying both himself and his environment according to his own changing purposes and within the limitations and opportunities of his changing capacities and changing environment. (51, p. 198)

The basic assumption is that there is not only an ability to change but an innate striving toward psychological growth in each person, and also a creative push toward a fuller, more integrated self. As the individual reaches toward growth and change, she fears and resists it because of the simultaneous pull in the opposite direction, toward the security and safety of the known: "Only at points of growth crisis, where the pressure for further development becomes strong enough to overcome the fear of change and disruption, is the ordinary individual brought to the necessity of enlarging his hard-won integration" (58, p. 5). The point at which a troubled client summons courage and resolve to seek help with an immediate problem is just such a point of growth crisis and, as such, provides the basic ingredient for the kind of mobilization toward self-help that functional casework offers. As each person is unique, so has each developed an individually peculiar pattern for meeting critical experiences; first through the particular weathering of what Rank refers to as the birth trauma, the first separation or beginning, and then through meeting every subsequent growth change. It is through relationships that these growth-producing or growth-limiting experiences are encountered: "The Ego needs the Thou in order to become the Self" (35, p. 290). If past relationships, particularly the earliest and most vital relationship with the mother, have been positive and constructive, the will has learned to accept the inevitability of separation and to adopt reality limitations as its own. If these formative experiences have been negative or destructive, the will has developed a pattern of refusing to accept separation and of repeated and futile attempts to complete the self through the other person in the relationship. Regardless of how negative a client's growth experiences may have been, however, the casework relationship, premised on an implicit trust in the growth potential, provides a unique opportunity for the release of that potential. It provides this opportunity through a consistent attitude of respect for and faith in the worth and strength of clients and a consequent creation of an atmosphere in which the clients can feel safe and free to be truly themselves (3, 4).

The concepts of conflict, counterwill, and resistance are to the functionalist not only inevitable but necessary for movement and growth. Conflict is inherent in the development of the human organism: conflict between the individual and others and with society. The counterwill (the negative aspect of the will) exists in opposition to the will of others and against reality in general, and carries with it a connotation of guilt. Resistance, an unavoidable phenomenon in the beginning casework relationship, is not only a natural and essential attempt on the part of the individual to maintain his personality, but is a sign of the strength of will indispensable to new growth. The caseworker-therapist represents not only a human counterwill, a needed reality, but perhaps for the first time in a client's experience offers almost no counterprojection, creating rather "a situation so safe, so reassuring that none of his defenses is needed and, therefore, fall away, leaving his underlying fears, loves and jealousies free to express themselves" (44, p. 113). As Angyal points out, the very foundations of a patient's neurosis begin to crumble when she learns to trust the worker's attitude of complete acceptance and the client can, therefore, no longer "uphold the fiction of being unloved and unworthy, undeserving of love" (31, p. 57). In being safe to express hitherto suppressed negative feelings, the client performs the valuable function of bringing "unconsidered isolated impulse" into relation with "conscious will and intelligence" (44, p. 139). Similarily, in the vital symbolic act of separation that takes place in a planned constructive way in the ending of the casework relationship, the client dares to trust his own will without feeling the need to justify it morally to the caseworker or to feel guilty about it as in previous encounters with other individuals. The client dares, in other words, to endure consciously the pain of separation resolutely, confidently, and guilt free: "The true self reveals itself . . . always only in the other self, that which we want to be, because we are not, in contrast to that which we have become and do not want to be" (31, p. 70). This discovery and reaffirmation of the true self, or at least a sufficient glimpse of it to remobilize coping resources within a limited piece of life, is the goal and substance of the helping relationship. There is in the entire functional approach an implicit faith in the innate striving of each person to be truly human, to be healthily social, and to act in a manner consistent with personal values and with confidence that a consciously controlled relationship or unqualified empathy and acceptance can and does provide a healthy basis for each client's social growth. As the term "functionalist" holds always before us, the therapeutic aspect of the service is inherently "incidentally, within the limits of a concrete function" (44, p. 157).

Major Concepts of Functional Social Work Practice

The major concepts of functional theory can also be concisely examined and described in terms of the importance of time, freedom of choice, and the place of the agency structure and authority in social work practice. All three of these key concepts play significant roles within the phases of the helping process from a functional approach (11).

Time

The universal reality of time, as identified by Rank and adopted by the functionalists, Taft saw as "only a name for the inmost nature of man, his own medium, which can sustain as well as confound him. It is his own element if only he will yield to it instead of fighting it" (44, p. 316). It is recognized in the functional approach that the client brings a dual attitude to the beginning phase of the process—a strength of will to grow or change in some degree through help, and a fighting resistance to the pain of growth and to accepting the needed help. The helping role of the social worker is, as noted, that of a counter will presented in such a way that it will strengthen, not break, the will of the client. The strengthening is effected through an acceptance of resistance, along with a firm faith in the client's ability to work through this resistance to a positive affirmation of the will to grow. It is helped further by a planned use of this particular time phase to overcome in the client the fear of the unknown, and to acquaint the client with the limits of the service offered and help in deciding, through partializing the problem, whether and how the service can be used, accepting the boundaries of time tentatively and judiciously set. Once this initial phase has been completed and the "climax of acceptance" passed, the direction of the helping process begins to veer toward preparation for the ending—the separation that, as we have seen, can complete the final and self-perpetuating therapeutic effect of the entire process by allowing the client to experience, perhaps for the first time, a guilt-free leaving of a significant other and of a self-willed growth phase propelled by a rediscovered strength to cope. The middle phase might be considered as comprising no more than the turning point between beginning and ending. The separation phase reintroduces in full force the struggle between wanting and not wanting and again, in order that this struggle may be carried out within the safety zone of a preestablished time limit, the skill of the worker is challenged to work out, not only for but with the client, an appropriate ending point. The therapeutic value of endings, as Taft identified it, "consists primarily in this fear-reducing heightening of the value of the present and the releasing discovery that an ending willed or accepted by the individual himself is birth no less than death, creation no less than annihilation" (44, p. 170).

Perhaps the most succinct summary of the meaning of consciously guiding the client's use of service phases is this quotation from Rank:

> Experience has taught . . . that as the therapist can only heal in his way, the patient also can only become well in his own way; that is, whenever and however he wills, which moreover is already clear through his decision to take treatment and often enough also through his ending of it. (36, p. 99)

Freedom of Choice

The cornerstone of the social work process from a functional point of view is the unshakable belief "in the existence of a natural impulse toward better organization of the self, which, however blocked or confused, provides the basis for a new orientation to living, once a situation is encountered which can disrupt the habitual pattern and release, for the formation of a new integration, the underlying growth tendencies" (44, p. 329). The growth-releasing situation is the helping relationship that either engages the voluntary commitment of the client or is rejected. It cannot be imposed from without if it is to be effective. The significance of choice and self-determination on the part of the client is central. Anita Faatz (10), who has written extensively about the nature of choice in social casework, points out that only when an individual chooses to grow or change can growth occur, and that self-chosen growth is possible only when an individual's inner strength remains intact. The decision to approach a social agency with a problem is already a choice to change, but the inevitable persistence, which further solidifies the internal strength to maintain, has first to be worked through in the process. The desire to change must be strengthened to the point of the second vital moment of choice, which is the climax of the beginning phase, the choice to accept and use the service personified by the worker in the casework relationship (12). In order that the ending, the crucial positive separation from the helping person, really frees the client to use rediscovered, newly mobilized inner resources, it is imperative that the client's choice be enlisted in the decision to end the process.

> What man resists, above all, is external interference with any phase of his living before he himself is ready to abandon it. It is not the leaving, but the lack of control over leaving, that he fears. If he can possess to some degree the ending phase of even the deepest relationship, so that he feels as part of himself the movement toward the new, then he cannot only bear the growth process, however painful, but can accept it with positive affirmation. (44, p. 106)

Agency, Structure, and Authority

In choosing to accept the limitations of an agency's service, the client identifies with the social purpose the agency represents and thus the client discovers, rediscovers, or confirms an ability to deal responsibly with reality in the pursuit of personal goals. Similarly, in the conscious decision to work within the parameters of a specific agency's function, the worker accepts a circumscribed area of service, not in resignation, chafing at the boundaries or secretly resolving to stretch them in the wider interests of the client, but recognizing and using them as the most valued, basic tool in the worker's armamentarium (26).

Arising from and determined by the function of the agency are the structure and form of service delivery, the conscious and knowing use of which is the principle dynamic in the helping process. The time structure, as we have seen, is neither mere expedience nor simple necessity, but a deliberate plan with a particular philosophical and psychological rationale. The form adopted for beginnings and endings—the way they are set up; the application, intake, registration, and assessment forms; the content—is consciously designed in functional practice for the maximum effectiveness of the social work processes. The form and structure of the place are regarded as a similar tool, affording, if truly suitable to discharging the particular agency's function, a center of stability that further facilitates the process. Agency policy, itself a structure, also provides a center from which all other form and structure arise. It is recognized, however, that structure faces the constant danger of rigidifying and so requires unceasing creativity and imagination in use and ongoing assessment. As the client in functional social work is helped to accept limitations and to exploit them creatively for personal purposes, so is the positive acceptance and use by the worker of form and structure seen to be the royal road to achievement of social work goals.

The relationship between choice and limitation is easy enough to see in situations where a client freely seeks out an agency service and as freely takes or rejects that service. Not so obvious, however, is the scope for free and voluntary engagement in an authoritarian setting, where the service must be seen by the uninitiated, at any rate, to be imposed by social rules enforcing conformity with no place for choice. Pray, whose experience was largely within just such settings in the field of corrections, has written a great deal about this apparent dilemma. He argues cogently that freedom and authority are not by any means mutually exclusive, but can, in the functionalist view, be seen to be completely compatible. Pray identifies two conditions in the authoritarian setting as essential and conducive to the potential success of the social work process. The first is that the authority reflects not an individual will but a social will. Second is the freedom to accept the authoritative bounds and so find fulfillment within them or to reject a service the captive client has not freely sought out.

> The function of social casework in facilitating social adjustment is not . . . to free the individual from all limitation; it is not to assist him to achieve, without hindrance, any or all of the ends to which he might aspire, but rather it is to help him to face, to understand, to accept, and to deal constructively and responsibly with certain realities of his own situation—his own capacities and also the facts of his social setting. (33, pp. 165–166)

The kind of authority embedded in social agencies is a rational authority that, as Fromm has defined it, "not only permits but requires constant scrutiny and criticism of those subjected to it. It is always temporary, its acceptance depending upon its performance. The source of irrational authority, on the other hand, is always power over people" (65, p. 13).

Functional Theory in Group Work and Community Organization

Clearly, although a generic application of the central concepts of functional theory has been implied throughout this review, the focus has repeatedly gravitated toward social casework where the principles can be most readily demonstrated. A brief examination, therefore, should be made of two other primary methods: group work and community organization in functional social work practice (7, 8).

Helen Phillips made a major contribution to the application of functional theory to social work practice with groups (32). The writings of Harold Lewis on community organization are significant in exploring the application of functional theory to community practice (20).

Ruth Smalley, in her definitive work pulling together the many threads of functional theory (50), carefully pointed out that group work and community organization must be understood as phenomena in their own right. The great parallel potential for functional application is seen to be the general recognition of the power within groups for defining a purpose and moving toward it. In other words, the group as an organism, whether it be a foster parent group in a child placement agency or a welfare rights group under the aegis of a governmental body, is essentially the same as a person, as an organism, or a microscopic cell. All are in process, striving toward fulfillment of a self-appointed purpose. The helping agent or worker is there to facilitate that process through a helping relationship that remains clearly within the limits defined by the function of the agency.

Pray reminds us that the objective of social work is not to make over environments or people but to introduce people to a process of dealing with problems of social relationships or social adjustment that would lead to "solutions satisfying to themselves and acceptable to the society of which they are a part" (33, p. 277). In group work, by and large, it is easy enough to see how agency purpose as it is embodied in the service might be clearly presented to the client unit and either accepted or rejected. The goal could be either social adjustment or social agitation. The responsibility of workers remains within the parameters of agency function and purpose. If the social worker believed the present agency function was not suited to the group goal, it would be necessary to work toward bringing desired changes to agency functions as part of the group process and work with clients.

In community organization it is equally easy to see a dilemma arising for the worker as the client group evolves its purpose, which may well be to make radical inroads on agency goals and structure, even to the point of seeking to overthrow them. It may be less easy to assume that such groups will always readily recognize the congruence of society's interest as the agency purports to represent it and their own. This may, of course, also happen with individuals and with small groups set up within the agency's purpose, but the self-perpetuating power evoked and fostered in a community group might conceivably end by biting the hand that feeds it. Certainly the functional approach can be seen as applicable to these two methods, and Smalley, as other functionalists before her, presents some quite telling arguments that it is.

Current and Future Perspectives

Much of the material covered so far in this chapter has described a dramatic dynamic debate in a particular period in the history of the social work profession. Newly trained social workers emerging from modern social work classrooms to practice in the agencies of today are finding that many concepts or principles of functional theory have been incorporated or even subsumed in the major theories of social work in the last decades of the twentieth century. The mid-century, almost heretical, argument for mankind as self-determining is, by and large, no longer an issue. The revolutionary key concepts brought forward by Taft, Robinson, and Smalley concerning process and time have been adapted and adopted over the years until they can be found deeply embedded in the major theories for practice today. Regardless of the theoretical model or the particular terminology used, theorists have incorporated ideas about freedom of choice, the human potential for change, and the use of time as a part of treatment. Whether one is reading about the ecological perspective of social work practice or studying family systems theory, one finds the authors assuming that interventions can be agents for change—in the goodness-of-fit between person, environment, or by entering the appropriate level of a family system.

What then of functional theory itself? Has it become extinct as the once lively debate has diminished? Writing in 1977, Smalley and Tybel Bloom were of the opinion that two major developments had added dimension to functional theory and its usefulness:

1. A comprehensive concept of social work practice, which encompasses the various methods, direct and indirect, not as specializations in themselves, but as interrelated modalities of a larger social process utilized to meet social needs. These modalities have both common and unique features, depending on the social unit served, its purpose, and configuration of relationships (practice with individuals, families, groups, communities, administration, consultation, planning, and so forth), but their utility is enhanced by their organic interconnection with the whole.
2. Specialization, no longer defined by method, is invested in the substantive areas of basic institutional arrangements of society: education, family, health, justice. Thus the social agency, still the locus of practice providing societal values, sanction, resource, and accountability, is also viewed within the larger context of its mission in relation to these allocations of major societal tasks and roles. Professional responsibility, values, knowledge, and skill are directed to processes of institutional as well as individual change, calling for an assertive stance in working to eliminate oppressive and discriminatory

policies and practices throughout the human services and in the broader society. (52, p. 1290)

It is precisely within the context of these developments that function as defined by functional theory remains a relevant and integral component of social work. In a sense, the functional approach has almost been rediscovered by some seeking to define practice with specific client groups (23, 27).

Indeed, David Howe, in responding to recent attempts by the British Association of Social Workers to establish a definition of social work, suggests that without agency function there is no social work: "There is no discernible and permanent entity, social work, although there is a particular way of doing some things. The things which are done and the areas in which they take place, though they may change with time and place, are encompassed within the notion of agency function. That is the home of the social worker" (16).

While this view of the importance of agency function may be seen as somewhat extreme, it serves to underline the current debate within the profession concerning the usefulness of function in establishing practice parameters. Harold Lewis, a leading contemporary proponent of this theory, reaffirms the functional position on the place of the agency in his book *The Intellectual Base of Social Work Practice*. He views them as the visible expression of a community's or some part of a community's wish to direct some of its resources, either public or private, to meet the identified needs of some groups of citizens. "The social agency constitutes the 'given,' the dynamic field of action within which the functional approach expects social work activity to occur" (22).

Lewis appears to agree with Smalley and Bloom that both integration and specialization of contemporary social work services have influenced the focus of the functional approach. In times that have been labeled as neo-conservative by political writers, one might speculate that this emphasis may become yet stronger. One could hypothesize that as society and the larger community face a scarcity of resources the mandate to agencies will be reexamined, and that this exercise in and of itself will have a profound effect on the social work practitioner. As the economic necessities compel agencies to maintain services strictly within budget realities, there must be for some functionalists a sense of déjà vu! Certainly the functional school evolved during a similar economic climate in the 1930s, and it may well prove to be that Taft's "revelation" in 1939 of agency differentiation of "the responsible and skillful exercise of a specific function" will turn out to be a "prophecy" for the final decades of the century (44).

The most important legacy of the functional school to modern social workers might well be seen in terms of two of Smalley's principles. The use of agency function to give focus, control, and direction to social work processes to assure accountability to society; and the conscious use of structure to reach social work objectives (50).

Conclusion

Although functional social work theory originated as an opposing force to the prevailing diagnostic school of thought in social work, its contribution to the conceptualization of practice must be seen in a broader perspective. The theory helped to widen the psychological and social bases for understanding man, the social environment, and the concept of the social agency. Throughout the history and development of functional theory the emphasis has remained on the refinement of the helping process of social work. The task of building a scientific theory base for social work practice is enormous. It calls for recognition of the contributions different theories can make to unraveling the phenomena called social work.

Functional theory has much to offer to the understanding of the complex realities of social work, and it would be a sad day for the profession if we failed to recognize the importance of this contribution.

References

1. Allan, Frederick. "Dilemma of Growth," *Archives of Neurology and Psychiatry*, Vol. 37 (1937). Reprinted in Frederick Allan, *Positive Aspects of Child Psychiatry*. New York: Norton, 1963.
2. Allport, Gordon W. *Becoming*. New Haven: Yale University Press, 1955.
3. Aptekar, Herbert. *The Dynamics of Casework and Counselling*. Boston: Houghton Mifflin, 1955.
4. ———. Book review of Ruth E. Smalley, "Theory for Social Work Practice," *Social Service Review*, Vol. 41, No. 3 (September 1967), pp. 342–344.
5. Briar, Scott, and Henry Miller. *Problems and Issues in Social Casework*. New York: Columbia University Press, 1971.
6. Corner, George W. *Ourselves Unborn*. New Haven: Yale University Press, 1944.
7. Coyle, Grace L. *Group Work with American Youth*. New York: Harper, 1948.
8. ———. *Social Science in the Professional Education of Social Workers*. New York: Council on Social Work Education, 1958.
9. Drucker, Peter. *Landmarks of Tomorrow*. New York: Harper and Row, 1959.
10. Faatz, Anita J. *The Nature of Choice in Casework Process*. Chapel Hill: University of North Carolina Press, 1953.
11. Faith, Goldie Basch. "The Elements of Functional Practice in Casework." Mimeographed, School of Social Work Library, University of Pennsylvania, 1961.
12. Gardner, John W. *Self-Renewal: The Individual and the Innovative Society*. New York: Harper and Row, 1964.
13. Gardner, John W., and Rosa Wessel. *Professional Education Based in Practice*. Philadelphia: School of Social Work, University of Pennsylvania Press, 1953.
14. Hoffman, Banesh. *The Strange Story of the Quantum*, 2nd edition. New York: Dover, 1959.

15. Hofstein, Saul. "The Nature of Process: Its Implications for Social Work," *Journal of Social Work Process*, Vol. 14 (1964), pp. 13–53.

16. Howe, David. "Agency Function and Social Work Principles," *British Journal of Social Work*, Vol 9 1979), pp. 29–47.

17. *Journal of Social Work Process*, Vols. 1–15. Philadelphia: University of Pennsylvania Press, 1937–1966.

18. Kasius, Cora (ed.). *A Comparison of Diagnostic and Functional Casework Concepts*. New York: Family Service Association of America, 1950.

19. Lee, Porter. *Social Work as Cause and Function and Other Papers*. New York: Columbia University Press, 1937.

20. Lewis, Harold. Outline Statement in Response to "Statement in Progress to Draft Statement Towards a Working Definition of Community Organization Practice." Mimeographed, Philadelphia, April 1961.

21. ———. "The Functional Approach to Social Work Practice—A Restatement of Assumptions and Principles," *Journal of Social Work Process*, Vol. 15 (1966), pp. 115–133.

22. ———. *The Intellectual Base of Social Work Practice: Tools for Thought in a Helping Profession*. New York: Haworth, 1982, pp. 207–221.

23. Lichtenstein, H., and C. H. Winograd. "Geriatric Consultation—A Functional Approach," *Journal of the American Geriatrics Society*, Vol. 32, No. 5 (1984), pp. 356–361.

24. Lynd, Helen Merrell. *On Shame and the Search for Identity*. New York: Harcourt Brace, 1958.

25. Marcus, Grace. "The Necessity for Understanding Agency Functions." Unpublished manuscript, School of Social Work Library, University of Pennsylvania, Philadelphia, 1937.

26. ———. "The Need and Value of Supervision for the Experienced Caseworker," *Journal of Social Work Process*, Vol. 10 (1959).

27. McGilloway, F. A., and L. Donnelly. "Religion and Patient Care—The Functionalist Approach," *Journal of Advanced Nursing*, Vol. 2, No. 1 (1977), pp. 3–13.

28. Mead, George Herbert. *Movements of Thought in the Nineteenth Century*. Chicago: University of Chicago Press, 1936.

29. ———. *Mind, Self and Society*. Chicago: University of Chicago Press, 1962.

30. ———. *On Social Psychology*. Chicago: University of Chicago Press, 1964.

31. Moustakas, Clark (ed.). *The Self: Explorations in Personal Growth*. New York: Harper and Row, 1956.

32. Phillips, Helen U. *Essentials of Social Group Work Skill*. New York: Association Press, 1957.

33. Pray, Kenneth L. M. *Social Work in a Revolutionary Age and Other Papers*. Philadelphia: University of Pennsylvania Press, 1949.

34. Rank, Otto. *The Trauma of Birth*. New York: Harcourt, Brace and World, 1929.

35. ———. *Beyond Psychology*. Published privately, 1941. New York: Dover, 1958.

36. ———. *Will Therapy and Truth and Reality*. New York: Knopf, 1945.

37. Rein, Martin. "Social Work in Search of a Radical Profession," *Social Work*, Vol. 15, No. 2 (1970), pp. 13–28.

38. Roberts, Robert W., and Robert H. Nee. *Theories of Social Casework*. Chicago: University of Chicago Press, 1970.

39. Robinson, Virginia P. *A Changing Psychology in Social Casework*. Chapel Hill: University of North Carolina Press, 1930.

40. ———. *Supervision in Social Case Work*. Chapel Hill: University of North Carolina Press, 1936.

41. ———. "The Administrative Function in Social Work," in *Four Papers on Professional Function*. New York: American Association of Social Workers, 1937.

42. ———. The Meaning of Skill," in Virginia P. Robinson (ed.), "Teaching for Skill in Social Casework," *Journal of Social Work Process*, Vol. 4 (1942), pp. 1–8.

43. ———. *The Dynamics of Supervision under Functional Controls*. Philadelphia: University of Pennsylvania Press, 1949.

44. ———. (ed.). *Jessie Taft, Therapist and Social Work Educator*. Philadelphia: University of Pennsylvania Press, 1962.

45. Selye, Hans. *The Stress of Life*. New York: Viking, 1961.

46. Sinnott, Edmund W. *Cell and Psyche*. New York: Harper and Row, 1950.

47. Smalley, Ruth E. "Distinctive Knowledge and Skills in Child Welfare: A Symposium," *Child Welfare*, Vol. 34, No. 4 (April 1955), pp. 10–16.

48. ———. "The Significance of Believing for School Counsellors," in Grace Lee (ed.), *Helping the Troubled School Child*. New York: National Association of Social Workers, 1959.

49. ———. "Freedom and Necessity in Social Work Education," *Proceedings Annual Program Meeting, 1963*. New York: Council on Social Work Education, 1963.

50. ———. *Theory for Social Work Practice*. New York: Columbia University Press, 1967.

51. ———. "Social Casework: The Functional Approach," in Robert E. Morris (ed.), *Encyclopedia of Social Work*, 16th issue. New York: National Association of Social Workers, 1971.

52. Smalley, Ruth E., and Tybel Bloom. "Social Casework: The Functional Approach," in John B. Turner (ed.), *Encyclopedia of Social Work*, 17th issue. Washington, D.C.: National Association of Social Workers, 1977.

53. Taft, Jessie. "The Relation of Psychiatry to Social Work." Address given at New York City Conference of Charities and Corrections, May 12, 1926.

54. ———. "Living and Feeling," *Child Study*, Vol. 10 (1933), pp. 105–109.

55. Taft, Jessie. "The Relation of Function to Process in Social Case Work," *Journal of Social Work Process*, Vol. 1, No. 1 (1937), pp. 1–18.

56. ———. "Function as the Basis of Development in Social Work Processes." Presented at Meeting of American Association of Psychiatric Social Workers, NASW, June 1939.

57. ———. "Some Specific Differences in Current Theory and Practice," in *Role of the Baby in the Placement Process*. Philadelphia: Pennsylvania School of Social Work, 1946.

58. ———. "A Conception of the Growth Process Underlying Social Casework Practice," *Social Casework*, Vol. 31 (1950), pp. 311–318.

59. ———. *Otto Rank, A Biographical Study Based on Notebooks, Letters, Collected Writings, Therapeutic Achievements and Personal Associations*. New York: Julian Press, 1958.

60. ———. *The Dynamics of Therapy in a Controlled Relationship*, 2nd edition. New York: Dover, 1962.

61. Wasserman, Harry. "Social Work Treatment: An Essay Review," *Smith College Studies in Social Work*, Vol. 45, No. 2 (February 1975), pp. 183–195.

62. Wessel, Rosa. "Training for Skill in Casework Through Professional Education in a School of Social Work," *Compass*, Vol. 25, No. 5 (September 1944).

63. ———. "Implications of the Choice to Work for Mothers in the ADC Program," in *Training for Service in Public Assistance*. Washington: U.S. Bureau of Public Assistance, 1961.

64. ———. "Family Service in the Public Welfare Agency—Focus or Shift?," *Public Welfare*, Vol. 22, No. 1 (January 1963), pp. 7–16.

65. Yelaja, Shankar A. *Authority and Social Work: Concept and Use*. Toronto: University of Toronto Press, 1971.

66. Younghusband, Eileen. "Foreword," in Francis J. Turner (ed.), *Social Work Treatment*. New York: Free Press, 1974.

Annotated Listing of Key References

LEWIS, HAROLD. *The Intellectual Base of Social Work Practice: Tools for Thought in a Helping Profession*. New York: Haworth, 1982.
This distinguished volume in the Hunter College Saul Horowitz Jr. Memorial Series provides an up-to-date view of functional social work practice. While the entire book will be of interest, Chapter 11 (pages 207–221) gives an excellent overview of the theory.

PRAY, KENNETH L. M. *Social Work in a Revolutionary Age and Other Papers*. Philadelphia: University of Pennsylvania Press, 1949.
A collection of papers, speeches, noted articles by Pray, a major exponent of functional theory. His contribution to functional theory is notable for its extension to other areas of social work practice, including administration, community organization, and social policy and planning.

ROBERTS, ROBERT W., and ROBERT H. NEE, *Theories of Social Casework*. Chicago: University of Chicago Press, 1970.
This collection of various theories for social casework contains a chapter on functional theory by Ruth Smalley. This chapter is more or less a condensed version of her book, *Theory of Social Work Practice*. However, this chapter must be considered an additional source of information on functional theory because of a section on unresolved issues in social work theory and practice.

ROBINSON, VIRGINIA P. (ed.). *Jessie Taft, Therapist and Social Work Educator*. Philadelphia: University of Pennsylvania Press, 1962.
A collection of papers by Jessie Taft, one of the major architects of functional theory. The book is a most comprehensive source of material on major concepts and ideas of functional theory. This can be used as a major reference book on functionalism.

SMALLEY, RUTH E. *Theory for Social Work Practice*. New York: Columbia University Press, 1967.
This book is a definitive source of an overview of functional theory, its historical background, development, and application to practice. In this scholarly book, Smalley sets forth the theoretical foundations of functional theory and explores its applications to social work practice.

SMALLEY, RUTH E., and TYBEL BLOOM. "Social Casework: The Functional Approach," in John B. Turner (ed.), *Encyclopedia of Social Work*, 17th issue. Washington D.C.: National Association of Social Workers, 1977.
A slightly revised and updated version of the functional approach to social casework, this is an excellent and detailed account of the historical origins and development of functional theory.

CHAPTER 4

Contributions of Gestalt Theory to Social Work Treatment

Michael Blugerman

Introduction

While there has not been a great deal written about the Gestalt approach in social work treatment, many social workers are becoming familiar with this point of view. There are some idiosyncratic parts of the system of Gestalt therapy that make this state of affairs no accident.

Fritz Perls, the major proponent of the Gestalt approach, once wrote: "What I do next year, I cannot tell. . . . I shall be very happy indeed if my paper has encouraged you to be benevolently sceptical towards both your own and my present convictions, and to make the transition from any compulsive dogmatism to the experimental, insecure, but creative pioneering attitude for which I can find no better example than the courage of Sigmund Freud" (28, pp. 55 and 68). These words, written two years after his arrival in New York from South Africa, very much understated Perls's relentless struggle to understand himself, therapy, and the human personality.

The colorful contours of this development have been well described by Perls himself (13) and others (21). Even if these works had not been written, Perls's reputation has spread through the professional community through his innumerable workshops, lecture tours, films, and through almost three generations of therapists whom he trained or influenced.

Perls grew suspicious of the value of concepts and "intellectual understanding." As we shall see, his view of human growth was predicated on principles antithetical to written work and the professional establishment. He attempted always to get beyond the false knowing of intellectualism and strived for understanding on a much more complete and organismic plane.

This kind of knowing emerges from a complete contact with our subject material—the human condition. It is an integration of cognitive, kinesthetic, and emotional material.

Historic Origins

Although Perls frequently dropped names of major theorists and philosophers, very little of his writing was intended to trace the roots of his thinking. Several authors have since tried to establish these important connections: Polster (19), Wallen (29, p. 8), Smith (26), and Kogan (7), to name a few. Some threads will presented here.

Smith (26) describes five main influences of Perls's thought: psychoanalysis, Reichian character analysis, existential philosophy, Gestalt psychology, and Eastern religion. Polster (19) adds the name of Otto Rank to this list.

Perls's early work, *Ego, Hunger and Aggression* (11), demonstrates the importance of his classical analytic training. In this work, Perls makes some major contributions that will continue to be the cornerstone of his development. According to Smith (26, p. 5):

> In terms of his revision of the psychoanalytic position, Perls (1947) set forth three criticisms of Freud: (1) The treatment of psychological facts as if they exist in isolation from the organism as a whole, (2) the use of a linear association psychology as a basis for a four dimensional system, (3) the neglect of the phenomena of differentiation. . . .
>
> As a result, Perls offered the following revisions: (1) replacement of the psychological by the holistic organismic content, (2) replacement of association psychology by the field theory of gestalt psychology and (3) application of a differential thinking based on Friedlander's notion of creative indifference.

In developing a perspective on human development based on *hunger* in contrast to Freud's *sexuality,* Perls laid the way for an integration between organismic assimilation of food and psychological symbolism and meaning.

These and other influences will be developed below as we discuss components and techniques flowing from this theory: particularly the disturbances of function at the contact boundary.

Smith describes Reich's influence on Perls, and their differences, in these ways: (1) remembrances must be accompanied by the appropriate affect; (2) it is essential to bring into therapy the body of the client through the understanding of retroflection, or turning back onto the self (often through the use of musculature); (3) there must be a frustrating and confronting style of the therapist in order to strike a balance between support and frustration; (4) it must be understood that the character resistance is revealed in the "how" of the patient's communication instead of the "what"; (5) Perls's description of the layer notion of working with the impasse has some correlation to the idea of the breaking down of "secondary narcissism"; (6) Reich maintains that there is only one technique for a patient at any time, that which flows from the uniqueness of the individual's circumstances, while Perls maintains that the role of the therapist is to promote growth of the individual and not to follow a formula or technical model; (7) there must be an appreciation of the political dimension of the life of the therapist in society; and (8) while Reich feels that the freeing up of character armor puts the patient into a better stance vis-à-vis the world, in which he can go beyond addressing particular symptoms, Perls sees the development of self—support of the individual through awareness and responsibility—as a path to a more creative interaction with the environment (26, pp. 7–13).

From existentialism, Perls developed the notion that one must take personal responsibility for one's own existence. Smith cites Perls's statement to the effect that no one can be different from what they are at that moment. "The model which Perls chose for the therapeutic relationship is one delineated by Buber as the 'I–Thou' relationship. . . . Gestalt therapy is based on the coming together of two persons in an atmosphere where the therapist respects the personhood of his patient" (26, p. 16).

As he continues to trace the roots of Gestalt therapy, Smith describes the contribution of the Gestalt psychologists to Perls:

> From the writings of Goldstein, Angyal, Lecky and Maslow, a coherent position of organismic theory evolved. These are the major facets of that position: (1) The normal personality is characterized by unity, integration, consistency and coherence. Pathology is defined as the converse. (2) Analysis of the person begins with the whole and proceeds by a differentiation of that whole into its aspects. (3) The individual is unified and motivated by a sovereign drive—self-actualization or self-realization. (4) The influence of inherent potentialities is emphasized, while the influence of external forces is minimized. (5) The vocabulary and principles of Gestalt psychology are used. (6) The emphasis in research is idiographic (the comprehensive study of a single case). (26, p. 31)

Finally, the principle of organismic self-regulation emerges from this rubric. The principle is that the need-motivation system of the individual determines the most relevant figure and its background formation, merging into a meaningful Gestalt at that point in time.

Perls's interest in Zen and other Eastern religious philosophy shows prominently in his work. Smith describes the paradox of the "likeness of the not alike." From Eastern thought and the work of S. Friedlander, there is a suggestion that if one slows down contact and increases experience with a primarily undifferentiated object and then progressively differentiates the feeling until both poles are recognized, one can learn that opposites within a context are more related than either of the opposites is to any other concept.

For example, love and hate are opposite polarities on one level. At the same time, they have more in common (involvement with the object) than with another polarity of each of them—indifference or apathy (no involvement with the object).

In working with these polarities, it is important that the poles be experienced and teased apart, so that each aspect can be seen for what it is and integrated into the personality.

Another central paradox is that of change (2). The notion here is that change is occurring all the time. We are often engaged in a process to manage change in ways that we can handle. In *Future Shock*, Alvin Toffler has described the effect of social change on the individual and the ways through which we try to maintain constancy in our lives. We often succeed in slowing down our experience of life's flow to the point that we think it is stuck, and then we try to get it going again. The paradox here is that change begins to flow when we allow ourselves to be where we are at that moment. From this identity, we can once again track the impulse and momentum of a natural tendency toward movement. Acceptance of oneself in the here and now is a first step toward allowing the organism to break up a stagnant process.

Polster adds this reference to the influence of the work of Otto Rank:

> The *constructive* view of resistance and its role in the resolution of disparate parts of oneself is a major theme in gestalt therapy. Gestalt therapy realizes the *power of creative resistance* mobilizing it into a major force moving beyond the mere resolution of contradiction and into a new personal composition.
>
> Finally, Rank's interest in the developing sense of individuality identity led to a change of focus in the interaction between patient and therapist. Acknowledgement of the human aspects of this interaction make him one of the major influences toward harmonistic orientation in psychotherapy—an important inheritance for gestalt therapy (19, p. 314 [italics mine]).

Principal Proponents

Shortly after his arrival in New York, Perls and his wife, Laura, developed an intellectual circle of colleagues and participated in some writing and teaching. Paul Goodman was a key figure in the development of this circle. He wrote much of "Gestalt Therapy: Excitement and Growth in the Human Personality (part 2)," and was part of the inner circle that developed the central ideas of the Gestalt approach into sound thought and practice. However, the massive explosion of Gestalt therapy as an influence in the helping professions did not really occur until Perls went to California. Shepard describes this conversation:

> "If you write a book about Fritz," said Wilson Van Dusen, a west coast phenomenologist who brought Fritz to California in 1959, "you must emphasize what things were like when he turned up on the scene. We were all imbued with psychoanalysis, we must get an extensive history of the person. We were all basically retrospective, strongly retrospective, in both our analysis and our ther-

apies. We couldn't conceive of understanding a patient without an extensive history. And for a man to just walk into a room and describe people's behavior so accurately added a whole new dimension. This is where I considered Fritz very great. His incomparable capacity to observe. He could see all that he needed to see in the present. He often said, 'I'm only trying to see the obvious. . . . ' It was dealing right here on the surface, the skin, the obvious. Yet all you needed to know was right there. The patient's history would only elaborate—repeat again—what you are seeing now.

This was illuminating. At the time I was well into existential analysis. I was drifting in the general direction of the *here and now*. We had gobs of Binswanger, Minkowski, Heidegger. But here was a man who could put into practice a rather tortured theory. So naturally, I studied and learned as much as I could from him."(21)

Perls broke into the professional system through the back door. He had a tremendous flair for drama, loved to be the center of attention, and delighted in illustrating his genius. The kicker was that he could do what he claimed his theory promised. Time after time, all manner of credentialed, "successful" but dissatisfied professionals, tired of the thin comfort of their well-learned dogma, saw in the work of Perls some hope for a different quality to *their* work with their clients: face-to-face and person-to-person.

Smith describes the growth of Gestalt therapy "to the extent that the *Directory* of the American Academy of Psychotherapists lists it as the sixth most common affiliation" (26, p. 3). This development occurred in spite of the fact that there were very few formal courses in professional schools teaching this system.

Impact on Social Work Practice

With philosophical roots in phenomenology and existentialism, Gestalt therapy can offer a great deal to social work. Beginning where the client is at is often a difficult task because of the difficulty in locating where the client is really at. Do we pay attention to the content the client brings? Do we notice that he is holding his breath now? Do we accept the tremor in the chin as indicating the holding back of tears? Do we consider the fact of this client's being a man or a woman?

The most effective answer lies in the understanding of the client's point of view or situation as it is experienced. Often a worker may listen to a client disclose painful detail after painful detail in his life situation. Asking the client what he is experiencing, what he wants, and what he feels at this moment may offer many of us quite a surprise. In many cases, we have been hearing the story from our own heads, with our own agendas, and embellishing it with our imagined pain.

Gestalt therapy offers a different map to the client's territory. It encourages acceptance in the fullest sense of the I–thou relationship. It demands our participation as another human being in order to keep from performing robotlike with a bag of cliché interventions and tricks.

Much of social work practice involves dealing with people as they experience difficulty in their environment. While some question the clinical value of dealing with intrapsychic difficulties, and suggest that the profession's responsibility is with the environmental end of this continuum, it will be seen that this artificial boundary makes less sense. If one deals competently with the environment, in a contactful way, personality integration and self-growth may be a large part of the outcome. This is especially the situation in the larger amount of relating to the environment that we do through the mechanism of projection. Social work has the opportunity to thaw out the process of movement from environmental support to self-support, interdependence, and dignity. Much of this facilitation can occur through the *how* of the helping process. In later sections, we can examine these ideas further.

General Therapeutic Concepts

We have looked at some of the assumptive roots of the Gestalt approach. Developed from these basic thoughts, we can identify several organizing principles to prepare for our work with clients.

First, we may consider the awareness continuum. Central to the work of Gestalt therapy is the use of the flow of conscious contact with the environment. The individual may be in touch with the inner zone, or how she experiences herself; the outer zone, or what she experiences as an object in the environment; or the middle zone, the thoughts and illusions modifying the clarity of contact with either the outer or inner zones. It should be clear that the problematic use of the middle zone doesn't allow contact between self and object or self and self.

Perls has said that the essence of Gestalt is the awareness process.

> Everything is in flux. Only after we have been stunned by the infinite diversity of processes constituting the universe, can we understand the importance of the organizing principle that creates order from chaos; namely the figure, background formation. Whatever is the organism's foremost need makes reality appear as it does. It makes such objects stand out as figures which correspond to diverse needs. It evokes our interest, attention, carthexis or whatever you choose to call it. (28, p. 51)

Further, in the same article, he states:

> The most important fact about the figure background formation is that if a need is genuinely satisfied, the situation changes. The reality becomes a different one from what it was as long as the situation was unfinished. . . .
>
> The healthy organism rallies with all its potentialities to the gratification of the foreground needs. Immediately as one task is finished, it recedes into the background and allows the one which in the meantime has become the most important to come to the foreground. This is the principle of organismic self-regulation. (28, pp. 51–52)

A second organizing principle is the value of the here and now. Whether the client remembers *now* what happened in the past, or anticipates *now* what may happen in a little while, or experiences his contact with the environment *now*, at this moment, the richness of experience is occurring here and now. This is not a metaphysical statement of truth as much as a workable reality. While we are striving to bring about integration of alienated parts of our clients, or address their apparent duplicity, it is most helpful to utilize the concerting function of the here and now. While we encounter them and engage at the contact boundary, the here and now remains the point of maximum contact possible.

A third assumption is that growth occurs at the contact boundary of systems. As difficult as it is, there is no more powerful level of analysis or focus of attention than the obvious or surface. Perls remarked that a neurotic is someone who cannot see the obvious. It may be that both the client and the worker have been avoiding the obvious, and instead dealing with much more "meaningful material": the client through his middle zone of cluttered self-doubt and the worker through her middle zone of "professional diagnosis or politeness."

The nature of disturbance between the organism and the environment can be observed and identified in definite ways. Let us consider these: *confluence, introjection, projection,* and *retroflection.*

Confluence is an agreement to maintain the status quo, to pretend that there are no differences, to avoid making waves, to emphasize the similarity or identification between two individuals or two systems. If you place your hand on the table in front of you, your experience in the first instance will probably be something like a feeling of temperature difference, a feeling of texture, a sense of pressure. If you let your hand move a little, some of these experiences may intensify. If, however, you leave your hand there for some time, much of your experience may diminish. You may feel some pressure and it may not be immediately clear where your hand stops and where the table surface starts and stops. If you stay with this notion a little longer, you may experience some restlessness and boredom.

This process happens just as easily between people, often marriage partners. Polster describes this scene:

> Indeed, someone can be involved in a confluence contact without ever having been consulted or having even negotiated its terms. One may buy into such an arrangement through indolence or ignorance and discover that such a contract existed to his surprise only by breaking or disturbing it. Even if vaguely sensed differences may never have erupted into overt argument, there are signs of disturbance in confluent relationships between husband and wife, parent and child, boss and underling, when one of them, knowingly or otherwise, breaches the contract terms. (19, p. 93)

The remedy is the reactivation of difference, through contact and awareness. Polster continues:

> Questions like, "What do you feel now?", "What do you want now?", or "What are you doing now?" can help him focus on his own directions. . . . Stating his

expectations aloud, first to the therapist, perhaps, and finally to the person from whom these satisfactions are demanded can be the first steps in sorting out covert attempts at confluent relationships. (19, p. 95)

Let us consider the other three: Introjection is the incomplete assimilation of what the environment has to offer. This may be due to the avoidance of meeting the material head on and breaking it down into digestible pieces. This may refer to physical or symbolic material. It is usually identifiable with language such as "I should . . .," "I ought to . . .," "I have to . . .," and so on. One source of much introjection material is parental messages. As a result of this type of disturbance at the contact boundary, growth is limited through incomplete digestion of the differential information. The antidote or action plan for this disturbance is the "spitting up" and "rechewing" of the introjected material. If, for example, one is carrying the voice of a parent around with them, and it is not yet clear how much of this voice is parent and how much is client, the client may be asked to become the voice and express it until some identification occurs with the voice. At that point the client can confront the speaker of the voice and meet him head on in a contactful battle.

Many students have reported that *Gestalt Therapy* is a difficult book to read. There is a popular story currently that the authors purposefully did not want to make the material too easy to swallow. They hoped that readers would have to struggle to digest the information in a form that enhanced their learning, not simply to reproduce the information back on an exam.

Although the risk is one of frustration and possible rejection, out of hand, by potential students, if one's goal is in fact the serious study of the subject, there must be this active interchange between the teacher and the student. This idea is actively promoted in the pragmatism of John Dewey: the notion of learning by doing, with a high quality of engagement in the process.

Perhaps it was a good thing that material such as the Gestalt approach to human growth wasn't taught in professional schools. In the struggle to digest material that I have outlined above, some heat is generated, and further, this kind of learning cannot be crammed or put on schedule. The demand is on the parties to provide some honest engagement. It may be that this kind of learning is better done in a setting compatible with these goals— a professional institute, for example.

Another style of disturbance at the contact boundary is projection. This approach is characterized by a disowning of some aspect of the personality, pleasant or unpleasant, and spotting it outward in the environment. This approach results in a personal depletion of energy insofar as the talent or power of the disowned aspect disappears from the psychic economy. Further, it is added to the supply of the environment in a way that the environment gains more influence and control over the individual's life. Because of the fact that projections often find appropriate screens, the individual may operate with some successful intuition.

The task in dealing with projection is to facilitate the reclaiming of the disowned aspect of the individual. Somewhere in the mechanism of the projection is some element of an introject directing the giving away of the projector's attributes. Sometimes a helpful route may be to assist the identification of the projected material and the client. If the client can appreciate *how* she gives away her capability and power, she may choose to use it in a different way.

The fourth of these patterns of disturbance of contact at the boundary of systems is retroflection. This may take the form of the self using itself as object of environment—either to avoid doing something to someone else or to replace that outside object and do something to the self that the self wishes the outside object to do.

This pattern is usually anchored in muscular activity. Consequently, some mobilization of physical energy may be necessary before redirection to the more appropriate environment may be possible. As in the previously described patterns, each of these in itself is not necessarily problematic. It is only when the pattern becomes fixed and preferred by the organism that a deceleration of growth occurs. Thinking and planning are a form of retroflection. There is no doubt that most of the time this is a healthy and helpful function. If, however, the individual didn't move to the environment now and then for nourishment and refueling, stagnation would be quickly evident.

Each of these patterns occurs often in combination with some of the others. In each there is often some central introjection that must be dealt with. The advantage of his conceptual map is that, at the same time, it offers a direction for action as well as a diagnostic aid. They are *process*-oriented labels rather than *event*-oriented labels. More clarification of this distinction will be made below.

Implications for History Taking and Diagnosis

In just the same way as we have been looking at principles for growth at the contact boundary between the individual and the environment, the same patterns hold true at the contact boundary between worker and client. In the interview, the worker becomes an active part of the environment, acting and challenging the client within a framework of support and frustration.

The material that is being obtained then may be seen as material from the client to the worker. What is the style of contact at this point? What would describe the quality of exchange occurring?

Instead of a diagnosis—usually in the form of a statement like "He is an X," where the X stands for a label, for example, neurotic, single parent, character disorder, welfare mother, and so on—we are looking for a description of process; that is, a pattern.

This would take the form, "When L, then M" or "When I want him to come home on time he dawdles," for example.

The advantage of this difference is the emphasis on "how" and "what" instead of on the more linearly causal "why." This allows movement from a therapy of explanation to a theory of action, where the pattern suggests an action plan for intervention.

In describing the tasks of the therapist, Fagan gives us this description:

> Of course, past events of much importance do arise from the process of exploring posture, gestures and dreams. However, the Gestalt therapist is not interested in the historical reconstruction of the patient's life, nor in focusing upon one specific behavior such as communication style. Rather, he is interested in a global way in the point of contact between the various systems available for observation. The interactions between a person and his body, between his words and his tone of voice, between his posture and the person he is talking to, between himself and the group he is a member of, are the focal points. The Gestalt therapist does not hypothesize nor make inferences about other systems that he cannot observe, though he may ask the patient to reenact *his* perceptions of them, as in a dialogue with his father, for example. Most Gestalt procedures are designed to bear upon the point of intersection, and the nature of the other system is viewed as less important than how the patient perceives or reacts to it. (4, p. 91)

This is not to say there is no room for educated hunches that could expand the possibilities surrounding the patterns that are discovered. In the same way that a figure and ground create a demand for understanding, the figure of a client in front of you demands some background to make the image or Gestalt sensible and complete. Often, the little missing pieces that come to mind as the worker sorts through her own process of understanding the client lay the groundwork for further intervention. This understanding need not be only intellectual or cognitive. It may be on any level of experience.

Part of the rationale for moving to patterns and here-and-now material as the basis for work is the notion that intervention begins at the first moment of contact with the client. The honest interaction between the two parties is the beginning of fostering a growth-producing relationship.

The concept of organismic self-regulation and the notion that the most valuable contact occurs at the surface of systems help support this point of view. The client is bringing you the most pressing material in his social system at that moment. He is, as well, showing you where to start work.

It is in the relation to work that a diagnostic statement is helpful. Current social work practice develops good assessments that are unrelated differentially to the provision of service. In the Gestalt view, the process of diagnosis (patterning) is already the beginning of the work. As a viable hypothesis, the pattern serves to close the gap between client and worker, rather than creating professional distance through "knowing about."

Treatment Methods and Techniques

Later in his life, Perls was convinced of the value of the workshop, commune, and multimedia approach to getting across his world view. Consequently, while some may miss a solid academic book from Perls, there is no shortage of transcripts, episodes, and fragments of his work with clients (12, 14, 15).

In addition to these, other workers have tried to share their integration of Gestalt theory and themselves (4), and statements on personal philosophy of practice (20). Gestalt therapy has developed a great number of "rules," "games," etc. These have been documented in several places (4, 5, 26, 27).

It must be remembered that many of these techniques were developed as much to illustrate the process of growth to an audience as to facilitate something for the client. Take Perls's use of drama—the hot seat was clearly more a way to show the audience the internal process of the client.

The only valid technique is one that grows out of the full I–Thou contact with the client in the here and now, and that is emerging from sound Gestalt principles.

Two points must be made here: the first is the value of the Gestalt approach as an orienting principle to the work, and the second is the notion of the experiment.

As an orienting principle, the Gestalt approach allows the worker to use himself in unique ways. The worker focuses on *how* the client makes contact with her as part of the environment. She looks for patterns. These data are available whether the client is filling out a housing application with the worker or is engaged in relating a heavily charged emotional incident in his life.

Zinker states that the Gestalt therapist is particularly interested in bridging blockages of the awareness–excitement–contact cycle within the individual (31, p. 97).

As the worker monitors the client's contact with the environment, including himself, she may see where in this rhythm of contact and withdrawal there is an interruption of flow. As well, the *how* of that disturbance of contact may be seen (e.g., confluence, retroflection, etc.). In utilizing this paradigm, Zinker moves into a nice piece of integration between Gestalt theory and psychoanalytic theory (31, pp. 98 ff.).

The point of interest for us here is that the worker can use herself to monitor the nature of disturbance of contact boundary work. She can see where the flow of experience is being broken and can attend to an active bridging of that avoidance.

John Enright (4, p. 108) states: "The task of the therapist is to help the patient overcome the barriers that block awareness and to let nature take its course (that is, to let awareness develop), so that he can function with all his abilities." Note that the therapist in this view does not help directly with the transaction—he does not help solve the problem—but helps reestablish the conditions under which the patient can best use his own problem-solving abilities.

Fagan and Shepherd (4, p. 82) describe how Gestalt deals with inconsistencies between theory and technique: "However, in Gestalt therapy the theory that people's problems arise from their lack of awareness and from the ways in which they block awareness leads directly to the therapist's fo-

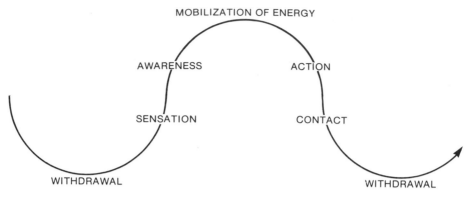

Figure 4-1. The awareness–excitement–contact cycle

cusing attention on this area and offering suggestions, tasks, exercises designed either to promote awareness in general or to assist an individual with his specific avoidances" (4, p. 82).

Both Polster and Zinker have developed the notion of the value of the experiment in Gestalt work. Perls stated that in the safe emergency of the therapeutic situation, the neurotic discovers that the world does not fall to pieces if he gets angry, sexy, joyous, mournful (28, p. 14).

The translation of the idea of a safe emergency into action leads us to the investigation of the experiment as a medium for growth. Polster states:

> The experiment in Gestalt therapy is an attempt to counter the aboutist deadlock by bringing the individual's action system right into the room. Through experiment the individual is mobilized to confront the emergencies of his life by playing out his aborted feelings and actions in relative safety. A safe emergency is thus created where venturesome exploration can be supported. Furthermore both ends of the safety-to-emergency continuum can be explored, emphasizing first the support and then the risk-taking, whichever seems salient at the time. (19, p. 234 ff.)

Zinker states that "Gestalt therapy bridges the gap between cognitive therapies and behaviour modification." He further states:

> Gestalt therapy is an integrated version of phenomenology and behaviourism. Our orientation is similar to phenomenology because we respect the individual's internal experience: Therapeutic work is rooted in the client's own perspective. At the same time, we modify concrete behaviour in a graded and carefully timed manner. Thus, a unique quality of Gestalt therapy is its emphasis on modifying a person's behaviour in the therapy situation itself. This systematic behaviour modification, when it grows out of the experience of the client, is called an experiment. The experiment is the cornerstone of experiential learning. (31, p. 122 ff.)

Zinker has identified and outlined a way of understanding and coming to terms with the development of the helpful experiment. (31, p. 128 ff.) The purposes of the experiment are to increase awareness and social competence. Specifically, Zinker addresses these goals:

1. to expand the individual's repertoire of behaviour;
2. to create conditions under which the person can see his life as his own creation (take ownership of therapy);
3. to stimulate the individual's experiential learning and the evolution of new self-concepts from behavioural creations;
4. to complete unfinished situations and overcome blockages in the awareness/excitement/contact cycle;
5. to integrate cortical understandings with motoric expressions;
6. to discover polarizations which are not in awareness;
7. to stimulate the integration of conflictual forces in the personality;
8. to dislodge and re-integrate introjects and generally place "misplaced" feelings, ideas, and actions where they belong in the personality;
9. to stimulate circumstances under which the person can feel and act stronger, more competent, more self-supported, more explorative and actively responsible to himself. (31, p. 126)

With these goals in mind, Zinker goes on to describe the process by which an experiment evolves.

LAYING THE GROUNDWORK.   It is important to develop an honest and contactful appreciation of where the client is at that moment. This requires the reconnecting of the relationship with the client at the beginning of the interview—a "warming-up process of re-establishing contact again and again."

As the interview progresses, themes emerge—some stronger than others. Through staying in contact with the client, the worker begins to visualize a unifying theme. Zinker states that for every learning process, there is the matter of preparation and timing. If one cannot take the time to establish a field within which the experiment can be done properly, the client will not learn very much, nor will he remember the substantive outcome of the experience.

Equally as important is the genuine curiosity and interest in the client as another human being. Without this aspect, a great amount of material will not enter the worker's experience. For that matter, the client requires this interest in order to share some cognitive and, more important, some feeling material.

NEGOTIATING A CONSENSUS BETWEEN CLIENT AND THERAPIST.   The worker addresses the responsibility and choice of the client and negotiates a common task for the next part of the interview.

GRADING.   An experiment is successful if it is within the client's ability to perform it successfully. Zinker states that considerable skill and experience in human understanding are necessary to tailor-make a situation that provides the proper balance of support and frustration. The goal is not explosion

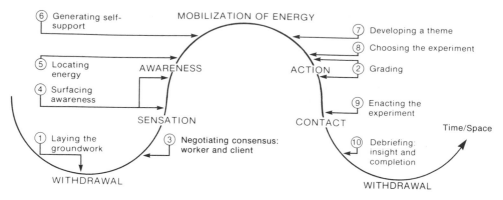

Figure 4-2. Tracing the development of an experiment along the awareness-excitement-contact cycle

or breakthrough, it is incremental learning. Consequently, experiments must be graded up or down to challenge the client's experienced difficulty.

SURFACING THE CLIENT'S AWARENESS.   The awareness the client experiences is preceded by an increase in sensation. As the worker monitors the client's process, he can check for incongruence or confusion. A successful intervention is continued through this experiment by close tracking of the client's movement experientially as indicated by his awareness.

LOCATING THE CLIENT'S ENERGY.   This process involves staying aware of changes in movement, breathing, and color of skin in order to track the building or diminishing of energy. In the next step, as we find support, this energy may be engaged in work.

GENERATING SELF-SUPPORT FOR BOTH CLIENT AND THERAPIST.   The client needs enough support to continue to contact the environment. Failure of establishing this support will draw attention away from the experiment and toward a search for this needed support. The worker can be helpful by attending to the client's usual support system, breathing, posture, or other muscular activity.

GENERATION OF A THEME.   Zinker describes the "focus" in the experiment as an indicator of the process and direction of the session. The theme is related to the content. There may be several themes that become material for possible synthesis. After the experiment, the client can often articulate how he understands or perceives the theme at another level.

CHOICE OF EXPERIMENT.   The client brings forth some themes. The worker develops some through his own process and through staying with the client's process. The particular experiment chosen will be a blending of these factors. The clearer a worker is, the more free he is to use what he feels, knows, or intuits with the client.

ENACTING THE EXPERIMENT. The experiment itself may address any of the goals listed above. It is a careful balance of ego-alien and ego-syntonic material, carefully graded up or down to challenge the client at his experienced level of support.

INSIGHT AND COMPLETION. The important point here is that the learning takes place for the client. It is true that the worker may have learned a great deal from remaining in contact with the client and the work. His learning, however, is separate from the learning of the client. The client may be asked to comment on his experience at this point. He may be directed to continue some form of the experiment on his own, outside the session, in order to enhance the integration of this new material.

Zinker summarizes this process by describing the experiment as a work of art, having elegance in the sense that it is easily observed or assimilated by the client. The flow of energy may follow the paradigm shown in Figure 4–1 (p. 80). In Figure 4–2, we can follow the course of an experiment through the "awareness–excitement–contact" cycle (with apologies to Zinker!). The reader is directed to Zinker for further elaboration of this conceptualization of the experiment and case examples (31).

Considerations in the Application of Methods

The Gestalt approach is as much a way of viewing the helping process as a body of methods. It is difficult to imagine a situation where the Gestalt perspective would not lend itself to social work.

Following its phenomenological roots, the Gestalt approach values the personal experience and existence of the client. Many of the techniques developed thus far may not be applicable to *this* client, *this* worker, or *this* agency setting. The essence of the Gestalt approach lies in the faithful attending to the emerging situation: client; agency or worker. From this process a relevant technique or method may be developed. If one wonders, however, how a particular technique that she has just seen at a conference, seminar, or workshop can be useful to her, we have a different question.

Passons states that a large part of the Gestalt method is addressed to develop self-knowledge and self-exploration on behalf of the client. (10, p. 28) He points out that self-awareness is a core ingredient in any theoretical approach. He states that it is in the enhancement of awareness that counselors from many schools of thought may borrow Gestalt techniques. He then identifies different theoretical frameworks and how they might benefit from this added perspective.

Utilization of the Gestalt approach makes different demands on client and worker. While some humanistic workers believe that growth can occur in any person regardless of how dysfunctional he is at that point in time, many of us have neither the patience, skill, nor personality to work in this way.

Demands of agency mandate, caseload, and client population may militate against working where the client is at. In many of these situations alternate conceptual frameworks are necessary.

In order to develop the working conditions that support the use of Gestalt methods, some goodwill between client, worker and agency is essential. Polster has stated that Gestalt therapy may be too good for sick people (19). In some way, his statement reflects the fact that much of the early work in this approach is geared to (a) mobilizing awareness of the client's experience, (b) encouraging a sense of his personal responsibility for the growth process, and (c) backing the client's acceptance of his self.

Not only is goodwill necessary to support this challenging process, but a geometric increase in benefit may be seen the more this early work is developed and the more the client is mobilized.

In some ways, Gestalt theory offers a method of discovering method. Based on the *how* of the helping process, it orients the worker to developing a technology that constantly stays in contact with the work. True adherence to the Gestalt approach may allow theory and practice to evolve unrecognizably past what we consider the method today. This can clearly be seen in the revisions over time in Perls's work. We can track his focus from the individual to the group, to the workshop, and finally to the commune or kibbutz.

Implications for Practice

Due to the organismic nature of Gestalt theory, there is a close connection with systems theory. We can consider the language of the Gestalt approach to be translatable across the range of macro- or microsystems. General systems theory suggests that there is an organismic tendency of systems to complicate themselves. This process of growth occurs at systems' boundaries. Consider the popular saying, "You are what you eat," or the title of Edmund Carpenter's book, *They Became What They Beheld*.

If we observe the nature of contact at the boundaries of systems, we can observe patterns of disturbance or enhancement of this contact. Some of these patterns have been described. In many situations, it is just as important to interfere in this growth process as to facilitate it. The important consideration here is whether this interference is done with awareness and a sense of responsibility, and whether we are willing to pay the necessary costs.

An example of interference with a growth process is the case of racial intermarriage. For the sake of cultural identity and values, contact between racial systems may be limited or even curtailed. The hidden emotional costs of this curtailment may never be fully known. The majority of people, how-ever, may never realize the costs and, consequently, may not make this choice in full awareness.

In working with individuals, our goal is often the reowning of disowned parts of the personality. In our attempts to strengthen the client's sense of competence and responsibility, we work with disturbances at the contact boundary between her and her environment. In the interview situation we are a large part of the environment. What is this client's pattern of making a disturbing contact with us? In dealing with the integration of projected parts or aspects of her personality, does the client utilize the cast of characters in her own repertory company or does she overuse one or two "stars," causing discontent in the others in the dressing room or wings of the theater of her mind?

When we work with a family the level of abstraction changes (6). We observe how the family subsystems make contact with each other at their boundaries. We may consider the parent-child system, the couple system, or the intergenerational system. Our task is to design experiments that will al-low for the discovery of new possibilities of relating: replacing learned lim-itations of experience and action.

As we stay in contact with the family, we obtain some hunch or hy-pothesis about the operating patterns between individuals or subsystems. The family is acting "as if" an unwritten script were being enacted. In the design of the helping experiment, we challenge the "unwritten script" and allow more contactful sequences to develop.

In working with groups, we are also faced with another collection of subsystems. We can examine what is going on between the leader and mem-ber(s). How is contact disturbed at this boundary? We can also look at in-termember boundaries, or look at contact between subgroupings or cliques. Much of Perls's work was done in a group format. We can see this as the interaction of a subsystem (leader–member) in front of the remainder of the group. Several authors have examined this and other uses of groups (3, 10, 31). It is also of interest to consider the boundary between the group and the host agency or wider parts of the environment.

This type of analysis can also be made at larger levels of abstraction. If our concern is organizational development in an agency, we may notice how the board of directors subsystem is kept, or keeping itself, from full contact with either the staff or the client subsystem. We can notice how line workers, middle management, and the agency director have designed their interac-tions to limit or prevent healthy contact.

In the professional school, we can examine the contact between the teacher and student subsystems. We can deal with the subsystems of theory and field practice and how they are in contact. Is there a flow across the boundary of theory and practice data, or are there two unrelated activities?

The community affords a look at interaction between subsystems or-ganized on socioeconomic, cultural, racial, or other variables. In all these situations growth occurs at the boundary between systems. Our task as social workers addressing these situations is to produce the same kind of safe emergency and constructive experimentation that we have arranged in aiding individual growth. Techniques, strategies, and methods will vary greatly, and are limited by the creativity of the worker.

The Gestalt perspective may be used to develop these techniques, provided the worker is available to enter the target system and develop the necessary groundwork and contract to work.

Counter Indications for the Use of Theory

Shepherd describes the limitations and cautions in the Gestalt approach (22, p. 728). Some of these are:

1. The therapist's capacity for I–thou, here and now relationships is a basic requisite and is developed through extensive integration of learning and experience. Probably the most effective application of Gestalt techniques comes with personal therapeutic experiences gained in professional training workshops and work with competent supervisors and therapists.
2. Gestalt therapy is most effective with oversocialized, restrained, constricted individuals—often described as neurotic, phobic, perfectionistic, ineffective, depressed, etc.—whose function is limited or inconsistent.
3. Work with less organized, more severely disturbed or psychotic individuals is more problematic and requires caution, sensitivity and patience. Such work should not be undertaken where long term commitment to the patient is not feasible.
4. Individuals whose problems center in lack of impulse control—acting out, delinquency, sociopathy, etc.—require a different approach.
5. Because Gestalt techniques, in general, facilitate the discovery, facing and resolution of the patient's major conflicts in often dramatically short time, the inexperienced therapist, observer or patient may assume the Gestalt therapy offers "instant cure."

Gestalt techniques were developed out of work with particular client groups. Many of the groups with which social work deals are different from these. It remains to be seen whether the principles of Gestalt theory can generate some methods to deal with these groups. Many of the current techniques have developed from Gestalt theory and contact with specific client populations. With the same principles of Gestalt theory and different client groups, the question becomes: What techniques can flow from interaction between workers and clients in these categories as they are involved in the helping process?

Implications for Social Work Research

It has been indicated that some of the contributions from phenomenology and Gestalt psychology have influenced the development of this approach.

In considering the connection between this approach and social work research, we need to discuss two of these contributions. The first is the focus on ideographic study of single cases, and the second is the replacement of stimulus response learning with field theory.

The study of single cases is important in focusing on how this client, with his experienced difficulty, can be helped by this worker through this method.

It is not enough to ask: Does aspirin cure a headache? At this time, science has identified over two hundred types of headaches. It is important to know how functional and meaningful this headache is in this client's life. Consider programs to provide service dealing with social concerns such as truancy, delinquency, and alcoholism. It may be demonstrated that at this level of abstraction we have created an event or noun that replaces a more complicated sequence of behavior or process. The Gestalt approach operates by reversing this abstracting process, once again finding the functional groundwork of events that led up to this labeling of an event.

In this process, truancy becomes more of an operational description than a label. We may find that the truancy is based on a mother who prefers the child at home, a family that requires the child to work, a peer group that demands allegiance in misdeeds, a sense of physical embarrassment at the thought of entering the common showers, and so on. In each of these examples, the details of the helping technique might be different. What is important is the personal meaning of the problem behavior and the reestablishment of a personal solution to this concern. This does not mean that we cannot generalize treatment methods. It does mean that through the detailed study of single cases we can answer the differential demand situation of a specific problem, a specific worker, a specific approach.

In just the same way a valid theory is that which is anchored in practice skills, meaningful research is most useful when it is grounded in the experienced phenomena that are being studied rather than in grand levels of abstraction.

The shift from stimulus response approaches to Gestalt field theory learning allows a shift from *why* to *how* as an operating principle. Our thinking on causality is best done when we can move from "A causes B" statements to statements describing the range of experienced vector forces brought to bear on a situation, together with the client's experienced perception of the meaning of these vectors.

Summary

Gestalt theory orients the worker toward encouraging the fullest expression of the client as a person. Application of Gestalt methods must go beyond techniques and gimmicks into the development of a safe emergency situation within which experiments designed to enhance functioning can be undertaken. Considerable skill on the part of the worker is one prerequisite. Another is the willingness of the worker to engage herself fully as a human being in the helping process.

This I–thou connection with the client is at the center of our work. In accepting the client where he is at, the worker sees the client's difficulty a positive and creative adaptation to the environment as the client experiences it. The task is to restore the awareness–excitement–contact cycle in a way that mobilizes the client's creative resources.

If one is faithful to Gestalt principles, one's techniques will continue to develop along lines based on client need and potential. Applications in social work will continue to need to be formally tested. Currently, some formal teaching of this approach may be just beginning in professional schools. It is quite encouraging to consider the number of people in the helping professions who have discovered the Gestalt approach as a perspective that "fits" and is helpful. It is particularly encouraging because of the grounding of the work in a natural, organismic approach to an interpersonal enterprise in human service.

References

1. Appelbaum, A. A. "A Psychoanalyst Looks at Gestalt Therapy," in C. Hatcher and P. Himelstein (eds.), *Handbook of Gestalt Therapy.* New York: Aronson, 1976, pp. 753–778.

2. Beisser, A. "A Paradoxical Theory of Change," in J. Fagan and I. L. Shepherd (eds.), *Gestalt Therapy Now: Theory, Techniques, Applications.* Palo Alto, Calif.: Science and Behavior Books, 1970, pp. 77–87.

3. Cohn, R. C. "Therapy in Groups: Psychoanalytic, Experiential and Gestalt," in J. Fagan and I. L. Shepherd (eds.), *Gestalt Therapy Now: Theory, Techniques, Applications.*, Palo Alto, Calif.: Science and Behavior Books, 1970, pp. 130–139.

4. Fagan, J., and I. L. Shepherd (eds.), *Gestalt Therapy Now: Theory, Techniques, Applications.* Palo Alto, Calif.: Science and Behavior Books, 1970.

5. Hatcher, C., and P. Himelstein (eds.), *Handbook of Gestalt Therapy.* New York: Aronson, 1976.

6. Kempler, W. *Principles of Gestalt Family Therapy: A Gestalt–Experiential Handbook.* Salt Lake City: Deseret Press, 1974.

7. Kogan, J. "The Genesis of Gestalt Therapy," in C. Hatcher and P. Himelstein (eds.), *The Handbook of Gestalt Therapy.* New York: Aronson, 1976, pp. 235–258.

8. Levitsky, A., and F. S. Perls. "The Rules and Games of Gestalt Therapy," in J. Fagan and I. L. Shepherd (eds.), *Gestalt Therapy Now: Theory, Techniques, Applications.* Palo Alto, Calif.: Science and Behavior Books, 1970, pp. 140–149.

9. Naranjo, Claudio. "Expressive Techniques," in C. Hatcher and P. Himelstein (eds.), *Handbook of Gestalt Therapy.* New York: Aronson, 1976, pp. 281–305.

10. Passons, W. R. *Gestalt Approaches in Counseling.* New York: Holt, Rinehart and Winston, 1975.

11. Perls, Frederick S. *Ego, Hunger and Aggression*. New York: Vintage Books, 1969.

12. ———. *Gestalt Therapy Verbatim*. Lafayette, Calif.: Real People Press, 1969.

13. ———. *In and Out the Garbage Pail*. Lafayette, Calif.: Real People Press, 1969.

14. ———. *The Gestalt Approach and Eye Witness to Therapy*. Palo Alto, Calif.: Science and Behavior Books, 1973.

15. ———. "Theory and Technique of Personality Integration," in John O. Stevens (ed.), *Gestalt Is*. Moab, Utah: Real People Press, 1975.

16. ———. *Legacy from Fritz*, and Baumgardner, P. *Gifts from Lake Cowichan*. Palo Alto, Calif.: Science and Behavior Books, 1975.

17. ———, R. F. Hefferline, and P. Goodman. *Gestalt Therapy: Excitement and Growth in the Human Personality*. New York: Dell, 1951.

18. Perls, L. "One Gestalt Therapist's Approach," in J. Fagan and I. L. Shepherd (eds.), *Gestalt Therapy Now: Theory, Techniques, Applications*. Palo Alto, Calif.: Science and Behavior Books, 1970, pp. 125–129.

19. Polster, E., and M. Polster. *Gestalt Therapy Integrated: Contours of Theory and Practice*. New York: Vintage Press, 1974.

20. Rosenblatt, D. *Opening Doors: What Happens in Gestalt Therapy*. New York: Harper and Row, 1975.

21. Shepard, Martin. *Fritz, An Intimate Portrait of Fritz Perls and Gestalt Therapy*. New York: Saturday Review Press, Dutton, 1975.

22. Shepherd, I. L. "Limitations and Cautions in the Gestalt Approach," in C. Hatcher and P. Himelstein (eds.), *Handbook of Gestalt Therapy*. New York: Aronson, 1976, pp. 725–731. (Also in J. Fagan and I. L. Shepherd (eds.), *Gestalt Therapy Now*. Palo Alto, Calif.: Science and Behavior Books, 1970.)

23. Simkin, J. S. "Mary, A. Session with a Passive Patient," in J. Fagan and I. L. Shepherd (eds.), *Gestalt Therapy Now: Theory, Techniques, Applications*. Palo Alto, Calif.: Science and Behavior Books, 1970, pp. 162–168.

24. ———. "The Use of Dreams in Gestalt Therapy," in C. Sager and H. S. Kaplan (eds.), *Progress in Group and Family Therapy*. New York: Brunner/Mazel, 1972.

25. ———. "The Development of Gestalt Therapy," C. Hatcher and P. Himelstein (eds.), *The Handbook of Gestalt Therapy*. New York: Aronson, 1976, pp. 223–234.

26. Smith, E. W. L. (ed.). *The Growing Edge of Gestalt Therapy*. New York: Brunner/Mazel, 1975.

27. Stevens, J. O. *Awareness: Exploring, Experimenting, Experiencing*. Lafayette, Calif.: Real People Press, 1971.

28. ———. *Gestalt Is*. Moab, Utah: Real People Press, 1975.

29. Wallen, R. "Gestalt Therapy and Gestalt Psychology," in J. Fagan and I. L. Shepherd (eds.), *Gestalt Therapy Now: Theory, Techniques, Applications*. Palo Alto, Calif.: Science and Behavior Books, 1970, pp. 8–13.

30. Yontef, G. M. "The Theory of Gestalt Therapy," in C. Hatcher and P. Himelstein (eds.), *The Handbook of Gestalt Therapy*. New York: Aronson, 1976, pp. 213–222.

31. Zinker, J. *Creative Process in Gestalt Therapy*. New York: Brunner/Mazel, 1977.

Annotated Listing of Key References

FAGAN, J., and I. L. SHEPHERD (eds.). *Gestalt Therapy Now: Theory, Techniques, Applications.* Palo Alto, Calif.: Science and Behavior Books, 1970.
This book developed from second-generation Gestalt therapists who saw a need to address the professional community in writing. It contains some very valuable work spelling out principles and applications in Gestalt work. At the same time it is faithful to feeling and experience.

HATCHER, C., and P. HIMELSTEIN (eds.), *Handbook of Gestalt Therapy.* New York: Aronson, 1976.
This large anthology contains several articles that are not available or published elsewhere. Many different therapists describe their personal integration of Gestalt in their work. There are several papers discussing the Gestalt approach in comparison with other theoretical frameworks.

PERLS, F. S., R. F. HEFFERLINE, and P. GOODMAN. *Gestalt Therapy: Excitement and Growth in the Human Personality.* New York: Dell, 1951.
Although this is a volume to be worked through slowly, it is a valuable piece. Paul Goodman wrote the second part from a manuscript by Perls. Many Gestalt therapists consider the first part a historic curiosity. This work is derivative of a great deal of philosophical, social, and political discussions among the first generation of Gestalt therapists surrounding Fritz and Laura Perls in New York. It was seen as an attempt to go beyond psychoanalysis toward a radically new approach.

PERLS, F. S. *The Gestalt Approach and Eye Witness to Therapy.* Palo Alto, Calif.: Science and Behavior Books, 1973.
Published after his death, this book presents a short synthesis of Perls's thinking about Gestalt therapy. In addition to a theoretical presentation in *The Gestalt Approach*, the second part of the book, *Eye Witness to Therapy*, is a transcription of films of some of Perls's seminars. The original films are available elsewhere, making this book a handy teaching aid.

SMITH, E. W. L. (ed.). *The Growing Edge of Gestalt Therapy.* New York: Brunner/Mazel, 1975.
This collection of articles traces many of the historic roots and parallel paths of Gestalt therapy. Connections are made with a wide range of philosophical thought, including Eastern religions. Gestalt practice and thought are the take-off point into many other directions.

ZINKER, J. *Creative Process in Gestalt Therapy.* New York: Brunner/Mazel, 1977.
This is a first-rate exposition of Gestalt therapy from someone who understands creativity and the human process. Zinker offers a refreshing formulation of some key ideas in therapy. This work moves a long way from the medical model of helping. Zinker's description of the creative experiment is clear and valuable.

CHAPTER 5

Cognitive Theory

Harold D. Werner

Summary of Theory

A cognitive approach holds that the principal determinant of emotions, motives, and behavior is an individual's thinking, which is a conscious process. The problems that clients bring to social workers are considered to be problems of consciousness. The essence of cognitive theory is that it requires the practitioner to discard the concept of an "unconscious" as the primary force in the psychic life.

It should be emphasized that cognitive theory is not a body of ideas created by one or two individuals. Rather, it is a general category that can be clearly defined and into which the concept systems of several theorists will fit. Each practitioner, on the basis of personality and style of work, can put together a personal treatment technique from components within the category. More use may be made of some components than of others, stressing or omitting particular aspects. All the concepts that are appropriately included in the category of cognitive theory are consistent with each other: the category does not have internal contradictions. As a result, this kind of choosing from within the category has nothing in common with the eclecticism of those social workers who try to combine contradictory elements from psychoanalysis, behavior modification, and other non-Freudian systems.

Included in cognitive theory are approaches that go by the names of "rational," "reality," or "phenomenological."

The main features of cognitive theory are:

1. Behavior is determined by thinking. We observe situations, other people and ourselves in action, arrive at conclusions or judgments about what we have observed, and act accordingly. In the words of Alfred Adler, "A person's behavior springs from his opinion." Inaccurate perceptions lead to inappropriate behavior.

2. An important kind of thinking that human beings do concerns their immediate and long-term goals. The goals we set up for ourselves in turn influence our lifestyle, our basic patterns of behavior. We develop the lifestyle we believe will bring us to our goals.

3. An individual's life is not controlled by unconscious forces. However, a person can be unaware of the origins of current attitudes, of the impression he is making, or of the effect of his behavior on others.

4. There are instinctual drives, but aggression is not one of them. Aggression is seen instead as a reaction to feelings of threat or frustration or as the life-style of a person who has chosen antisocial goals that cannot be attained without it.

5. An individual is not doomed to be dominated by instinctual drives. When important goals provide sufficient incentives, he defuses or modifies those drives that are inconsistent with her chosen objectives.

6. Most behavior is not a manifestation or sublimation of the sex urge. The sex drive is just one of several, and should not be automatically assumed to underlie a particular problem.

7. Emotions also trace back to thinking. The conclusions we draw about something we have perceived decide whether our emotional response will be fear, anger, guilt, love, or joy. By definition, an unconscious emotion cannot exist. Unconscious guilt, for example, is not possible because the development of guilt is a conscious process requiring a judgment.

8. Motives likewise cannot be unconscious. A motive is a goal or objective that we choose on the basis of a personal conception of what is necessary for our welfare, happiness, or success. Motives (called goals in No. 2) can come into being only through a cognitive—that is, conscious thinking—process.

9. Treatment focuses on the thoughts, emotions, expressed motives, and behavior of the client. No unconscious content is postulated.

10. Cognitive theory is socially oriented. The principal determinant of emotions, motives, and behavior is thinking, which in turn is primarily influenced by an individual's society, immediate environment, human relationships, and experiences in general.

11. Every person is inherently creative, has resources of strength and courage, with a basic tendency to strive for competence and a sense of completion. Abraham Maslow referred to this tendency as a need for self-

actualization, a need "to become everything that one is capable of becoming."

12. Change consists of expanding or modifying individual consciousness until perception more nearly approximates reality. This is done by talking to the client and/or guiding her into direct experiences that will alter her distorted thinking.

Historical Origins

It might be said that cognitive theory began around 1911, when Alfred Adler and Sigmund Freud went their separate ways after a close association in Vienna for many years. Fundamental differences arose between them, and Adler proceeded to develop his own conceptual framework, which he named "individual psychology." Adlerian theory was in disagreement with Freud's division of the psyche into sections and Freud's concept of the continual war going on between the id and the superego. Adler saw the human personality as a unified whole never in conflict with itself. (This came to be known later as the "holistic" approach.) Conflicts in people were not within themselves but with the world around them and resulted from antisocial or distorted thinking.

Adler seems to have been the original proponent of the cognitive approach, by virtue of his contention that each person's behavior was shaped by notions of what constituted success and by the goals set up to achieve it. We have here, in elementary form, the main tenet of cognitive theory: thinking shapes behavior. In the 1920s and 1930s, Adler's ideas were widely accepted in many parts of Europe, and also had some following in the United States. For about twenty years after his death in 1937, there was a decline of interest, but this has been increasing steadily again since the publication in 1956 of a collection of his writings (5).

Principal Proponents

The decade of the 1950s saw the appearance of other writings that made contributions in varying degrees to the substance of cognitive theory. A synonym for the cognitive approach is "rational psychotherapy," and perhaps the first use of this term in a book was made by Joseph Wortis in 1953 (71).

Joseph Furst, in a work published in 1954, viewed neurosis as a distortion or limitation of consciousness (20).

The year 1955 witnessed the first issue of *Psychotherapy*, the journal of the Robbins Institute in New York City. The Institute was made up of psychiatrists who had received orthodox psychoanalytic training but were moving away from Freud. An article in this publication stated: "Cure is change;

cure is the development of rational consciousness. The Institute does not subscribe to the thesis that consciousness is a knowledge of the 'unconscious'."

It was in 1956 that the American Psychological Association heard a paper on rational psychotherapy for the first time at one of its annual meetings. It was in this presentation that Albert Ellis described emotion as a "strongly evaluative kind of thinking," a result of the sentences we say to ourselves. Formulating it another way, he viewed thought as taking the form of "self-talk," "internationalized sentences," or "self-verbalization." Irrational or unrealistic thought produced distorted and disturbed emotions and behavior.

From the 1960s up to the present time (1984), the earlier literature has been augmented by additional works that elaborated on cognitive theory, expanded it, and specified additional treatment techniques. Albert Ellis enlarged upon his preliminary ideas in two books: A Guide to Rational Living (co-authored with Robert A. Harper, 1961) and Reason and Emotion in Psychotherapy (17). William Glasser published Reality Therapy: A New Approach to Psychiatry (22) and postulated two basic human needs: to give and receive love, and to behave in such a manner as to feel worthwhile to oneself and to others. Glasser believed that clients seeking professional help are people who through their actions have failed to satisfy these needs. He did not regard them as sick but as weak and requiring assistance in order to change. The reality therapist's task was to force the client to judge his behavior for what it was, and then to educate him to take responsibility for fulfilling the aforementioned needs.

The author of this chapter was responsible for A Rational Approach to Social Casework (65), New Understandings of Human Behavior (67), and Cognitive Therapy: A Humanistic Approach (68). The first was a preliminary sketch of cognitive theory with treatment procedures for social workers; the second volume was a collection of non-Freudian readings for practitioners and students in all the treatment professions, with major emphasis on cognitive theory; the third was the author's updated and complete exposition of theory and practice.

The eminent psychologist Abraham Maslow died in 1970 shortly before the appearance of a book summing up his major ideas. This was Frank G. Goble's The Third Force (23). A brilliant thinker, Maslow's original ideas ranged far and wide, did not usually have a treatment orientation, and were not well systematized. Goble was able to simplify and structure Maslow's concepts, drawing them together from all of Maslow's complex writings. As a result, it has become clearer that Maslow belongs in the cognitive camp.

We came full circle with the publication of Techniques for Behavior Change, edited by Arthur G. Nikelly (1971). The book's basic premise is that maladjustment stems from an incorrect evaluation of oneself and others, from excessive striving and mistaken goals, from discouragement and an inadequate interest in cooperation with others.

Maxie Maultsby's Help Yourself to Happiness (42) reinforced previous writings by himself and others on the importance of mental imagery in cognitive treatment. Maultsby pointed out that people do not see and react to actual external events, but to the image of them that our brain makes in the neocortex. The brain does not automatically distinguish between images it makes of real external events and images it makes from our imagination or memory of old happenings. A person can react to memory or an imagined image of an event with as much intensity of emotion as to the actual event itself (42, p. 88). For example, an individual can become very upset by a radio report of a tragic accident. Maultsby has his clients use what he calls "rational emotive imagery" to practice correct thinking, feeling, and acting. In his view, it is the brain's mental image, from whatever source, that controls emotional and physical reactions. Therefore, he will instruct people to imagine systematically and repeatedly, acting effectively and feeling calm in anxiety-provoking situations.

In *Multimodal Behavior Therapy* (37), Arnold Lazarus described imagery as various "mental pictures" that exert an influence upon our lives. He recommended utilizing imagery as an aid in assessing a client's problems. He himself asks clients to picture three things in their mind: their childhood home, a tour from room to room in this childhood home, and a special safe place. He probes for details, information about other people involved, and associated feelings, (37, pp. 37–38). In general, Lazarus ascribed great importance to imagery: "It must be stressed that image formation is a crucial component of thinking. In other words, cognitive processes involve various levels of construct formation, abstract reasoning, intentions, plans, decisions, expectancies, values, belief systems, internalized rules, and mental imagery—innumerable events, scenes, people, and places drawn from past experience. Any cognitive schema that ignores imagery is bound to be incomplete" (37, p. 90).

In addition to Lazarus's book, the year 1976 also witnessed the publication of Aaron Beck's *Cognitive Therapy and the Emotional Disorders* (7). Written by a leading psychiatrist who was originally trained as a psychoanalyst, this is one of the definitive works on cognitive theory. Beck pulled together the ideas and formulations of many who preceded him. He set down in succinct but scientific fashion a body of principles and the cognitive therapeutic techniques appropriate for each of the major emotional disorders. In all cases he held that thought shapes emotion and behavior, and that the task of therapy was to reshape the erroneous beliefs that produced inappropriate emotions and behavior. He contended that the concept of "free-floating anxiety" was a fallacy, since anxiety was the consequence of a specific thought.

Until the 1980s, the only books by a social worker on cognitive theory as a distinct, identified entity were authored by this writer. Howard Goldstein joined him with the publication of *Social Learning and Change: A Cognitive Approach to Human Services* (24) and *Creative Change: A Cognitive-Humanistic Approach to Social Work Practice* (27). The book ends with a concise statement of eighteen basic principles. In *Creative Change*, Goldstein serves as both author and editor. In three chapters written by himself, he restates the philosophical and theoretical foundations of a cognitive approach, with emphasis on the subjective, unmeasurable, and uncategorizable aspects of personality. He also sums up some of the implications of the other eight chapters, contributed by various practitioners and dealing with the ways they apply a cognitive approach in working with specific client groups. Goldstein describes a cognitive-humanistic orientation to social work practice as "an unpretentious way of working with other human beings as colleagues and not as experts. The primary intent is to enter into and attempt to fathom the subjective world of our client" (27, p. 280). Attention should be paid not only to the client's definition of the problem but also to those purposes that the client's solutions may serve. In regard to a client's version of past personal history, whether or not the events actually occurred is not as important as "how the meanings that are given to these experiences may be employed to explain or justify the person's current way of life" (27, p. 44).

The task-centered approach of William Reid and Laura Epstein, while not formally allied to any particular theoretical system, seems to be essentially cognitive. Reid viewed people as less prisoners of unconscious drives than Freudians believe and less prisoners of environmental forces than orthodox behaviorists contend (52). Clients therefore had the ability to make their own free choices about what their problems were and what they wished to achieve. His book focused on the steps and procedures to be used in helping clients solve their problems by working on specific tasks. Similarly, Epstein placed emphasis on the client's definition of the problem, which the client was helped to solve through a series of client and practitioner tasks mutually agreed upon (18). She described her approach as a structured one, involving a number of specified steps such as problem identification, contracting, and problem-solving.

Path into Social Work; Principal Social Work Proponents

Many social workers use aspects of a cognitive approach in their daily practice, and some have written about these cognitive techniques in social work journals. However, until the late 1970s, neither the practitioners nor the writers seemed aware of the larger identity of these components, seldom designated them as cognitive, and did not realize they were actually part of a theoretical system. It is the intent of this chapter to delineate that system.

Meanwhile, it may be of interest to review how cognitive theory has gradually been extending its path into social work through two types of articles in social work journals: those dealing with cognitive techniques as fragments without awareness of their larger identity, and more recent papers that identify cognitive approaches as part of a distinct theoretical system.

Following are brief summaries of several articles of the first type, beginning with Werner Gottlieb and Joe Stanley, who stated: "Treatment in casework should be based on goals that are consciously established and mutually agreed upon by the client and the worker. . . . This process occurs within the framework of the caseworker-client relationship on a conscious level. . . ." (28, p. 471). These authors went on to warn against situations in which the worker's set of goals and the client's set of goals are not even remotely connected: "If the worker sets up objectives for treatment without sharing them with the client, he runs the risk of losing the client or of losing the focus of treatment because the client does not know why he is in treatment or has unrealistic expectations" (28, p. 472). Gottlieb and Stanley declared that the responsibility of the worker in treatment was to "feed back" pertinent diagnostic data, to help the client achieve new perceptions of herself and her situation, and to enable her to reformulate or expand goals (28, p. 473).

This paper further recognized the importance of working with consciousness, helping the client to achieve new perceptions of herself and her situation, and dealing with the client's strengths rather than with her pathology. The authors seem to be well aware of the part goals play in shaping relationships, and they anticipate that personality growth will result from a process that occurs on a conscious level. These techniques and beliefs all flow directly out of cognitive theory.

According to David Hallowitz, Ralph Bierman, Grace Harrison, and Burta Stulberg, there can be an assertive counseling component in therapy (30). One of its elements is confronting the client with disparities between perception and reality and offering alternatives to inaccurate perception. Another element involves showing the client discrepancies between stated goals and actual behavior, caused by shortsighted, impulsive, pleasure-seeking acts that block the attainment of desired long-term goals. In assertive counseling, the therapist may suggest concrete measures by which the client might achieve her objectives. Thus, the worker gives the client "homework" to do between interviews, guiding her into growth-producing experiences. Always, the client's own ideas are elicited and utilized.

Robert Sunley was the first to use the term "cognitive casework" (61). However, in so doing, he did not refer to an overall treatment approach but, rather, to a limited helping process dealing specifically with clients who exhibited cognitive deficiency.

Sunley believes caseworkers should take responsibility for developing new ways of reaching out to clients, and one of these new dimensions he designates cognitive casework, which should deal with those early-level cognitive deficits that deprive individuals of the basic tools or skills necessary for thinking. It should deal with the *processes* of thinking and the use of language, rather than with the *content* of thinking (opinions, conclusions, etc.). The goal of cognitive casework should be the improvement of the client's thinking processes. Specifically, those with cognitive deficiency lack the ability to find the right words for naming and classifying things. They have much difficulty in transferring what they have learned in one situation to another that is similar. It is hard for them to put problems into words and to see alternative solutions. Sunley takes the position that it is valid for casework to concern itself with teaching clients how to use language, how to think systematically, how to observe, remember, and generalize. Thus, he affirms some of the main tenets of cognitive theory: language is the unique possession of man, which sets him apart from all other animals; mastery of language makes possible rational thought; expansion of consciousness, which includes how an individual goes about his thinking, is required when limitations in the thinking process produce problems in living.

Norman Epstein discussed brief group therapy for parents in a child guidance clinic, describing a philosophical orientation that fits into the cognitive category, but not identifying it as such (19). He referred to the great amount of time and energy that was being spent elsewhere, with questionable returns, in attempts to resolve infantile conflicts.

Epstein explained that treatment in his clinic was geared to helping people live more comfortably. The therapist did not focus on transference, countertransference, and the working out of problems through resolution of a countertransference relationship. The agency's follow-up program found no evidence that symptom removal necessarily led to symptom substitution, a formulation that is central to the more traditional analytical conceptualizations.

Colby White described casework with reluctant welfare clients and how to circumvent hindrances to effective casework (69). He favored the experiential approach to therapy, in which *why* questions are never asked. The orientation is to the client in the interview here and now: what she is doing, how she is acting and feeling, what she dislikes about her current situation, how she is trying to solve her problem, and what prevents her from solving it. "The primary function of the caseworker is to present the client with the opportunity to consider his behavior and to decide whether this behavior is in his best interest" (69, p. 617).

White's approach contains the essence of cognitive theory, which deemphasizes probing for the *origin* of current feeling and behavior. Instead, it emphasizes understanding the *quality* of that feeling and behavior: are they constructive or destructive, appropriate or inappropriate, effective or ineffective? Cognitive theory and White are in agreement in relating better emotional health to the expanded consciousness that results from accurate perception.

Max Siporin urged social workers to adopt a situational perspective in their efforts to help the client (58). He states that behavior change requires, among other things, "change in a person's situational attitudinal definitions" (58, p. 99). Personality change likewise "concerns a new consciousness and definition of one's life situation (58, p. 99). He concluded by urging social workers to adopt "an explicit and conscious situational perspective" that will enable them to "achieve a richer and more valid understanding of clients in the context of the social realities of their lives and problems" (58, p. 109).

Siporin pointed out that this would represent a return to a psychosocial outlook in social work that was lost for a while when psychoanalytic theory became dominant. He noted that the return to situational approaches in social work has in part been stimulated by "phenomenological, existentialist trends in philosophy and psychology" (58, p. 93). (The reader is reminded that "phenomenological" is a synonym for "cognitive.") Siporin's situational perspective fits completely into the cognitive framework, with its focus on the close relationship between a person's behavior and personality and that person's perceptions of reality.

Up to this point cognitive theory was not identified as such in articles appearing in social work journals. However, in the mid-1970s the situation began to change. Maultsby described how to diagnose and treat neurotic adolescents within a framework of rational-emotive therapy, which is one form of cognitive treatment (43). Veronica Snyder, a supervisor of therapy in an alcoholism treatment program, discussed cognitive approaches in the treatment of alcoholism (60). She identified cognitive approaches by that name and encouraged their use in work with alcoholics.

James Lantz published a landmark article entitled "Cognitive Theory and Social Casework" in which he stated that "The primary concept held by cognitive practitioners is that most human emotion is the direct result of what people think, tell themselves, assume, or believe about themselves and their social situations" (36, p. 361). He concluded that cognitive theory had generally been ignored in the casework literature and hoped that his presentation would result in more systematic use of cognitive theory in the practice of social casework.

Hanna Zacks proposed a general outline of an educational program for groups of middle-aged people to help them develop problem-solving techniques for problems typical of their age group. She declared that "the proposed program is cognitively oriented; it focuses on developing a rational approach to dealing with personal difficulties" (72, p. 232).

Terri Combs examined the theory, method, and clinical outcomes of cognitive therapy as applied by Aaron Beck to the treatment of depression (13). Combs also reviewed the relatively small number of existing experimental studies of the effectiveness of cognitive therapy in treating depression, concluding that it showed promise, especially in combination with other modalities. Recommendations were made as to some of the areas that needed special attention in future research on the cognitive treatment of depression.

Sharon Berlin discussed the recent development of a "cognitive-behavioral hybrid" to deal with the inadequacy of traditional separate learning theory formulations, which held that responses are regulated by environmental consequences without requiring cognitive involvement of the responders (8). She then presented what she called a cognitive-learning perspective for social work, which was primarily a cognitive approach. However, she did not regard a cognitive approach as able to stand alone and independent as a treatment modality.

Charles Zastrow advanced a new child-abuse theory derived from the rational therapy of Albert Ellis, a variation of cognitive therapy (73). His theory took the position that the reasons for any abusive act can be determined by examining what the offender was telling herself before or during the time the abuse was being committed. Zastrow claimed that rational therapy has demonstrated that the primary cause of all our emotions and actions is what we tell outselves about the events that happen to us.

In 1982, Berlin continued the discussion begun in her 1980 paper. In this one she again merged cognitive and behavioral modalities into what she designated as cognitive behavioral interventions (9). She emphasized that these represented a psychosocial orientation. Two detailed case studies were presented. In the first, a combination of both cognitive and behavioral techniques were utilized, each category clearly recognizable as distinct from the other. The second client was treated with an almost exclusively cognitive approach. Nevertheless, Berlin did not choose to regard cognitive therapy and behavior therapy as separate entities. This issue will be explained more fully later in this chapter.

One of the principles of cognitive treatment is to help the client see reality as accurately as possible. To accomplish this, the perceptions of the practitioner about the client and her world also need to correspond closely to the facts. Stanley Witkin examined how faulty cognitive processes of practitioners can lead to erroneous judgments and inappropriate practice decisions (70). He cited errors in the assigning of causes and reasons and in the assessment of strengths and weaknesses. He noted the strong persistence of inaccurate judgments even in the face of new information. Recommendations were made as to how to prevent or minimize biased and irrational thoughts that might creep into a social worker's orderly thinking.

Harvey Weiner and Sonja Fox sought to expose clinicians to the use of a cognitive approach with substance abusers (64). They suggested a combination of cognitive therapy, setting up goals that could be used to measure progress, relaxation and assertiveness training, and daily task assignments. They took the position that, while physiological detoxification can occur in a relatively brief period of time, little has been accomplished if the client retains the faulty cognitions that originally led to the addiction. They described common cognitive distortions about substance abusers that occur among staff who work with them, and then presented a case in which treatment emphasized changing the client's distorted cognitions. Weiner and Fox chose to designate their treatment as cognitive-behavioral therapy.

Showing its relation to other treatment systems, Howard Goldstein offered a lucid description of the fundamentals of cognitive theory (25), tracing its origins and development, and viewing this theory as having two separate tracks: the mediational model (reality constructs the person), and the phenomenological model (the person constructs reality). Goldstein pointed out that practitioners more and more are recognizing cognitive functions as critical media for change, and that various treatment approaches partly utilize a cognitive orientation without designating it as such. He concluded with the ways cognitive principles are actually translated into direct practice by different practitioners, noting that the mediational view is basic to the practice of the recent hybrid known as cognitive-behavior therapy, a fusing of cognitive and behavioral techniques. (This development will be examined further on.) The phenomenological perspective seems to be associated by Goldstein with the practice of cognitive therapy as a separate entity with a humanistic orientation.

"Starting where the client is," according to Goldstein, can best be understood and accomplished within a cognitive approach to direct practice (26). In this article, he went on to examine some of the factors that can limit the worker's understanding of the client's reality. Early interviews with a social worker are often such a new experience for the client that, struggling with this novel event, the client initially does not come across to the worker as he really is in daily life. The client will need time to develop trust in the helper before risking self-disclosure. Cultural differences of which the worker is not aware can distort the practitioner's cognitions, as can meanings attached by clients to words and sentences they use that are different from the meanings the worker attributes to those words. The practitioner's theoretical orientation can restrict her from paying attention to all aspects of the client's state of being. Goldstein recommended looking at the purposes served by client behavior as one way of knowing where they were, at the same time bearing in mind the selective nature of their perceptions and the tendency of people to disregard events that contradicted what they already believed. Finally, Goldstein saw "starting where the client is" as useful only when the client's own story was not challenged or judged to be true or false, but utilized as a way to enter into the client's present actual world of experience.

Pranab Chatterjee published a highly theoretical article (12) acknowledging the recent impact of cognitive theories on social work practice, but disagreeing with Goldstein's discussion (25) of the roots of modern cognitivism in social work. He claimed that Goldstein and social workers in general have ignored the influences and contributions of various psychologists, sociologists, and anthropologists, especially George Kelly. Chatterjee questioned the validity of Goldstein's phenomenological model of cognitive theory.

Present Status and Influence on Current Social Work Practice

Cognitive theory is a general category within which are included Adler's individual psychology, Ellis's rational-emotive psychotherapy, Glasser's reality therapy, this writer's rational casework, and the ideas of others who regard emotions and behavior as the products of thinking. Philosophically, it is closely related to Mary Richmond's psychosocial orientation, which insisted that the caseworker had to understand both the individual he sought to help and the situation in which that client lived.

In the 1920s, Mary Richmond's ideas were washed away by the tide of psychoanalysis, whose focus was entirely on the client's inner dynamics. This concentration on the individual psyche was fostered in part by the prevailing political climate in the United States at that time, characterized by illusions that this was the best society possible and by resentment against any efforts to criticize or change that society. In such an atmosphere, personal problems and breakdowns were regarded as the consequence of individual weakness or pathology; the possibility of societal defects as a causal factor was not given much consideration. Herman Borenzweig has supported this interpretation:

> Concern with sexual behavior and the unconscious led to the neglect of balancing psychological theories, particularly those concerned with the more rational cognitive processes of mind. Finally, the repudiation of social reform caused by the political climate of the 1920s reinforced a preoccupation with the individual psyche. (10, p. 16)

Following twenty years of psychoanalytic domination, there was a shift in emphasis again in the 1940s, after the depression and World War II made it clear that preoccupation with the unconscious was ineffective in helping people deal with massive pressures and anxieties generated by the world around them. The shift was to "ego psychology." The new emphasis on the "nonconflicted ego functioning" of the client was testimony to the fact that social work intuitively had moved back to working with the consciousness of people. The conceptualization of consciousness as "nonconflicted ego functioning" was an attempt to preserve Freudian terminology and framework. Nevertheless, this represented recognition of Adler's view that personality is a holistic phenomenon, that the psyche functions as a unit. Thus, the cognitive orientation made itself felt in the 1940s, although the new adherents of ego psychology never called it by that name.

From that time until now, cognitive theory has continued to influence social work practice, sometimes in the same anonymous way, but more recently with increasing frequency of identification. While many workers still use cognitive techniques on the sole basis that they make "common sense," others are now able to identify a treatment method as coming from Adler, Ellis, Glasser, Beck, or others.

Whether identified or not, methods flowing out of cognitive theory are widely used by social workers today. This is true when a worker does any one of the following things:

1. Relates to the client on the basis of his behavior and his stated thoughts, emotions, and goals, without postulating unconscious forces.

2. Makes a diagnosis in terms of the distortions or limitations in the client's thinking.
3. Looks for the client's strengths rather than his pathology and puts those strengths to use.
4. Guides the client into trying selected experiences that may alter his inaccurate perceptions.
5. Recognizes that each client's behavior is shaped by his personal goals rather than by universal biological drives.
6. Works to achieve changes the client wants by expanding this consciousness of self, others, and the world around him.
7. Requires the client to take responsibility for his behavior, not allowing the past or the "unconscious" to excuse present conduct.

At the present time, the professions of psychiatry and psychology pay more attention than does social work to cognitive theory as a well-defined theoretical system. For example, in 1984 the Commission on Psychiatric Therapies of the American Psychiatric Association published *The Psychiatric Therapies* (2). It examines the major therapies and places them in perspective, giving historical background, basic theoretical issues, strategies and techniques, indications and limitations, and developmental and age-related issues for each. The purpose of this volume is to present the state of the art of all therapies practiced in this country, and serve as a guide to clinicians as to which therapy is appropriate for a particular disorder. Cognitive therapy is one of the approaches included.

Connection with Other Theories

Existential and functional theory have elements that are compatible with the cognitive orientation. In fact, existential theory would seem to fall completely within the cognitive category. It has not been so classified in this chapter only because it is the subject of a separate chapter in this volume.

According to Adrian Van Kaam, the existential viewpoint holds that the essential difference between one individual and another is the degree of readiness that each has developed to be open to whatever she encounters in her environment. The whole life of a person is built upon the decision she makes either to face or to avoid the truth about herself—e.g., her weaknesses and limitations. Only when an individual opens herself to all of significant reality and to the many modes of her existence can she understand her authentic self and fulfill her potentials and responsibilities (63).

Thomas Hora, in explaining existential psychotherapy, states that complete understanding of one's mode of being tends to bring about a changed attitude toward life. Change occurs when a person can see the totality of her situation. Hora contends that "change is the result of expanding consciousness" (32, p. 37).

The existential therapist and the cognitive therapist thus share an identical conviction: change in the client results from being helped to perceive herself, her world, and her relationship to that world more fully and more accurately.

Functional (Rankian) theory insists, as does cognitive theory, on the primary importance of consciousness. Ruth Smalley tells us that the push toward growth and fulfillment is primary in human beings; the innate purpose in each of us is to grow (59). This conception is shared by Adler, Maslow, and others in the cognitive category. Otto Rank himself was especially interested in the will, which he considered to be a significant component of consciousness. Functionalists believe their task is to help the client use his will positively toward his own self-chosen ends. The cognitive practitioner has in mind a similar concept when she helps the client to understand his situation, assert himself, and confront whatever needs to be faced. Rank maintained that individuals are understood through their present experience, where their whole reaction pattern, past and present, is apparent. The cognitive practitioner uses the same kind of "here-and-now" approach. Finally, Rank placed considerable emphasis on the process of choosing between alternatives, a conscious act that each person carries out repeatedly throughout his lifetime.

For Rank, will and consciousness were primary. We remember what we *will* to remember. We will unconsciousness to escape facing the present (51). Cognitive theory, with its view that the *content* of a person's behavior is usually based on what he thinks, recognizes that the *intensity* of his acts depends on the strength of his will. Adler, for example, gave much importance to the cultivation of courage in the client.

With the coming of Freud, thinking and reasoning were relegated to a minor role in the mental life of human beings. As Charles Brenner stated, Freud believed that "the majority of mental functioning goes on without consciousness and that consciousness is an unusual rather than a usual quality or attribute of mental functioning" (11, p. 15). Interestingly, John B. Watson's behaviorism took the same stance and regarded behavior not as a product of conscious thinking, but mainly as the conditioned consequences of external events.

Psychoanalysis and behaviorism had their first major impact on this side of the Atlantic at about the same time in the 1920s, and they became the dominant psychological trends. This meant that social work, in its formative years, had a choice between two theories, both of which emphasized the animal nature of man. Freud saw man's behavior as controlled by inner biological drives; Watson saw it as conditioned by external events. Both regarded thinking as a minimal factor in determining behavior, and therefore in effect ignored the unique characteristic that sets a human being apart from, and above, other animals: language. Behaviorism also minimized the importance of emotions in human behavior, which may have been one of the reasons why social work was not attracted to it at that time and chose psychoanalysis for its theoretical framework.

The cognitive approach is based entirely on the fact we do have language. It is language that makes it possible for us to reason, calculate, think abstractly, solve problems, recapture memories, describe emotions, formulate goals, make predictions, generalize, and communicate conclusions to others. In sum, it is language that makes thinking possible, and it is thinking that brings into being behavior, emotions, and motives. Change in a person's behavior, emotions, or motives is accomplished by effecting change in his thinking.

To use Maslow's phrase, cognitive theory is therefore a "third force," a psychological approach that does not see behavior as shaped either by unconscious biologically determined inner drives or by externally conditioned habits. The cognitive approach asserts that thinking intervenes continuously to deactivate or modify instinctual drives and learned responses. Heinz Ansbacher confirmed this in a paper on Adler:

> Today the entire movement of humanistic and existential psychology and psychotherapy is founded on this "third force," namely, the self-determination of the individual, as opposed to the other two determining forces: Freud's psychogenetic determinism and the environmental determinism of behaviorism. While Adler was far from denying the importance of biological determinants or environment, he insisted that the individual is not passively shaped by them but "uses" them in accordance with his style of life. (4, p. 779)

The reader may question this cognitive premise that instinctual drives and entrenched habits do not shape behavior because it appears to be self-evident that they do. In this chapter, the word *shape* is used in the sense of "having the critical influence upon" behavior. Obviously, an inner urge or a strongly conditioned response starts us moving in a particular direction, but, except for those with psychoses, phobias, or severe addictions, the movement or action is not completed unless our conscious thought processes support it. It is for this reason that cognitive theory maintains that thinking is the principal determinant of behavior.

In recent years, Arnold Lazarus, a principal figure in contemporary behavior therapy, and other behaviorists have moved away from the school of orthodox stimulus-response-oriented behavior therapists. In 1979, Lazarus wrote about classical behaviorism as being too limited in its approach to solving human problems, with its belief in automatic and autonomic conditioning and its eschewal of most cognitive processes. He summed up his position as follows:

> But our current view is that in humans, conditioning does not occur automatically and is in fact cognitively mediated. The non-mediational model cannot account for vicarious learning, semantic generalization, and other "exclusively human" functions such as imaginal response patterns and symbolic processes. . . . To account for behavior solely in terms of external rewards and punishments overlooks the fact that human beings can be rewarded and punished by their *own thinking*. (38, p. 552)

Lazarus also asserted that, while orthodox behaviorists remained opposed to the idea that behavior can be influenced by cognitions, the field of behavior therapy was currently becoming increasingly "cognitive." He regarded the stimulus–response "learning theory" basis of behavior therapy as passé, claiming that a distinctly cognitive orientation now prevailed, which did not deny consciousness and recognized that conditioning was produced through the operation of higher mental processes. Meanwhile, Lazarus himself had moved ahead to develop a more comprehensive framework for assessment and treatment, which he named "multimodal" and which included cognition and several other modalities in addition to behavior per se (37). When focusing on the modality of cognition with clients, Lazarus recommended emphasis on exploring the categorical imperatives ("shoulds" and "musts") that people impose on themselves, perfectionism and refusal to accept fallibility, and tendencies to attribute to external events.

Lazarus's observation in 1977 that the field of behavior therapy was becoming more and more "cognitive" has been fully confirmed by the literature published from that time until the present (1984). We now have a large number of books and articles about "cognitive-behavior therapy," written mostly by psychologists.

This conceptual merging of the two approaches by some practitioners represents a realization that behavior modification techniques need to be based on the fact that humans are thinking and feeling beings who are not to be mechanically manipulated. In that sense, the partial blending is a positive and necessary development. However, it obscures the reality that they are still fundamentally different theoretical systems with separate identities. It will be more useful and less confusing for behaviorists to continue seeing behavior as influenced by cognition, for cognitists to utilize behavior modification methods whenever indicated, as they have been doing, and for both to avoid a blurring of basic premises by the creation of a new label.

The results of research done by Robert Kaplan, Sharon McCordick, and Mark Twitchell showed that a cognitive-only treatment for test anxiety was more effective than desensitization only or a combination of cognitive treatment plus desensitization (33). This would indicate that cognitive therapy can stand alone as a separate entity.

R. Christopher Miller and Jeffrey Berman conducted an analysis of forty-eight studies of cognitive behavior therapies (47). The studies in this review encompassed a broad spectrum of treatments, ranging from therapies sometimes labeled cognitive to therapies explicitly combining cognitive and behavioral techniques. The researchers were able to compare the efficacy of primarily cognitive approaches with therapies that explicitly emphasized the use of behavioral techniques, recognizing their separateness. They found no difference in effectiveness between cognitive behavior therapy explicitly stressing the behavior component of treatment and a primarily cognitive approach.

Giovanni Liotti and Mario Reda discussed the increasing efforts to integrate behavior and cognitive therapy, as exemplified by the cognitive behavior modification (CBM) developed by Meichenbaum. They warned that "we must approach this integration with extreme caution in order to avoid the possible theoretical and methodological confusion" (40, p. 235).

Traditional or pure kinds of behavior therapy such as desensitization, operant conditioning, or biofeedback differ from Meichenbaum's CBM, which has been presented as a newer and different technique. In CBM, cognitive change rather than behavior change is supposed to be the focus of treatment. Barry Ledwidge contended that "cognitions are not behaviors; they are constructs . . . and CBM is not behavior modification. . . . Failure to distinguish the two kinds of therapy could have unfortunate theoretical as well as practical consequences" (39, p. 138).

While the psychotic, phobic, and severely addicted constitute exceptions to the "rule" that thinking is the principal determinant of behavior, they do not invalidate the concept. Maslow made an important contribution to the process of theory building in dealing with this same point; you cannot understand very disturbed people until you first understand more healthy functioning. Goble stated that Maslow himself wrote: "It becomes more and more clear that the study of crippled, stunted, immature, and unhealthy specimens can yield only a cripple psychology and a cripple philosophy" (11, p. 180). Maslow believed that a healthy individual's motivation was stronger than most instinctual drives. He felt that the power of these drives had been overestimated, and reclassified them from "instincts" to "instinctoid impulses" (41, pp. 77–95).

Donald Krill supported the same view when he concluded:

> For the existentialists, man's biological drives are important and must be understood, but they do not fully explain man's nature. As a matter of fact, emphasis on the primacy of instinctual drives is a way of viewing human beings at their minimum level of functioning rather than their maximum level. At this maximum level man has freedom, the power to transcend his egotistical strivings, courage to venture, and a capacity to endure (35, p. 49).

The aforementioned three special situations in which the axiom "thinking shapes behavior" does not apply will be more fully examined further on in the section entitled "Counterindications for Use of Theory."

The cognitive practitioner sees each client as a person who perceives himself, other people, his world, and his relationship to that world in his own special way. Experience consists of sensory inputs that the client interprets and evaluates. The combination of sensing and judging is what we call "perception." If perception is accurate, emotions and behavior will be appropriate. If perception is not accurate, emotions and behavior will be inappropriate. This is illustrated by the child who sees a friendly dog, perceives it accurately, reacts with a happy feeling, and goes over to play with it. Perception, emotions, and behavior are appropriate, but they would not be if the child perceived the same dog as dangerous, felt frightened, and began to cry.

It is perception, a conscious thinking process, that generates emotions and behavior. Thinking is also necessary for the development of motives, which in cognitive terms are defined as objectives or goals chosen by the client out of his conception of necessity. Emotions, behavior, and motives are, therefore, all viewed as conscious phenomena. In the cognitive framework, it is not possible for a person to have unconscious fear because the emotion of fear is the product of the conscious processes of becoming aware of something and evaluating it.

A complete definition of emotion also takes into account the individual's physical reactions to a given object or situation. In cognitive theory, then, a full definition of emotion would be: emotion is the feeling a person experiences after estimating what an event means to him and reacting with a set of involuntary physiological responses. Such responses include flushing, sweating, trembling, stiffening, relaxation, increasing of heart rate, and many more. The more pronounced the physiological responses are, the stronger the emotion is considered to be.

Magda Arnold supported this concept when she wrote:

> We have seen that emotion is an experience in which the person appraises the object as affecting himself. Such an appraisal of the object results in a felt attraction or aversion, and eventually (if no other motive interferes) in approach or avoidance. Perception is completed by an intuitive appraisal that arouses emotion. . . . Summing up our discussion, we can now define emotion as the felt tendency toward anything intuitively appraised as good (beneficial), or away from anything intuitively appraised as bad (harmful). This attraction or aversion is accompanied by a pattern of physiological changes organized toward approach or withdrawal. The patterns differ for different emotions. (6, Vol. I, p. 182)

Confirming the cognitive view of emotion as a conscious phenomenon, Arnold also stated: "We can like or dislike only something we know. We must see or hear or touch something, remember having done so or imagine it, before we can decide that it is good or bad for us" (6, Vol. II, p. 33).

As we have said, inaccurate perceptions or appraisals generate inappropriate emotions. Ellis stated this another way when he maintained that man's "emotional or psychological disturbances are largely a result of his thinking illogically or irrationally; and that he can rid himself of most of his emotional or mental unhappiness, ineffectuality, and disturbance if he learns to maximize his rational and minimize his irrational thinking" (17, p. 36). Ellis went on to specify a number of irrational ideas that can lead to emotional disturbances. These irrational ideas are taught and transmitted either by the culture as a whole, the family, and/or significant others:

1. It is a dire necessity for an adult to be loved and approved by most of the significant people in his environment.

2. One is not worthwhile unless he is virtually perfect in all respects.
3. Certain people are bad and should be blamed and punished for their badness.
4. It is terrible when things are not the way one would like them to be.
5. Human unhappiness is externally caused and people have little ability to control their sorrows.
6. One should keep dwelling on the possibility of dangerous things happening and be deeply concerned (e.g., being in a car accident).
7. It is better to avoid difficult situations or responsibilities than to face them.
8. One should depend on someone else, for we each need someone stronger on whom to rely.
9. One's past history is an all-important determiner of present behavior, and a significant past event will indefinitely continue to influence us.
10. We should become quite upset over other people's problems or disturbances.
11. There is a correct and perfect solution to human problems and it is catastrophic if this perfect solution is not found. (17, pp. 60–88)

Within the cognitive framework, aggression is not regarded as inherent in a human being. Cooperative behavior is not regarded as something that can only be achieved by one's repression of her true nature, because cognitive theory does not view her true nature as aggressive. On the contrary, cooperative behavior is seen as an inborn potential that, if cultivated by family and society, brings one to her highest level of functioning. Bertha Reynolds, the great social work teacher, wrote after her retirement: "I have come to challenge too much reliance on Freudian psychology with its assumption that neurosis is preconditioned by civilized society. A different view of history is that man is a part of nature and healthy adjustment to it is 'natural' for man" (53, p. 16).

In examining Adler's ideas about aggression, Ansbacher stated:

Adler was fully aware of the frequently observed aggressive and hostile behavior of men toward one another. However, he did not see this behavior as one of the signs of an instinct of destruction that must find an outlet. Rather, he saw aggression as a way in which the individual mistakenly pursues the goals of personal superiority and power. Far from assuming an innate aggression and hostility, Adler assumed that a positive capacity for social living is an innate component of human nature. Once this capacity has been properly developed, beginning in early childhood, it becomes social interest that assures a constructive life. (3, pp. 269–270)

In recent years, Lorenz, Ardrey, Morris, and others have been affirming their support of the "naked ape" concept: a human being is just another savage animal who kills to get what he wants. This is the modern version of Freud's contention that man is born "a wolf unto other men," driven by the same biology as jungle animals. On the other hand, it has been pointed out for a long time by many other investigators, of whom Alland is one of the latest, that the evidence is against the theory of inherent aggression. For example, if all individuals are born aggressive, then all societies should be aggressive, but they are not. There are many nonviolent societies. Alland contends that a person is born with the biological *capacity* for aggression. However, he claims that the major determinant of behavior is culture, which has the decisive effect on whether or not aggressive behavior actually occurs, and on the form in which aggression is expressed. "The evidence tells us that man is not driven by instincts but rather that he is born with a set of capacities, potentials which are developed or thwarted and given direction by early learning and the cultural process" (1, p. 165).

The cognitive approach to aggression, therefore, is to consider it not an inborn quality but a reaction or a chosen life-style. It is a reaction to feelings of threat or frustration: one responds forcefully if she thinks she is in actual danger, may attack first to secure an advantage over potential aggression from another, asserts herself if she believes she is being deprived of what is due her, or explodes when pressures become too great. Aggression becomes a life style for those whose greed for possessions or power is so great and so in conflict with the environment that their goals cannot be attained without aggression.

From the cognitive point of view, neurosis is a way of living based on unrealistic fear, guilt, or anger. The individual is aware of these emotions, which are not necessarily associated with sexuality, but can relate to any of several important aspects of life. The neurotic person is saturated with anxiety, a state of apprehensiveness accompanied by somatic tensions, which is actually, as Herbert Krauss expressed it, "the dread of a future event" (34, pp. 88–93). Some of the future events that people commonly dread are rejection by others, loss of self-control, physical harm, failure, deprivation of power, and exposure of their weaknesses. Rollo May saw anxiety as "the apprehension cued off by a threat to some value which the individual holds essential to his existence as a personality" (4, p. 191). Theodore Sarbin further enriched the concept of anxiety by depicting it as cognitive strain. He defined "cognitive strain" as large increases in cognitive activity produced by a person's inability to fit a new situation or object into his perceptual framework, find his place in society, or evaluate his performance of life tasks (55, pp. 635–638).

Finally, the concept of a substantive "unconscious" plays a minor role in cognitive theory. It is not seen as the controlling force of our mental lives. One can be unconscious—that is, unaware—of certain facts, of the impression she is making on others, of the origins of her current ideas, of her own potentialities, or of a thought she has forgotten or deliberately put out of her mind. However, in the cognitive view, material out of awareness does not exert any influence over our behavior. Consciousness is not a knowledge of the "unconscious" but of the realities of our world and ourselves.

This new way of regarding the unconscious has considerable support. May wrote: "The 'unconscious,' then, is not to be thought of as a reservoir of impulses, thoughts, wishes which are culturally unacceptable; I define it rather as those potentialities for knowing and experiencing which the individual cannot or will not actualize" (45, p. 688). Rado described the unconscious as a "nonreporting (in contrast to the conscious mind which is reporting) organization of causative links between processes of which we are aware" (50, p. 182). Adler concluded: "The unconscious is nothing other than that which we have been unable to formulate in clear concepts" (5, p. 232).

The cognitive attitude toward the concept of an unconscious has important immediate theoretical consequences. As the author has written elsewhere, "This viewpoint does not recognize the existence of an 'unconscious' serving as a repository of ideas, emotions, drives, and conflicts of whose existence we are unaware but which determine our behavior without our knowing it" (65, p. 21). Consequently, the cognitive practitioner cannot regard anxiety as a danger signal warning that repressed material is breaking out of the unconscious. Dreams are not what Freud called "the royal road to the unconscious," but instead are seen as reflections of situations or problems we fail to master in our waking existence. Montague Ullman suggests that the distorted content of dreams is due to the fact that parts of the brain which select, organize, and systematize stimuli are inactive when we sleep (62, pp. 30–60).

In addition to dreams, Freudians view behavior under hypnosis and multiple personalities as further evidence of the existence of a substantive unconscious. Ernest Hilgard, however, claims that his studies of people under hypnosis suggest that what takes place is a division of consciousness into parallel parts instead of higher and lower levels. He finds that, under hypnosis, consciousness is split vertically, so that the hypnotized part can be instructed to become deaf or feel no pain, while a parallel process in another part of consciousness, "the hidden observer," registers spoken words or physical discomfort. Hilgard refers to Pierre Janet's theory of dissociation in characterizing dual personalities a similar division of consciousness, a dissociation of some part of the personality from the primary personality, but on a single level. The secondary or hidden personality manifests itself in conscious behavior exactly as the normal one usually does, and knows all about the primary personality, although the primary persona has no awareness of the second one. The barrier between the two parts is interpreted as an inability to recall, an amnesia by the conscious part for the split-off part that on occasion may become conscious. It does not seem necessary to postulate the existence of the unconscious on a different, deeper level. In cases where the hidden personality is healthier, therapy attempts to bring about an integration based on the secondary personality, not the primary one.

Hilgard believes that the mind as a whole has unity, though one's acquaintance with it is always partial. He concludes from his studies that in hypnosis the experimenter can deliberately inhibit certain cognitive systems. These systems, although they are not now represented in consciousness, continue to register and process incoming information. "When such a system is released from inhibition, consciousness uses this information as though it had been conscious all along. This is the clinical picture we find in cases of multiple personality; it is the laboratory picture when the hidden observer is brought to light" (31, pp. 49).

Ansbacher has provided the following succinct summary of cognitive therapeutic concepts: "It follows directly from man's creative power that he is not blindly driven by instincts, but is guided by his goals or anticipations. Psychotherapy is not as concerned with discovering causes as with changing the individual's goals and interpretations, and thereby his actions. . . . Successful therapy is based on a cognitive reorganization; the criterion is a change in behavior" (3, p. 779).

Theoretical Concepts: The Therapeutic Relationship

An experience reported by John Mayer and Noel Timms illustrates one of the key issues regarding any therapeutic relationship. They described a British family agency where social workers were trying to provide clients with some psychological insight into their difficulties. The clients were working-class people complaining about another member of the family. They were not interested in the causes of their problems but in obtaining specific advice or in getting their worker to take steps to reform the offender. However, the workers took a nonactivist approach and probed into the past. The clients found this strange and puzzling, and interpreted is as a lack of interest or understanding. Many dropped out. Mayer and Timms made the following comment:

> It is our impression that the social workers were unaware that the clients entered the treatment situation with a different mode of problem-solving and that the clients' behavior during treatment was in part traceable to this fact . . . there is a pervasive, although possibly decreasing, tendency in the field of social work to rely on psychodynamic concepts in explaining behavior. As a consequence, cognitive elements (beliefs, thoughts, opinions) receive little attention and are apt to be viewed as epiphenomena, as derivatives of something deeper, and therefore unlikely to produce any decisive effects of their own on behavior. (46, pp. 37–38)

Since cognitive theory holds that cognitive elements are in fact the decisive influences on behavior, its practitioners as a matter of principle would have easily avoided the client disappointment and treatment termination mentioned above. The cognitive practitioner deals with the client's view of the situation, not his own. He establishes a therapeutic relationship based on working as a partner with the client to achieve the client's goals and to provide the type of help the client wishes. If the cognitive worker believes that the client's goals or the type of help requested will not serve the client's own interests, this becomes a matter of open discussion between them until the matter is resolved.

Cognitive theory regards the goal of treatment to be the expansion and changing of consciousness so that the client's perceptions more closely approximate reality. Accurate perceptions of reality, plus the ability to act on the basis of this accurate understanding, are the prime components of mental health. Therapeutic relationships should be of such a nature as to facilitate the expansion of consciousness and the performance of rational behavior.

Since the cognitive approach is reality-oriented, it calls for a therapeutic relationship in which the client perceives the social worker realistically. The worker should discourage any tendency on the part of the client to perceive the worker either as a parent/lover symbol who is omniscient and virtually perfect or a symbol of others in his life who have been too controlling or rejecting. Such fantasies should be challenged immediately. It is more fundamental to deal with the client's misperceptions about himself and his real world than with transference reactions to the worker that have been deliberately allowed to develop.

The worker should become a friend the client can trust, with all the implications this has for mutual respect, complete openness and informality. As a part of the therapeutic relationship, the client needs to have complete confidence in the worker, who in turn must exemplify any positive concept or quality she discusses. This applies particularly to courage, to which social workers have not paid sufficient attention in the past. If the therapeutic relationship is to enable the client to see things more accurately and to undertake difficult action that may be necessary, it must include the cultivation of courage within the client. Confronting reality and attempting acts that previously were feared can be extremely painful, and require courage.

The therapeutic relationship should be based on consciousness. The ideas the client expresses, the emotions she describes, the motives she states, and the behavior she exhibits are true delineators of what she is. It is not necessary to speculate about unconscious conflicts, forces, or problems. It has become fashionable in recent years to declare that psychoanalytic concepts apply to working-class clients as much as they do to the so-called upper classes, that poor people have an unconscious just like the more affluent have. The cognitive practitioner would claim that the reverse is true: all clients have a consciousness and can be understood only in terms of their consciousness.

The final important element in the therapeutic relationship is the professionalism of the worker. While conducting himself with warmth, spontaneity, and friendliness, the worker must always maintain the maximum objectivity. What he does should always flow out of a sound knowledge of the theory of his choice, and out of his experience with other clients. When theory or past experiences do not apply or are lacking, he needs the courage to utilize his intuition, so that in the end his treatment of the client becomes a blending of science and art. The professionalism of the worker also must include a full understanding of the client's world. Since cognitive theory emphasizes the client's perceptions of reality, the worker will be unable to judge the accuracy or significance of these perceptions unless he knows the culture from which the client comes. In principle, a worker should disqualify himself in favor of another more appropriate colleague if he does not have an essential grasp of the life situation of his client.

Theoretical Concepts: The Nature of Personality*

If we synthesize cognitive concepts about the nature of man into a systematic presentation, we emerge with the proposition that a person's behavior is mainly determined not by unconscious forces but by her thinking and willing. She evaluates herself, others, and the world around her; sets up goals to achieve; and behaves in ways she thinks will attain her objectives and otherwise give her maximum satisfaction. The strength of an individual's will, and the direction in which it is applied, affect the amount of effort she expends and the progress she makes toward her goals. She has the ability to control and deactivate instinctual drives that interfere with her purposes. She normally feels and acts according to the thoughts she presently holds concerning significant factors in her environment.

People have to make choices all their lives: between dependence on others and independence; between clinging and separating; between conformity and originality; between accepting and challenging limits; between goals on the destructive and on the useful side of life; between avoiding and facing all the implications of their existence.

Emotional distress can develop in various ways. A person's goals may be destructive or antisocial, in which case the life-style he evolves to reach these goals will bring pressure, rejection, or retaliation from his society. If an individual is afraid to reveal his authentic self for fear of being found imperfect by others, he erects defensive structures behind which to hide what he really is, becoming anxious and draining his emotional energy in the process. Emotional strain may be experienced in making any of the crucial choices listed in the preceding paragraph. In other cases, individuals become upset as a result of blaming themselves too severely for mistakes they commit just by virtue of being human. Some of us suffer acutely when significant people do not approve of us, or when we encounter disagreement in the world at large. Some of us become disturbed when we are unable to give love, receive love, or behave so as to feel worthwhile to others and to ourselves. There are all kinds of fears and guilt feelings, realistic and otherwise, that prevent people from enjoying a measure of inner peace. Finally, strongly conditioned responses that a person cannot stop even though he knows they are inappropriate can cause great distress.

The cognitive conception of man's nature views the individual as not born either good or evil but trainable in either direction. A person is not seen as inherently aggressive; cooperation with a society in which he believes does not repress his true nature but develops it. He is creative, possesses an innate purpose to grow, and has a basic tendency to strive for competence and a sense of completion. His sex drive is not primary but just one of several drives. Attachments or hostilities to parents, neurosis, and anxiety do not inevitably

---

*The text of this section originally appeared in the writer's *New Understandings of Human Behavior* (New York: Association Press, 1970). It is reproduced with the kind permission of the publishers. A few minor changes have been made.

trace back to sexuality and are more often reactions to all types of life situations. Each person is unique, differing in some ways from all other persons,
and comprehensible only in his own terms. Diagnoses and labels can at most
contribute only a partial understanding of an individual.

Theoretical Concepts: The Nature of Personality Change

Man's principal activities are the pursuit of chosen goals, dealing with new
situations according to the way he perceives them, and solving problems.
Choosing goals, evaluating events, and solving problems are conscious cognitive processes intimately associated with personality. Change in goals, in
perceptions of reality, or in degree of success in problem-solving—that is,
cognitive reorganization—result in personality change.

A client whose goal in life is success in a highly competitive business
exhibits a belligerent personality that would undergo a change if this goal
were replaced by one completely different. Another client, convinced other
people are all potential enemies ready to take advantage of her, presents a
suspicious type of personality that can change if her perceptions of people
change. A third client, whose personality is withdrawn because she fails frequently in her living or job situation, can experience personality change if
she begins to have more success in solving her problems.

When a client changes her goals or perceptions, her behavior changes,
and she engages in experiences that she avoided before due to ignorance, lack
of interest, or fear. The client who overcomes a basic distrust of others is able
to try reaching out to people. A client, whose success after previous failure
engenders new confidence and self-esteem, has a changed perception of herself, is likely to revise her goals and can be encouraged to try unfamiliar
experiences. Change in behavior is not a superficial result in treatment. New
behavior leads to new experiences that can reinforce the client's recent insights, make her future thinking more realistic and thus alter basic personality attributes.

Implications of Theory for Psychosocial History and Diagnosis

Diagnosis asks the question: What is the problem? Cognitive theory implies
that the answer should be given in terms of the client's goals, her perceptions
of reality, and her life-style. This means that the cognitively oriented worker
tries to determine whether the client's goals are constructive or destructive,
what distortions or limitations there are in her evaluations and judgments,
and what the nature of her life-style is. In order to accomplish this, the worker

will be interested in the kind of psychosocial history that provides material in these areas.

In that part of the history-taking that focuses on the client's goals, the worker can utilize the projective technique of Early Recollections (ER), which is economical in terms of time and cost. Arthur Nikelly and Don Verger believe ERs can help the therapist understand the client's purposes, repetitive patterns of behaving, and unity of life. The client is simply asked to think back as far as he can and state the earliest memory from his childhood (49, p. 55). In assessing the client's goals, it is important to find out who are the principal opponents in his life and whether the goals represent an attempt to compensate for a lack or an inferiority feeling.

If the worker observes that the content of the client's evaluations of himself, others, and his world are distorted or limited, part of the psychosocial history should contain information about the family atmosphere, which can be a prime cause of maladjustment. Edith Dewey has worked out the following classifications of family atmosphere: rejective, authoritarian, matyrdom, inconsistent, suppressive, hopeless, indulgent, pitying, high standards, materialistic, competitive, disparaging, and inharmonious (14, pp. 41–45).

Another cause of distorted perceptions of reality is what Adler called "private logic," a faulty *process* of thinking that leads to inaccurate conclusions. This is related to the "cognitive deficiency" described by Sunley earlier in this chapter. In taking the history, the worker should be alert to any evidences of a faulty private logic.

Other factors in distorted perceptions for which the worker should probe in taking a history include severely traumatic experiences, the client's ordinal position in the family (first, middle, last, only child), physical unattractiveness or handicap at any time, and what being a male or female of a certain color, nationality, and religion has meant to the client within his particular family and surrounding environment.

Life-style, the third basis for diagnosis, is the way the client goes about her quest for personal significance, her pattern of living, her "style of acting, thinking and perceiving" (Adler). Nikelly, in discussing psychotherapy from the Adlerian point of view, stated: "Instead of deciphering unconscious wishes and motives, as the psychoanalyst would do, the therapist looks for the basic pattern by which the client moves through life" (48, p. 31). The psychosocial history should include sufficient clues from the past so that the worker, by combining these data about past behavior with his own observations of the client's current behavior, can reach an assessment of the client's life-style. Some varieties of life-style are; pampered, withdrawn, self-sacrificing, controlling, inadequate, joyful, obsequious, and altruistic.

To sum up with an illustration, a cognitive practitioner takes a psychosocial history on a new client to arrive at a working diagnosis, which, of course, is always subject to revision. The client comes for help because he feels tense, overwhelmed, and anxious. The history the worker takes is designed to elicit goals, distortions of perception, and life-style. They are the three bases of diagnosis. She may ask the client for early recollections. She will probe for indications as to the client's chief opponents in life. She will look for evidence that goals which are based on the client's conception of success may have developed out of a strong need to compensate for a specific lack or a specific kind of inferiority feeling. The worker will obtain data about the family atmosphere, any handicaps the client has suffered, his ordinal position, traumatic events, and any problems created by gender, race, or other ethnic characteristics. Finally, the worker will evaluate the soundness of the client's private logic.

In this case, the worker obtains a picture of a man who, because of a sickly childhood, fell behind in school and never matched the educational achievements of his four siblings, among whom he was the middle child. His parents, who overvalued both college education and material possessions, did not conceal their disappointment, and the client developed feelings of failure and inferiority. His earliest recollection was being left behind for misbehaving while all his siblings were taken on a special family trip. Because of the family atmosphere, he came to equate success with monetary wealth, and he set up for himself the compensatory goal of making lots of money in business any way he could. His private logic permitted bending or breaking the law, taking advantage of associates, cheating customers, and using people for his own purposes. Anyone who stood in his way was his opponent. He used the fact that he was a member of the majority ethnic and religious group in his community to beat out business competitors by appeals to bigotry. His manipulating life-style finally became clear to a significant number of people, who began to challenge him, block him, and retaliate with all kinds of pressures. He sought professional help when he could no longer cope with his increasing anxiety, which was triggered by the threat to one of his essential values—business success.

The diagnostic impression of this client is anxiety reaction in a person with antisocial goals whose manipulating life-style has finally evoked from society retaliation, which he cannot handle. Impelled by an urgent need to overcome his feelings of inferiority through the attainment of a family-approved type of success, a limited and distorted perception of himself and his situation has led to equating self-worth and success with the accumulation of wealth in any way possible. Cognitive teatment will include helping the client to adopt a more constructive life-style by having him reevaluate his goals. The reevaluation of goals, however, can only take place when, through the treatment process, the client alters his perceptions of his world to approximate reality more closely.

Treatment Methods and Techniques

The treatment methods and techniques that flow out of cognitive theory can be described simply and clearly. This writer, in a previous work, began such a description this way: "I ask my client to pinpoint his problems and goals. Then I work with him to accomplish the changes he chooses. I show him when his behavior defeats his own stated purposes. I try to help him reach the point where he can see things as they really are and act on the basis of his correct understanding. The focus is on the present and on what the client himself can do to overcome his difficulties" (67, p. 267).

In the process of treating a client, the cognitively oriented worker bases her activity on these premises:

1. Change in perception alters emotions, motives (goals), and behavior.
2. Change in goal is especially influential in altering behavior.
3. New activities and new kinds of behavior alter perception.

As can be seen, there are reciprocal relationships among perception, emotions, goals, and behavior. It follows logically that treatment techniques include contradicting the client whose perceptions of self, others, and society are not accurate. Evidence supporting more realistic appraisals is introduced whenever necessary. When the client's problems are the consequences of antisocial or self-destructive goals (e.g., the case presented in the previous section), the worker points out the connection between the client's distress and his choice of goals. The worker then has the therapeutic task of helping the client to reorient himself with a different set of goals. Finally, since the client himself has chosen the objectives he wishes to achieve in treatment, the worker does not hesitate to recommend new experiences or behavior that may bring him closer to those objectives.

This last point was given strong support by Martin Shepard (who was trained in traditional psychoanalysis) and Marjorie Lee:

> Nonbehavioral therapists are apt to forget or overlook the importance of activity and to lapse into the role of pseudo-philosopher or emotional historian, devoting unnecessary time to the study of feelings and their place in the life of man. Regardless of what patients bring to their therapeutic sessions, the antiaction therapist, feeling safe in the rut of his classical training, invariably directs the discussion to one of emotional reaction. (57, pp. 58–59)

Designating a similar type of practitioner as a Tell Me Why therapist, Shepard and Lee went on to say:

> Yet the TELL ME WHY therapist is not interested in the facts. He is concerned with proving that he is one step ahead of the patient. He can hide his ignorance of life-solutions by relying on a long analysis of Why, rather than launching into WHAT and WHAT-TO-DO-ABOUT-IT. (57, p. 62)

Glasser, one of the new cognitive theorists, who calls his treatment technique "reality therapy," also emphasized behavior, believing that it is much more important than feelings. He stated that the emphasis in treatment should not be on the client's attitudes and feelings but on what she is doing at present and what she is planning for the future. He contended that feelings will change when behavior changes; they do not change merely by discussing them. Glasser's treatment technique focuses on compelling the client to judge her own behavior realistically and to determine if it is meeting her basic human needs: giving and receiving love, achieving self-respect and respect from others. The therapist then has the task of educating the client to adopt better behavior; that is, to take responsibility for fulfilling those basic needs that she has not yet met. A client knows that a therapist cares about her when the therapist demands responsibility and a high standard of behavior from her (22).

Consciousness-altering activity is also part of the "rational–emotive psychotherapy" practiced by Ellis, who gives his clients "homework" to do between interviews. This might involve participating in a social activity about which the client has been apprehensive, confronting a spouse with a grievance or taking a job for which one feels inadequate. Successful self-assertion is also very effective in diminishing anxiety.

The cognitive practitioner does not postulate unconscious emotions, conflicts, or ideas. Remembering that the unique characteristics of human beings are language and the ability to think and reason, she makes use of these in the way she conducts her treatment. The client is asked to put into words what he has been saying to himself about significant events and problems. He is encouraged to describe his emotions, his goals in life, and his current behavior. What the client says combined with what the worker observes is considered to be a valid basis upon which to develop a treatment plan. As treatment progresses, the client will be making basic decisions about his future. It is one of the responsibilities of the worker to be sure that the client has all the facts and concepts necessary to make judgments that correspond to reality.

Most people have untapped strength and courage. Under conditions of stress, they need to discover these resources within themselves and use them. It is most important in treatment that the therapist put the client in touch with this aspect of herself. This can be done only if the therapist concerns himself primarily with the client's strengths rather than her pathology. Such a treatment orientation is called for by the emphasis cognitive theory places on the potential for growth inherent in every person. The cognitive worker uses what the client reveals about herself to foster a sense of worth, pointing to past accomplishments or successes to give her courage for the future. However, as we know, the client often denies that she has any competence.

Scarbrough discussed this issue in an article concerning his treatment of depressed and phobic patients. He reported very effective results in overcoming impasse situations when he shifted tactics from a neoanalytic approach to one in which he allied himself with unrecognized strengths the patient already possessed. An analytically oriented clinical psychologist, Scarbrough commented that "the historical development of psychoanalysis and psychology had understressed the competent side of the personality" (56, p. 298). He described his treatment technique as follows: "Whenever the patient pauses to take a breath, I interrupt him, seeking to uncover and dig out any elements of competence in his history, everything surrounding whatever successes he has had. In some patients previous competent functioning has not been very great; in others it is striking, and the patient works hard to deny the extent of it. Whether the history of competence is striking or minimal, I begin to dig it out" (56, p. 297). Scarbrough suggested some reasons why an individual might refuse to admit previous success or to seek future success: success may be equated with perfectionism or having to achieve a paralyzing level of ability; with aloneness due to abandonment by the parent who wants him to be helpless; with disapproval by significant others; or with conformity to a parental ideal. The cognitive worker helps the client either to correct any such perceptions that are inaccurate or to take action on those situations that the client has evaluated realistically.

For further information about cognitive treatment techniques, the reader is referred to the annotated bibliography.

Types of Clients, Problems, and Settings
Most Appropriate for This Theory

Cognitive theory is a psychosocial theory, viewing each person on his own terms and simultaneously as a reflection of his environment. It is oriented to each individual's particular reality. It would therefore seem to have an across-the-board validity that makes it equally appropriate for most types of clients, illiterate or educated, naive or sophisticated, poor or affluent, presenting a long-standing problem or reacting to an immediate situation. However, there will be difficulty with the nonverbal client, both child and adult, who cannot talk about his reality perceptions, emotions, goals, or the way he behaves.

The cognitive worker is not required to fit the client into a preconceived universal blueprint. The uniqueness of each individual is stressed, instead of the concept that there are universal characteristics common to all. Cognitive theory holds that we are all different rather than we are all the same: each client presents a different combination of goals, perceptions, and life-style.

Since each individual is unique, the dynamics of each case are different. The nature of the problem and what needs to be done will vary infinitely from person to person. One of the aims of cognitive treatment is for the client to achieve insight into the realities of her world, other people, and herself. A further aim is to enable the client to decide what she should do about her problem and then to do it. These aims are in sharp contrast with other schools of thought, in which the aim of treatment is for the client to achieve insight into her unconscious and/or accept one of two or three universal explanations for her problems. Such theories do not work well with many types of clients, because they simply cannot meet these criteria for successful treatment.

As indicated previously, phobias, addictions, and psychoses are types of problems best treated by other approaches. (See Counterindications for Use of Theory.) Otherwise, cognitive theory is applicable to all other types.

In regard to the settings that are most suitable for applying cognitive theory, we would say that the reality orientation of the theory makes it appropriate to use in any kind of social or mental health agency. With its focus on understanding reality and taking action on problems, it is fully compatible with the functions of social workers in public assistance agencies, child-placing organizations, psychiatric clinics, hospitals, schools, probation departments, family casework agencies, and social action programs.

Although cognitive theory is mainly a clinical theory, it also provides a rationale for social action. Consciousness is held to be the primary determinant of behavior, but consciousness itself is formed by the larger society, the immediate environment, interpersonal relationships, and individual experiences. To the extent that social action changes the external happenings in people's lives, their consciousness changes and produces alterations in emotions, goals, and behavior. Positive environmental modifications make possible better human lives, in regard to both physical health and personal happiness. It is implicit in the theory that the worker should make accessible to the client, either directly or by referral, those concrete services needed to relieve any external stresses that have a destructive effect on the inner life. Counseling plus concrete services is a higher level of treatment than counseling alone.

Implications for Various Treatment Modalities

Because cognitive theory is reality-oriented, it can serve as a guide to all forms of treatment: individual, family, group, or community. Every treatment modality is concerned with people-in-situations, with the interplay between reality and perception, and with the resolution of problems through taking action. Not only individuals, but small groups and large groups are most clearly understood in terms of their perceptions, goals, and basic patterns (life-styles). Perceptions, goals, and patterns are the principal concerns of the theory.

Counterindications for Use of Theory   + nonverbal clients

A cognitive approach is not applicable to the treatment of phobias, addictions, or psychoses.

A phobia is a specific fear that a person knows is irrational but cannot control. A phobia of elevators may have developed out of a traumatic incident in which the individual was trapped between floors for many hours under frightening conditions. Although the person now recognizes that incident to have been an atypical one not likely to recur, the phobia has become entrenched and is not subject to removal by reasoning. Realistic thinking does not produce realistic behavior because the phobic reaction bypasses the higher cortical centers, the thinking parts of the brain. It has become an automatic physiological phenomenon, a conditioned reflex built into the nervous system. This concept was summarized by Hans Gerz: "Since the nervous system in itself is well known for its repetitious qualities, and since our feelings are carried and expressed through nerve tissue, namely, the autonomic nervous system, a once-established neurotic feeling pattern will tend to repeat itself and become a sort of reflex, even when the causes of the neurotic systems have been resolved and removed" (21, p. 207). Phobias are best treated by a behavior modification approach. This writer once treated a client with an elevator phobia by gradually desensitizing him, at first accompanying the client in an elevator, than later having him ride alone on increasingly longer trips.

Joseph Wortis noted that "a rational psychotherapy . . . can be successfully applied to those psychic disorders which do not have prominent physiological components" (71, p. 181). The strong organic factors in drug, alcohol, overeating, and smoking addictions place them outside the scope of cognitive treatment because the body's physical needs are too powerful. They first need to be brought under control by medical, pharmaceutical, or behavior modification means. Likewise, the organic component in the schizophrenias and other psychoses and the separation of the person from reality render cognitive theory ineffective for these conditions.

An encouraging exception to this position was taken by Snyder, who asserted that cognitive therapy could be employed with other means in treating drinking problems (60). She saw the alcoholic client as able to assume responsibility for his thinking, motives, and behavior, and in need of the help to change his life-style to one the cognitive approach provided.

Implications for Social Work Research

Cognitive theory has definite implications for social work research, especially the efforts to compare the effectiveness of different treatment approaches and the attempts to measure client change after treatment.

The theory maintains that a person can be understood accurately in terms of her stated thoughts, goals, emotions, and experiences, and in terms of his manifest behavior. From the research point of view, these are objective items because different observers are bound to record them in essentially the same way. They leave little room for personal judgment or guesswork by the observer. If these items are the ones that are utilized to match sets of controls and sets of experimental subjects, we avoid the hazards of matching that is done on the basis of presumed unconscious dynamics. If these items are the ones that are used for studying the same client before and after treatment, we are again on solid research ground. We make no guesses about unconscious phenomena, but compare the client as she is now with the way she used to be, in relation to certain objective items.

Thus, cognitive theory lends itself readily to objective, scientific research. A great deal of such research has been carried out in recent years on the effectiveness of cognitive treatment, primarily by psychologists, although social workers could do likewise if so inclined.

Gaps in Knowledge from Social Work Viewpoint

It has been stated elsewhere that there is general agreement in social work on the following: case work should promote mutual adjustment between individuals and their environment; each person is unique; the difficulties of our clients are psychosocial problems; individuals cannot be understood in isolation but only in relationship to society; and helping people requires both art and science (66, p. 16). It is our contention that cognitive theory provides the knowledge and the concepts necessary to understand these principles and put them into practice.

This theory points out the crucial influence of environment on thought and the primary effect of thought on emotions and behavior. Nevertheless, many people living under healthy and desirable social conditions exhibit emotional and behavioral difficulties. This is not necessarily indicative of a gap in the theory. As Berthe Gronfein suggested: "Regardless of what societal alterations take place, some persons in all classes will continue to have problems of interpersonal relations and faulty self-management. This is in the nature of the human condition. There are no utopias!" (29, p. 655).

Case Vignettes Exemplifying Treatment

HELEN

Helen, a married woman with children entered treatment still maintaining the inaccurate perception of herself that began in childhood. Constantly criticized and rejected by her parents, she came to feel that she had no value as a person and was not entitled to have any wants of her own. In her marriage, she was dominated by an insensitive husband who insisted she confine herself exclusively to the roles of housekeeper and always available sex partner. As the years passed, Helen began to feel trapped by this constricted existence and wanted to satisfy some of her cultural and intellectual interests. However, her husband had no such interests himself and opposed her joining any community group, not wishing to lose any of his control over her.

In treatment she was depressed and anxious. She needed to enrich her life, but had doubts about her right to assert herself. She could not tolerate the current situation, yet her goal was to continue the marriage. The worker's approach was to try to understand Helen in terms of her reality perceptions and her goal: she inaccurately saw herself as having no worth and no right to fulfill her own needs. She wanted relief from the depression and anxiety associated with her marital relationship, yet did not want to solve the problem by leaving her husband.

Helen was helped to achieve the treatment objective she herself formulated: overcoming her depression and anxiety. This was accomplished by challenging her inaccurate evaluation of herself both in individual and then in group treatment. She was finally able to stand up to her husband and gradually acquired the freedom to attend various cultural activities in the community, in which her husband later began to join her. At the end of treatment she was demonstrating courage and confidence in handling her situation. She had no expectations that her husband would change very much, but he no longer controlled her life. The satisfactions from outside activities gave her the strength to cope with the incompatibilities existing between herself and her husband.

ARNOLD

Arnold was a young man who asked for professional help with his sexual problem. He had been engaging in overt homosexual acts, but at the same time was repelled by this kind of life and wanted very much to move in the other direction. He expressed a strong wish to become heterosexually oriented so that he could have a wife, family life, and children, yet he feared he was doomed to be a permanent homosexual.

Cognitive theory holds that the worker's task is not deep exploration of the client's drives. Rather, the focus should be on helping the client acquire accurate perceptions and constructive goals. The client can and will control his drives if his goals require it. (An obvious example is the celibacy of men who enter the priesthood.)

In Arnold's case, the worker, after consultation with a psychiatrist, assured him he was not doomed to be a homosexual if he was willing to struggle against these tendencies. Such a struggle would involve self-control and avoidance of homosexual contacts, combined with seeking out relationships with women. If he could find physically and emotionally satisfying relationships with the opposite sex and continue them, he might be able to weaken the tendencies he wished to abandon. Fortunately, Arnold met a girl with whom a close relationship quickly developed, and he began to report satisfaction from their growing physical intimacies. He stated that he gained the confidence to approach this girl only after his worker had told him that he was not necessarily destined to remain homosexually oriented. Later, Arnold and his girlfriend started to talk about marriage and the kind of life they wanted together.

SANDRA

Sandra, a young adult, came for help with a problem of compulsive-obsessive behavior that had begun to interfere with getting to her job on time and doing her work properly. Brought up in a family with a phobic mother who was hospitalized twice for mental breakdowns, she was strongly conditioned to view the world as a dangerous and insecure place. Because the world was so full of hazards, she took great pains to make no mistakes.

In treatment, she talked about her compulsions to triple-check household applicances to be sure they were turned off, to try the front door over and over as she left for work for fear it might not be locked, and to wash her hands many times during the day at the office as a precaution against germ infection.

Treatment was based on Leon Salzman's concept of the compulsive-obsessive person as someone with excessive feelings of insecurity who requires absolute guarantees of safety (54, pp. 1139–1146). The problem was considered to be a consequence of Sandra's particular perception of reality, in contrast to the psychoanalytic view that behavior such as compulsive handwashing is a ritual to deal with unconscious sexual guilt and unconscious feelings of dirtiness. The cognitive worker saw Sandra's extreme insecurity as a result of all kinds of life experiences, possibly but not necessarily including sexual ones. In her case, by performing her rituals, Sandra believed she was following a proven, automatic procedure that would eliminate possible dangers.

The cognitive worker had to teach Sandra that there are no absolute guarantees in life, that we have to live with a small element of risk in everything we do. A cognitive approach to treatment is not considered successful unless the client is enabled to take action on the stated problem. Therefore, the worker, through a warm and supporting relationship, helped her to find the courage to live normally by accepting the small risks in her daily life.

BUDDY

Buddy, a twelve-year-old-boy, was a good student who had no difficulties with his academic work. He spoke up in class, conversed easily with his school peers, and had no trouble keeping up with them in sports or other types of play. In his neighborhood he kept busy with many friends. At home, he was engaged in a fierce rivalry with his brother and was often punished by his parents for fighting and minor misconduct. His parents brought him for help with a problem of speech blocking, which occurred only in the home during clashes with his brother or in the presence of his parents.

On the premise of cognitive theory that perception determines functioning, the worker hypothesized that Buddy's view of the significance of speech had a great deal to do with his blocking. He further hypothesized that Buddy regarded his spoken words at home as a danger to himself, since quarreling with his brother or talking back to his parents usually resulted in harsh punishments. The parents were therefore asked to discontinue punishing Buddy for any spoken word. They could continue to penalize him for his behavior, but not for anything he said. The new arrangement at home was then explained to the boy.

Almost immediately, there was a marked decrease at home in Buddy's stuttering and blocking. A great deal of work was done with the parents to encourage them to avoid punishing or hitting Buddy when he spoke disrespectfully, and they were able to maintain their self-discipline. Meanwhile, the worker pointed out to Buddy the need for self-control on his part to avoid the parents' returning to stern punishments for what he said. The boy was finally able to meet this responsibility, aided greatly by the father's becoming less critical of him and recognizing that sometimes Buddy's brother was the real instigator of the fights between them. At the termination of treatment, Buddy's speech at home was still continuing to improve.

Summary

The approach of these cases discards the concept of an "unconscious" as the primary determinant of the psychic life. It illustrates the basic premise of cognitive theory: emotions, motives, goals, and behavior are conscious phenomena that are usually the consequences of thought.

References

1. Alland, Alexander, Jr. *The Human Imperative*. New York: Columbia University Press, 1972.

2. American Psychiatric Association, Commission on Psychiatric Therapies, Chaired by Toksoz Byram Karasu, M. D. *The Psychiatric Therapies*. Washington, D.C.: American Psychiatric Press, 1984.

3. Ansbacher, Heinz L. "Ego Psychology and Alfred Adler," *Social Casework*. Vol. 45, No. 5 (May 1964).

4. ———. "Alfred Adler: A Historical Perspective," *American Journal of Psychiatry*, (Vol. 127, No. 6 (December 1970).

5. ———, and Rowena Ansbacher. *The Individual Psychology of Alfred Adler*. New York: Basic Books, 1956.

6. Arnold, Magda B. *Emotion and Personality*. 2 vols. New York: Columbia University Press, 1960.

7. Beck, Aaron T. *Cognitive Therapy and the Emotional Disorders*. New York: International Universities Press, 1976.

8. Berlin, Sharon B. "A Cognitive-Learning Perspective for Social Work," *Social Service Review*, Vol. 58, No. 4 (December 1980).

9. ———. "Cognitive Behavioral Interventions for Practice," *Social Work*, Vol. 27, No. 3 (May 1982).

10. Borenzweig, Herman. "Social Work and Psychoanalytic Theory: A Historical Analysis," *Social Work*, Vol. 16, No. 1 (January 1971).

11. Brenner, Charles. *An Elementary Textbook of Psychoanalysis*. New York: Doubleday, 1957.

12. Chatterjee, Pranab. "Cognitive Theories and Social Work Practice," *Social Service Review*, Vol. 58, No. 1 (March 1984).

13. Combs, Terri D. "A Cognitive Therapy for Depression: Theory, Techniques, and Issues," *Social Casework*, Vol. 61, No. 6 (June 1980).

14. Dewey, Edith A. "Family Atmosphere," in Arthur G. Nikelly (ed.), *Techniques for Behavior Change*. Springfield, Ill.: Charles C. Thomas, 1971.

15. Directors of the Robbins Institute. "An Integrated Psychotherapeutic Program,"*Psychotherapy*, Vol. 1, No. 1 (Fall, 1955).

16. Ellis, Albert. "Rational Psychotherapy," *The Journal of General Psychology*, Vol. 59 (1958).

17. ——. *Reason and Emotion in Psychotherapy*. New York: Stuart, 1962.

18. Epstein, Laura. *Helping People: The Task-Centered Approach*. St. Louis: C. V. Mosby, 1980.

19. Epstein, Norman. "Brief Group Therapy in a Child Guidance Clinic," *Social Work*, Vol. 15, No. 3 (July 1970).

20. Furst, Joseph B. *The Neurotic—His Inner and Outer Worlds*. New York: Citadel Press, 1954.

21. Gerz, Hans O. "The Treatment of the Phobic and the Obsessive-Compulsive Patient Using Paradoxical Intention Sec. Viktor E. Frankl," in Viktor E. Frankl (ed.), *Psychotherapy and Existentialism: Selected Papers on Logotherapy*. New York: Simon and Schuster, 1968.

22. Glasser, William. *Reality Therapy: A New Approach to Psychiatry*. New York: Harper and Row, 1965.

23. Goble, Frank G. *The Third Force: The Psychology of Abraham Maslow*. New York: Grossman, 1970.

24. Goldstein, Howard. *Social Learning and Change: A Cognitive Approach to Human Services*. Columbia: University of South Carolina Press, 1981.

25. ——. "Cognitive Approaches to Direct Practice," *Social Service Review*, Vol. 56, No. 4 (December 1982).

26. ——. "Starting Where the Client Is," *Social Casework*, Vol. 64, No. 5 (May 1983).

27. ——. *Creative Change: A Cognitive-Humanistic Approach to Social Work Practice*. New York: Methuen, 1984.

28. Gottlieb, Werner, and Joe H. Stanley. "Mutual Goals and Goal-Setting in Casework," *Social Casework*, Vol. 68, No. 8 (October 1967).

29. Gronfein, Berthe. "Should Casework Be on the Defensive?" *Social Casework*, Vol. 67, No. 10, (December 1966).

30. Hallowitz, David, Ralph Bierman, Grace P. Harrison, and Burta Stulberg. "The Assertive Counseling Component of Therapy," *Social Casework*, Vol. 68, No. 9 (November 1967).

31. Hilgard, Ernest R. "Hypnosis and Consciousness," *Human Nature*, Vol. 1, No. 1 (January 1978).

32. Hora, Thomas, "Existential Psychotherapy," in *Current Psychiatric Therapies*, Vol. 2. New York: Grune and Stratton, 1962.

33. Kaplan, Robert M., Sharon M. McCordick, and Mark Twitchell. "Is It the Cognitive or the Behavioral Component Which Makes Cognitive-Behavior Modification Effective in Test Anxiety?," *Journal of Counseling Psychology*, Vol. 26, No. 5 (September 1979).

34. Krauss, Herbert H. "Anxiety: The Dread of a Future Event," *Journal of Individual Psychology*, Vol. 23, No. 1 (May 1967).

35. Krill, Donald F. "Existential Psychotherapy and the Problem of Anomie," *Social Work*, Vol. 14, No. 2 (April 1969).

36. Lantz, James E. "Cognitive Theory and Social Casework," *Social Work*, Vol. 23, No. 5 (September 1978).

37. Lazarus, Arnold A. *Multimodal Behavior Therapy*. New York: Springer, 1976.

38. ———. "Has Behavior Therapy Outlived Its Usefulness?," *American Psychologist*, Vol. 32, No. 7 (July 1977).

39. Ledwidge, Barry. "Cognitive Behavior Modification: A Rejoinder to Locke and to Meichebaum," *Cognitive Therapy and Research*, Vol. 3, No. 2 (1979).

40. Liotti, Giovanni, and Mario Reda. "Some Epistemological Remarks on Behavior Therapy, Cognitive Therapy and Psychoanalysis," *Cognitive Therapy and Research*, Vol. 5, No. 3, (1981).

41. Maslow, Abraham H. *Motivation and Personality*, 2nd edition. New York: Harper and Row, 1970.

42. Maultsby, Maxie C., Jr. *Help Yourself to Happiness*. New York: Institute for Rational Living, 1975.

43. ———. "Rational Behavior Therapy for Acting-Out Adolescents," *Social Casework*, Vol. 56, No. 1 (January 1975).

44. May, Rollo. *The Meaning of Anxiety*. New York, Ronald, 1950.

45. ———. "Existential Bases of Psychotherapy," *American Journal of Orthopsychiatry*, Vol. 30, No. 4 (October 1960).

46. Mayer, John E., and Noel Timms. "Clash in Perspective Between Worker and Client," *Social Casework*, Vol. 50, No. 1 (January 1969).

47. Miller, R. Christopher, and Jeffrey S. Berman. "The Efficacy of Cognitive Behavior Therapies: A Quantitative Review of the Research Evidence," *Psychological Bulletin*, Vol. 94, No. 1 (July 1983).

48. Nikelly, Arthur G. "Basic Processes in Psychotherapy," in Arthur G. Nikelly (ed.). *Techniques for Behavior Change*. Springfield, Ill.: Charles C. Thomas, 1971.

49. ———, and Don Verger. "Early Recollections," in Arthur G. Nikelly (ed.), *Techniques for Behavior Change*. Springfield, Ill.: Charles C. Thomas, 1971.

50. Rado, Sandor. *Psychoanalysis of Behavior*. New York: Grune and Stratton, 1956.

51. Rank, Otto. *Will Therapy*. New York: Knopf, 1936.

52. Reid, William J. *The Task-Centered System*. New York: Columbia University Press, 1978.

53. Reynolds, Bertha C. "The Social Casework of an Uncharted Journey." *Social Work*, Vol. 9, No. 4 (October 1964).

54. Salzman, Leon. "Therapy of Obsessional States," *American Journal of Psychiatry*, Vol. 122, No. 10 (April 1966).

55. Sarbin, Theodore R. "Anxiety: Reification of a Metaphor," *Archives of General Psychiatry*, Vol. 10, No. 6 (June 1964).

56. Scarbrough, H. E. "The Hypothesis of Hidden Health in the Treatment of Severe Neuroses," *Social Casework*, Vol. 49, No. 5 (May 1968).

57. Shepard, Martin, and Marjorie Lee. *Games Analysts Play*. New York: Putnam's, 1970.

58. Siporin, Max. "Situational Assessment and Intervention," *Social Casework*, Vol. 53, No. 2 (February 1972).

59. Smalley, Ruth. *Theory for Social Work Practice*. New York: Columbia University Press, 1967.

60. Snyder, Veronica. "Cognitive Approaches in the Treatment of Alcoholism," *Social Casework*, Vol. 56, No. 8 (October 1975).

61. Sunley, Robert. "New Dimensions in Reaching-out Casework," *Social Work*, Vol. 13, No. 2 (April 1968).

62. Ullman, Montague. "The Dream Process," *Psychotherapy*. Vol. 1, No. 1 (Fall 1955).

63. Van Kaam, Adrian, *The Art of Existential Counseling*. Wilkes-Barre, Pa.: Dimension Books, 1966.

64. Weiner, Harvey, and Sonja Fox. "Cognitive-Behavioral Therapy with Substance Abusers," *Social Casework*, Vol. 63, No. 9 (November 1982).

65. Werner, Harold D. *A Rational Approach to Social Casework*. New York: Association Press, 1965.

66. ———. "Adler, Freud, and American Social Work," *Journal of Individual Psychology*, Vol. 23, No. 1 (May 1967).

67. ———. *New Understandings of Human Behavior*. New York: Association Press, 1970.

68. ———. *Cognitive Therapy: A Humanistic Approach*. New York: Free Press, 1982.

69. White, Colby L. "Untangling Knots in Casework with the Experiential Approach," *Social Casework*, Vol. 51, No. 10 (December 1970).

70. Witkin, Stanley L. "Cognitive Processes in Clinical Practice," *Social Work*, Vol. 27, No. 5 (September 1982).

71. Wortis, Joseph. "Comments and Conclusions," in Joseph Wortis (ed.), *Basic Problems in Psychiatry*. New York: Grune and Stratton, 1953.

72. Zacks, Hanna. "Self-Actualization: A Midlife Problem," *Social Casework*, Vol. 61, No. 4 (April 1980).

73. Zastrow, Charles. "Self-Talk: A Rational Approach to Understanding and Treating Child Abuse," *Social Casework*, Vol. 62, No. 3 (March 1981).

Annotated Listing of Key References

BECK, AARON T. *Cognitive Therapy and the Emotional Disorders*. New York: International Universities Press, 1976.
A definitive formulation of the principles of cognitive theory, with emphasis on their practical application to the treatment of the major emotional disorders. Many case illustrations are provided and specific treatment techniques are spelled out.

ELLIS, ALBERT. *Reason and Emotion in Psychotherapy*. New York: Stuart, 1962.
A complete discussion of the theory and practice of the writer's "rational-emotive psychotherapy."

GLASSER, WILLIAM. *Reality Therapy: A New Approach to Psychiatry*. New York: Harper and Row, 1965.
The concepts and techniques of "reality therapy," an approach that views human problems as irresponsibility rather than illness.

GOLDSTEIN, HOWARD. *Creative Change: A Cognitive-Humanistic Approach to Social Work Practice*. New York: Methuen, 1984. In three chapters, Goldstein examines how to go about understanding a person's cognitive processes as an intertwining of thought with subjective attitudes and beliefs. The other eight chapters by various contributors are devoted to applications of a cognitive approach with particular client groups, including the abusing family, the chronically ill patient, the alcoholic, the battered woman, the rural poor, self-help groups, the mentally ill, and the Vietnam veteran.

NIKELLY, ARTHUR G. *Techniques for Behavior Change*. Springfield, Ill.: Charles C. Thomas, 1971.
The author has edited thirty papers, some written by himself, that succinctly outline Alfred Adler's principal ideas and practical treatment techniques derived from Adlerian theory. Included are assessment methods, individual and group treatment techniques, ways of treating specific problems, and educational techniques.

WERNER, HAROLD D. *Cognitive Therapy: A Humanistic Approach*. New York: Free Press, 1982.
The theory, philosophy, and specific techniques of an approach based on the premise that thinking shapes emotions and behaviors. Many case illustrations are presented, situations for which behavioral methods seem appropriate are noted, but essentially the system is viewed as a main current in psychotherapy that has a separate existence.

WERNER, HAROLD D. *New Understandings of Human Behavior*. New York: Association Press, 1970.
A collection of twenty-five articles by psychiatrists and psychologists explaining behavior in non-Freudian terms. In addition to serving as editor, the author has supplied an introduction and a final chapter dealing with non-Freudian treatment methods, most of them cognitive.

CHAPTER 6

Behavior Therapy in Social Work Practice

Ray J. Thomlison

A Historical Perspective

The knowledge explosion that has confronted the helping disciplines in the past decade has, to a large extent, been fueled by the clinical and research activities reported under the rubric of behavior therapy or behavior modification.* As one observer recently commented, behavior therapy has had an impact on the helping disciplines that has been unprecedented since the impact of Freud in the early years of this century (42, p. 219). Interestingly, however, this impact has been, in large part, felt by psychology and psychiatry to a greater extent than social work. For example, K. O'Leary summarized the results of surveys of practicing psychologists in various fields by stating that:

> With children, a behavioral orientation seems to be a clearly dominant trend with approximately half of all child clinicians identifying with this orientation. With adults, no single theoretical orientation is ascribed to by most profession-

---

*It is acknowledged that in some quarters the concepts of behavior therapy and behavior modification are differentially applied (78). For the purposes of this chapter they will be used synonymously.

als; eclecticism is the most popular identification and a wide variety of orientations are mentioned. However, a behavioral orientation is clearly emerging as one of the top three ranked orientations. (42, p. 221)

Complete and accurate data regarding the incorporation of behavior therapy in social work practice is not available. In an earlier edition of this book, Richard Stuart referred to behavior modification as a "Technology for social change" and supported its importance for social work (62). There is, however, a respectable behavioral social work literature that has contributed to the continued growth of behavior therapy in social work (13, 16, 50, 52, 55, 56, 57, 61, 67, 69, 71, 79). Given its compatibility with social work values (72) and its demonstrated effectiveness (70), there is little doubt that behavior therapy will impact social work practice with greater force in the next years. This chapter is, therefore, written with the primary objective being to enhance this development by acquainting the reader with the breadth of behavior therapy, its history, its conceptual framework, and its basic procedures and techniques.

What Is Behavior Therapy?

It is probably more appropriate to refer to the behavior therapies rather than to imply that a single method of behavior therapy exists. In this respect behavior therapy shares with the other "therapies"—psychotherapy, marital therapy, family therapy—a pluralism of theory and technique. Generally speaking, behavior therapy refers to the systematic application of techniques intended to facilitate behavioral change and which are based principally, but not exclusively, on the conditioning theories of learning. Historically, behavior therapy can trace its beginnings to the first quarter of this century in the well known work of Ivan Pavlov. Interestingly, however, while Pavlov's name is often used almost synonymously in the popular press with conditioning theory, his contribution to behavior therapy was not nearly as significant as such conditioning theorists as Thorndike, Watson, Hull, and, most importantly, B. F. Skinner.

The Development of Behavior Therapy

The contributions of Pavlov and Skinner are well documented in both the behavioral and social work literature and will not be reviewed here (15, 59). It is important, however, to identify that these two fathers of modern behavior therapy identified and studied two distinct behavioral processes.

Pavlov's studies of the salivation reflex of dogs are familiar to most students of human behavior. The basic experimental procedure for the learning process involved placing food within the view of the dog. Salivation was elicited and the relationship between the unconditioned stimulus (food) and the unconditioned response (salivation) was established. An arbitrary event (stimulus), for example a bell, was then caused to occur at the same time as

Pavlov — Respondent Conditioning

the presentation of the food. Over a number of such pairings, the bell (the conditioned stimulus) took on the power to elicit the response of salivation (the conditioned response). This behavioral learning process is referred to as respondent conditioning and remains as a foundational theoretical explanation for a variety of anxiety and phobic disorders in contemporary behavior therapy (71).

Skinner's contribution to behavior therapy was initially motivated by a different set of objectives than those of Pavlov. Skinner was dedicated to the objective of the scientific study of human behavior. While he did not deny the possibilities of the internal mechanisms postulated by other theorists, he argued that human behavior could only be empirically investigated through the measurement of observable behavior. Underlying his approach was the belief that "If we are to use the methods of science in the field of human affairs, we must assume that behavior is lawful and determined. We must expect to discover that what a man does is the result of specifiable conditions and that once these conditions have been discovered, we can anticipate and to some extent determine his actions" (59, p. 6). It is necessary to understand that this commitment to science set relatively stringent requirements on the pursuit of knowledge within the behavioral school, not the least of which was the need to develop techniques of measurement compatible with the exploration of human behavior.

True to his commitment, Skinner evolved one of the most empirically based theories of human behavior and set the foundation for contemporary behavior therapy. At the heart of this Skinnerian theory was the concept of reinforcement. Operant behavior (voluntary behavior) emitted by an individual could be increased in frequency of occurrence if such behavior was positively or negatively reinforced. Alternatively, the frequency of occurrence of a behavior could be decreased by either administering punishment or withholding reinforcement; this latter process being referred to as extinction. In other words, the essence of the Skinnerian or operant model of conceptualizing human behavior relied heavily upon an understanding of the environmental (behavioral) events that preceded and/or followed the behavior(s) under scrutiny. This theoretical explanation of human behavior acquisition has been refined and elaborated as the results of clinical experience and research have been incorporated. Importantly, however, the interaction of behavior, its prior and consequent events, remains the foundation of most contemporary behavior therapy.

operant model of conditioning

Social Learning Theory and Behavior Therapy

Elements of Social Learning Theory

Social learning theory is comprised of three major elements. First are those behaviors that are the focus of the behavioral analysis. These are often identified during the period of assessment as undesirable or problematic. When they become the focus for change they are often referred to as the target behaviors. A second category are those behaviors or environmental events that precede or follow the problemetic or target behaviors. These are referred to as antecedent behaviors or events (those that precede) and consequences (those that follow). They are often identified as the controlling or maintaining conditions for the problem behaviors. These problem behaviors serve as the focus of the behavioral assessment. The interaction of these three elements is represented in Figure 6–1. It must be noted that this paradigm serves to label one exchange in an ongoing sequence of exchanges between people. In order for the therapist to determine the antecedents and consequences, a decision as to the problem or target behavior must first be made. With this target behavior in mind, the therapist then identifies those events or behaviors that precede or follow the target behavior. To illustrate the application of this social learning paradigm as it might be operationalized into a behavior therapy assessment and change program, a short vignette is presented.

A Parent–Child Illustration (73)

Suppose that a father, Mr. S., registers the complaint that his child, John, will "never do what he is told." For the sake of illustrative simplicity, imagine that among other complaints the father's greatest concern centers on the child not coming to the dinner table when he is called. An observation of the behavioral exchanges between father and child might show the following sequence of exchanges:

1. "John, come to dinner." | No observable response from John. | "John, didn't you hear me?"

2. "John, get in here for dinner before I come in there and get you!" | "Just wait a minute." | "I said now!"

(after some elapsed time)

3. "John, this is your last chance. Get in here. If I have to come in there, you are going to be in trouble!" | John presents himself angrily at the table and begins to eat. | Father is silent and appears angry.

What is depicted in this brief exchange is not an atypical parent-child exchange. However, it may often become a behavioral pattern which, in as-

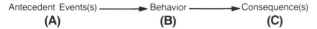

(A)   **(B)**   **(C)**

Figure 6-1. Behavior therapy paradigm

sociation with other noncompliant behaviors, becomes the focus for a great deal of frustration and anger between parent(s) and child(ren).

From the social learning perspective, in this example the noncompliant behavior appears to be maintained by the father's commands and threats at the antecedent level, combined with the threats and lack of parental acknowledgment at the consequence level. For example, when John finally arrived for dinner, his father ignored him.

In order to assess the behavioral exchange further, it is necessary to examine, generally, the nature of the consequences that might be provided for John. Behavioral consequences differ in terms of quality and purpose. Some are of a positive (pleasing) nature, while others are of a negative (displeasing) variety.

This latter category is usually referred to as punishment and is frequently observed when a parent attempts to prevent the recurrence of an undesired behavior by spanking the child; that is, physical punishment. While the use of physical punishment as a consequence is acknowledged as a means of decreasing the frequency of a behavior, it is viewed among behavioral social workers as an unacceptable means of altering behavior. In addition to humanitarian reasons, physical punishment is generally considered unacceptable because in many instances it suppresses a behavior without providing an alternative, more desirable behavior. Behavior therapy requires that any agreed behavioral change must be defined in terms that are recognized to be desirable and to be increased in frequency by the participants. This requires that all parties to a behavioral change contract define what behaviors are desired, not simply what is undesired. This is often a difficult requirement as it is almost always easier to tell someone to stop doing something that is considered undesirable as opposed to asking them to engage in a desired behavioral alternative.

The use of positive consequences to increase desirable behavior is the strength of the social learning approach to behavior therapy. The research in the clinical arena strongly supports the use of positive consequences as a means of facilitating desired behavior. Few would find this an unacceptable research finding and, indeed, might see it as axiomatic. Interestingly, however, it is not always easy to put this principle into practice. For example, if we return to John and Mr. S. for a moment, it is likely that Mr. S. would readily accept this statement. However, he would probably counter by saying that "if John would do what he was told then all would be okay, but until he changes I can't give him any positive strokes!" Unfortunately, John and his father have reached a stalemate wherein even if they agree that change is desirable, it is difficult because they are into a "coercive exchange" (46).

Attempting control another person's behavior by command and threat is familiar to most of us. In many instances, however, it has the effect demonstrated by John and his father. The commands and threats escalate until finally the child complies in order to terminate the threats and/or yelling. By the time the child obeys the parent's command, the parent has become agitated enough to lose any motivation to acknowledge, in positive terms, the child's compliance. This coercive process, then, can be conceptualized using Skinner's notion of a negative reinforcement process—that is, the termination of a behavior (threats) upon the occurrence of the desired behavior (compliance); an extinction process—that is, the withholding of a positive reinforcer upon the occurrence of the desired behavior (compliance); as well as a positive reinforcement process—that is, Mr. S. achieves what he set out to get (compliance).

In other words, when John did sit down at the table, his father chose to ignore his compliant behavior. On the other hand, Mr. S. achieved his objective and to some degree was positively reinforced, save for the feelings of frustration and anger. The difficulty is that one person (John) is being negatively reinforced and the other (Mr. S.) is being positively reinforced. This behavioral exchange will therefore be strengthened and can be predicted to increase in frequency unless an alternative exchange can be identified and practiced by both.

In order to help John and his father alter their undesirable behavioral interaction, the therapist will need to devise a program by which the father can give positive consequences for John's compliance upon arriving at the dinner table at the desired time. Intervention requires that a target behavior for desired change be identified. In this case such a target might be labeled as "John coming to the table when called." New antecedents would be identified, as well as new consequences for this new target behavior. An agreement to change might well be formalized in a contractual statement detailing the new behavioral target, its antecedents, and its consequences (see Figure 6–2).

This brief example serves to demonstrate the basic procedures of assessment and intervention in accordance with the A-B-C paradigm. While the overall behavior therapy program would require a greater detailed assessment and a more comprehensive intervention strategy, behavior, its controlling antecedents, and consequences, remains the focus of this approach.

Cognitive-Based Behavior Therapy

Elements of Cognitive Theory

Returning briefly to the developmental history of behavior therapy, there has always been some question raised, both within and outside the behavioral school, regarding the place of human "internal mental" processes. For example, the relatively potent technology of systematic desensitization used in

Participants:	Mr. S. and John
Target Behavior:	John comes to the dinner table when called.
Antecedents:	Father agrees to call John for dinner by saying, "John, it is time for dinner; please come to the table" (or some approximation to this verbal request). Father must call only once and he agrees not to repeat the request by yelling at John.
Consequences:	When John arrives at the dinner table as requested, his father agrees to verbally express his positive acknowledgment (praise) and to place a check mark on John's tally sheet.
	If John chooses not to respond to his father's request, Mr. S. will begin eating alone, ignoring John's absence. John will forego the opportunity for his father's praise and tangible, positive acknowledgment for this dinner time.

Figure 6–2. Agreement to change contract

the treatment of anxiety reactions and phobic disorders has always depended heavily on a classical (Pavlovian) learning theoretical explanation. However, the actual procedures of desensitization developed by Joseph Wolpe required the anxiety-ridden client to learn a relaxation response that is then called forth in association with mental images of the client's anxiety-provoking situations. Simply speaking, the client is instructed to imagine a hierarchy of increasing anxiety-provoking scenes while in a state of relaxation.

The degree to which this approach to behavior therapy can be theoretically explained on the basis of either classical or operant learning theory has been the subject of considerable debate (58). For many behavior therapists this reliance on visual imagery to facilitate the therapeutic process has lent considerable support to the exploration of the place of cognition in behavioral change. For some this seems to be the natural next phase of development for behavior therapy, while for others it represents a basic violation of the principles underlying empirically based behavior therapy.

Whatever the final resolution of this debate, there is no doubt that a cognitively based behavior therapy has developed, one that is quite compatible with social work practice. In its broadest definition, cognition incorporates many of the elements of human thought processes characteristically of concern to social work. Such a broad definition would include the processes by which information (input) from the environment is translated, considered, integrated, stored, retrieved, and eventually produced as some form of personal activity (output). Cognitive theory is in a relatively early phase of development and naturally there are a variety of perspectives. The cognitive behavior therapists have, however, selected and explored certain cognitive elements in behavior change. In a recent consideration of cognitive behavior modification, Robert Schwartz identified the following elements of cognitive theory used in behavior modification:

Cognitive Behavior Therapy

(1) information processing—this involves the acquisition, storage and utilization of information and encompasses attention, perception, language and memory;
(2) beliefs and belief systems—ideas, attitudes and expectations about self, others and experience;
(3) self statements—private monologues that influence behavior and feelings;
(4) problem solving and coping—conceptual and symbolic processes involved in arriving at effective responses to deal with problematic situations. (58, p. 269).

Classification of the various cognitive behavioral approaches at this juncture is somewhat difficult because of the variety of new and empirically untested techniques that have developed in the past decade. In order to meet the objectives of this chapter, a brief overview of some of the major cognitively based behavior therapy approaches is provided.

Systematic Desensitization

Since the late 1950s the treatment of choice for many professionals working with anxiety and phobic disordered clients was Joseph Wolpe's systematic desensitization (81, 82). This approach was compatible with social work practice, and in later years the approach was recommended for use in social work practice by some prominent authors in the field (12, 57). In recent years, variations on this approach have been developed (18, 37), but the original approach has remained quite valid as evidenced by the publication of the third edition of Wolpe's *Practice of Behavioral Therapy* (82).

At the base of this approach is the theoretical postulation that anxiety is an autonomic response learned in a situation perceived by the individual to have been anxiety provoking. Wolpe argued that in order to reduce or alleviate this anxiety the individual must learn a new response to the anxiety-provoking situations, one that would be incompatible with the anxiety response. Of course, a logical alternative to an anxiety response is relaxation; therefore, the desensitization approach requires that the person learn relaxation techniques, such as deep muscle relaxation or relaxation through imagery.

Procedurally, the client's anxiety is explored during the assessment period with the goal of establishing a list of anxiety-provoking situations arranged under specific situational theme areas. The situations in each theme area are arranged in a hierarchy so that the least provoking imagined situations may be presented to the person in a successive graded fashion. The imagined situations move from the least anxiety provoking to the most. The therapist helps the individual to imagine each situation while she is in the learned relaxed state. The hierarchy is confronted systematically, with the client nonverbally signaling the therapist if and when any imagined scene elicits undue anxiety. If this occurs the imagined scene is withdrawn and the individual is instructed to return to the state of relaxation. This procedure is repeated over successive sessions until the client has successfully dealt with the hierarchies within each theme area.

The following summary of one of the author's actual cases is illustrative of the systematic desensitization behavior therapy approach:

> Ann, a 53-year-old woman, was referred to the social worker by a psychiatrist whom Ann had consulted regarding her fear of elevators and restaurants. Early in therapy Ann had mentioned that her ultimate goal was to have dinner with her husband in a revolving restaurant atop an extraordinarily high local tower.
>
> Ann dated the onset of her problem to an episode that had occurred some eight years earlier, when she was living on a West Indian island. Ann's husband had achieved a high social status on this island and was regularly entertained by business leaders and political dignitaries. At one function, Ann found herself in a crowded, warm room with many persons to whom she felt quite inferior. Sometime during the evening, she was asked to join a group of people at a table; her husband was to be seated at another table. She sat down at the table but midway through dinner Ann suffered a panic attack. She abruptly left the table with no explanation. Later, she was severely criticized by her husband. The problem continued over the next few years, but Ann managed to avoid most potentially problematic situations by feigning illness or otherwise excusing herself.
>
> When Ann and her husband moved to a large metropolitan area in Canada, her phobic anxiety increased dramatically. Her husband insisted that she secure help because Ann would not accompany him to any social engagements.
>
> Assessment indicated that Ann's phobic anxiety was associated with three major situational themes: restaurants, elevators, and social situations (e.g., cocktail parties). Ann's hierarchy for the restaurant phobia began with a scene in which her husband would telephone to say he was entertaining an associate and would like her to join them. The hierarchy moved through a scene in which Ann was in a restaurant near an exit door, to a scene in a crowded restaurant, and to the most anxiety-provoking scene— a very noisy, crowded restaurant with no visible exit and Ann's husband not available. Similar hierarchies were compiled for the elevator phobia and the social situation phobia.
>
> Ann was seen weekly over a three-month period. Ann's first recognition of her beginning improvement came when she was able to take the elevator to the fifth-floor office of the therapist. This event took place at the sixth week of intervention. At the point of termination Ann had encountered each of the hierarchy situations and was planning the dinner at the revolving restaurant (71, pp. 302–303).

Other Cognitive Behavior Therapies

The cognitive behavioral approaches all appear to share one common element; that is, they attempt to help the client to construe her problem in some other fashion, through some modification in cognitive processing, that is subsequently validated in actual behavioral assignments. There is an ever-increasing number of approaches appearing to facilitate these cognitive shifts. The main efforts at this time are based upon the work of such pioneers as Aaron Beck (4), Albert Ellis (11), M. Goldfried (18,19), M. Mahoney (32, 33), and D. Meichenbaum (38).

Each of these approaches requires a depth of exploration that space does not permit here. However, at the risk of oversimplification, all require the therapist and client to identify negative self statements, private thoughts, or self talk that in some manner inhibit the individual's performance. These statements or thoughts have to be confronted because of their "irrationality" and inhibiting effects. The "cognitive restructuring" of these thoughts is then accomplished by helping the client identify positive, constructive self statements combined with a redefinition of the client's perception of the reality of the inhibiting situation. In addition, there is a greater requirement on the part of the client to learn how to use positive self statements to reinforce positively himself as various behavior change goals are achieved.

By way of a simple illustration of this approach, imagine for a moment a situation that provokes, for you, a disconcerting level of anxiety. For many, such an example is making a public speech or even a seminar presentation. With your example firmly in mind, recall as many of your private thoughts concerning this situation as you can. How many of these private thoughts are actually statements you make to yourself regarding the reasons why this is a threatening situation; one in which you cannot possibly succeed and one in which, if you entered it, would no doubt have devastingly embarrassing results? These are negative self statements and are seen as a cognitive process that must be restructured before behavior change can take place; that is, giving the public presentation.

In terms of the procedures for how this cognitive restructuring can take place, the three principle proponents of cognitive therapy have differing approaches. To illustrate, Meichenbaum has compared his approach to that of Ellis and Beck:

> In Ellis' form of cognitive therapy the client views his behavior as influenced by maladaptive beliefs and the challenging of these beliefs is the central task of therapy. Beck's focus on irrational beliefs is in the context of a host of cognitive therapeutic tactics such as reality testing, authenticating observations, validating conclusions, and distancing (i.e., regarding thoughts objectively). . . . Beck's focus is more on the specific self statements that occur in particular situations (usually graded task assignments) and how the client can test the validity of these self statements.

He goes on to describe his own approach by stating that it is closer to the Beck approach as he attemtpts:

> to have clients increase their awareness of the negative self statements and images they emit but without formally doing a rational analysis of the so-called

irrational belief system. Instead, the focus is on the client's learning to employ specific problem-solving and coping skills. (38, pp. 197–198)

In each approach the negative statements are viewed as essential for change, with alternative thought processes being substituted to provide the foundation for a successful "I can do it!" confrontation to the situation.

Cognitive behavior therapy is the result of a concerted effort to integrate two important theories of human functioning, and it should offer a viable alternative to those social workers who have been attracted to the behavioral focus of behavior therapy but who have felt it did not adequately deal with the individual's internal processes.

The Effectiveness of Behavior Therapy

The effectiveness of the various approaches to helping is increasingly a concern for practioners. Much of the literature supporting the relative success of various therapies depends on anecdotal material from the case materials of practitioners. Very few of these accounts are based on empirical findings, with before and after measures, with clear relationships being established between the therapeutic intervention and client change.

The behavior therapies have, on the other hand, a built-in opportunity for data collection. The procedures comprising most of the behavior therapies involve the systematic application of specific techniques intended to facilitate observable behavior change. Measurement of change is therefore an integral part of behavior therapy. This has led to an extensive amount of research data demonstrating the effectiveness of the behavioral approaches to most client problems.

An impressive number of outcome research studies (28, 51) are available attesting to the effectiveness of behavior therapy in producing individual change with problems of anxiety disorders (3, 17), sexual problems (13), psychosis (20), gerontology (48), depression (24, 29, 77), obesity (66), and alcohol and drug addiction (8, 30, 34, 39). The research evaluating behavior therapy with marital and family problems began to appear in the early 1970s. The results of this research has evidenced the impact of behavior therapy with couples and families (1, 2, 5, 6, 16, 25, 26, 27, 43, 47, 61).

By far one of the most important areas of behavior therapy research is that dealing with parenting, parent training, and child management and skill acquisition (21, 22, 40, 45, 49, 54). Using the basic A-B-C paradigm, many childhood problems have been reconceptualized as behavioral problems resultant from interactional exchanges between children and parents. By systematically altering these exchanges in the context of behavior therapy, it has repeatedly been demonstrated that both parental and child behavior can be altered toward their desired objectives (14).

This same model has been used effectively as a training approach for developmentally handicapped children (9, 83), children in residential treatment (7), as well as those diagnosed as autistic (23).

Another group that remains a challenge to work with has been the adolescent client group, particularly those judged to be delinquent. Again, behavior therapy both within treatment centers such as Achievement Place (80) and within the adolescent's own community has shown impressive outcomes (10, 64, 65, 76).

Those clients suffering the inhibitory effects of phobic disorders have been the subjects of a great deal of effective intervention by behavior therapists. Combined with the basic systematic desensitization, new cognitive behavioral approaches are promising even more effective outcomes. In fact, it is now to the point where a practitioner would be hard pressed to make an argument for an alternate treatment method for any of the phobic disorders. The outcome effectiveness data strongly favor behavior therapy (35, 36, 70, 71).

Behavior approaches to group work have a recognized place in social work primarily due to the excellent ongoing work of Dr. Sheldon Rose. Rose and others have used the behavioral approach successfully with a variety of groups including adults and children (31, 52, 53).

Finally, applications of behavior therapy principles to community practice have been somewhat more limited. Importantly, however, there are numerous examples of community projects based on behavioral principles reported in the literature (41, 75).

Overall, and relative to other approaches, behavior therapy has an attractive record of success with a wide variety of human problems. The future will see a greater emphasis on determining which behavioral approaches work most effectively with what kind of problem in what context. Findings from these studies will enhance the differential application of techniques for specific problems.

The Outline of a General Approach to Behavior Therapy

Throughout this chapter, reference has been made to a systematic approach to intervention. Indeed, there are specific stages through which all behavior therapy must proceed. While there are a range of activities that are specific to each of the different behavior therapy approaches, there is also a basic set of procedures that serve as a skeletal framework. Such a framework is outlined in the following presentation. It is important to remember, however, that this framework is essentially a summary of a behavior therapy approach and is based primarily on the social learning paradigm.

The procedural outline is based on the author's practice and research with married couples (74) and families. Since much of social work practice is carried out within the context of the family, the outline is presented as an approach to working with the family system.

Beyond the procedural steps identified here, it is important to emphasize that behavior therapy depends heavily upon a positive therapeutic relationship being created. Often the importance of this relationship is underestimated as it is rarely the focus of attention in the behavioral literature (68). However, where this element of therapy has been measured using the genuineness, warmth, and empathy scales, the behavior therapists evidence relatively high levels (60, 74).

Procedures During the Assessment Phase

1. Compilation of the problematic behavior inventory.
   (a) Begin by asking for one member of the family group to identify his perception of the problems that have resulted in the meeting.
   (b) Clarify these perceived problems by asking for behaviorally specific examples. Most perceived problems can be translated into statements of who does what to whom within what context.
   (c) As each family member offers their perception of the problem, there is a high probability that the ensuing discussion will stimulate disagreements among family members. It is important to observe who disagrees with whom, and over what behavioral statements. Therefore, these interchanges must be allowed to occur; however, they can become counterproductive to the objective of the assessment. When this occurs, the therapist should intervene, requesting the family members to terminate the debate, yet acknowledging that differences of opinion are expected. Assure all family members that their perceptions of the problems are important and that each member will have an opportunity to present personal views.
2. Identifying priority behavioral problems and their maintaining conditions.
   (a) Attempt to identify the antecedent events of at least those behaviors that arouse the highest level of intensity of feeling among family members. Antecedent events are those conditions existent immediately prior to the occurrence of a target behavior; e.g., what other members of the family are doing or not doing prior to the occurrence of an undesired behavior.
   (b) Identify the consequences of those problem behaviors that elicit the more intense family feelings. Identify the consequences of those events that occur after a target behavior; e.g., what other family members do after one of the problem behaviors has occurred.
3. Identify the contingencies existent for the provision of consequences; that is, what rules appear to govern the conditions under which these consequences are provided—for example, when a child is

spanked versus when he is not, or when privileges are withdrawn versus when they are not.

4. Identify recurrent behavior patterns in the exchanges among the family members. Observe and record behavioral exchanges; e.g., coercive exchanges, shouting, avoidance responses, excessive demands, etc.

5. Secure a commitment from each member of the family system, ensuring that they wish to work toward change. This commitment should clearly explicate: (a) that they will work as a unit on these family problems, and (b) they, as individuals, will work toward behavioral change.

At this point in the assessment phase, the therapist should be able to demonstrate to the family the interconnections of their individual behaviors in that when one individual behaves, all family members must respond in some manner; that is, behaviors do not occur in isolation. For example, when the adolescent child repeatedly violates her curfew, the resultant parent-child conflict affects all members of the family.

6. Begin to identify possible behavior targets for change. These target behaviors should be "desirable behaviors" with the objective of increased frequency of occurrence. This identification is often assisted by asking each family member to answer two questions: How could you behave differently to make this a happier family? How would you like to see others behave differently to make this a happier family?

These questions may be given as homework assignments, with the instructions that each person provide as many answers as possible to each question. The therapist should point out to the family members that this assignment is a challenge as it requires the identification of desired behaviors. Individuals are more often accustomed to identifying what behaviors they do not like to see, as opposed to those they prefer.

7. On the basis of the family's homework assignment, discuss possible appropriate behavioral targets for change.

   (a) Select behaviors that are to be accelerated in frequency in order to maximize the opportunities for positive consequences.

   (b) Select behaviors that appear to be most relevant to enhancing this family's definition of its own happiness.

   (c) Strive to select behaviors that are incompatible with the occurrence of undesirable (problematic) behaviors.

   (d) For each child, select at least one behavior that is "low risk" for change. A low-risk behavioral target is one that can be easily attained by the child and one that, if performed by the child without positive reinforcement (a violation of the change contract), will not jeopardize the growing trust of the child. An example of a child's low-risk target behavior change might be combing her hair in the morning, or taking the garbage out each evening.

(e) Attempt to select behaviors that are commonly identified among family members; e.g., dinner time behavior, family "get togethers," doing the dishes cooperatively, playing with all siblings.

(f) Remember that a behavior must be observable to all and therefore it is necessary to explicate the indicators of some behaviors in order to minimize debates over whether the behavior has actually occurred. For many parents, the behavior "cleaning up his room" is a desired behavior change objective. Interestingly, what appears to be a very clear behavior has a great deal of opportunity for individual interpretation. It is therefore necessary to pinpoint such behaviors as picking up clothes, placing them in the appropriate locations, making the bed, etc.

8. Allow time for all family members to present their concerns and their support for the target behaviors. Certain behavior choices will elicit strong feelings from some family members. Negotiation must take place before selected behaviors are settled upon and must always take place within the spirit of the agreement or commitment for change. If one or more family member wishes to reevaluate this commitment in light of the selected targets for change, then this request must be honored. Such reevaluation may have to take place within the context of the consequences of no change; that is, all persons have a right not to be required not to change. There are, however, certain consequences for not changing. What are they for the individual and the family?

9. When target behaviors have been agreed upon, set the conditions for a baseline measure.

(a) Before instructing the family to change, request that the parents monitor the frequency of occurrence of the target behaviors. This will allow for some "before" behavior frequency measures. These measures should be recorded and can be used at a later date to assess the ongoing behavioral change within the family.

(b) Appoint the parents as the monitors of the behavior targets. Give the parents a tally sheet and instructions to record the frequency of occurrence of each target behavior.

10. During the assessment phase, the therapist may identify problems with an individual or the marital couple that require specific attention. On occasion, the assessment period indicates that the change process should be focused on the marital couple rather than on the child. Behavioral marital intervention is compatible with the as-

sessment in progress. With the couple's agreement, the intervention may be temporarily suspended in light of the recognized need to concentrate on the couple's problems.

Implementation Phase Procedures

The implementation phase of a behavioral therapy program is marked by the identification of new contingencies between identified behaviors and their consequences. To this point the focus has been on the appropriate targeting of behaviors for change. At the time a program for change is to be implemented, a contingency contract might be formulated in order to facilitate a systematic, cooperative effort on the part of the family in facilitating change.

1. Clearly identify the target behaviors that have been agreed upon as the focus for change.
2. Establish new antecedent events for each of these target behaviors.
3. Establish new consequences that are to be provided for each occurrence or nonoccurrence of a targeted behavior.
4. Formulate a written contract specifying the following conditions:
   (a) The target behaviors for change and their pinpointed elements.
   (b) New antecedents. If these are to be instructions, then specify by whom these instructions are to be given.
   (c) New positive consequences that might include the tangible checkmarks and/or tokens provided upon behavioral occurrence, as well as social reinforcers such as affection and praise.
   (d) Specify what is to happen if there is a violation of the contract; that is, if a behavior does not occur or an undesired behavior occurs, then it must be clear as to what others in the family are to do. For example, if a target behavior focuses on "good dinner time behavior" and one or more of the children violate this agreement, then all family members must be clear as to what is to happen when unacceptable behavior occurs at the dinner table.
   (e) Specify those positive consequences that are to act as bonus reinforcers, particularly when certain behavioral objectives are accomplished. For example, it is often helpful to include special privileges, such as family outings, as bonus reinforcers for a designated behavioral achievement; e.g., a target behavior that occurs at the desired level for a period of one week or more.
   (f) Specify those persons in the family unit who are to be responsible for recording the frequency of behavioral occurrences. This is usually one or both of the parents. These tally records are important in communicating to the family members the degree and intensity of change.

(g) Contracts may be written in a variety of ways, but they must all contain the condition: Who does what to whom under what conditions! Many different examples of contracts may be found in the literature (6, 44, 63, 76).

5. After a program has been implemented, it is necessary to follow up with a series of telephone calls to ensure that the program is implemented. In addition, these telephone calls provide the opportunity for members of the family, particularly the parents, to ask any questons that might have arisen as a result of implementing the program for change. These calls need not take long and should be limited only to the pragmatics of the program implementation. Any conflict among family members reported at this time should be directed back to the family for resolution. If resolution is not possible, the persons in charge of recording should make note of the nature of the conflict and the context in which it occurs. This will be dealt with at the next meeting with the therapist.

6. Difficulties in implementing the program are inevitable. These problems usually pertain to such things as tally recording, differences in target behavior definitions, and lack of "cooperation" on the part of certain family members. In order to deal with these problems, the therapist must remember that the contract is the reference point. Once agreed to, all problems arising with the behavioral changes must relate to the original document. Changes in the contract must be negotiated by all members of the family. Remember that all problems related to the implementation of and adherence to a contract for family interactional modification may eventually have to be related back to the original commitment for change agreed to by the family during the assessment period.

7. Each interview with the family after implementation should begin with an examination of the tally recording provided by the family members. Where change is evident in these data, the therapist must provide positive reinforcement by acknowledging the change and the hard work of all family members.

8. Discussion must then shift to focusing on problems arising between sessions. These discussions may flow to more general aspects of the family's functioning, and special techniques such as role playing, modeling, and behavioral rehearsal may be introduced in an effort to assist the family in dealing with these problems.

9. Since much of the family's energy goes into problem-solving activity and conflict resolution, the therapist must spend time on these areas of family life. One of the advantages of having required the family to negotiate a contingency contract is that they have experienced a process of successful problem-solving and negotiation. Examples derived from that process can be utilized in the ongoing problem-solving and conflict-resolution training.

10. Where the monitoring of change has indicated that little if any change is taking place, it is necessary to examine certain aspects of the program design. Depending on the area in which the program is failing, it will be necessary to consider changes in: target behaviors, consequences, violations in the contract. It is often necessary to assess whether people are in fact following through on the requirements of the contract. For example, it might be that a parent has agreed to read a bedtime story for successful achievement of a behavioral objective during the day, but fails to deliver.

11. When target behaviors have been achieved at the desired level of frequency: identify new behaviors for change, or move toward termination of the behavioral therapy program.

Termination Phase Procedures

1. Together with the family system, evaluate the progress in relation to the objectives of the contract.
2. If the decision is to terminate, then set the conditions for behavioral maintenance.
3. Behavioral maintenance requires the therapist to review with the family the basic learning principles identified during the modification of the target behavior—e.g., positive consequences versus punishment.
4. Instruct the family to continue the tally recording over the next four weeks but without the regularly scheduled appointments.
5. Set up an appointment for four weeks from the last interview for the purposes of termination and follow-up.

Follow-Up Procedures

The follow-up interview should be an assessment interview related to whether or not the behavioral changes have been maintained. If these changes have not been maintained at a level consistent with the expectations of the therapist and/or the family, it will be necessary to reinstitute the program structure. If, on the other hand, the therapist and family feel that the behavioral changes have been maintained within desired parameters, then termination may take place. Termination, of course, does allow for the family to contact the therapist at any point in the future where they feel the necessity.

From the perspective of clinical evaluation, it is important that the therapist analyze the results of the behavioral change program. Further, it is helpful for the therapist to assess the maintenance of change by contacting the family members at a three-month and six-month interval to ascertain the degree to which the behavioral changes have been maintained.

Conclusion

Behavior therapy, as it has been presented here, is comprised of a variety of distinctly different approaches to facilitating behavioral and in some cases cognitive changes. It has developed from a strong commitment to planned and systematic assessment and intervention within a context of empirical inquiry. Its impact on social work practice continues to be felt both directly (e.g., clinical practice) and indirectly (e.g., task-centered approaches, as well as single subject designs in research). Behavior therapy has been demonstrated to be effective in almost all areas of social work practice and with some human problems it is argued to be the most advisable therapeutic option. There is little doubt that its place within eclectic social work practice has been assured.

References

1. Alexander, J., and C. Barton. "Systems—Behavioral Intervention with Delinquent Families," in J. Vincent (ed.), *Advances in Family Intervention, Assessment and Theory*. Greenwich, Conn.: JAI Press, 1980.

2. Alexander, J., and B. Parsons. *Functional Family Therapy*. Monterey, Calif.: Brooks/Cole, 1982.

3. Barlow, D., G. O'Brien, and C. Last. "Couples Treatment in Agoraphobia," *Behavior Therapy*, Vol. 15 (1984), pp. 41–58.

4. Beck, Aaron. *Cognitive Therapy and the Emotional Disorders*. New York: International Universities Press, 1976.

5. Birchler, G., and S. Spinks. "Behavioral-Systems Marital and Family Therapy Integration and Clinical Application," *American Journal of Family Therapy*, Vol. 8 (1980), pp. 6–28.

6. Blechman, E. "Objectives and Procedures Believed Necessary for the Success of a Contractual Approach to Family Intervention," *Behavior Therapy*, Vol. 8 (1977), pp. 275–277.

7. Brown, B., and M. Christie. *Social Learning Practice in Residential Child Care*. New York: Pergamon Press, 1981.

8. Callner, D. A. "Behavioral Treatment Approaches to Drug Abuse: A Critical Review of the Research," *Psychological Bulletin*, Vol. 82, No. 2 (March 1975), pp. 143–164.

9. Carr, J. *Helping Your Handicapped Child: A Step-by-Step Guide to Everyday Problems*. Hardmondsworth: Penguin Books, 1980.

10. Douds, A., M. Engelsgjerd, and T. Collingwood. "Behavior Contracting with Youthful Offenders and Their Parents," *Child Welfare*, Vol. 56, No. 6 (June 1977), pp. 409–417.

11. Ellis, Albert, and R. Grieger (eds.). *Handbook of Rational-Emotive Therapy*. New York: Springer, 1977.

12. Fischer, J. *Effective Casework Practice: An Eclectic Approach*. New York: McGraw-Hill, 1978.

13. ——, and H. Gochros (eds.). *A Handbook of Behavior Therapy with Sexual Problems*, 2 vols. New York: Pergamon Press, 1977.

14. Forehand, R., and R. McMahon. *Helping the Noncompliant Child: A Clinician's Guide to Parent Training*. New York: Guilford, 1981.

15. Franks, C. (ed.). *Behavior Therapy: Appraisal and Status*. New York: McGraw-Hill, 1969.

16. Gambrill, E. "A Behavioral Perspective of Families," in E. Tolson and W. Reid (eds.), *Models of Family Treatment*. New York: Columbia University Press, 1981.

17. Gelder, M. "Behavior Therapy for Neurotic Disorders," *Behavior Modification*, Vol. 3, No. 4 (October 1979), pp. 469–495.

18. Goldfried, M., and G. Davison. *Clinical Behavior Therapy*. New York: Holt, Rinehart and Winston, 1976.

19. Goldfried, M., and M. Merbaum (ed.). *Behavior Change Through Self-Control*. New York: Holt, Rinehart and Winston, 1973.

20. Gomes-Schwartz, B. "The Modification of Schizophrenic Behavior," *Behavior Modification*, Vol. 3, No. 4 (October 1979), pp. 439–469.

21. Gordon, S., and N. Davidson. "Behavioral Parent Training," in A. Gurman and D. Kniskern (eds.), *Handbook of Family Therapy*. New York: Brunner/Mazel, 1981, pp. 517–555.

22. Graziano, A. "Parents as Behavior Therapists," in M. Hersen, R. Eisler, and P. Miller (eds.), *Progress in Behavior Modification*, Vol. 4 (1977), pp. 251–298.

23. Harris, S., and R. Milch. "Training Parents as Behavior Therapists for Their Autistic Children," *Clinical Psychology Review*, Vol. 1, pp. 49–63.

24. Hersen, M., and A. Bellack, "Perspectives in the Behavioral Treatment of Depression," *Behavior Modification*, Vol. 6, No. 1 (January 1982), pp. 95–106.

25. Jacobson, N. "A Component Analysis of Behavioral Marital Therapy: The Relative Effectiveness of Behavior Exchange and Communication/Problem-Solving Training," *Journal of Consulting and Clinical Psychology*, Vol. 52 (1984), pp. 295–305.

26. ——. "Behavioral Marital Therapy," in A. Gurman and D. Kniskern (eds.), *Handbook of Family Therapy*. New York: Brunner/Mazel, 1981, pp. 556–591.

27. ——, and G. Margolin. *Marital Therapy: Strategies Based on Social Learning and Behavior Exchange Principles*. New York: Brunner/Mazel, 1979.

28. Kazdin, A., and G. Wilson. *Evaluation of Behavior Therapy: Issues, Evidence, and Research Strategies*. Cambridge, Mass: Ballinger, 1978.

29. Kovacs, M. "Treating Depressive Disorders," *Behavior Modification*, Vol. 3, No. 4 (October 1979), pp. 496–517.

30. Krasnegor, N. "Analysis and Modification of Substance Abuse: A Behavioral Overview," *Behavior Modification*, Vol. 4 (January 1980), pp. 35–55.

31. Lawrence, H., and C. Walter. "Testing a Behavioral Approach with Groups," *Social Work*, Vol. 23, No. 2 (March 1978), pp. 127–133.

32. Mahoney, M. *Psychotherapy Process: Current Issues and Future Directions*. New York: Plenum, 1980.

33. ——. *Cognition and Behavior Modification*. Cambridge, Mass.: Ballinger, 1974.

34. Marlatt, G., and P. Nathan (eds.). *Behavioral Approaches to Alcoholism*. Rutgers, N.J.: Center of Alcohol Studies, 1978.

35. Mathews, A., M. Gelder, and D. Johnston. *Agoraphobia: Nature and Treatment*. New York: Guilford, 1981.

36. Mavissakalian, M., and D. Barlow (eds.). *Phobia: Psychological and Pharmacological Treatment*. New York: Guilford, 1981.

37. McGlynn, F., W. Mealiea, and D. Landau. "The Current Status of Systematic Desensitization," *Clinical Psychology Review*, Vol. 1 (1981), pp. 149–179.

38. Meichenbaum, D. *Cognitive-Behavior Modification: An Integrative Approach*. New York: Plenum, 1977.

39. Miller, P. *Behavioral Treatment of Alcoholism*. New York: Pergamon Press, 1976.

40. Moreland, John R., Andrew I. Schwebel, Steven Beck, and Robert Wells. "Parents as Therapists: A Review of the Behavior Therapy Parent Training Literature—1975 to 1981," *Behavior Modification*, Vol. 6, No. 2 (April 1982), pp. 250–276.

41. Nietzel, M., R. Winett, M. MacDonald, and W. Davidson. *Behavioral Approaches to Community Psychology*. New York: Pergamon Press, 1977.

42. O'Leary, K. "The Image of Behavior Therapy: It Is Time to Take a Stand," *Behavior Therapy*, Vol. 15 (1984), pp. 219–233.

43. ———, and H. Turkewitz, "Marital Therapy from a Behavioral Perspective," in T. Paolino and B. McCrady (eds.), *Marriage and Marital Therapy: Psychoanalytic, Behavioral and Systems Theory Perspectives*. New York: Brunner/Mazel, 1978, pp. 240–297.

44. Patterson, G. *Families: Applications of Social Learning to Family Life*. Champaign, Ill.: Research Press, 1971.

45. ———, P. Chamberlain, and J. Reid. "A Comparative Evaluation of a Parent-Training Program," *Behavior Therapy*, Vol. 13 (1982), pp. 638–650.

46. Patterson, G., and J. Reid. "Reciprocity and Coercion: Two Facets of Social Systems," in C. Neuringer and J. Michael (eds.), *Behavior Modification in Clinical Psychology*. New York: Appleton-Century-Crofts, 1970, pp. 133–177.

47. ———, R. Jones, and R. Conger, *A Social Learning Approach to Family Intervention: Families with Aggressive Children*. Eugene, Ore.: Castalia, 1975.

48. Patterson, R., and G. Jackson. "Behavioral Approaches to Gerontology," in L. Michalson, M. Hersen, and S. Turner (eds.), *Future Perspectives in Behavior Therapy*. New York: Plenum 1981, pp. 293–313.

49. Phillips, J., and R. Ray. "Behavioral Approaches to Childhood Disorders," *Behavior Modification*, Vol. 4, No. 1 (January 1980), pp. 3–34.

50. Pinkston, E., J. Levitt, G. Green, N. Linsk, and T. Rzepnicki. *Effective Social Work Practice*. San Francisco: Jossey-Bass, 1982.

51. Rimm, D., and J. Masters. *Behavior Therapy: Techniques and Empirical Findings*, 2nd edition. New York: Academic Press, 1980.

52. Rose, Sheldon. *Group Therapy: A Behavioral Approach*. Englewood Cliffs, N.J.: Prentice-Hall, 1977.

53. ———. *Treating Children in Groups*. Washington: Jossey-Bass, 1973.

54. Ross, A. "Behavioral Therapy with Children," in S. Garfield and A. Bergin (eds.), *Handbook of Psychotherapy and Behavior Change*, 2nd edition. New York: Wiley, 1978, pp. 591–620.

55. Schinke, S. (ed.). *Behavioral Methods in Social Welfare*. Hawthorne, N.Y.: Aldine, 1981.

56. Schwartz, A. *The Behavior Therapies: Theories and Applications*. New York: Free Press, 1982.

57. ———, and I. Goldiamond. *Social Casework: A Behavioral Approach*. New York: Columbia University Press, 1975.

58. Schwartz, Robert. "Cognitive-Behavior Modification: A Conceptual Review," *Clinical Psychology Review*, Vol. 2 (1982), pp. 267–293.

59. Skinner, B. F. *Science and Human Behavior*. New York: Macmillan, 1953.

60. Sloane, R. B., F. R. Staples, A. H. Cristol, N. J. Yorkston, and K. Whipple. *Psychotherapy vs. Behavior Therapy*. Cambridge, Mass.: Harvard University Press, 1975.

61. Stuart, Richard B. *Helping Couples Change a Social Learning Approach to Marital Therapy*. New York: Guilford, 1980.

62. ———. "Behavior Modification: A Technology of Social Change," Francis Turner (ed.), *Social Work Treatment*, 2nd edition. New York: Free Press, 1979, pp. 433–448.

63. ———. "Behavioral Contracting with Families of Delinquents," *Journal of Behavior Therapy and Experimental Psychiatry*, Vol. 2 (1971), pp. 1–11.

64. Stumphauzer, J. *Progress in Behavior Therapy with Delinquents*. Springfield, Ill.: Charles C. Thomas, 1977.

65. ———. "Modifying Delinquent Behavior: Beginnings and Current Practices," *Adolescence*, Vol. 11, No. 41 (Spring 1976), pp. 13–28.

66. Stunkard, A., and M. Mahoney. "Behavioral Treatment of the Eating Disorders," in H. Leitenberg (ed.), *Handbook of Behavior Modification and Behavior Therapy*. Englewood Cliffs, N.J.: Prentice-Hall, 1976, pp. 45–73.

67. Sundel, M., and St. Stone. *Behavior Modification in the Human Services: A Systematic Introduction to Concepts and Applications*. New York: Wiley, 1975.

68. Sweet, A. "The Therapeutic Relationship in Behavior Therapy," *Clinical Psychology Review*, Vol. 4 (1982), pp. 253–272.

69. Thomas, E. *Marital Communication and Decision Making: Analysis, Assessment, and Change*. New York: Free Press, 1977.

70. Thomlison, Ray J. "Something Works: Evidence from Practice Effectiveness Studies," *Social Work*, Vol. 29 (1984), pp. 51–56.

71. ———. "Phobic Disorders," in Francis Turner (ed.), *Adult Psychopathology: A Social Work Perspective*. New York: Free Press, 1984, pp. 280–315.

72. ———. "Ethical Issues in the Use of Behavior Modification in Social Work Practice," in Shankar Yelaja (ed.), *Ethical Issues in Social Work*. Springfield, Ill.: Charles C. Thomas, 1982.

73. ———. "Behavioral Family Intervention with the Family of a Mentally Handicapped Child," in D. Freeman and B. Trute (eds.), *Treating Families with Special Needs*. Ottawa: Canadian Association of Social Workers, 1981, pp. 15–42.

74. ———. *A Behavioral Model for Social Work Intervention with the Marital Dyad*. Unpublished doctoral dissertation, University of Toronto, 1972.

75. ———. "An Introduction to the Sociobehavioral Approach in the Community Context." Unpublished paper, University of Toronto, 1970.

76. Weathers, L., and R. Liberman. "Contingency Contracting with Families of Delinquent Adolescents," *Behavior Therapy*, Vol. 6 (1975), pp. 356–366.

77. Whitehead, A. "Psychological Treatment of Depression: A Review," *Behavior Research and Therapy*, Vol. 17, No. 5 (1979), pp. 495–509.

78. Wilson, G. T. "On the Much Discussed Nature of the Term 'Behavior Therapy,' "*Behavior Therapy*, Vol. 9 (January 1978), pp. 89–98.

79. Wodarski, J., and D. Bagarozzi. *Behavioral Social Work*. New York: Human Sciences Press, 1979.

80. Wolf, M., E. Phillips, D. Fixsen, C. Braukmann, K. Kirigin, A. Willner, and J. Schumaker. "Achievement Place: The Teaching Family Model," *Child Care Quarterly*, Vol. 5 (1976), pp. 92–103.

81. Wolpe, Joseph. *The Practice of Behavior Therapy*. New York: Pergamon Press, 1969.

82. ———. *The Practice of Behavior Therapy*, 3rd edition. New York: Pergamon Press, 1982.

83. Yule, W., and J. Carr (eds.). *Behavior Modification for the Mentally Handicapped*. London: Croom Helm, 1980.

Annotated Listing of Key References

ALEXANDER, J., and B. PARSONS. *Functional Family Therapy*. Monterey, Calif.: Brooks/Cole, 1982.

This volume clearly and concisely outlines a behavioral approach to family therapy and provides a nice introduction to this particular model.

MAHONEY, M. *Cognition and Behavior Modification*. Cambridge, Mass.: Ballinger Press, 1974.

Read in conjunction with the Meichenbaum book (38), this volume provides an excellent perspective on the role of cognition in behavior therapy.

ROSE, S. *Group Therapy: A Behavioral Approach*. Englewood Cliffs, N.J.: Prentice-Hall, 1977.

This is one of the few books applying the behavioral approach to work with groups. Rose has extensive experience with groups and has expertly woven this experience into a solid behavioral approach to group therapy.

SCHINKE, S. (ed.). *Behavioral Methods in Social Welfare*. New York: Aldine, 1981.

This edited volume offers the reader an excellent overview of the principles of behavioral therapy and their impact on a wide range of social work issues.

SCHWARTZ, A. *The Behavior Therapies: Theories and Applications*. New York: Free Press, 1982.

Schwartz provides an excellent overview of the behavioral approach. This book could well serve as an easily read introduction to this subject matter.

CHAPTER 7

Meditation and Social Work Treatment

Thomas Keefe

Meditation is an ancient discipline wedded to several major psychophilosophical systems arising from diverse cultures. Among others, American Indian, Central Asian Sufi, Hindu, Chinese Taoist, widespread Buddhist, and some Christian traditions have cultivated forms of meditation as a source of spiritual enrichment and personal growth. Now, meditation has begun its marriage to the rational-empirical tradition of Western science. In this most recent alliance it will be tested, objectified, stripped of its mystical trappings, and enriched with empirical understanding.

Although testing is under way and final acceptance is some time in the future, the potential of meditaton in psychotherapy and social work treatment has already been recognized by some. Meditation is a method that is adjunctive to social work treatment. Its potential in treating a variety of problems and persons is becoming clear. Yet meditation as a method will demand much from, and occasionally will challenge, the theories underlying social work treatment for its full description and explanation.

Description and Explanation: The Mind as an Open Hand

Meditation is a set of behaviors. Some of the consequences of meditation are directly observable; others can be indirectly inferred. Meditation here does not refer to the mind's wandering and floating in fantasy, or to the mind's

155

laboring along a tight line of logic toward a solution. In contradistinction to these common Western notions, meditation is the deliberate cultivation of a state of mind exclusive of both fantasy and logic. While there are several varieties of meditation, they all share some common characteristics that shall be described in detail to provide an overview of the method.

In essence, meditation is the development—or discovery, depending on your orientation—of consciousness independent of visual and verbal symbols that constitute what we call thought. It is the deliberate cultivation of a mental state conducive to intuition. Meditation usually pairs a relaxed state of the body with an attentive focus of the mind. A brief description of this common process in meditation will help orient us to the method.

One meditates by focusing attention upon a single thing while physically relaxed. This may be a sound (mantra), a design (mandala [24]), an object, a part of the body, a mental image, or a prayer. This ostensibly simple task is in fact extremely difficult for most people. Noises, bodily stimuli, internal dialogues, monologues, images, and emotions constantly interrupt the task to break one's attention. Meditation then becomes a task of first, continually noticing a distraction; second, recognizing or naming the loss of attention—e.g., "thinking," "feeling," "remembering," etc.; and third, letting go of any resulting chain of associations to return to the meditation object. This task of refocusing attention and cultivating an attitude of noninvolvement to the distracting chains of association that would pull the meditator from his object of attention constitute meditation for the beginner. I like to use the analogy that *the mind becomes like an open hand. Nothing is clung to, nothing is pushed away.*

Some theorists and practitioners distinguish two basic forms of meditation. One is a concentrative form in which the meditator's attention is riveted to the meditation object—e.g., mandala, mantra, etc.—to the exclusion of other stimuli. In contrast, insight meditation described in this chapter stresses the examination of the randomly occurring mental contents often with a naming of each—e.g., memory, fantasy, fear, etc. There are many variations on these two themes. Interestingly, studies of electroencephalographic changes accompanying representative variations on these two themes indicate changes in brain activity that parallel the form of meditation underway (2, 25). For advanced meditators, easy attention to the meditation object actually facilitates the examination of randomly occurring internal and external stimuli when they adopt the mental attitude of an "open hand."

Most meditators initially find that their attention is disrupted by a stream of thought. Distractions by the stream of thought seem to present themselves in a hierarchy of personal importance. Those incidents of the recent past evoking the most anxiety or anger seem to intrude first. These are followed by memories or anticipations of increasingly remote concern. Thoughts, images, and feelings well up, momentarily distract, and if not clung to or elaborated upon, burn themselves out. When paired with the relaxed state of the body and followed by refocusing upon the pleasantness of the meditation object, a *global*, that is, total *desensitization* (18) of cathected thoughts and images occurs. Increasing equanimity and objectivity secure the meditator in an attitude of observation of the thoughts that make up the symbolic self and its constituent concerns.

The meditation behaviors of focusing attention, recognizing when attention is interrupted, sometimes naming the nature of the interruption— e.g., "thinking," "feeling," "remembering," etc.—and deliberately refocusing attention are forms of discrimination learning (21). Perceptions, thoughts, and feelings are discriminated from the meditation object. Slowly, the capacity to discriminate thoughts and feelings from any focus of attention is developed. The meditator descriminates memory and anticipation, fear, and guilt from the immediate focus of attention. He cultivates a *present centeredness*. As this learning to discriminate the ingredients of consciousness or contents of mind becomes easier, an *observer self*, also called *watcher self* (10, p. 135) or *witness* (20, p. 178), emerges. The observer self is helpful in a variety of areas of functioning.

We must be very clear that the observer self is not an alienated, depersonalized, or neurotic self sustained by dissociative processes or suppression of thought and emotion. It is, instead, a secure subjectivity that allows full experience without judgment, defense, or elaboration. In the cultivation of this observer self of meditation, there emerges several psychofunctional capacities that are taken up below and further elaborated on as we examine meditation as a techinque in personality change.

Capacities Learned in Meditation

For those of us involved in social work treatment, examining the learnings transferred from meditation practice into the psychosocial functioning of the meditator may prove valuable. This is one of our own cultural mechanisms for integrating meditation behavior within our own psychophilosophical traditions. The learnings transferred from meditation can be termed "capacities," and there are several of them.

The capacity to *focus attention on a single thing* or *task* is enhanced. This is called "one-pointedness-of-mind." When carried over into everyday life, tasks undertaken with this state of mind are completed with less distraction and with the expenditure of less wasted energy. The Buddhists call this state of mind, carried into everyday life, *right mindfulness* (7, p. 30).

The *capacity to discriminate among internal stimuli*, such as memories, fears, anger, etc., provides a measure of enhanced self-awareness useful in empathic relating and communicating of one's responses in social situations. The capacity to view with a degree of objectivity and nonattached concern these internal processes allows enhanced performance in complex behaviors. Consider the snow skier: Skiing requires concentration. As speed increases and the slope becomes steeper and the surface more varied, concentration must intensify. If the skier suddenly becomes preoccupied with a distant drop-off, or with an intruding and distracting fear of falling, his concentration is broken and the possibility of his falling is more likely. The clutched athlete, the self-conscious speaker, the ego-involved attorney are all momentarily off their present-time center—far from their observer self.

Finally, the capacity for an *altered mode of perception* is cultivated in the meditation process. The passive-receptive phase of perception, wherein one allows the senses to be stimulated, delaying cognitive structuring and allowing the things perceived to speak for themselves, is enhanced in meditation. Psychologist Sidney Jourard (23) and Abraham Maslow (17) both described this form of perception as necessary to supplement the more active, structured, need-oriented perception typical of Western consciousness. Nyanaponika Thera described the Buddhist view of this perceptual mode generated in meditation as *bare attention*. Thera elaborated:

> It cleans the object of investigation from the impurities of prejudice and passion; it frees it from alien admixtures and from points of view most pertaining to it; it holds it firmly before the eye of wisdom, by slowing down the transition from the receptive to the active phase of the perceptual or cognitive process, thus giving a vastly improved chance of close and dispassionate investigation. (49, pp. 34–35)

In sum, we see the results of meditation behaviors as including such global capacities as relaxation, desensitization of charged stimuli, enhanced discrimination, concentration of attention, self-awareness, intentional present centeredness, development of a secure observer self, and augmented perceptual modes.

Each of these factors has implications for enhanced personal and interpersonal functioning. Moreover, meditation behaviors are used to counter specific behaviors seen as symptomatic or problematic for clients. These include anxiety, some forms of depression, phobic reactions, interpersonal difficulties, and others. Generally arising from traditions that are unhampered by notions of health and illness in relation to human behavior, meditation has been used in the personal growth and consciousness development of both the average lay person and the select initiates of particular religious orders. Used as a tool to extend the potential of its practitioners, meditation has been oriented toward the possible rather than the merely adequate or healthy in human functioning. Consequently, there are several ramifications for social work treatment. Meditation has, as shall be seen later, potential for the social work practitioner as well as for the client. It requires no predisposing diagnosis for its use—although there are definite contraindicators. It has potential for use with individuals, families, groups, and in community settings.

Origins and Paths into Social Work Treatment

Meditation comes to us from diverse cultures and traditions. Yet the various forms, whatever their source, express a common origin in man's intuitive modes of thought. As an example, the *zazen* meditation of Zen Buddhism has its origin with the intuitive enlightenment of Siddhartha Gautama, Buddha in about 544 B.C. (7, p. 21). Siddhartha was said to have led a life of wealth and indulgence and then a life of asceticism in his spiritual quest to find the cause of suffering in this world. After relinquishing these extremes of self-preoccupation, his answer and enlightenment came. His Four Noble Truths together with his Eightfold Path served as vehicles for transmission of insight into his wisdom for centuries. The Buddha's Eightfold Path includes meditation as one of the paths to spiritual freedom from suffering (4, p. 30). Thus it is a central practice in all branches of Buddhism, although characteristic variations have developed in each tradition.

Buddhism is thought to have been carried from the northern India of Siddhartha to China in A.D. 520 by Bodhidharma (30, p. 302). There the Indian *dhyana* became the Chinese *Ch'an*. Influenced by Taoism in China, meditation was transmitted to medieval Japan, where it is referred to as *Zen*, which literally means "meditation." Zen found its way to the West by several routes and has been popularized by D. T. Suzuki (48), Allen Watter (53), and others.

But Zen is only one form of meditation that has ancient and divergent cultural origins. In fact, meditation has been an important practice in the major world religions: Hinduism, Confucianism, Taoism, Buddhism, Judaism, Islam, and Christianity.

For centuries in India, meditation was taught in the oral traditions of the Hindu Vedas. Then, sometime before 300 B.C., some of these traditions of meditation were written in the *Yoga Sutras* of Patanjali (55). The techniques used in yoga include mantras, visualizations, breath control, and concentration on various postures or parts of the body. The purpose of yoga meditation is to unify the body, mind, and spirit allowing an individual to become whole, integrated, and functioning as Atman, a godlike higher self (40). Ultimately, union with Brahman, or God, is achieved. The *Bhagavad-Gita* (c. 200 B.C.) suggests meditation as one of the three main ways to achieve freedom from karma (40) or the world of cause and effect.

In China, Confucius recommended meditation as a part of personal cultivation. Later it became the central feature of the Lu Chiu-Yuan school of Neo-Confucianism. Taoists during the same period in China also used meditation to facilitate mystical harmony with the Tao (54).

Some types of Jewish mysticism incorporate meditation to achieve metaphysical insights. Philo of Alexandria (c. 15 B.C.–A.D. 50) and other Jewish scholars in the Middle Ages used this type of meditation (11, P. 183).

From the twelfth century A.D., Sufism, a popular folk Islam, has encouraged various types of meditation as well as other techniques such as whirling to induce trance. Meditation is considered to be an important rememberance of God. It is also used to facilitate perceptions of inner reality (1).

Christianity, too, is rich in traditions using a variety of meditative techniques, from the early Christian Gnostics to the medieval monasteries to eighteenth-century Greek orthodox teachings. Some original training manuals include *The Philokalis* (Greek Orthodox) and *The Way of Perfection* by St. Theresa of Avila (23, p. 26).

Interestingly, the philosophies of the Yogic and Buddhist meditators are reflected in their contrasting meditation behaviors. For example, most Yogic meditators seem to cultivate a *habituation effect* (39, pp. 52–56, 178) to the object of meditation and experience a loss of perception of the object or a "blending" with it. This subjective experience of habituation corresponds with the brain's productivity of electromagnetic alpha waves that accompany relaxed awareness. These Yogic meditators reduce awareness of outside stimuli and experience a blissful indifference sometimes called *samadhi*. For the Yogi, *samadhi* is a high state of self-transcendent consciusness, a link with the godhead or universal consciousness to be attained through rigor and single-minded devotion.

Like the Yogic meditators, advanced Zen meditators undergo the habituation effect and record increased alpha wave productivity. However, when exposed to outside stimuli while meditating, they respond with sharp, momentary attention as evidenced by corresponding short bursts of beta wave productivity. These meditators seem to be able to respond repeatedly to external stimuli without habituating to them. Psychologist Robert Ornstein suggests that they are responding without constructing a visual model or verbal label for the intruding stimulus, perceiving it clearly each time (39, p. 179). For Buddhist, the state of nirvana, analogous to *samadhi*, is attained but rejected by the protagonists in favor of an act of compassion. This act is to enter the world in a state of wisdom, or *prajna*, there to undertake the work of bringing other sentient beings—or aspects of the larger consciousness—to enlightenment. In interesting ways, then, the responses of meditators parallel the doctrines of their traditions. Given these parallels found in other traditions, it seems natural that meditation should become a part of Western therapeutic traditions. The reciprocal influences between meditation and social work should be exciting.

While meditation comes to the West by many paths, it has far from penetrated to all parts of our industrial culture. Professional social work, a by-product of the industrial market system, is itself relatively new in man's endeavors. The path of meditation is a new trail in social work. It comes to the profession at a time when variety and eclecticism are the norm. As the instability, contradictions, and stresses of the socioeconomic structure create a frenetic search for relevant modes of treatment, meditation will perhaps be another technique to be taken up in the interest of more effective practice.

This vision of the reasons for the profession's interest in meditation is not meant to be derogatory. Basically because of the contradictions and instability of the economic system, we live in an age of anxiety. Meditation may fill a symbolic and practical need in our personal and professional psyches. To face the fragmentation and contradictions of our lives, a safe and quiet place to recollect, sort out, and relax is a natural balm. Moreover, if meditation is more than a clinical adjunct technique, but also a facilitator of other social work skills and a precursor to action as well, it has relevance for the profession as a whole.

Meditation is used or discussed by various psychologists and psychiatrists. Citing ten studies conducted in the last ten years, Jack Engler notes that techniques from all the major meditative traditions have been incorporated or adopted for use in psychiatric treatment settings (12, p. 51). Psychologists using biofeedback apparatus are naturally drawn to meditative techniques and their work influences social work colleagues. They do the lion's share of research on meditation (45).

Meditation as an aid for psychotherapists themselves (28) and in the development of empathic skill (26) has been proposed and examined. Both endeavors have generated interest among clinical social workers and social work educators. The author's interest was spurred by his own experience with meditation. Other workers have had experience with meditation, especially Transcendental Meditation (6), and have incorporated it into their work. While a good fix upon the extent of its use is difficult without a study, one can assume that as more findings are reported in the literature, more interest will be generated in the social work profession.

As noted in the historical origins of meditation, the technique has been refined for personal growth and positive behavior change in several cultural traditions. In each of these traditions, meditation is linked to conceptualizations that explain the subjective experiences of meditation and the behavioral and psychosocial outcomes for practitioners. Each culture has placed meditation within its own context. To use meditation as an adjunct to psychotherapy and social work treatment is to place it within a Western rational, technological, cultural context. In so doing, we can refine and extend meditation technique and at the same time enrich our own tradition.

Meditation, the Personality, and the Conditioned Self

The experience and outcomes of meditation related to the organization of the personality extend Western psychodynamic conceptualizations. We will be concerned with those areas relevant to psychodynamically oriented social work treatment where modifications or extensions of theory are suggested.

The ego or symbolic self in traditional Freudian theory is thought to develop out of the necessity to symbolize real objects that meet our needs. Our capacity to symbolize allows deferred gratification in keeping with social reality. Thus, symbol formulation is seen as necesary to creation of meaning and social interaction. Meditation experience does not refute these perspectives, but it does challenge certain assumptions underlying them.

The symbolic self or ego is experienced as a network of verbal and visual symbols linked to emotional or physiological responses. However, as already described, the meditator can develop a capacity to observe the symbolic self as if from a vantage point of equanimity. In meditation, the emotions, internal dialogue, and visualizations are recognized, experienced vividly, and sometimes labeled, but they do not become a self-perpetuating stream of thought.

As suggested earlier, the advanced meditator generalizes certain capacities learned in meditation to daily functioning. These include the capacities to discriminate memory, fantasy, worry, the accompanying emotional content, and present time perceptions, and to decide which cognitive or emotional responses will become stimuli to further responses and which will not. In learning these two faculties, the meditator cultivates the observer self. In describing a form of Zen breath meditation useful in psychotherapy, psychologist Gary Deatherage suggests:

> If a patient is taught over time to note interruptions in breath observation and to label each interruption with neutral terms such as "remembering," "fantasizing," "hearing," "thinking," or "touching," he will quickly discover a rather complicated, but comforting, situation where there is one aspect of his mental "self" which is calm and psychologically strong, and which can watch, label, and see the melodramas of other "selves" which get too involved in painful memories of the past or beautiful and escapist fantasies of the future. By helping the patient to identify for a time with a strong and neutral "watcher self" there begins to develop with him the strength, motivation, and ability to fully participate in, and benefit from, whatever other forms of psychotherpay are being provided to him. (10, p. 136).

For the meditator, then, the ego or symbolic self is not the only locus of experience. There is an undifferentiated or unconditioned awareness upon which the symbols and felt physiological responses play—like a drama before a mirror.

The process of meditation occupies the focal attention of the rational, linear, verbal (usually left hemisphere) function of the personality. Meanwhile a diffuse, nonlinear awareness emerges before the observer self. The mediator experiences the larger linkages of his symbolically constructed self with the past, present, and future world. This experience of the "larger self" has again and again been described as ineffable, uncommunicable. This is because our verbal, logical self must focus on single components of what is a panorama of perception and experience undifferentiated in time—past, present, or future—and space—here, elsewhere, etc. Because only portions of our more diffuse, intuitive (usually right brain lobe) awareness can be the focus of the narrow beam of our focal attention, only portions of our larger consciousness are immediately accessible to our verbal-logical, verbal-conscious self. This notion of a larger self separate from what we have called our conscious self has recently provoked much interest.

In 1977, in "Meditation and the Unconscious: A New Perspective," John Welwood hypothesized that the "unconscious" of traditional Freudian and Jungian theory limited our understanding of human functioning. In essence, Welwood postulated that the phenomena defined as evidence of an unconscious—forgetting, slips of the tongue, laughter, habit, neurotic symptoms, and dreams—are evidence that we function outside our ordinary focal attention (54). Rather than postulate an internal, unknowable psychic region inhabited by instincts, Welwood suggested that we might envision a focal attention that defines the *figure* in a universal *ground* of perception and awareness. For Welwood, the ground is not simply an internal structure. Instead, the ground is comprised of felt meanings, patterns of personal meanings, ways the organism is attuned to patterns and currents of the universe, and the immediate present.

While Welwood's particular definition of ground is very different from traditional concepts of the unconscious, the conceptualization of ground is descriptive of the way in which the meditator experiences those aspects of awareness not labeled conscious in traditional psychodynamic terms. In meditation, the ego or symbolic self does not dissolve. The meditator does not become "egoless."

Meditation, instead, facilitates the realization of the socially conditioned nature of the self. That each person has a history of conditioning by the interpersonal context of his world, that he can attend to or be conscious of only a small part of his own social programming at a given time, and that meditation is a means of liberation from social conditioning are realized in meditation. These are the sources of personality change in meditation.

In light of meditation, then, the personality is not structured into conscious-unconscious components. Rather, it is a web of interlacing symbolic meanings, each rooted in the social world. The self is like an eddy in a stream. In a sense, it is illusory.

In cultivating an observer self, the meditator grasps the illusory nature of the symbolically constructed self. Conflicts, anxiety arousing ideas, and repetition compulsions are the experienced components of this symbolic self. Seen from the vantage of an observer self, their power and control of response are rendered less ominous. This is because the advanced meditator discriminates the sources of problems and decides, with a degree of neutrality, alternative lines of action. As the anxiety or anger related to particular incidents or situations is desensitized in the relaxed state of meditation, their power and control are further diminished as the capacity for intentional decision about behavior and responses is increased. These behaviors can enhance treatment. As Deatherage puts it: "By becoming aware of the intentional process, one can then intercept and cancel unwanted words or deeds before they are manifested in behavior—something many patients find useful since it places control of their own behavior back at the conscious level" (10, p. 136).

These experiences and outcomes of meditation, therefore, extend and modify traditional psychodynamic perspectives, particularly with regard to the nature and function of the unconscious.

The traditional cultural contexts of meditation universally interject their own myths to supplant critical observaton of what exactly comprises the conditioning of the psychosocial self. Communication science, ego psychology, symbolic interactionism, sociology, and other Western sciences fill the void in traditional understating of the processes that actually condition the self. However, even Western psychologists and therapists who have taken up the practice and systematic study of meditation fall back to philosophical musings when the parameters of the interpersonal ground are defined. Some use the language of mysticism and speak of the larger self or cosmic consciousness, to which each small ego is linked and of which each person is a small manifestation. This language is very global and a more precise and critical view of the social realities should not be abandoned for a blind belief or mystification of social realities.

Social work, with its particularly broad orientation toward human behavior and the social environment, has a special contribution to make toward an understanding of this larger ground of the self. Social workers are cognizant of the extent to which social conditions interact with the individual psyche and condition its nature, prospects, and levels of awareness. Briefly extending this orientation, Karl Marx postulated that the economic organization or structure of society conditions the social and ideological life of a society (36, p. 159). We might caution, then, that the global language of mystical traditions must not supplant critical analysis of the experiences of meditation, for these experiences are behaviors that may carry over into daily functioning with positive benefit to the practioner's personality and social functioning.

Personality and Other Applications

Physical relaxation, concentration of attention, desensitization of anxiety-arousing thoughts, discrimination of thoughts from other stimuli, insight into behaviors and events, and cultivation of an observer self are outcomes of meditation that enhance psychosocial functioning and help in the treatment of problems.

First, learning to be more self-aware—aware of feelings and motivations—can inform one's responses to interpersonal situations. As we shall learn later, the self-awareness of meditation facilitates sensing and then communicating one's responses to others—both behaviors conducive to empathy. Bernard Glueck and Charles Stroebel, in their study of the effects of meditation and biofeedback in the treatment of psychotherapy patients, made detailed observations of the physiological changes occurring during meditation. They found that Transcendental Meditation generated recordable electroencephalographic changes in the brain that parallel relaxation. They think that the repeated sound, mantra, is the direction of relaxation that eventually involves both the dominant and nondominant hemispheres of the brain. This response is functional to self-understanding and psychotherapy by allowing "repressed" material to come into consciousness more quickly, permitting more rapid recovery of patients than therapeutic treatment would allow (16).

Second, learning to relax through meditation is conducive to managing anxiety-related problems. For example, Deane Shapiro found Zen meditation combined with behavioral self-control techniques effective in reducing anxiety and stress in a client experiencing generalized anxiety and a feeling of being controlled by external forces (47). In overcoming insomnia in patients, Robert Woolfolk and his colleagues, Lucille Car-Kaffashan, Terrance McNulty, and Paul Lehrer, found that meditation derived attention-focusing techniques as effective as progressive relaxation exercises in reducing the onset of sleep. Both meditation and relaxation were effective in improving patients beyond controls on six-month follow-up (56).

Third, traditional therapy for anxiety-related problems like those discussed above has been broadened in recent years to the domain of ordinary stress. Stress is a field of inquiry that promises to enrich our ability to prevent more serious symptoms and mental disorder. The present author defines stress as *the physical and psychosocial response of a person who perceives external and/or internal demands as exceeding her capacity to adapt or cope.* Some stress, of course, challenges or interests. Overstress, however, is a common problem in our industrial society.

Meditation and various forms of relaxation training have been studied for their potential in reducing the physical effects of stress and in helping people self regulate aspects of their behavior or consciousness related to stress. In the early 1970s, research conducted by Robert Wallace, Herbert Benson, and Archie Wilson suggested that meditation might produce unique physiological and other changes (50). Later, other studies suggested that relaxation and various relaxation strategies and hypnosis may have effects similar to meditation (3, 13, 38, and 51). Some studies are clear in indicating that meditaton is at least as good as relaxation strategies in helping relieve stress and in lowering autonomic indicators of stress (20, 35). For example, in their study, Woolfolk, Lehrer, Barbara McCann, and Anthony Rooney compared meditation, progressive relaxation, and self-monitoring as treatments for stress. Meditation and progressive relaxation significantly reduced stress symptoms over time (57). I should note here that in all comparative research, the "halo" effect may make a given technique appear effective or may make "controls" improve as well.

The advantage of meditation as a strategy in helping clients deal with stress lies in the cognitive domain. What causes a person stress is determined in large part by the perceptions of an event or situation. Events viewed as threats are more stressful than those viewed as challenges in which one will grow. Meditation allows the individual to discover the symbolic meanings, the subtle fears, and other internal stimuli evoked by the event. Strategies, opportunities for coping, calm decisions, and previous successes can be distinguished in the mental contents and consciously enlisted in coping strategies. Moreover, one case study and some theorists support the aforementioned idea that meditation behavior may be transferred to other aspects of life and consciously enlisted to meet stressful events as they occur (46, 58). Maladaptive coping occurs when stress is responded to in ways that cause more problems for the stressed individual than they help. Meditation may help prevent these maladaptive responses, such as substance abuse, which relieve immediate stress but generate long-term physical, psychological, and even interpersonal problems. Indeed, there is some evidence that meditation can help treat these maladaptive problems once they have developed.

A fourth outcome, therefore, combining self-awareness and the capacity to relax intentionally, permits an individual to transfer behaviors learned in meditation to other realms of life where there is stress or excessive stimulation that would hamper objective or reasoned functioning. Some studies suggest that meditation may be useful for alcohol and drug abusers to reduce anxiety, discriminate stimuli that evoke the problematic habits, and cultivate an "internal locus of control" (5, 14, 35). One might reason that anxiety-arousing stimuli are less likely to become self-perpetuating in the symbolic system if they are discriminated and desensitized in the meditative process. For example, some individuals have associated worry over coming events with positive outcomes of those events. Worry, intermittently rewarded, is likely to persist, complete with fantasized negative outcomes, anxiety, and preoccupation (8, p. 94). Meditation enables the individual to discriminate worrisome fantasy and to observe its impact upon the body and overall functioning. Desensitization and a secure observer self enable the individual to recognize worry, minimize its effects, and allow worrisome thoughts to burn themselves out without negative consequences. As the observer self is cultivated, the normal state of consciousness of modern Westerners, complete with split attention, worry, preoccupation, and anxiety can be sharpened to a mindfulness in which attention is voluntarily riveted to the action at hand. Preoccupation with oneself and how one is performing, worry over consequences, and wandering attention interfere less in the tasks one has decided to do. In a sense, the self is lost in the activity.

Fifth, observation and discrimination of one's thoughts in meditation enable the meditator to use thoughts and images more as tools to represent reality, to communicate, and to serve as intentional guides to action than as illusory and unintentional substitutes for real circumstances. Symbols and cognitive constructs no longer interfere with clear present-time perceptions.

Finally, meditation as discrimination training may have specific usefulness in managing depression. In her article, "Learned Helplessness," social worker Carol Hooker reviewed literature suggesting that reactive depression is dynamically similar to experimentally induced states of learned helplessness in experimental animals (22). The works of Martin Seligman (43, 44) and others suggests that one may learn, in effect, not to learn when repeatedly subjected to noxious circumstances over which one can find no mastery or control. Under such conditions, one learns that there is no escape, no solution other than unresponsive withdrawal with little or no mobility, eye contact, or normal need-fulfilling behaviors. Hooker, drawing on the work of Beck (4), sees this learned helplessness as having cognitive components in humans wherein all known avenues of mastery and solution have been tried or rehearsed to no effect. Action and effort have no effect on circumstances. Beliefs about one's effectiveness sustain a depressive reaction. Loss of a loved one to death, for example, is an insoluble trauma. Repetition of guilt-evoking thoughts, self-deprecation, and beliefs that there is no future without the deceased may in some cases sustain depression for extended periods. Meditation may help the depressed person regain a sense of self separate from the dilemma, partially sustained in the symbol system. Traumatic thoughts associated with the event are desensitized and one learns increasing mastery over the contents of one's depression sustaining ruminations. Eventually, thoughts that constitute new tasks and new opportunities for mastery and rehearsal of new roles to play can be sustained intentionally and used as guides for action and mastery. Similar processes used with caution, elaborated below, may be therapeutic for persons with thought disorders. In other words, observaton of thinking, not building upon associations and becoming "lost in thought," is the intent of meditation for enhanced discrimination.

In summary, meditation is an adjunct to treatment of a potentially wide variety of problems. There are, as suggested in the discussion of depression, certain problems that should not be approached with meditation except with intense supervision by workers skilled in treatment of the problem and in meditation. While much-needed definitive studies that show direct contraindications for the use of meditation are not available at this time, some guidelines are emerging.

Cautions and Contraindications

In the author's experience, some people find meditation more suited to their temperament than others. Also, certain severe disorders make the correct practice of meditation difficult or impossible.

Anxious but organized persons seem to take to meditation quickly. Relaxation and learning control over focal attention is rewarding and rather immediate. With very anxious, driven people, however, a caution is in order. Meditation of the Zen type, which requires a continued refocusing to the breath of another object of attention, or of those Yogic types that require strict postures and attention, can become a do-or-die endeavor for these persons. Individuals may incorrectly feel compelled to suppress thoughts and emotions. Or they may force their breath in an unnatural way rather than following their natural breathing systems. Often this response is not unlike their life-style, in which they constantly push themselves to perform or conform without attention to their own desires and physical needs. The attitude of wakeful awareness is misinterpreted as rigid attention where all interruptions are excluded before their full perception. Sometimes the body is not held relaxed, but rigid and tense. With such persons, the point must be made clear that they are to let go of interrupting thoughts, not push them away or compulsively follow them. The author uses the analogy of the mind as an open hand, neither pushing away nor grasping, in interpreting the correct mental attitude. In any case, the worker or therapist must make sure that the client is *meditating* and not *magnifying* anxiety, building anxiety-provoking images, or obsessing along an improbable chain of associations about hypothetical, destructive interpersonal events or outcomes.

Two authors have discussed use of meditation by persons who suffer severe mental problems or who are labeled psychotic or schizophrenic. Deatherage, in discussing limitations on the use of Buddhist mindfulness meditation in psychotherapy, cautions, "While this psychotherapeutic approach is extremely effective when employed with patients suffering from depresson, anxiety, and neurotic symptoms, a caution should be issued regarding its use with patients experiencing actively psychotic symptoms such as hallucinations, delusions, thinking disorders, and severe withdrawal" (10, p. 142). He goes on to note that the particular meditation technique for self-observation requires "an intact and functional rational component of mind, as well as sufficient motivation on the part of the patient to cause him to put forth the effort to do that observation" (10, p. 142). Arnold Lazarus, discussing psychiatric problems possibly precipitated by Transcendental Meditation, cautions that his clinical observations have led him to hypothesize that T.M. does not seem to be effective with people classified as hysterical reactions or strong depressive reactions. He speculates that "some" 'schizophrenic' individuals might experience an increase in 'depersonalization' and self preoccupation" (32).

As an activity derived from religious traditions, meditation is associated with notions of self-transcedence. Observation of the conditioned self or ego from a perspective of dispassionate neutrality can be confused with several problematic behaviors. Engler, for example, cautions that borderline personalities and others without a well-developed self may be attracted to meditation. Also, persons in developmental stages struggling with identity may find meditation an unfortunate substitute for dealing with their developmental tasks or discovering "who they are" (12). Persons with very fragile identities, symptoms related to depersonalization, and inadequate ego development are not good candidates for meditation except under close supervision. Put very simply, "You have to be somebody before you can be nobody" (12).

In general, therefore, clients or patients with severe disorders, whose reality testing, perception, and logical thinking are such that they cannot fully understand meditation instructions or follow through with actual meditation under supervision, are poor candidates for its successful use in treatment. Just as the anxious client may build upon anxiety-arousing associations or the depressed client may ruminate on ineffectiveness and despair instead of actually meditating, clients with severe thought disorders and problems with reality testing may substitute hallucinations, delusions, withdrawal, depersonalization, and catatonic responses for meditation, thereby aggravating their problems. Glueck and Stroebel (16), however, found Transcendental Meditation effective as adjunctive treatment with a sample of ninety-six psychiatric patients who would have been expected to have the kind of difficulties outlined here. Preliminary investigation indicated that the higher the level of psychopathology, the greater the difficulty patients had producing alpha waves. Testing Transcendental Medication against autogenic relaxation and electroencephalogram (EEG) alpha wave biofeedback training, Glueck and Stroebal found T.M. to be the only one of the three experimental conditions that patients could persistently practice. Consequently, the authors match-paired their meditation sample with a comparison group and found their meditating patients to have higher levels of recovery than both their twins and the general patient population. Controls for "halo" effect and other factors render the research strictly preliminary. But the research does suggest that testing varieties of meditation with the severely disturbed is in order if the supervisory precautions outlined earlier—and noted by Glueck and Stroebel (16, p. 307)—are followed. Treatment of the severely depressed and psychotic patients with meditation without close supervision nad immediate post-meditation checks is contraindicated until further research is done.

Psychosocial History and Diagnosis

One phenomenon occurring in most forms of meditation is the intrusion of the memory of events in the meditator's life into the meditative state. Meditators employing Zen and similar concentration techniques usually experience mental images of significant and emotionally intense events replayed before their relaxed mind. Desensitization of these memories has been discussed. But intentional use of meditation to allow significant facts and events of the psychosocial history is possible. Requesting the client to record these memories following meditation, for use in the context of treatment and for rounding out a more complete psychosocial history, may be helpful to workers with psychodynamic and psychoanalytic orientations.

The diagnostic value of meditation, implicit in earlier discussions, lies in the nature of the difficulty that the client has in meditating correctly. Elsewhere, the author has discussed optimal psychosocial functioning based upon Eastern conceptualizations related to and developed from meditation

(27). Briefly stated, the capacity to attend to activities one is about without interference by irrelevant ideation, worry, and guilt suggests a positive level of functioning. Meditation evokes memories and worries that intrude upon the meditation task. Repetitive anxiety-, anger-, or guilt-associated thoughts will indicate to the meditator and the worker or therapist those areas of conflict of "unfinished business" that hinder the client's functioning. Repetitive self-destructive images will indicate disturbed role rehearsal or depression. Conflicts from pushing or driving oneself will manifest themselves in forced breath or lack of relaxation in meditation.

The Therapeutic Relationship

There are several behaviors learned in meditation that would theoretically contribute to enhance empathic functioning on the part of the meditating social worker. Some preliminary study suggests that this notion should be researched further (26).

First, learning increased voluntary control over one's attention permits one to shift from attending to the various verbal and nonverbal communications of the client to one's own emotional responses to the client. This ability to sense one's own emotional reactions from moment to moment facilitates sensing and verbalizing feelings that parallel those of the client. Accurate reflection of these feelings to the client, of course, is a major component in therapeutic empathy (41), a worker skill conducive to positive behavior change for the client.

Second, learning to discriminate internal or cognitive stimuli from perceptual stimuli in meditation and learning to gain a measure of voluntary control over cognitive processes can enhance empathic functioning in another way. The worker can hold complex cognitive elaboration in abeyance and allow himself to perceive the client as she is, without premature diagnosing or other cognitive elaboration coloring his bare attention to the client as she is. This intentional slowing of the perceptual process that allows the client to speak for herself holds the worker in the present time—where emotions are felt, where the worker can be fully with the client, and where behaviors are changed.

Third, the meditating worker is likely to have cultivated a strong centeredness or observer self not easily rattled by the stresses or intense emotional interaction. Therefore, staying with the client in her deepest feelings, as Carl Rogers described high-level empathy (41), becomes more likely. And because such a worker has a perspective on his own reactions, countertransference responses may be more accessible.

Meditation as an adjunctive technique to treatment has a virtue common to all profound and shared experiences. It is an experience a worker can impart and then share with the client that may serve as a basis for communication, trust, and mutual discovery when other bases for relationships are less productive. In this sense, meditation can be a common ground of mutual experience that can strengthen a therapeutic relationship.

Teaching Meditation: One Technique

There are several techniques for meditation useful as adjuncts for treatment. Among the more prominent are Yogic mantra techniques, Benson's relaxation technique (16, p. 314), Transcendental Meditation (6), and Zen techniques. The technique to be briefly detailed here is a form of Zen. The general instructions are readily found in a variety of texts. Expert instruction and a good period of time meditating are recommended for workers considering meditation as an addition to their repertoire of techniques.

The client is instructed to meditate half an hour each day in a quiet place where she is unlikely to be interrupted. The client is asked to briefly record in a log her meditation experiences for later discussion with the worker. The meditation posture as suggested by Kapleau (24) is as follows:

1. A sitting position with the back straight.
2. Sitting cross-legged on a pillow is ideal
3. If uncomfortable, sit in a straight wooden chair without allowing the back to come to rest against the back of the chair.
4. The hands should be folded in the lap.
5. The eyes may be open or closed; if open, they are not to focus on any particular thing.
6. The back must be straight for comfort since slumping causes cramping.
7. Loose clothing around the waist is suggested.

The client is instructed to focus on the breath manifest in the rising and falling of the abdomen and to begin the first three sessions by counting each exhalation up to ten and beginning again. In the fourth session and thereafter, the client may simply follow the natural—unforced, uncontrolled—breath for the duration of each session. The attention should be focused on the surface of the center of the body about an inch below the navel.

The client is told that there will be frequent intrusions of thoughts, feelings, sounds, and physical responses during her concentration. The response to these is in every case an easy recognition that attention has wandered and refocusing to the breath is necessary.

Repressed material will usually emerge as insights. These are automatically paired with a relaxed state. The client should be instructed that, if the meditation becomes upsetting or frustrating, she should stop and resume the following day or wait until the next appointment with the therapist. Particular cautions with special clients were enumerated above. Generally, if the experience is not pleasant and rewarding, it may be evidence the client is pushing rather than allowing mental content to flow.

Settings and Levels of Intervention

Meditation is a worldwide phenomenon. It is practiced in settings as varied as Japanese corporate offices, quiet monasteries in all parts of the world, downtown apartments, and mental health centers. Most physical settings where social workers practice would be conducive to meditation. While each agency has its own major theoretical orientation or admixture of orientations, few would preclude meditation as an appropriate technique if thoughtfully and systematically introduced. While a psychodynamically oriented worker would define and describe meditation behavior and results differently than a behaviorist or an existentialist, the technique is not tied to a single system. Therefore, agency acceptance hinges more upon tolerance for innovation, interest in research, and openness to new ideas. Meditation as a social work technique was thought to be well out of the mainstream and esoteric a few years ago, but it has gained wide acceptance in related disciplines and promises to become a more common technique in work with individuals, families, and groups.

Because meditation tends to be an individual activity, it is naturally thought of as a mode for individual treatment only. However, in additon to its use and ramifications for individual treatment, meditation is of use for certain kinds of groups, including families.

Group meditation can enhance group processes. Beginning and ending a group with a meditation session can enhance group feeling and mellow out intense feelings enough to allow their sharing, analysis, and discussion. A unison group chant of a mantra such as *Om*, pronounced "aum," evokes a sense of group unity and feeling with a lessening of feelings of isolation and egocentrism by individual members. A group meditation sets the atmosphere for constructive interaction. Meditation to end a group meeting has similar effects and supports solidarity and identity within the group.

Receptivity to meditation a few years ago was largely restricted to young people and the religiously or spiritually oriented. But over the years the various forms—and Transcendental Meditation in particular—have crossed many class and age barriers and is widely practiced (6). Increasingly, meditation can be introduced into group work with a variety of people. The author has used individual meditation to begin and group chants to end treatment groups for college-age youth and for sex-role-consciousness-rising groups for married persons ranging in age from twenty-two to forty-five. Meditation for family treatment may help to reduce conflict and give the family a positive, common experience to share and discuss.

Claims of increased harmony and lower crime rates have been made as resulting from certain percentages of meditation in given communities (6, pp. 283–284).Obviously, if meditation contributes to personal functioning, certain aspects of community life will be enhanced.

But much research must be done to determine the long-term effects of the various forms of meditation on individuals, groups, families, and communities. Optimal personal and group functioning does not lead directly to more harmonious community life if the social order is fundamentally exploitive and contradictory. As with many forms of treatment techniques, the gaps in our knowledge about meditation, as an adjunct to treatment at whatever level of intervention, are many, and considerable research is in order.

Implications for Research

Meditation is a widely studied behavior. Nevertheless, our understanding is still far from complete. As a treatment technique, it has been found valuable in a variety of situations. However, there is growing knowledge of the appropriate forms of meditation, precise contraindications, the relative value of meditation and other relaxation techniques, and even the effects of meditation upon the nervous system, psyche, and social life.

Transcendental Meditation has in recent years inspired much research. As more of these findings are reported in referenced professional journals, the research base related to this particular technique will become more familiar to social workers and allied professionals. Much research is in order for assessing other techniques, including Zen meditation, also in increasing use as a treatment adjunct. Well-controlled outcome studies comparing meditation with autogenic relaxation, biofeedback, and similar techniques followed the works of Glueck and Stroebel, and more recently Woolfolk and others (16, 55). In addition, some preliminary research suggests that there is potential for the careful matching of meditation and relaxation techniques with the primary systems activated by anxiety (9, 42). So, for example, somatic arousal might be more amenable to autogenic training while concentrative meditation may be more appropriate for relief of anxiety-arousing ruminations.

Although there is much clinical evidence and intuitive exploration, the research concerning subset meditation phenomena is sparse. These include the desensitization, discrimination, and observer self mentioned earlier. Clinicians must begin to refine the appropriate use of meditation for particular kinds of clients and particular kinds of problems. Together with researchers, we must deduce where it helps and where it does not. Use of meditation with groups and families needs more study. Researchers also have rich opportunities to follow the differential effects of meditation used with various clinical problems and various personalities.

Being a technique of potentially great value for social work, meditation must be examined empirically. Hopefully, it will not be picked up "whole hog" and incorporated into practice without critical evaluation. This would render it, like some other techniques, a passing fancy, soon discarded in favor of new approaches. Nor should meditation be disregarded as the esoteric product of foreign and bygone cultures. Despite barriers that exclude the wisdom of other cultures and other lands from our consideration, a critical openness is in order. We must try out, test, and incorporate meditation as an adjunct to treatment where it benefits our clients, our practice, and ourselves.

Conclusion

Meditation is, of course, more than just an adjunct to social work treatment. Meditation must flourish in our culture independent of the helping professions and their practice. If we in social work and others in related professions find it a powerful adjunct to treatment, we should not attempt to subsume it as ours alone. Meditation is unique because it is a vehicle of consciousness. We must not pretend to bring what is a powerful vehicle under our hegemony to enhance our own power and prestige. Most forms of meditation are public domain; they must remain so in our society. This is all the more important precisely because meditation is a vehicle of consciousness. It can be used to liberate, to extend individual functioning, to help create social change in the democratic interest. It could also be used to mystify, to distract people from their social concerns related to their personal problems. How the technique will be used is related to the conscience, wisdom, and position of the profession in the years of profound social change ahead. This author hopes that what has been presented here will be used in the development of critical consciousness, and that it will encourage and facilitate constructive involvement in the world by workers and clients alike.

A BRIEF CASE EXAMPLE: THE USE OF MEDITATION IN THE TREATMENT OF FUNCTIONAL BOWEL DISEASE

A thirty-six-year-old woman, married and the mother of three children—ages three, seven, and twelve—living in California was referred by her physician. She was suffering abdominal pain. Extensive physical examinations and tests had all been negative, although she had recently had an increase in pain when she was under stress. She wanted to understand why she was having these troubles and how she could control them.

She had been experiencing an increase in pain over the past year. She had gone on special diets, consulted several health care professionals, and taken many different medications, but there was no change in her distress, which was becoming overwhelming. She said she was becoming increasingly depressed, anxious, and overly self-critical as her symptoms continued and there seemed no hope for any change in them. Psychological tests completed at the time of the initial evaluation confirmed that she was indeed severely depressed, with little energy. There seemed to be emotional overlay to her pains.

The client was quick to agree to short-term outpatient treatment of eight weekly sessions. The goals would include developing some understanding of her emotions, the stresses in her life, her coping skills and difficulties, and learning various types of relaxation techniques. It was also agreed that the results of the psychological tests would be fully reviewed with her in the third session. In addition, she was helped to work through some unresolved feelings from earlier years that were related to her parents' divorce and the death of her first husband. She explored how she could utilize some of her past coping skills with some of her present difficulties.

The client was experiencing many stressful and unstable living conditions at the present time while her husband was building their new home. This necessitated their living in a series of different friends' homes. Her husband had been so involved in building their dream home that he had not involved her in the process. He was included in one of the outpatient sessions in order to increase communication between them and to help them to reinstitute their previous level of positive interactions, which had been present in the year previous to all of these changes.

In the second treatment session the client was taught a passive, modified hypnotic, relaxation technique that was tape-recorded for her daily use at home. She was quite pleased with her ability to immediately relax and experience a definite decrease in her abdominal pains. She was instructed to listen to the tape recording of the relaxation four times a day and to record her responses each time in a "Relaxation Log" that she was to bring with her to each session.

The following week the patient had several days without any pain until she would forget to use the technique because she felt "so good." The patient continued with the passive-therapist-directed relaxation techniques by listening to the tape recording daily. The worker was very directive with this technique. The client was slowly encouraged to try the relaxation technique on her own, without using the tape. She quickly became able to do this.

After the fourth treatment session, the client was introduced to a new technique designed to help her relax on her own, to become more comfortable with her own body, and to learn how she could help herself on an ongoing basis. It was presented to her as a new coping skill that she could continue to utilize after the termination of treatment. Since the client was now feeling much better, she was eager to increase her skills in this area. She was therefore given oral and written instructions for meditation. She was asked to take the instructions home and read them and to try to implement them into her daily routine. Initially she had some difficulty in being totally comfortable with the technique, so she continued listening, once a day, to the relaxation tape. However, she found less need to rely on the tape recording as she increased her ability to relax with the meditation. After one week, the client found that she was able to relax just as fully as she had with the tape recording. Further, she felt quite proud of her ability to do it on her own. By the last session she reported that she was able to relax without any reliance on the tape. She found that if she meditated once a day, she had no pain, and could reduce any stresses that arose by short relaxation techniques, which she would go over in her mind. At that point she had been totally pain-free for three weeks. Follow-up contacts with the patient one month after formal termination of treatment showed that she continued to do her daily meditation, was pain-free, felt much more confident in her abilities and coping skills, and felt that all aspects of psychotherapy, relaxation, and finally meditation had been quite beneficial to her. She recognized the benefits of continuing to practice what she had learned, and her family was quite supportive.

References

1. Al-Ghazzali (Bankey Behari, trans.). *The Revival of Religious Sciences.* Farnham, Surrey, Eng.: Sufi, 1971.

2. Anand, B. K., G. S. Cchhina, and Baldev Singh. "Some Aspects of Electroencephalographic Studies in Yogis," in Deane H. Shapiro and Roger N. Walsh (eds.), *Meditation: Classic and Contemporary Perspectives.* New York: Aldine, 1984, pp. 475–479.

3. Beary, J. F., and Benson, H. "A Simple Psychophysiologic Technique which Elicts the Hypometabolic Changes of the Relaxation Response," *Psychosomatic Medicine,* Vol. 36 (1974), pp. 115–120.

4. Beck, Aaron T. *Depression: Clinical Experimental and Theoretical Aspects.* New York: Harper and Row, 1967.

5. Benson, Herbert, and Keith Wallace, with technical assistance of Eric C. Dahl and Donald F. Cooke. "Decreased Drug Abuse with Trancendental Meditation— A Study of 1,862 Subjects," in Deane H. Shapiro and Roger N. Walsh (eds.), *Meditation: Classic and Contemporary Perspectives.* New York: Aldine, 1984, pp. 97–104.

6. Bloomfield, Harold H., and Robert B. Kory. *Happiness.* New York: Pocket Books, 1977.

7. Burt, E. A. (ed.). *The Teachings of the Compassionate Buddha.* New York: New American Library, 1955.

8. Challman, Alan. "The Self-Inflicted Suffering of Worry," cited in "Newsline," *Psychology Today,* Vol. 8, No. 8 (January 1975), p. 94.

9. Davidson, Richard J., and Gary E. Schwartz. "Matching Relaxation Therapies to Types of Anxiety: A Patterning Approach," in Deane H. Shapiro and Roger N. Walsh (eds.), *Meditation: Classic and Contemporary Perspectives.* New York: Aldine, 1984, pp. 622–631.

10. Deatherage, Gary. "The Clinical Use of 'Mindfulness' Meditation Techniques in Short-Term Psychotherapy," *Journal of Transpersonal Psychology,* Vol. 7, No. 2 (1975), pp. 133–143.

11. *Encyclopaedia Britannica,* Macropoedia. Vol. 10. London: Benton, 1974, p. 183.

12. Engler, Jack. "Therapeutic Aims in Psychotherapy and Meditation: Develop-

mental Stages in the Representation of Self," *Journal of Transpersonal Psychology*, Vol. 16, No. 1 (1984), pp. 25–61 and p. 31.

13. Fenwick, P. B. C., S. Donaldson, L. Gillis, J. Bushman, G. W. Fenton, I. Perry, C. Tilsley, and H. Serafinovicz. "Metabolic and EEG Changes During Transcendental Meditation: An Explanation," in Deane H. Shapiro and Roger N. Walsh (ed.), *Meditation: Classic and Contemporary Perspectives*. New York: Aldine, 1984, pp. 447–464.

14. Ferguson, Marilyn (ed.). "Valuable Adjuncts to Therapy: Meditation, Relaxation Help Alcoholics Cope," *Brain-Minded Bulletin*, No. 7 (February 20, 1978), p. 2.

15. Fromm, E., D. T. Suzuki, and Richard DeMartino. *Zen Buddhism and Psychoanalysis*. New York: Harper and Row, 1970.

16. Glueck, Bernard C., and Charles F. Stroebel. "Biofeedback and Meditation in the Treatment of Psychiatric Illness," *Comprehensive Psychiatry*, Vol. 16, No. 4 (1975), p. 316.

17. Goble, Frank. *The Third Force*. New York: Pocket Books, 1970.

18. Goleman, Daniel. "Meditation and Consciousness: An Asian Approach to Mental Health," *American Journal of Psychotherapy*, Vol. 30, No. 1 (January 1976), pp. 41–54.

19. ———. "Mental Health in Classical Buddhist Psychology," *Journal of Transpersonal Psychology*, Vol. 7, No. 2 (1975), pp. 176–183.

20. ———, and Gary E. Schwartz. "Meditation as an Intervention in Stress Reactivity," *Journal of Consulting and Clinical Psychology*, Vol. 44, No. 3 (1976), pp. 456–466, and in Deane H. Shapiro and Roger N. Walsh (eds.), *Meditation: Classic and Contemporary Perspectives*. New York: Aldine, 1984, pp. 77–88.

21. Hendricks, C. G. "Meditation as Discrimination Training: A Theoretical Note," *Journal of Transpersonal Psychology*, Vol. 7, No. 2 (1975), pp. 144–146.

22. Hooker, Carol E. "Learned Helplessness," *Social Work*, Vol. 21, No. 3 (May 1076), pp. 194–198.

23. Jourard, Sidney. "Psychology of Transcendent Perception," in H. Otto (ed.), *Exploration in Human Potential*. Springfield, Ill.: Charles C. Thomas, 1966.

24. Kapleau, Philip. *Three Pilars of Zen*. Boston: Beacon Press, 1967.

25. Kasamatsu, Akria, and Tomio Hirai. "An Electroencephalographic Study of the Zen Meditation (Zagen)," in Deane H. Shapiro and Roger N. Walsh (eds.), *Meditation: Classic and Contemporary Perspectives*. New York: Aldine, 1984, pp. 480–492.

26. Keefe, Thomas W. "Empathy: The Critical Skill," *Social Work*," Vol. 21, No. 1 (January 1976), pp. 10–15. "The Development of Empathic Skill: A Study," *Journal of Education for Social Work*, Vol.15, No. 2 (1979), pp. 30–37.

27. ———. "Optimal Functioning: The Eastern Ideal in Psychotherapy," *Journal of Contemporary Psychotherapy*, Vol. 10, No. 1 (Fall 1978), pp. 16–24.

28. ———. "Meditation and the Psychotherapist," *American Journal of Orthopsychiatry*, Vol. 45, No. 3 (April 1975), pp. 484–489.

29. ———. "A Zen Perspective on Social Casework," *Social Casework*, Vol. 56, No. 3 (March 1975), pp. 140–144.

30. Kennett, Jiyu. *Selling Water by the River: A Manual of Zen Training*. New York: Vintage Books, 1972, p. 302.

31. Kohr, Richard L. "Dimensionality in Meditative Experience: A Replication," *Journal of Transpersonal Psychology*, Vol. 9 (1977), pp. 193–203.

32. Lazarus, Arnold A. "Psychiatric Problems Precipitated by Transcendental Meditation," *Psychological Reports*, Vol. 39 (1976), pp. 601–602.

33. LeShan, Lawrence. "The Case for Meditation," *Saturday Review*, Vol. 2, No. 11 (February 22, 1975), pp. 25–27.

34. Linden, William. "Practicing of Meditation by School Children and Their Levels of Field Dependence-Independence, Test Anxiety, and Reading Achievement," *Journal of Consulting and Clinical Psychology*, Vol. 41, No. 1 (1973), pp. 139–143, and in Deane H. Shapiro and Roger N. Walsh (eds.), *Meditation: Classic and Contemporary Perspectives*. New York: Aldine, 1984, pp. 89–93.

35. Marlatt, Alan C., Robert R. Pagano, Richard Rose, and Janice K. Marques. "Effects of Meditation and Relaxation Training Upon Alcohol Use in Male Social Drinkers," in Deane H. Shapiro and Roger N. Walsh (ed.), *Meditation: Classic and Contemporary Perspectives*. New York: Aldine, 1984, pp. 105–120.

36. Marx, Karl. *Preface to Contribution to the Critique of Political Economy*, as cited in Edgar Allen, *From Plato to Nietzsche*. New York: Fawcett, 1966, p. 159.

37. Miller, William R., and Martin E. P. Seligman. "Depression and the Perception of Reinforcement," *Journal of Abnormal Psychology*, Vol. 82 (1973), pp. 62–73.

38. Morse, Donald R., and John S. Martin, Merrick L. Furst, and Louis L. Dubin. "A Physiological and Subjective Evaluation of Meditation, Hypnosis and Relaxation," in Deane H. Shapiro and Roger N. Walsh (eds.), *Meditation: Classic and Contemporary Perspectives*. New York: Aldine, 1984, pp. 645–665.

39. Ornstein, Robert E. *The Psychology of Consciousness*, 2nd edition. New York: Harcourt, Brace Jovanovich, 1977.

40. Prabhupada, Swami A.C.B. *Bhagavad Gita as It Is*. New York: Bhaktivedanta Book Trust, 1972.

41. Rogers, Carl R. "The Necessary and Sufficient Conditions for Therapeutic Personality Change," *Journal of Consulting Psychology*, Vol. 21, No. 2 (1957), pp. 95–103.

42. Schwartz, Gary, Richard Davidson, and Daniel Goleman. "Patterning of Cognitive and Somatic Processes in the Self-Regulation of Anxiety: Effects of Meditation Versus Exercise," *Psychosomatic Medicine*, Vol. 40 (1978), pp. 321–328.

43. Seligman, Martin E. P. *Helplessness: On Depression, Development, and Death*. San Francisco: Freeman, 1975.

44. ———. "Depression and Learned Helplessness," in Raymond J. Friedman, and Martin M. Katz (eds.), *The Psychology of Depression: Contemporary Theory and Research*. New York: Halstead Press, 1974, pp. 83–107.

45. Shapiro, Deane H., and Roger N. Walsh (eds.), *Meditation: Classic and Contemporary Perspectives*. New York: Aldine, 1984.

46. Shapiro, Deane H., and Steven M. Zifferblatt. "Zen Meditation and Behavioral Self-Control: Similarities, Differences, and Clinical Applications," *American Psychologist*, Vol. 31, No. 7 (July 1976), pp. 519–532.

47. Shapiro, Deane H. "Zen Meditation and Behavioral Self Control Strategies Applied to a Case of Generalized Anxiety," *Psychologia: An International Journal of Psychology in the Orient*, Vol. 19, No. 3 (September 1976), pp. 134–138.

48. Suzuki, D. T. *An Introduction to Zen Buddhism*. New York: Grove Press, 1964.

49. Thera, Nyanaponika. *The Heart of Buddhist Meditation*. New York: Weiser, 1970.

50. Wallace, Robert K., Herbert Benson, and Archie F. Wilson. "A Wakeful Hypometabolic State," *American Journal of Physiology*, Vol. 221, No. 3 (1971), pp. 795–799.

51. Walrath, Larry C., and David W. Hamilton. "Autonomtic Correlates of Meditation and Hypnosis," in Deane H. Shapiro and Roger N. Walsh (eds.), *Meditation: Classic and Contemporary Perspectives*. New York: Aldine, 1984, pp. 645–665.

52. Walsh, Roger."Initial Meditative Experiences: Part I," *Journal of Transpersonal Psychology*, Vol. 9, No. 2 (1977), p. 161.

53. Watts, Allen. *Psychotherpay East and West*. New York: Ballantine, 1961.

54. Welwood, John. "Meditation and the Unconscious: A New Perspective," *Journal of Transpersonal Psychology*, Vol. 9, No. 1 (Spring 1977), pp. 1–26.

55. Wood, Ernest. *Yoga*. Baltimore: Penguin, 1959.

56. Woolfolk, Robert L., Lucille Car-Kaffashan, Terrence McNulty, and Paul Lehrer. "Meditation as a Training for Insomnia," *Behavior Therapy*, Vol. 7, No. 3 (May 1976), pp. 359–365.

57. Woolfolk, Robert L., Paul M. Lehrer, Barbara S. McCann, and Anthony J. Roonoy. "Effects of Progressive Relaxation and Meditation on Cognitive and Somatic Manifestations of Daily Stress," *Behavior Research and Therapy*, Vol. 20, No. 5 (1982), pp. 461–467.

58. Woolfolk, Robert L. "Self-Control Meditation and the Treatment of Chronic Anger," in Deane H. Shapiro and Roger N. Walsh (eds.), *Meditation: Classic and Contemporary Perspectives*. New York: Aldine, 1984, pp. 550–554.

59. Yu, Lu K'ann (Charles Luk, trans.). *The Secrets of Chinese Meditation*. New York: Weiser, 1972.

Annotated Listing of Key References

Deatherage, Gary. "The Clinical Use of 'Mindfulness' Meditation Techniques in Short-Term Psychotherapy," *Journal of Transpersonal Psychology*, Vol. 7, No. 2 (1975), pp. 133–143.
Deatherage provides five interesting and useful case examples in his lucid description of the use and limitations of "mindfulness meditation" in short-term psychotherapy. This article is of value to workers and therapists who are using or considering using meditation as an adjunct to treatment.

Engler, Jack. "Therapeutic Aims in Psychotherapy and Meditation: Developmental Stages in Representation of the Self," *Journal of Transpersonal Psychology*, Vol. 16, No. 1 (1984), pp. 25–61.
Traces the different perceptions of the self in meditation traditions and ego psychology and resolves some seemingly conflicting views.

Glueck, Bernard C., and Charles F. Stroebel, "Biofeedback and Meditation in the Treatment of Psychiatric Illness," *Comprehensive Psychiatry*, Vol. 16, No. 4 (1975), p. 316.
This article is an important pioneering study that compared meditation and similar treatments for psychotherapy patients. In addition to the study's partially successful major thrust, other insights, including the function of meditation in mental health and indications for its use, are provided.

Keefe, Thomas W. "Meditation and the Psychotherapist," *American Journal of Orthopsychiatry*, Vol. 45, No. 3 (April 1975), pp. 484–489.
This article describes a form of meditation and hypothesizes ways in which behavior learned in meditation can enhance the skill of the psychotherapist in the therapeutic relationship.

Shapiro, Deane H., and Roger N. Walsh (eds.). *Meditation: Classic and Contemporary Perspectives*. New York: Aldine, 1984.
This volume is a collection of the major theoretical and empirical articles on meditation. It constitutes a collection that represents the state on meditation, our knowledge about it, and its uses in treatment.

Shapiro, Deane H., and Steven M. Zifferblatt. "Zen Meditation and Behavioral Self-Control, Similarities, Differences and Clinical Applications," *American Psychologist*, Vol. 31, No. 7 (July 1976), pp. 519–532.
A systematic description of Zen meditation and its effects upon functioning as followed by a comparison with the behavioral self-control approach. The article represents a useful advance for behaviorally oriented therapists interested in meditation.

Welwood, John. "Meditation and the Unconscious: A New Perspective," *Journal of Transpersonal Psychology*, Vol. 9, No. 1 (Spring 1977), pp. 1–26.
Welwood's article is a provocative critique of traditional Western perspectives of the conception of the unconscious. The article provides the foundation for a theoretical understanding of human consciousness based upon meditation.

CHAPTER 8

Existential Social Work

Donald F. Krill

The impact of existential philosophy upon the social work profession remains unclear. The first article on the subject appeared in social work literature in 1962, and three books by social workers delineated existential perspectives in 1969, 1970, and 1978. The topic of existentialism has yet to make entry into a national conference of social workers.

On the other hand, those social workers familiar with the existential viewpoint emphasize that this perspective speaks to the profession's most pressing needs: for more effective treatment of the poor and minorities; for more present-focused, experiential, task-oriented short-term work with families and individuals; for a more flexible and eclectic use of varied treatment techniques; for a lessening of categorization of people and of paternalistic efforts by therapists to adjust the values of clients to those of their therapist or those of the established society. The existential perspective is even seen as providing an important humanizing effect to social workers' present experimentation with social change.

The failure of the existentialist to attract major attention among social work professionals may be twofold. In the first place, writings of this type by philosophers, psychologists, theologians and social workers tend to present a terminology that seems foreign to the average practitioner (Being, Nothingness, the Absurd, Dread, I–Thou, Bad Faith, etc.). Social workers have tended to be doers rather than theoreticians and even the theorists tend to be pragmatic rather than philosophical. Second, existential social work writers have proposed a more philosophical perspective rather than specific working techniques. This is primarily because there does not really seem to be an existential psychotherapy per se. To be more accurate, one might say there is an existential philosophical viewpoint of how one sees oneself, one's client system, and what can happen between them. Various theoretical approaches may then be used to provide techniques compatible with this philosophical perspective.

The Existential Stance

Modern existentialism was born in the ruins, chaos, and atmosphere of disillusionment in Europe during and following World War II. Earlier existential writers, such as Kierkegaard and Dostoevsky, reacted against what they believed to be false hopes for the salvation of men and the world through a philosophy and politics of rationalism in their times. In the United States, with its boundless faith in achieving the good life through continued growth in economic productivity and scientific advancement, the interest in existentialism has been slower in coming.

The disillusioning events of the sixties (assassinations, generation gaps, protest movements, Vietnam War) continued into the early seventies (Watergate, economic instability, mounting divorce and crime rates, failures of psychotherapy hopes). Energy shifted somewhat from outside to inside, from rebellious protest to the "age of narcissism."

Existentialism has been termed a "philosophy of despair," partially because of the fact that it seems to emerge from disillusionment. But we may view this emergence as the origin and rooting of existentialism and a turning away from a primary allegiance to those idols and values that have fallen. Where it goes beyond this point depends upon which particular writer, theologian, philosopher, or film director one chooses to follow.

In most of the philosophical literature on existentialism, four themes seem to recur: the stress upon individual freedom and the related fundamental value of the uniqueness of the person; the recognition of suffering as a necessary part of the ongoing process of life—for human growth and the realization of meaning; the emphasis upon one's involvement in the immediate moment at hand as the most genuine way of discovering one's identity and what life is about (not in any finalized sense but, rather, in an ongoing, open way); and the sense of commitment that seeks to maintain a life of both discipline and spontaneity, of contemplation and action, of egolessness and an emerging care for others.

The existentialists disagree with those who hold human beings to be either essentially impulse-driven animals or social animals of learned conditioning. Both of these ideas deny the individual what is, for the existentialists, her source of dignity: the absolute value of her individual uniqueness. A person discovers her uniqueness through the way she relates to her own subjective experience of life. Sartre points out that this subjectivity is a person's freedom; it is something that is there; it cannot be escaped from or avoided; one can only deny one's own responsibility for choices made within this freedom. From the existential view, psychoanalytic theory is sometimes misused by encouraging the individual's denial of responsibility on the basis of impulsiveness forces; similarly, sociological and learning theory may be misused by excusing a person on the basis of totally determining social forces.

Characters from fiction, drama, mythology, and philosophical tradition have portrayed the existential posture. Stoicism, courage, and individualism are common attributes. The existentialist hero is often characterized as living on the edge of the traditions, values, and enticements of his society, prizing the preservation of his own uniqueness and authenticity above all else. He commonly suspects the motives of others, bordering on the cynical, and therefore avoids complete identity with any group espousing a "good cause." He is tough-minded in holding to his own code, evaluating it and preserving its integrity. He refuses to be "put down" by dehumanizing social forces through conformity or by selling himself out to their rewards. He is against system efforts to suppress the individuality of others in his society. His values are concrete and inseparable from situations: certain arising social or political issues, loyalty to friends, unfolding creative potentials, honesty and sincerity in relationships. He lives forever with a clear awareness of life's limits, the absurd, the tragic, yet maintains a committed faith in his groundings of freedom—the springboard for unique assertion. His interaction with life defines who he is rather than the acceptance of some definition of himself imposed by an outside authority, such as family, church, or economic system. The rhythm of responsive life-swinging-in-situation is his sole guide.

Existentialism is rejected by many as a narcissistic withdrawal from life when disappointments arise. At first glance, this might appear true as we hear the existentialist proclaim her own consciousness, subjectivity, uniqueness as the sole absolute: "truth is subjectivity," said Kierkegaard. The existentialist does reject the world, in one sense, in her new commitment to her own deepest self. What she rejects, however, is not life—its conditions, limits, joys, and possibilities—but the mistaken hopes and expectations she had held about life, which, under closer examination, failed to fit with the reality of her life.

What is real does shatter cherished yearnings in us all—about love, about divine protection, about our own abilities and goodness. Yet in surveying the landscape of rubble from broken aspirations and beliefs, we find that we still have a choice of how to relate to these realities. We can allow ourselves to be driven to despair, or to choose new illusional hopes, or we can accept the reality and go from there.

The Hemingway hero is a portrayal of this. We might expect him to say, "We lose in the end, of course, but what we have is the knowledge that we were going great." One's manhood, the sense of realistic pride, comes from the engagement with, and assertion of, one's own uniqueness. Each must discern what is right for him in terms of talent and skill, what is of value, and what is enjoyable. This becomes his own private personal perspective for which he alone is responsible. It changes throughout life, but it remains always his own, and hence truly unique.

The black concepton of "soul" has been defined as "the force which radiates from a sense of selfhood, a sense of knowing where you have been and what it means. Soul is a way of life—but it is always the hard way. It essence is engrained in those who suffer and endure to laugh about it later."* Soul is the beauty of self-expression, of self-in-rhythm. One swings from inside and in response to what is outside as well. Soul is mind operating free of calculation. It is humor and spontaneity and endurance. This concept of soul is consistent with the existential aim of authenticity.

Subjectivity

What is this subjectivity, this freedom, that holds the devotion and loyalty of a person? To Sartre, freedom is "no-thingness." For Kierkegaard, it is the human encounter with the Transcendent—one's "moment before God." Buber sees this as the "I" meeting the "Thou" of life. Kazantzakis speaks of the cry from deep within the human personality. To respond to it is our sole possiblity of freedom.

Yet this subjectivity, while termed by some as an encounter with the transcendent, cannot be considered as God itself. Each of us is all too soon aware of the finite nature of subjectivity. It is not all-knowing, and subjectivity is different in each person and constantly in the process of change within the same person. Subjectivity exists as a unique responsive relation to the world. Its primary activity is the conveyance of meaning through thought and feeling, intuition and sensation, and the assertion of this unique perspective through creative acts. Some would term this the activity of spirit, a divine possibility available to human beings. Yet divine and human remain intertwined.

It is this relationship between one's own subjectivity and the outside world that is the basis for responsible freedom instead of narcissistic caprice. One's inner subjectivity encounters outer reality again and again in the form of limits set up by life that challenge certain beliefs and meanings one has concluded about oneself. One experiences failures, misjudgments, hurt of others, neglect of self, conflict, and guilt. There is inevitable death, uncertainty, and suffering. These limiting situations, this suffering, becomes a revealing, guiding force of one's life. In a similar way, one realizes one's

*"Lady Soul: Singing It Like It Is" (article on Aretha Franklin), *Time*, June 28, 1968, p. 26.

potentials. A person senses in the world some expectation of response from herself. She feels called upon to choose, to act, to give, and to imprint herself upon the world. This awareness of both limits and potentials is the foundation upon which one can judge one's own unique perspective and readjust it when necessary. The ongoing encounter between subjectivity and the outside world may be looked upon as a continuing dialogue, dance, responsive process of inner and outer reality, continually affecting and being affected by the uniqueness of all forms involved.

Each must assume the burden of responsibility for his own freely chosen perspective and the associated consequences of his actions. To be a person is to assert one's uniqueness, knowing that one does not have an absolute knowledge of truth and that one may hurt others or oneself; one's efforts will often end in mistakes or failure. One must assert this uniqueness again and again—choosing courage or cowardice and knowing that suffering is often inevitable as one's perspective conflicts with the limits of life.

We fail, finally, in our resurging hopes, the existentialist might say, but then we are a brotherhood in this—not only with others, but with all of nature. For there is a striving everywhere, a fight, and, in the end, only the remnants of our struggles—and a little later there are no longer even the remnants. Our loyalty is to the thrust behind this struggle in all things. What is this thrust? A mystery! A meaningful silence! Can we be sure it is meaningful? Who is to know? The questions of salvation or an afterlife must be held in abeyance. They can no longer be certainties. For many, these very uncertainties become the springboard to religious faith.

The mystical flavor of life is shared by both existential believers and nonbelievers alike. It affirms life as meaningful, not because it has been clearly revealed as such through science or Scripture, but rather because one has sensed a deeper or clearer experience of reality in certain moments. These moments are not dismissed lightly, but are preserved as precious and illuminating even though the full meaning of their revelation may be unclear. Such experiences as love, beauty, creative work, rhythm, awe, and psychic phenomena, suggest seeing "through a glass darkly." Those followers of religious faiths may find a "rebirth," an adult reorientation to the message of revelation in religious writings.

The Bond with Others

If subjectivity and its uniqueness development and expression is valued in oneself, it must be valued in others as well. Since there is no absolute subjective perspective, each person's unique view and contribution contains an intrinsic value. The existentialist feels a bond with others and is responsive to their needs and to friendship, for she respects their subjectivity as being as valid as her own. She also knows that the assertion of courage is difficult and often impossible without occasonal affirmation from others. Human love is the effort to understand, share, and participate in the uniqueness of others. It is validating in others that which one also values within oneself. Love is sometimes an act of helping, at other times a passive compassion. At times it reaches a total merging that takes one beyond the fundamental awareness of isolation.

The existentialists realize, too, the dangers in human relationships. Just as one guards against self-deceptions that tempt one toward a narcissistic idolizaton of oneself, so one remains on guard in relation to the institutions of society. The assertion of individual uniqueness is often a threat to others and to a smoothly functioning social group. This is because such assertion will frequently defy those rules, patterns, habits, and values that are sources of defined security for others, or a group. Thus society and subgroups within a society will again and again attempt to suppress arising individual uniqueness out of a sense of threat or an inability to comprehend. Conformity is urged. It happens with family, friends, neighborhoods, church, professional, and political groups. The existentialist often finds himself estranged from others because of his own creativity and authenticity. Even when there is a relationship of mutual respect, with moments of unity through love, there will also come the moments of threat and misunderstanding because of the impossibility of one person's subjectivity fully comprehending that of another.

Yet conflict and threat in relationships do not move the existentialist into a schizoid withdrawal. She may display a touch of cynicism as she hears others identify themselves wholly with some group effort or as they proclaim the hope of humanity to be in her sensitive and loving interchange with her fellowman. But she knows that her own growth depends upon both affirmation from others and their occasional disagreement with her. The same interchanges are true for their growth. She believes in the beauty and warmth of love even though it is momentary. She knows that people must stand together in respecting and validating the uniqueness of one another and resisting the forces of those who believe themselves blessed with an absolute truth that justifies their using other people as things instead of as valued, unique personalities.

The philosophical position described has stressed both faith and commitment to a perspective of life deemed valid as a result of one's direct and sensitive involvement in the life process. It is in opposition to establishing a life perspective by accepting some theoretical explanation of life as defined by some outside authority—whether parental, religious, scientific, or political. The subjective involvement of the whole person is essential to the life perspective one finally concludes is her reality. This perspective is also in opposition to those who use fragmented life experiences as the ground for a total life perspective (as is sometimes found in the superficial assessments of the meaning of a weekend sensitivity group experience, or the realization of the "rightness" of a cause by a budding social activist). Human life is highly complex and one must seek an openness to its totality of experiences if her search is to be legitimate. This effort should not neglect an opening up of oneself to the meaning of experience as described by others as well.

What becomes apparent is a movement in personal awareness—from egotistical strivings to self-understanding; then to I–thou relationships with one's immediate surroundings; and finally, in the incorporation of some over-all principle where humanity and universe are joined. Both discipline and spontaneity are essential elements on this road of increasing awareness. Dis-illusionment, freedom, suffering, joy, and dialogue are all important hap-penings along the way. The end of this process does not really arrive until death. It is a continuing way that requires again and again the reaffirmation of that personal perspective called "truth."

Professional Contributions

These ideas can be found in philosophical and religious writings as well as in motion pictures, plays, novels, and poetry labeled "existential." One of the earliest examples of existential literature is the Book of Ecclesiastes in the Old Testament. From the Orient, Zen Buddhism is often compared with Western existential thinking.

Existential philosophy as we know it today had its initial comprehensive presentation by Soren Kierkegaard (1813–55), whose writings were a pas-sionate reaction to the all-embracing system of Hegelian philosophy. Later developments included the thought of Friedrich Nietzche and Henri Bergson. Modern-day existential philosophers include Martin Heidegger, Jean-Paul Sartre, Albert Camus, Simone de Beauvoir, Miguel de Unamuno, Ortega y Gasset, Nicholas Berdyaev, Martin Buber, Gabriel Marcel, and Paul Tillich. This array of names suggests the widespread interest in existentialism among several European countries.

Much of existential psychology had its ideological rooting among the phenomenologists, most notably Edmund Husserl. Two European analysts, Ludwig Binswanger and Medard Boss, were constructing an existential psy-chology during Freud's lifetime.

Viktor Frankl, a Viennese psychiatrist, developed his "logotherapy" fol-lowing his imprisonment in a German concentration camp during World War II. Logotherapy is based upon existential philosophy, and Frankl remains one of the most lucid writers in conveying existential thinking to members of the helping professions.

Rollo May's monumental work *Existence* (50), published in 1958, was the first major impact of existential psychology upon American psychiatry and psychology. May presented the translations of existential psychologists and psychiatrists from Europe, where such thinking had become popular and in many places had replaced psychoanalytic thought. There was a readiness in America for existential thinking and it quickly became part of the third force or humanistic psychology movement. This group included people such as Karen Horney, Carl Jung, Clark Moustakas, Carl Rogers, Abraham Maslow, Gordon Allport, Andras Angyal, and Prescott Lecky.

Two journals devoted specifically to existential psychology and psychotherapy began quarterly publication in the United States in the early 1960s.

Existential thought was related to Gestalt therapy (Frederick Perls), the encounter movement (Carl Rogers and Arthur Burton), rational–emotive psychotherapy (Albert Ellis), and R. D. Laing's provocative writings labeled "antipsychiatry." Thomas Szasz pursued a similar attack upon psychiatry, particularly in relation to the "therapeutic state," the insanity plea, and the dehumanizing use of clinical diagnostic categories. Ernest Becker and Irvin Yalom presented challenging reappraisals of psychoanalytic thinking from existential postures.

Perhaps the earliest social work writings with a decided existential flavor were by Jessie Taft of the functional school, which had its roots in the psychology of Otto Rank. In his Pulitzer prize–winning book, *The Denial of Death*, Becker produced a monumental integration of the thought of Rank and Freud (5). Social workers, who once avidly debated the "dynamic" versus the "functional" schools of social work theory, appear to have totally ignored Becker's incisive thought as to how these two systems of thought could be effectively wedded.

In 1962, David Weiss's article appeared in *The Social Worker* (81) and Gerald Rubin's paper in *Social Work* (63). Andrew Curry was publishing articles in the existential psychiatry journals. In the late 1960s, several articles appeared in various social work journals written by John Stretch, Robert Sinsheimer, David Weiss, Margery Frohberg, and myself. These papers were specifically related to the application of existential philosophy in social work thought and practice.

There were also several social work papers published during this period that did not specifically emphasize existentialism but were related to similar concerns of the existential social work group. These writers included Elizabeth Salomon, Mary Gyarfas, and Roberta Wells Imre. The first book on the subject of existentialism in social work was published in 1969 by Exposition Press. It was Kirk Bradford's *Existentialism and Casework* (10). Its subtitle expresses its intent, *The Relationship Between Social Casework and the Philosophy and Psychotherapy of Existentialism*. It should be considered an introductory and integrative work rather than a comprehensive or prophetic book. In 1970, Alan Klein related existential thinking to social group work in his book *Social Work Through Group Process* (39). A second book was published in 1975 by Dawson College Press of Montreal authored by David Weiss and titled *Existential Human Relations*. This was a more comprehensive work applying existential thought to various aspects of social work practice. In 1974, James Whittaker's book *Social Treatment* legitimized existential thinking as one of the four major theories contributing to social work practice. An effort to clarify both spiritual and systemic ideas for social workers appeared in *Existential Social Work* (44) by myself. Other social work writers related the existential view to child abuse (11), to social work education (72), and to cross-cultural counseling (79).

While there appears a rising, if somewhat limited, interest in existential philosophy in social work literature, it would seem that the interest is far more widespread among social work students and younger professionals. Many of the newer therapeutic approaches being performed by social workers are closely akin to the existential view of the therapeutic process. Such points of emphasis as choice and action, here-and-now problem orientation, dispensing with the use of diagnostic categories, stressing the expression of the worker as a vital, human person, and recognizing the connection of personal identity with the quality of significant other relationships all have their existential linkages.

Therapeutic Concepts

The philosophical perspective discussed earlier suggests five organizing concepts of existential thought: *disillusionment, freedom of choice, meaning in suffering, the necessity of dialogue,* and *a stance of responsible commitment.* These same concepts can provide a way of viewing the therapeutic process (43).

DISILLUSIONMENT.   In existential thinking, one can move from a life of "bad faith" to one of authenticity. To do this one must risk the pain of disillusionment. Similarly, in psychotherapy, change can be viewed as a result of giving up those very defensive beliefs, judgments, symptoms, or manipulations that interfere with the natural growth process. This growth process would be seen as the emergence of unique personhood through responsive acts in relation to one's surroundings. Realistic needs and potentials begin to be the source of choice and action instead of neurotic, self-deceptive security needs.

An important therapeutic task, then, is to help a client experience disillusionment with those various security efforts that block his own growth. Disillusionment will seldom result from a rational exploration of one's past with the hope of realizing causal factors of present defensive behavior. It is rare that one gives up security patterns because they are viewed as irrational, immature, or no longer applicable. Disillusionment occurs through the pain of loneliness and impotence. On the far side of such despair arise the possibilities of new values and beliefs. It is the therapist's concern that these be more human values than those abandoned. The therapist acts as a midwife for the release of the natural growth energies within personality so that what is wholly and individually unique may emerge. Any tampering with this natural direction, once begun, is likely to do more harm than good.

FREEDOM OF CHOICE. Sartre characterizes consciousness as "no-thing-ness," for it is an awareness of oneself that transcends or goes beyond any fixed identity one might have concluded about oneself. Personality is always emerging. To view it as static or secured is an act of self-deception (bad faith). This conception of consciousness as freedom is a break with conceptions of personality as being totally ruled by "unconscious" or by early learned behavior.

Despite one's past, despite any diagnostic label pinned upon a person, he always has the capacity to change himself. He can choose new values, or a new life-style. This does not always necessitate years or months of "working something through"; it may occur within days or weeks.

Choice is for action and differs from intellectual meandering or good intentions. Chosen actions occur in the present. Therapy is, therefore, present-focused and task- or action-oriented. People learn from experience, not from reason alone.

The critical ingredient for change is the client's wish to do so. Therapy must, therefore, be designed to clarify quickly the nature of change sought by the client and the therapist must be able to work within this framework, rather than seek to convince or seduce the client into redefining his problems and aiming for some type of change goal that pleases the therapist but is only vaguely understood by the client.

A therapist's belief in the client's capacity for change is a message of positive affirmation conveyed throughout treatment. There is no question but that a therapist's focus upon unraveling the intricacies of past relationships conveys a deterministic message that is a commentary upon the weakness and helplessness of a client.

MEANING IN SUFFERING. Just as existentialists see suffering as an inherent part of a life of authenticity based upon responsibility and freedom, so, too, the existential therapist does not seek to discredit or eliminate anxiety and guilt in her clients. She, instead, affirms such suffering as both necessary and directional for a person. She will help reveal what real anxiety and guilt may lie disguised behind neurotic (unrealistic) anxiety and guilt. But she would not seek to minimize or eradicate realistic anxiety and guilt. Such efforts would themselves be dehumanizing, unless used to prevent decompensation.

NECESSITY OF DIALOGUE. A person does not grow from within herself alone. Her emergence happens in responsive relation to her surroundings. She creates her own meaning in response to situations, and these meanings become the basis for choices and actions. However, her own meanings are no more absolute than those of any other person. Her own growth has to do with the continued reassessment of personal meanings, and she depends upon feedback from her environment (particularly human responses) for this reassessment activity. In order to gain honest feedback, one must allow others to be honest and free in their own expression. In therapy, therefore, it is critical to help a person open herself to relationships with others wherein she gives up her manipulative or "game" efforts in order to invite free responses from others. In doing this she not only allows herself experiences of intimacy, but she also realizes that her own emerging sense of self requires such honest transactions with others.

COMMITMENT. A client's recognition of and commitment to his own inner emerging unique life-style is a hope of the existential therapist. The client realizes this commitment through his experience of the therapist's own affirmation of the client's worldview. This unique worldview is affirmed from the beginning in the therapist's acceptance of how the client perceives his symptoms, problems, conflicts—how he perceives change and what he wants changed. His uniqueness is also affirmed during the course of treatment by the way a therapist relates to "where a client is" in each interview. The theme of a session comes as an emerging force from the client, rather than as a rationally predicted starting point made in advance by the therapist. Both the goal-setting process and the activity of centering upon and working with an interview theme are therefore client-centered rather than therapist-centered. This in no way crimps the therapist's operation as a skilled professional with "expertise," but he acts out of this expertise rather than displaying it in a manner that will inhibit the process of therapy.

The client's awareness of and respect for his own unique life-style might be described as a turn away from self-pity and impotence. Rather than complaining about his lot in life, he discovers that he is intricately involved in the life process itself. He learns to listen to what life says to him and finds meaning in the response that is unique to himself. This is what is meant by the existential concept of dialogue and commitment.

Related Therapeutic Approaches

As suggested earlier, there are obvious differences among those therapists claiming the existential label. This becomes more understandable if we consider the above therapeutic principles and note how they may be activated in a number of differing ways. A consideration of the ranging techniques that may fit with the principles outlined will also clarify how other treatment theories tend to be compatible with the existential view. Existentialism claims no technique system of its own and needs none. Its affirmation of the uniqueness of each client results in a perspective of each treatment situation being also unique. Whatever techniques can be used, from whatever treatment theory, become the tools toward accomplishment of the unique goal chosen. In this sense existentialism is thoroughly eclectic. Techniques are always placed secondary to the uniqueness of the client and the puzzle he presents to the therapist.

Several therapeutic systems are compatible with existential thinking. Some are not, and these will be considered later. The reality-oriented therapists (Glasser, Ellis, O. Hobart Mowrer, and Frankl) all stress choice and specific behavior change. William Reid, Laura Epstein, and Harold Werner have described similar cognitive-oriented approaches in social work literature. They are present-focused and commonly propose specific tasks for clients wherein the client is expected to put into immediate practice a decision for change. They tend to use reason to aid the decision for change, but then stress action. The action is usually expected to occur outside of the therapy interview (often as homework assignments) but its results are brought back for further discussion. The reality therapist focuses upon the disillusionment process by clearly identifying "faulty or irrational beliefs" that are responsible for problematic behavior. She affirms the client's freedom to choose and encourages a value shift through action.

Gestalt therapy, psychodrama, client-centered therapy and provocative therapy techniques all stress a heightening of a client's awareness through action in the here and now. They seek the immediacy of experience as a thrust for change rather than a rational process of analyzing causal connections. They differ from the reality therapies in that the stress is upon choice and action that is more immediate; it is to occur in the here and now of the therapy meeting itself. Whether the client seeks to make use of this experience in his outside daily life is usually left up to him. There is less effort to deal rationally with the disillusionment process of beliefs and manipulations. These are dealt with experientially as group members are encouraged to give direct and open feedback to the attitudes and behavior expressed by others. The activity of dialogue is stressed.

Family systems approaches, like those of Virginia Satir, Salvador Minuchin, and Murray Bowen, combine awareness heightening with choices and tasks yet add the ingredient of activating the significant other system in the helping process. Here the dimension of dialogue and intimacy is at last addressed within its daily living context. Bowen and Satir emphasize individuation, while Minuchin focuses more upon action tasks.

There are a few therapists to whom the term "existential" fits more accurately than any other: Carl Whittaker, Frank Farrelly, Lester Havens, William Offman, Walter Kempler. Their common attribute is an intense, often surprising use of their personal self-expression combined with a general disdain for conceptualization about clients from theory. Here the subjective emphasis of existentialism reaches its height of therapeutic expression. When these therapists are paradoxical in their actions, it is seldom as a result of planned strategy. Paradox results from their intuitive response to the client and often expresses the paradoxical life stance of the therapist himself.

From the foregoing comparisons of therapeutic approaches, as they relate to existential thought, several areas of existential theory become more clear cut. We shall look at these in more detail, considering the therapeutic relationship, nature of personality, concept of change, use of historical data and diagnosis, and treatment methods.

The Therapeutic Relationship

The therapist's use of himself and the type of relationship he seeks to foster with a client will be considered from two vantage points. First, the attitude of the therapist toward the client and her problems; and second, the behavior of the therapist as he interacts with the client—his use of himself as a unique person in her own right.

There is a critical difference between a therapist who sees the client as a complex of defenses or learned behaviors that are dysfunctional and a therapist who views the client as a unique, irreplaceable worldview that is in the process of growth, emergence, and expansion. The latter is an existential position. It views the problems and symptoms of a client as her own efforts to deal with the growth forces within herself and the risks these pose to her in relation to her self-image, relationship with significant others in her life, and her role in society.

The writings of R. D. Laing are aimed at clarifying the critical differences between the two types of therapists (48). He points out that the therapist who sees the client as a mass of complexes, defenses, and dysfunctional learnings sees himself as the authority. His task is to diagnose the nature of these "dynamics" and convey these insights to the client either through verbal commentary or through specific behavioral tasks he gives the client. But in doing so, he also acts as another societal force that seeks to adjust the client to someone's definition of the functional personality. Such a therapist tends to support the view that the client's symptoms and problems identify her as ill (even "dysfunctional" implies that she is out of step with her surroundings). The therapist often becomes another dehumanizing force in the client's life in the sense of urging the "patient" to adjust to her family, her instincts, her needs, society's needs, etc.

In contrast to this position, the existential therapist has no prescriptions of how the client should live. He sees his task as that of a midwife, an agent who has knowledge and skills to aid in the unblocking process that will allow the client to resume her own unique growth and emergence—whether or not this puts her in further conflict with her family, friends, and society. While the therapist may point out the potential risks and consequences of an emerging life-style, he will not negate its potential value.

The existential therapist's attitude affirms the inherent value of the client as a unique person with a very special worldview or life-style that is hers alone to charter. The client is also aware that the therapist sees in her the power of free choice. Instead of being helplessly at the mercy of forces beyond her consciousness, she can see the significant choices in her present life situation and has the power to decide which way she will proceed in the shaping of her life.

In one sense the existential therapist does stand for a particular life-style, but it is one based upon his belief in the nature of humanness rather than a cultural viewpoint of how a person should pursue her role in her family or her society. The values conveyed by the existential therapist are these: human beings have the capacity for free choice; they are of fundamental worth in their own unique perspective of life and their assertion of this perspective; they require an open interaction with their surroundings in order to grow—emergence is a responsive and interactive process; suffering is an inevitable part of the growth process for emergence involves risks and unknowns, and self-deception is a potent force.

These values are in opposition to several values supported by society at large; that an individual is a helpless creature both at the mercy of an unknown unconscious and of utter insignificance in the complex mechanisms called society; that one can and should find happiness through avoidance of suffering and pain and by means of the distractions and pleasures offered at every turn; that a person is what he is, so he should fulfill his role in his family or social system as best he can and be satisfied with his already finished identity; and that since there are groups of men considered ultimately wise in politics, universities, at the executive level of business and the military, in churches, and in medical buildings, Mr. Citizen should essentially consider a conforming obedience to what these soothsayers say is best for him.

The existential value perspectives of the worker also differ significantly from "value life models" all too often conveyed by "therapist gurus." These models have been described by the author in three forms: the hope of enlightening reason, the hope of flowering actualization, and the hope of satisfying mediocrity (46). The therapist-guru enjoys a priestly role of telling people how to attain happiness, enlightenment, or maturity. While the existential worker sometimes addresses value issues, as they relate to the presenting problems, she is unwilling to represent a value life model, or ideal, to the client. She prefers that the client seek such ultimate definitions and commitments through his own significant others and/or support groups. Counseling is neither a truth search (guru model) nor an exercise in symptom alleviation (technician model). Problems are addressed in such a manner as to invite the client to consider the relationship of his current value framework and life-style as possibly problem-related. Problems are not merely annoyances to be discarded, but may be signposts for self-examination.

The behavior of the existential therapist reflects her philosophical–psychological attitudes toward the client. If she is not the authority with the answers, what is she? The therapist does see herself as an expert, but her expertise has to do with her skills and talents of empathy; understanding; appreciation of/and compassion for individual human beings and their struggles; experience in the process of self-deception, having struggled with the growth–defensive process within herself; and affirmation of the value of the unique soul, having herself been disillusioned with all the society-made authorities who offer solutions, happiness, etc.; and an open honesty that offers the client the possibility of genuine dialogue, if the client seeks to engage in such. The worker, then, seeks to normalize the problems of the client by reference to the struggles of the human situation. She avoids paternalistic conclusions about the client, viewing both problem and person exploration as a mutual process. Clients' self-conclusions are also challenged in light of the human activity of ongoing change (becoming). Another way by which the worker avoids paternalism is by being honest and clear, rather than hidden and deceptive, in relation to strategies utilized.

She may exhibit a type of detachment. But this detachment is not the cool aloofness of the objective mechanist who is dissecting and reforming the patient. The detachment of the existential therapist is an expression of her profound belief in the freedom of the client. The client has a right to his own life-style. If he chooses not to follow a direction of personal growth, but chooses to maintain his defensive posture for security or other reasons, so be it. The therapist's sense of worth is not in the client's hands but within herself. Her detachment is from results, even though her actual activity in the helping process will be quite open and involved.

Detachment must not impair vitality and therefore cannot take the form of intellectual aloofness, analyzing the client from afar. Vital engagement through spontaneity, surprise, and unsettling responses is one of the valued methods of the existential worker. Genuine dialogue calls for an immediacy of feedback in many cases, and considered responses in others. Habitual mind sets and communication patterns of clients require interruption and jostling, on occasion, in order for the new, the creative, to be brought to awareness.

The relationship between therapist and client is seen by many existential writers as the essential ingredient of change. The concepts of individual growth and genuine encounter with others are interdependent in the thought of Martin Buber. David Weiss emphasizes this same connectedness in his discussion of healing and revealing (86). This I–thou relation need not be seen as mystical. Carl Rogers's description of this activity suggests that the therapist provides an atmosphere for growth by means of a nonthreatening, affirming, understanding responsiveness (61). But this does not mean the therapist remains passive. On the contrary, Rogers emphasizes the importance of the therapist being himself in the expression of important arising feelings. To offer a dialogue is at least to present one side of it in an open, honest fashion. The therapist reveals himself in another manner at times. He shares some of his own struggles, disillusionment, and experiences wherein he, too, sought growth in the face of pain. In both these examples of the therapist's openness, we see that the therapist sees his own unique worldview as an important experience to share with his client—not in a "go and do likewise" spirit, but rather showing himself as a fellow traveler on the rocky road of human existence.

Human Personality

Freudian theory proposed the ego as a balancing, organizing, controlling, harmonizing agent among the demands of the superego, the pressures of the "outside world" and the cravings of the id. Behavior theory suggests a passive psyche that is primarily molded by outside forces. What one learns from others is what one is. Both roles render the individual practically helpless to resist the many forces that work upon him.

Two key concepts differentiate the existential view from those above. The first is the idea of an integrating, creative force for growth at the core of the personality. The second is the belief that every individual has the capacity to shift his style of life radically at any moment.

In terms of the human dynamo, the existentialists would not disagree with Freud's formulation of the id as a composite of Eros and Thanatos, or life and death instincts. To this is added, however, the notion of a force that moves one toward meaning and toward relations with his surroundings on the basis of meanings concluded. There is an integrative, unifying, creative force within a person that synthesizes his experiences, potentials, and opportunities and provides him with clues for his own direction of growth. No matter how emotionally disturbed a patient may seem, there is this integrative core within him that prompts him in the direction of experiencing and expressing his own uniqueness (realistic needs and potentials). He may shut himself off from such integrative promptings; he may refuse to listen or mislabel such messages as dangerous. But they are with him always.

The existential idea of a core of integration and creation suggests a conflict-free portion of personality that survives and transcends any dysfunctioning that may possess a person.

Such a force toward integration and meaning need not be considered separate from id. It is an expression of id activity. Teilhard de Chardin posits such a force as existing in all forms of existence: animals, plants, and even inanimate matter. Chardin sees in man the fruition of this drive toward complexity, and it is experienced in man's need for meaning and for love. Martin Buber, too, suggests a force in man that permits him to enter the realm of relation with nature, ideas, other men, and God. This is a force that transcends what otherwise appears to be his limited, finite, individual self. This thinking helps distinguish the existential view of the creative force in man from what the ego psychologists have attempted to add to basic Freudian theory to explain creative functioning through certain basic powers of the ego.

The second major distinction has to do with the power of free choice possessed by every person. Even the most disturbed individual is not solely at the mercy of chaotic, irrational, destructive forces—an id gone wild. Nor is he at the total mercy of environmental forces that seek to identify, coerce, dehumanize, conform, or destroy him. The individual pesonality is always in the process of change and emergence. Sartre defined human consciousness as a "no-thingness." Since it is always in the process of becoming, it is never fixed and completed. This no-thingness is an openness to the new, the unknown; it is forever moving beyond whatever identity one has concluded about oneself. Sartre sees this as an essential human construct. One may deny one's freedom and find ways of avoiding responsibility for this very process of change and emergence, but the process itself goes on. Pathology is not the arrestment of growth but the self-chosen distortion of growth (3).

Human consciousness is itself freedom—for it is a force that moves forever beyond whatever one has become as a fulfilled identity. As such, it is the power within man to change, to alter his life-style, his direction, and his sense of identity. It is an ever-present potential for a conversion experience. "To find one's self, one must lose one's self."

If one has the capacity for free choice and also some awareness of integrative promptings toward growth from the very core of his psyche, then why should one choose dysfunctioning, defensive symptomatology, or madness?

Freud's concept of the superego and his view of defense mechanisms and pathological symptomatology are seen by the existentialist in a more holistic manner. The existential idea of bad faith is a person's activity of denying his nature of freedom and emergence for the sake of a sense of security and identity. He deceives himself by a set of beliefs that define specifically who he is and what he can expect from others. This belief system contains both positive and negative judgments about oneself and suggests how one must relate to other people. It is the center of one's defensive control efforts, of his symptomatology, of his manipulatons of relationships, and of his fostering myths about who he is. He *chooses* to believe certain notions about himself when he is quite young and undergoing the socialization process with his parents, teachers, peers, etc. The beliefs he holds to are used to maintain a sense of secured identity. He is tempted somehow to reassure himself of the solidity of his identity whenever he feels threatened. This he can do through manipulations of others, physical or psychological symptomatology, and reassuring beliefs about himself. The belief pattern may change over the years, so that ideas implanted by parents may become more personalized beliefs, but it is the rigidity and response to threat that characterize his security image, rather than the nature of the beliefs themselves.

This defensive belief system, or security image configuration, has its values, too. It helps the young, developing ego with limited experience and judgement conclude a manner of survival in a family constellation. The beliefs concluded about self and others provide habit patterns that furnish a sense of security so that one can use one's energy for other achievements as well. Even the adult ego is occasionally on the verge of exhaustion and needs to resort to the security image patterns of reassuring contentment. One will at times choose security image behavior, even when one knows it to be irrational and defensive, simply as a means of enduring and managing under considerable stress.

Security image patterns take the form of outer identifications, as well as inner passions. Outer identification includes all ways by which a person uses others to conclude who she is as a fixed identity—using her parents, spouse, children, friends, employer, profession, politics, church, race, social norms, etc. Inner passions have to do with feeling responses to life's situations that also fulfill a sense of identity, so that certain feelings become fanned into possessing passions. For the self identified as "Top Dog," irritation can become rage. For the self identified as "Don Juan," sensual excitement can become lust. For some people, competition becomes greed. For others, pride becomes a quest for power. In the outer identifications, one identifies with beliefs and roles; in the inner passions, one identifies with specific feelings. In either case, the sense of self is experienced as fixed, solidified, defined, rather than flowing, free, and emerging.*

The Process of Change

If you want to know who you are, don't conceptualize upon it. Look at your actions, your behavior, your choices. Existentialism is a philosophy rooted in personal experience. "Truth is subjectivity," Kierkegaard's slogan, and "existence precedes essence," Sartre's assertion, are both ways of rooting identity in personal experience—one's active and unique response in a situation. Being-in-the-world is a concept of Heidegger's that asserts the same notion.

There are two components commonly accepted as necessary for the change process, one rational and the other experiential. Almost every form of psychotherapy includes both these components, despite their occasional assertions to the contrary.

The experiential component has to do with the client experiencing herself in a new and different way. She may discover that she is being dealt with differently by a significant other person in her life. She may also find new kinds of feelings or symptoms arising within herself. The rational component has to do with self-understanding through the process of reflecting and conceptualizing about oneself—the cause-effect relationships in her background, evaluating how she handled recent situations, considering the meaning to her of a new way she has experienced herself, etc.

The existentialists see values in both components of change—one reinforces the other when both occur. The existentialists, however, are particularly wary of the common self-deception of intellectualizing about oneself—of dwelling on self-evaluation and introspection in a manner that negates any

---

*This description of security image operation is similar to other conceptions of defensive functioning: Perls's "maya" and "hole" and associated "top dog and underdog" behaviors; Berne's life script with its games played out of certain "parent and child" ego states; Horney's "self idealization" and "self glorification."

action or choice in the here and now. The existentialists, therefore, stress the experiential component of change as of primary importance. The rational component is secondary and is most useful in either preparing oneself to act now in a new way, or else in evaluationg the meaning of an experience wherein one did act differently. Several forms of experiential activities can occur in therapy:

1. The attitude of the therapist toward the client can present a new type of affirmation by a significant other person that the client has never experienced.

2. The therapist's skill with empathy may provide the client an experience of being understood more intensely than by others in his life.

3. The openness of the therapist about himself as a revealing, engaging person provides an invitation for the client to the dialogical experience. It can also offer an experience of an authority figure as human and of equal status. Such openness by a therapist may constructively take the form of provocative, negative feedback to the client about his appearance, attitudes, feelings, and behavior. Here the client experiences a candid honesty that may be otherwise denied in him in his everyday world of interactions.

4. Techniques designed for here-and-now heightening of awareness, such as in Gestalt, psychodrama, and encounter groups or the dealing with "transference" interactions between therapist and client, are obviously aimed primarily at the experiential component of change. Similarly, efforts to vitalize new interactions between group or family members quickly stir new areas of individual awareness.

5. Action tasks for the client to perform outside of therapy sessions provide new behavioral experiences.

Compatible with the existential therapist's emphasis upon experiential change is his lack of interest in historical data. Some history may be of value in the early interviews to help the therapist see the client in a more human, better rounded perspective, so that the therapist is less inclined to make superficial judgments about the client in response to the stereotype the client usually presents to other people. But the therapist often does not even need this aid. It is far more important to understand the dynamics of the client's present struggle, and what her symptoms or complaints reveal about her efforts to grow and meet her own needs (the present beliefs and activities of her defensive belief system).

If the client herself brings up historical material, the existential therapist will often seek to make it immediately relevant. He may do this by relating the past experience to present choices, or else (using Gestalt techniques) by asking the client to bring the early parent figure into the present interview session by role playing the past interaction that the client is describing.

The existential therapist is in agreement with Glasser's position that an intent focus upon early historical material plays into the client's feelings of helplessness and her efforts to rationalize her own impotence.

Dynamics, Diagnosis, and World View

Clinical diagnosis has its value as a shorthand way of communicating to peers about clients, in terms of areas of conflict and types of defenses. Other than this, it is of questionable value in the eyes of the existential therapist and commonly results in more harm than good. The danger of diagnosis is the categorization of a client, so as to provide the therapist some "objective" way of defining prognosis, goals, the role she must play as she interacts with the client and her decision about termination. Such "objective" efforts based upon generalizations about clients with a similar history-symptomatology-mental status constellation miss what is unique about a particular client. A further danger described by Laing is that diagnosis is often used as a way of agreeing with the family that this client is "sick" and in need of readjustment to the demands and expectations of the family.

This depreciation of the value of clinical diagnosis, however, does not suggest a disregard for understanding the nature of a client's present struggles, conflicts, strivings, and fears. Dynamic understanding remains of key importance. Here the existentialist differs with the behavioral modifier who relates himself only to a specific symptom without regard for its meaning and the client's present life-style.

It is critical to understand the unique "worldview" of the client. This consists of patterns of relating to meaningful others and expectations of them. It also includes beliefs about oneself, both positive and negative judgements, and assumptions about oneself and how these affect the way one meets one's own needs and handles one's frustrations of need satisfaction. It is important to see how the client is interfering with his own growth, and this includes both the beliefs he holds about the sort of person he is and the notions he has about how he must deal with the significant people in his life. It may even include how he evaluates forces of society that play upon him and attempt to conform his behavior into some stereotype that is useful to society's needs (employers, church, racial attitudes, etc.). Normalization in the assessment phase conveys this message: given your special way of viewing the world and your patterns of affecting it and responding to it, your problem is perfectly understandable—it is a natural expression of you. This is not to say that he created the problem; nor, on the other hand, is he a total victim of it.

This type of dynamic formulation stresses the here-and-now life-style— the client's present being-in-the-world. How he gets this way is of questionable significance. The values of dynamic formulations are twofold. First, they provide the therapist with an understanding of her unique client and how his present symptoms are ways of handling a particular stress or conflict area. Second, dynamics give the therapist somewhat of a guideline to assess her own work with the client, particularly when she discovers that her therapeutic efforts are bringing no results.

The dynamic formulation of the existential therapist will emphasize family dynamics (interactions, scapegoating, alliances, etc.). For these usually make up the most significant area of the client's life-style functioning. Intervention efforts will frequently involve other family members for the same reason. The existential understanding of the person as "being-in-the-world" is wholly compatible with the dual focus model of social work. The personal, unique truth of the individual is known best through his relation with others and forces beyond his own ego—usually social but at times, perhaps, transcendental in nature.

Even when the problem is not set forth as family or marital in nature, the therapist will tend to see the presenting symptom as a means of dealing with significant others in his life. An interpersonal appraisal of symptoms is attuned to the absence, loss, breakdown, or dysfunctioning of important human relationships in the person's life. Therapeutic work will commonly be addressed to the creation, the restoration, or the improvement of such relationships. This interpersonal focus upon symptomatology need not neglect the individual's subjective experience of attitudes, values, and feelings. The two are obviously interdependent. However, the existential therapist sees catharsis and self-understanding as a vehicle for altering the person's world of human relationships, which is the fundamental goal.

Treatment Methods

It is difficult to talk of treatment methods without first considering the types of clients and problems for which the methods are used. In one sense, the existential perspective is loyal to no particular treatment system. It is eclectic and uses whatever techniques will best meet the needs of a particular client. In another sense, the existential therapist may be considered best equipped to work with clients whose problem involves a loss of direction, a value confusion, a shaken identity in a swirling world of anomie. For these clients, certain techniques have been developed to focus precisely on such difficulties. However, it should be clearly understood that the existentialist works out of his unique philosophical perspective with all clients, and he should not be viewed only as a specialist with clients experiencing personal alienation.

There are three principles of treatment that clarify the therapeutic approach of the existentialist. These are:

1. A client-centered orientation
2. An experiential change emphasis
3. A concern with values and philosophical or religious perspectives

A Client-Centered Orientation

The client-centered focus has already become apparent in our introductory comments on the existentialist's antiauthoritarian stance. Client-centeredness was also the major issue in the discussion on diagnosis and dynamic formulation. Two other areas exemplify client-centeredness: goal formulations, and work with an emerging theme in any given interview.

Goal formulation involves the therapist and client working out a mutual agreement in the early interviews as to the purpose of future treatment. What must be guarded against here is the type of therapeutic dogmatism that seeks to convince the client as to the "true implications" of her symptoms or problem, so that she will work in the manner the therapist wishes. The most important initial step in treatment, following the age-old social work principle, is to "start where the client is." This adage refers to focusing on how the client is experiencing her problem, what it is she wants changed, and other ideas as to the type of help she is seeking.

Elsewhere, I enumerated a framework of possible goals from which social workers may proceed with treatment (42). These are: *provocative contact; sustaining relationship; specific behavior (symptom) change; environmental change; relationship change; directional change;* and combinations of the above.

The type of goal left off this list is the extensive insightful analysis that a client who enters psychoanalysis may be seeking. Whether or not he ends up with any more significant change through insightful analysis than in some of the above-mentioned goals is highly questionable at this point in time, considering research efforts into the effects of treatment.

The above-stated goals can be briefly differentiated by considering the client's view of change in each category.

PROVOCATIVE CONTACT.   The client seeks neither change nor help of any kind. The caseworker assertively seeks to provoke a client into wanting change. This occurs often in protective services, in residential treatment centers for children, and in the "back wards" of psychiatric hospitals and institutions for the retarded. It is also common with the "hard-to-reach" families who present various problems to the community via the schools and police departments. Just how far a caseworker should go in her provocative efforts is itself an ethical decision related to the right of a client to his own unique life-style. Nevertheless, provocative efforts are often justified insofar as they provide an outreach effort and offer an opportunity that the client might otherwise never consider.

SUSTAINING RELATIONSHIP.   Here the client seeks help, in that he is lonely and wants an affirmative, interested contact in his life. But he has no hope for changing his life-style in any way and will resist any such efforts. His need is for an affirming relationship without expectations of changed behavior.

SPECIFIC BEHAVIOR (SYMPTOM) CHANGE.   The client is distressed with a particular troublesome behavior. He has no interest, however, in widening his problem area by seeing how this particular symptom is related to his past or present life-style and system of relationships. His motivation is restricted to symptom alleviation.

ENVIRONMENTAL CHANGE.   The client sees his difficulty in relation to the environment beyond his family. The problem may have to do with employment, education, social contacts, community forces that he experiences as dehumanizing. He does not see himself as part of the problem. He seeks help in dealing with social institutions and systems.

RELATIONSHIP CHANGE.   Here the client experiences difficulties in relationships with significant others in his life—his spouse, children, parents, relatives, friends. He realizes his own involvement and wants to alter a relationship pattern.

DIRECTIONAL CHANGE.   The client's sense of identity, of values, of personal direction is confused. He has difficulty in making choices and feels impotent in relation to his immediate future. The conflict is experienced as within himself.

The mode of therapy used (individual, couple, group, family) or the types of techniques (reality, behavioral modification, encounter, psychoanalytic ego, Gestalt, etc.) will vary, of course, in accordance with the interest of the client, the skills of the therapist, and the nature of the treatment setting itself. However, certain techniques are obviously more appropriate for certain goals. Behavior modification would be particularly useful with the goals of provocative contact and specific behavior (symptom) change. Social work literature provides many useful approaches to accomplishing the goal of environmental change. The goal of relationship change can be dealt with using communications theory (Satir, Haley, Jackson) and other family and marital therapy models. Directional change can be effected by techniques described by Rogers, Farrelly, the Gestaltists, reality therapy, cognitive therapy, task-centered casework, and psychoanalytic psychotherapy. The critical point here is that the therapeutic approach must fill the unique goal and needs of a client rather than fitting clients into some pet system of psychotherapy, and dismissing the misfits as "unmotivated."

What is important to understand in this goal framework is that it provides a starting point for treatment in a manner that recognizes the unique experience of the client as valid. The goal may change during treatment as the client begins to experience her problems in some other light. The goal must also be tested out in early interviews so as to ascertain whether the goal agreed upon is merely a verbalized goal of the client, or whether it is indeed the way in which the client experiences the need for help and hope for change. With this framework, the therapist engages the client in a manner by which they can both "talk the same language" and have similar expectations for what is to follow.

There would appear to be a contradiction between some of the above-mentioned goals and what has previously been described as the existential focus upon disillusionment, freedom of choice, finding meaning and suffering, discovering the growth value of dialogue and coming to a sense of personal commitment in relation to one's future. Such a focus seems most applicable to the goal category of directional change. The existential therapist, however, is not bound to pursue such a focus, it is does not seem appropriate. The existentialist's concern with client-centered treatment and an emphasis upon experiential change enables him to assert his philosophical perspective to a degree in all goal categories described.

The other client-centered activity deals with the interview theme of any given session. The client is not a problem to be solved, a puzzle to be completed. She is a person who is undergoing constant change from week to week, day to day. Change occurs in her life for both the good and the bad apart from what happens during her therapy sessions. For the therapist to preplan an interview, picking up where the last one ended or getting into what the therapist considers to be an area of increasing importance, is often presumptuous.

The interview begins and the therapist listens to both verbal and nonverbal expressions of the client. He is alert to possible inconsistencies among what the client says, her feeling state and behavior. The therapist's most important listening tool is his capacity for empathy. In the initial stages of the interview, the therapist must free himself of preconceptions about the client and preoccupations with himself in order to open himself to the whole person before him.

How the theme is made known as well as how it is dealt with are related to the goal of therapy (thinking in terms of the goal framework described earlier) and what particular therapeutic approach a therapist favors for work on such a goal. The therapist and client work together from the point of theme clarity. Techniques aimed at experiential insight, self-understanding, or both, may be used depending upon the goal, therapeutic approach, and needs and capacities of the client at that particular moment.

An Experimental Change Emphasis

The experiential emphasis has already been discussed. The activities encouraging experiential change included: attitude of therapist, empathy, therapist's openness or transparency, heightening of here-and-now awareness, tasks for choice, and action. In the earlier discussion of how various theories of therapy reflected various existential points of emphasis, it was apparent that techniques could be tapped from many theoretical sources.

It is clear by now that the existentialist is radically concerned with the here-and-now encounter between a person and his world. For it is in this moment of responsiveness, of being in-the-world, that one experiences her freedom of choice and meaning making. Who she is stems from what she does—the choice she activates—and does not stem from the intellectual conceptualization she holds about herself, nor from any dogmas or groups to which she holds allegiance in exchange for some bestowed identity.

A Concern with Values and Philosophical or Religious Perspectives

The concern with pinpointing, challenging, clarifying values, and philosophy or religious perspectives is also dealt with by various writers. There are strong similarities between the rational–emotive psychotherapy of Albert Ellis and the morita therapy of Japan. Both pinpoint "irrational" or "unrealistic" beliefs that holds to and specifically propose other more realistic and human beliefs in substitution for the dysfunctional beliefs. Hobart Mowrer's integrity therapy follows a similar course, where the emphasis is upon helping the client see that there is a contradiction between the values he holds in common with his "significant others" and his behavior or actual life-style. Frankl has developed two techniques, dereflection and paradoxical intention, that are designed to help a client reexamine and alter his philosophical perspective so as to affirm a new way of viewing himself in relation to his symptoms, choices, and life direction.

These "reality-oriented" approaches include four common ingredients:

1. Pinpointing specific values (attitudes, beliefs, judgments about self and others) manifested by the client's life-style.
2. Clarifying how these very values are interfering with his own growth and intimacy needs or efforts.
3. Helping him substitute more realistic, human values and beliefs for the dysfunctional ones so his realistic growth and intimacy needs can achieve more direct satisfaction.
4. Encouraging decisions, choices, and actions (often as homework assignments) in order to activate the new values concluded to be more valid.

This therapeutic emphasis upon values and philosophical perspective is designed for certain types of clients—those whose working goal is directional change. There is a growing recognition of the effects of anomie in modern culture with resulting personal alienation from the roots of human needs and human strivings. Jung reported this phenomenon forty years ago and existential novelists, philosophers, and psychologists have been emphasizing the extent of alienation ever since.

The American culture has finally felt the same impact of alienation that shook Europe during and after World War II. In America, this awareness was helped along by the revolt of the youth, minority groups, and poor people. At this point, it is unclear whether alienation is a problem of a particular client population or whether it is really at the root of all emotional distress.

The writings of Laing, Becker, and, recently, Irvin Yalom are certainly weighted toward the latter view.

Considering the three therapeutic principles discussed (the client-centered orientation, focus upon experiential change, and concern for values and philosophical perspectives), it becomes clear that the existential caseworker seeks to work with all types of clients and human problems and that she could function with any kind of social agency or therapeutic setting, provided she was given the administrative approval to work as she wished. It is also clear that the existential position is in opposition to those therapeutic practices that seek to adjust clients to family and social norms or to those prognostic nòrms stemming from the rigid use of diagnostic categories. The authoritative misuse of behavior modification and psychoanalytic theory is a major concern of the existential social worker.

Considering the eclectic use of treatment approaches suggested by the existential perspective, it is also apparent that social workers can make more creative and varied use of the existential perspective than can either psychiatrists, psychologists, ministers, or nurses. This is because of the wide-ranging problem activities that engage the efforts of social workers, necessitating a manner of work that includes multiple skills. While there is still a lack of research verification, it appears that work with a middle-class clientele will commonly involve techniques aimed at heightening here-and-now awareness, as well as dealing with values and philosophical perspectives. Clients from the lower classes, who are considered unresponsive to traditional treatment approaches, would appear most responsive to task-oriented techniques emphasizing choice and action.

The modes of therapy (individual, couple, family, and group) are all effective ways of conducting an existential-oriented treatment. Application to individual counseling has been elaborated upon, particularly by Rogers, Farrelly, May, Frankl, and Perls. Work with groups with an existential perspective has been described by Helen Durkin, Carl Rogers, Arthur Burton, and Irvin Yalom. Social work writer Alan Klein relates the group work approach to existential thinking. Family therapists whose approaches are highly compatible with the existential perspective include Jay Haley, Virginia Satir, John Bell, and Carl Whittaker.

The existential approach fulfills two major needs of modern social work practice. First, it is the only social work approach that emphasizes value issues related to the client's problem. With the apparent increase of alienation and anomie, social work may require methods of response to value questions. Second, the existential view of clients and their problems bridges the gap in current social work theory between the intrapsychic emphasis on the one hand, and the behavioral-systemic emphasis on the other. Using the person-problem-situation perspective of social work assessment, the existentialist would agree with the behavioral-systematic emphasis upon both a here-and-now and a social interactional focus as the characterization of social work practice. She would further agree that the diagnostic, or medical model, is not only ineffective, for the most part, but that it produces negative results with too many clients. Labeling, prognosis, and prescription are means by which the mental health hierarchy seeks means of control over the lives of citizens of Szasz's "therapeutic state." Yet she would agree with the intra-psychic-focused worker that the risk of the behaviorist-systemic approach is to eliminate symptoms without either care or understanding of the person who has the problem. A problem is not a simple irritant; it is a message to the person about his present life orientation, some indicator of personal truth.

Case Example

The following could be considered an example of the existential social work approach. The case described is short-term casework with an individual from the goal framework of specific behavior change. It should be clear from the previous discussion about differing goals and the eclectic use of treatment techniques, that other case examples would take much different forms from the one described. The three existential principles of client-centered focus, experiential change, and value focus are illustrated in this case.

> An attractive Spanish-American woman, aged thirty-four, came to me complaining of a severely inhibiting depression. In the course of the evaluation, it appeared that she had little interest or sensitivity for seeing any connection of her symptoms to her past or present living situation. She was somewhat troubled over a divorce of a year ago. There was also a problem with her mother (living across the street) who tried to dom-inate her and provoke her guilt, and who often took care of her two teenage daughters. Some rebellion in the older daughter was apparent. She also believed herself "hexed" by her mother-in-law. These were areas of complaints, yet she saw no prospects for changing them. Her concerns for change were very concrete: she could not do her housework or cook the meals or discipline the children, for she would usually go to bed soon after she returned from work. In bed, she would either sleep or fantasize about how bad off she was, and the running of the house was left to the children, particularly the rebellious older one. She feared losing her job as a nurse's aide at the local hospital and had already missed several days of work because of feeling too tired. She had given up going out with her boyfriend and felt extremely alone and worthless.
>
> Within ten interviews, seen on an alternate week basis, the depres-sion had lifted. She managed her housework well; disciplined the chil-dren—the older one was much less rebellious; she could stand up to her mother on a realistic basis; she was dating again; and she was taking a training course to become a practical nurse. The goal was specific be-havioral change although its successful accomplishment resulted in a broadening of this woman's constructive activity in several areas of her

life. My techniques dealt primarily with the symptoms of depression and helplessness. In the second interview, I emphasized what I sensed to be her inhibited potential: I said that she could make herself get out of bed (or refuse to enter it) by performing the tasks of her housework and by going to her hospital work every day, no matter how tired she felt. I recognized that feelings of depression were strong within her, but pointed out that they represented a part of herself that seemed to be trying to convince her that she was no good. In the third interview, I dealt actively with a defensive belief, challenging its validity and questioning her need to be dominated by it. She thought the depression resulted from being "hexed." I told her that I did not believe in the magic of hexing and if there was anything to it, it had to do with her own reaction to the notion that she had been "hexed." I linked this belief with the part of her that was trying to convince her that she was helplessly useless and inadequate. As sessions went on, she did bring up material about her mother, husband, children, job, and relatives, but this was more from the standpoint of content for discussion in what she felt to be a positive, affirming relationship. The actual therapeutic effort, in terms of pinpointing her problem and a way of dealing with it, was primarily in relation to the depressive symptom described. The techniques used were my ways of responding to her area of concern and view of change. We could communicate through the goal of specific behavior change. She was able to see the depression as being a self-defeating part of her. This freed her from the belief that the depressive symptom was a condemnation and failure of her *whole* personality, which had been implied in her notion of "being hexed." While this was a limited shift in the belief system of this woman, it could still be a significant one. Furthermore, her resumption of responsibility in the family had its rewarding feedback responses from the children, as well as from her own mother who was closely involved with her family.

Note the three principles involved: a client-centered focus in terms of goal selection and interview management; emphasis upon experiential change through use of task assignment as well as through the attitude of the therapist regarding the client's potential strengths; and finally, an effort to deal with the woman's value system, specifically suggesting that she did have some capacity for free choice and need not identify herself completely with her symptom (feelings of fated helplessness).

This case raises an interesting cultural issue in relation to the client's view of the change process and how she views change as possibly occurring. An alternative approach might have been a referral of this woman to a *curandero* to handle the "hexed" issue. Had she been unresponsive to my rational efforts to deal with her belief about "being hexed," I would have considered such a referral. Since she had sought out my help, I chose to deal with this belief issue in this more personal, challenging way.

In retrospect, my expression of disbelief in the magic of hexing was an example of value imposition, and therefore contrary to an important existential concern. A better way to handle this matter might have been to say that the worker knows of some Chicano people who don't believe in hexing and have a different way of thinking about such matters. This is true and sidesteps the potential problem of imposition.

Existentialism and the Community

Existentialism is sometimes criticized as an individualistic philosophy lacking a social ethic. This is a misnomer. Philosophers such as Camus, Berdyaev, Tillich, and Buber have written extensively on the application of existential thinking to social issues. Members of the helping professions have also related existential philosophy to social concerns. Edward Tiryakian, a sociologist, compares existential thought with that of Durkheim. Lionel Rubinoff's *The Pornography of Power* (64) is a critique of modern philosophical, psychological, and sociological thought on the subject of the individual and his relationship to society. Rubinoff's basic premises are existential. R. D. Laing also uses an existential framework in his critique of society and of the helping professions as dehumanizing extensions of society's values.

Beginning with the existential belief that truth is not found in any objective fashion, within a doctrine or within a group of people, we find some implications for a view of society and social change.

In the first place, the existentialist stands against tyranny in any form—not only by politically conservative, status quo-oriented leaders, but also by the rational social engineers who would seek to establish the utopian society necessitating many controls and committed to adjustment of individuals to a "properly functioning" society. The existentialists are a prime opponent of B. F. Skinner in his appeal for a society that meets humanity's needs by limiting freedom and nonconformity.

The existentialists know that power corrupts and that much of the evil perpetrated is unpredictable at the moment of its inception. If, on the other hand, there is an effort to decondition evil-producing behavior, this effort itself, if successful, would result in the most profound evil of all: the dehumanization of people by depriving individuals of freedom—the only valid source of their sense of personal meaning and dignity.

On the other hand, an appeal for a completely free and open society, such as proposed by Charles Reich's *Greening of America* (58), is again a naive position founded upon a disregard for the self-defeating, the aggressive, and the evil-producing behavior of people. Spontaneous "doing one's own thing" is too simple a commitment. We can be defeated by our own instincts and self-deceptions as easily as by our efforts to organize and construct the happy state.

Power itself results in an increased effort toward solidification and self-perpetuation. Society must be a dynamic, growing system, just as an individual is a being of responsive emergence. The healthy society is one attuned to the creative ideas and efforts of individuals and groups within its structure that propose change and new ideas. A participatory democracy is an expression of the existential affirmation of the unique perspective of each individual. In a participatory democracy, groups are seen to possess their own truths, which will differ from the attitudes and values of others who have not had the same life experiences. The minority groups are correct in claiming the right to speak for themselves. On the other hand, this does not mean that any single minority group possesses the final truth and wisdom for all men either, as many guilt-ridden whites seem to believe.

The direction for a society's emergence stems from the sufferings and potentials of its people, and not from an elite group of rebels or social organizers. Eric Hoffer was right in saying that the most creative and innovative shifts in a society stem from its outcasts, nonconformists, and those who experience the failures of its present functioning. The existential model for social change would be one wherein the very people who suffer from dehumanizing social forces would be the indicators of what sorts of changes are needed. The community organization social worker would have a facilitating, clarifying, enabling role here, perhaps, and once a direction is clear she may use her knowledge of power structure and change tactics in order to mobilize the social change effort.

The "antiexistential" community organizer would be one who decides for himself what change other people really need and then uses his knowledge and skills to "educate," seduce, and pressure a disadvantaged group into deciding what their problems are and the change indicated. The worker's basic notions of change, here, come either from his own needs, or his rational, analytical conclusions of what this group or community lacks in comparison with some ideal he holds about how people should live. The impetus for change is worker-oriented rather than community-oriented.

The opposite extreme, also antiexistential, is sometimes seen in community mental health clinics. Although such clinics are committed, by their very purpose (and federal funding), to a community outreach stance, there is little genuine effort at dialogue with those needy members of the community who do not enter the portals of the clinic itself requesting some specific help. In contrast, the genuinely committed community mental health clinic is actively seeking contact with those groups in its community who are known through police, welfare and schools to have problems but who are not availing themselves of any helping services. Primary prevention at times of family or neighborhood crisis becomes a major way of help, and this most often takes the form of consultation with police, welfare workers, teachers, nurses, ministers, and doctors.

As discussed earlier, the existentialists see many of the forces of society as being in opposition to the individual's effort at an authentic life-style—

establishing her unique direction out of an awareness of her own freedom, responsibility, and what she learns through personal suffering. Modern society encourages anomie and personal alienation by its forces of seduction and oppression. Insofar as the economic–political system uses people as objects in order to preserve its own efficient functioning, it may be said to be dehumanizing. Various social institutions combine their efforts to achieve this goal. Certain roles in the system are rewarded with status, financial remuneration, and prestige while others are ignored. Happiness is defined in such a way as to keep the public at large an active consumer of economic goods. An attunement to personal suffering is discouraged through the various tranquilization forms of drugs, alcohol, treadmill activities, and a work ethic that implies a solution to all one's problems with the purchase of the next automobile, house, or packaged vacation plan. Such writers as Erich Fromm and Henry Winthrop have elaborated upon the multiple forms of social dehumanization that are too numerous and complex to mention here (26, 90).

The helping professional is faced with a critical choice in relation to social dehuminization. He can become a part of this system that is a purveyor of anomie by the very way he performs his helping role. Or, on the other hand, he can be a member of a vanguard actively in touch with many of society's victims, who can help bring individuals and groups to an active awareness of themselves as free and responsible beings despite the negative forces bestowed upon them by society. Beyond such awareness, he will help them toward personal direction and action that affirms human dignity in the face of tyrannical and dehumanizing social forces.

The institutions of society can and do provide constructive, affirming forces for individuals and groups, or course, through education, employment, protection, health, and welfare care as well as valued traditions, a sense of history, and a national spirit that affirms a set of values that is generally accepted and may be quite compatible with the freedom, responsibility, and valuing of uniqueness and personal dignity that characterize existentialism. The existential helping professional realizes, however, that the constructive forces of society cannot in themselves bring an individual to authenticity. The matter of personal choice and acceptance of responsibility for one's own worldview and life-style remain essential. The existentialist is, therefore, cynical in response to social utopians who seek to construct a society of need-met, happy people.

Research and Knowledge Gaps

The existential approach eludes research. Its lack of a specific theory of personality, its emphasis upon subjectivity and uniqueness, its eclectic use of multivaried techniques, and its concern about values are all factors that make structured studies difficult. On the other hand, the existential perspective extends the hand of gratitude to the numerous research studies that have clearly unseated dogmatic-authoritative assumptions proselytized by "sophisticated" adherents to the varied theories of personality. For example, the fact that medical, legal, insurance, and institutional systems want to uphold psychoanalytic theory as true and necessary does not in the least impress the existential worker—for she knows that the results of research say otherwise (46). When it comes to practice, the existential worker tends to agree with the behaviorist: we should utilize what was proven effective in practice to avoid forcing clients to submit to our favored (though ineffective) methods. Effective treatment includes a combination of general attributes and conditions and specific techniques: client-worker liking of one another; use of "placebo" effect in structuring the treatment process; core conditions (warmth, genuineness, empathy) when combined with attitude change; attitude change when accompanied with emotional change as well as task assignments; and the use of significant others in the assessment and treatment process wherever possible.

Another important conclusion from practice research has been that no theory of treatment has proven itself superior to any other model. The existentialist sees this as a crucial statement about the place of theory in practice. Theory does not seem to be the important ingredient in helping people, and is therefore considered of secondary (informative) value. While it is not clear what then is the magic ingredient, the existential worker would suggest it to be human sensitivity as developed over time through both self-awareness and learning from many experiences with clients. The better one comes to know oneself, the more clearly is one able to see oneself within the client's experiences as well. This is a most important area for future research study.

How are social work education programs preparing students for present practice? Do they foster those ingredients that may eventually result in a wise practitoner, given a few years of additional experience? Here the existentialist has serious concerns. An educational tradition has existed for many years in social work that has emphasized the analytic, diagnostic, rational-authoritarian approach. Teachers have often viewed students in this categorical manner and have in turn urged students to view their clients in a similar manner. This has been the phony guise of "scientism" that has sought to identify social workers as "scientific" when in fact the "objective nature" of most of their knowledge would be scoffed at by physical scientists. Many students, in their insecurity, seek comfort in categorizing clients according to the knowledge system taught them. Other students, rebelling against what feels like a rigid authoritarianism, will completely abandon dynamic understanding of any type and naively seek to provide "band-aid" answers to problems posed by clients. It would appear that students need to be somehow "humanized" rather than "objectified." Self-awareness has been a goal of social work education, but it would seem that new educational approaches need to be devised to achieve this goal more effectively. Only by an appreciation of one's own personal complexity can one begin seriously to understand the complexities of others.

Human sensitivity is a bed partner of humility. Humility results from personal disillusionment, or humiliation, providing the student is warned against too quickly attaching oneself to the notion that one has now achieved some "sophisticated maturity" as a result of personal insights. Humility can be also the springboard toward creativity. As one realizes one's personal blind spots, gaps in awareness, withdrawal from knowledge and situations posing threat, the student finds a personalized direction for his reading and openness to new experience. He senses, too, that his search for expanding truth will enable him to understand and help more clients.

I have found the classroom situation a useful "experimental lab" for generating human sensitivity among students. Assessment of clients is dealt with simultaneously with students' self-exploration. Personal exercises to promote such examination are used in class as well as through homework assignments. Peer sharing in small groups engenders honesty, spontaneity, and supportive feedback in relation to results of exercises (46). Exercises explore dimensions of personal problem-emotion-attitudes-values interplay, of roles with family and significant others, of trouble spots in personal response to certain clients. Reading of theory is encouraged, then, as the student's means of building upon and expanding self-knowledge in the directions necessary to handle areas of confusion, insufficient self-client understanding, and intrigue with new ideas. Values need to be clarified by both the instructor and students in terms of how they are used constructively with clients. Vitality and spontaneous engagement with clients are demonstrated and practiced in role plays of common client-worker situations.

In conclusion, the existential stance provides a philosophical perspective that can be related to the many avenues of social work practice. One does not need a profound acquaintance with existential philosophy in order to benefit from the perspective. One might, instead, view the existentialists as emphasizing a sense of direction and a style of working that are primarily concerned with a greater humanization of the social work profession. From their emphasis upon the value of the uniqueness of the individual there comes an affirmation of a client-centered focus and an awareness of the dangers of anomie in a mechanistic society. From their view of growth through choice and action there comes a primary effort aimed at experiential change with clients. From their model of man as a meaning-making being there comes a recognition of the importance of values, philosophy, and religion as ingredients of the casework process. From their emphasis upon dialogue there comes the concern for therapist transparency and authenticity as well as the valuing of a participatory democracy. And from their appreciation of the powers of self-deception at work with human beings, there comes an emphasis upon personal commitment in the face of suffering and uncertainty, as well as a suspicion about any authority that establishes itself as knowing how other people should live their lives.

References

1. Allport, Gordon. *Letters from Jenny*. New York: Harcourt, Brace and World, 1965.
2. Angyal, Andras. *Neurosis and Treatment*. New York: Wiley, 1965.
3. Barnes, Hazel. *The Literature of Possibility: A Study of Humanistic Existentialism*. Lincoln: University of Nebraska Press, 1959.
4. Barret, William. *Irrational Man*. New York: Doubleday, 1958.
5. Becker, Ernest. *The Denial of Death*. New York: Free Press, 1975.
6. Berdyaev, Nikolai. *Slavery and Freedom*. New York: Scribner, 1944.
7. Binswanger, Ludwig. *Begin in the World*. New York: Basic Books, 1963.
8. Borowitz, Eugene. *A Layman's Guide to Religious Existentialism*. New York: Delta, 1966.
9. Boss, Medard. *Psychoanalysis and Daseinsanalysis*, New York: Basic Books, 1963.
10. Bradford, Kirk A. *Existentialism and Casework*, Jericho, N.,Y.: Exposition Press, 1969.
11. Brown, J. A. "Child Abuse: An Existential Process," *Clinical Social Work Journal*, Vol. 8, No. 2 (1980), pp. 108–114.
12. Buber, Martin. *Between Man and Man*. Boston: Beacon Press, 1955.
13. ———. *The Knowledge of Man*. New York: Harper and Row, 1965.
14. Burton, Arthur (ed.). *Encounter*. San Francisco: Jossey-Bass, 1969.
15. Camus, Albert. *The Rebel*. New York: Knopf, 1969.
16. Curry, Andrew. "Toward a Phenomenological Study of the Family," *Existential Psychiatry*, Vol. 6, No. 27 (Spring 1967), pp. 35–44.
17. Durkin, Helen. *The Group in Depth*. New York: International Universities Press, 1964.
18. Ellis, Albert. *Reason and Emotion in Psychotherapy*. New York: Stuart, 1962.
19. Farber, Leslie. *The Ways of the Will*. New York: Harper Colophon Books, 1966.
20. Farrelly, Frank, *Provocative Therapy*. Madison, Wis.: Family, Social and Psychotherapy Service, 1974.
21. Ford, Donald, and Hugh Urban. *Systems of Psychotherapy*, New York: Wiley, 1964, Chapter 12.
22. Frankl, Viktor E. *Man's Search for Meaning: An Introduction to Logotherapy*. Boston: Beacon Press, 1962.
23. ———. *The Doctor and the Soul: From Psychotherapy to Logotherapy*. New York: Knopf, 1965.
24. ———. *Psychotherapy and Existentialism: Selected Papers on Logotherapy*. New York: Simon and Schuster, 1967.
25. Frohberg, Margery. "Existentialism: An Introduction to the Contemporary Conscience," *Perceptions* (School of Social Work, San Diego State College), Vol. 1. No. 1 (Spring 1967), pp. 24–32.
26. Fromm, Erich. *The Sane Society*. New York: Rinehart, 1955.
27. Glasser, William. *Reality Therapy*. New York: Harper and Row, 1965.

28. Gyarfas, Mary. "Social Science, Technology and Social Work: A Caseworker's View," *Social Service Review*, Vol. 43, No. 3, (September 1969), pp. 259–273.

29. Haley, Jay. *Strategies of Psychotherapy*. New York: Grune and Stratton, 1963.

30. ———. *Problem-Solving Therapy*. San Francisco: Jossey-Bass, 1976.

31. Heinecken, Martin J. *The Moment Before God*. Philadelphia: Mulenberg Press, 1956.

32. Hoffer, Eric. *The True Believer*. New York: Harper, 1951.

33. Imre, Roberta Wells. "A Theological View of Social Casework," *Social Casework*, Vol. 52, No. 9 (November 1971), pp. 578–585.

34. James, Muriel, and Doroghy Jongeward. *Born to Win: Transactional Analysis with Gestalt Experiments*. Reading, Mass.: Addison-Wesley, 1971.

35. Jourard, Sydney. *The Transparent Self*. Princeton, N.J.: Van Nostrand, 1964.

36. Jung, Carl G. *Modern Man in Search of a Soul*. New York: Harcourt, Brace, 1933.

37. Katz, Robert L. *Empathy*, New York: Free Press, 1963.

38. Kazantzakis, Nikos. *The Saviors of God*. New York: Simon and Schuster, 1960.

39. Klein, Alan F. *Social Work Through Group Process*, Albany: School of Social Welfare, State University of New York, 1970.

40. Krill, Donald. "Psychoanalysis, Mowrer and the Existentialists," *Pastoral Psychology*, Vol. 16 (October 1965), pp. 27–36.

41. Krill, Donald F. "Existentialism: A Philosophy for our Current Revolutions," *Social Service Review*, Vol. 40, No. 3 (September 1966), pp. 289–301.

42. ———. "A Framework for Determining Client Modifiability," *Social Casework*, Vol. 49, No. 10 (December 1968), pp. 602–611.

43. ———. "Existential Psychotherapy and the Problem of Anomie," *Social Work*, Vol. 14, No. 2 (April 1969), pp. 33–49.

44. ———. *Existential Social Work*. New York: Free Press, 1978.

45. ———. *The Beat Worker*. Lanham, Md.: University Press of America, soon to be published.

46. Kuckelmans, Joseph J. *Phenomenology: The Philosophy of Edmund Husserl and Its Interpretation*. New York: Doubleday, 1967.

47. Laing, R. D. *The Divided Self*. Baltimore: Penguin, 1964.

48. ———. *The Politics of Experience*. Baltimore: Penguin, 1967.

49. Maslow, Abraham H. *Toward a Psychology of Being*, Princeton, N.J.: Van Nostrand, 1962.

50. May, Rollo, E. Angel, and H. F. Ellenberger (eds.). *Existence: A New Dimension in Psychiatry and Psychology*. New York: Basic Books, 1958.

51. May, Rollo (ed.). *Existential Psychology*. New York: Random House, 1961.

52. ———. *Psychology and the Human Dilemma*, Princeton, N.J.: Van Nostrand, 1967.

53. Moustakas, Clark (ed.). *The Self: Explorations in Personal Growth*. New York: Harper and Row, 1956.

54. Mowrer, O. Hobart. *The Crisis in Psychiatry and Religion*. Princeton, N.J.: Van Nostrand, 1961.

55. Nuttin, Joseph. *Psychoanalysis and Personality*. New York: Mentor-Omega, 1962.

56. Perls, Frederick S. *Gestalt Therapy Verbatim*. Lafayette, Calif.: Real People Press, 1969.

57. Picardie, M. "Dreadful Moments: Existential Thoughts on Doing Social Work," *British Journal of Social Work*, Vol. 10 (1980) pp. 483–490.

58. Reich, Charles. *The Greening of America*. New York: Random House, 1970.

59. Reid, William. *The Task-Centered System*. New York: Columbia University Press, 1979.

60. Reinhardt, Kurt F. *The Existentialist Revolt*. New York: Unger, 1952.

61. Rogers, Carl. *On Becoming a Person*. Boston: Houghton Mifflin, 1961.

62. ———. "The Group Comes of Age," *Psychology Today*, Vol. 3, No. 7 (December 1969), p. 29.

63. Rubin, Gerald K. "Helping a Clinic Patient Modify Self-Destructive Thinking," *Social Work*, Vol. 7, No. 1 (January 1962), pp. 76–80.

64. Rubinoff, Lionel. *The Pornography of Power*, New York: Ballantine, 1969.

65. Ruesch, Jurgen, and Gregory Bateson. *Communication: The Social Matrix of Psychiatry*. New York: Norton, 1968.

66. Salomon, Elizabeth. "Humanistic Values and Social Casework," *Social Casework*, Vol. 48, No. 1 (January 1967), pp. 26–32.

67. Satir, Virginia. *Conjoint Family Therapy*. Palo Alto, Calif.: Science and Behavior Books, 1964.

68. Sinsheimer, Robert. "The Existential Casework Relationship," *Social Casework*, Vol. 50, No. 2 (February 1969), pp. 67–73.

69. Skinner, B. F. *Beyond Freedom and Dignity*. New York: Knopf, 1971.

70. Stretch, John. "Existentialism: A Proposed Philosophical Orientation for Social Work," *Social Work*, Vol. 12, No. 4 (October 1967), pp. 97–102.

71. Sutherland, Richard. "Choosing as Therapeutic Aim, Method, and Philosophy," *Journal of Existential Psychiatry*, Vol. 2, No. 8 (Spring 1962), pp. 371–392.

72. Swaine, R. L., and V. Baird. "An Existentially Based Approach to Teaching Social Work Practice," *Journal of Education for Social Work*, Vol. 13, No. 3 (Fall 1977), p. 99–106.

73. Szasz, Thomas. *The Therapeutic State*. New York: Prometheus Books, 1984.

74. Taft, J. "A Conception of the Growth Underlying Social Casework Practice," *Social CAsework*, Vol. 21, No. 5 (1950), pp. 311–316.

75. Teilhard de Chardin, Pierre. *The Phenomenon of Man*. New York: Harper and Row, 1959.

76. Tillich, Paul. *The Courage to Be*. New Haven, Conn.: Yale, 1952.

77. ———. *Love, Power and Justice*. New York: Oxford, 1960.

78. Tiryakian, Edward A. *Sociologism and Existentialism*. Englewood Cliffs, N.J.: Prentice-Hall, 1962.

79. Vontress, C. E. "Cross-Cultural Counselling: An Existential Approach," *Personnel and Guidance Journal*, Vol. 58, No. 2 (1979), pp. 117–122.

80. Watzlawick, Paul, John Weakland, and Richard Fisch. *Change: Principles of Problem Formation and Problem Resolution*. New York: Norton, 1974.

81. Weiss, David. "The Ontological Dimension—Social Casework," *Social Worker*, C.A.S.W., June 1962.

82. ———. "The Existential Approach to Social Work," *Viewpoints*, Montreal, Spring 1967.

83. ———. "Social Work as Authentication," *Social Worker*, C.A.S.W., February 1968.

84. ———. "Self-Determination in Social Work—An Existential Dialogue," *Social Worker*, C.A.S.W., November 1969.

85. ———. "Social Work as Encountering," *Journal of Jewish Communal Service*, Spring 1970.

86. ———. "Social Work as Healing and Revealing," *Intervention*, No. 50 (Summer 1970).

87. ———. "The Existential Approach to Fields of Practice," *Intervention*, No. 55 (Fall 1971).

88. ———. "The Living Language of Encountering: Homage to Martin Buber 1878–1965," *Intervention*, No. 57 (Spring 1972).

89. Wheelis, Allen. *The Quest for Identity*. New York: Norton, 1958.

90. Winthrop, Henry. "Culture, Mass Society, and the American Metropolis; High Culture and Middlebrow Culture: An Existential View," *Journal of Existentialism*, Vol. 8, No. 27 (Spring 1967), p. 371.

91. Yalom, Irvin D. *Existential Psychotherapy*. New York: Basic Books, 1980.

Annotated Listing of Key References

BRADFORD, KIRK A. *Existentialism and Casework*. Jericho, N.Y.: Exposition Press, 1969.
A short review of existential thought in terms of its philosophical development and its entry into the field of psychology. A comparison and integration of existential psychology and social case work concepts.

BUBER, MARTIN. *The Knowledge of Man*. New York: Harper and Row, 1965.
Articles relating Buber's philosophy of dialogue to the psychotherapeutic relationship.

CURRY, ANDREW. "Toward a Phenomenological Study of the Family," *Existential Psychiatry*, Vol. 6, No. 27 (Spring 1967), pp. 35–44.
The effects of existential despair upon family life, described as a "web of unrelatedness."

FRANKL, VIKTOR E. *The Doctor and the Soul. From Psychotherapy to Logotherapy*. New York: Knopf, 1965.
A very readable development of existential psychology in comparison with other psychologies and its application in therapeutic practice.

KRILL, DONALD F. *Existential Social Work*. N.Y.: Free Press, 1978.
A delineation of existential and related thought to both theory and practice in social work. An eclectic-interpersonal perspective is emphasized.

SINSHEIMER, ROBERT. "The Existential Casework Relationship," *Social Casework*, Vol. 50, No. 2 (February, 1969), pp. 67–73.
Concepts from existential psychology are related to the casework relationship in terms of the I–thou dialogue and encounter.

STRETCH, JOHN. "Existentialism: A Proposed Philosophical Orientation for Social Work," *Social Work*, Vol. 12, No. 4 (October 1967), pp. 97–102.
Existentialism provides a view of life that accepts the perennial crises of people as opposed to utopian hopes of a secured society.

SUTHERLAND, RICHARD. "Choosing as Therapeutic Aim, Method and Philosophy," *Existential Psychiatry*, Vol. 2, No. 8 (Spring 1968), pp. 371–392.
The applicability of the concept of freedom of choice in specific techniques of psychotherapy.

WEISS, DAVID. "Social Work as Healing and Revealing," *Intervention*, No. 50 (Summer 1970). Development of Buber's philosophy of dialogue according to the concepts of Being, Becoming, Belonging and Sympathy, Empathy and Compathy.

CHAPTER 9

Communication Theory and Social Work Treatment

Judith C. Nelsen

Communication theory is not really a single theory but rather a designation covering a number of loosely related areas of study. Some of these are concerned with ways in which information is transmitted, while others consider the effects of information on mechanical or human systems. Since social workers are primarily interested in human functioning, this chapter addresses only those areas of communication theory that examine how people are influenced by information from within themselves and their environments, and how they communicate or exchange information, thus influencing each other. Emphasis in the latter discussion is on interpersonal influence in face-to-face interaction rather than mass communication or the technical study of language as in linguistics or semantics. Consideration is given to both verbal and nonverbal communication and to the influence of the context in which communication occurs.

Communication theory has had considerable impact on the social work treatment of marital pairs and families. Development of the theory and its applications in marital and family work still continues at an exciting pace. Beyond this, some social workers have been interested in using communication theory as a metatheory to conceptualize diverse influences on human functioning and generic practice processes. A few have picked up specific aspects of the theory to elucidate specific aspects of individual, group, or community work, such as by examining messages clients may receive from the physical settings in which practice occurs (56). By and large, however, social workers' use of communication theory other than in marital and family treatment is a promising potential still to be realized.

Some of the assertions of communication theory to be discussed below have been validated through research, while others have not. The theory can be useful in generating research hypotheses as well as in offering new insights to practitioners abut general and selected aspects of their work.

Theoretical Concepts and Principles

The study of how information available to human beings affects their functioning has, in a sense, been ongoing since the dawn of man. Authors developing theory about this influence in the 1940s and 1950s broadly took as their domain of interest all internal or external stimuli that can affect people in any way. The further emphasis of social and behavioral scientists utilizing the theory has been on the cognitive processes through which people often mediate their response; that is, it is on understanding how people receive information from their own feelings, thoughts, memories, physical sensations, and environments; how they evaluate this information; and how they subsequently act.

Communication theorists have also moved to examine more closely the question of how people immediately influence each other. Some have focused attention on the patterns of communication or behavior that tend to develop when people interact over time and on the impact these patterns can have on participants. Some have looked at the effectiveness of people's communication in conveying needed information. Still others have noted the special impact of nonverbal communication and of the context within which any communication occurs.

Since communication theory looks at individual and social system functioning as well as the influence of the environment, it can be compared with the personality theories, theories of social interaction, and ecological theories social workers currently use. Further, communication theory seeks to explain what causes people to change either naturally or in response to therapeutic intervention. Social work practice models must also inevitably be concerned with this issue.

Why Individuals Function as They Do

Drawing upon earlier, more complex formulations about the effects of information on any system (6, 58, 63), social and behavioral scientists—especially Jurgen Ruesch (49, 51), Gregory Bateson (3, 51), and Karl Deutsch (8, 9)—have written specifically about how information influences human functioning. They define *information* very broadly as including anything people perceive from their environments or from within themselves. All that one sees or hears is information, including observations of the world, what one reads, one's own image in a mirror, one's own voice and the voices of others, sounds of machines, and so on. Whatever people taste or smell and their bodily sensations—such as hunger, pain, or sexual satisfaction—are information. Perceptions of one's own feelings, thoughts, and knowlege stored in memory are considered to be information as well. People need not be conscious of their perceptions to receive information from them, and in any given instance the information received may or may not be accurate. A five-year-old who hears his parents say that the police will take him to jail if he misbehaves may believe them even though their statement is untrue.

The way people *process information* determines its ultimate effect on their functioning. First, they perceive only some of the vast amounts of potential information available to them at a given time. But as they constantly receive perceptions, they evaluate each against all other incoming information and relevant data stored in memory and decide whether to reject, store, or immediately act on it. A driver who sees a light turning yellow evaluates this information against other immediate perceptions and past experiences with yellow lights. Within an instant, he chooses to respond by disregarding the light or by braking or accelerating. As people act, they perceive and evaluate the effects of their actions on their environment and themselves as *feedback*, further information that they will use to determine how to behave next. All these processes are ongoing as people keep having access to potential new information, perceive some of it, think, act, and evaluate the results of their actions.

Over time, people store in memory not only vast amounts of information about themselves and the world, but also what they have learned about how to process information. Their implicit *rules for information processing* help them determine what potentially available data they will perceive or ignore, what new information they will accept and use rather than reject, and the like. These rules influence their ways of dealing with information stemming both from their environments and from within themselves. A father does or does not notice his children's expressions of need for his support. A woman with anorexia nervosa does not perceive or accurately evaluate her physical sensations of hunger and perhaps her sexual feelings as well. People mainly learn their rules for information processing from past and present interpersonal experiences, which are in turn strongly influenced by the values of their sociocultural groups and of the larger society. How much a woman is aware of dust in her home probably depends on how much her past and current relatives and friends, influenced by their own cultural values, have inculcated the idea that a dust-free house is "good" and is her responsibility.

CONDITIONS FOR HEALTHY FUNCTIONING. These ideas suggest that people should be able to function adequately when certain conditions obtain.

One is that information available from their environments and from within themselves be such that reasonable adaptation or coping is possible; that is, people should not be faced with overwhelming or unmanageable environmental information—they will have to go without shelter or food—or overwhelming information from within themselves—their feelings are out of control. Sometimes it is the combination of external and internal information that may be overwhelming, as when a pregnant teenager does not believe in abortion but will lose her parents' love if she keeps the baby.

In addition, effective functioning depends on people having sufficient accurate information stored in memory to guide them appropriately in new situations, and on their being able to reasonably and accurately perceive and evaluate available information that could be useful to them. Their prior life experiences will largely govern the amount of accurate information they have stored in memory. A young married woman may contemplate having an affair to "let my husband know he's not giving me enough attention" because she has not heard about or thought about the possibility of openly discussing her need for attention with him. However, her learned rules for information processing might determine whether she could accurately hear or constructively react to a suggestion that she proceed differently. For example, she might have learned not to be conscious of her own feelings of anger, even though they play a significant role in her wish to have an affair. When people are not conscious of particular information they have on hand or have stored from the past, they may reject new information that conflicts with it, to the detriment of their coping. The man who learned in childhood that women will reject him if he allows himself to be dependent on them yet who is not conscious of this belief may never test its validity or may not "see" evidence to the contrary.

Material reviewed so far does not constitute a personality theory per se, but it is concerned with why people function as they do and why their functioning may change; that is, theory articulated by Ruesch and others posits that people act based on available information as they perceive and evaluate it. They will change their function when available information suggests the desirability of doing so as long as they can perceive and evaluate this information accurately. Ruesch draws the further implication that therapeutic help involves offering people new information that they can use to solve their problems or teaching them to process information differently (49, 50).

Comparison to other practice theories and models.   The theories of human functioning and practice models most social workers use are compatible with this conceptual framework, supplementing rather than contradicting it. Thus, psychodynamic theory highlights the kind of troubles people can have when their rules for information processing do not allow certain information stored in memory to be retrieved and examined, especially if the earlier learning is inapplicable in present circumstances. The woman who learned in childhood that assertiveness was dangerous may not even be aware of or may reject later evidence contradicting this belief. Psychodynamic therapy, by removing clients' blocks to consciousness, allows them to begin to process information differently. Psychosocial treatment adds to this perspective the idea that practitioners need to assess information clients are receiving from their current environments and often must make new information available to them. Behavioral or learning theories (55) suggest that people may have problems due to insufficient or inaccurate knowledge about how to behave more effectively, old learning that stands in the way of new, or their behavior actually being adaptive to information they are receiving in their environments. Helping professionals using a treatment model based on learning theories may give new information that clients can use to function differently, may try to remove information processing blocks, or may try to change what is happening in clients' environments.

These and other concepts of communication theory also build on general systems theory, an overarching or metatheoretical framework much favored by social workers in recent years. If human systems are influenced by their environments, including other systems, this influence occurs largely through the input of information. If such systems influence their environments in turn, there has been an exchange of information. Elements within a social system, including individual human beings, also influence each other through exchanging information or communicating. Social systems, in fact, maintain organization and equilibrium in their functioning through communication, a matter we now address.

Communication in Small Social Systems

People who interact influence each other through the information they exchange. Important further ideas about how they do so have been put forth by theorists examining the rules or norms that come to govern interaction. Pioneers in this area of theory development have been Gregory Bateson, Don D. Jackson, Jay Haley, Paul Watzlawick, John Weakland, and Virginia Satir, all participants in either or both of two interrelated projects carried out in Palo Alto, California, in the 1950s and 1960s (18, 23, 24, 61). The Palo Alto theorists' beginning premise was that "One cannot *not* communicate" (61, p. 49). Whenever people are aware of each other's presence, their behavior conveys information even if they do not speak. In fact, these theorists use the terms "communication" and "behavior" synonomously. They contrast digital or speech communication, which is precise but abstract, with analogic communication, that occurring through behavior, which is more compelling but also more ambiguous.

A key notion of the Palo Alto theorists is that all communication between people conveys not only its obvious content but also implicit or explicit messages attempting to define the nature of the participants' *relationship*. If a woman comments that a friend is wearing eye makeup, she has not only conveyed that she sees the makeup. Her statement tends to define their relationship as one in which she is allowed to comment on such intimate aspects of her friend's appearance. The content of any communication, verbal or nonverbal, implies, "I am allowed to say this to you in this way," or "I am allowed to act in this way while we are together." The receiver of the communication may then accept it, reject it, or make an ambiguous response.

Much of people's communication merely redundantly confirms long-established rules about what can go on in a relationship. But one's words or actions may also seek to broaden or challenge the definition of an existing relationship. For example, if topics of conversation in the friendship mentioned above had so far been limited to events in the two women's work setting and public events such as the weather, the comment about the eye makeup would have proposed that their relationship include discussion of more personal content than before. At such times the response of the relationship partner is especially noteworthy. The second woman saying "That's none of your business" would be a clear rejection of the new relationship definition. But a "yes" offered in a disapproving tone and followed by a quick change back to a more public topic could get the same message across only slightly less clearly.

One aspect of a relationship that may be especially important to define is people's relative power or control. The statements "Take out the garbage" and "Would you mind taking out the garbage" convey very similar content, but the implied relationship definition is quite different in the two instances. The Palo Alto theorists posit that at any given time, communication tends to define a relationship between two people as *symmetrical*, with the two having equal power, or *complementary*, with one party in the one-up position and the other one-down. Some relationships, such as that of a parent with a young child, appropriately are complementary although the parent and child should move toward being more symmetrical as the child grows up. No relationship is defined entirely in one way or the other. For example, the relationship between two marital partners may usually be symmetrical. But each may have more power in regard to certain aspects of their life together and each will probably assume a benign parental role at times, as by comforting the other.

In continuing relationships involving more than two people, everyone's verbal and nonverbal behavior tends to define what each participant is allowed to say and do and what power each has in regard to all the others. In fact, the members of any ongoing dyad or other small social system develop regular patterns or sequences of behavior that can be objectively observed. From these, inferences can be made about who can do what when; that is, about the system's operating norms or rules. Since all members of a social system participate in its behavior patterns, all can be seen as upholding its operating rules. Based on these notions, the Palo Alto theorists have made highly significant contributions to the conceptualization of family system processes. Don D. Jackson especially has elaborated ideas now widely accepted and used about patterns of family interaction, family operating rules, and how communication tends to maintain homeostasis in the family system (22, 23).

DYSFUNCTIONAL COMMUNICATION AND ITS TREATMENT. A specific concern of the Palo Alto theorists was to understand how family communication patterns might be related to schizophrenia. Their early observations spawned the famous double bind theory (23, 24), about the inherent destructiveness of someone offering two contradictory messages combined with a third that prohibited the recipient from noticing the contradiction or leaving the field. As their interest in patterns of family interaction grew, they noted that everyone in a family with a schizophrenic member may participate in creating double binds. Eventually, as the double-bind theory was questioned, these theorists focused less on the idea that family interaction patterns cause schizophrenia and more on stating how they seem to maintain it. For example, the schizophrenic individual often produces symptoms when the parents have been made anxious, as if the operating rule is that he must protect them by diverting attention from them at such times.

The Palo Alto theorists' search to understand the function of pathological symptoms in human relationships also led to their identification of *paradox* as a major therapeutic strategy (18, 61). If communication within any relationship serves to define who is in control, they reasoned, symptoms allow people to maintain control of certain aspects of their relationships with others without having to assume responsibility for doing so. A woman's hand-washing compulsion, which she really cannot help, may nonetheless prevent her from being able to clean the house as thoroughly as her overbearing husband wishes. A further implication of this idea is that when clients enter a relationship with a psychotherapist, whose sole purpose is to help them change, their inability to get over their symptoms could tend again to place them in control. Haley deduced, however, that all effective therapists confound this control mechanism by allowing or even encouraging clients to continue having their symptoms. For example, psychoanalysts may tell patients that they will not lose their symptoms for quite a while; indeed, that it will be important to observe the symptoms to see when they occur. By such means, clients are placed in a therapeutic paradox. If they continue manifesting their symptoms, they are obeying the therapist and therefore have given up being in control. The symptoms are no longer serving their purpose and can disappear. If they stop showing their symptomatic behavior to defy the therapist, they have changed as the therapist obviously ultimately wishes.

While some of the Palo Alto theorists were interested in syntactic and semantic qualities of family communication such as its clarity, directness, and completeness in conveying given information, most eventually looked more at family interaction patterns and rules. The exception was Virginia Satir, a social worker, who has continued to emphasize the importance of "good" or constructive communication to healthy family functioning. Early on, Satir began to identify a compendium of communication problems marital pairs and families often show and to describe effective communication (53). Her later works, including a book with linguistic experts Richard Bandler and John Grinder (2), have explored further the properties of problematic and successful family communication and have suggested how family therapists can promote the latter.

In recent years many marital therapists and, to a lesser degree, family therapists besides Satir have used an understanding of the formal qualities of effective or dysfunctional communication in deciding how to help their clients. A number of concepts introduced by the original Palo Alto theorists have also been developed further by Jay Haley, John Weakland and Richard Fisch, a group led by Mara Selvini Palazzoli in Milan, and others. These later contributions, including several by Satir and other social workers, will be elaborated below.

COMPARISON WITH GROUP AND ORGANIZATIONAL THEORIES.   Theories social workers have traditionally used to understand the functioning of small groups and organizations again supplement or parallel many of the Palo Alto theorists' ideas. The notion that patterns of interaction, implicit rules or norms, homeostatic mechanisms, and power negotiations are important aspects of system functioning is not new to group and community practitioners. The value of the communications concepts in such practice may be twofold, however. For one thing, the Palo Alto theorists' ideas about symmetry, complementarity, and paradox may offer group and community practitioners some new ways of looking at their work. For another, the communications terms provide a common vocabulary into which the different languages of casework, group work, and community practice can be translated to highlight their generic base. More will be said shortly about these possibilities.

Nonverbal Communication and Context

People's nonverbal communication through such means as facial expression, gesture, and posture can be considered as a context within which verbal messages are offered and interpreted as well as being a potent form of communication in itself. Voice tone and such sounds as laughter or sighs, technically classified as nonlexical rather than nonverbal communication, also tend to modify speech. Additional aspects of context that communication theorists have identified as having an impact on people's interpersonal interaction are their use of space and time, how they look, and attributes of the physical setting in which they meet. Finally, in a larger sense, all that people do during an interaction and all that they bring to it, including their understanding of what has already happened between them, serves as a context within which they interpret continuing messages.

Those who have pioneered in the study of nonverbal and nonlexical communication include especially Ray Birdwhistell (4), Albert Scheflen (54), and Jurgen Ruesch and Weldon Kees (52). These theorists posited that members of a given culture unknowingly learn a common system of paralinguistic modifiers and an entire nonverbal language of gestures, postures, and facial expressions in which "every little movement has a meaning of its own." One of the major functions of body movement and paralinguistic verbalizations is to accompany speech (26). Gestures may illustrate something that is being said. Facial expressions that convey emotion can augment verbal statements about feelings. Movements of the head, face, and hands, as well as voice tone can accent speech or regulate turn-taking in a conversation. Interestingly, however, people tend to view voice tone and body movement as more honest and trustworthy forms of communication than speech because they assume these cannot be fabricated as easily as words can be (61). The declaration "I love you" is not likely to be believed if it is accompanied by a posture of leaning away, a cold or "shifty-eyed" expression, or the like. On the other hand, warms looks, touching, a trembling smile, and other nonverbal communication that constitutes "the language of love" will make the words believable or even convey that strong affection or love probably exist when nothing is said.

Unfortunately, people's nonverbal communication is ambiguous in many situations and is actually quite subject to being misunderstood. A head may be bowed in sorrow, suppression of a laugh, or sleepy disinterest. When participants in an interaction come from different sociocultural backgrounds, the potential for misunderstandings is even greater (28, 35, 44). The Hispanic boy learns at home to show parents or other authority figures respect by never looking them in the eye (54). When the same boy looks down while being addressed by a non-Hispanic teacher, the teacher labels him as deliberately evasive and disrespectful.

Troubles can also arise when people do not attend to all aspects of each other's verbal and nonverbal communication or when what is conveyed via these communication modes is contradictory. Bandler, Grinder, and Satir (2) have suggested that individuals develop preferred "representational systems" that make them pay attention to what others convey mainly through one of three major communication channels: auditory, visual, or kinesthetic (tactile). A visually oriented wife may complain to her husband, "You always look bored when I'm talking to you," and may incorrectly infer his lack of interest and his lack of love for her. Her more "kinesthetic" husband may believe she does not love him because she rarely touches him except during sexual encounters. Satir, both with Bandler and Grinder and in her other writings, further sees incongruity between verbal and nonverbal communication as a major reason why members of some families cannot get along. A primary goal of her family therapy is "congruent communication" in which people's verbal and nonverbal messages are not contradictory.

SPACE, TIME, AND OTHER ASPECTS OF CONTEXT.   The study of nonverbal communication also includes attention to people's use of interpersonal space and time. Theorists Edward Hall (20, 21) and Albert Scheflen (54) have made important original contributions here. How close to another person one is comfortable standing or sitting depends partly on whether one views the relationship as a public or impersonal one, as businesslike, as more personal such as with most friends and family members, or as intimate. However, one's use of interpersonal space is often socioculturally determined. A Jew is comfortable standing closer to a friend in conversation than is a WASP, so much so that the issue of appropriate distance between them may create discomfort until it is worked out. Social class and gender differences can also be found (26, 34). Within situations where space is limited yet relationships between people are not personal or intimate, members of a culture learn rigid rules as to how available space is to be managed, although most have never thought about these rules consciously. Human behavior in an elevator as it becomes more and more crowded illustrates this assertion.

People's use of time is influenced by culture as well. As Hall points out, the majority culture in the U.S. tends to think of time as a ribbon stretching from the past into the future, to be cut into pieces and used for specific purposes (21). People of many other cultures are more oriented to activities and human relationships, with less attention to the time these occupy.

A number of theorists (26, 31, 45) have examined the ways in which people's physical appearance and the immediate physical surroundings in which interaction occurs communicate something and serve as a context in which verbal and other nonverbal communication can be understood. For example, people interpret from others' dress and grooming whether they are seeking a more casual or more formal relationship, whether they "cared enough" to dress neatly, and even whether they may be sexually available. Even relatively immutable physical characteristics may be taken as communicating something about people's personalities or functioning, as when a redhead is expected to have a strong temper. When one participant in an interaction presumably has arranged or decorated a space, inferences may also be drawn as to her temperament, approachability, or the like. Certainly an individual's immediate physical surroundings influence her interaction. Communication theorists as well as interior designers and architects know that arrangements of chairs and tables in a room, the brightness of light, and so on can strongly affect how people behave.

Some social work authors have recently attempted to add to systems theory an ecological perspective, concerned with "the structure of the environment and the nature of its . . . influence" (16, p. 8). Those aspects of theory about nonverbal communication that address the influence of the immediate physical setting on human interaction are especially compatible with this ecological approach.

In fact, people probably consider all of their own and each other's attributes, circumstances, and behavior as well as what has already occurred between them in interpreting any new communication (61). The woman who touches the arm of a man and says, "Thank you, that meant a lot to me," might be perceived as more or less likely to be making a sexual advance depending on the tone of voice, facial expression, posture, the nature of the touch, what she was wearing, the time of day, and the place. But their prior interaction and all of their other circumstances would certainly have an influence as well. If what the man had just done was to offer the woman sympathy for the recent death of a family member, the touch is less likely to be interpreted as a sexual advance. If the man were her relative, minister, or physician, such an interpretation would be even less likely.

Uses of Communication Theory in Social Work

Social work practitioners have used or can use communication theory in a number of ways. One is as a metatheory conceptualizing generic elements of social work assessment and treatment, especially for teaching purposes. Then, already highly developed is use of the theory in understanding and treating marital couples and families. A number of particular communications concepts can also illuminate specific aspects of social work practice that are important to the whole, such as that of cross-cultural understanding.

Communication Theory as a Conceptual Framework for Social Work Practice

The concepts and principles of communication theory elaborated so far can be used to conceptualize generically why social workers' clients may have trouble functioning and what can be done to help them (39).

As noted earlier, people sometimes have problems because information available to them from their environments or within themselves is overwhelming or otherwise such that they should not be expected to manage it. Examples are an individual feeling an irresistible urge to commit suicide, a family lacking enough money for food, or a group facing discrimination based on race, sex, or age. Here, social workers may try to intervene directly in clients' environments to make more benign information available or to ensure environmental protection, such as through hospitalization, when clients cannot manage internal information in any other way.

As a second possibility, clients may not be able to function effectively because they do not have sufficient accurate information about how to do so. A teenage mother may not know how to care for her baby. A man may not know how to deal with anger except through fighting, which loses him jobs. A family may not know how to cope with the mother's alcoholism, or a community group may not know how to get adverse zoning laws changed. In each of these instances, social work interventions may be designed, at least in part, to give clients new information they can use to function better or to direct them to where they can find the new information they need. One area of communication theory is how people are influenced by information from their environments. Here are instances where individuals do not know how to obtain information from their environments, and the social worker then aids clients in obtaining it. Sometimes, practitioners' interventions take the form of questions that focus clients' attention on data they already possess but have not used in resolving a problem. A client who feels uncomfortable dealing with his new female boss may, when asked, realize his discomfort stems from a belief that he should not be taking orders from a woman. He may be able to lessen the influence of this belief once he becomes aware of it.

When clients are unable to make use of their own information or of new information made available to them, the problem may lie with their rules for information processing, with operating rules in their small social systems, or both. Social workers may help in some cases by offering ideas about how clients can process information differently or how a social system can change its operating rules. For example, a woman who did not know how to perceive what her own feelings were might be taught to do so. Parents perpetuating the family operating rule that children are given attention only for negative behavior could be helped to change. Such efforts may involve helping clients examine conflicts between new information they are having trouble using and their feelings, what they have learned in the past, or what they think others in their social systems will tolerate. A man whose fiancée wants to be closer to him may need to become aware that he evaluates this information as dangerous because he learned from early childhood experiences with women that attempts at dominance inevitably accompany closeness.

Social work interventions include more than changing clients' environments and offering them new information verbally. Since people's nonverbal communication or behavior conveys information in a more compelling way than their words, clients learn further from what practitioners do. For one thing, they will judge practitioners' sincerity by the practitioners' tone of voice and facial expressions as well as by their words. Then, clients gain new information when practitioners model how another human being can process information and act. Many a mother has learned how to be more nurturing toward her children by observing her social worker interact with her. Clients also learn through being able to try different behaviors with social workers and evaluating how they respond. The woman who tries to be more assertive and perceives her social worker's acceptance of this may be able to take a small step toward becoming more assertive in other relationships.

Finally, clients, with the encouragement of the social worker, sometimes can best receive new information by risking change in role plays or in real life and receiving feedback from others and from within themselves that promotes further change. Techniques like having group members touch or family members "sculpt" ways they would like to interact can promote new experiences. Or social workers may themselves behave in ways designed to bring about changes in family or group operating rules, such as by talking about forbidden topics.

The Communications Framework as a Teaching Tool

A generic communications framework for practice can be especially useful as a teaching tool. Students can be helped to see that clients' problematic functioning is not random or foolish but must in some way "make sense" based on information available to the clients, their ways of processing that information, or the rules of the small social system to which they belong. Key questions for assessment are: What information may clients have stored in memory or might they be presently receiving that could lead to the kind of behavior they show? Are their ways of processing information or operating rules in their small social system perhaps preventing their receiving new information that should be useful to them, including information offered by the social worker? When these questions have been answered, some intervention possibilities should be implied; that is, practitioners should have some idea of whether to intervene with clients' environments to change information available to them there, to offer clients new information directly, or to try to help them change their information processing or small system operating rules. An important further issue is how any new information the social worker intends to offer can best be gotten across, verbally or through behavior. A case vignette may illustrate some of these points.

> Mrs. J., thirty-eight, came for social work help because her teenage daughter was defiant and having trouble in school. The daughter, Sandy, sixteen, refused to come in. Mrs. J. was dealing with Sandy by threatening to make her go live with her father even though the father had proven to be an unreliable caretaker in the past. Mother and daughter were living at just about the poverty level, with Mrs. J. working long hours as a waitress even to manage that.
>
> After learning more about what went on between Mrs. J. and Sandy, the social worker assigned to the case asked herself what information Mrs. J. might be operating on to be coping with Sandy as she was. For one thing, while information from this client's environment was not totally unmanageable, to deal with it was probably sapping some of the energy she might otherwise have had to better cope with Sandy. The social worker asked Mrs. J. how she decided to deal with Sandy by threatening to send her to her father. The immediate response was "She deserves it," indicating that Mrs. J. was, at least in part, being influenced by internal information that she was very angry at her daughter. Further probing revealed that Mrs. J. had already tried other ways to deal with Sandy, such as the kinds of severe punishment her

mother used to give to her, and these had not worked. Besides, a friend had suggested Sandy might be better off with her dad.

Believing that part of Mrs. J's problem was inaccurate or insufficient information about how to deal effectively with her daughter, the social worker offered her some new ideas on how to try to talk to Sandy about what was happening between them. Mrs. J. rejected this new information outright and when asked why responded that Sandy did not deserve being talked to because she was bad. The social worker decided Mrs. J. was having trouble processing the new information the social worker had offered because it conflicted with ideas Mrs. J. already had on hand and with her anger. Mrs. J. perhaps, had to become more aware of these conflicting factors to make a sound decision about how to proceed.

Use of Communication Theory in Marital Treatment

Interestingly, the use of communications concepts in work with couples and with families has for the most part been divergent. Marital therapists from social work and other disciplines almost always assess how effective or dysfunctional a couple's communication is. Whether their primary orientation is psychodynamic (1), behaviorist (60), or eclectic (29), most believe that a major source of marital partners' troubles is their inability to communicate well enough to solve the problems people who live together in an intimate relationship must manage. For example, couples may be too involved in attaching blame for what has gone on between them as well as labeling each other's character traits as bad than in saying specifically, in behavioral terms, what they do not like about each other's behavior and how they want it to be different. What they do say may be ambiguous or confused. They may make too few positive statements about each other and too many negative ones, and so on.

After determining how marital partners' communication is dysfunctional, a practitioner may initiate their setting a goal, if the couple has not done so already, of "better communication." This outcome need not be vague and general but can be spelled out in very specific terms. Most marital therapists make the assumption, at least until proven otherwise, that a couple is likely to be having trouble partly or wholly because they do not know how to communicate more effectively; that is, it is assumed that the spouses lack sufficient accurate information about how to communicate well enough to accomplish problem-solving. The prescribed intervention strategy is for a practitioner literally to teach new comunication skills. He may verbally offer the couple information about how to communicate differently, may model the new skills, and may ask the couple to try using the new skills, with coaching in treatment interviews and later by themselves at home.

Bill and Joan were arguing about how much time she spends with her family, with Bill claiming she is still tied to her mother's apron strings and Joan disagreeing. I stopped them and asked what was it about Joan being with her family that upset Bill. He said, "She always goes over there . . ." and I stopped him again, reminding him to talk about a specific instance and not in generalities. Finally it came out that Joan went to her folks this week on an evening when Bill had hoped to have some quiet time with her. She fired back, "You were just reading the paper—how did I know you wanted to spend time with me?" I suggested we play out what they both could say to each other to be clearer when such an evening came up again.

If couples balk at learning new ways to communicate, some marital therapists then focus treatment on individuals' intrapsychic issues. A possibility favored by behaviorists is to help the pair find a more constructive marital quid pro quo (55), Don D. Jackson's notion of a compromise based on "I'll do something for you if you do something for me." Some marital therapists also take into account the Palo Alto theorists' (61) belief that the content of a couple's communication may be less important then their use of it to regulate power in their relationship. Problems can result when the partners try to best each other or when one is almost always ahead in the one-up game to the extent that the other begins to lose personal identity or becomes seriously depressed.

Communications Concepts in Family Treatment

Practitioners who see families, as opposed to marital pairs, are less likely to make more effective family communication their main treatment goal. In fact, Virginia Satir (2, 53) is perhaps the only well-known family therapist who still focuses extensively on improving the quality of family members' communication—its clarity, specificity, and the like. Her techniques for doing so include directly teaching new communication skills, modeling these, giving family members tasks requiring them to communicate differently in sessions and at home, and "sculpturing" family members into body postures and movement caricaturing their problematic communication patterns to make them more aware of these. A number of practitioners, among them structural family therapists (36) and those doing family crisis treatment (43), do advocate helping families with their communication as a secondary focus of treatment.

The greater influence of communication theory on family practitioners has resulted from their picking up and expanding the two concepts of family rules and paradox. Most people doing family treatment deal with the family as a system and see the system's functioning as regulated by its operating rules, or members' implicit agreements about who can do what when. They may differ on which of these rules are most important to understand and influence in treatment, but not on the existence or significance of the rules. Psychodynamic theorists may examine and try to change family interaction patterns reflecting members' rules about the handling of dependency, anger, sexuality, closeness, and the like. Salvador Minuchin (36) and his followers are interested in rules governing family structures: who is enmeshed with or disengaged from whom, who can form coalitions, and who has what amount of power. Jay Haley and other strategic family therapists (19, 32) have been especially concerned with rules governing cross-generational coalitions and power hierachies. In all these instances, goals of treatment are to change existing dysfunctional family operating rules.

Many therapists try to do so through the use of paradox. A current generation of practitioner-theorists writing out of Palo Alto rely at least partly on paradoxical interventions in brief therapy with individuals, couples, and families (12). Jay Haley and Cloe Madanes's strategic family therapy model, often used along with structural family treatment, uses paradox as a main intervention strategy. So does an approach described by a social worker Peggy Papp of the Ackerman Institute for Family Therapy (41). Finally, the Milan group led by Mara Selvini Palazzoli (40) relies almost exclusively on paradox to free families with a schizophrenic member from operating rules that apparently perpetuate the identified patient's symptoms.

These therapists have developed, much further than the original Palo Alto theorists did, notions of when and how to use paradoxes effectively to alter dysfunctional family operating rules. The current Palo Alto group believe that it is people's attempts to solve problems that may not really have been so major in the first place that get them into more serious trouble. Thus, they paradoxically direct clients to try to bring on their problems. Since the clients usually cannot, they improve. Haley's use of paradoxes has been similar although he designs these to alter dysfunctional family hierarchies as well as to reduce symptoms. Madanes has broadened what Haley does to include encouraging one family member to pretend to have her symptoms and the others to pretend to respond as they usually do. Palazzoli and Papp redefine one individual's symptom and the family's operating rules that seem to require it as everyone's positive attempts to help each other, then prescribe that all continue as before.

Use of Theory on Nonverbal and Cross-Cultural Communication

Experienced social workers certainly pick up much that is meaningful in clients' nonverbal communication and are at least somewhat aware of how their own nonverbal communication and the immediate physical surroundings of an interview influence their interaction with clients. Those working with clients whose sociocultural backgrounds differ from their own usually know about some of the clients' different use of nonverbal communication. Still, practitioners' awareness of these matters is often more superficial and incomplete than it should be. Recent texts on basic social work practice skills (14, 25) have recognized this deficit and provided more discussion of nonverbal communication and contextual factors than earlier ones usually did. Beyond this, practitioners who do not have the time to become experts can still learn enough to offer service much more closely geared to clients' needs.

As one example, researchers have identified a type of nonverbal communication called an "adaptor" (26, p. 8), thought to develop in childhood as a means to try to handle emotions, social situations, and the like through bodily motion. Some adaptors apparently have similar meanings for many people. Covering the eyes seems to be associated with shame or guilt while scratching or picking at one's clothing may signal hostility. Restless movements of the hands or legs may reflect an impulse to take flight from closeness in an interpersonal relationship. Practitioners aware of these possibilities or of the fact that clients' idiosyncratic body movements may have symbolic meaning are in a position to understand their clients more fully than if they attend closely only to their words. While some authors have described potential meanings of nonverbal communication in psychotherapy (59), only a few (27, 33, 56) have attempted to suggest what social workers could benefit by knowing from the vast material available on nonverbal communication and context.

The field has paid more attention to verbal, and to some extent nonverbal, communication between practitioners and clients whose race, ethnic background, or social class differs. A number of books (14, 25) and articles (15, 35, 57) caution against the use of words that may mean different things to practitioners and clients or that may have no meaning to clients, simply confounding them and increasing their sense of powerlessness. Several of these works also note that practitioners and clients can misread each other's nonverbal communication. For example, black clients may be comfortable with less eye contact than white practitioners or may distrust while practitioners who smile at them before they get to know them (35). One text that addresses the area of interracial communication (47) relies extensively on communication theory to consider how different life experiences and language usage may shape the way members of different races perceive and evaluate new information. Ths author makes the further important point that members of different races, whose opportunities for verbal interaction may be limited or fraught with distrust, may especially search each other's nonverbal communication to try to understand what the other is "really" like. Yet their nonverbal "languages" may be different and subject to misunderstandings. Social work practitioners need to be highly cognizant of such data.

Understanding Operating Rules in Treatment

While group and community practitioners have had theories highlighting the importance of group norms, those who work with individual clients have had only the very limited theory of transference to help them examine operating rules that develop in the dyadic treatment relationship. Utilizing the Palo Alto theorists' ideas, such practitioners can recognize that all they do with clients, and their responses to what clients do, is to propose rules as to what can go on in treatment. For example, do workers explicitly state that clients can ask questions about what is happening in treatment or that the clients can object if they disagree? Does a caseworker's response when clients do ask questions, disagree, talk about their and the caseworker's racial differences, or bring up other touchy matters convey that such discussion really is allowed?

Then, both in dyadic treatment relationships and in groups, the concepts of symmetry and complementarity can clarify power issues that inevitably arise. Many clients have considerable aversion to being in a one-down position to an authority figure—adolescents and individuals diagnosed with borderline personality disorder especially come to mind. Their fears can often be prevented or at least calmed if the social workers who see the clients project expertise in areas of the interaction that are rightly within their domain, but speak from a symmetrical or even one-down position. Doing so suggests an operating rule that the treatment relationship will not be one in which the social workers will use their expertise to dominate or control clients. To convey such a proposed operating rule, a worker might say something like, "This is what I think, but it's up to you whether you want to accept it."

At the opposite extreme, some clients present themselves in such a one-down way that they seem to want to place all responsibility in the hands of their social workers to run the treatment interviews and even, at times, to make important life decisions for them. Passive, dependent, and depressed clients and some schizophrenic clients can present this problem. Social workers may be very good at telling clients that they will have to take a more active role if they want to help themselves in treatment, but a knowledge of theory about symmetry and complementarity can assist them in figuring out how to convey the same message through their actions, a medium clients are more likely to believe. Thus, to name only a few possibilities, the social worker with a passive, dependent client might need to hold back from offering suggestions, reward any reasonably constructive actions by the client with considerable attention, and, if they can be genuine, make comments such as, "I couldn't have thought of that." When it becomes necessary to offer some new ideas to such a client, the social worker might do so from as one-down a stance as possible, as in, "This may not be much help but. . . ."

Clients whose personality style is to be one-down are sometimes more expert than their social workers can be at co-opting this stance in a dyadic relationship. One possible solution is to place them together in a group, where not all can succeed at being the most one-down. When some clients therefore become more assertive, they and others may learn that doing so does not lead to the dire results they feared. Although not conceptualized in communication theory terms, this approach to group treatment of depressed clients is well illustrated in an article by social workers Baruch Levine and Judith Schild (30). Further discussion of how social workers' communication in interviews serves to define operating rules of their relationships with clients, including rules about symmetry and complementarity, may be found in *Communication Theory and Social Work Practice* (39).

More Attention to the Use of Paradox

Another important application of communication concepts to social work treatment can be in the use of paradoxes with individuals, groups, and community groups rather than just with families. Lynn Segal, a social worker, is one of the current Palo Alto therapists using paradoxical interventions with individuals as well as families. Behavioral social workers also employ paradoxes with clients in other than family treatment (55). Otherwise, this possibility remains largely unexplored. The reason may be that most caseworkers and group workers use more traditional practice models and have other means with which to deal with clients' resistance or recalcitrance to change. Some also question the ethics of prescribing symptoms or otherwise telling clients to keep behaving in ways that are obviously dysfunctional for them. Perhaps what should occur is not the more widespread use of the type of paradoxes family therapists employ but an adaptation of the technique to work with individuals and groups.

Further, it may be useful to recognize that traditional social work interventions can have a paradoxical element at times and to explore when and how this element might be maximized. For example, psychosocial caseworkers may be very comfortable telling clients things like, "You're not going to be able to change overnight," or "Maybe we've been trying to move along too fast; let's slow down a little and see if that helps." Both these statements are at least mildly paradoxical because they encourage clients not to try to change just then. Developing a better understanding of such statements as paradoxes might be a step toward knowing better when and how to use them.

Research on Communication Theory

The merit of any social or behavioral science theory is demonstrated not only by its apparent utility to those who seek to understand and influence human functioning. Valid further questions are whether assertions of the theory have been tested through research or, if not, whether the theory at least can generate interesting and testable hypotheses.

Research on the Effects of Information

The basic concepts and principles of communication theory discussed above vary widely in how much they have been tested in methodologically sound research. The framework developed by Jurgen Ruesch and others to conceptualize how information and information processing affect human functioning is at too high a level of abstraction to be proven or disproven empirically. However, it can help researchers generate testable hypotheses.

For example, based on such theory, a social worker planning a single-subject multiple baseline design study might generate a hypothesis that several clients were behaving in a particular dysfunctional way because they lacked certain information that could help them see how to behave differently. The practitioner might further speculate that the clients would be able to process this new information if it was offered to them. Having measured the frequency of the clients' dysfunctional behavior over time, the social worker might offer them the new information and continue measuring as before. A significant decrease in the rate of the behavior for each client just after the new information was offered would suggest that the hypothesis was correct. I have elsewhere suggested a number of ways in which use of communication theory as a metatheory for understanding clients' functioning and generic practice processes can help practitioners identify potential study variables for single-subject research (38).

Of course, while communication theory cannot be claimed as the impetus, thousands of studies within psychology, medicine, and related fields have examined how people perceive new information, what influences their perceptions, how they evaluate incoming information, and so on.

Research on Interpersonal Communication

In the 1950s and early 1960s, theorists associated with the original Palo Alto projects counted research on family communication as one of their major endeavors. Much of what was done was in the style of other family research going on at the time; that is, it consisted of careful clinical observation but no objective measurement of variables. However, attempts eventually were made (23) to find valid and reliable ways to study both selected qualities of family communication, such as its clarity, and family interaction variables, such as symmetry and complementarity. Jay Haley even found a way to measure coalitions in families with and without a schizophrenic member by having the parents and child press buttons in a coalition "game." Most of these efforts, except for Haley's, did not result in actual studies but the researchers' excitement in looking at whole families rather than at individuals and their creative attempts to objectify important family interaction variables were apparent.

Many others have since done research on family communication and have obtained some interesting results, often replicated reasonably closely over several studies (10). Families without a symptomatic member and who are therefore presumed healthier have shown certain characteristic patterns distinguishing them from families in which at least one member has identifiable problems. The healthier families tend to agree more with each other's statements, offer each other more support, and show more use of humor or laughter. They also show fewer cross-generational coalitions when coalitions are defined through such measures as who speaks most to whom. In families with a schizophrenic member, there are more confused messages than in other families. Of course, one must keep in mind that the direction of these associations has not been established.

Some studies have examined symmetry and complementarity in marital pairs and in groups (7, 11, 13, 42, 48). Studies of marital communication problems also abound, although it is less clear that most of these have been stimulated by communication theory per se. Fairly numerous are research reports supporting the notion that teaching couples new communication skills during treatment increases their marital satisfaction (17). Consistent with enhancement of family communication skills not being a significant focus of most family treatment, virtually no major studies have been done to determine the value of helping families improve their communication.

Much of the large body of research studying how treatment processes affect clients seen individually, as families, or in groups is concerned with "communication" between practitioners and clients or among clients. But again, concepts actually derived from communication theory do not generally seem to have influenced study hypotheses. Some studies done by social workers do examine symmetrical and complementary relationship messages exchanged between clients and practitioners (46) or between students and field instructors (37). In these, congruence or agreement between role partners about how symmetrical or complementary their relationship will be seems to be correlated with other measures of their comfort or compatibility in working together. In spite of the widespread use of paradox by family practitioners, there have been no methodologically sound major research studies on the use of this technique with families. Some studies have examined the use of paradox with individuals undergoing behavioral treatment (62). Given the potential power of practitioner relationship messages in general and of paradoxes in particular to influence clients, further research examination of these variables would seem to promise useful results.

Of the several areas of communication study reviewed earlier, theory about nonverbal communication has directly stimulated by far the greatest amount of research (5, 26, 44). Essentially, this has substantiated the contention that people learn and use, largely unknowingly, an entire nonverbal language of facial expressions, gestures, postures, and so on and that those from different cultures employ partially different nonverbal languages. Minute methods of analysis have been developed and used in studies with quite interesting, but also quite technical results. Many studies of the influence of people's immediate surroundings on them and on their interaction hve also been undertaken within sociology, social psychology, architecture, and interior design.

Conclusions

Where does all this leave communication theory as a theory for use by social work practitioners? Perhaps it can represent a metatheory or generic conceptual framework for understanding assessment and treatment processes. This framework probably has its greatest utility as a teaching tool. Communication theory certainly is not the only theory base a competent practitioner needs. It can serve to help social workers organize the theories they use to understand personality, family, group, and community functioning and can clarify commonalities and differences in interventions espoused by different practice models.

In addition, some of the communications concepts and principles can provide useful insights into specific aspects of clients' functioning and social work practice. The Palo Alto theorists' notions about operating rules in small social systems, already applied within family treatment, could be within individual treatment as well. Social workers can make fruitful use of the concepts of symmetry and complementarity to understand better the power or control dimension of their relationships with clients and to plan which relationship stances they can most constructively convey to which clients. The idea of paradox can be developed for more widespread use in individual, group, and perhaps community work.

Those aspects of communication theory that have been most tested through research can be picked up and used with the greatest assurance that they are valid. One of these is a theory that suggests certain family communication problems are associated with poor family functioning. Another is the use of communication skills training with couples. Finally, the nonverbal communication "language" used by their clients warrants social workers' special attention and understanding.

References

1. Ables, Billie S., with Jeffrey M. Brandsma. *Therapy for Couples*. San Francisco: Jossey-Bass, 1976.
2. Bandler, Richard, John Grinder, and Virginia Satir. *Changing with Families: A Book About Further Education for Being Human*. Palo Alto, Calif.: Science and Behavior Books, 1976.
3. Bateson, Gregory. *Steps to an Ecology of Mind*. New York: Chandler Publishing, 1972.
4. Birdwhistell, Ray. *Kinesics and Context: Essays on Body Motion Communication*. Philadelphia: University of Pennsylvania Press, 1970.

5. Burgoon, J. "Nonverbal Communication Research in the 1970s: An Overview," in D. Nimmo (ed.), *Communication Yearbook 4*. New Brunswick, N.J.: Transaction, 1980.

6. Cherry, Colin. *On Human Communication*. New York: Science Editions, 1961.

7. Courtright, John A., Frank E. Miller, and L. Edna Rogers-Millar. "Domineeringness and Dominance: Replication and Expansion," *Communication Monographs*, Vol. 46, (1979), pp. 179–192.

8. Deutsch, Karl. "Communication Theory and Social Science," *American Journal of Orthopsychiatry*, Vol. 22 (1952), pp. 469–483.

9. ———. "A Simple Cybernetic Model," in Theodore Mills and Stan Rosenberg (eds.) *Readings on the Sociology of Small Groups*. Englewood Cliffs, N.J.: Prentice-Hall, 1970.

10. Doane, Jeri A. "Family Interaction and Communication Deviance in Disturbed and Normal Families: A Review of Research," *Family Process*, Vol. 17 (1978), pp. 357–376.

11. Ellis, D. G. "Relational Control in Two Group Systems," *Communication Monographs*, Vol. 46 (1979), pp. 153–166.

12. Fisch, Richard, John H. Weakland, and Lynn Segal. *The Tactics of Change: Doing Therapy Briefly*. San Francisco: Jossey-Bass, 1982.

13. Fisher, B. Aubrey. "Content and Relationship Dimensions of Communication in Decision-Making Groups," *Communication Quarterly*, Vol. 27 (1979), pp. 3–11.

14. Garvin, Charles D., and Brett A. Seabury. *Interpersonal Practice in Social Work: Processes and Procedures*. Englewood Cliffs, N.J.: Prentice-Hall, 1984.

15. Gelman, Sheldon R. "Esoterica: A Zero Sum Game in the Helping Professions," *Social Casework*, Vol. 61, No. 1 (1980), pp. 48–53.

16. Germain, Carel B. (ed.). *Social Work Practice: People and Environments, An Ecological Perspective*. New York: Columbia University Press, 1979.

17. Gurman, Alan S., and David P. Kriskern. "Research on Marital and Family Therapy: Progress, Perspective, and Prospect," in Sol L. Garfield and Allen E. Bergin (eds.), *Handbook of Psychotherapy and Behavior Change: An Empirical Analysis*, 2nd edition. New York: Wiley, 1978.

18. Haley, Jay. *Strategies of Psychotherapy*. New York: Grune and Stratton, 1963.

19. ———. *Problem-Solving Therapy*. San Francisco: Jossey-Bass, 1976.

20. Hall, Edward. *The Hidden Dimension*. New York: Doubleday, 1969.

21. ———. *The Silent Language*. New York: Doubleday, 1980.

22. Jackson, Don D. "The Study of the Family," *Family Process*, Vol. 4 (1965), pp. 1–20.

23. ——— (ed.). *Communication, Family, and Marriage*, Human Communication, Vol. 1. Palo Alto, Calif.: Science and Behavior Books, 1968.

24. ——— (ed.) *Therapy, Communication, and Change*. Human Communication, Vol. 2. Palo Alto, Calif.: Science and Behavior Books, 1968.

25. Kadushin, Alfred. *The Social Work Interview*, 2nd edition. New York: Columbia University Press, 1983.

26. Knapp, Mark L. *Essentials of Nonverbal Communication*. New York: Holt, Rinehart and Winston, 1980.

27. Lackie, B. "Nonverbal Communication in Clinical Social Work Practice," *Clinical Social Work Journal*, Vol. 5 (1977), pp. 43–52.

28. LaFrance, Marianne, and Clara Mayo. "Cultural Aspects of Nonverbal Communication," *International Journal of Intercultural Relations*, Vol. 2 (1978), pp. 71–89.

29. Larsen, Jo Ann. "Remedying Dysfunctional Marital Communication," *Social Casework*, Vol. 63, No. 1 (1982), pp. 15–23.

30. Levine, Baruch, and Judith Schild. "Group Treatment of Depression," *Social Work*, Vol. 14, No. 1 (1969), pp. 46–52.

31. Lurie, Alison. *The Language of Clothes.* New York: Random House, 1981.

32. Madanes, Cloe. *Strategic Family Therapy.* San Francisco: Jossey-Bass, 1981.

33. Marcus, Lotte. "Emotional Perceptivity in Social Work," *Intervention*, Vol. 28 (1970), pp. 15–19.

34. Mayo, Clara, and Nancy M. Henley. *Gender and Nonverbal Behavior.* New York: Springer-Verlag, 1981.

35. McNeely, R. L., and Mary Kinny Badami. "Interracial Communication in School Social Work," *Social Work*, Vol. 29, No. 1 (1984), pp. 22–26.

36. Minuchin, Salvador. *Families and Family Therapy.* Cambridge, Mass.: Harvard University Press, 1974.

37. Nelsen, Judith C. "Relationship Communication in Early Fieldwork Conferences," *Social Casework*, Vol. 55, No. 4 (1974), pp. 237–243.

38. ———. "Use of Communication Theory in Single-Subject Research," *Social Work Research and Abstracts*, Vol. 4 (1978), pp. 12–19.

39. ———. *Communication Theory and Social Work Practice.* Chicago: University of Chicago Press, 1980.

40. Palazzoli, Mara Selvini, Luigi Boscolo, Gianfranco Cecchin, and Guiliata Prata. *Paradox and Counterparadox: A New Model in the Therapy of the Family in Schizophrenic Transaction.* New York: Aronson, 1978.

41. Papp, Peggy. *The Process of Change.* New York: Guilford, 1983.

42. Parks, Malcom R. "Relational Communication: Theory and Research," *Human Communication Research*, Vol. 3 (1977), pp. 372–381.

43. Puryear, Douglas A. *Helping People in Crisis.* San Francisco: Jossey-Bass, 1979.

44. Ramsey, Sheila J. "Nonverbal Behavior: An Intercultural Perspective," in Molefi Kete Asante, Eileen Newmark, and Cecil A. Blake (eds.), *Handbook of Intercultural Communication.* Beverly Hills: Calif. Sage Publications, 1979.

45. Rapoport, Amos. *The Meaning of the Built Environment: A Nonverbal Communication Approach.* Beverly Hills, Calif: Sage Publications, 1982.

46. Rhodes, Sonya L. "Communication and Interaction in the Worker-Client Dyad," *Social Service Review*, Vol. 52, No. 1 (1978), pp. 122–131.

47. Rich, Andrea L. *Interracial Communication.* New York: Harper and Row, 1974.

48. Rogers Millar, L. Edna, and Frank E. Millar III. "Domineeringness and Dominance: A Transactional View," *Human Communication Research* Vol. 5 (1979), pp. 238–246.

49. Ruesch, Jurgen. *Semiotic Approaches to Human Relations.* The Hague: Mouton, 1972.

50. ———. *Therapeutic Communication*. New York: Garden City Books, 1973.

51. Ruesch, Jurgen, and Gregory Bateson. *Communication: The Social Matrix of Psychiatry*, 2nd edition. New York: Norton, 1968.

52. Ruesch, Jurgen, and Weldon Kees. *Nonverbal Communication: Notes on the Visual Perception of Human Relations*. Berkeley: University of California Press, 1956.

53. Satir, Virginia. *Conjoint Family Therapy: A Guide to Theory and Technique*, 2nd edition. Palo Alto, Calif.: Science and Behavior Books, 1983.

54. Scheflen, Albert. *Body Language and Social Order: Communication as Behavioral Control*. Englewood Cliffs, N.J.: Prentice-Hall, 1972.

55. Schwartz, Arthur. *The Behavior Therapies: Theories and Applications*. New York: Free Press, 1982.

56. Seabury, Brett. "Arrangements of Physical Space in Social Work Settings," *Social Work*, Vol. 26, No. 1 (1971), p. 43–49.

57. ———. "Communication Problems in Social Work Practice," *Social Work*, Vol. 25, No. 1 (1980), pp. 40–44.

58. Shannon, C., and W. Weaver. *The Mathematical Theory of Communication*. Urbana: University of Illinois Press, 1949.

59. Steere, David A. *Bodily Expressions in Psychotherapy*. New York: Brunner/Mazel, 1982.

60. Thomas, Edwin J. *Marital Communication and Decision-Making: Analysis, Assessment, and Change*. New York: Free Press, 1977.

61. Watzlawick, Paul, Janet Beavin, and Don D. Jackson. *Pragmatics of Human Communication: A Study of Interactional Patterns, Pathologies, and Paradoxes*. New York: Norton, 1967.

62. Weeks, Gerald R., and Luciana L'Abate. *Paradoxical Psychotherapy: Theory and Practice with Individuals, Couples, and Families*. New York: Brunner/Mazel, 1982.

63. Weiner, N. *Cybernetics or Control and Communication in the Animal and the Machine*. Cambridge, Mass.: M.I.T. Press, 1948.

Annotated Listing of Key References

BANDLER, RICHARD, JOHN GRINDER, and VIRGINIA SATIR. *Changing with Families: A Book About Further Education for Being Human*. Palo Alto, Calif.: Science and Behavior Books, 1976.
The first part of this book identifies several types of problematic communication troubled family members often show and suggests how therapists can get families started on the right track in treatment. The four communication stances Satir finds that people often take under stress (placating, blaming, superreasonable, and irrelevant) are reviewed.

KNAPP, MARK L. *Essentials of Nonverbal Communication*. New York: Holt, Rinehart and Winston, 1980.
One of the many reviews of the status of theory and research on nonverbal communication, this book offers a good introductory overview. In nontechnical language, it considers what is known about facial expressions, body movement, touching, vocal cues, and the effects of physical appearance and the immediate environment on human interaction. The last chapter suggests a relatively simple coding scheme for use in research or clinical observation of nonverbal behavior.

NELSEN, JUDITH C. *Communication Theory and Social Work Practice*. Chicago: University of Chicago Press, 1980.
This book reviews basic concepts of communication theory and suggests how they can be used to develop a generic conceptual framework for social work assessment and intervention. The framework is then applied to illuminate practice processes with individuals, families, groups, and other professionals. Several chapters especially analyze what can cause worker-client communication blocks and how to deal with these.

RAMSEY, SHEILA J. "Nonverbal Behavior: An Intercultural Perspective," in Molefi Kete Asante, Eileen Newmark, and Cecil A. Blake (eds.), *Handbook of Intercultural Communication*. Beverly Hills, Calif.: Sage, 1979.
After some brief comments about the relationship between verbal and nonverbal communication, Ramsey provides a review of research on nonverbal communication in different cultures. The material is useful both as an overview and as a bibliographic source for finding more material on nonverbal communication in particular cultures, ethnic groups, or social classes.

WATZLAWICK, PAUL, JANET BEAVIN, and DON D. JACKSON. *Pragmatics of Human Communication: A Study of Interactional Patterns, Pathologies, and Paradoxes*. New York: Norton, 1967.
This classic, highly readable work details the Palo Alto theorists' original thinking about such matters as the impossibility of not communicating, content and relationship messages in communication, differences between digital and analogic communication, pathological communication, and therapeutic paradox.

CHAPTER 10

The Problem-Solving Model

Helen Harris Perlman

Because I have set forth and explained the problem-solving model several times before I shall take another perspective here. I shall focus upon "how it got that way" to trace its theoretical sources and the practical considerations that were spur to its development.

When I first put forward my formulation of the underlying structure and principles of problem-solving in social casework it was considered a radical departure from the established Freudian-based psychodynamic "diagnostic" school of thought in which, as a caseworker, I had been born and reared. I had, in fact, so thoroughly digested the then major concepts of Freudian psychology tht I could not have shed them even had I consciously determined to do so. But for a number of reasons I had been drawn to some other thinkers on the human condition—a disorderly mélange, I confess, of some social philosophers, of psychoanalytic rebels against Freud, of psychoanalytic heirs who carried forward, expanded, and sometimes revised his essential formulations, chiefly the ego psychologists, and of the ideas and practices of the newly emergent "functional school" of social work. Of which more to follow.

Today, as a result of many changes both inside and outside of social work, many modifications and cross-fertilizations have occurred in all the psychologically oriented professions, including social casework. What was once considered new or even rank heresy (no pun intended!) has become "business-as-usual." Thus, many of the notions and procedures I first put forward in the problem-solving model are today to be found settled comfortably in many forms of casework practice and theory, no longer a "problem."

It was no air-spun theoretical formulation, this mode. It was a process that had evolved out of both "book learning" and of my many years of direct work with clients in a range of settings: family service agencies, a child guidance clinic, a psychiatric teaching hospital, a school social work setting. My clients were of every class and age; among them they had suffered every sort of problem to which we human beings are subject. And while, during those eighteen years of practice I became a supervisor, both of students and staff, an administrator, a part-time classroom teacher, I always carried a few cases. I wanted to keep a finger in the hot water of daily practice, not to forget how hot it can be at times.

Growing older and presumably wiser I became increasingly sensitive to what a multiplex situation every caseworker faced every day as he entered into the lives of his clients. So I was both pushed and pulled to search for ways by which we could more effectively bring order into our efforts to understand how people live and love and work and need and want and cope or fail—and beyond that how to engage and perhaps teach our clients some more effective and satisfying ways of dealing with the problems of everyday life. (A big order!)

Freud once said (paraphrasing Sir Isaac Newton) that most innovators are dwarfs who, standing upon the shoulders of giants who preceded them, are able to see further or in some different perspectives. I could not presume to stand upon the shoulders—but I listened to the pronouncements of some giants and read some of what they wrote, and often those who did stand on their shoulders—my teachers both in social work and psychiatry—gave me a good strong hand and boost-up to catch a glimpse of what they saw.

"To whom do I owe?" is a question that pricks at me often. Sometimes just one idea sets off a sunburst of thought. For instance, Gordon Hamilton was one of my most influential teachers when I was her student and later her part-time colleague. If I were asked what I had learned from her I would be hard-put to list it all.[1] Two single ideas that were hers I know: that of the "person-in-a-situation" always in transactional connectedness, obvious now, but freshly stimulating those many years ago; and the statement that casework lies midway between therapy and education. Yes! I said to both; they opened doors for me. I know there is more. But the fact is, that when one encounters ideas that are immediately consonant with one's own bents there occurs a spontaneous ingestion, a sense that "Of course—I've known that all along!" Which leads me back to Freud.

Until we stop to carefully consider the idea, it is probably impossible for any of us to realize how deeply we have been permeated by Freudian thought.

He was a giant whose seminal and diversified thought bred other giants—and some dwarfs, too! He was a major source of ensuing explorations of man's intrapsychic being and becoming within the society of the family and then outwards into the civilization and its discontents.

It does not matter whether we became Freud's orthodox adherents or the rebellious sons who were determined that "the king must die." What he set forward over half a century of remarkable productivity served as the starting place for further explorations. He was not guilty of what Emerson called "a foolish consistency" that is characteristic of "the little mind." Many times he revised his earlier hypotheses. The corpus of his work stands with that of great philosophers and literary geniuses.

"Where id was, there shall ego be" said he, of the goals of psychotherapy. He was more prophetic than he knew because it was to that very progression that those who stood on his shoulders moved. His daughter was the first to attempt to limn the ego's unconscious mechanisms. From her work or simultaneously with it there streamed out a brilliant company who turned to study the conflict-free functions, the congnitively directed coping strategies of the ego. Of whom more below.

Meantime, back in America (which Freud opined had no virtue except as a source of tobacco) was a social psychologist and educator-philosopher giant, John Dewey. It was to explore some of the terra incognita of how people learned and figured things out and managed to cope that I began to riffle through his heavy pages.

It was from Dewey that I caught on to the fact that if a person's motivation and abilities are to be engaged in learning, he must *feel* and *see* that there is a problem to be solved—and, of course, that the problem in some vital way involves him. For his learning was "problem-solving."[2] His delineating of "how we think" included perceptions of inner wants and needs and the outer realities, of mediation between them, of consideration of choices and alternatives, of anticipation of outcomes and their costs and rewards—all cognitive processes that were always infused with affects. He saw that mental and emotional factors were continuously in transaction, each affecting the other in two-way channels.

Most thought-provoking in what I drew from him was the idea of the place of action—of making something happen, of *doing* something as a way of actualizing what had been thought and felt, as a way of experiencing the self. Action, he postulated, and its outcome makes thought and feeling tangible, real, experiential, and thus may change thought and feeling as vitally as the other way around.

Some years later, when the psychoanalytically oriented ego psychologists set forth their studies and speculations, they spoke a different language but said, it seemed to me, essentially many of the same things. Thus, from his meticulous observations of infants learning, Jean Piaget averred that "thought proceeds from action."[3] Heinz Hartmann, countering the resistance of some more rigid theorists, wrote, "We do not share the malaise of our time . . .

the fear that a surfeit of intelligence and knowledge will impoverish and de-naturalize man's relationship to the world. We have no traffic with those who bemoan the mind as the 'adversary of the soul' "[4] From her studies of young children's coping, Lois Barclay concluded that action, the realization that "I *do*," is the precondition to the sense of "I am."[5] (Descartes notwith-standing!) And Erik Erikson postulated that identity formation is the product of active involvement in appropriate tasks.[6] Later, Robert W. White, lucidly and engagingly, drawing from his own and other researchers, argued that a person's sense of competence and confidence rises from experiencing the self as effective in action.[7] And, back to Hartmann, "action is also one of our most efficient instruments for the development of insight or knowledge."[8]

So—of what import was this to me as a caseworker? The fact was that in my own first ten years or so of practice (in well-respected agencies) I had grown increasingly uncomfortable with a number of the then usual perspec-tives and practices. There was among us an all-but-unquestioning acceptance of the iron determinism of the person's past, and very little recognition of the moving forces in his current life experiences. There was overemphasis on his "sickness" or failures, little observation or grasp of his "health." Our inter-viewing focused upon the client's recounting of his problems, his history, along with the ventilation of the emotional freightage that accompanied them; our responses were compassionate and supportive, which often served some heal-ing purposes, to be sure, but scarcely prepared the client for grappling with his present-day difficulties. In many instances the client's sense of psycho-logical dependency grew.

As I took stock I began to be struck with some of the remarkable survival strengths and management capacities in clients who had experienced what in theory should have left them devastated. I was by no means alone in this questioning of our practices, as I will indicate later. But I was highly mo-tivated to *do* something about it. (Question: Did Dewey—and those who were at one with him—push me to action? or was I action-oriented and thus pushed to Dewey? The larger question: What preconditions of discomfort and hope and of mind-set propel us into connecting with or drawing back from new ideas?)

It was Dewey's term "problem-solving" that I took on as the name for what I now saw social casework to be. I saw it clearly as a *process*, not necessarily as a goal, though the latter was much to be desired. How, then, to make that process happen? How to engage the client actively from the first in some aspect of his problem, past his recounting it, past ventilating his feelings, past vaguely hoping for some fortuitous solution? How, from the first hoping for some fortuitous solution? How, from the first, to involve the applicant in feeling himself to be a participator in dealing with his problem?

I recalled that this was the very same question that the thoughtful mem-bers of the Milford Conference, back in 1929, had asked themselves when, having delineated the valued aims of social casework, they ruefully and honestly added that it was easier to desire participation than to know how to achieve it.

It was from the practice and its supporting theory of the "functionalists," the so-called "Rankians," that I derived my next spur and sustenance for the slowly developing problem-solving process.[9] I had been exposed to them first in discussions with some of my skilled and respected colleagues in the New York Jewish Family Service Agency. A few of them were graduates of the functionalist school, others were commuting to Philadelphia to take part-time courses there. I began to read this school's publications, finding their literary quality pleasurable, but, more, finding myself excitedly at-one with many of their formulations about the nature of the life process, and thence, in its encapsulated form, the nature of the "helping process."*

Herewith the most useful ideas I drew from the functionalists and incorporated into my practice without violation of my cherished beliefs.

• *A focus upon the "here-and-now,"* based on the recognition that each help-seeker comes to us at a point of what *he* feels to be a crisis; and that potential powers for change and movement are mobilized best when the "iron is hot." Rather than beginning with the logic of study-diagnosis as precedent to treatment one must begin where the applicant/client *is.* There was behind this an existential assertion that the person is always in a process of being and becoming, not just of having been. And that immediate movement to change was to be set in motion.

The connection between this view and its consequences for practice and the later-to-be-developed "crisis intervention" strategies is readily to be seen.

• The reality and impact for the applicant of *the agency itself.* This was something to which we of the diagnostic school had given scant attention. We knew ourselves to be *for* the applicant, eager and ready to serve his best

---

*Many years later I learned that Jessie Taft—co-leader with Virginia Robinson of the functionalist school had taken her Ph.D in the University of Chicago's department of Social Sciences. Among a remarkable group of seminal thinkers there—George Mead and W. I. Thomas among them—was John Dewey. Although he had left the University of Chicago before Jessie Taft arrived, there is no question but that his thought still permeated that of his former colleagues. I guessed then that it was no accident that I was finding strong traces in Taft's writings not only of Rank's existential philosophy but also of John Dewey's action-experiential philosophy of learning.

In the almost two decades of hot war between the diagnostic and functional schools of social casework, I was frequently caught in the crossfire. When, in 1949, in an effort to suggest some ameliorative perspectives on both sides, I published "A Parable of the Workers of the Field" (*Social Service Review* Vol. 23 [March 1949], and reprinted in my *Perspectives on Social Casework*, Philadelphia: Temple University Press, 1971), I was deluged by responsive letters. From one leader of each school came a reproach. One adjured me not to be "too clever"; the other admonished me not to "deny our differences." From the "workers in the field," however, the letters all expressed gratitude, cheer, and relief.

Enough here to say that a theory system is often more "pure" and intransigent than is its practical application. For a number of reasons, Hegelian and others, many modifications and syntheses have occurred since then.

interests. But we had rarely recognized how unknown, even unfathomable and threatening we could be to persons who entered our doors for the first time. Nor did we regularly get at what his preconceptions were of what we would ask of him, do to him. What the functionalists saw was that the agency itself might pose a first (and recurring) problem, one that might loom large. So the client's perceptions and expectations of the agency, in line with or in contrast to the reality were to be subject for discussion with him.

The connection between this and the much later introduction of "contracts" and agreements between applicant and agency may be apparent.

• *The uses of relationship*, its tremendous powers for motivation or deterence. It was to the latter that the functionalists gave fresh understanding and practice attention. Of course relationship, in its empathic, caring, supportive, enhancing aspects had been the stock-in-trade of traditional psychodynamic casework. Its characteristics and powers had been clearly set forth by casework's leaders over some years.[10] But it was largely the "good" relationship that was discussed. That worked remarkably well at times, especially with those clients who came with some trust, who were responsive to warmth, who reached out for help. But our goodwill and ready compassion cut little ice with the resistive client, the nonvoluntary "applicant," and only rarely did we face the rise of resistance in continuing cases when the client found he was not getting what he had expected. Of course, too, the concept of resistance had been introduced and discussed by Freud, but his focus was largely upon intrapsychic resistance, unconscious defenses against knowing the self.

What the functionalists dared to face and uncover was the underbelly of relationships, the natural ambivalences that occur in even the best of them. Further, they recognized the natural negative feelings that must arise when expectations are not fully met, when no magic salves are available, when hard work may be involved in the change that is sought. I, then, began to take as natural and understandable such resistance as I saw in distrustful, nonvoluntary help-needers (often not help-seekers!). Thus from the first, often as the first problem-to-be-worked, I drew out such attitudes and feelings, as my first demonstration of being able to accept and bear anger or suspician projected at me.

The connection between this and the methodology later used in projects with the "hard-to-reach" is manifest.

• *Time*—that ineffable and fleeting reality that is life itself—this the functionalists grasped and used as a central consideration in the helping process. They were the first to recognize the impetus to self-mobilization inherent in time limitations (except, perhaps, for Bertha Reynolds who in 1926 and again in the early thirties wrote on short-term treatment.[11] But Reynold's insights were lost sight of, partly because "sophisticated" caseworkers had subconsciously begun to take the long-term case as proof of therapeutic skill.)

Beyond recognition of time limits as inherent in all life experiences the functionalists stressed the idea that any living experience which was meaningful had a beginning, middle, and end. The "middle" was generally unexplored, even by them. But heightened attention was paid to the beginnings and endings of the helping process. They saw that ends are inherent in beginnings; the planning together with the client about the time and terms of termination took the place of ambiguous, trailing-off closures. Termination became a period of stock-taking—with perhaps movement to another area of difficulty.

The connection with much later "planned short-term treatment" is plain to be seen.

• *Partialization*—that is, the cutting down of a complex problem to such size and specificity as to make it manageable for discussion and work-over by the client at a given time. Any effective problem-solving in the ordinary course of a day, whatever the problem, requires focus, selection, postponement of the less urgent, and so on. The "part" to be chosen may be self-evident or selected from the "blooming buzz" of problems that assail the client, chosen for its crucialness, or for its being most readily workable, most amenable to change, and for its being connected, of course, with the larger problem. As one goes forward it is not difficult to move from one part to another. What is desirable is that the helper be able to show the client the connections not only between the problems but also between the behaviors that he may transfer from work on one problem to another.

The idea of partialization is obviously in complete consonance with all effective ego functioning. As is the idea of partialization and that of the "problem-to-be-worked" at a given time.

These, in too-brief-sum, were among the salient ideas of the functional school that I found compatible with my already ingrained psychodynamic practice and thought.

When, late in 1945, I joined the faculty of the University of Chicago's School of Social Service Administration, I found myself in what was both an invigorating and benign climate. Most influential was my senior colleague and mentor with whom I worked closely for almost twenty years—that small-in-physique but large in mind-and-spirit giant, Charlotte Towle. We were in immediate rapport on several bases. Both reared in psychodynamically oriented casework, we had never lost sight of the sociodynamics of everyday life.[12] Further, in several years of practice in Philadelphia she had come to know and respect several of the persons who were later to found the functional school of thought. She had a kind of wisdom that includes a tolerance for difference, an openness, at once critical and supportive, to another's exploratory thinking. Her already many publications were both with and beyond their time—many as relevant today as they were years ago. For me she was a continuous source of nurture.

It was Towle who, in the malaise shared in our faculty with the then practice of diagnostic study as the prelude to "treatment," formulated a different framework appropriate to immediate engagement with applicants. It was an assessment, from the first and ongoing, of the client's motivation, his capacity, and the opportunities available and applicable to the presented problem; its acronym was M-C-O. Its purpose: to engage, as quickly and relevantly as possible, the client's wanting and willing (M) his ego operations (C) strong or frail as they may be, in connecting with casework services and the other resources (O) relevant to dealing with his problem.

The M-C-O assessment fit readily into the still-to-be-written (but being taught) problem-solving model, and was taken as the central proposition in the research of our colleague Lilian Ripple and her associates. It was this: ". . . the client's use of casework service is determined by his motivation, his capacity, and the opportunities afforded him by his environment and by the social agency from which he seeks help." (Note: "by the social agency" in no sense meant *confined* to that agency. It implied the caseworker's active intervention, when appropriate, in corralling such significant other persons and services and such material means as are called for by the problem in work.) The assessment of these factors was to start from the first encounter between caseworker and applicant, and to be continuously guaged in on-going.[13]

Diagnosis was not abandoned. We used the term "diagnostic assessment" for the M-C-O. In situations when the client's character structure and/or mental-emotional disabilities were part of the problem, perhaps causal to the malfunctioning, we expected that these would be revealed in the active interchange between him and the caseworker. Our emphasis, however, was upon the simultaneous stimulation and assessment of the person's "work-ability" within the boundaries of the problem-at-hand, whether of interpersonal relationships or of role-task performance or of deficits in social provisions. We "palpated," so to speak, for what motivational coping capacities were alive and working within him, not in his totality but as seen within the for-the-time partialized problem.

Yes, the person was "whole." That is why we could believe that what he learned and experienced in one segment of living might (with help) be transferred to another, and that what he found rewarding in the coping work on one piece of his problem might be shifted (with guidance) to another. And yes, the person could be viewed holistically, as a biopsychosocial being in continuous transaction with a complex living environment (and the greater one's knowledge the more dynamically complex this interaction among systems became!) But when *doing*, not just viewing, is required, and the person's sense of immediate needfulness is high, the parameters must be narrowed (this the ego decrees) for clarity of vision and concentration of efforts.

In these think-and-try-out sessions in which our research, casework, and human development faculty collaborated, we drew, with gratification and gratitude, upon the swelling tide of thought roughly subsumed under ego psychology. I have already named the several we found most enlightening or supportive: Erik Erikson, whose developing thought about the impact of social roles and life-phase tasks was all but ready-made for social work considerations; Heinz Hartmann, who emerged from depth psychology to assert that the ego was more than a derivative of the id, and to point the inter-penetration between conscious cognition and the sub- and unconscious; and, markedly, Robert W. White, who turned his inquiring and fertile mind to examining conscious intent and motivation as movers and shakers of human behavior, and who, based upon observations and studies of infants, adults, and humanoid animals, saw aggressive drives as the inborn push for "ef-fectance," toward "mastery"—and more for which I do not have space here.[14]*

From these and fellow-thinkers there emanated a kind of optimism, an existential affirmation of the human being's being-and-becoming that was the product not just of faith or wishful thinking but of clinical observation and research. They provided an open door, a breath of fresh air from what had become an Escher-like no-exit position of determinism. It was reinvigorating for us.

Increasingly evident were some stubborn problems in the state of case-work. Among them was the increasing evidence of high numbers of drop-outs of persons who had voluntarily applied to be and had been accepted as clients. Intake and its outcomes was becoming a costly and fruitless opera-tion. Indicative of our maturing ability to take stock of ourselves was the rise of new research that asked, in effect, what was the matter with what we did, in what ways were we failing. The best of the research revealed what many of us had long and uneasily observed: that in many places study and diagnostic explorations preparatory to treatment left most clients at sea; that the caseworker's goals and those of the client rarely met, and were rarely put on the table between them; that the problem presented by the client was seen as a kind of ticket of admission to a process that would try to guide him into his "basic" problems; and so on.[15]

A second problem to which many social workers were giving fresh and concerned attention was that of the large numbers of persons and families who needed but did not—or would not—use social agency services—or the medical or educational or psychiatric services—they needed but somehow avoided or bypassed. Labeled the "hard-to-reach" or "multiproblem" fam-ilies as indeed they were, they were also largely the long-disadvantaged, long-victimized by impulse and chance, undereducated, innocent of knowledge about "talking cures," suspicious of the rules and arrangements that governed educational and health and welfare organizations.

Several demonstration projects (among which New York's Mobilization for Youth and the St. Paul Family-Centered Project were outstanding) re-vealed what is by now obvious: that to engage those who are perhaps most needful not only economically but culturally and psycholgically too, there would have to be some radical changes made, not only in the policies and provisions of human welfare programs, but, when dealing with individuals, in our casework strategies. To those of us involved in these projects it became

*See Annotated Bibliography under each of these authors.

swiftly manifest that even if long-term services were necessary it would have to be offered in small-piece parts; that intertwined with drawing out and listening to angry complaints and projected blame there would need to be consistent and genuine empathy with how it seemed and felt to the "victim." (Later, once that victim felt some trust, those perceptions might be subject to challenge and change.) The focus would have to be upon the immediate *felt* need, and the offer of such help as was wanted would need to come as close to it as possible, as soon as possible. The question for thinking out together was repeatedly "What's in it for *you?*"—What is it worth to *you*— how does it feel to *you?*" Rehearsal for action (such as a parent's going to see his child's teacher) and, following that, an assessment together of "how come it worked" or "did not work"—these were ways by which behaviors were learned and incorporated or, if unsuccessful, thought over and rejected. Such limitations as realistically existed were not simply explained but were accompanied by the recognition of how frustrating they must feel. Not infrequently we saw heartening spurts of fresh motivation, along with evidences of greater self-dependence and self-regard. At the least, "I tried my best!"

One further small facilitating step in the use of the problem-solving process: as a teacher of casework both in practice settings and the classroom I was continuously awed by the complexities of human living and aware of the many diversities that every practitioner must shuffle and put in order every day. So, to help organize our thought and labors I hit on a mnemonic device as a reminder in every case: that there is always a *Person* (or several) beset by a *Problem* (or several) who comes to a *Place* (which may in itself present a problem) for help, which is given by a *Process*, called casework. "Always," as one of my students put it, "Four Ps in a Pod."

I wish I had added two more Ps: the *Professional* person, is one. He/she is, of course, a representative of the Place. But he/she is himself/herself too, and no easy part of being a professional helper is maintaining a balance between one's personal-emotional-mental freedom and one's disciplined, responsible self-management in the interest of the client.

The other would perhaps be *Provisions*, to identify those "opportunities" which must so often be found, invented, and made accessible to the client for the meeting of his material needs and those relationship supports and activity satisfactions that existed but remained unutilized within his social milieu.

The "four Ps" have been analyzed for their assumptions, implications, and interrelationships in previous publications, so I shall not repeat myself or resort to pale paraphrase.[16] Instead I shall briefly try to exemplify the process with commentary.*

---

*I have used this case before, in "In Quest of Coping," *Social Casework* Vol. 56, (April 1975), pp. 213–225. Though it was many years ago that this interview took place, I recall it with fair accuracy, because it was my first conscious attempt to "rehearse" a client in the action she was being prepared to take.

Referral: Mrs. M., mother of fifteen-year-old Mark, has been referred to the family service agency by Mark's teacher-counselor because of the boy's deteriorating work at school, his occasional truancy, his general unresponsiveness. The counselor had called Mark in to ask what was troubling him, since he had formerly been an adequate-to-good student, but Mark shrugged and denied any difficulty. When she sent a note to Mrs. M., the mother appeared at once. She was having the same problem with Mark. "Can't get a word out of him"—whereas they used to be "good friends." She felt she was "licked." Mark is an only child. His parents had separated about three years earlier. Mrs. M. was glad for the referral.

The Place: a private family agency, a pioneer in family therapy. Usually the family members immediately involved are dealt with in a two-or-more-some group, but individual interviews may be used when needed. When she phoned, an appointment was made to see Mrs. M. alone.

The Person: presents herself well, eager to talk, vital, quick, both angry and anxious. She is at her "wit's end"—and she hopes something can be done about Mark. Asked to tell me the trouble, she gives essentially the same information as was given to the counselor, with considerable detail, in a rush, as if to unload it. To which I listen with responsiveness to her concern and her reactions.

The Problem: As above. It started about a year ago, worsened gradually. In response to my question: Mark's father left the home about three years ago—"no big fight—he just sort of drifted out." He is an accountant, regularly pays for her and Mark's support "but just barely." Mark sees his father on weekends—they go to a movie, bowling, "nothing much." She doubts that the father means much to Mark—he's always been "sort of a piece of milk toast."

The Process: I interrupted what promised to be a long string of pent-up anecdotes to ask if Mrs. M. would tell me what she had tried to do since she became aware of Mark's withdrawal. (It was already clear to me that she had alternately pleaded, threatened, coaxed, bribed—but I wanted *her* to hear it.) When she said that lately she had been "screaming my fool head off" and that she had "put my whole life into that boy" I said I could see how rough it had been for *her*. But I could also see that nothing had been gained. She ruefully agreed.

What, I asked, did she hope we could do? To this Mrs. M. quickly proposed that we call Mark in—see him—tell him to shape up—explain to him—find out—.

I said that in our experience when two people are tied in knots it takes two to untangle. Both need help—maybe together, maybe separately. She nodded understandingly. "There's also a father," I added. Now she shrugged, impatiently. So I suggested that deciding whether and when Mark's father should be drawn in could wait.

But I wondered whether Mrs. M. was expecting that we could make Mark over? It would only be natural for her to wish that we had some magical formula—Mrs. M. smiled broadly in assent. Natural but not possible, I went on. I said that since she and Mark are the two chief actors in this problem right now both of them might have to be involved in work on it. Could she see that? She supposed so—reluctantly.

I said I thought I'd like to see Mark alone at first—to get his version of the story. What did she think? She could see that. But, I admitted, I wasn't sure how best to get through to him. I wondered aloud: Should I ask the school counselor to refer him? Should I write to Mark? I wanted to make sure that Mark didn't think this was to be a punishment. Had Mrs. M. told Mark about her coming here? No, she had not. Could she? Well—she'd try. Now I could take no more time—my next appointment was due. So I faced this honestly with Mrs. M.

I said the first problem we had to tackle was how to get Mark to want to come here—or at least to agree he would. And probably she and I ought to talk this over, so I could help her to face it. Did she see the point? She was silent. I said I knew she hated to put all this off. But that was better, wasn't it, than our failing with Mark? She agreed, reluctantly. I asked her to think it over—and I would too. We had a real job to do next week.

Assessment: Mrs. M.'s *motivation* is charged with the essential ingredients of *discomfort* (with Mark and flickers of discomfort with her own handling of him) and *hope* that help may be available. She makes peace with— or at least can tolerate—the procedures that are something less than she wished for. Her *capacities* seem good—she is responsive to clarifying questions, to empathic comments, seems to trust. She recounts a range of efforts (none successful) to deal with the boy, and shows some ability to perceive herself as actor, and a "foolish one." Impulse control is seen in her apparent willingness to take some frustrations under consideration. Much warmth, free feeling. *Opportunities*—unknown until problem is clarified—except for casework help, cooperation with the school, and, later, involving the father.

Questions on nature of the problem: Is this a "normal" identity crisis of adolescence? complicated by what may be a too powerful and possessive mother (both loving and demanding)? exacerbated by the parental separation? by a swing to identification with a passive-resistive father? Might this be the onset of mental illness in the boy?—a clinical depression? All this yet to be explored. But first things first.

Second interview: Mrs. M. reports. "Nothing's new." She kind of kept out of Mark's hair this week, because she wasn't sure what she should say or do.

I asked her what she'd thought to do about getting Mark in here. Several times, she said, he had mumbled something about quitting school and going to work. So she thought she might say maybe we had a job for him—or could get him one?

W: But is that true?

C: No—but . . .

W: Then let's not say it. Let's think together now about what would really be true.

Mrs. M. agrees but lapses into silence. I suggest that we suppose that she's Mark. What would she want to hear? She enters in, saying "No hollering—that's for sure!" We laugh together about that. She tentatively suggests, "Maybe something like I'm sort of worried about him?" I said that's a good idea—instead of being just mad at him. And that she feels he's not very happy? She says it's true. She does feel that—she feels *bad* for him. I acknowledged that she's put a lot of feeling into Mark, to which she says, "That's for sure! And, brother, what a pay-off!" I accredit how rough it's been for her, and that we want to talk more about that. But now we've got to get back to how to get Mark here.

C: Okay. So—I'll say I feel for him. And I feel for myself too. But maybe I don't do right. So I came here for both of us."

W: (I warmly accredit this gambit.) You're saying maybe the trouble is me as well as you! (She grimaces.) "That's hard medicine to swallow." But could you go on from there to say something like maybe *both* of you have your faults? Most human beings do! But you're trying to work out a little truce.

C: Well—I can *say* it.

W: Try it, on me

She does so, haltingly, using my exact words. I encourage her to try to put it in her own way. She giggles with embarrassment. I say I know it feels silly. But these things are really hard to do. So it's usually better to work them out in advance. She enters in-

C: Uh—well—look, Mark . . . I want to tell you something if you'll please listen (Her affect has become one of personal discomfort rather than irritation.) I took myself today to a place where I could get somebody to help me—maybe being a better mother to you—or whatever. You're mad at me—and I guess I've been mad at you too—so I want us to try for a little peace. So they said—um—they want to hear *your* side of the story.

W: That sounds very good to me! It's good, and it's true. Does it feel honest-to-God to you? Could you try it?

She agrees. I forewarn her. It may not work at all. If it doesn't—come back, or call me, and we'll figure out some other ways. It's agreed and we shake hands on it.

(Because I know that every caseworker wants to know "how it came out": Mrs. M. called to say she did it! Mark said he'd come! She was tremendously pleased with herself, and I said she had every right to be.)

Assessment of the transaction: The applicant has become a client, that is, a person ready to employ the services of the agency. She has been helped to move from being a complainant, a recounter of victimization, to accepting (perhaps only tentatively) that she is a participant, if not in creating the difficulty at least in involvement in its present status and outcome. She has had put before her one of the agency' procedures relevant to the problem's management and has seemed to accept it (for the time being). There is no hidden agenda on the caseworker's part. Reasons for procedures have been briefly explained, along with open recognition of the frustration that must inevitably arise when there is a big gap between what one would wish for and what the realistic situation is.

A participatory working relationship has been established. In part this is the product of the applicant's own motivation for help, in part to her capacity to connect and trust, in part to the caseworker's responsiveness and feeling with the "naturalness" of her "bad" feelings.

The total problem is complex in its ramifications. But here-and-now is a preliminary problem-to-be-worked. Pointed up by the caseworker, it constitutes the major focus of the first two interviews: how to draw the problem-creator (or is it victim?) into the orbit of change.

To this end the active participation of the "partner" is drawn into thinking and planning about the next steps. (Her own inclination was to unload the burden). But her capacity is perhaps heightened by the evidence that the caseworker was understanding of her so she moves to respond to questions about what *she* thinks, how *she* reacts, what *she* might say or do to make something different happen. To more fully realize her thoughts she is encouraged to rehearse, act out, her possible moves. That affords the opportunity to question and halt possible missteps, and also to reward her by affirmation of what she does that is actually "good."

For any one of us a rehearsal for some difficult action, whether within a discussion with another person or within our own mind, is an exercise of the ego "muscles." All mental or fantasied rehearsals are interiorized coping, preparations for action. If, as here, the work is rewarded by a desired outcome, or even only by recognition from a significant other that one's intention and effort were good, there ensues both a sense of support and of greater self-esteem. Which is no small thing when one feels "licked."

Finally, the client is prepared for possible failure, of which she need not be afraid. The caseworker herself is openly uncertain about what next move is best. She stands by, unfazed, ready to share the responsibility, and to plan another try. This is the psychological equivalent of "contract."

"But," you may protest, "this is an ideal client! No wonder what the caseworker did seemed to work!" It's true. Mrs. M. is one of those persons whose spirit and intelligence (motivation and capacity) readies her to take and use help. And I know all too well how many others resist, detour, vacillate in their willingness and understanding. With them the movement must be slower, often with the need to retrace the same territory and always with the open reconition and understanding of resistance, reluctance, and so on. But the essential process is the same: a responsiveness to feeling; its acceptance, along with the expectation that it may need to change; the stimulation of consideration and reflection on behaviors as they affect the problem; the examination of possible alternatives and the anticipation of their "pay-off"; and the making of some decision or choice, miniscule though it might be, about who is to do what, and how.[17]

Several widely used present-day modes of casework may be subsumed under the problem-solving model. I do not say that they are derivative from it. They represent yet again, perhaps, the phenomenon of separate but like thought and innovation that so often occurs when a general problem becomes manifest and a search for its solutions is set off in various places. As I suggested earlier, there rises a kind of "thought-dust" in the air that mingles and generates similar conclusions.

Crisis intervention is one of these modes. This form of short-term, focused treatment was first set forth by two psychiatrists. It found quick responsiveness in the group of social workers who learned from them. One of the first social work expositions of crisis intervention was published in 1962.[18] Its treatment principles were in complete consonance with those of the problem-solving process set forth in 1957: the approach was to be "task-oriented," that is, focused upon a problem-to-be-worked; "broken down into its component parts," that is, partialized; "mental work" was to be intertwined with the ventilation and responsiveness to affect; "anticipation of outcomes," and "rehearsal for reality" were among other similar principles.

Short-term treatment on a planned basis follows close on the crisis mode. And with considerable validity. The fact is that most persons who present themselves at the door of a social agency, or who are brought there by the scruff of their necks, so to speak, *feel* themselves to be in a crisis. Some last straw has broken the back of their own good or bad coping, and they are at the point of high motivation to get and use the help of another, or to flee from it. Either way, it is a point of potential engagement.

Task-centered casework is another variant of short-term, planned casework.[19] While today it is more closely allied with behavioral modification than with the problem-solving model, it began with emphasis upon precise problem identification between caseworker and client, with partialization of the problem, and with the client's active participation in planned coping efforts from the first. Its design is determined by the goal of measuring both the efficiency and effectiveness of its methodology. (A persistent problem-to-be-solved by every helping profession!)

In our present-day fascination with abbreviated forms of treatment we must not lose sight of the fact that there remain in social work's bailiwick many kinds of cases in which long-term care, or extended "middle" phases, are necessary. They are cases of hurt children, of their often all-but-intractable parents, of the aged, of the physically or emotionally mentally frail or disabled. They present situations where a kind of long-term overseeing, protection, standing-by, and occasional swift intervention is necessary, and also cases where changes and modifications of behavior and attitudes are only slowly won, a small part at a time.

I do not know of studies of such cases—of the differences among them, of whether some could desirably be "closed" with careful stock-taking prior to termination, and with the assurance of the agency's open-door at any point of crisis; which of them should desirably be kept open but with frequency of contact tapered off according to plan; and whether some of them simply "mark time." I wish there were some research designed to tease out and identify the structure and process of casework in both long-term protective (sometimes called "preventive") casework and in regularized and extended psychotherapy.

One further side light on the application of the problem-solving model:

In that "midway between education and therapy," group work has long operated as another of social work's methods. Closer to the education end of the continuum than casework, more indebted to the theories of the social sciences than to those of psychodynamic psychology, group work began, several decades ago, to recognize its frequent therapeutic by-products and therapeutic potentials, and thence to incorporate some selected knowledge from the ego-psychologists.

Somewhat earlier, casework thinkers had begun to venture into dealing with two-or-more-somes especially when problems were those of interpersonal transactions. Marital pairs, parent-child, or parent-children constellations became the units of treatment. Later, caseworkers began to form groups of unrelated persons whose similar and delimited problems served temporarily to bind them together in that "company" that misery is said to love—and often need. (Some examples: parents of handicapped children, in need of learning to cope and to tolerate, patients in a mental hospital, facing the hopes and fears of imminent discharge; and so on.). Caseworkers, on their part, moved to understand and to use more of the psychology of social groups and social meanings in everyday life—such as the place and powers of roles. Today, with many kinds of problems and persons, there is an area of considerable overlap between casework and group work.[20]

That the problem-solving model is readily applicable to groups as well as to work with individuals seems manifest. Further, long overdue, in my opinion, is the recognition of its applicability to good teaching of emotionally laden subject matters, as in courses in casework and group work, and certainly in field work.) Transferrable are such principles as clear and agreed upon delineation of the problem-to-be-worked at a given time or phase; a focus upon how that problem is perceived, felt, thought about; considerations of the outcomes sought, their realistic or wishful aspects, their pay-offs for the problem-carrier; considerations of alternative ways and means, their costs and rewards; decisions about actions to be taken—by individuals or by the group, and so forth. Of course, the management of group sessions and that of sessions with individual clients will pose many differences, both for the involved clients and for the helper, differences of kind and degree. But the guiding principles of relationship management, focus, partialization, rehearsal, exercise of coping capacities, stock-taking, and so on remain basic.

The problem-solving model has concentrated upon the beginning phase of casework help for several reasons. Along with many of my fellow workers I had grown increasingly aware of how crucial to continuance and ongoing was the engagement of the applicant from the first; how important it was to move him from the role of applicant (tentative, wishing, uncertain, trying to assess the place and the person called caseworker) to that of client, which is to say one who agrees to employ the services offered on the basis of having had a supportive, clarifying, next-stop, anticipated experience.

Second, my focus upon that beginning phase was in the effort to partialize the problem of treatment, in order to be able to examine in specific detail and depth its component parts. I hope it was not a case of self-hypnosis that made me believe (still!) the essential elements of the total helping process and the client's participation are to be found and experienced within the first few hours of transactions between caseworker and the applicant. Of course, there will be variations of emphasis, timing, and services determined by the nature of the person-problem-place and assessment of "workability," but the essential elements of process will be the same and ongoing.

One goes forward, past the beginning phase, with some agreed-upon part of the problem (or it may be a sought-after-goal). It may shift to another area, it may broaden or deepen in import. If so, the move is to once again clarify what the new or different problem-to-be-worked consists of, its causes, and its effects upon the client; his feelings, thoughts, and actions in regard to it; what he would want to make happen (realistically, beyond the wish), what *if*—what possible ways of dealing with it may be drawn upon or learned, what would their rewards be—and on. In short, within the boundaries of this new problem, big or small, the caseworker and client begin again to exercise the ego capacities to perceive, to reflect, to figure out, to choose between alternatives—all buffered and underpinned in the safety island of the casework relationship. It is a repeated process in which working on new material entrenches learning—repeated in the sense of involving some of the same coping operations but in a kind of upward spiral rather than in remaining in the old groove. Isn't that what occurs in effective if unassisted problem-solving of everyday life?

In sum: the problem-solving model is an eclectic construct. Its theoretical roots lie in psychodynamic ego psychology, in selected existential life-views, selected ideas from learning theory, enriched by social science hypotheses and social work's own observations of the continuous interpenetrations between man and his sociopsychological environment.

Selection was governed by the criterion of "fit," which is to say by the coherence and connectedness among essential ideas and principles. And by their applicability to casework practice, undergirding it, giving it reason and order.

In one of his latter-day essays, Freud commented that psychoanalysis did not promise to rid a person of his problems; it aimed, rather, at enabling the patient to deal with his problems—and those he would inevitably encounter in the course of living—with a modicum of comfort and competence.[21]

So with social casework. Its idealized aim, we have reiterated, is to enable its clients to achieve and maintain "personally satisfying and socially constructive" living. The problem-solving process focuses upon one or more way stations toward that goal. Its aim is to help its clients deal with such here-and-now problems as undermine or constrict their personal satisfaction and social adequacy. Even within those limits such help may run a broad and varied continuum. It includes the provision or the making available of necessary social and material resources. In tandem with that or separate from it, it includes the provision of psychological nourishment and supports to the client's spirit, while stimulating, flexing, and exercising his own (meager or strong) coping capacities—mental-emotional-behavioral.

Even when it is only partially successful, the goal and the process are as one; the means and ends are indivisible.

Notes

1. But I know where to reach for it—on the center shelf! Gordon Hamilton's *Theory and Practice of Social Case Work* (New York: Columbia University Press, 1940; rev. ed. 1951) was the first complete book on modern casework. See also her "Basic Concepts in Social Case Work," *Family*, Vol. 18 (July 1937).

2. See John Dewey's *How We Think*, revised edition (New York: Heath and Co., 1933), especially "Analysis of Reflective Thinking." See also *Art as Experience* (New York: Putnam and Sons, 1934). Dewey is hard reading. At times his prose is like a dense underbrush, but it is punctuated by sudden upthrusts of great trees. If you are interested in how you—and others—problem-solve, and how you—and others—fully "experience," he is worth looking into.

3. through 8. Re ego psychologists, quoted and referred to are:

    Jean Piaget, as quoted in Henry Maier's *Three Theories of Child Development* (New York: Harper and Row, 1965).

    Heinz Hartmann, *Ego Psychology: the Problem of Adaptation* (New York: International Universities Press, 1958), p. 65.

    Lois Barclay Murphy, *The Widening World of Childhood* (New York): Basic Books, 1962). See especially chapters 14 to 17.

    Erik Erikson, "Identity and the Life Cycle," in *Psychological Issues* (New York: International Universities Press, 1959).

    Robert W. White. See note 14c.

    Heinz Hartmann, *Essays in Ego Psychology* (New York: International Universities Press, 1964), p. 39.

9. For a succinct summary of the essentials of the functional school's theory see Ruth Smalley, "The Functional Approach to Casework Practice," in Robert Roberts and Robert Nee (eds), *Theories of Social Casework* (Chicago: University of Chicago Press, 1970). Note especially the suggested readings authored by Taft, Robinson, and Faatz, as well at the chapter in this book.

10. Re relationship: Several of the earliest and still apt articles are: Charlotte Towle, "Factors in Treatment" (1936) and "Some Uses of Relationship" (1940). The former appears in the *Proceedings: National Conference of Social Work*, 1936, the latter is part of "The Social Worker and the Treatment of Marital Discord Problems," *Social Service Review*, Vol. 14, (June 1940). Both are reprinted in Helen Harris Perlman, (ed). *Helping: Charlotte Towle on Social Work and Social Casework* (Chicago: University of Chicago Press, 1969).

    Annette Garrett's "The Worker-Client Relationship" is one of the clearest and most cogent expositions. *American Journal of Orthopsychiatry*, Vol. 9, No. 2 (April 1949).

    Actually, no book on casework omits this vital "factor in treatment." See especially Gordon Hamilton, op cit., and Florence Hollis in *Casework: A Psychosocial Therapy* (New York: Random House, 1964).

    The problem of establishing a working relationship with "unlovable" or "hard-to-reach" clients is to date most fully dealt with in Helen Harris Perlman, *Relationship: the Heart of Helping People* (Chicago: University of Chicago Press, 1979).

11. Bertha Reynolds, "An Experiment in Short Contact Interviewing," *Smith College Studies in Social Work*, Vol. 3, (September 1932).

12. Re the "social" in social casework: Space limitations preclude discussion within this chapter's text of those aspects of casework practice that engage, modify, and activate the social resources that may constructively affect the client's life. Briefly:

    Towle's writings were permeated with social concerns and perspectives, as may be seen in the collection of her papers, *Helping: Charlotte Towle on Social Work and Social Casework*, op cit. See also "Putting the Social Back into Social Casework," *Child Welfare*, Vol. 31 (1952), and "Social Components of Case work Practice," *Social Welfare Forum*, N.C.S.W., 1953, both reprinted, along with other articles on this subject by Helen Harris Perlman, in *Perspectives on Social Casework* (Philadelphia: Temple University Press, 1970) and *Social Work Practice: the Changing Landscape* (New York: Free Press, (1976).

    Today's clearest voice on this aspect of casework is that of Carol Meyer. See her *Social Work Practice: a Response to the Urban Crisis* (New York: Free Press, 1970), and *Social Work Practice: the Changing Landscape* (New York: Free Press, 1976).

    There remains the dilemma in casework—that there is more lip- than head-heart-hand-service (to use Charlotte Towle's phrase) in dealing with the social circumstances and opportunities affecting the client's life. The multiple reasons include, it seems to me, our failure to identify what skillful processes are involved in dealing with the "social" in individual casework, and claiming those skills with pride.

13. For specifics and clarifications re M-C-O: See Lilian Ripple, Ernestina Alexander, Bernice W. Polemis, *Motivation Capacity, and Opportunity: Studies in Casework Theory and Practice*, (Social Service Monographs, School of Social Service Administration, University of Chicago, 1964) especially chapter 3.

See also chapter 12, "The Client's Workability and the Casework Goal" in Helen Harris Perlman (ed.). *Social Casework: a Problem-Solving Process*, (Chicago: University of Chicago Press, 1957).

14. Further re the postulates of ego psychology:

a. The most recent, lucid, carefully summarized and documented presentation of the thought and work of the ego psychologists is Eda Goldstein's. *Ego Psychology and Social Work Practice* (New York: Free Press, 1984).

b. For an excellent presentation of the work of Erikson, Hartmann, and Piaget see Henry Maier's *Three Theories of Child Development*, op cit.

c. Robert W. White was thoroughly steeped in the work of Freud and the subsequent ego psychologists. White's research and probing thought yielded some fresh questions and stimulating perspectives about the human personality. In "Motivation Reconsidered: the Concept of Competence," *Psychological Review*, Vol. 66 (1959), and "Ego and Reality in Psychoanalytic Theory," in *Psychological Issues* (New York: International Universities Press, 1963), White sets forth the argument for the human being's push for mastery and effectiveness, for the adaptive powers inherent in cognition; he opens considerations of the mysteries of human curiosity, hope, intention, and of self-actualization via the responsivity of the environment. His *Lives in Progress* (New York: Holt, Rinehart and Winston, 1966) examines and analyzes both in depth and longitudinally the healthy as well as the destructive forces that determined the fate of three people. It is presented in a provocative, thought-stimulating study that is also a pleasure to read.

d. Last (but first, except for her father): Anna Freud, *The Ego and the Mechanisms of Defense* (New York: International Universities Press, 1936). Her focus was on the strategies of the *un*conscious (sometimes *sub*conscious) layers of the ego, by which human beings strive to maintain internal equilibrium and to gain gratification. This presentation was germinal to the thought, observations, and research of a host of students of ego functioning who followed her and moved into consideration of conscious—and thus more open to modification—functions.

15. Among the most telling studies:

1949: "The Functioning of Psychiatric Clinics in New York City. . . . Towards the Prevention of Waste" (New York State Charities Aid Association). The findings: Of patients whose first four interviews were focused on history taking for purposes of diagnosis, almost half dropped out. Of patients who from the first were engaged in discussion of their present-day feelings, actions, and circumstances, fewer than one-sixth discontinued.

1957: "What Research Tells Us About Short-Term Cases in Family Agencies" by Ann Shyne, *Social Casework* Vol. 38. (Note: "Short-term" here was unplanned; it was the drop-out client who made it so.) These findings spurred the study published in 1969 by Reid and Shyne.

1969: *Brief and Extended Casework* by William Reid and Ann Shyne (New York: Columbia University Press). This illuminating research was based upon an ingeniously designed and carefully worked out experiment. It compared a group of cases in *planned* short-term treatment with a group of like cases in "open-ended" treatment. These findings strongly supported the better outcomes in short-term cases. Those outcomes were not attributable to the time limits per se. Rather, they revealed the structuring, focus, partialization of problems, goals, etcetera that time limits impose, and along with these, the treatment conditions preferable to most of the clients. The procedure in the short-term cases were in all but full consonance with the problem-solving model as well as with the emerging crisis-intervention and short-term treatment modes.

16. See Helen Harris Perlman:

1953: "The Basic Structure of the Casework Process," *Social Service Review* September 1953; reprinted in *Perspectives on Social Casework*, op cit. This article was a "trial balloon" suggesting that problem-solving as a process in casework parallels the "normal problem-solving processes of the ego."

1957: *Social Casework: a Problem-Solving Process* (Chicago, University of Chicago Press).

1970: "The Problem-Solving Model in Social Casework," in *Theories of Social Casework*, op cit.

1977: "Social Casework: the Problem-Solving Approach" in *Encyclopedia of Social Work* (New York: National Association of Social Workers).

17. For examples of the application of problem-solving principles with less competent clients see Katherine Lloyd's "Helping a Child Adapt to Stress," *Social Service Review*, Vol. 31 (1957). Lloyd and Jean Tarrant, the caseworker, were both students of mine when the problem-solving approach was evolving. "The aim of casework here," wrote Lloyd, "is not treatment of the child per se, but rather treatment of a child in relation to facing a particular ordeal. . . . " And "such help may be seen to strengthen the ego's capacity to endure and adapt to frustration."

See also the case of Mr. Grayson, and the commentary which follows in *Social Casework—A Problem-Solving Process* (Chicago: University of Chicago Press, 1957). Mr. G's caseworker is guided by the functional school's principles.

18. Lydia Rapoport, "The State of Crisis: Some Theoretical Considerations," *Social Service Review*, Vol. 36 (1962). A later presentation by Rapoport appears in *Theories of Social Casework* op cit. For more recent developments and applications see Naomi Colan's *Treatment in Crisis Situations* (New York: Free Press, 1973) and *Passing Through Transitions* (New York: Free Press, 1983), as well as her chapter in this book.

19. William Reid (co-author of the 1968 study of brief and extended casework) and Laura Epstein, *Task-Centered Casework* (New York: Columbia University Press, 1972).

20. For a more complete discussion, including some questions yet to be answered on the overlap between case and group work, see Helen Harris Perlman, "Social Work Method: a Review of the Past Decade," *Social Work* Vol. 10 (October 1965); reprinted in *Perspectives on Social Casework*, op cit.

21. Sigmund Freud (I touch base yet once again!) How shall one select from a continuously re-fresheting source? There stand the formidable twenty-four volumes of the *Standard Edition of the Complete Works of Sigmund Freud*, edited by James Strachey (London: Hogarth, 1966). Turn to any page and find food for thought. But perhaps most accessible to new acquaintanceship and most engaging by its clarity is that small volume, *New Introductory Lectures in Psychoanalysis*, edited by James Strachey (New York: Norton, 1964). From there—let interest be your guide.

Annotated Listing of Key References

DEWEY, JOHN. *How We Think*, rev. ed. New York: Heath, 1933.
Although difficult reading this is a useful presentation of how we experience and problem-solve.

HALEY, JAY. *Problem Solving Therapy: New Strategies for Effective Family Therapy*. San Francisco: Jossey-Bass, 1976.
Haley's problem-solving approach to therapy focuses on "solving a client's presenting problems within the framework of the family. The emphasis is not on a method but on approaching each problem with special techniques for the specific situation."

HALLOWTIZ, DAVID. "The Problem-Solving Component in Family Therapy," *Social Casework*, 51 (February 1970), pp. 67–75.
Family therapy usually has a practical and realistic problem-solving component that is embedded in and grows out of deeper-level discussion of breakdowns and conflicts in intrafamilial relationships. The therapist provides guidance and leadership in helping the family members work out different ways of handling issues that have previously driven them apart.

PERLMAN, HELEN HARRIS. *Social Casework: A Problem-Solving Process*. Chicago: University of Chicago Press, 1957.
This book is a classic in the social work literature and stands as the cornerstone presentation of the problem-solving approach.

PERLMAN, HELEN HARRIS. "Social Casework: The Problem-Solving Approach" in *Encyclopedia of Social Work*. New York: Association of Social Workers, 1977, Vol. II, pp. 1290–1300. A succinct presentation of the principal concepts of problem-solving.

SPITZER, K., and B. WELSH. "A Problem Focused Model of Practice," *Social Casework*, Vol. 50 (June 1969), pp. 323–329.
A conceptualization is presented of a problem-focused approach to social work practice designed to deal with the rapidly changing demands and needs of today's fast-moving society.

SPIVACK, G., J. PLATT, and M. SHURE. *The Problem Solving Approach to Adjustment: A Guide to Research and Intervention*. San Francisco: Jossey-Bass, 1976.
This book proposes a beginning statement about the nature of healthy human functioning and a set of working postulates relevant to social adjustment and the ways in which certain cognitive skills function in social adjustment.

CHAPTER 11

Task-Centered Social Work

William J. Reid

Task-centered social work evolved from a model of casework tested in the mid-sixties at the Community Service Society of New York. The results of that test suggested that brief psychosocial casework might provide a more efficient means of helping individuals and families with problems in family relations than conventional, long-term forms of psychosocial practice (50). Using that brief service approach as a starting point the author, in collaboration with Laura Epstein, attempted to develop a more comprehensive, systematic, and effective model of short-term treatment (47). In its initial conception, the task-centered approach utilized the time-limited structure and techniques of short-term psychosocial casework as a means of helping clients devise and carry out actions or tasks to alleviate their problems. Helen Perlman's view of casework as a problem-solving process (39, 40), and Eliot Studt's (61) notion of the client's task as a focus of service were particularly influential in this beginning formulation.

Since its inception, the task-centered system has continued to grow and change. In fact, our intent was to create an approach to practice that would continue to evolve in response to continuing research and to developments in knowledge and technology consonant with its basic principles. The model was designed to be an open pluralistic practice system that would be able to integrate theroretical and technical contributions from diverse sources. In keeping with this design feature the model is not wedded to any particular theory of human functioning or to any fixed set of intervention methods. Rather, it provides a core of value premises, theory, and methods that can be augmented by compatible approaches.

This core incorporates a number of basic principles that continue to evolve. A current summary of the basic principles is:

Empirical Stance	Research-based knowledge has highest priority; hypotheses and concepts about client system need to be grounded in case data; speculative theorizing is avoided; stress placed on developmental research to improve model.
Consumer Orientation	Focus of help is on client-defined problems and goals; practitioner open and above-board about purposes and nature of service, eschews hidden agendas.
Problem Focus	Intervention concentrated directly on resolving specific problems of concern to client.
Role of Context	Problems occur in a context of individual, family, and environmental systems that may block or facilitate their resolution; change in the problem may bring about, or require, contextual change, which may have benefits for clients beyond resolution of the target problems.
Planned Brevity	Brief, planned services are generally as effective as long-term or open-ended approaches, but principle needs to be used flexibly with judicious extensions of service limits when appropriate.
Collaborative Relationship	Relationship is caring but collaborative. Practitioners and clients expected to work together to achieve agreed upon goals; extensive use is made of the client's input in developing problem-solving strategies.
Structure	The intervention program, including treatment sessions, is structured into well-defined sequences of activities.
Problem-Solving and Action	Change is brought about primarily through problem-solving in the session culminating in external actions (tasks) undertaken by clients and practitioners.

During the past decade the evolution of the model has been characterized by developments in theory and method as well as by the generation of various adaptations for particular settings and populations. Among major sources for development of the model as a whole have been learning theory and related behavioral techniques, cognitive theory and methods, and structural and other family therapy approaches. Variations of the model have been devised for work with groups (17, 19, 20, 21, 22, 52) family units (45, 46), and as a method of agency management (38). In the course of this evolution the model has maintained a social work focus, with attention to the distinctive functions and needs of that profession.

Specific adaptations have been developed for most settings in which social workers practice, including child welfare (54, 55, 56, 57), public social services (55), school social work (11, 51), corrections, (1, 29, 32), medical (67), industrial (62, 68), geriatric (9, 10, 41), family service (28, 43, 70), and mental health (7, 13, 36). The bulk of recent work on the model can be found in a series of volumes that have appeared during the past decade (12, 16, 24, 38, 44, 46, 48).

In this chapter a review of the task-centered system of practice will be presented. The review will encompass the major theoretical formulations that underlie the practice model; the model itself—that is, the strategy and methods that guide work with clients; and research evidence relating to the efficacy of the model. The chapter will conclude with an illustrative case and a brief consideration of the range of application of the task-centered approach.

Theoretical Foundations

Both our initial and subsequent theoretical work have been based on the premise that the essential function of task-centered practice is to help clients move forward with solutions to psychosocial problems that they define and hope to solve. The primary agent of change is not the social sorker but the client. The worker's role is to help the client bring about changes the client wishes and is willing to work for.

The theoretical base of the model consists largely of formulations concerning the nature, origins, and dynamics of psychosocial problems. A problem classification defines the types and range of difficulties considered to be targets of the model, included are problems in family and interpersonal relations, in carrying out social roles, in decision-making, in securing resources, and emotional distress reactive to situational factors. At the same time, target problems are part of a larger context that must always be taken into account. The context of a problem can be seen generally as a configuration of factors that may interact with the problem. The context includes obstacles to solving the problem and resources that can be applied to work on it. These obstacles and resources in turn can reflect almost any aspect of the multiple systems of which the client is a part.

It is assumed that problems generally reflect temporary breakdowns in problem coping that set in motion forces for change. These forces, which include the client's own motivation to alleviate his distress as well as resources in the client's environment, operate rapidly in most cases to reduce the problem to a tolerable level, at which point the possibility of further change lessens. If so, then clients might be expected to benefit as much from short-term treatment as from more extended periods of service. Placing time limits on the brief service might be expected to enhance effectiveness by mobilizing efforts of both practitioner and client. Effectiveness would be further augmented by concentrated attention on delimited problems in which practitioners would help clients formulate and carry out problem-solving actions.

The planned brevity of the model is then based on the proposition that effectiveness of interpersonal treatment is relatively short-lived; that is, that the most benefit clients will derive from such treatment will be derived within a relatively few sessions and a relatively brief period of time. The proposition has been supported by a large amount of research evidence that suggests: first, recipients of brief, time-limited treatment show at least as much durable improvement as recipients of long-term, open-ended treatment (27, 31, 33, 49, 50); second, most of the improvement associated with long-term treatment occurs relatively soon after treatment has begun (34, 60); and third, regardless of their intended length, most courses of voluntary treatment turn out to be relatively brief—the great majority of such treatment courses probably last no longer than a dozen sessions or a three-month time span—a generalization that suggests most people may exhaust the benefits of treatment rather quickly (3, 18).

The psychosocial problems that make up targets of intervention are always the expression of something that clients want that they do not have; problems are ultimately defined by the self-perceived motivations of the client rather than by constructs in the mind of the practitioner. The usual and most effective way to obtain what one wants is to take action to get it. Since clients are human beings, their actions are guided by sophisticated sets of beliefs about themselves and their worlds, beliefs that help them form and implement plans about what they should do and how they should do it. Since their problems are psychosocial, their plans and actions will usually involve others—the individuals, groups, and organizations that make up their social systems. These actions will in turn be shaped by their evaluation of the responses of these systems. This theory does not attempt to deal with remote or historical origins of a problem, but rather with current obstacles that may be blocking the resolution or with resources that may facilitate it.

These formulations, more than some others that guide social work practice, stress people's autonomous problem-solving capacities—their ability to initiate and carry through intelligent action to obtain what they want (25). In this conception, the person is seen as less a prisoner of unconscious drives than in the theories of the psychoanalyst and less a prisoner of environmental contingencies than in the views of the behaviorist. Rather people are viewed as having minds and wills of their own that are reactive but not subordinate to internal and external influences. We think those human problem-solving capacities—complex, ingenious, and, in the main, quite effective—deserve more prominence than they have received in theories of helping. We have tried to build our theory accordingly.

The Practice Model

The basic strategy and selected methods of the task-centered model will be presented as they are used in work with individual clients. Variations for family and group treatment will then be taken up.

Strategy

Guided by the foregoing theory, the practitioner helps the client identify specific problems that arise from unrealized wants and are defined in terms of specific conditions to be changed. Work proceeds within the structure of contracts in which the client's problems, goals, and the nature and duration of service are explicitly stated and agreed upon by both practitioner and client. Analysis of a problem leads to consideration of the kinds of actions needed to solve it, what might facilitate those actions, and obstacles standing in the way of their implementation.

Change is affected primarily through problem-solving actions or tasks the client and practitioner undertake outside the interview. The practitioner helps clients select tasks. She facilitates task work through assisting the client in planning task implementation and establishing his motivation for carrying out the plan.* She helps him rehearse and practice the task and analyze obstacles to its achievement. Reviews of the client's accomplishments on each task allow the practitioner to provide corrective feedback on the client's actions and serve as the basis for developing new tasks.

To supplement the client's problem-solving efforts, the practitioner may carry out tasks within the client's social system. These tasks are usually designed to assist others in facilitating the client's task or to secure resources from the system that the client cannot readily obtain on his own. Although a client's problem may be resolved exclusively through practitioner tasks, the theory and methodology of the system are obviously oriented toward problems in which at least some client initiative is indicated and will be of the most value when such problems are at issue.

The central and distinctive strategy of the present system is found in its reliance upon tasks as a means of problem resolution. The client's and practitioner's efforts are devoted primarily to the construction, implementation, and review of tasks. The success of these tasks largely determines whatever benefit results from application of the model.

The stress on tasks is an attempt to build upon the considerable capacity of human beings to take constructive action in response to difficulty. In effect, we have modeled our intervention strategy after the way the majority of people resolve most of their problems—by doing something about them.

*I use the indefinite pronoun "she" to refer to professionals; "he" for all other persons.

To be sure, the problems brought to the attention of social workers have usually not yielded to the client's problem-solving initiatives. Nevertheless, we assume that a capacity for problem-solving action is present. It is the social worker's responsibility to help the client put this capacity to work.

The strategy we advocate leads to a parsimonius form of intervention that respects the client's right to manage his own affairs. If the client is clear about what is troubling him and has a reasonable plan for resolving the difficulty, the practitioner's role may be limited largely to providing encouragement and structure for the client's problem-solving efforts. If more is needed, more is supplied, to the extent necessary to help the client resolve his difficulties. Even when the practitioner's involvement is great, her purpose is to develop and augment the client's own actions. Thus, the practitioner may need to help the client determine what he wants and in the process may need to challenge wants that are unrealizable. She may need to help the client identify and modify action and interaction sequences contributing to the difficulty, to provide corrective feedback on his action, to teach him necessary skills, to work with him to alter beliefs that are interfering with problem-solving, to bring about changes in the social system and to secure resources from it, and even to suggest specific tasks for him to carry out. But whatever is done is done collaboratively and leads to actions that must be agreed to by the client. The decisive actions in most cases are those that clients themselves perform in their own way and on their own behalf.

Enabling clients to take constructive and responsible action in their own interests has an important corollary: the action so taken is likely to be incorporated as part of their strategies for continued coping with their problems. Since the client has participated in its planning, has an understanding of its rationale, agreed to carry it out, actually implemented it and reviewed its results, one can assume that the action is more a part of him and, if successful, is more likely to be used again with appropriate variations, than if he were simply following the practitoner's instructions or unwittingly responding to contingencies arranged by others.

While the distinctive strategy of the model flows from its task structure, other elements are needed if the approach is to work successfully. Two merit discussions at this point: the practitioner-client relationship, and the social agency.

The relationship between the practitoner and client provides a means of stimulating and promoting problem-solving action. Their sessions together do not provide the essential ingredients of change; rather, they serve to set in motion and guide subsequent actions through which change will be effected. It is assumed, nevertheless, that this purpose will be facilitated through a relationship in which the client feels accepted, respected, liked, and understood. This kind of relationship is considered fundamental in most forms of interpersonal practice, although it has been difficult to define and measure the various quantities it is supposed to contain. Perhaps the most promising work in this regard has consisted of efforts to isolate and study what have been called the "core conditions" of an optimal therapeutic relationship: empathy, nonpossessive warmth, and genuineness (66). While research on the core conditions has usually lacked adequate controls and has produced mixed results, the evidence on the whole suggests that these conditions do contribute to successful treatment outcomes (35).

The strategy of the task-centered model calls for the actualization of these conditions within the context of a treatment relationship that is problem-focused, task-centered, and highly structured. This means that the expression of these conditions must be fitted to the requirements of the model. It is assumed that this fit can be made without unduly sacrificing either those relationship qualities or the essential structure of the treatment program. But in so doing it may not be feasible, or desirable, to push the core conditions to the limits possible in less-structured forms of treatment. Thus, the task-centered practitioner may bring a client back to focus on an agreed-upon problem and not simply respond at a high level of empathy to a tangential communication. Nevertheless, ways can be found, I think, to maintain a reasonably high level of the core conditions and keep at the business of the contract.

Perlman has described a good treatment relationship as containing both support and expectancy (39). Its supportive elements, which assume specific expression in the core conditions, have perhaps been given the greater weight in social work practice theory. Within the task-centered system, the expectations the practitioner conveys to the client are viewed as a therapeutic force of at least equal importance. The practitioner expects the client to work on agreed-upon problems and tasks and communicates these expectations to the client both explicitly and implicitly. While she respects the client's decision to reject her services, she also holds the client accountable for following through once a contract has been established. These positions are not inconsistent: they both reflect an acceptance of the client as a person who can make responsible decisions. Expectations, if clearly communicated, serve to influence the client's reactions, since the client is likely to regard the practitioner as an authority who can be trusted to advance his interest and whose approval is important. The practitioner's reaction, which is likely to be more approving if the client makes an effort to resolve his problem than if he does not, serves to strengthen the force of these expectations. This is as it should be if the practitioner-client relationship is to be used to full advantage on the client's behalf. But if clients are to be helped to resolve problems, qualities of the relationship must be fused with specific problem-solving methods. The relationship provides the raw material but not the finished product.

Behind any social work practice model stands a social agency. The intervention strategy of a model can be seen, in fact, as an expression of the agency's purposes. One often gets the impression from the direct practice literature that the main function of the agency is to provide office space and salary for the practitioner and a sanction for her work. Too little attention has been paid to the agency's contribution to the potency of a treatment approach.

The agency's role in task-centered practice is twofold. First, it provides a variety of resources, including supervision (particularly for inexperienced workers), staff training programs, and tangible services. Second, the agency confers on the practitioner an "authority of office" critical to the helping process. In order to be helped a client must be willing to place himself under the influence of a helper. The client must then perceive the practitioner as someone who has the capacity to help him and is worthy of his trust. In some professions, such as law or medicine, the practitioner relies on the image of his profession to provide this aura of authority and competence. The social worker, whose profession has a less clear-cut image, is more dependent on an agency to perform this function.

The immediate purpose of the model is to help the client resolve problems through enabling him to plan and execute necessary problem-solving actions. An effort is made, however, to help clients alleviate target problems in ways that will exert a positive influence on the context of the problem. Whereas significant contextual change is not a fixed objective in all cases, it is generally sought after as a means of facilitating solutions, of preventing recurrences and side effects, and of strengthening the client's problem-solving abilities. Contextual change is essentially defined and limited by the nature of the target problem. It is not just any change that would help the client. Practitioners move from the target outward by degrees, giving priority to contextual change most directly relevant to the problem at hand. Two major ways of achieving such change have been identified.

First, contextual change can occur as a direct consequence of alleviation of a target problem. Changes in target problems can produce "ripple effects." Improvement in a child's grades may lead to a positive change in his teachers attitudes toward him, which in turn may result in more cooperative behavior on the child's part.

Second, contextual change may occur in the process of working through the obstacles that prevent resolution of target problems. For example, in order to help a withdrawn adolescent make friends, the practitioner may need to deal with the youngster's depreciated self-image. Unlike some approaches, the manifest problem is not seen as a point of entry to the "real difficulties" underneath. Although the problem remains the focus of attention, its resolution may require considerable change in its context.

The treatment strategy is guided by principles that maximize the client's own problem-solving activities and potentials. It is assumed that, in general, clients can be best helped if they are provided with an orderly, facilitative structure in which to work out immediate problems and to develop problem-solving skills, with the practitioner in the roles of guide and consultant. Although the client's limitations are realistically appraised, emphasis is placed on identification of his strengths, competencies, and resources. Accordingly, clients are helped to devise their own solutions with the practitioner's assistance. Should these efforts be blocked by obstacles, increased attention is paid to contextual factors that may be responsible for the obstacles. The practitioner assumes more of a leadership role and pushes for greater contextual change as is necessary in order to help the client work through the obstacles preventing problem resolution. These principles serve to organize contributions from a broad range of treatment approaches.

Practitioner-Client Activities

The central strategy of the model is effected through a series of activities carried out in a collaborative manner by the practitioner and client. Although specific practitioner techniques, such as encouragement, advice giving, role playing, and exploration, are important in this process, stress is placed on the practitioner's and client's joint problem-solving efforts. The major activities are outlined briefly below.

PROBLEM EXPLORATION AND SPECIFICATION.   Problems are explored and clarified by the social worker and the client in the initial interview. As suggested, the focus is on what the client wants and not on what the practitioner thinks the client may need. However, the practitioner may point out potential difficulties the client has not acknowledged or the consequences that may result if these difficulties are allowed to go unattended. In other words, the target problem is not necessarily defined by what the client initially says he wants, but rather by what he wants after a process of deliberation in which the practitioner contributes her own knowledge and point of view. As a result, the client may alter his conception of his problem or, as in the case of an "involuntary client," may realize he does have difficulties he may wish to work on. At the end of this process, normally at the close of the first or second interview, the practitioner and client must come to an explicit agreement on the problems to be dealt with. These problems are defined as discrete, numerable entities and are specified in terms of specific conditions to be changed. The problem is generally summarized in a single sentence (the problem statement) and then specified.

For example, the case of Mrs. N. who was seen concerning difficulties in caring for her two-year-old daughter, Ann, produced the following problem statement and specification.

Problem: Mrs. N. constantly loses her temper with Ann, frequently shouting at her and slaping or shaking her.

Mrs. N. becomes quickly irritated whenever Ann "gets into things," spills food, cries, or won't obey. Mrs. N. generally starts shouting at her when these things happen. If Ann then persists in the behavior or starts to cry, Mrs. N. usually will scream at her and then slap her or shake her. During

the past week, Mrs. N. lost her temper with Ann on the average of about
five times a day and slapped her at least once a day.

As this example illustrates, problems are spelled out in concrete terms
and in language the client can understand. Estimated frequencies of problem
occurrence over a specified period add additional precision to the problem
description and provide a baseline against which change in the problem can
be measured. The problem of most concern to the client normally becomes
the primary focus in treatment, although usually more than one problem is
defined and worked on.

Exploration of the context of the problem is concentrated upon identifying the manipulable causes that are contributing to it or resources that can
help solve it. What are the immediate causative factors in the client's beliefs,
actions, or environment that we or the client can do something about? We
are interested in causal analysis only as a means of arriving at possible solutions. Exploration may also include pertinent history and general contextual factors involving health, family, work, school, and other relevant aspects
of the client's situation.

Studies of the process of task-centered practice have made it clear that
exploration and specification of the problem continue to be major activities
over the life of a case (14, 15, 44). At first the findings were interpreted to
mean that practitioners were spending too much time discussing the problem. It subsequently became apparent that sustained emphasis on these activities served necessary functions: to enable practitioners and clients to
deepen their understanding of the problem, to examine new developments,
and to deal with potential shifts in problem focus. This reconceptualization
of the workings of the model provides an example of the usefulness of a
research-based approach to model development.

CONTRACTING.   We insist on an oral or written contract in which the
client agrees to work with the practitioner on one or more explicitly stated,
acknowledged problems. The contract may also include a statement of the
client's goals in relation to the problem; that is, what kind of solution of the
problem does he want to achieve? The client needn't be highly motivated to
solve his problems, but must at least agree to work on them. Once the contract is formed we try to hold to its terms. We try to avoid the kind of practice
in which the client has agreed to see the social worker for one kind of problem
but the social worker attempts covertly to treat him for another.

The contract then states at least one problem that the practitioner and
client will begin to work on. The contract also includes an estimation of the
limits of treatment, usually expressed in terms of an approximate number of
sessions and length of time. We normally limit treatment to eight to twelve
interviews, weekly or twice weekly, over a one- to three-month time span.
The contract is open to renegotiation at any point to include new problems

or longer periods of service, but we insist this process be carried out explicitly with the client and that his explicit agreement to any revisions be secured.

TASK PLANNING.   Once agreement has been reached on the targets and duration of treatment, tasks are formulated and selected in collaboration with the client and their implementation is planned. A task defines what the client is to do to alleviate his problem. The task may be what we call a "general" one, cast in realtively general terms, giving the client a direction for action but no specific program of behavior to follow—for example, Mrs. B. is to develop a firmer, more consistent approach to handling her child's behavior; Mr. and Mrs. C. are to develop a plan for the care of their mentally retarded daughter. Or a task may be very specific, what we term "operational." Operational tasks require the client to undertake a specific action—for example, Mr. A. is to apply for a job at X employment agency within the next week, or Johnny is to volunteer to recite in class on Monday. The push in the model is toward task specificity. Thus an effort is made to spell out broadly defined tasks in terms of specific operational tasks. In order for a proposed course of action to be considered a task, the client must agree that he will try to carry it out. The client's express commitment to try to achieve the task is crucial.

In some cases the nature of the problem and the client's circumstances may point to a particular course of action, which can then be developed. In others, alternative actions need to be considered and appraised. The process works best if both the practitioner and the client can freely suggest alternatives as they come to mind without too much consideration initially as to their appropriateness. Research on problem-solving indicates that this kind of brainstorming is an effective means of devising solutions, perhaps because it stimulates imaginative thinking about a wide range of approaches to a difficulty (37). The best alternatives can then be selected for more serious consideration. In addition to suggesting alternatives, the practitioner tries to encourage the client to generate his own. At this stage, practitioner criticism of particular client proposals is kept to a minimum.

Often the practitioner is the primary generator of alternatives because the client may not be able to produce much on his own. Moreover, the practitioner may have special knowledge about kinds of tasks that generally work well for particular problems. To date, our research does not indicate a relationship between who originated the idea for the task and task accomplishment. Tasks initially proposed by practitioners tend to show about the same amount of progress as those suggested by clients. It should be kept in mind, however, that the practitioner proposes *ideas* for tasks that are then gone over with the client. The client's contributions normally become a part of the task plan. She does not "assign" the task to the client.

An agreement between practitioner and client on the client's task—that is, on what he is to do—may occur after alternatives have been sorted out and the best selected. Generally, an agreement at this point concerns the global nature of the client's proposed action and not the detail, which is developed subsequently. In some cases the practitioner may prefer to explore in some depth the strategies and tactics of carrying out a possible task before reaching agreement on it with the client. This option may be used when extensive planning of a possible task may be necessary before a judgment can be made about its usefulness. In any event, a final agreement on the task is made at the end of the planning process, *after* it is determined what the execution of the task will involve.

Once an action alternative has been selected for consideration as a task, the practitioner and client work on the plan for its execution. Most tasks involve hierarchies or sequences of operations, or sub-tasks. A task can be carried out in an endless variety of ways depending on which operations are selected and how they are ordered and executed. Generally, planning proceeds by breaking the task down into sequences or operations that may be required to carry it out. Suppose the client's proposed task is to look for a job. The question then becomes: How can he proceed to do this? As this question is answered, a number of immediate steps become apparent. He may need to decide what kind of work he wants to look for; he may want to consult the want ads; contact friends or acquaintances who might be able to inform him about job openings; look up employment agencies and make arrangements to visit one; and so on. The question of how to proceed may be meaningful for some of these steps. For example, the client may have a friend who might be able to give him a job. He may want to approach the friend but may be uncertain about how to do so without jeopardizing the friendship. Even tasks that are specific to begin with can profitably be broken down in this manner. A client's task may be to initiate a conversation with a co-worker. Whom should he select? What might he say? How? When?

Whatever the level of client action under consideration, the process proceeds until a plan is developed that the client *can begin to execute prior* to his next visit with the social worker. The plan may consist chiefly of a general task (to look for a job) together with one or more operational tasks that he can carry out in the interim (to contact an employment agency). Or it may be built around one or more operational tasks. The plan always contains at least one operational task. In addition, it generally includes some guidelines for the execution of the operational task(s).

Regardless of the form of the plan, the practitioner attempts to make sure that it calls for initial actions the client will be able to carry out. We have found that it is better to err on the side of having the first task be too easy rather than too difficult, since it is important, we think, that the client experience initial success in his work on the problem. There is empirical evidence to support this position. It has been found, for example, that subjects in laboratory experiments will do better on a second task if advised their completion of the first was successful (59). The impression that one has performed successfully can create a sense of mastery and self-confidence that can augment problem-solving efforts. The actual experience of success is perhaps the best way to acquire this impression.

For the plan to work, it is essential that the client emerge with a clear notion of what he is to do. To ensure that he does, the practitioner and client go over the plan in summary fashion, normally at the end of the interview. This final wrap up may be preceded by summarizations of parts of the plan during the process of its formulation. An important part of this procedure is to elicit from the client the essentials of the plan. The client is asked to present the plan as he sees it. The practitioner can then underscore the essential elements of it or add parts the client has left out. Summarizing the plan gives the practitioner the opportunity to convey to the client her expectations that it will be carried out and that his efforts will be reviewed. "So you will try to do————. We'll see how it worked out next time we meet."

The same principles are applied to planning of practitioner tasks or actions the practitioner will take outside the session in an attempt to bring about desired changes in the client's social system. Although such actions may not be planned in detail with the client, their consideration as tasks not only enables the client to understand and perhaps help shape the worker's environmental interventions, but makes the worker accountable, as is the client, for task performance.

ESTABLISHING INCENTIVES AND RATIONALE. The worker and client develop a rationale or purpose for carrying out the task if it is not already clear. Either the worker or the client might first consider the potential benefit to be gained from completing the task. What good will come of it? The practitioner reinforces the client's perception of realistic benefits, or points out positive consequences that the client may not have perceived.

Anticipating Obstacles

An important practitioner function in task planning is to help the client identify potential obstacles to the task and to shape plans so as to avoid or minimize these obstacles. This function is implicitly addressed when the practitioner presses for specificity in the task plan. As details of how the task is to be done are brought out, possible obstacles can be identified and dealt with. A more explicit approach is to ask clients to think of ways that a task might fail (5). If substantial obstacles appear, techniques of contextual analysis (below) can be used. Alternatively, the task can be modified or another developed.

SIMULATION AND GUIDED PRACTICE. The practitioner may model possible task behavior or ask the client to rehearse what he is going to say or do. Modeling and rehearsal may be caried out through role play if appropriate.

For example, if the client's task is to speak up in a group, the practitioner may take the role of the leader of the group and the client could rehearse what he might say if called on, or the roles could be reversed, with the worker modeling what the client might say. Guided practice is the performance of the actual (as opposed to simulated) task behavior by the client during the interview; thus, a child may practice reading or a marital pair more constructive forms of communication, with the worker taking a coaching or teaching role. Guided practice can also be extended to real-life situations; for example, a practitioner might accompany a client (who has a fear of going to physicians) to a medical clinic.

PROBLEM AND TASK REVIEW.   The client's progress on problems and tasks is routinely reviewed at the beginning of each session. The review covers developments in the problem and what tasks the client has and has not accomplished to resolve it. Practitioner tasks are reviewed in a similar manner. What the practitioner does next depends on the results of the review. If the task has been substantially accomplished or completed the practitioner may formulate another task with the client on the same problem or a different one. If the task has not been carried out, or only partially achieved, the practitioner and client may take up obstacles, devise a different plan for carrying out the task, or apply other task implementation activities. The task may be revised or replaced by another or the problem itself may be reformulated

CONTEXTUAL ANALYSIS.   During the course of the review of tasks and problems, obstacles to task achievement and problem change are usually encountered. The essential difference between a target problem and an obstacle is that the former is a difficulty that the client and practitioner have contracted to change, and the latter is a difficulty standing in the way of progress toward resolution of a target problem.

Whereas obstacles block progress, resources facilitate it. Resources are usually found in strengths and competencies of individual clients, in the ties of loyalty and affection that hold families together, and in the intangible and tangible supports provided by external systems. However, a given characteristic may serve as either an obstacle or resource depending on its function in relation to the problem.

In *contextual analysis* the practitioner helps her clients identify and resolve obstacles as well as locate and utilize resources. The discussion is led by the practitioner, who relies on focused exploration, explanations, and other methods designed to increase the client's understanding. When obstacles and resources emerge and are explored, the process may overlap with the problem and task reviews. The practitioner may help clients modify distorted perceptions or unrealistic expectations. Dysfunctional patterns of behavior or interactions may be pointed out. Obstacles involving the external system, such as interactions between a child and school personnel or the workings of a recalcitrant welfare bureaucracy, may be clarified or resources within these systems may be searched for.

TERMINATING. The process of terminating is begun in the initial phase when the duration of treatment is set. In the last interview, the practitioner and client review progress on his problems. The client is helped to plan how he will continue work on his tasks or develop new ones he might undertake on his own. What the client has achieved is given particular stress. Extensions beyond agreed-upon limits are normally made if the client requests additional service. Extensions, which usually involve a small number of additional sessions, occur in only a minority of cases, less than twenty percent in most settings.

Work with Families and Formed Groups

The strategy that has been outlined for treatment of the individual client is applied, with certain modifications, to work with clients in groups. Specific adaptations have been developed for two types of groups: families (or individuals who live together), and groups assembled expressly for the purpose of helping members work on individual problems.

From its beginning, the task-centered approach has been used as a method of helping families. Early efforts emphasized work with family dyads, marital and parent-child pairs. Recently, attention has been given to treatment of larger family units (16, 45, 46).

Treatment of a family unit, like treatment of the individual client, focuses on resolution of specific client-acknowledged problems and associated contextual change. Problems are seen as occurring in a multisystems context in which the family is a major, though not always the most critical, system. To understand problems and their contexts use is made of research and theory on family interaction as well as specific contributions from behavioral, structural, strategic, and communications schools of family therapy.

In most cases, family members are seen together and to the extent possible problems are defined in interactional terms. In addition to tasks carried out by individual family members and the practitioner, as in the general model, use is made of tasks undertaken jointly by family members, either in the session or a home. Tasks within the session (session tasks) generally involve family members in face-to-face problem-solving efforts, structured and facilitated by the practitioner, who may in addition help family members improve skills in problem-solving communication. Additional kinds of session tasks involve use of role play and live enactments of family interactions. Possible solutions devised by family members in their problem-solving work in the session are used as a basis for tasks to be carried out at home.

The theme of collaborative effort is continued in these home tasks. Shared tasks, those family members do together, provide a means for continuing at home problem-solving and communication tasks worked on in the session, for enabling family members to work together on practical projects, such as home improvements, and for affecting relationships among family members.

Reciprocal tasks make use of the principle of reciprocity in arranging for exchanges between family members. These exchanges may involve comparable behaviors or rewards (or noncompliance for penalities)—the form reciprocal tasks usually take between unequals, such as parents and children.

Whatever their form, reciprocal tasks require that participants express a willingness to cooperate and regard the exchange as equitable. Although it is important to work out the details of the exchange during the session, a "collaborative set" (30) is essential to ensure that participants are prepared to accept reasonable approximations or equivalents of expected behavior rather than letter-of-the-law performance and are willing to adjust expectations in the light of unanticipated circumstances. All of this suggests that work in the session toward clarifying and negotiating conflicts around particular issues precede the setting up of reciprocal tasks to deal with the issues at home. If reciprocal tasks are "tacked on" at the end of a session without sufficient preparatory work, they are likely to fail.

Session and home tasks are used to bring about contextual change. Frequently such change is necessary to resolve obstacles in family interaction that may be blocking solutions to problems. For example, a coalition between mother and son may be undermining the father's attempt at discipline. Session and home tasks may be designed to weaken the mother-son coalition and strengthen the parental alliance. In this way, as well as in others, the model draws on the strategies of systems-based—especially structural—family therapy.

A fundamental principle, however, is to concentate on alleviating target problems through relatively simple, straightforward tasks. These tasks may be designed to effect contextual change in passing, but the target problems should be the first priority. Structural dysfunctions, underlying pathologies, and so on, are left alone unless they intrude as obstacles. To the extent they do, practitioners can then shift toward tasks more directed at contextual change—tasks, including paradoxical varieties, that may be aimed at structural modifications. This progression from the simple to the not-so-simple fits the needs of social workers who deal with a wide range of family types, from normal to highly disturbed, across a wide variety of problems and settings, and who may not be expert in family therapy. Many families do not want a change in structure, many problems do not require it, and many practitioners lack the skill to effect it.

The family treatment variation is viewed as part of a more comprehensive system of task-centered practice. Although work with the family as a unit is generally seen as the treatment of choice when target problems consist of difficulties in family relationships, this method must be evaluated against other options when the target problem involves the behavior of a member outside the family context, such as a child's difficulty at school. Although family treatment may be indicated if the problem is reactive to family processes or if the family can be used as a resource for solving it, work focused on the individual and the setting in which his difficulty occurs may prove to be a more effective alternative. By incorporating within a single framework methods for work with individuals, family units, and the environment, the model facilitates flexible, combined approaches to helping client systems resolve problems.

The principles of conjoint treatment that have been presented can be applied to any situation in which target problems involve interaction of members of natural groups; that is, groups that have a life apart from the treatment session. Somewhat different principles apply when clients are treated for individual problems within the context of a formed group; that is, a group created to help individuals with their own concerns. The ultimate change target against which success is measured is not interaction of group members outside the session but rather resolution of the separate problems of each. Within the task-centered framework, the term "group treatment" is used to describe this form of intervention. The strategies and methods of task-centered group treatment have been presented elsewhere in detail (17, 21, 22).

In task-centered group treatment, the group process is used to further the basic activities of the model. Group members, guided by the leader, help one another to specify problems, plan tasks, rehearse and practice behavior, analyze obstacles to task achievement, review task progress, and so on. The leader's role is to make effective use of this process through orchestrating his own interventions with the contributions of group members.

In order for the contribution of members to be used to best advantage, groups are made relatively homogeneous in respect to target problems. Thus, a group may be formed around problems of academic achievement or post-hospitalization adjustment. As a result, group members have firsthand knowledge of the kind of problems others are experiencing and are thus in a good position to provide support and guidance. Moreover, members can more readily apply to their own situations lessons learned from the task work of others.

While it does not permit the kind of sustained, focused attention on individual problems and tasks possible in one-to-one treatment, the group mode has certain distinct advantages. Group members in the aggregate may possess more detailed knowledge than the leader about intricacies of the target problems. Given this experiential knowledge base, the group can often suggest task possibilities that may not have occurred to either the leader or the member being helped at the moment. Gaining recognition from a group provides an incentive for task accomplishment not available in individual treatment; in particular, a member who carries out a task successfully can serve as a model to others. These advantages are not always realized, however. Groups may become unfocused and discordant. Members may become competitive and overly critical. Certain participants may become objects of group hostility—the well-known scapegoating phenomenon. In order to exploit the potentials of this medium and avoid its pitfalls, the group leader needs to exert a constructive influence on the dynamics of the group. The general purpose of the group—to help individual members with their target problems—needs to be clarified and kept in view. The communications of the participants must be channeled in relation to the purpose.

Beliefs that members have about one another and about appropriate behavior in the group influence the sociometric and normative structures of the group. The practitioner attempts to encourage beliefs that are functional for the group's purpose; for example, that each participant is a worthwhile person who deserves help in working out his problems, that each has to find a solution that is right for him, that each has a right to his fair share of attention and assistance from the leader and the group. Shared beliefs about how the group should conduct itself become the basis for group control of the behavior of its members. The practitioner attempts to foster group-control efforts that will maintain focus on problems and tasks, that will facilitate sharing of relevant information (but discourage prying into aspects of the members' lives not germane to the work on their problems), and that will stress positive reactions to task accomplishment over negative responses to task failure.

Leadership within the group is an additional facet that needs to be attended to and used constructively. Although the practitioner normally assumes the primary leadership role in task-centered groups, she may use members as co-leaders for particular purposes—one member may be particularly adept at reducing tension in the group, another at keeping the group focused on the business at hand.

While procedures for forming and conducting groups vary, the following format is typical. Preliminary individual interviews are held with prospective group members to determine primarily if the applicant has at least one problem that would fall within the prospective focus of the group, and to orient him to the general structure and purpose of the group treatment model. In the initial group meeting, clients are asked to state the problems they wish to work on and to assist one another in problem exploration and specification. A contractual agreement is reached on the purpose of the group and its duration, which is planned short-term as in individual treatment. In subsequent sessions, each member, in turn, formulates, plans, practices, and reviews tasks with the help of the practitioner and other group members. In addition, the practitioner may undertake tasks outside the session on behalf of a single client or the group as a whole, or group members may perform extrasession tasks to help another with their problems.

Effectiveness of the Task-Centered Approach

Numerous uncontrolled studies of the outcomes of the task-centered model have been conducted in a variety of sites, including medical, family, child guidance, psychiatric, school, corrections, and public welfare settings. In these studies data have been collected on such factors as characteristics of clients and problems treated, types of tasks attempted, task progress, problem change, and client satisfaction with the model (47, 48). The results have suggested that test-centered methods appear to work in a broad range of situations and are generally well received by clients. Outcome data in the form of measures of task progress and of problem change have suggested that the great majority of clients studied received some benefit from the approach.

Since control groups were not used in these studies, it was not possible to determine the extent to which the task-centered model was responsible for the outcomes observed; other factors that might have produced change, such as tendencies for problems to dissipate with the passage of time, could not be ruled out. Studies in which controls were employed have provided more definitive evidence on the impact of the model.

The first of these studies suggested that the use of methods to help clients plan and implement tasks resulted in more task progress than occurred when clients were not given such help (42). The experimental task-centered methods were limited, however, to a single interview occurring in cases involving largely children in a school setting.

The first major controlled study of the effectiveness of the model (43, 44) consisted of an experimental test of the activities related to task planning, implementation, and review as described in the preceding section (47). The test was conducted in two settings primarily: a public school system and a psychiatric clinic, both located in an inner-city area on the south side of Chicago. Eighty-seven families, predominantly black and low-income, were seen by social work student practitioners who were trained and supervised in the use of the model.

Following procedures set forth in the model, problems were specified with relevant family members who became the actual clients of the project. Problems relating to school adjustment of children and interpersonal difficulties of adults were the most common. When the problem specification phase was completed, clients were randomly divided into two comparable groups. One group (the experimental group) received three weeks of intensive task-centered treatment, consisting of six interviews per case plus related environmental work. The other group (the control group) was given three weeks of placebo treatment in which there was client-practitioner contact but no use made of task-centered or other forms of problem-solving intervention. The amount of problem alleviation that occurred in each case during this period was rated by "blind" judges who were given tape-recorded problem reviews conducted with clients and collaterals.

The control group then received the three-week, task-centered intervention package that had previously been used to treat the clients in the experimental group. A second comparison was then made: The amount of problem alleviation shown by the clients in the control group during the period in which they received the placebo treatment was compared with the amount of problem alleviation they experienced during the period in which they received task-centered treatment. From one to three months following termination of treatment follow-up interviews were conducted with clients in both groups.

The findings revealed that the amount of problem alleviation experienced by clients in the experimental group during task-centered intervention was significantly greater than the amount of experienced by clients in the control group while they were receiving the placebo treatment. Moreover, problem alleviation for clients in the control group showed a significant acceleration when they received task-centered service. Data obtained at follow-up suggested that gains achieved by clients in both groups had been mair-tained following termination of service. There was no evidence that these gains had been affected by the emergence of problems in other areas. We were not able to identify from the data particular characteristics of clients, problems, or workers that strongly affected the apparent effectiveness of the model, although task-centered intervention seemed to be somewhat more effective with adults than children.

Because the impact of the model appeared to be less for children than adults, an effort was made to improve the effectiveness of task-centered methods with children. The revised model was tested in a school setting with twenty-one children who were referred for academic and behavior problems and were treated by student practitioners. In each case two problems were identified; problems were randomly assigned to treatment and control conditions of three-week's duration. At the end of this period, the focus of intervention was shifted from the treated to the untreated problem. Ratings of change in the problems during treated and untreated periods were made by judges following procedures used in the first experiment. Analysis indicated that problems showed the greatest gain during periods in which they were actively treated, thus providing clear evidence of the effectiveness of the model in direct treatment of children. Best results were obtained for academic problems and problems regarded as "important" by the children.

The most extensive controlled study of the model was a suicide prevention experiment conducted in England (23, 24). Four hundred patients who had taken drug overdoses in apparent suicide attempts were randomly allocated to experimental (task-centered) and control (routine service) groups. Difficulties in "continuing personal relationships," usually problems with a spouse, were reported in two-thirds of the cases. Research interviews were conducted with the patients four and eighteen months following termination of service. Measures of change in personal relationships favored the experimental group at both follow-ups, with statistically significant differences obtained at the second follow-up. There were no differences between experimental and controls in respect to recurrence of suicide attempts, which happened infrequently in both groups.

Two studies of the effectiveness of group treatment variations of the model used nonrandomly assigned control groups. In one study a group of delinquent youngsters who received task-centered treatment showed greater gains in self-concept and performance than a control group (32). In the other study (36), chronic mentally ill clients who received an approach combining task-centered group treatment and practitioner tasks outside the session scored higher on a goal attainment instrument and were less likely to be hospitalized than a group of control clients. Finally, a series of single case studies using within case controls have provided evidence for the effectiveness of the model in treating communication problems of a marital pair (65), in helping parents with children in placement (56), in enabling a mother to improve her communication with her young child (17), and avoiding self-destructive behavior in elderly ill clients (63).

Although all controlled studies conducted thus far have provided support for the effectiveness of the model, they have also indicated considerable room for improvement in the magnitude of the effects. There is still a lack of evidence about the effectiveness of the model with larger family units and many unknowns remain about the relationship between task attainment and problem change.

Case Illustration

The following case illustrates basic features of the model as well as recent developments of the use in conjoint work with families.

> Mrs. Johnson contacted a family agency because of problems concerning her sixteen-year-old daughter, Nancy, and the resulting fighting in her family. In an initial interview with the parents, Nancy, and her fourteen-year-old brother, Mark, the family members presented their views of their problems. Mr. J. began the session with a stream of complaints about Nancy. Her "attitude" toward him and his wife was "hostile." She did not accept his beliefs or standards and any attempt to communicate with her was futile. He then turned to the problem that precipitated their contact with the agency: Nancy's insistence that her boyfriend, Mike (age nineteen), be allowed to visit in their home over the weekend.
>
> Mr. J. had objected to Nancy's relationship with Mike ever since Nancy's pregnancy and abortion about six months earlier, but had accepted it because Nancy was determined to see him anyway. He even tolerated Mike's coming to their home but did not want him there all weekend (Mike would stay over Friday and Saturday night, using a spare room). He saw Mike as an unwelcome intruder whose presence deprived Mr. J. of his privacy.
>
> Joining in, Mrs. J. complained of Nancy's nagging her to get permission to do things her father might not allow. If Mrs. J. refused, Nancy would become belligerent and insulting. On top of this, Mrs. J. would usually be the one to patch things up between Nancy and her father. Nancy said little but expressed bitterness that her parents were trying

to disrupt her relationship with Mike. When asked about his views of the problem, Mark commented in a somewhat detached way that the fighting between his mother and Nancy was the main difficulty.

From the family's presentation of the problems and their interactions in the session, the practitioner was impressed with the father's lack of real control and Nancy's efforts to get what she wanted through her mother, who was put in the middle. Further exploration made clearer the mother's peacekeeping role and her discontent with it. The practitioner presented this picture as an additional problem to be considered.

In ranking the problems that had been brought up, the family agreed that the issue of greatest priority concerned the conflict over Mike's visiting. They accepted the practitoner's formulation of "mother's being in the middle" as a second problem.

The family was seen for seven additional sessions. The main interventions were structured around problem-solving tasks in the session and at home. These tasks were designed to achieve a compromise around Mike's visiting and, in the process, to work on the dysfunctional interaction patterns that had been identified. Initially, these tasks were designed to bring about more direct communication between Nancy and her father as well as more cooperation between the parents. It became apparent, however, that the interaction pattern was more complex than originally thought. Mrs. J. was not the only peacemaker. Mr. J. frequently assumed this role with Nancy and her mother. The parents were then coming to each other's rescue without taking responsibility either individually or jointly for dealing with Nancy's behavior. In subsequent family problem-solving tasks, each parent agreed to take responsibility for settling his or her differences with Nancy without trying to rescue the other. At the same time, an effort was made to encourage the parents jointly to develop rules that each could apply consistently in dealing with Nancy.

Midway in treatment, a compromise was reached on Nancy's relationship with Mike. Mike could spend one night a week at the J.'s home but would not be there on the weekend. Interestingly enough, the solution was suggested by Mark who had remained somewhat on the sidelines in the family discussions. The plan was implemented, and, perhaps to everyone's surprise, held up.

The case ended on a positive note. The immediate problem had been worked through and the family members, in their evaluation of treatment, indicated that their situation was as a whole better. In her consumer questionnaire, Mrs. J. commented that the experience had been a "good lesson in problem-working."

This case illustrates several features of the model. Focus was on the specific problem the family wanted most to solve. The major intervention strategy was based on tasks in which family members struggled toward a solution in their own way. At the same time, dysfunctional patterns of intervention that might underlie this and other problems were expicitly identified with the family or worked on as a part of the problem-solving tasks. Not all cases present such opportunities to achieve contextual change within the context of family problem-solving. In this case, they were present and were well utilized by the family and practitioner.

Range of Application

A question inevitably asked of any treatment system, in one form or another, is, "For what kind of case is, and is not, the system applicable?" In answering this question, it is important to distinguish between use of the system as a whole and use of activities for task planning, implementation, and review. The latter have of course a much wider range of application than the former. In fact, sequences of task-centered activities can be used in almost any form of treatment to enable clients to define and carry through particular courses of action. Thus, a practitioner might use task-centered methods during the course of long-term psychosocial treatment to help the client translate into action some aspect of insight into his problems.

When the task-centered system is used in full as the sole or primary method of treatment, its range of application, while narrower, is still broad enough to serve as a basic approach for the majority of clients served by clinical social workers. However, the majority is not all. It is possible to identify certain types of clients for whom the model in full may not provide the optimal mode of practice. Such types would include: (1) clients who are not interested in taking action to solve specific problems in their life situations, but who instead want help in exploring existential issues, such as concerns about life goals or identity, or who wish to talk about stressful experiences, such as loss of a loved one, with an accepting, empathic person; (2) clients who are unwilling or unable to utilize the structure of the model—for example, clients who prefer a more casual, informal mode of helping, or clients faced with highly turbulent situations in which it is not possible to isolate and follow through on specific problems; (3) clients who wish to alter conditions, such as certain psychogenic and motor difficulties, for which it is not possible to identify problem-solving tasks that the client is able to carry out; and (4) clients who wish no help but may need to be seen for "protective reasons."

Although all these categories merit elaboration, the last in particular requires additional comment because of frequent misunderstandings concerning the use of the model with involuntary clients. The task-centered approach can be used with many persons who may not have sought the social worker's help or who may be initially reluctant to accept it since the social worker, as noted, does have the opportunity to influence the client's conception of his problems. Many of these cases involve "mandated" problems, which are essentially problems that are defined not by the client but by the community and its representatives, including the practitioner. Essentially, the social worker needs to reveal to the client at the outset the general shape of these mandated problems (54). As Tina Rzepnicki (56) has suggested and demonstrated, a reasonable next step is work with the client and relevant community agencies in an effort to negotiate problem definitions that are acceptable to those involved. In our experience such problem definitions can usually be found. In some cases the most honest and viable formulation is that the problem is the practitioner's and agency imposed presence in the client's life; the client and practitoner can then work collaboratively to accomplish what is needed to eliminate this instrusion.

Summary

Task-centered treatment is a system of brief, time-limited practice that emphasizes helping clients with specific problems of their own choosing through discrete client and practitioner actions or tasks. Service interviews are devoted largely to the specification of problems, and to the identification and planning of appropriate tasks, which are then carried out between sessions. Although there are limits on its range of application, it is offered as a basic service for the majority of clients dealt with by clinical social workers. The core methods of the approach, notably activities designed to help clients plan and implement problem-solving tasks, can be used within most practice frameworks.

References

1. Bass, Michael. "Toward a Model of Treatment for Runaway Girls in Detention," in William J. Reid and Laura Epstein (eds.), *Task-Centered Practice*. New York: Columbia University Press, 1977.

2. Beck, Aaron T. *Cognitive Therapy and the Emotional Disorders*. New York: International Universities Press, 1976.

3. Beck, Dorothy Fahs, and Mary Ann Jones. *Progress on Family Problems: A Nationwide Study of Clients' and Counselors; Views on Family Agency Services*. New York: Family Service Agency of America, 1973.

4. Bergin, Allen E., and Michael J. Lambert. "The Evaluation of Therapeutic Outcomes," in Sol L. Garfield and Allen E. Bergin (eds.), *Handbook of Psychotherapy and Behavior Change*, 2nd edition. New York: Wiley, 1971.

5. Birchler, Gary R., and Suzanne H. Spinks. "Behavioral-Systems Marital and Family Therapy: Integration and Clinical Application," *American Journal of Family Therapy*, Vol. 8 (1981), pp. 6–28.

6. Bogatay, Alan, and Frank Farrow. *An Assessment of the Management Impact of the Task-Centered Model in Public Welfare Agencies*. Washington, D.C.: Lewin and Associates, 1975.

7. Brown, Lester B. "Client Problem-Solving Learning in Task-Centered Social Treatment." Ph.D. dissertation, University of Chicago, 1980.

8. Butcher, James N., and Mary P. Ross. "Research on Brief and Crisis-Oriented Psychotherapies," in Sol L. Garfield and Allen E. Bergin (eds.), *Handbook of Psychotherapy and Behavior Change*, 2nd edition. New York: Wiley, 1978.

9. Cormican, Elin J. "Task-Centered Model for Work with the Aged," *Social Casework*, Vol. 58 (1977), pp. 490–494.

10. Dierking, Barbara, Margot Brown, and Anne E. Fortune. "Task-Centered Treatment in a Residential Facility for the Elderly: A Clinical Trial," *Journal of Gerontological Social Work*, Vol. 2 (1980), pp. 225–240.

11. Epstein, Laura. "A Project in School Social Work," in William J. Reid and Laura Epstein (eds.), *Task-Centered Practice*. New York: Columbia University Press, 1977.

12. ———. *Helping People: The Task-Centered Approach*. St. Louis: The C.V. Mosby Co., 1980.

13. Ewalt, Patricia L. "A Psychoanalytically Oriented Child Guidance Setting," in William J. Reid and Laura Epstein (eds.), *Task-Centered Practice*. New York: Columbia University Press, 1977.

14. Fortune, Anne E. "Communication in Task-Centered Treatment," *Social Work*, Vol. 24 (September 1979), pp. 390–396.

15. ———. "Problem-Solving Processes in Task-Centered Treatment with Adults and Children," *Journal of Social Service Research*, Vol. 2 (1979), pp. 357–371.

16. ———. *Task-Centered Practice with Families and Groups*. New York: Springer, 1985.

17. ———. "Treatment Groups," in Anne E. Fortune (ed.), *Task-Centered Practice with Families and Groups*. New York: Springer, 1985.

18. Garfield, Sol L. "Research on Client Variables in Psychotherapy," in Sol L. Garfield and Allen E. Bergin (eds.), *Handbook of Psychotherapy and Behavior Change*, 2nd edition. New York: Wiley, 1971.

19. Garvin, Charles D. "Task-Centered Group Work," *Social Service Review*, Vol. 48 (1974), pp. 494–507.

20. ———. "Strategies for Group Work with Adolescents," in Willian J. Reid and Laura Epstein (eds.), *Task-Centered Practice*. New York: Columbia University Press, 1977.

21. ———. "Practice with Task-Centered Groups," in Anne E. Fortune (ed.), *Task-Centered Practice with Families and Groups*. New York: Springer, 1985.

22. ———. William J. Reid, and Laura Epstein. "Task-Centered Group Work," in Robert Roberts and Helen Northen (eds.), *Theoretical Approaches to Social Work with Small Groups*. New York: Columbia University Press, 1976.

23. Gibbons, James S., Janet Butler, Paul Urwin, and Jane L. Gibbons. "Evaluation of a Social Work Service for Self-Poisoning Patients," *British Journal of Psychiatry*, Vol. 133 (1978), pp. 111–118.

24. Goldberg, E. Matilda, Jane Gibbons, and Ian Sinclair. *Problems, Tasks and Outcomes*. Winchester, Mass.: Allen and Unwin, 1984.

25. Goldman, Alvin I. *A Theory of Human Action*. Englewood Cliffs, N.J.: Prentice-Hall, 1970.

26. Gurman, Alan S., and David Kniskern. "Research on Marital and Family Therapy," in Sol L. Garfield and Allen E. Bergin (eds.), *Handbook of Psychotherapy and Behavior Change*, 2nd edition. New York: Wiley, 1971.

27. ———. "Family Therapy Outcome Research: Knowns and Unknowns," in A. S. Gurman and D. P. Kniskern (eds.), *Handbook of Family Therapy*. New York: Brunner/Mazel, 1981.

28. Hari, Veronica. "Instituting Short-Term Casework in a 'Long-Term' Agency," in William J. Reid and Laura Epstein (eds.), *Task-Centered Practice*. New York: Columbia University Press, 1977.

29. Hofstad, Milton O. "Treatment in a Juvenile Court Setting," in William J. Reid and Laura Epstein (eds.), *Task-Centered Practice*. New York: Columbia University Press, 1977.

30. Jacobson, Neil S., and Gayla Margolin. *Marital Therapy: Strategies Based on Social Learning and Behavior Exchange Principles*. New York: Brunner/Mazel, 1979.

31. Johnson, Deborah H., and Charles J. Gelso. "The Effectiveness of Time Limits in Counseling and Psychotherapy: A Critical Review," *Counseling Psychologist*, Vol. 9 (1982), pp. 70–83.

32. Larsen, JoAnn, and Craig Mitchell. "Task-Centered Strength-Oriented Group Work with Delinquents," *Social Casework*, Vol. 61, No. 3 (1980), pp. 154–163.

33. Luborsky, Lester, Barton Singer, and Lise Luborsky. "Comparative Studies of Psychotherapy," *Archives of General Psychiatry*, Vol. 32 (1975), pp. 995–1008.

34. Meltzoff, J., and M. Kornreich. *Research in Psychotherapy*. New York: Atherton Press, 1970.

35. Mitchell, Kevin M., Jerold D. Bozarth, and Conrad C. Krauft. "A Reappraisal of the Therapeutic Effectiveness of Accurate Empathy, Nonpossessive Warmth and Genuineness," in Alan S. Gurman and A. M. Razin (eds.), *Effective Psychotherapy: A Handbook of Research*. New York: Pergamon, 1977.

36. Newcome, Kent. "Task-Centered Group Work with the Chronic Mentally Ill in Day Treatment," in Anne E. Fortune (ed.), *Task-Centered Practice with Families and Groups*. New York: Springer, 1983.

37. Osborn, Alfred F. *Applied Imagination: Principles and Procedures of Creative Problem Solving*, 3rd edition. New York: Scribner's, 1963.

38. Parihar, Bageshawari. *Task-Centered Management in Human Services*. Springfield, Ill.: Charles C. Thomas, 1983.

39. Perlman, Helen Harris. *Social Casework: A Problem-Solving Process*. Chicago: University of Chicago Press, 1957.

40. ———. "The Problem-Solving Model in Social Casework," in Robert W. Roberts and Robert H. Nee (eds.), *Theories of Social Casework*. Chicago: University of Chicago Press, 1970.

41. Rathbone-McCuan, Eloise. "Intergenerational Family Practice with Older Families," in Anne E. Fortune (ed.), *Task-Centered Practice with Families and Groups*. New York: Springer, 1985.

42. Reid, William J. "A Test of a Task-Centered Approach," *Social Work*, Vol. 20 (1975), pp. 3–9.

43. ———. *The Characteristics and Effectiveness of Task-Centered Methods*. Report

of the Task-Centered Services Project, Vol. 2. Chicago: School of Social Service Administration, 1977.

44. ——. *The Task-Centered System*. New York: Columbia University Press, 1978.

45. ——. "Family Treatment Within a Task-Centered Framework," in Eleanor R. Tolson and William J. Reid (eds.), *Models of Family Treatment*. New York: Columbia University Press, 1981.

46. ——. *Family Problem-Solving*. New York: Columbia University Press, 1985.

47. Reid, William J., and Laura Epstein. *Task-Centered Casework*. New York: Columbia University Press, 1972.

48. —— (eds.). *Task-Centered Practice*. New York: Columbia University Press, 1977.

49. Reid, William J., and Richard O'Connor. "Client Acceptance and Brief Treatment." Paper presented at Annual Program meeting of Council on Social Work Education, Detroit, Michigan, March 1984.

50. Reid, William J., and Ann Shyne. *Brief and Extended Casework*. New York: Columbia University Press, 1969.

51. Reid, William J., Laura Epstein, Lester B. Brown, Eleanor Tolson, and Ronald H. Rooney. "Task-Centered School Social Work," *Social Work in Education*, Vol. 2 (1980), pp. 7–24.

52. Rooney, Ronald H. "Adolescent Groups in Public Schools," in William J. Reid and Laura Epstein (eds.), *Task-Centered Practice*. New York: Columbia University Press, 1977.

53. ——. "Separation Through Foster Care: Toward a Problem-Oriented Practice Model Based on Task-Centered Casework." Ph.D. dissertation, University of Chicago, 1978.

54. ——. "A Task-Centered Reunification Model for Foster Care," in Anthony A. Maluccio and Paula Sinanoglue (eds.), *Working with Biological Parents of Children in Foster Care*. New York: Child Welfare League of America, 1981.

55. ——, and Marsha Wanless. "A Model for Caseload Management Based on Task-Centered Casework," in Anne E. Fortune (ed.), *Task-Centered Practice with Families and Groups*. New York: Springer, 1985.

56. Rzepnicki, Tina L. "Task-Centered Intervention in Foster Care Services: Working with Families who have Children in Placement," in Anne E. Fortune (ed.), *Task-Centered Practice with Families and Groups*. New York: Springer, 1985.

57. Salmon, Wilma. "A Service Program in a State Public Welfare Agency," in William J. Reid and Laura Epstein (eds.), *Task-Centered Practice*. New York: Columbia University Press, 1977.

58. Sloane, R. Bruce, Fred R. Staples, Allen H. Cristol, Neil J. Yorkston, and Kathrine Whipple. *Psychotherapy Versus Behavior Therapy*. Cambridge, Mass.: Harvard University Press, 1975.

59. Stotland, Ezra. *The Psychology of Hope*. San Francisco: Jossey-Bass, 1969.

60. Strupp, Hans H., Ronald E. Fox, and Ken Lessler. *Patients View Their Psychotherapy*. Baltimore: Johns Hopkins Press, 1969.

61. Studt, Eliot. "Social Work Theory and Implication for the Practice of Methods," *Social Work Education Reporter*, Vol. 16 (1968), pp. 22–46.

62. Taylor, Carvel. "Counseling in a Service Industry," in William J. Reid and Laura

Epstein (eds.), *Task-Centered Practice*. New York: Columbia University Press, 1977.

63. Thibault, Jane M. "The Analysis and Treatment of Indirect Self-Destructive Behaviors of Elderly Patients." Ph.D. dissertation, University of Chicago, 1984.

64. Thomas, Edwin J. *Marital Communication and Decision-Making: Analysis, Assessment, and Change*. New York: Free Press, 1976.

65. Tolson, Eleanor. "Alleviating Marital Communication Problems," in William J. Reid and Laura Epstein (eds.), *Task-Centered Practice*. New York: Columbia University Press, 1977.

66. Truax, Charles B., and Kevin M. Mitchell. "Research on Certain Therapist Interpersonal Skills in Relation to Process and Outcome," in Sol L. Garfield and Allen E. Bergin (eds.), *Handbook of Psychotherapy and Behavior Change*. New York: Wiley, 1971.

67. Watzlawick, Paul, Janet Helmick Beavin, and Don D. Jackson. *Pragmatics of Human Communication*. New York: Norton, 1967.

68. Weissman, Andrew. "In the Steel Industry," in William J. Reid and Laura Epstein (eds.), *Task-Centered Practice*. New York: Columbia University Press, 1977.

69. Wexler, Phyllis. "A Case from a Medical Setting," in William J. Reid and Laura Epstein (eds.), *Task-Centered Practice*. New York: Columbia University Press, 1977.

70. Wise, Frances. "Conjoint Marital Treatment," in William J. Reid and Laura Epstein (eds.), *Task-Centered Practice*. New York: Columbia University Press, 1977.

71. Wodarski, John S., Marcy Saffir, and Malcolm Frazer. "Using Research to Evaluate the Effectiveness of Task-Centered Casework," *Journal of Applied Social Sciences*, Vol. 7 (1982), pp. 70–82.

Annotated Listing of Key References

EPSTEIN, LAURA. *Helping People: The Task-Centered Approach*. St. Louis, Mo.: C.V. Mosby Co., 1980.
The basic methods of the model are presented within the context of the realities of agency practice and the social welfare system.

FORTUNE, ANNE E., with contributors. *Task-Centered Practice with Families and Groups*. New York: Springer, 1985.
The author and her contributors examine applications of task-centered practice in family, group, and organizational contexts. Chapters cover adaptations of the model for work with older persons, the mentally ill, married couples, single parents, and families in child welfare settings.

REID, WILLIAM J. *Family Problem-Solving*. New York: Columbia University Press, 1985.
The book presents developments in task-centered family practice. Drawing on contributions from behavioral communications, structural and other family therapy approaches,the volume shows how tasks within the session and at home can be used to resolve specific problems, enhance family problem-solving skills, and strengthen family functioning.

REID, WILLIAM J. *The Task-Centered System*. New York: Columbia University Press, 1978.
Developments in the task-centered model since its original formulation are set forth. The theory underlying the model is enlarged, new methods of intervention are described, and research on its effectiveness is presented.

REID, WILLIAM J., and LAURA EPSTEIN. *Task-Centered Casework*. New York: Columbia University Press, 1972.
The original formulation of the task-centered system of practice is presented together with studies of preliminary trials of the model.

REID, WILLIAM J., and LAURA EPSTEIN (eds.). *Task-Centered Practice*. New York: Columbia University Press, 1977.
This edited volume reports on applications of the task-centered model with individuals, families, and groups in a variety of settings, including child guidance, mental health, medical, school, public welfare, family service, and correctional.

CHAPTER 12

Crisis Theory

Naomi Golan

Summary of Theory

Over the past thirty-odd years, a number of theoretical formulations, reports of therapeutic innovations, and research studies have been loosely drawn together under the rubric of "crisis theory." The parameters are probably too broad and too amorphous to grant it recognition as a systematic theory in the sense of its being an internally consistent body of verified hypotheses, as discussed by Francis Turner in Chapter 1. Nevertheless, enough generalizations and conclusions have coalesced to recognize the emergence of a discernible framework wthin which to examine stressful situations, to offer a body of guidelines and techniques for intervention at such times, and to distinguish between crises and other forms of stress.

The crisis approach is rooted in several disparate bodies of theory and practice, some of which developed quite independently and others which have converged, fused, and sometimes separated again to go off in diverse directions. No one particular discipline can lay claim to ownership, although the Harvard Schools of Psychiatry and Public Health have probably been most active in pioneering the theoretical framework, while the Benjamin Rush Center of Los Angeles has undoubtedly developed the practice application most fully, at least within the mental health field. However, for more than

296

ten years, its usage has broadened until today it is widely accepted by a broad range of helping professions. A prolific body of professional literature accumulated around two foci: the nature and process of crisis and stress situations, and the utilizaton of these formulations to deal with a broad spectrum of psychosocial difficulties.

Although crisis theory is essentially eclectic in nature, certain basic assumptions, hypotheses, and concepts appear to form the core approach. These can be summarized in a set of statements gleaned initially from the work of Erich Lindemann and Gerald Caplan and developed and expanded by Lydia Rapoport, Howard Parad, David Kaplan, Gerald Jacobson, Martin Strickler, Peter Sifneos, Naomi Golan, and others:

1. An individual (or family, group, or community) is subjected to periods of increased internal and external stress throughout his normal life span that disturb his customary state of equilibrium with his surrounding environment. Such episodes are usually initiated by some *hazardous event* that may be a finite external blow or a less bounded internal pressure that has built up over time. The event may be a single catastrophic occurrence or a series of lesser mishaps that have a cumulative effect.

2. The impact of the hazardous event disturbs the individual's homeostatic balance and puts him into a *vulnerable state*, marked by heightened tension and anxiety. To regain his equilibrium, he goes through a series of predictable phases. First, he tries to use his customary repertoire of problem-solving mechanisms to deal with the situation. If this is not successful, his upset increases and he mobilizes heretofore untried emergency methods of coping. However, if the problem continues and can neither be resolved, avoided, nor redefined, tension continues to rise to a peak.

3. At this point, a *precipitating factor* can bring about a turning point, during which self-righting devices no longer operate and the individual enters a state of *active crisis*, marked by disequilibrium and disorganization. This is followed by a period of gradual *reorganization* until a new state of equilibrium is reached.

4. As the crisis situation develops, the individual may perceive the initial and subsequent stressful events primarily as a *threat*, either to his instinctual needs or to his sense of autonomy and well-being; as a *loss* of a person, an attribute (status or role), or a capacity; or as a *challenge* to survival, growth, or mastery.

5. Each of these perceptions calls forth a characteristic emotional reaction that reflects the subective meaning of the event to the individual: threat elicits a heightened level of anxiety; loss brings about feelings of depression, deprivation, and mourning; challenge stimulates a moderate increase in anxiety plus a kindling of hope and expectation, releasing new energy for problem-solving.

6. Although a crisis situation is neither an illness nor a pathological experience and reflects a realistic struggle to deal with the individual's current life situation, it may become linked with earlier unresolved or partially re-

solved conflicts. This may result in an inappropriate or exaggerated response. Crisis intervention in such situations may provide a multiple opportunity: to resolve the present difficulty, to rework the previous difficulties, and/or to break the linkage between them.

7. The total length of time between the initial blow and final resolution of the crisis situation varies widely, depending on the severity of the hazardous event, the characteristic reactions of the person, the nature and complexity of the tasks that have to be accomplished, and the situational supports available. The actual state of active disequilibrium, however, is time-limited, usually lasting four to six weeks.

8. Each particular class of crisis situation (such as the death of a close relative or the experience of being raped) seems to follow a specific sequence of stages that can be predicted and mapped out. Emotional reactions and behavioral responses at each phase can often be anticipated. Fixation and disequilibrium at a particular point may provide the clue as to where the person is "stuck" and what lies behind his inability to do his "crisis work" and master the situation.

9. During the unraveling of the crisis situation, the individual tends to be particularly amenable to help. Customary defense mechanisms have become weakened, usual coping patterns have proved inadequate, and the ego has become more open to outside influence and change. A minimal effort at such time can produce a maximal effect; a small amount of help, appropriately focused, can prove more effective than extensive help at a period of less emotional accessibility.

10. During the reintegration phase, new ego sets may emerge and new adaptive styles may evolve, enabling the person to cope more effectively with other situations in the future. However, if appropriate help is not available during this critical interval, inadequate or maladaptive patterns may be adopted that can result in weakened ability to function adequately later on.

After the first flush of controversy, during which proponents of the crisis approach seemed to advocate its usage as a universal panacea and opponents damned it as ineffective symptom removal, the theory and its application have entered the mainstream of social work knowledge. Currently it is being used discriminately by practice theoreticians to explain certain types of phenomena encountered throughout the life span of individuals, families, and groups during period of enhanced stress. It has become an important transitional theory, binding traditional casework practice to new developments in ego psychology, learning theory, and the role and systems approaches.

For practitioners, it provides the conceptual frame of reference for brief, focused intervention in a wide range of pressureful situations and is being offered as the treatment of choice for a considerable part of the activities within family agencies, public welfare offices, medical facilities, mental health clinics, school services, and community development programs, among others. Social workers in traditional primary agencies, in complex secondary settings, and in special crisis and emergency management outposts now tailor their practice toward helping clients deal with problems generated by antic-ipated and unanticipated stress, according to guidelines set down by crisis theory.

Historical Origins

Present-day crisis theory can be viewed as the merging of two mainstreams of developments since World War II: psychological and sociological theory and experimentation, on the one hand, and social work practice theory, on the other.

Psychological Developments

In the field of psychodynamic theory, while classical psychoanalytic theo-reticians continued to concentrate on unconscious processes and the psycho-pathology of patients, significant segments of second- and third-generation metapsychologists, such as Heinz Hartmann, Ernst Kris, Rudolf Loewen-stein, Ives Hendrick, Abraham Kardiner, Bela Mittelmann, David Rapaport, Sandor Rado, Franz Alexander, and Abraham Maslow, turned their atten-tion to the executive, conflict-free areas of the ego. Hartmann's concept of ego autonomy (82), amplified and developed by Rapaport (65), spurred in-terest in the autonomous role of the ego in personality formation. Functions such as cognition, perception, intention, motility, motivation, and mastery began to be studied in detail and a far more optimistic view of personality growth and development started to supplant the earlier, more deterministic id psychology.

Meanwhile, Erik Erikson, working independently, developed his eight-stage epigenetic approach to the life cycle (46). He postulated that, as the person passes through the various stages in his life span, he faces key problems ("psychosocial crises") in reorientation. His ability to solve each successive crisis either enhances or weakens his ability to master problems in subsequent stages. At this same time, child psychologist Jean Piaget was examining min-utely children's intellectual and motor processes to determine at which levels they developed their cognitive capacities to organize and incorporate new experiences and to solve problems (150).

Sibylle Escalona investigated the normal developmental patterns of in-fants (49) and Lois Murphy mapped the unfolding abilities of children and adolescents to evolve coping and master patterns (133). The new field of life-span developmental psychology began to view the individual's normative life span from the dual perspective of his unfolding personality and his sociali-zation to his environment (9), with special attention paid to the transitional phases between developmental stages (38, 161).

Parallel to this, laboratory experimenters were studying stress from quite a different point of view. Using Cannon's concept of homeostasis and Herrick's theory of systemic equilibration as a starting point, Hans Selye (171) began in the 1950s to observe the individual's performance under various stress-inducing conditions. He proposed a series of three stages: first, an *alarm reaction*, consisting of successive shock and countershock phases; then, *resistance*, during which maximal adaptaton is attempted; and finally, *exhaustion*, when adaptive mechanisms collapse.

Experimental psychologists examined reactions under naturally stressful conditions such as isolation in the Antarctic or in prison camps, or through laboratory studies during which stress-producing variables were systematically introjected. Of particular interest are Richard Lazarus's studies on cognitive factors underlying stress (113) in which he emphasizes the need to appraise both the threatening condition and the potential avenues for solution and mastery. Irving Janis's original interest in patients' response to high-threat situations such as impending surgery (99) has more recently broadened to the decisions individuals make under stressful conditions (100). He sees such decision-making as involving appraisal of the challenge posed by the stress situation, evaluation of recommended alternatives, reaching a tentative decision as to the best available policy, commitment to the new policy, and adherence to it despite challenge.

Learning theorists were also looking at coping and decision-making, using a cognitive approach with its emphasis on information processing. Thus Julian Taplin (192) sees the person experiencing a crisis as having his processes of perception, cognition, and decision-making interrupted as the result of some physical or psychological "overload"; he now needs new information to build new cognitive maps and to develop his capacity to design and select new coping strategies. Even after the crisis peak is passed, these can stand him in good stead in the future.

Behavioral modification advocates stress the need, during periods of crisis, to unlearn old, unsuccessful, or damaging patterns of interaction and to learn new, constructive ones. Emphasis is placed on teaching the person how to change and to recognize how others perceive him. Behavior is shaped toward helping him to engage in more socially acceptable and less pain-producing activities and learn more productive ways to deal with problems (31).

Sociological Studies

Sociologists have been studying crises in two main areas: family stress situations and reactions to community disasters.

Pioneer work on family responses was carried out by Reuben Hill and his associates (87) who investigated stress reactions of family members during various stages in the family life cycle. He found three interacting elements that appeared to determine whether a given event would bring about a family crisis—the external hardship or crisis-precipitating event ("stressor"), the internal organization of the family, and the family's definition of the event as stress-inducing—and developed his "ABCX" family crisis model. Customary adequacy in family functioning was contrasted with crisis proneness in multiproblem families. Ernest Burgess (23) noted that sudden changes in family status and conflict among family members as to their roles added to family crises.

Other researchers examined the impact of various types of family developmental and transitional crisis such as marriage (155), parenthood (166), and old age (117), as well as viewing the entire process of change and development within the life cycle (119). The effect of stressful life events such as physical and emotional illnesses (39) and poverty, deprivation, and alienation (145) on both individual and family functioning were also studied.

Extensive attention has been paid by sociologists and "disasterologists" to large-scale disasters (8, 32) and field studies have been carried out on community behavior during tornadoes (193), floods (194), mine collapses, (198) etc. James Tyhurst (198) noted that community disasters produced three overlapping phases: *impact, recoil,* and *post-trauma.* Other researchers found that, while each disaster followed its own unique pattern, seven common stages could be discerned: *warning, threat, impact, inventory, rescue, remedy,* and *recovery* (172). Much of the more recent work on emergency and disaster management (142), (183) has been built upon this foundation.

Psychiatric Developments

Since the mid-forties, military psychiatrists, as the result of experiences in the armed forces during and after World War II (73), the Korean conflict (79), and the Vietnam War (26), attempted to predict the performance of soldiers who might later break under field pressures. Early theories of a "stress personality profile" turned out to be unpredictive under subsequent tests and were eventually revised to include current situational factors that could mitigate underlying pathology. Ruth Jaffe (98) found the need for self-preservation, libidinal ties with friends in the army, identification with his nation's ideals, an intact body image, and ego-controlled aggression were predominant characteristics of Israeli soldiers in the Six-Day War, while Michael Merbaum and Albert Hefez (126) were able to isolate common personality characteristics of Israeli and American soldiers who broke under extreme stress.

As an offshoot of the Vietnam War and its aftermath, the plight of families of prisoners of war and servicemen missing in action began, in the late 1960s, to receive particular attention for the first time (120). Special counseling services were set up to discuss with families problems arising out of the incipient and subsequent reunion with their long-separated husbands and fathers.

In Erich Lindemann's seminal study on grief reactions to the Coconut Grove nightclub fire in Boston in 1943, (118), he found that the duration and severity of bereavement depended upon the extent to which each survivor or relative could successfully carry out his "grief work"; that is, the degree to which he was able to achieve emancipation from his bondage to the deceased, to readjust to an environment in which the deceased was missing, and to be able to form new relationships over time.

Lindemann noted that certain inevitable events in the individual's life cycle generate emotional stress and strain, which are countered by a series of adaptive mechanisms that can either lead to mastery of the new situation or failure, with impairment of functioning. While some situations may be stressful to all persons, they become crisis for those who are particularly vulnerable because of personality factors or whose emotional resources are unduly taxed. This theoretical formulation led to the establishment, in 1948, of the Wellesley Human Relations Service, a community-based project aimed at preventive intervention in typical hazardous family situations (108).

Parallel to and interwoven with Lindemann's work, Gerald Caplan, whose early interest in crisis situations grew out of his work with immigrant mothers and children in Israel after World War II (27), began to develop his own approach, which was set in the public health format of primary, secondary, and tertiary levels of intervention (28). He defined a crisis as occurring when a person faces an obstacle to important life goals that is, for a time, insurmountable by means of customary methods of problem-solving. He identified two types of crisis situations: those precipitated by changes in the normal course of living, such as entry into school, birth of a sibling, marriage, retirement, and death; and those occasioned by accidental hazardous events, such as acute or chronic illness, accidents, or family dislocation.

During the 1950s and early 1960s, a series of investigations was carried out by the Harvard School of Public Health, under Caplan's direction, at the Family Guidance Center and elsewhere in the Boston area on various types of situational maturational crises such as the premature birth of a child (30) and adjustment to marriage (155). Much of the core theory on crisis intervention was developed within this framework.

The public health model questioned use of the traditional treatment model of sickness and cure and offered, as an alternative, the concept of the "acute situational disorder," in which crises are seen as similar to infectious disease states, which are usually self-limiting and are often superimposed upon healthy personalities or on long-term chronic conditions (101). Intervention in such cases becomes limited to alleviation of the acute reactive condition without dealing with the underlying pathology.

More recently, Caplan and his colleagues at the Harvard Department of Psychiatry's Laboratory of Community Psychiatry carried out studies on widowhood (179) and reactions to death (104). During the 1970s, Caplan focused his attention upon the natural and mutual support systems in the community that can be used to prevent and/or ameliorate the destructive aspects of crisis situations (29).

On the West Coast, Gerald Jacobson and his colleagues opened the Benjamin Rush Center for Problems of Living as part of the Los Angeles Psychiatric Service, using Caplan's framework to offer brief, immediate crisis intervention in a wide range of social and emotional problems (2, 97). As their contribution to crisis theory, they differentiated between two approaches, the *generic*, which emphasizes classes of situational and maturational crises that occur to significant population groups and can be dealt with by paraprofessionals and volunteers as well as professionals, and the *individual*, which stresses the patient's specific intrapsychic and interpersonal processes and requires more intensive treatment (96).

As a special development within the mental health field, the suicide prevention movement, largely in the hands of clinical psychologists, developed with astonishing rapidity in the late 1950s and in the 1960s (122). Much of the pioneering work was carried out, first by Louis Dublin (41) and then by Edwin Shneidman, Norman Farberow, and Robert Litman (175), who contributed the concept of the "psychological autopsy." In recent years, suicide prevention centers have broadened their scope to cover other types of crisis and emergency situations, such as alcohol and drug abuse and psychiatric difficulties, and have merged into "crisis centers."

Path into Social Work

Social workers have been confronted with clients seeking help because of acute, stress-generated problems since the early days of the "friendly visitor." Bertha Reynolds recalled that the first summer course in psychiatric social work at Smith College in the summer of 1918 was set up "to contribute to the war effort by training workers for the rehabilitation of shell-shocked soldiers" (160).

Involvement on a broad scale, however, probably started during the Great Depression of the 1930s with its widespread economic and social dislocations that forced numerous individuals and families, for the first time, to turn to public and private social agencies for help. Gordon Hamilton (76) noted that caseworkers, drawn from private and voluntary services, were initially bewildered and overwhelmed by the staggering caseloads. Under the pressure of necessity, however, they learned to combine mass assistance with "reasonable individualization."

It was during this period that the Travelers Aid, which primarily operated in railway stations and bus terminals, developed its special approach, backed by intuitive and skillful practice, for dealing with frightened, upset, disheartened clients:

> A crisis which has just developed is far easier to resolve than one less abrupt in development. . . . The sudden crisis presents a challenge to the client; friends and family recognize the need to rally to his reinforcement. But the problem which has been slowly developing over a period of months or years requires a different attack. While the latest point of difficulty may be treated in the short contact, the more fundamental problem may have to remain untouched. (206, p. 64)

Trained caseworkers were purposely placed within easy reach of the public under the agency's firm conviction that it was possible to provide fundamental help in one or several interviews (197).

World War II, following closely after the depression, eased some of the economic pressures but brought other family disruptions, separations, and difficulties. This resulted in both increased pressures and new opportunities for family agencies that undertook to help mothers take necessary jobs in defense industries and to develop child care services for their children. Agencies also became concerned with men rejected for service for physical and emotional reasons. Family breakup as the aftermath of separation, war tensions and anxieties, and hasty war marriages called for quick, skilled casework services (162). Within the armed forces, psychiatric social workers, rapidly trained to meet the burgeoning needs, focused on short-term treatment of service-connected problems (35).

During this period, social work theoreticians were attempting to reconcile two divergent viewpoints; the *diagnostic* approach, which emphasized the importance of a careful, all-encompassing evaluation of the total person-in-his-social-situation, and the *functionalist* outlook, which emphasized the special needs of the client under pressure and the importance of time as a factor in the casework relationship (96).

Charlotte Towle (195) was one of the first to bring out the rehabilitative goal in helping people in periods of trouble as a way of meeting their common human needs. During the Korean conflict, she observed:

> Social work has always served families whose individual worlds have been stressful. The noteworthy features today are the totality of life's uncertainty and the facts that parents and children have grown up during precarious times—war, inflation, depression, war, inflation, and now a defense economy. Many are vulnerable by reason of long-standing strain. . . . Stresses become traumatic through repetition. (162, p. 163)

Helen Perlman described the client coming to a social agency as being under a twofold stress; the problem itself is felt as a threat or actual attack, and his inability to cope with it increases his tension. She also pointed out that "the greater the client's sense of duress and tension, the more overwhelmed and helpless he may feel. The problem-solving functions of his ego are likely to be at least temporarily disabled or constricted. . . . Relief from stress in one aspect of living may lighten the burden in another (147, pp. 25–26).

She observed that, while not every problem brought to an agency may be an actual crisis at the point of calling or walking in, the applicant feels that it is. Thus the chance to provide the "little help at the strategic time" is lost if the applicant is asked to wait (148).

By the early 1960s, social workers were becoming increasingly concerned over lengthening waiting lists and staff shortages, on the one hand, and frequent dropouts and unplanned terminations, on the other. Research studies brought out the startling information that one out of three cases did not return to family agencies after the first interview (11) and four out of five discontinued by the fifth (164). A series of research investigations at the Community Service Society of New York (158) and at the University of Chicago (156) led to the development of a short-term, time-limited model of focused treatment, which was subsequently tested in a wide range of settings (157).

Much of the traditional dichotomy between "treatment aimed at maintaining adaptive patterns" and "treatment aimed at modifying adaptive patterns" (52) had broken down by this time and a far more eclectic approach to clients in acute stress was emerging. By the 1980s, both crisis intervention and planned short-term treatment had become assimilated into social work practice as an appropriate approach to clients in high-stress situations. One recent textbook on practice offers this point of view:

> Individuals and families frequently come to the attention of social workers when they are in crisis and at that time they are frequently most ready to develop new and more differentiated means of responding to the demanding events and changes. The events precipitating these crises may be developmental, occasioned by rapid growth and changes in members of the family. For example, in many families the onset of adolescence in a child is experienced as a crisis; in others, the departure of the first grown child from the home. Other potential precipitants include painful and disrupting events such as illness, accidents, personal losses, or economic reverses. (81, p. 66)

Principal Social Work Proponents

Social Work Theory in Crisis Intervention

Much of the early adaptation of crisis theory to social work practice was developed by Howard Parad (137), Lydia Rapoport (152), and David Kaplan (102) through their participation in the School of Public Health program at Harvard, and by Martin Strickler and his colleagues at the Rush Center in Los Angeles (189). More recently, Golan (69), Smith (184), and Parad (139) have attempted to place the theory in the context of current approaches to practice.

In evaluating the current status of crisis theory in social work, we note that its development has passed through three stages. First, a number of theoretical, experiential, and research formulations on crises and the related areas of stress, disasters, and emergencies were gathered together. Next, these ideas were woven into a theoretical framework that was applied, tested, and modified to meet the specific conditions and needs of a wide variety of clients, workers, and settings. Finally, selected elements from both theory and practice were integrated into a series of models that became integrated into the matrix of practice and accepted as part of the armamentarium of strategies and techniques that practitioners could call upon. (These will be developed in detail later on.)

Strickler and Margaret Bonnefil (191) see similarities between crisis intervention and traditional casework as it is currently being practiced. Treatment goals in both instances are aimed at enhancing the client's ability to cope with current problems in living. Treatment is focused on specific problems of interpersonal conflict and role dysfunction; it is concentrated on the problem to be solved and is largely geared to the conscious and near-conscious levels of emotional conflicts. The practitioner recognizes transference aspects but moves to replace them with analogous feelings related to the client's current situation and significant relationships. The worker in both types of treatment must be able to make a diagnostic evaluation based on the client's position in his intrafamilial and extended social relationships.

Nevertheless, they find significant differences between the two approaches. In the traditional psychosocial viewpoint, the practitioner seeks to help the client gradually sort out and clarify her feelings; in the crisis approach, he works at an intense pace, sharing the client's sense of urgency as they work together to resolve the problem at hand. Treatment is based on the client's readiness to risk herself in order to gain a sense of mastery, of being once more in control of his life, and on the worker's alertness to forestall or minimize the client's dependent or regressive fantasies. The need to make quick, independent decisions and to take an activist stance makes many caseworkers uneasy and uncomfortable.

Social Work Practice in Crisis Situations

Even before crisis theory reached its present level of extrapolation, social work practitioners were beginning to use elements inherent in the theory to resolve some of the unresolved difficulties encountered in their ongoing practice. Starting in the late 1950s, reports began to appear at national and regional conferences and in the professional literature, ranging from simple experiential accounts on the "we-did-it-and-it-worked" level to highly sophisticated evaluations, complete with research components, of crisis-oriented service programs.

As might be anticipated, much of the innovation initially developed in the mental health field. In some instances, special programs, such as the Benjamin Rush Center described above, were set up where walk-in patients were helped to regain psychic equilibrium by reducing their anxiety over a particular difficulty in their current life situation. In pilot projects, such as the Emergency Psychiatric Service experiment at Massachusetts General Hospital in Boston, alcoholics and other types of patients were offered immediate, round-the-clock help with social and emotional problems as part of an intensificaton of admissions arrangements. In traditional psychiatric clinics, such as the Madeline Borg Child Guidance Institute of the Jewish Board of Guardians in New York City and the Langley-Porter Neuropsychiatric Institute in San Francisco, theoretical frameworks of practice were modified to pave the way for the use of the crisis approach. In psychiatric hospitals, crisis intervention with patients' families was used profitably as an alternative to admission.

Since the mid-sixties, these innovative programs have increased and proliferated, with social workers often acting as prime movers in offering direct service to patients and their families, individually and in groups. The offering of social service in the emergency room at Temple University Hospital in Philadelphia on weekends (185) and at the Cult Clinic of the Los Angeles Jewish Family Service (1) are current examples of new modes of practice in stressful situations.

Some of the early projects in family service agencies were simply modest efforts to modify the ways in which traditional help was offered (42). It took the national survey of family services and psychiatric clinics for children in 1965–66 to bring widespread attention to the extent and relative success of crisis-oriented programs in this area (141). This project, as well as the Reid research studies mentioned earlier, were undoubtedly instrumental in encouraging the shift in practice in short-term, focused intervention, often with a crisis orientation. Family agencies began to hold staff development seminars to update workers' orientation (45) and in recent years, crisis intervention has become the treatment of choice for many cases seen in family agencies (110).

Services for the aged, in children's courts, and in legal conciliation programs were all accustomed to dealing with clients at points of high urgency; they now adopted the crisis approach as a theoretical justification for what they had already been doing on a *de facto* basis. Even public welfare agencies began to shift to the crisis intervention framework for part of their services. Basing their practice on the premise that a family's request for financial assistance often implies other needs as well, workers in a special counseling project at the New York Bureau of Child Welfare used reaching-out techniques to help clients restore coping capacities temporarily impaired by stress situations (131).

Child welfare workers have become active in using the crisis approach, both in foster home placements (181) and in providing services to children in their own homes to enable families experiencing severe crises to stay together despite disruptions and pressures (107). When children have had to be cared for outside of the home, innovative programs like the twenty-four hour Emergency Crisis Care Center in Madison, Wisconsin, were developed (57). The stress inherent in the pregnancy of unwed college students were used to teach them new, growth-producing coping skills (168).

Since medical situations, by their very nature, tend to generate crises, hospital social workers have always spent a major part of their practice in-dealing with them (169). Other reports of work in a neonatal intensive-care nursery service (174) and with families of patients undergoing kidney trans-plants (25) reflect efforts to deal with the stress induced by diagnosis of the illness or defect. In cases of terminal illness, helping parents anticipate the death of their child (104) or working to keep communication open between patient and spouse (114) demonstrate the sensitive, crisis oriented practice taking place in these highly traumatic situations. Social workers on contin-uous call in emergency services make immediate psychosocial assessments and rapid dispositions of nonmedical problems as part of admission service staffs (13, 75, 94).

Rape victims are being seen in a special program in a community mental health center and are helped, through crisis intervention techniques, to pass through the sequential phases of acute reaction, outward adjustment, and final resolution of the experience (55). Sometimes several agencies band to-gether to provide comprehensive service for rape victims (78). Sometimes so-cial workers and police form special teams to deal with these and other violent situations in which crisis intervention is deemed necessary (24, 208). In other instances, new structures of services have been set up, such as a special run-away center to provide emergency service for youngsters unwilling to use established services (209).

Assistance during and after periods of community and social disasters had formerly been given in an informal, unplanned, spontaneous way (74). During the 1970s, following implementing federal legislation, disaster aid has become an established form of social intervention (142). A pattern of disaster service has emerged in which public and voluntary programs com-bine in a delicate balance (58). Short-term ameliorative help, often carried out by social workers "on the front line," is provided on a crisis-intervention basis while longer range prevention and amelioration programs are being developed on the administrative and policy-making level within governmen-tal frameworks (22).

Despite the wide variations in structure, clientele, and service affilia-tion, all these recent programs show a common orientation rooted, to a greater or lesser degree, in crisis theory.

Today, crisis intervention has become an accepted approach, both for new situations with clients struggling with anticipated or unanticipated changes in their life patterns and in long-term cases where sudden deepen-ing—or heightening—of clients' stress enables the practitioner to take ad-vantage of the opportune moment to centralize his focus and intensify the pace of treatment. Much of the current interest in crisis intervention as a mode of treatment has become merged into experimentation with task-centered models of practice (157).

Social workers' adoption of the crisis approach is undoubtedly due to a large extent to the fact that much of the theory is in general agreement with their own value systems and because it tends to supplement and flesh out their own practice experience. Lydia Rapoport (154) points out that this theory incorporates a great deal of familiar and accepted knowledge and clinical concepts, as well as relevant principles and techniques. Nevertheless, its actual application is often capricious and halfhearted.

Part of the difficulty, on the practice level, lies in the setting up of telephone "hot-lines" and special crisis centers, often manned largely by volunteers and paraprofessionals, who have reduced its application to a rigid and often ritualistic formula, which is against basic social work principles of treating each client as an individual. A second, major area of confusion, on the theoretical level, lies in the ambiguous application of the term "crisis." This stems, to a large extent, from the idiosyncratic definition used by Erikson. He called a psychosocial crisis "not a threat or catastrophe but a turning point, a crucial period of increased vulnerability and heightened potential" (47, pp. 95–96).

This usage enabled others to speak of a whole developmental stage as a period of crisis. Frances Scherz (170), for example, referred to the "crisis of adolescence," while Barbara Fried (61) described the "middle-age crisis." Others spoke of transitional periods, which sometimes lasted for years, as the "crisis of divorce" (207) or the "crisis of migration" (88). This is a far cry from Caplan's tight definition of a crisis as lasting no longer than six weeks and made up of definable elements. It becomes particularly confusing for practitioners when trying to apply a crisis model of treatment.

Within the last decade, several theoreticians have attempted to deal with this contradiction. Gerald Jacobson (95, pp. 8 9), for one, proposes the concept of a *crisis matrix*, a period in the life span during which a person is more likely to become upset or may require a prolonged period of adjustment. While such situations are not, in and of themselves, crises, individuals and families during such periods tend to find themselves in a precarious state of equilibrium and more vulnerable to a number of hazards, each of which may trigger a crisis, each limited to four to six weeks.

Golan (71) and others have suggested viewing developmental and transitional changes in a broader theoretical context, which will be discussed below.

Connection with Other Theories

Crisis theory as presently formulated has its primary roots in psychodynamic personality theory, in stress theory, and in learning theory, with sideshoots reaching into systems theory, role theory, and gratifications theory. While much of recent thinking in ego psychology has fundamental pertinence, several concepts have proved particularly useful.

In his later writings, Freud (60) suggested, but did not develop, the concept of *signal anxiety*. He noted that the young child, in the course of growing up, learns to anticipate a traumatic situation and to react to it with anxiety before it becomes traumatic; its producton in a situation of actual or anticipated danger is an ego function that serves to mobilize the forces at the ego's command to meet or avoid the impending peril. Hartmann (83) adds that signal anxiety is paramount among those forms of anticipation that makes organized action possible, helping to master an inner danger before it becomes an external threat. Erikson (46) differentiates between *fears*, which are states of apprehension that focus on isolated and recognizable dangers so that they may be judiciously appraised and realistically countered, and *anxieties*, which are diffuse states of tension that magnify and even cause the illusion of an outer danger, without pointing to any avenue of defense or mastery. Robert White, however, sees the avoidance of anxiety as equivalent to effectance, an independent ego energy. He uses it to explain the transformation of rigid defensive arrangements into more flexible ones (205, pp. 155–156).

In discussing the *mechanisms of defense*, Anna Freud (59) points out that, when persons are subject to the same real danger, those who have had no opportunity to master their tension by fulfilling some overt task are more likely to react with panic. Hartmann (82) points out that not every adaptation to the environment or every learning or maturation experience is a conflict; defense mechanisms can have a positive, reality-adaptive component. With change in function, the activity can become pleasurable in its own right.

White feels that one should pay careful attention to the way in which defenses adopted at time of crisis lead to "actions of an efficacious sort which work well upon the particular environment and thus become the basis for the continuing growth of competence and confidence" (205, p. 193). It is this temporary weakening of the defense mechanisms during the crisis situation that led Caplan to suggest that this period offers a time-limited opportunity to intervene effectively.

The third concept has been variously called "coping devices," "problem-solving activities," or "grappling patterns"; this refers to the way in which individuals learn to adapt and master internal and/or external pressures. Lois Murphy distinguishes between two kinds of coping: "the capacity to make use of the opportunities, challenges, and resources of the environment and to manage the pain, frustration, difficulties, and failures with which he (the child) is confronted," and "the capacity to maintain internal integration along with the resilience or potential to recover after a period of disintegrative response to stress" (132). The development of these coping patterns as ways of dealing with anxiety and reducing tensions are highly individual and related to the child's or family's basic life-style.

As noted earlier, learning to cope more successfully with stressful situations is one of the keystones of crisis theory. Caplan (28) outlines three general patterns for healthy crisis resolution: correct cognitive perception of the situation, management of affect through awareness of feelings and appropriate verbalization leading to tension discharge and mastery, and development of patterns of seeking and using help with actual tasks and feelings by using interpersonal and institutional resources.

Finally, John and Elaine Cumming maintain that the ego develops through a series of disequilibrations and subsequent reequilibrations between the person and her environment. Successful crisis resolution promotes ego growth by increasing the repertoire of ego sets available and the ability of the individual to cope with future crises. Thus crisis becomes an opportunity for growth and change. While ordinary problem-solving demands new uses or combinations of existing ego sets, a crisis requires the learning of new sets and their integration into the personality (37, pp. 54–57).

Many of the concepts taken from stress theory have already been described. The term "stress" itself has been used variously to describe three kinds of phenomena: (1) the noxious, stimulating condition, the stressful event or situation—sometimes called the "stressor"; (2) the state of the individual who responds to the stressful event (who is considered to be "in stress"); and (3) the relation between the stressful event, the individual's reaction to it, and the events to which it leads (154, pp. 273–274).

In its original engineering usage, the term "stress" was often given a negative connotation and linked with "strain"; this has carried over into the psychological research in this area. (This is in contrast to the term "crisis," which has been given a positive, challenging connotation. Charlotte Babcock points out that stress is handled by the ego. Its determinants, like those of ego strength, can be found in the person's biological matrix, in his environmental structures, and—in the case of illness or disability—in the scope and ramifications of the particular disease process (5, p. 47). Evaluating these structures later led to the building of an ecologic model for the assessment and design of services in stress situations (80, p. 280).

The attempt to establish a relationship between stressful events and their consequences spurred efforts by Thomas Holmes, Richard Rahe, and their associates to build scales to measure *susceptibility to stress* at various points in the life cycle (92). A long series of studies attempted to apply this type of classification to a wide range of stressful life events (39). While such a summation of values attached to various incidents can appear to have an arithmetic summation leading up to a danger point (in one study, of 300 points in one year), the Dohrenwends point out that distinctions must be made between objective and subjective events, gain and loss events, and events for which the individual may or may not be responsible. Differentiation needs to be made between physiological, psychological, and social processes that mediate the individual's response to stressful situations.

Most recently, Hamilton McCubbin and Joan Patterson (121) expanded the Hill family crisis model—ABCX (87, p. 141) in which A, the stressor event, interacts with B, the family's crisis-meeting resources, and with C, the definition the family makes of the event, to produce X, the crisis—into the Double ABCX model that focuses upon family efforts over time to recover from a crisis situation. The new elements are: *a*, the additional life stressors and changes that may influence the family's ability to achieve adaptation; *b*, the critical psychological and social factors families use in managing crisis situations; *c*, the processes families engage in to achieve satisfactory resolution; and *x*, the outcome of adaptation or maladaptation. These are then used to examine both normative family transitions and familial and community catastrophes (53).

Developments in learning theory have been concerned with cognitive processes and functioning. Much of the recent thinking on motivation and ego autonomy in psychodynamic theory has been paralleled and overlapped by that in learning theory (93). Franz Alexander (4), for example, suggests that the therapeutic process contains two components: the motivational factor and the acquiring of new patterns of behavior. Every change in the total situation requires the unlearning of old patterns and the learning of new and more adequate responses. Cognitive and learning elements in actual life experiences (and in the therapeutic interaction) result in "emotional insight," which is motivated by some kind of urge for mastery and accompanied by tension resolution as a reward.

This is very similar to the position of behavioral modification theorists who say that treatment consists of unlearning old, unsuccessful, or damaging patterns of interaction and learning new, constructive ones. Emphasis is placed on the cognitive aspects of experience, on learning how to change and how others perceive the individual who needs to change. By stressing the cause-effect aspects of behavior, the worker gets the client to see that, if she modifies what she does, others, too, will change in response. Her shaping or relearning of behavior is directed toward helping her engage in more socially acceptable and less pain-producing activity and in learning more productive ways of dealing with the problem situation (31). This is very close to what appears to take place in the resolution phase of crisis intervention.

Taplin (192) advocates the use of a cognitive perspective in crisis situations, with the emphasis on information processing. He advocates the acquisition of new information, the building of cognitive maps, and the learning of new means of adaptaton in order to develop his capacity to design and select among competing strategies. Successful crisis resolvers are those who have learned to call upon such strategies to solve problems at times of disequilibrium and can stand him in good stead in the future.

Crisis, in this approach, is defined as a breakdown in thinking through a physical or psychological overload. At the peak of the crisis, too much dissonant information prevents the usual planning and executive processes from functioning normally. Once the peak is passed, all strategies, both those leading to good and those leading to bad outcomes, result in the restoration (adaptation) process, with a consequent decreased sensitivity to intervention.

Experiments by behavioral modification proponents suggest that coping behaviors reinforced at the time of crisis tend to be stronger and those extinguished weaker at times of subsequent crisis (35). It is suggested that family caseworkers who work with parents train them to expose their children to a series of varied, real-life crises, systematically graduated in difficulty, to help them develop flexible coping repertoires that will be resistant to extinction. Peter Alevizos and Robert Liberman (3) find that, in family crisis intervention, instruction and feedback can be used to point out confused or discrepant communication and to show the family, as a unit, how to solve their problems more effectively.

Separating Acute and Developmental Changes

To clarify the relationship between active, unanticipated, or situational crises, which result in disequilibriation, and developmental and transitional changes, theoreticians have been examining the similarities and differences between the two (70). Robert Weiss (203) recommends that the term "crisis" be used to refer to situations of sudden onset, limited duration, and considerable severity in the stress that they impose on those involved. They often begin with brief periods in which the individual's emotions seem suspended while, at the same time, a sudden mobilization of new energy occurs. The crisis ends either in a return to the previous, precrisis situaton or in a persisting disruption, which Weiss calls a "transition state." This leads to permanent change in which new coping patterns are employed, new relationships developed, and a new, stable life organization established along with a new identity. In some situations, particularly where the change has emerged as the outcome of a significant loss, a new stable state of permanent *deficit* may occur.

C. Murray Parkes, a social psychiatrist, notes that whether a transition is defined as a loss or a gain depends on the person's perception of the final outcome of change (144). The area in which change occurs lies, first of all, in that part of the external world that impinges upon the self, the person's *life space*. This includes those parts of the environment with which the self interacts: other persons, material possessions, the familiar worlds of home and work, and even her own body and mind. The second area of change is in the person's internal *assumptive world*, the total set of assumptions and interpretations that she builds up on the basis of her past experiences and expectations for the future. If the change takes place slowly, as in maturational changes, the person has time to prepare gradually for the restructuring process. If, on the other hand, the change is sudden and surprising, as in the unexpected loss of a spouse, it is likely to be felt as a major disruption (and, by inference, a crisis).

Much of the theory on developmental and transitional changes can be found within the recently expanding field of adult life-span psychology, in which developmental changes are viewed longitudinally in the context of the life course. Its origins are usually attributed to Erikson, whose last three stages are concerned with adulthood, a subject upon which he has devoted much of his recent thinking (48). At the same time, within an educational psychology context, Robert Havighurst (84) postulated a series of developmental tasks that the individual needed to master if he was to mature successfully. Evelyn Duvall (44) used this approach within the field of family sociology to plot the eight stages in the family life cycle, enumerating the individual and family tasks that must be carried out.

Klaus Riegel (163) has pointed out two contrasting approaches to developmental changes. The first sees the life cycle as a continuous process of development and evolution, in which sudden changes are viewed as disruptions and crises are seen as unpredictable interruptions that do not necessarily play a significant role in the person's long-term maturation and achievement. The second approach views the life course as progressing through discrete, qualitative leaps and reorganizations of the life structures; crises and catastrophes thus become necessary steps in moving the process forward.

Bernice Neugarten (135) has become an outstanding advocate of this first approach to the life cycle. She finds individuals engaged in an ongoing process of socialization, during which they develop a sense of the normal, expectable life course, an anticipation and acceptance of the inevitable sequence of events that will occur over time, and a recognition that turning points are part of the process. Normal expectable life events do not in themselves constitute crises nor are they trauma-producing, although they call forth changes in self-concept and in sense of identity and mark the incorporation of new social roles and new adaptations.

On the other hand, unanticipated traumatic events upset the sequence and rhythm of the life cycle, such as when a parent dies during childhood and a baby is born too early or too late. When events occur "off-time" or not in their expected sequence, they become major stresses. Timing, says Neugarten, is the key factor.

Typifying the second approach is Daniel Levinson (116), who divides the life cycle into five *eras*, each lasting twenty to twenty-five years and encompassing a transitional interval of about five years. An era consists of a six- to eight-year period of relative stability during which the person lays down and develops his life structure, then a five-year mid-era transition during which the first structure is altered in response to changing need, followed by another six- to eight-year period of stability and growth.

The transitional intervals are often characterized by periods of crisis during which the person finds his current life structure intolerable yet feels unable to form a better one. Making the choice to change is often triggered by a specific *marker event*, such as a divorce or major job change, which may last for only a few days or weeks but is embedded within an ongoing process that may have started some time before and may continue for some time after the specific crisis. The transitional phase ends when the tasks of questioning and exploring choice lose their urgency and the individual starts the change process.

Within recent years, social workers who had earlier attempted to fit developmental and transitional changes into the crisis framework, now make a distinction. Thus Carel Germain and Alex Gitterman, in discussing their life model of practice, point out that developmental changes pose particular demands and create varying degrees of stress for both individuals and families. Transitional shifts in role and status can also be stressful, particularly when they occur too early or too late in the life cycle. They point out that not all stress partakes of the nature of crisis, although all crises are stressful. For example: "The crisis cause by the death of a spouse is time-limited, but the long and stressful process of mourning will continue for a year or more. The stressful tasks involved in the new status of widower and the role changes involved, will continue long after the crisis of bereavement has subsided" (63, p. 98)

General Therapeutic Concepts

The basic precepts of crisis theory have been listed in the first part of this chapter and need not be recapitulated. We might emphasize again that intervention in a crisis situation is predicated, not on the traditional psychiatric or surgical model of sickness and cure, but, to a large extent, on the public health approach to "populations at risk." The practitioner may attempt to intervene at several levels: on the primary prevention level to keep a potential situation from developing into a crisis; on the secondary level, once the client has experienced the hazardous blow and while the acute stage is developing, to minimize the effects of the impending disequilibrium; or on the tertiary level, once the client has "fallen apart" and after maladaptive or even destructive adjustment to the situation has occurred, to halt further deterioration and deal with the debilitating aftereffects of the active crisis.

Crisis theory operates, not according to a normalcy-abnormalcy dichotomy, but on the presumption that all persons tend to be subjected to various internal and external stresses at various stages in their life cycle. As part of their ego development, they assemble a repertoire of coping devices and problem-solving techniques. While these may suffice for the usual tasks of daily living, sometimes, because of an increase in pressure, both internal and external, or of a decrease in their ability to handle such pressure, their self-righting homeostatic devices fail and disequilibrium results. Korner (109) points out that two different etiological processes can precipitate the crisis. In the *exhaustion crisis*, the individual may have coped effectively under prolonged conditions of stress but suddenly reaches the point where he no longer has enough strength to continue to cope. In the *shock crisis*, a sudden change in the social environment creates an explosive release of emotions that overwhelms his available coping mechanisms. Without forewarning, which would have given him time to prepare for the impact, he goes into emotional shock.

At the point of disequilibrium, if help is offered within the time-limited period when anxiety is high and motivation great, when defense structures have been weakened or shaken, "a little help, rationally directed and purposefully focused . . . is more effective than more extensive help given at a period of less emotional accessibility" (153, p. 38).

Two therapeutic concepts closely allied to this last idea have been receiving increasing attention in recent examinations of the outcome of short-term treatment: hope, and expectation. Ezra Stotland (188) emphasizes that hopefulness is a necessary condition for action; the motivation to achieve a particular goal is partly a function of the perceived probability that the goal can be achieved and the importance attached to it (pp. 7–27). Research on the role of hope in psychotherapy showed that aspects of the treatment that aroused and strengthened the patient's hope of relief were found to be positively correlated with short-term improvement. The essential ingredient was the therapist's ability to stimulate the patient's expectation of relief and to convey confidence in his ability to help (56).

Expectations, both on the part of the client and of the practitioner, emphasize the power of the present and the future to mold, influence, and modify behavior, and they can become a significant force in determining the outcome of treatment. It was found that successful crisis intervention not only helped to solve persons' current situations but altered some of their negative expectations of what the future would hold. Brief treatment, with its focus on realistic, time-limited goals, affirms some expectations of what can be accomplished in treatment and removes others that are unrealistic and fantasy-linked.

The aspect of hope is also tied to the practitioner's degree of therapeutic enthusiasm, notes Lydia Rapoport. Both are necessary, particularly in the initial stage, to produce the desired therapeutic climate. To effect rapid reintegration, the worker needs to play an active role, both in conveying the expectation that things can be changed and in creating confidence in his own active investment in the process. Anthony Maluccio (124) points out that crisis intervention (as well as behavior modification, Gestalt therapy, family treatment, and milieu therapy) emphasizes experiential learning and the use of action in the here-and-now situation.

The nature of the worker-client relationship assumes a different dimension in crisis intervention. By definition, Naomi Brill points out, a helping relationship is purposeful and goal directed; otherwise there is no reason for its existence. It is aimed at enabling one of the participants—the client—to achieve a more satisfactory degree of functioning. When the purpose is served and the goal achieved, the specific relationship is terminated (20, p. 50).

In crisis intervention, as in other forms of brief treatment, the worker needs to establish quick rapport in order to elicit needed information quickly and to inspire confidence that he can help. The traditional concept of a "meaningful relationship," based largely on a leisurely exploration and testing over time and often deepens into regressive transference, has little place in this form of intervention. It may very well be that emphasis on active involvement of both the client and the worker, rather than passive attachment, is the significant factor here. The worker's authority, based on professional competence and expertise, can be enlisted to capitalize on the client's readiness to trust him during this period of confusion, helplessness, and high anxiety. Thus, his ability to engage the client in taking an active role in resolving his current impasse is a crucial step in involving him in crisis work.

One concept that takes on a different aspect in crisis intervention is that of *insight based on self-understanding*, considered to be a prerequisite to significant change in traditional practice. Lydia Rapoport shrewdly points out that sometimes insight is no more than hindsight, of little relevance to the current situation. Except insofar as it breaks the links to the present conflict, she sees crisis-oriented brief treatment, which seeks to deemphasize the past, as requiring a more appropriate goal—that of *foresight*. This she defines as the enhancement of anticipatory awareness of what can be expected in the future and how stress can be handled more adequately (153, pp. 42–43).

In a further effort to resolve some of the built-in inconsistencies in crisis theory, a new concept has recently been introduced by David Kaplan (103), one of the early social work theoreticians in the crisis area. He proposes a new classification of human disturbances, *disorders of change*,* which he defines as "brief personal struggles to adapt to changes in the psychological and social phenomena that affect individuals." Intervention in these disorders must be addressed to both the individual who undergoes the change and to significant persons and social systems that are part of her immediate environment.

Kaplan sees this classification as an elaboration of crisis theory and disorders of change as having the following characteristics: they involve problem-solving struggles in which successful outcomes are linked to the resolution of common, specific tasks of coping; they are concerned with cognitive, affective, and decision-making elements; although they are brief and bring about their own resolutions, persons who undergo them often suffer lasting complications and sequelae; observable outcomes may be normal (adaptive) or morbid (maladaptive); individuals' struggles to resolve the coping tasks are profoundly affected by current relationships and by impinging social systems; they are quite distinct from chronic mental and emotional disorders; they can be described in a "psychosocial history" of the disorder; and they represent critical interludes between previously existing steady states and new, perseverating conditions.

*I would prefer the term "disruptions of change" since "disorders" smacks too much of pathology and the medical approach.

Kaplan points out that, during the brief tenure of the disturbance, critical decisions are made that have far-reaching and sometimes irreversible negative effects on the individuals involved. He stresses the importance of early intervention to assess prior problem-solving efforts and to be prepared to move in rapidly should these attempts prove ineffective.

Implications for Practice

Within the past several years, serious attempts have been made to apply crisis theory to the field of practice by developing various types of models for intervention in different settings. Some have been tailored to the training of crisis counselors who operate as part of mixed professional-semiprofessional teams in community crisis centers or in emergency rooms of general hospitals (140). Often these services are geared to a special type of clientele, such as rape victims or battered wives, where definition of the situation as a crisis is taken for granted. In other situations, the service is structured to offer aid within the crisis format, as at the Rush Center in Los Angeles (129) or the Crisis Hostel in Denver (21).

The selection of the crisis approach as the treatment of choice, in juxtaposition to other practice modalities, as part of the service offered by social workers in multifaceted settings, is more complex. It calls for an early determination of whether, in fact, a crisis situation exists, and at what stage the individual or family is being seen. Since different persons faced with the same circumstances, or the same persons at different stages of life or in other circumstances, may react differently, a careful, individualized evaluation of the total field of social forces is needed. The traditional phases of the casework process—study, diagnosis, treatment planning, treatment, and evaluation—tend to be inapplicable since the sometimes extreme nature of the situation, the client's* high level of anxiety, and the strong involvement of interested others provides an atmosphere of urgency and requires immediate action.

Parad, Lola Selby, and James Quinlan have offered a "patterned approach" based on four basic steps (143, pp. 320–321):

1. The search for the precipitating event and its meaning to the client.
2. The search for coping means utilized by the client.
3. The search for alternate ways of coping that might better fit the current situation.
4. Review and support of client's efforts to cope in new ways; evaluation of results.

Golan (68, pp. 80–95), using somewhat the same frame of reference, offers a basic treatment model for use by practitioners in a range of primary

---

*The term "client" may be taken to refer to an individual, family, group, or even community as the situation demands.

and secondary settings. It is rooted in the problem-solving theory of casework and was developed as part of the short-term, task-centered approach to practice. Intervention is divided into three phases. The beginning phase aims at *formulation* and assessment of the present situation, with determination of whether a crisis exists and what its current status is, and with setting up a working arrangement. The middle phase concentrates on *implementation*, on the identification and execution of tasks designed to solve specific problems in the current situation, to modify previous inadequate or inappropriate ways of functioning, and to learn new coping patterns. The ending phase deals with *termination* and building new ties with persons and resources in the community. Although couched in quite a different framework, this model bears some similarity, at least in its general format and progression of steps, to the "focused problem resolution" model of family therapy developed at the Brief Therapy Center in Palo Alto (202).

Assessment of the Situation

Five components of a client's situation must be evaluated at the outset to determine the nature and extent of the crisis: *the hazardous event, the vulnerable state, the precipitating factor, the state of active crisis,* and *the extent of reintegration.* While these are diagnostic abstractions, sometimes hard to isolate or describe, their determination is a necessary precondition to effective intervention.

The *hazardous event* is a specific, stress-producing occurrence, either an external blow or internal change, that occurs to an individual or family in a state of relative stability in terms of biopsychosocial situation, initiating a chain of reverberating actions and reactions. Such events can be classified as anticipated and predictable, or as unanticipated and accidental.

Anticipated events are generally of two kinds, the normal developmental critical periods, such as adolescence or middle adulthood, when a person is particularly vulnerable, and transitional stages, such as getting married or moving to a new place, when the person passes from "one condition of certainty through uncertainty to another condition of certainty" and has to take on new roles, learn new tasks, and adjust to new circumstances (127, pp. 72–74).

Unanticipated events are the unpredictable changes that can occur to anyone, at any stage in life, with little or no advance warning. They usually involve some actual or threatened loss (to the person or a significant other) of a person, a capacity, or a function, such as the sudden loss of a spouse or a debilitating heart attack; conversely, they may entail the sudden introduction of a new person into the social orbit, such as the premature birth of a child or the unexpected repatriation of a prisoner of war. These may be totally unexpected or merely not anticipated at this particular time; they may

happen to one person or family or involve entire communities and populations as in the case of natural disasters, such as tornadoes and floods, sociopolitical events, such as civil wars or atomic bombings, or economic–environmental catastrophes, such as the wiping out of a community by an urban renewal program or the gutting of a neighborhood by fire.

Although a client seen for the first time may not be able to pinpoint "when it all started," this information is important in determining the baseline for subsequent changes in the person and the situation.

The vulnerable or upset state refers to the subjective reaction of the individual or family to the initial blow, both at the time it occurs and subsequently. Lydia Rapoport has noted that each person tends to respond in his own way, depending on whether he perceives the event as a threat to instinctual needs or to emotional or physical integrity, as a loss of a person or an ability, or as a challenge to survival, growth, mastery, or self-expression (154). Each reaction calls forth a primary characteristic affect: threat is usually accompanied by a high level of anxiety; loss brings out feelings of depression and mourning; challenge stimulates a moderate degree of anxiety plus elements of hope, excitement, and expectation. We also find elements of shame, guilt, anger, and hostility, with some cognitive and perceptual confusion.

Questioning about the vulnerable state also includes queries as to how the individual attempted to grapple with the difficulties posed by the hazardous event prior to coming, and the extent to which such efforts were effective.

The precipitating factor or event is the link in the chain of stress-provoking happenings that brings tension to a peak and converts the vulnerable state into one of crisis. It may coincide with the initial hazardous event or it may be a negligible incident not even directly or consciously linked to it. It becomes, however, the "straw that breaks the camel's back," the final push that overloads the system and serves to tip the balance. It is often viewed as the presenting problem and thus becomes the immediate focus for engagement of the client, since it has motivated her to seek some form of help (177, pp. 34–35).

Some practitioners feel there is little need to go beyond working on the precipitating event and the thoughts and feelings behind it in order to restore equilibrium. David Hoffman and Mary Remmel (89) call these thoughts and feelings the "precipitant" and see them as connected with some earlier unresolved core conflict, which becomes the focus of treatment.

The state of active crisis refers to the individual's subjective condition, once tension has stopped, her homeostatic mechanisms no longer operate, and disequilibrium has set in. It is the key element in crisis theory and the criterion for determining whether or not to use the crisis intervention approach. During this time-limited period, often only four to six weeks, Caplan describes the person as passing through a predictable series of reactions: psychological and physical turmoil, including aimless activity or even mobilization, disturbances in body functions, mood, mental content, and intellectual functioning. This is followed by a painful preoccupation with events leading up to the state of crisis. Finally comes a time of readjustment and remobilization (28, pp. 39–44).

The state of reintegration or reorganization occurs gradually and is an extension of the previous one. As the disequilibrium gradually subsides, some form of adjustment, either adaptive and integrative or maladaptive and destructive, takes place. Richard Pasewark and Dale Albers (145) find that initially the problem is maintained at a conscious thinking level, with cognitive perceptions corrected. Next, affect is managed through awareness of feelings and an appropriate acceptance and release of emotions associated with the crisis, such as remorse, guilt, and hostility. Finally, the client develops new behavioral patterns of coping as she begins to deal constructively with the problems that arise and to utilize other persons and organizations to help her carry out prescribed tasks.

This period of learning to cope has become the focus, in recent years, for some of the most creative thinking on how to help clients (149). Perlman calls it the "person's effort to deal with some new, and often problematic, situation or encounter or to deal in some new way with an old problem." She sees partialization, the carving out of some piece that can be coped with, as the way to deal with such stress. In crisis intervention, the problems-to-be-worked-through in the formulation and implementation stages become tied in with the psychological tasks described by Kaplan (102) and by Golan (68).

Operationally, in terms of the intake process, the initial interview becomes crucial. Armed with her knowledge of the nature and process of the crisis situation, the worker focuses immediately on the "here and the now," finding out the essential details of the precipitating event, its scope and severity, and the persons involved. She does a preliminary sweep of the applicant's current condition, both subjectively as reported by the client and/or collaterals, and objectively as observed in the interview: his dysfunctions in feelings, thoughts, behavior, and physical condition. She checks out the significant role networks to determine how widespread the disturbance is, and its main effects are, and what previous efforts have been made to deal with the situation.

She then attempts to identify the original hazardous event and to trace the subsequent blows that may have aggravated the effects of the initial impact. She encourages the client to ventilate his feelings of loss, guilt, fear, anxiety, sadness, etc. She probes the particular significance of the crisis to the client and what links, actual or symbolic, have been made to previous unresolved conflicts. Once the emotional tone is lowered and the client's anxiety has been somewhat abated, he and the worker get down to discuss resolution of the crisis situation.

Setting Up Treatment Goals

The goals in crisis intervention are primarily aimed, says Parad, to cushion the impact of the stressful event by offering immediate emotional first aid and by strengthening the person in his coping and integrative struggles through on-the-spot therapeutic clarification and guidance (139, p. 237).

More specifically, Lydia Rapoport lists six goals for this kind of treatment. Four of them may be considered minimal: (1) relief of symptoms; (2) restoration to the optimal precrisis level of functioning; (3) understanding of the relevent precipitating events that contributed to the state of disequilibrium; and (4) identification of remedial measures that can be taken by the client and his family or that are available through community resources. In addition, where the individual's personality and the social situation are favorable and the opportunity presents itself or can be created, work can be done on (5) recognition of the connection between the current stress and past life experiences and conflicts, and (6) initiation of new models of perceiving, thinking, and feeling and development of new adaptive and coping responses that can be useful beyond the immediate crisis situation (154, pp. 297–298).

In planning treatment, Jacobson and his associates (96) suggest two treatment approaches. The *generic* approach emphasizes specific situational and maturational crises occurring to significant population groups, with no attempt made to assess the particular psychodynamics of the individuals involved. Intervention is often carried out by a paraprofessional, a nonmental health professional, or a community care-giver, focusing on the characteristic course that the crisis situation will probably take. It concentrates on the acute crisis episode and treatment consists of specific interventive measures aimed at the target group as a whole.

The *individual* approach, designed to be used by mental health professionals, emphasizes assessment of the interpersonal and intrapsychic process of each person in crisis, with particular attention paid to the unique aspects of the particular situation and the solution specifically tailored to help the client return to a new steady state.

Donald Langsley and Kaplan (112) suggest two models for crisis treatment: the *recompensation* model, which sees the person as "falling apart" and in need of treatment geared to helping her pull herself together again in order to return to her prestress level of functioning; and the *limited psychotherapy* model, which considers the individual as decompensating as a result of the reactivation of old conflicts. Treatment consists in interpreting and helping her understand some of these earlier conflicts.

Similarly, Sifneos (177) distinguishes between *anxiety-suppressive* treatment, for disturbed persons with weakened egos, which aims to decrease or eliminate anxiety through the use of supportive techniques and environmental manipulation during the acutely traumatic phase of the situation, and *anxiety-provoking* treatment, for persons with some ego strengths and capacities, which makes use of rapport and transforms treatment into a learning experience. It challenges past actions and teaches the client to anticipate situations likely to produce unpleasant consequences. By stimulating a certain degree of new anxiety, the worker motivates the person to understand her emotional conflicts, recognize and deal with her reactions, and engage in a corrective emotional experience.

As part of treatment planning, time limits may be set by using the three dimensions—number of interviews, spacing of intervals, and total span of time—flexibly as the situation demands. Some services specifically limit intervention to a set number of meetings—say, six, eight, or ten.

Implementation of Treatment

As mentioned, the implementation phase of crisis intervention usually deals with setting up and working out specific tasks, primarily by the client, but also by the worker and significant others, designed to solve specific problems in the current life situation, to modify previous inadequate or inappropriate ways of functioning, and to learn new coping patterns. Treatment becomes keyed to the achievement of limited goals previously decided upon or implied by the nature of the initial contract. These may be simply relief from the pressures built up during the development of the crisis or arriving at a clearer understanding of what has been going on and what are the options open.

The concept of *task* opens up many possibilities. In crisis intervention, tasks are specifically couched in terms of what must be done in order to achieve reequilibration, the equivalents of Rapoport's "useful next steps." Golan sees them as divided into two categories, which may be carried out concurrently, the *material-arrangemental tasks* concerned with the provision of concrete assistance and services, and *psychosocial tasks* concerned with dealing with clients' feelings, doubts, ambivalences, anxieties, and despairs, which arise while trying to carry out what both worker and client agree needs to be done.

Treatment techniques are, for the most part, similar to those used in other types of social work practice (90), with the terminology determined largely by the worker's frame of reference. During the initial phase, sustainment techniques, designed to lower anxiety, guilt, and tension and to provide emotional support, are frequently employed, with *reassurance, encouragement,* and the *offering of "gifts of love,"* to use Hollis's term, predominant. Procedures of direct influence, designed to promote specific kinds of change in the client's behavior, are probably used more often in crisis work than in other types of of direct treatment. Of these, *giving advice,* particularly when the client is feeling overwhelmed and needs help in choosing a course of action, *advocating a particular course of action,* and *warning clients of the consequences* of maladaptive resolutions of the situation, are most often used. In extreme situations, where suicide may have been threatened or attempted or where the client is deteriorating rapidly, *direct intervention* may be necessary. As the client becomes more integrated, techniques of reflective discussion, particularly of her current and recent past situation and patterns of interaction, are appropriate.

Techniques geared to learning how to change behavior become important tools. *Anticipatory guidance, role rehearsal,* and *rehearsal for reality* are three closely allied procedures that emphasize the learning component in crisis treatment. Among behavioral modification techniques, those aimed at *positive reinforcement* and *shaping* of new behavior through a step-by-step approximation of the desired action are probably the most frequently used, as well as *modeling, teaching, coaching,* and *prompting.* (These last tools have long been used by social workers under different labels.) Employment of *assertive training* and *desensitization* programs have also been reported, and, most recently, *provision of feedback and instruction.* In recent years, a number of Gestalt and Transactional Analysis techniques have added a new vocabulary to treatment (19, 136), although the usefulness of some of the devices may be questioned. In general, the level of effectiveness tends to reflect the particular commitment of the advocators of the technique.

An integral part of treatment in a crisis situation, as part of the "broad push" to achieve rapid reintegration, is *environmental work* and *activity with collaterals*—within the agency itself, with other professionals in the community, and with various types of natural and mutual support systems. Sometimes the worker may choose to leave direct treatment to others and to act as consultant to an agency or to diverse elements in the total ecological system (36). At times, he becomes an advocate on behalf of crisis victims (91).

Termination of Intervention

In crisis work, termination of a case assumes unique importance. Worker and client, once the agreed-upon time limit approaches, review their progress since the client first came in terms of key themes and basic isues with which they struggled. Emphasis is placed on the tasks accomplished, the adaptive coping patterns developed, and the ties built with persons and resources in the community. Future activity, when the client will be on his own, is planned. Often the case ends on an "as needed" basis as the worker closes the door but leaves a crack open for further reapplication, should the situation change or new crisis situations develop. (This is based on the presupposition that crises are part of the normal life pattern of individuals and families and can be expected to recur episodically.)

Throughout the case, the worker's stance is active, purposive, and committed, conveying the message that she knows what she is doing and is willing to take risks. However, as the client becomes more integrated, he tends to become more active in seeking his own solution. At such points, the worker becomes correspondingly less active. A fairly frequent occurrence is for the client to take the lead and inform the worker, even before the time limit is up, that he is ready to "take charge of himself" once more, thus terminating on his own.

Types of Clients Best Treated

If we look upon the crisis approach as a formulation to be used selectively, as one of a variety of interventive strategies, a central question to be posed is: For whom? What should be the criteria for its application?

The answer is complex since two separate issues are involved: who experiences the crisis, and who needs help in dealing with the situation created. As mentioned, crisis theory states that anticipated crises, of both the developmental and transitional kinds, can arise throughout the life span; thus, crisis intervention would seem appropriate for everyone at some point. From another angle, unanticipated crises are so varied and unpredictable that, unless the service is available at points where such situations, by definition or prediction, can be expected to turn up—such as the emergency ward of a general hospital or the waiting room of a police station—the crisis aspects of the situation may come to light only after a different type of intervention has been started or the client has been sent away.

Some years ago it was recommended that the crisis orientation might be appropriate for the very strong or the very weak, for those requiring only short periods of help or for those not motivated for continued service (138, p. 279). Since then we have become much more flexible in its application and more broad-based in our outlook. If we use the nature of the request for service and the extent to which the applicant wants to change as the criteria, we would probably find that a large majority of clients asking for help at moments of stress are asking for relief of discomfort and reduction of external pressures—two of the goals of crisis treatment.

One of the after-the-fact sets of criteria that might have some bearing could be to look at those persons or families that have demonstrated ability to cope with crisis-producing events in the past. Successful crisis coping was found to be associated with behavioral adaptability and flexibility within a family, affection among family members, good marital adjustment between husband and wife, companionable parent–child relationships, family members' participation in decision-making, wife's participation in husband's social activities, nonmarginal economic status, individual or family previous experience (direct or vicarious) with the type of crisis encountered, objective knowledge of the facets of a specific crisis before it occurs, and established patterns of interaction with the extended family, neighbors, and friends (145, p. 74). The obvious difficulty in using such a checklist is that precisely these types of clients are not usually the ones who come to the attention of professionals. Probably, would-be clients would have a negative prefixed to each attribute.

An extension of this approach might be to ask, along with Rapoport (154), for which clients would the crisis approach not be appropriate? It has been found that the large group of clients frequently seen in social agencies who seem to live in a chronic state of crisis are not good candidates since, to them, a self-generated crisis state is a life-style. While they manifest the overt symptoms of urgency, disordered affect, disorganized behavior, and ineffectual coping, closer examination shows that the basic character structure may have suffered severe and chronic ego depletion and damage. To many in this group, the crisis appearance is not a reaction to the original hazardous event, but a maladaptive attempt to ward off underlying personal disturbance or even psychosis. Such persons, often classified as borderline personalities or character disorders, may need help in emergencies but do not seem to be able to engage in the active participation and task resolution involved in the crisis approach. A typical example of this type of personality are those clients seen in Travelers Aid Offices who engage in "crisis flight" (79).

As a corollary to this group of clients, some persons may or may not themselves demonstrate overt symptoms of disequilibrium but lead such disordered, chaotic lives that they tend to produce crisis states in others—in their families, neighbors, teachers, public health nurses, and police with whom they come in contact and, eventually, in the professionals to whom they are, often unwillingly, referred. Those who tend to exhibit this "crisis-inducing" syndrome are usually quite resistant to change.

A further group of clients who may not be amenable to this approach are those persons who exist marginally in a state of chronic inability to cope with life's demands, such as the discharged mental patient, the physically or mentally handicapped, and the aged ill. Providing continuous support is probably a necessary attribute to their continued functioning, even in a limited way. Nevertheless, even this group can probably respond to short-term crisis support (111).

Although we broadened our concept of crisis to include a large proportion of life events, we have probably merely sketched out the outlines of the possibilities for use of this approach. Practically, it seems that the three pivotal indicators that can offer keys to the extent to which it should be offered as the treatment of choice are: *evidence of a clearcut hazardous event* that has direct bearing on the client's present state of disequilibrium; *a high level of anxiety or pain*, coupled with demonstrated motivation and potential capacity for change; and *evidence of breakdown in problem-solving in the recent past* (67).

Implications for Work with Families, Groups, and Communities

Crisis situations, by definition, usually involve family role networks; in fact, much of the basic theory dealt with families in disequilibrium (66, 77). In terms of its application, most of the Harvard Public Health studies concentrated on the family as the basic unit of service (30). Langsley and Kaplan (112) see the family as experiencing a crisis when an important role is not being filled. If agreement cannot be reached as to who should fill the role, the family pressures build up and the susceptible member may choose to escape through psychotic symptoms, seemingly irrational behavior, suicide attempts, or a request for sanctuary in a hospital. His refusal to undergo role change may be enough for the family to demand hospitalization for him as a maladaptive way of maintaining their equilibrium. Thus the goal of intervention becomes the restoration of the entire family unit to an acceptable level of functioning without the need to resort to hospitalization of the "sick" member.

In general, whether the family is considered initially to be in a state of collective crisis because of some role disruption of a member, or whether the state of crisis in one member acts as a hazardous blow to the rest of the family, disrupting their usual balance, the total upset situation calls for careful examination, sometimes on a concerted basis (62). An evaluation of the family's strengths and weaknesses, their capacities and motivation for change, and the resources at their disposal builds the foundation for treatment planning and execution. Restoring and augmenting family communication patterns becomes a particularly important treatment goal. At times, entire family networks, actual or simulated, have been activated as a treatment strategy to enable distressed persons to regain their equilibrium (167, 175).

In addition to use of the crisis approach with nuclear and extended families, which are natural small groups, it has also been applied to friendship and common interest groups, including gangs and clubs that are not family-related (143). According to Parad (139), crisis intervention can be applied to a broad spectrum of formed groups as well, including groups of children and teachers in school settings, work groups, and therapy groups.

Groups are also being used as treatment tools when a number of people are simultaneously experiencing a common crisis. In the case of community disasters, the group provides a quick, economical means of reaching large numbers of victims to provide psychological first aid and to inform them of the details of the catastrophe, the resources available, and the means of minimizing disruptive aftereffects, as in the case of the Chicago train crash (74) and the San Fernando Valley earthquake (16). Recent developments include the use of crisis intervention groups in protective service settings and the rapid spread of self-help groups for a wide range of problem situations, some of which reach crisis proportions. Ever since the 1973 war in Israel, social interest groups have been used to help widows of soldiers share their experiences in learning to overcome the transitional problems of widowhood.

One of the first uses of crisis groups occurred at the Rush Center in Los Angeles, where they still form one of the main instruments for treatment (190). Opinion as to their utility, however, fluctuates. People seem willing to accept help in a group who might not otherwise do so. Support to members, particularly from disadvantaged elements, appears to be significant; social relationships often grow out of group contacts; and the group provides a vehicle for encouraging expression of significant feelings and developing desensitization to disturbing topics. Members often suggest new coping mechanisms to help others overcome their own difficulties. On the other hand, some individuals find it difficult to focus on resolution of their own crises in the open-ended group setting, where each member may be at a different stage of grappling with his specific situation. Sometimes coping mechanisms may be suggested that are more maladaptive than adaptive. Groups are often hard to fill, and much time must be spent on matching and sorting out membership. Finally, little professional treatment time seems to be gained (124).

On the community level, use of the crisis approach in widespread disasters has already been discussed. In many instances the hazardous event and the collective reactions of shock, loss, and concern for others have resulted in the breakdown of defensive barriers of race prejudice and economic self-interest and the development—for a short while—of altruisic communities of voluntary cooperation and mutual goodwill (183, pp. 281–282). Professional activity at this level is frequently linked with programs for primary prevention or early intervention; enabling federal legislation has provided the impetus to develop imaginative, far-reaching approaches. While social workers have long been experts in building up to-and-from referral systems within their communities, they are only now beginning to envisage the posibility of viewing the community as a client in its own right. Crisis and disasters may thus provide the springboard for increased cooperation or even restructuring of welfare services.

Much of the earlier research interest in crisis intervention was practice-oriented and aimed at answering the basic question, "Do crisis services work?" (125) An allied interest has been to study the specific conditions, in terms of presenting problems, client populations, and structure of services, which provide the maximal return. In addition to the basic research in life span psychology and stress situations cited earlier, some work is being done on examining specific types of crisis situations (151) and on developing new tools by which to measure crisis dimensions or the clarification of methodological issues (40). Unfortunately, the rapid pace of crisis intervention and the committed, partisan dedication of staff members tend to run counter to the careful, meticulous planning and rigorous controls needed to carry out well-conceived and well-executed research projects.

Implications for Further Use

Several years ago, when the first edition of this volume was written, it was felt that, despite its wide dissemination and general acceptance, the application of crisis theory seemed to have approached the boundaries of its usefulness, that a lull had occurred in its application. Since then, a resurgence of interest and the taking over of the approach by multidiscipline crisis teams and suicide prevention centers seem to have given it new life; certainly, its usage appears to be increasing and spreading into new types of settings. Restructuring of services and broadening the roles of social workers has overcome the built-in difficulty of not having crisis interventors posted in places and at times when crisis-pressured clients can make quick use of them (134).

The separation of crisis treatment from other forms of services in an agency, however, brings about an artificial distinction between treatment offered during periods of high anxiety and increased pressure and other forms of service, and runs counter to the historical foundations upon which the social work profession has been built. If crisis intervention is to become a viable practice modality, it must be considered part of the practice repertoire of *all* social workers, to be offered differentially and as the treatment of choice under conditions where it appears to promise the maximal return. It should be usable at specific periods in long-term cases of chronic and recurrent crises as well as in short-term, limited problem situations. Hopefully, clarification of the differences between acute, time-bounded crises and longer-term developmental and transitional stresses will reduce some of the inconsistencies in the theory and lead to its more appropriate application.

References

1. Addis, Marsha, Judith Schulman-Miller, and Meyer Lightman, "The Cult Clinic Helps Families in Crisis," *Social Casework*, Vol. 65 (November 1984), pp. 515-522.

2. Aguilera, Donna C., Janice M. Messick, and Marlene S. Farrell. *Crisis Intervention: Theory and Methodology*. St. Louis: Mosby, 1970.

3. Alevizos, Peter N., and Robert P. Liberman. "Behavioral Approaches to Family Crisis Intervention," in Howard J. Parad, H. L. P. Resnik, and Libbie G. Parad, (eds.), *Emergency and Disaster Management: A Mental Health Sourcebook*, Bowie, Md.: Charles Press, 1976, pp. 129-143.

4. Alexander, Franz. "Psychoanalytic Contributions to Short-Term Psychotherapy," in Lewis R. Wolberg (ed.), *Short-Term Psychotherapy*. New York: Grune and Stratton, 1965, pp. 84-126.

5. Babcock, Charlotte G. "Inner Stress in Illness and Disability," in Howard J. Parad and Roger R. Miller (eds.), *Ego-Oriented Casework: Problems and Perspectives*. New York: Family Service Association of America, 1963, pp. 45-64.

6. Baldwin, Bruce A. "Crisis Intervention in Professional Practice: Implications for Clinical Training," *American Journal of Orthopsychiatry*, Vol. 47 (October 1977), pp. 659-670.

7. ———. "A Paradigm for the Classification of Emotional Crises: Implications for Crisis Intervention," *American Journal of Orthopsychiatry*, Vol. 48 (July 1978), pp. 538-551.

8. Barton, Allen. *Communities in Disaster*. New York: Doubleday, 1969.

9. Bates, Paul B., and K. Warner Schaie (eds.). *Life Span Developmental Psychology: Personality and Socialization*. New York: Academic Press, 1973.

10. Beatt, Earl J. "The Family Developmental Approach: A Program for Coping with Transitional Crises," in Howard J. Parad, H. L. P. Resnik, and Libbie G. Parad (eds.), *Emergency and Disaster Management*. Bowie, Md.: Charles Press, 1976, pp. 395-406.

11. Beck, Dorothy F. *Patterns in Use of Family Agency Services*. New York: Family Service Association of America, 1962.

12. ———, and Mary Ann Jones. *Progress on Family Problems: A Nationwide Study of Clients' and Counselors' Views on Family Agency Services*. New York: Family Service Association of America, 1973.

13. Bergman, Anne. "Emergency Room: A Role for Social Workers," *Health and Social Work*, Vol. 1 (February 1976), pp. 32-44.

14. Berren, Michael R., Allan Beigel, and Gypsy Barker. "A Typology for the Clas-

sification of Disasters: Implications for Intervention," *Community Mental Health Journal*, Vol. 18 (Summer 1982), pp. 120–134.

15. Birnbaum, Freda, Jennifer Coplon, and Ira Scharf. "Crisis Intervention After a Natural Disaster," *Social Casework*, Vol. 54 (November 1973), pp. 545–551.

16. Blaufarb, Herbert, and Jules Levine. "Crisis Intervention in an Earthquake," *Social Work*, Vol. 17 (July 1972), pp. 16–19.

17. Bonnefil, Margaret C. "Crisis Intervention with Children and Families," in Gerald F. Jacobson (ed.), *Crisis Intervention in the 1980s*. San Francisco: Jossey-Bass, pp. 23–34.

18. Borgman, Robert D. "Crisis Intervention in Rural Community Disasters," *Social Casework*, Vol. 58 (November 1977), pp. 562–567.

19. Brechenser, Donn M. "Brief Psychotherapy Using Transactional Analysis," *Social Casework*, Vol. 53 (March 1972), pp. 173–176.

20. Brill, Naomi I. *Working with People: The Helping Process*. Philadelphia: Lippincott, 1973.

21. Brook, Bryan D., Michael W. Kirby, Paul R. Polak, and Rita Vollman. "Crisis Hostel: An Alternative to the Acute Psychiatric Ward," in Howard J. Parad, H. L. P. Resnik, and Libbie G. Parad (ed.), *Emergency and Disaster Management*. Bowie, Md.: Charles Press, 1976, pp. 67–73.

22. Brown, Vivian B. "The Community in Crisis," in Gerald F. Jacobson (ed.), *Crisis Intervention in the 1980s*. San Francisco: Jossey-Bass, 1980, pp. 45–56.

23. Burgess, Ernest W. "Family Living in the Later Decades," in Marvin B. Sussman (ed.), *Sourcebook on Marriage and the Family,*. 2nd edition. Boston: Houghton Mifflin, 1963, pp. 425–431.

24. Burnett, Bruce B., John J. Carr, John Sinapi,and Roy Taylor. "Police and Social Workers in a Community Outreach Program," *Social Casework*, Vol. 57 (January 1976), pp. 41–49.

25. Cain, Lillian P. "Casework with Kidney Transplant Patients," *Social Work*, Vol. 18 (July 1973), pp. 76–83.

26. Caldwell, J. M. "Military Psychiatry," in A. M. Freedman, H. I. Kaplan, and H. S. Kaplan (eds.), *Comprehensive Textbook of Psychiatry*. Baltimore: William and Wilkins, 1967.

27. Caplan, Gerald. "A Public Health Approach to Child Psychiatry," *Mental Health*, Vol. 35 (1951), pp. 235–249.

28. ———. *Principles of Preventive Psychiatry*. New York: Basic Books, 1964.

29. ———. *Support Systems and Community Mental Health*. New York: Behavioral Publications, 1974.

30. ———, Edward A. Mason, and David M. Kaplan. "Four Studies of Crisis in Parents of Prematures," *Community Mental Health Journal*, Vol. 2 (Summer 1965).

31. Carter, Robert, and Richard B. Stuart. "Behavior Modification Theory and Practice: A Reply," *Social Work*, Vol. 15 (January 1970), pp. 37–50.

32. Chapman, Dwight W. "A Brief Introduction to Contemporary Disaster Research," in George W. Baker and Dwight W. Chapman (eds.), *Man and Society in Disaster*. New York: Basic Books, 1962, pp. 3–22.

33. Cohen, Nathan E. *Social Work in the American Tradition*. New York: Holt, Rinehart and Winston, 1958.

34. Cohen, Raquel E., and Frederick L. Ahern, Jr. *Handbook for Mental Health Care of Disaster Victims*. Baltimore: Johns Hopkins University Press, 1980.

35. Cohen, Shlomo I., and Leopold O. Walder. "An Experimental Analog Derived from Crisis Theory," *American Journal of Orthopsychiatry*, Vol. 41 (October 1971), pp. 822–829.

36. Collins, Alice H., and Diane L. Pancoast. *Natural Helping Networks*. Washington, D. C.: National Association of Social Workers, 1976.

37. Cumming, John, and Elaine Cumming. *Ego and Milieu*. New York: Atherton Press, 1966.

38. Datan, Nancy, and Leon H. Ginsberg (eds.). *Life-Span Developmental Psychology: Normative Life Crises*. New York: Academic Press, 1975.

39. Dohrenwend, Barbara S., and Bruce P. Dohrenwend. *Stressful Life Events: Their Nature and Effects*. New York: Wiley, 1974.

40. ———. "Stressful Life Events: Research Issues," in Gerald F. Jacobson (ed.), *Crisis Intervention in the 1980s*. San Francisco: Jossey-Bass, 1980, pp. 57–65.

41. Dublin, Louis I. *Suicide: A Sociological and Statistical Study*. New York: Ronald Press, 1963.

42. Duckworth, Grace L. "A Project in Crisis Intervention," *Social Casework*, Vol. 48 (April 1967), pp. 227–231.

43. Duggan, Hayden A. *Crisis Intervention: Helping Individuals at Risk*. Lexington, Mass.: Heath, 1984.

44. Duvall, Evelyn. *Marriage and Family Development*, 5th edition. Philadelphia: Lippincott, 1977.

45. Einstein, Gertrude. *Learning to Apply New Concepts to Casework Practice*. New York: Family Service Association of America, 1968, pp. 9–49.

46. Erikson, Erik H. *Childhood and Society*. New York: Norton, 1950.

47. ———. *Identity, Youth and Crisis*. New York: Norton, 1968.

48. ———. *Adulthood*. New York: Norton, 1976.

49. Escalona, Sibylle K. *The Roots of Individuality: Normal Patterns of Development in Infancy*. Chicago: Aldine, 1968.

50. Ewalt, Patricia L. "The Crisis Treatment Approach in a Child Guidance Clinic," *Social Casework*, Vol. 54 (July 1973), pp. 406–411.

51. ———. "The Case for Immediate Brief Intervention," *Social Work*, Vol. 21 (January 1976), pp. 63–65.

52. Family Service Association of America. *Scope and Method of Family Service*. New York: Family Service Association, 1953.

53. Figley, Charles R., and Hamilton L. McCubbin (eds.). *Stress and the Family. Vol. I: Coping with Normative Transitions. Vol. II: Coping with Catastrophe*. New York: Brunner/Mazel, 1983.

54. Fischer, Joel, and Harvey L. Gochros. *Planned Behavioral Change: Behavior Modification in Social Work*. New York: Free Press, 1975.

55. Fox, Sandra S., and Donald J. Scherl. "Crisis Intervention with Victims of Rape," *Social Work*, Vol. 17 (January 1972), pp. 37–42.

56. Frank, Jerome. "The Role of Hope in Psychotherapy." *International Journal of Psychiatry*, Vol. 5 (May 1968), pp. 383–395.

57. Franz, John. "Being There: A 24-Hour Emergency Crisis Care Center," *Children Today*, Vol. 9 (1980), pp. 7–10.

58. Frazer, James R., and Douglas A. Spicka. "Handling the Emotional Response to Disaster: The Case for American Red Cross/Community Mental Health Collaboration," *Community Mental Health Journal*, Vol. 17 (Winter 1981), pp. 255–264.

59. Freud, Anna (1936). *The Ego and Mechanisms of Defense*. New York: International Universities Press, 1946.

60. Freud, Sigmund (1923). *The Ego and the Id*. London: Hogarth, 1961.

61. Fried, Barbara. *The Middle-Age Crisis*, revised edition. New York: Harper and Row, 1976.

62. Garrison, Christine, and Janet Weber. "Family Crisis Intervention Using Multiple Impact Therapy," *Social Casework*, Vol. 62 (December 1981), pp. 585–593.

63. Germain, Carel B., and Alex Gitterman. *The Life Model for Social Work Practice*. New York: Columbia University Press, 1980.

64. Getz, William, Allen E. Weisen, Stan Sue, and Amy Ayers. *Crisis Counseling*. Lexington, Mass.: Heath, 1974.

65. Gill, Merton M. *The Collected Papers of David Rapaport*. New York: Basic Books, 1967.

66. Glasser, Paul H., and Lois N. Glasser (eds.). *Families in Crisis*. New York: Harper and Row, 1970.

67. Golan, Naomi. "When Is a Client in Crisis?," *Social Casework*, Vol. 50 (July 1969), pp. 389–394.

68. ———. *Treatment in Crisis Situations*. New York: Free Press, 1978.

69. ———. "Crisis Theory," in Francis J. Turner (ed.), *Social Work Treatment*, 2nd edition. New York: Free Press, 1979, pp. 499–533.

70. ———. "Using Situational Crises to Ease Transitions in the Life Cycle," *American Journal of Orthopsychiatry*, Vol. 50 (July 1980), pp. 542–550.

71. ———. *Passing Through Transitions: A Guide for Practitioners*. New York: Free Press, 1981.

72. ———. "The Influence of Developmental and Transitional Crises on Victims of Disaster," in Charles D. Spielberger, Irwin G. Sarason, and Norman A. Milgram (eds.), *Stress and Anxiety, Vol. 8*. Washington, D.C.: Hemisphere Press, 1982, pp. 123–131.

73. Grinker, Roy R., and John P. Spiegel. *Men Under Stress*. New York: Blackeston, 1945.

74. Grossman, Leona. "Train Crash: Social Work and Disaster Services," *Social Work*, Vol. 18, (September 1973), pp. 38–44.

75. Grumet, Gerald W., and David L. Trachtman. "Psychiatric Social Workers in the Emergency Department," *Health and Social Work*, Vol. 1 (August 1976), pp. 114–131.

76. Hamilton, Gordon (1940). *Theory and Practice of Social Case Work*, 2nd edition. New York: Columbia University Press, 1951.

77. Hansen, Donald A., and Reuben Hill. "Families Under Stress," in Harold T. Christensen (ed.), *Handbook of Marriage and the Family*. Chicago: Rand McNally, 1964, pp. 787–792.

78. Hardgrove, Grace. "An Interagency Service Network to Meet Needs of Rape Victims," *Social Casework*, Vol. 57 (April 1976), pp. 245–253.

79. Harris, F. G., and R. W. Little. "Military Organizations and Social Psychiatry," *Symposium of Preventive and Social Psychiatry*. Washington, D.C.: Walter Reed Army Institute of Research, 1957, pp. 173–184.

80. Harshbarger, Dwight. "An Ecologic Perspective in Disaster Intervention," in Howard J. Parad, H. L. P. Resnik, and Libbie G. Parad (eds.), *Emergency and Disaster Management*. Bowie, Md.: Charles Press, 1976, pp. 271–280.

81. Hartman, Ann, and Joan Laird. *Family-Centered Social Work Practice*. New York: Free Press, 1983.

82. Hartmann, Heinz (1939). *Ego Psychology and the Problem of Adaptation*. New York: International Universities Press, 1958.

83. —— (1947). *Essays in Ego Psychology*. New York: International Universities Press, 1964.

84. Havighurst, Robert. *Human Development and Education*. London: Longman, Green, 1953.

85. Henderson, Howard E. "Helping Families in Crisis: Police and Social Work Intervention," *Social Work*, Vol. 21 (July 1976), pp. 314–315.

86. Hiatt, Catherine C., and Ruth E. Spurlock. "Geographical Flight and Its Relation to Crisis Theory," *American Journal of Orthopsychiatry*, Vol. 40 (January 1970), pp. 53–57.

87. Hill, Reuben. "Generic Features of Families Under Stress," *Social Casework*, Vol. 39 (February–March 1958), pp. 139–150.

88. Hoff, Lee Ann. *People in Crisis: Understanding and Helping*. Menlo Park, Calif.: Addison Wesley, 1978.

89. Hoffman, David L., and Mary L. Remmel. "Uncovering the Participant in Crisis Intervention," *Social Casework*, Vol. 56 (May 1975), pp. 259–267.

90. Hollis, Florence, and Mary E. Woods. *Casework: A Psychosocial Therapy*, 3rd edition. New York: Random House, 1981.

91. Holmes, Karen A. "Services for Victims of Rape: A Dualistic Practice Model," *Social Casework*, Vol. 62 (January 1981), pp. 30–39.

92. Holmes, Thomas H., and Richard H. Rahe. "The Social Readjustment Rating Scale," *Journal of Psychosomatic Research*, Vol. 11 (1967), pp. 213–218.

93. Holt, Robert R. "Ego Autonomy Revisited," *International Journal of Psychoanalysis*, Vol. 46 (1965), pp. 151–167.

94. Houston, Mary K. "The Role of the Social Worker in Emergency Medical Services." Ph.D. dissertation, School of Social Work, University Southern California, September 1984.

95. Jacobson, Gerald F. "Crisis Theory," in Gerald F. Jacobson (ed.), *Crisis Intervention in the 1980s*. San Francisco: Jossey-Bass, 1980, pp. 1–10.

96. ——, Martin Strickler, and Wilbur E. Morley. "Generic and Individual Approaches to Crisis Intervention," *American Journal of Public Health*, Vol. 58 (February 1968), pp. 338–343.

97. Jacobson, Gerald F., D. M. Wilner, Wilbur E. Morley, S. Schneider, Martin Strickler, and G. J. Sommer. "The Scope and Practice of an Early Access Brief Treatment Psychiatric Center," *American Journal of Psychiatry*, Vol. 121 (June 1965), pp. 1176–1182.

98. Jaffe, Ruth. "Psychoanalytic Implications of Reactions of Israeli Soldiers to the Six-Day War," in Heinrich Z. Winnik, Rafael Moses, and Mortimer Ostrow (eds.), *Psychological Bases of War*. New York: Quadrangle, 1973, pp. 89–110.

99. Janis, Irving. *Psychological Stress*. New York: Wiley, 1958.

100. —— and Leon Mann. *Decision Making*. New York: Free Press, 1977.

101. Kaplan, David M. "A Concept of Acute Situational Disorders," *Social Work*, Vol. 7 (April 1962), pp. 15–23.

102. ——. "Observations on Crisis Theory and Practice," *Social Casework*, Vol. 49 (March 1968), pp. 151–155.

103. ——. "Interventions for Disorders of Change," *Social Work*, Vol. 27 (September–October 1982), pp. 404–410.

104. ——, Aaron Smith, Rose Grobstein, and Stanley E. Fischman. "Family Mediation of Stress," *Social Work*, Vol. 18 (July 1973), pp. 60–69.

105. Kasius, Cora (ed.). *A Comparison of Diagnostic and Functional Casework Concepts*. New York: Family Service Association of America, 1950.

106. Keith-Lucas, Alan. "Structures in Traditional Agencies for Crisis Intervention to Aid the Dependent Child in Trouble," *Child Welfare*, Vol. 48 (July 1969), pp. 420–422, 431.

107. Kinney, Jill. "Homebuilders: An In-Home Crisis Intervention Program," *Children Today*, Vol. 7 (1978), pp. 15–17, 35.

108. Klein, Donald C., and Erich Lindemann. "Preventive Intervention in Individual and Family Crisis Situations," in Gerald Caplan (ed.), *Prevention of Mental Disorders in Children*. New York: Basic Books, 1961, pp. 283–305.

109. Korner, I. N. "Crisis Reduction and the Psychological Consultant," in Gerald A. Specter and William L. Claiborn (eds.), *Crisis Intervention*. New York: Behavioral Publications, 1973, pp. 30–45.

110. Lang, Judith. "Planned Short-Term Treatment in a Family Agency," *Social Casework*, Vol. 55 (June 1974), pp. 369–374.

111. Langsley, Donald G. "Crisis Intervention and the Avoidance of Hospitalization," in Gerald F. Jacobson (ed.), *Crisis Intervention in the 1980s*. San Francisco: Jossey-Bass, 1980, pp. 81–90.

112. ——, and David M. Kaplan. *Treatment of Families in Crisis*. New York: Grune and Stratton, 1968.

113. Lazarus, Richard S. *Psychological Stress and the Coping Process*. New York: McGraw-Hill, 1966.

114. Lebow, Grace H. "Facilitating Adaptation in Anticipatory Mourning," *Social Casework*, Vol. 57 (July 1976), pp. 456–465.

115. LeMasters, E. E. "Parenthood as Crisis," *Marriage and Family Living*, Vol. 19 (1957).

116. Levinson, Daniel J., with Charlotte N. Darrow, Edward B. Klein, Maria H. Levinson, and Braxton McKee. *The Seasons of a Man's Life*. New York: Knopf, 1978.

117. Lieberman, Morton A., and Sheldon S. Tobin. *The Experience of Old Age: Stress, Coping, and Survival*. New York: Basic Books, 1983.

118. Lindemann, Erich. *Beyond Grief: Studies in Crisis Intervention*. New York: Aronson, 1979.

119. Lowenthal, Marjorie F., Majda Thurnher, David Chiriboga, and Associates. *Four Stages of Life: A Comparative Study of Women and Men Facing Transitions*. San Francisco: Jossey-Bass, 1975.

120. McCubbin, Hamilton I., Barbara B. Dahl, Philip J. Metres Jr., Edna J. Hunter, and John A. Plag (eds.). *Family Separation and Reunion: Families of Prisoners of War and Servicemen Missing in Action*. San Diego: Center for Prisoners of War Studies, Naval Health Research Center, 1974.

121. McCubbin, Hamilton I., and Joan M. Patterson. "Family Transitions: Adaptation to Stress," in Charles R. Figley and Hamilton I. McCubbin (eds.), *Stress and the Family, Vol. I; Coping with Normative Transitions*. New York: Brunner/Mazel, 1983, pp. 5–25.

122. McGee, Richard K. *Crisis Intervention in the Community*. Baltimore: University Park Press, 1974.

123. Madonia, Joseph F., "Clinical and Supervisory Aspects of Crisis Intervention," *Social Casework*, Vol. 65 (June 1984), pp. 364–368.

124. Maluccio, Anthony N. "Action as a Tool in Casework Practice," *Social Casework*, Vol. 55 (January 1974), pp. 30–35.

125. Maris, Ronald, and Huell E. Connor. "Do Crisis Services Work? A Follow-Up of a Psychiatric Outpatient Sample," *Journal of Health and Social Behavior*, Vol. 14 (December 1973), pp. 311–322.

126. Merbaum, Michael, and Albert Hefez. "Some Personality Characteristics of Soldiers Exposed to Extreme War Stress," *Journal of Consulting and Clinical Psychology*, Vol. 44 (1976), pp. 1–6.

127. Meyer, Carol H. *Social Work Practice*, 2nd edition. New York: Free Press, 1976.

128. Moos, Rudolf H. (ed.). *Coping with Physical Illness*. New York: Plenum, 1977.

129. Morley, Wilbur E. "Crisis Intervention with Adults," in Gerald F. Jacobson (ed.), *Crisis Intervention in the 1980s*. San Francisco: Jossey-Bass, 1980.

130. ———, and Vivian B. Brown. "The Crisis Intervention Group: A Natural Mating or a Marriage of Convenience?" *Psychotherapy: Theory, Research, and Practice*, Vol. 6 (Winter 1969), pp. 30–36.

131. Morris, Betty. "Crisis Intervention in a Public Welfare Agency," *Social Casework*, Vol. 49 (December 1968), pp. 612–617.

132. Murphy, Lois B. *The Widening World of Childhood*. New York: Basic Books, 1962.

133. ———, and Alice E. Moriarty. *Vulnerability, Coping, and Growth: From Infancy to Adolescence.* New Haven: Yale University Press, 1976.

134. Nacman, Martin. "Reflections of a Social Work Administrator on the Opportunities of Crises," *Social Work in Health Care*, Vol. 6 (Fall 1980), pp. 11–21.

135. Neugarten, Bernice L. "Adaptation and the Life Cycle," *Counseling Psychologist*, Vol. 6 (1976), pp. 16–20.

136. O'Connell, V. F. "Crisis Psychotherapy: Person, Dialogue, and the Organismic Event," in J. Fagen and I. L. Shepherd (eds.), *Gestalt Therapy Now.* New York: Harper and Row, 1970.

137. Parad, Howard J. "Preventive Casework: Problems and Implications," *Social Welfare Forum, 1961.* New York: Columbia University Press, 1961, pp. 178–193. Reprinted in Howard J. Parad, *Crisis Intervention.* New York: Family Service Association of America, 1965, pp. 284–298.

138. ———. "The Use of Time-Limited Crisis Intervention in Community Health Programming," *Social Service Review*, Vol. 40 (September 1966), pp. 275–282.

139. ———. "Crisis Intervention," in John B. Turner, (ed.), *Encyclopedia of Social Work*, 17th issue, Vol. 1. Washington, D.C.: National Association of Social Workers, 1977, pp. 228–237.

140. ———. "Role of the Social Worker in Emergency Medical Care." Summary of Project Findings and Recommendations, School of Social Work, University of Southern California, September 1984. Reproduction.

141. ———, and Libbie G. Parad. "A Study of Crisis-Oriented Short-Term Treatment," *Social Casework*, Vol. 49. Part I, June 1968, pp. 346–355. Part II, July 1968, pp. 418–426.

142. Parad, Howard J., H. L. P. Resnik, and Libbie G. Parad (eds.). *Emergency and Disaster Management: A Mental Health Sourcebook.* Bowie, Md.: Charles Press, 1976.

143. Parad, Howard J., Lola Selby, and James Quinlan. "Crisis Intervention with Families and Groups," in Robert W. Roberts and Helen Northen (eds.), *Theories of Social Work with Groups.* New York: Columbia University Press, 1976, pp. 304–330.

144. Parkes, C. Murray. "Psycho-Social Transitions," *Social Sciences and Medicine*, Vol. 5 (1971), pp. 101–115.

145. Pasewark, Richard, and Dale A. Albers. "Crisis Intervention: Theory in Search of a Program," *Social Work*, Vol. 17 (March 1972), pp. 70–77.

146. Pavenstedt, Eleanor, and Viola W. Bernard. *Crisis of Family Disorganization.* New York: Behavioral Publications, 1971.

147. Perlman, Helen H. *Social Casework: A Problem-Solving Process.* Chicago: University of Chicago Press, 1957.

148. ———. "Some Notes on the Waiting List," *Social Casework*, Vol. 44 (April 1963), pp. 200–205.

149. ———. "In Quest of Coping," *Social Casework*, Vol. 56 (April 1975), pp. 213–225.

150. Piaget, Jean. *The Origins of Intelligence in Children.* New York: Norton, 1963.

151. Polak, Paul R., Donald J. Eagan, Richard L. VandenBergh, and Vail Williams. "Crisis Intervention in Acute Bereavement: A Controlled Study of Primary Pre-

vention," in Howard J. Parad, H. L. P. Resnik, and Libbie G. Parad (eds.), *Emergency and Disaster Management*. Bowie, Md.: Charles Press, 1976, pp. 443–457.

152. Rapoport, Lydia. "The State of Crisis: Some Theoretical Considerations," *Social Service Review*, Vol. 36 (June 1962), pp. 211–217.

153. ———. "Crisis-Oriented Short-Term Casework," *Social Service Review*, Vol. 41 (March 1967), pp. 31–43.

154. ———. "Crisis Intervention as a Mode of Brief Treatment," in Robert W. Roberts and Robert H. Nee (eds.), *Theories of Social Casework*. Chicago: University of Chicago Press, 1970, pp. 267–311.

155. Rapoport, Rhona. "Normal Crisis, Family Structure, and Mental Health," *Family Process*, Vol. 2 (1963), pp. 68–80.

156. Reid, William J., and Laura Epstein. *Task-Centered Casework*. New York: Columbia University Press, 1972.

157. ——— (eds.). *Task-Centered Practice*. New York: Columbia University Press, 1977.

158. Reid, William J., and Ann W. Shyne. *Brief and Extended Casework*. New York: Columbia University Press, 1969.

159. Resnik, H. L. P., and Harvey L. Ruben (eds.). *Emergency Psychiatric Care: The Management of Mental Health Crises*. Bowie, Md.: Charles Press, 1975.

160. Reynolds, Bertha C. *An Uncharted Journey*. New York: Citadel Press, 1963.

161. Rhodes, Sonya L. "A Developmental Approach to the Life Cycle of the Family," *Social Casework*, Vol. 58 (May 1977), pp. 301–311.

162. Rich, Margaret E. *A Belief in People*. New York: Family Service Association of America, 1956.

163. Riegel, Klaus R. "Adult Life Crises: A Dialectic Interpretation of Development," in Nancy Datan and Leon H. Ginsberg (eds.), *Life-Span Developmental Psychology: Normative Life Crises*. New York: Academic Press, 1975, pp. 99–128.

164. Ripple, Lilian, Ernestina Alexander, and Bernice W. Polemis. *Motivation Capacity, and Opportunity: Studies in Casework Theory and Practice*. Chicago: School of Social Service Administration, University of Chicago, 1964.

165. Rosenberg, Blanca N. "Planned Short-Term Treatment in Developmental Crises," *Social Casework*, Vol. 56 (April 1975), pp. 195–204.

166. Rossi, Alice S. "Transition to Parenthood," *Journal of Marriage and the Family*, Vol. 30 (1968), pp. 26–39.

167. Rueveni, Uri. "Network Intervention with a Family Crisis," *Family Process*, Vol. 14 (June 1975), pp. 193–203.

168. Russell, Betty and Sylvia Schild. "Pregnancy Counseling with College Women, "Social Casework, Vol. 57 (May 1976), pp. 324–329.

169. Sands, Roberta G. "Crisis Intervention and Social Work Practice in Hospitals," *Health and Social Work*, Vol. 8 (1983), 253–261.

170. Scherz, Frances H. "The Crisis of Adolescence in Family Life," *Social Casework*, Vol. 48 (April 1967), pp. 209–215.

171. Selye, Hans. *The Stress of Life*. New York: McGraw-Hill, 1956.

172. Shader, Richard I., and Alice K. Schwartz. "Management of Reaction to Disaster," *Social Work*, Vol. 11 (April 1966), pp. 99–105.

173. Shaw, Robert, Harry Blumenfeld, and Rita Senf. "A Short-Term Treatment Program in a Child Guidance Clinic," *Social Work*, Vol. 13 (July 1968), pp. 81–90.

174. Sheridan, Mary S., and Doris R. Johnson. "Social Work Services in a High-Risk Nursery," *Health and Social Work*, Vol. 1 (May 1976), pp. 86–103.

175. Shneidman, Edwin S., Norman L. Farberow, and Robert E. Litman. *The Psychology of Suicide*. New York: Science House, 1970.

176. Sifneos, Peter E. "A Concept of Emotional Crisis," *Mental Hygiene*, Vol. 44 (April 1960), pp. 169–179.

177. ———. "Two Different Kinds of Psychotherapy of Short Duration," *American Journal of Psychiatry*, Vol. 123 (March 1967), pp. 1069–1073.

178. ———. *Short-Term Psychotherapy and Emotional Crisis*. Cambridge, Mass.: Harvard University Press, 1972.

179. Silverman, Phyllis R. "Widowhood and Preventive Intervention," *Family Coordinator*, January 1972, pp. 95–102.

180. ———. "Bereavement as a Normal Life Transition," in Elizabeth Prichard *et al. Social Work with the Dying Patient and the Family*. New York: Columbia University Press, 1977, pp. 266–273.

181. Simonds, John F. "A Foster Home for Crisis Placements," *Child Welfare*, Vol. 52 (February 1973), pp. 82–90.

182. Siporin, Max. *Introduction to Social Work Practice*. New York: Macmillan, 1975.

183. ———. "Disaster Aid," in John B. Turner (ed.), *Encyclopedia of Social Work*, 17th issue, Vol. 1. Washington, D.C.: National Association of Social Workers, 1977, pp. 277–288.

184. Smith, Larry L. "Crisis Intervention in Practice," *Social Casework*, Vol. 60 (February 1979), pp. 81–88.

185. Soskis, Carol. "Emergency Room on Weekends: The Only Game in Town," *Health and Social Work*, Vol. 5 (August 1980), pp. 37–43.

186. Speck, Ross V., and Carolyn L. Attneave. *Family Networks*. New York: Pantheon, 1973.

187. Specter, Gerald A., and William L. Claiborn (eds.). *Crisis Intervention*. New York: Behavioral Publications, 1973.

188. Stotland, Ezra. *The Psychology of Hope*. San Francisco: Jossey-Bass, 1969.

189. Strickler, Martin. "Applying Crisis Theory in a Community Clinic," *Social Casework*, Vol. 46 (March 1965), pp. 150–154.

190. ———, and Jean Allgeyer. "The Crisis Group: A New Application of Crisis Theory," *Social Work*, Vol. 12 (July 1967), pp. 28–32.

191. Strickler, Martin, and Margaret Bonnefil. "Crisis Intervention and Social Casework: Similarities and Differences in Problem Solving," *Clinical Social Work Journal*, Vol. 2 (Spring 1974), pp. 36–44.

192. Taplin, Julian R. "Crisis Theory: Critique and Reformulation," *Community Mental Health Journal*, Vol. 7 (March 1971), pp. 13–23.

193. Taylor, James B., Louis Zuicher, and William H. Key. *Tornado: A Community Responds to Disaster*. Seattle: University of Washington Press, 1970.

194. Titchener, James L., Frederic T. Kapp, and Carolyn Winget. "The Buffalo Creek Syndrome: Symptoms and Character Change after a Major Disaster," in Howard J. Parad, H. L. P. Resnik, and Libbie G. Parad (eds.), *Emergency and Disaster Management*. Bowie, Md.: Charles Press, 1976, pp. 283–294.

195. Towle, Charlotte. *Common Human Needs*. Washington, D.C.: Federal Security Agency, 1945. Reissued, New York: National Association of Social Workers, 1957.

196. ———. "Reinforcing Family Security Today," *Social Casework*, Vol. 31 (February 1950). Quoted in Margaret E. Rich, *A Belief in People*. New York: Family Service Association of America, 1956.

197. Townsend, Gladys E. "Short-Term Casework with Clients Under Stress," *Social Casework*, Vol. 34 (November 1953), pp. 392–398.

198. Tyhurst, James. "The Role of Transition States—Including Disaster—in Mental Illness." *Symposium on Preventive and Social Psychiatry*. Washington, D.C.: Walter Reed Army Institute of Research, 1957, pp. 149–169.

199. Vera, Maria I. "Rape Crisis Intervention in the Emergency Room: A New Challenge for Social Work," *Social Work in Health Care*, Vol. 6, No. 3 (1981), pp. 1–11.

200. Walfish, Steven. "Crisis Telephone Counselors' Views of Clinical Interaction Situations," *Community Mental Health Journal*, Vol. 19 (Fall 1983), pp. 219–230.

201. Wasserman, Sidney. "The Middle Age Separation Crisis and Ego Supportive Casework Treatment," *Clinical Social Work Journal*, Vol. 1 (September 1973), pp. 38–47.

202. Weakland, John H., Richard Fisch, Paul Watzlawick, and Arthur M. Bodin. "Brief Therapy: Focused Problem Resolution," *Family Process*, Vol. 13 (June 1974), pp. 141–168.

203. Weiss, Robert S. "Transition States and Other Stressful Situations: Their Nature and Programs for Their Management," in Gerald Caplan and Marie Killilea (eds.), *Support Systems and Mutual Help: A Multidisciplinary Exploring*. New York: Grune and Stratton, 1976, pp. 213–232.

204. White, Robert W. "Motivation Reconsidered: The Concept of Competence," *Psychological Review*, Vol. 66 (September 1959), pp. 297–333.

205. ———. *Ego and Reality in Psychoanalytic Theory*. Psychological Issues No. 11. New York: International Universities Press, 1963.

206. Wilson, Robert S. *The Short Contact in Social Case Work*, Vol. 1. New York: National Association for Travelers Aid and Transient Service, 1937.

207. Wiseman, Reva S. "Crisis Theory and the Process of Divorce," *Social Casework*, Vol. 56 (April 1975), pp. 205–212.

208. Woolf, Donald A., and Marvin Rudman. "A Police-Social Service Cooperative Program," *Social Work*, Vol. 22 (January 1977), pp. 62–63.

209. Zastrow, Charles, and Ralph Navarre. "Help for Runaways and Their Parents," *Social Casework*, Vol. 56 (February 1975), pp. 74–78.

Annotated Listing of Key References

CAPLAN, GERALD. *Principles of Preventive Psychiatry*. New York: Basic Books, 1964.
Basic presentation of Caplan's approach to crisis intervention, with emphasis on various levels of intervention, according to public health model. Important reference, although the theory has moved beyond this point.

CAPLAN, GERALD. *Support Systems and Community Mental Health*. New York: Behavioral Publications, 1974.
First essay is extremely important, signifying basic change in Caplan's orientation, with increased emphasis on use of natural and mutual help systems.

GOLAN, NAOMI. *Tratment in Crisis Situations*. New York: Free Press, 1978.
Attempts to place crisis intervention within framework of social work practice and presents a basic treatment model to be used flexibly in different settings. This is an outgrowth of task-centered model.

KAPLAN, DAVID M. "Observations on Crisis Theory and Practice," *Social Casework*, Vol. 49 (March 1968), pp. 151–155.
Discussion of early Harvard studies, using public health framework. Presents important concept of acute situational disorder and psychological tasks to be mastered, with implications for agencies and practitioners.

PARAD, HOWARD J. "Crisis Intervention," in *Encyclopedia of Social Work*, 17th issue. Washington, D.C.: NASW, 1977, pp. 228–237.
Crisp, concise presentation of basic crisis theory and its current research and practice applications, including future trends.

PARAD, HOWARD J., H. L. P. RESNIK, and LIBBIE G. PARAD (eds.). *Emergency and Disaster Management*. Bowie, Md.: Charles Press, 1976.
Important sourcebook of recent developments in the field, including reports of disaster work. While the quality of articles is uneven and some are repetitious, it reflects current emphases and preoccupations in crisis area.

RAPOPORT, LYDIA. "Crisis Interventions a Mode of Brief Treatment," in Robert W. Roberts and Robert H. Nee (eds.), *Theories of Social Casework*. Chicago: University of Chicago Press, 1970, pp. 267–311.
Presents Rapoport's last analysis and interpretation of crisis theory and its application to the field of practice. Excellent historical summary and perspective.

SIPORIN, MAX. "Disaster Aid," in *Encyclopedia of Social Work*, 17th issue. Washington, D.C.: NASW, 1977, pp. 277–285.
Careful, detailed analysis of recent developments in this area, including review of theory and discussion of governmental policies and programs.

CHAPTER 13

The Neurolinguistic Programming Model

Mary MacLean

An Overall Summary of the Thought System

Neurolinguistic programming is a new and exciting model of human communication and behavior. It is a different way of thinking and is concerned with the structure of subjective experience, the evolution of ideas, and with advancing practical skills. NLP is a system of highly pragmatic intervention that is readily compatible with methods of traditional social work practice. It respects the practice wisdom of therapists but seeks to enrich this practice by adding to the repertoire of therapeutic skills. Its distinguishing feature is its focus on the neurological base of communication as a way of achieving a more effective strategy of client change.

The overall objective of neurolinguistic programming is to provide us with more behavioral choices, since the more choices we have, the more we will move forward as a society. It is a model of the process of modeling—in meta model rather than a theory. Modelers are more interested in what people *do* than in what people *say* they do and in building descriptions that seem to work and are *useful* in terms of how to do something. The neurolinguistic programming model does not explain *why* things work, but it does have a lot to offer in terms of *how* things work.

Theorists explain what they do, but they do not always provide steps on

341

how you can do it yourself. This is what neurolinguistic programming does: it offers specific techniques by which practitioners may organize and reorganize their subjective experiences or the experiences of a client to secure a desired behavioral outcome.

Virginia Satir effects dramatic changes in families, yet, even if you knew everything there is to know about her theoretical formulations, you might not be able to accomplish the same results. Satir picks up on unconscious factors and immediately achieves a rapport. She tells us to listen to the family with our body. But this can prove to be an insurmountable task unless you are as sensitive as Virginia Satir (46). Milton Erickson (26) achieved similar results by using a hypnotic pattern. What neurolinguistic programming can do is to make conscious many of the steps Satir, Erickson, and other powerful communicators used when they were most effective. Practitioners do not have to give up any part of their practice skills to become neurolinguistic programmers. Everything that you have learned in order to be effective in the helping process is recognized and respected.

Many of us in Western society go through life repeating a remarkably small number of patterns that have resulted in positive outcomes in past social contexts. The purpose of neurolinguistic programming is to *add* to the number of available patterns so that desired behavioral outcomes can be reached in a variety of ways; that is, to expand therapeutic effectiveness, to help practitioners generate more choices.

This practice methodology is not only concerned with the observation of facts, but with the form and sequence of data, which interact subjectively with our neurology to form different meanings. It places much greater stress on our own and our clients' physical responses. The inclusion of the perceptions, actions, and responses of the observer in describing patterns of human communication systems greatly increases the descriptive power of the model. The requirement that description of the pattern be represented in sensory-grounded terms, which are available to the user, ensures usefulness and begins to close the gap between theory and practice. Neurolinguistic programming deals with material that practitioners do not usually attend to consciously, and as a result, its vocabulary includes terms that are not directly observable and address the individual's internal structure (e.g., representational systems, strategies). The NLP vocabulary provides a powerful set of behavioral organizing principles.

For the neurolinguistic programmer, all human behavior is the result of systematically ordered sequences of internal neurological processes; that is, behavior is programmed by combining and sequencing the sensory representational systems of hearing (auditory), seeing (visual), feeling (kinesthetics), and smelling and tasting (olfactory). An internal or external stimulus is processed through some sequence of internal representations and a specific behavioral outcome results. This process can be organized to obtain the desired state. Since all behavior is in some way communication about the neurological organization of the individual, *one cannot not communicate.*

The rather imposing name, neurolinguistic programming, simply means that all behavior is neurologically based: neural processes are represented, ordered, and sequenced into models and strategies through verbal and nonverbal communication, and there is a process of organizing sensory representations to achieve desired states. NLP has a broad range of practical applications and its technology can be used in behavioral interactions in any area of human endeavor. Truth is perceived as a metaphor and NLP is less interested in this than in whether patterns work and are useful. There is a real world out there but how we perceive that world is one of the most important variables that govern our lives.

The Historical Origins

Neurolinguistic Programming has been in existence since the early 1970s and is still only at the beginning of an evolving process. The model was founded by John Grinder, a linguist, and Richard Bandler (5–8), a mathematician, through their systematic study of therapists Virginia Satir, Milton H. Erickson, and Fritz Perls in actual therapy with individuals, couples, and families. Leslie Cameron-Bandler, Robert Dilts (13), and Judith DeLozier (15) have since made significant contributions.

Initially, Bandler and Grinder applied their abilities in detecting and utilizing patterns of human behavior to create change and constructed a therapeutic model of the English language that came to be known as the "meta model," a specific set of linguistic strategies for responding in a useful way to the form of verbalizations presented by people (12).* With NLP tools, Bandler and Grinder were able to secure quick, lasting, and amazing results: a "cure" for phobias and other long-term problems in less than an hour; resolution of deadlocked negotiations in business; and success in teaching children with learning difficulties.

Although their model was originally developed for use in therapy, it soon became apparent that NLP had the potential for a much broader application in that it offered explicit steps anyone could follow to make any desired changes in behavior. Subsequently, Bandler and Grinder turned their attention to the study of people with unusual talents in order to determine the structure of that talent. They found that the structure can be taught to others to give them the foundation for that same ability. This kind of intervention is known as *generative* change, in which people learn to create new talents and behaviors for themselves and others.

Many physical symptoms have their roots in behavioral patterns and can be alleviated by changing the way people neurologically guide and organize their behavior. Until very recently, we believed that blood pressure and heart

*A distillation of the Meta Model can be found in Appendix I of Leslie Cameron-Bandler, *They Lived Happily Ever After*, (Cupertino, Calif.: Meta Publications, 1978) and in detail in Richard Bander and John Grinder, *The Structure of Magic I* (Palo Alto: Calif. 1975).

rate were beyond the individual's control. Now, with biofeedback, we know that the locus of behavioral control of these functions is in the individual. Thus, sickness can be a decision variable for the individual. If your body knows how to get sick, it may also know how to get well. If the behavior of those who respond well to placebos and recover rapidly from a particular illness can be modeled, their strategies for self-healing might be taught to others. John Grinder claims that in his therapeutic work, people have had their physical symptoms improve, clear up, or go into remission when they have modified, changed, or acquired new strategies.

Changing an old strategy, installing a new one, and utilizing a forgotten resource are more profound and inclusive than attitude change, which has long been recognized as a contributor to health and disease. Nor are strategies merely cognitive activities within our representational systems, which interface with other neural systems so that neurological outcomes of our strategies affect body functions and body chemistry including the immune system.

Path into Social Work

Neurolinguistic programming addresses elements social workers are not accustomed to considering. All models of practice are linked with the social conditions out of which they emerge. Historically, in social work, there has been a broad swing back and forth between concern with social reform and concern with the relief of personal suffering. During certain periods of history there has been support for one approach over another, although professional social work practice must be concerned with both. In contrast to the radicals of the sixties who tried to revolutionize the "state" from without, there is a move in the eighties to work within the "system" for social change. As a consequence, today's activists see themselves as part of the establishment, and have a deep commitment to what the "system" ought to be. Out of this political climate has emerged the neurolinguistic programming model. NLP is a different way of thinking and reflects the current trend toward brief, planned intervention where the client (individual, family, group, or organization) is placed in the center of the helping process and is empowered to take a much more autonomous role. The belief is that each individual, family, group, or organization has the potential for development of positive resources and this potential is perceived to exist in both positive and negative experiences. The environment can retard or complicate but usually cannot control individual growth.

Neurolinguistic programming is, therefore, a new form of brief intervention and reflects the times in which we live—with agency cut-backs and reduced funding—as well as the North American propensity for wanting quick results.

Brief planned intervention provides both the practitioners and the clients with a unique opportunity to work on a single aspect of problematic functioning. This short-term framework is well-known to social work. As early as 1920, Bertha Reynolds pointed out the positive value of the single-contact interview that focused on the most pressing problem at the time. All brief intervention, regardless of the approach, is based on the rapid development of a positive working relationship. In all short-term work, it is essential to avoid regression in the client.

Provided the first experience in short-term intervention is successful, the client is likely to seek further help perhaps months or even years later, from the same trusted worker. In this manner, intermittent, short-term work can lead to long-term relationships. Unfortunately, the bureaucratic policies of many social agencies mitigate against such occurrences. Intermittent, brief intervention is more characteristic of private practitioners who are forging ahead and experimenting with new forms of social work practice.

Neurolinguistic programming does not pit idea against idea or method against method, but rather reflects the position that all important concepts and techniques complement or overlap each other as they attempt to deal with the complexities of the person in social context.

In the past, the many and diverse models of practice have often been taught as if these concepts arose from mutually exclusive, incompatible, and even competing schools of thought when, in fact, we need all the models of practice that are available to us, for each model addresses a different outcome. As soon as we adopt one model, we drastically limit our experience with the world. The more effective and useful a model of practice is, the more we are inclined to regard it as *the* model. NLP is particularly seductive in this regard because its techniques are powerful and work. By focusing on process and form rather than on content, the neurolinguistics programmer is not inundated and swamped by the story the client presents, and desired outcomes can be achieved more quickly. NLP can be considered an extension of social work, linguistics, neurology, and psychology.

Present Status and Influence on Current Social Work Practice

Many social work practitioners attend NLP workshops , which are being offered throughout the United States and Canada, and find this a most enjoyable way to learn the NLP model. In addition, some universities are beginning to offer courses in neurolinguistic programming in their schools of social work.

Connection with Other Theories or Systems

Neurolinguistic programming has combined knowledge and experience from such divergent fields as the neurosciences, psychophysiology, linguistics, cybernetics, communication theory, and the information sciences. It draws information from wherever it can.

General Therapeutic Concepts

The neurolinguistic programming model is a positive outcome frame. Life may be a problem-solving process, as Helen Harris Perlman maintains, but the danger is that, in the process, people may somehow perceive themselves as "a problem." In tracking the patterns of behavior of highly creative and successful people, it has been observed that they set positive goals for themselves. Once these goals are attained, new ones are set, or they come to find that the desired goal is not what they expected, or they are not prepared to make the investment necessary to achieve the desired state and decide on a new one. A goal can be as simple as wanting to have a friendly conversation with someone or as complex as wanting to become a neurosurgeon, something that would probably need to be chunked down into smaller, more manageable parts in order to be achieved. The positive outcome frame is what people do naturally to attain their goals and this is the frame used in NLP.

Neurolinguistic programming aims at transforming experiences previously regarded as environmental constraints into *decision strategies* in order to achieve *desired outcomes*. Resources within the person and in the external world are accessed and applied to the present state to help the individual, group, or organization achieve the desired state. Getting congruent representations of the desired state in all sensory neurological systems is a powerful resource in helping people attain their goal.

A neurolinguistic programmer needs:

1. Open sensory channels (sensory acuity); that is, an ability to detect verbal and nonverbal cues and to be able to discriminate,
2. To be clear about the positive outcome desired by the client(s) and to define this in sensory-grounded terms in order to reduce the possibility of miscommunication occurring, and
3. Behavioral flexibility; that is, being able to get to the same place in many different ways.

If these elements are present, there is perfect communication. This applies as much to business management as to therapy.

In any human interaction, people are offering you a great deal of information. The more information you can connect with, the more effective you will be. Most practitioners limit their attention to material that is in conscious awareness. Yet conscious awareness is one of our most limited channels and is not essential to human drives. George Miller (1956) maintains that we are only capable of keeping in conscious awareness seven plus or minus two chunks of information (39, 40). Fortunately, anything you have learned really well has also been learned by your unconscious mind. In learning to type or to drive a car, at first every action had to be attended to consciously; but soon many of the required skills became unconscious and reflex.

In learning any new, complex perceptual motor skill—whether it's driving a car, riding a bicycle, skiing, dancing, or skating—what is required is that the task be organized into small chunks so that each small chunk can be practiced individually until achieving the status of an unconscious perceptual-motor pattern. This unconscious learning of patterns of behavior is essential, otherwise our consciousness would be cluttered and unable to attend to the complex demands of each new day.

Consciousness is what we are aware of at any given moment. The *unconscious* is everything else. Information originating in the unconscious is often more valid, since that is the part which generates behavior—e.g., overeating, smoking.

Most of the things that are learned, are learned unconsciously. NLP offers patterns that are initially produced consciously, but as the learning is strengthened, they drop out of the conscious into the unconscious, yet are available almost automatically whenever needed. They no longer clutter the limited channels of conscious awareness. Consciousness in NLP is an emergent property of neural system activity rather than an initiator of the activity. Consciousness is a side effect, an indicator of a portion of what is going on during sensory, neurological systems processing. A sensory representation becomes conscious only when it reaches a certain level of intensity. A major portion of our lives is spent operating tremendously complex patterns of unconscious behavior (41–43).

Modeling

Everything we do is learned and in NLP the learning process is an ongoing process of change called "Modeling," occuring at both the conscious and unconscious levels of behavior. Modeling is a process of eliciting and utilizing the successful behaviors of other people. Learning to speak our native tongue is an example of the process of unconscious modeling. Learning to read and spell is usually an example of conscious modeling, although even these are dependent on the sequencing and organization of lower-level patterns of behavior at the unconscious level.

Our culture does not encourage following patterns. Patterns are like basic maps—we use them to be creative in our own activities and particular social context. In our culture, we are taught to pay attention to words; we are *not* taught to use our eyes, ears, sense of touch, feel, smell, and taste. However, we use them all unconsciously.

Presuppositions of NLP

There are a number of presuppositions in NLP. One is: *you already have all the positive resources to deal with any situation and to achieve your desired goals.* This is because we all have access to our sensory neurological systems; this presupposition assumes the absence of severe organic damage. As Milton Erickson has stated: "There is a great deal that you already know, that you don't know." The question is how to make the internal resources available to the conscious awareness and how to organize them in the appropriate context.

A second presupposition in NLP is: *the meaning of your communication is the response you get.* If I keep on doing what I am doing, I will get the same response. In fact, it will amplify the response. But if I take the responsibility for my communication not being accepted as I intended, I can change the response I receive. I am not a victim.

If I accept an irresponsible response as something *you* did, there is nothing I can do about it except label you "pig-headed" and "stubborn." If I vary what I have done, I have a better opportunity of getting what I want. For example, if I call, "Tom, come to lunch," and he does not come, the usual response would be to amplify the message and add a derogatory tone: "Tom, did you hear me? I said, 'Come to lunch'!" If Tom did not come with the first request, it is doubtful that the second will get the desired result. I would have a better chance of getting Tom to come to lunch if I did something different.

A third presupposition, then, is: *the element in a system that has the most flexibility will be the controlling or catalytic element.* This is the Law of Requisite Variety (2) and assumes that no element has a structurally dominant position. If what you are doing is not eliciting the desired response, do something different.

A fourth presupposition is: *the map is not the territory or don't eat the menu.* If we act on the belief that words mean the same thing to all people, we will make mistakes. When I asked a number of people at an Introductory Workshop to think about the word *cat,* some formed an internal picture of a cat while others pictured internally a particular cat. Some accessed the word *cat* by an internal sound, "meow," others experienced an internal sensation of the soft fur of a cat, and still others had a polarity response with the internal verbalization "dog" and through a crossover connection called "synesthesia" created an internal image of a dog. Such different ways of responding to one word illustrate that it is quite remarkable that any sentence is heard as the sender intended.

We do not experience the world directly; our primary experience is through our sensory channels, our sensory perception of the world around us. We represent, order, and sequence these neural processes to access and to understand the world as we experiment. Language is only a secondary experience, and we are all taught to use words differently. A word only has meaning when it triggers an individual's primary sensory neurological systems and a great deal of distortion and slippage occurs during the process of encoding primary experience into language.

A fifth presupposition is: *mind and body are an interconnected part of the same biological system and influence each other*. We are our body. We cannot even utter a sentence without activating organic nerve impulses.

A sixth presupposition is: *individual behavior is a function of the representation, order, and sequencing of sensory neurological systems or strategies.*

A seventh presupposition is: *human beings are capable of one-trial learning*. Anchors, or learned associations, presuppose single-trial learning. Anchors become established without positive reinforcement or direct reward for the association.

An eighth presupposition is: *any behavior is the best choice available to the individual in that particular social context; if a better choice had been available, it would have been taken.*

A ninth presupposition is: *there is no substitute for clean, active, open sensory channels in order to know what response you are eliciting*. A great deal of therapy is psychotheology. The experts theorize about it but do not tell us how to do what they do when they are most effective. Theoreticians explain how communication takes place, yet in actual management, none of this is visible. It is all internal processing in any kind of exchange and what is going on internally goes very quickly.

Representational Systems

Neurolinguistic programming is more concerned with form than content and with the representation of experience at the neurological level. We do not operate directly on the world but through sensory transformations of that world. NLP examines the correlations between what we experience as the external environment and our internal representations of that experience. We experience the world through a sensory-motor complex that NLP has termed "representational systems," comprising auditory, visual, kinesthetics (feelings, body sensations), and olfactory (smell and taste). These are the structural parameters of our knowledge. The abbreviated version is known as the 4-tuple (A^{ei}, V^{ei}, K^{ei}, O^{ei}). The superscripts "e" and "i" indicate whether representations are coming from external ("e") or internal ("i") sources. Sensory information received through each of these systems initiates or modifies, through neural interconnections, an individual's behavioral processes and output. For example, a person labeled schizophrenic usually has difficulty in knowing what information is generated internally and what is generated externally and how to make the distinction.

In contrast to more traditional models, the sensory systems are not regarded as passive input mechanisms. Each representational system involves *input, representation/processing*, and *output*. The acts of seeing, listening, or feeling are behavioral in the NLP model, and range from microbehavior outputs—such as blinking, tonal changes in the voice, skin color changes, eye movements, and breathing rates—to macrobehavior outputs—such as arguing, disease, running away from home, and playing baseball.

The representational system with the highest relative intensity, regardless of whether it is out of awareness or in consciousness, has the greatest behavioral significance. If the signal valves are close enough, it is possible for a multiple response to occur where the person signals both a "yes" and "no" message. It is also possible for two strategies to occur simultaneously causing split responses and behavioral incongruence.

Strategies

The models that we use to guide our behavior are developed from the ordering of representational systems into patterned sequences called "strategies." The rule of modeling elegance applies and models are preferred that employ the fewest number of distinctions and still are able to secure outcomes at least equal to more complex models.

All overt behavior in the human species is controlled by internal processing strategies. Each of us has a specific strategy for making decisions, for being creative, for delegating responsibilities, for motivation, and for learning among others. Strategies are formal operations of behavior, and a person is able to use a strategy regardless of the content of the situation encountered because they simply provide the framework within which we combine and ascribe meaning to the content of our sensory experience.

A strategy can be operative even when all the steps are not in conscious awareness. At each step of a strategy the 4-tuple is acted upon by a lead representational system, through accessing cues and synesthesia patterns, giving one representational system more behavioral significance than others.

One strategy we use is *uptime*, when all our external sensory channels are open, operational, and alert, allowing us to respond readily and immediately to appropriate external cues. *Downtime* is also a resource strategy and refers to the process of eliciting resources in terms of reference experiences. These patterns apply as powerfully to negotiation, mediation, teambuilding, education, and managment as they do to therapeutic contexts.

Each step in a strategy consists of a *congruent, polarity,* or *meta* response. A congruent response is an agreement with the representation before it but in a different modality. A polarity response is a representation reversal in content of the step preceding it. A meta response is a message about the step before it.

Eliciting Strategies Through Predicates

People talk about what they are doing and in so doing reveal which representational system they are using to make sense of the world and to organize their experience. The class of words known as *predicates* (adjectives, verbs, adverbs) are translations or modifiers of the way you represent your experience and are used to identify the steps in an individual's strategy. Which one has the most priority in consciousness? Which one is easiest to list? The following words are indicative of the representational system being described.

Visual	Auditory	Kinesthetic	Smell	Taste
Picture	Hear	Feel	Pungent	Bitter
Blue	Scream	Warm	Stale	Salty
Vague	Shout	Touch	Fresh	Sweet
Clear	Loud	Handle	Fragrant	Sour
See	Tune	Grasp	Fishy	Juicy
Focus	Tone	Soft	Rancid	Spicy

Smell and taste are not given great importance in our culture and are used primarily as triggers for accessing past 4-Tuples rather than for organizational strategies. Thus, the smell of a fish shop, the taste of honey, the smell of a hospital, the taste of cod liver oil, the smell of a former lover's perfume can trigger a transderivational search, that is, take us from the original sense experience to one we relate with it.

A high external signal tends to mask internal experience in the same representational system and vice versa since they share the same neural pathways to the brain. The meta-model in *The Structure of Magic I* provides the best tools for decoding such verbalizations into primary sensory experiences and for gathering high-quality information about how verbalizations and sensory experiences are connected in particular instances.

Language—that is, auditory digital representation—tends to be primarily organized by neurological systems localized in the dominant hemisphere of the brain, while the nondominant hemisphere seems to be specialized for organizing the tonal and rhythmic portions of our auditory experience.

NLP operators use *nonspecific* words when they want their clients to go into particular representational system.

Nonspecific Words

Think	Learn	Chance	Believe
Know	Intuit	Consider	Remember
Understand	Trust	Experience	Respect
Nice	Appreciate	Sense	

It is important to remember that the verbal portion of our communication is often the least important aspect. A large amount of information is transmitted nonverbally, outside the awareness of most people.

The TOTE

The basic format used to describe a specific sequence of behavior is the TOTE (test-operate-test-exit) and the general description of NLP as applying resources to a present state of behavior to achieve a new outcome state can be considered an example of the TOTE process. A TOTE is a sequence of activities in a representational system that has combined into a unit of behavior that is usually below the threshold of consciousness. A simple example would be a handshake; a more complex example, a musician's performance of a concerto. The operant phase of one TOTE may include other TOTEs, with their own tests and operations. TOTEs exhibit a hierarchical structure. NLP specifies the components of TOTEs in terms of representational systems and strategies. The purpose of TOTE and representational systems analysis is to provide the most appropriate representational systems for the TOTE steps to achieve a particular goal and to attain ability in using all representational systems as resources for learning and doing.

We are not accustomed to making assessments on sensory-grounded information. Actions are determined by the unconscious, therefore, if conscious output and unconscious output are not congruent, what the person does will come from the unconscious. We usually do not confront people with unconscious material, because they are not aware of it. Most therapists aim at giving the client a conscious understanding of what the problem is but do not let the unconscious know that they are aware of that.

Eliciting Strategies Through Accessing Cues

Accessing cues are subtle behaviors that help indicate which representational system a person is activating in his thought processes. These behavioral cues accompany the sensory representational steps of our strategies.

One method is to use *Calibration*, the process of learning to tune in to another person's interactional responses by pairing observable behavioral cues with a specific internal response.

Accessing Eye Movements and Other Nonverbal Cues

Throughout the world (except the Basques) the eye movements people make as they think and process information are systematic and provide reliable indicators of representational system activity. Eye-scanning patterns in the nonverbal system offer quick ways of determining which sensory neurological system the client is using and, therefore, tells the worker how to respond creatively and in a useful way. The eye-movement patterns of left-handed people are often reversed from that of right-handed people—left to right. In some cultures, it is considered polite to maintain eye contact when communicating, such people may access visual images by defocusing while maintaining their eyes in a level position.

Other equally useful cues are tonal qualities of a person's voice, the tempo of speech, the fullness of the lower lip, and the color of a person's skin. People will often consciously or unconsciously point to or touch with their hands the sense organs for the particular representational system that they are using, or these gestures may occur without verbalizations. Thus a person may tap her nose, or touch his ear, or tap with the fingers, indicating which sense organ is involved. Accessing cues may become specialized and when repeated over long periods of time, will begin to shape a person's body.

Elicitation

Elicitation is the procedure used to gather the necessary information to make explicit the ordered sequence of representational systems activity that comprises a specific strategy. The most useful strategies are those for *learning, motivation, creativity, belief, decision-making,* and *remembering.*

The first step is elicitation of the strategy you wish to model, utilize, and/or modify. This can be accomplished by placing the person in the same social context in which the strategy developed with the use of psychodrama and role-playing, by asking the person to exaggerate some portion of the strategy to gain access to the whole, or by direct questioning—e.g., Have you ever made a decision where you were absolutely delighted with the outcome? What do you need to do to learn? What is it like when you are motivated?

People explicitly demonstrate verbally and nonverbally the steps of the strategies used to access and explain their experiences to themselves and others. As the person accesses the satisfactory experience, the strategy useful in obtaining the desired state will be demonstrated. This can be compared to the present experience and the difference between the successful and unsuccessful strategy determined.

Utilization

This is the process of turning an environmental limitation into a decision strategy in order to achieve a desired outcome. What is important in reaching an outcome is not so much what resources are available but how these resources are *used.* Utilization, then, is the technique of applying a strategy sequence or pattern of behavior in order to influence the response of an individual, family, group, or organization to achieve some desired outcome or to secure some outcome for yourself. A content is only useful if processed through a strategy to achieve some goal. The process of utilization provides explicit ways of applying to current situations strategies and resources used successfully in past contexts. Having the part to repair a bicycle is useless if we do not know what to do with it. By recognizing the social context and by packaging experience in terms of the most appropriate strategies for each situation, we can greatly increase our behavioral choices. The more behavioral choices we have, the more liberated we will become.

Pacing

The best place to meet anyone is on their own ground. Pacing is a quick method to establish rapport and is done by matching your behaviors with those of the person with whom you are communicating. The effect of verbal pacing is strengthened by adding nonverbal pacing, such as using your hands to direct the person into the appropriate accessing posture. We have successfully paced a person's strategy when we have organized our presentation so that its form matches the step-by-step sequence of representations the person uses in a particular strategy. The more skilled we are at pacing a person's thinking processes with our communication, the more likely we are to achieve the desired outcome since, *a person cannot not respond to his own strategies.*

Nature and Process of the Helping Relationship

Nothing can happen without rapport. Therefore, a person can be helped to find new behavioral choices, it is essential for the worker to establish rapport. This is accomplished relatively quickly and easily in NLP through *pacing* and *leading*, since whether applied consciously or unconsciously, rapport is probably the basis for many of the experiences we label "relationship" or "the helping relationship."

The strongest form of rapport occurs when communication is presented in step-by-step sequences that mirror the unconscious processes or strategies of the person with whom you are communicating. Matching voice tone and tempo, vocabulary, posture, gestures, and breathing pattern to those of the other person can quickly establish rapport covertly. Yet it is important to test whether rapport exists by attempting to *lead* the person into a different behavior, which can be something as subtle as a change in breathing pattern, a change in body posture, a shift in eye gaze, or a change in the tone or tempo of the voice. If the person does not follow the change, return to *pacing* until the required rapport is established. Even after this has been accomplished, it is useful to test periodically to make sure rapport is maintained.

Nature of Personality Structure and Nature of Personality Change

Neurolinguistic programming provides useful insights into such complex behavioral structures as "personality." We are all multiple personalities because we behave differently in different social contexts. The difference between a person with a pathological diagnosis of multiple personality and everyone else is that most people *know* they are different personalities in different social circumstances, while the person with a pathological diagnosis does not. In addition, people have choices about how they will respond in a particular social context.

Position and Importance of the Person-Environment Continuum

The primary aim of NLP is to continue the evolutionary process of challenging environmental constraints, including culturally and institutionally structured limitations, and to transform these environmental variables into decision variables that are within personal control. When given the option, the NLP programmer would choose the path that would emphasize internal personal control and give the client power over those involving external factors that are outside their control.

Specific Approaches to Treatment

Neurolinguistic programming offers patterns and strategies that some people do naturally and others need to be taught.

Patterns to Establish Rapport

MIRRORING. *Direct mirroring* and *crossover mirroring* are two kinds of nonverbal pacing. Mirroring is a matter of style and elegance. If you offer a person something she wants, she will accept it. Because you are addressing the unconscious in your responses to the client, it is more easily accepted. Mirroring a person's unconscious patterns is like entering their world. You begin by exercising what you do most easily and calibrate it with the part you find more difficult.

Direct mirroring begins subtly from the neck up and proceeds to the lower body, with any cultural or social mores respected. In direct mirroring, you mirror the opposite side of the person with whom you are communicating; thus if the person were tugging at his right ear you would touch your left ear. If discovered, stop and mirror the breathing pattern; people are not conscious of that yet it has a profound impact on them.

CROSSOVER MIRRORING. This is another way to do nonverbal pacing and involves substituting one nonverbal channel for another. Crossover mirroring is a particularly useful pattern in working with someone like an asthmatic, who has an unusual breathing pattern.

There are two kinds of crossover mirroring, one is to crossover in the same channel and the other is to switch channels. If I use a foot movement or a small sway of the body to pace a person's rate of breathing, even though the movement is subtle, it will still have the same effect. In this instance, I am using a different aspect of the same kinesthetic channel. If I switch channels and match the tempo of my voice to the person's breathing pattern, that is a different kind of crossover. Both are very effective in establishing rapport.

Nonverbal mirroring is a powerful unconscious mechanism that every member of the human species uses to communicate effectively. Nonverbal mirroring can prevent "burn-out" by offering practitioners an alternative way to attempt to empathize with phobics, diseased and dying persons, and those experiencing extreme pain and suffering.

Successful matching of a person's verbal and nonverbal behavior is called pacing his experience. You can mirror the other person's predicates, strategies, gestures, posture, breathing, voice tone and tempo, facial expression, and eye blinks. It is essential to pace or establish rapport before attempting to lead the other person into new behavior.

When working with more than one person—a couple, for example—to maintain neutrality, a therapist can breathe with the wife while talking with the husband.

The Pattern Called Anchoring

Anchoring and *change personal history* are patterns of "first order change" to be used when the goal is to change behavior that does not have secondary gain. Anchoring is the procedure that allows you to access positive experiences by making existing resources available in a context where they previously were unavailable.

An anchor is any internal or external representation that triggers another representation; that is, they are learned associations between a stimulus and a response. For example, a couple walking past a fish store may respond very differently to their experience. One person may complain about the unpleasant aroma of decaying fish; for the other, the smell may evoke warm memories from the past. In other instances, a therapist's office frequently becomes an anchor for people to unload their negative feelings. The meaning of any representation depends solely on the response it elicits in a particular person.

Any part of a particular experience or 4-tuple—visual, auditory, kinesthetic, or olfactory—may be used as an anchor to access another portion of that experience. Establishing an anchor requires a synesthesia pattern, where representations in two different sensory channels become associated. Language is one of the most common anchoring systems, as are facial expressions, voice tone and tempo, touch, odor, and taste. Internal sounds, sights, feelings, and smells are also anchors. Anchoring creates a bridge between two totally distant experiences.

Although it is possible to anchor through any sensory channel, in the beginning it is recommended that kinesthetic anchors be used since these are the easiest to learn and the most useful.

Anchoring and "Collapse Anchors"

Anchoring can be used to access positive internal resources. Collapsing anchors is used as an integrative device to break down dissociation and to ensure a full range of response in that area.

To demonstrate anchoring and collapse anchors in an introductory workshop, I enlisted the assistance of a young woman. I instructed the other participants to carefully watch for any changes in the woman's facial expression, breathing rate, muscle tone, skin color, body posture, tightness of lips, and eye movements as I gave her the following instructions:

I whispered in her right ear to remember a time when she was absolutely delighted with her own performance. When I observed her eyes move up and down to the right, her skin flush, her lower lip enlarge, her posture become erect with shoulders back, her breathing relaxed, I touched her on the right shoulder for thirty to sixty seconds.

I released the anchor by removing my hand from her right shoulder and whispered in her left ear that I would like her to access the opposite to that first experience. When I observed her eyes shifting down and to the right, her face drop, lips tighten, shoulders slump forward, skin pale, and breathing become lower in the abdomen, I touched her on the left shoulder for thirty to sixty seconds.

By simply touching the right shoulder, I could now elicit the first non-verbal responses and by touching the left shoulder the other nonverbal responses.

I then collapsed anchors by asking her to experience both situations together while I touched both shoulders (anchors) at the same time for thirty to sixty seconds. The woman responded that she felt confused. She could remember the more negative experience but no longer felt "badly" about it.

By collapsing anchors two different representations were forced into the same time and space neurologically. The woman now had the choice of the positive feelings of the first experience or the negative feelings of the second *or any combination of the two.*

It is important to anchor when the experience or memory is at its highest point. It is best to have anchors established in all representational systems, for example, auditorily, through voice tone, and visually, through gestures, as well as kinesthetically. This is called "redundancy" and increases the chance of success.

The verbal portion of our communication is probably the least significant. It is *how* we say things and *what* we are doing when we say it, that gives meaning to communication. Thus it is important to have a well-developed repertoire of anchors.

Our memory of the past has very little to do with the past because there is much distortion and slippage and we remember so selectively. Through anchoring memories can be used as a resource instead of a limitation. Made-up memories can change a person just as well as perceptions made up at the time of the actual events. Anchoring is a powerful form of classical conditioning. You can anchor overtly or covertly: if you want to involve the person's consciousness, anchor in all systems; if the goal is to anchor covertly to go around a resistant conscious mind, then anchor in any system that is not represented in consciousness.

The Pattern Called "Change Personal History"

For many people, their personal history is a set of limitations on their experiences and behavior in the present. The construction of new possibilities using anchoring can actually convert personal histories from a set of limitations to a set of resources. Even if the person has not had the personal experience required as a resource, if she has some representation of what it is, through other people's behavior, it could be as real as any other behavior and can be anchored if accessed fully. The pattern for "change personal history" is:

1. Anchor the unwanted, unpleasant feeling, the limitation.
2. Use this anchor to assist client to go back in time, finding other times when she felt "this" way.
3. Reorient client, release anchor, and bring back to present.
4. Ask what resource was needed in the past for that to have been a satisfying experience. Access resources and anchor.
5. You can fire off another anchor; that is, a second experience where the person experienced her power and competency.
6. Using resource anchor, go back and change history with the new resource. (If not satisfied, repeat from step 4 on.)
7. Test—remember past experiences with no anchors.
8. Future pace—imagine the next time this situation may come up, reminding the person to take this resource with her.

If change personal history does not produce the desired outcome, it is usually an indication that there is secondary gain and the use of a pattern called "reframing" is indicated. Reframing will be dealt with in more detail in the section on "second order change."

Anchoring and change personal history are painless ways of working through patterns.

Visual-Kinesthetic Dissociation

This pattern is used when feelings are overwhelming or in the case of a phobia.

1. *Establish a powerful anchor.* The client is given instructions along these lines:

"Think of a situation in which you expressed yourself with what you regard as a fine representation of your full capacities as an adult human being. Take your time and think about a situation when you behaved in a way you found particularly satisfying. When you *see* the image clearly, step inside that image, as if you were pulling on a wet suit, and be back again in that situation. When you actually feel again those feelings of competence and strength that you associate with that experience, reach over with your left hand and hold my wrist. [Anchor positive resources.]

"A phobia can be thought of as one-trial learning that was never updated and it worked! I want to reassure that part of you that has been making you phobic all these years that I respect what it has done and I regard it as a valid response. You survived. If there had not been a part to keep you out of certain situations, you might not be here. My desire is not to take away the choice of being phobic but to update it so you can make other responses that are more congruent with your resources as a fully grown adult. I am going to use the same capacity for one-trial learning to help you to learn to do something else.

"I am going to ask you to go back in time and I want you to increase pressure on my wrist at any point you need to be reminded of your competence and strength as a fully grown person. This is your connection with the present time and all the powerful resources that you have as a mature person.

"Do you know what the feelings of phobia are? Touch arm. [Anchor phobia.]

"Your holding my wrist constitutes your connection to the strengths and resources you have as a fully grown person.

"There were experiences in your past, namely those connected with this phobia, that we are going to go back and relive but in a way that involves total comfort. Close your eyes. You can vary the pressure on my wrist any time you need more strength."

2. *Holding anchor, instruct "see a younger you, form a snapshot."*

"When I touch you on the arm, it is going to help you remember some of the phobic feelings. I do not want you to go through all the feelings again. I want you to take only as much of these feelings as you need and drift back in your mind's eye until there comes before you a scene in which you see yourself *over there*, a younger you, in a snapshot with a frame around it, in a situation that has some connection with how you first learned to respond in that way.

"When you can see these snapshots, which are connected intimately with your phobic feelings, I want you to stabilize an image and hold it steady. You can modulate how much of these feelings [touch phobic anchor on arm] you are going to use to help you drift back to the point when you see a focused image that is connected with these feelings. This image represents where the original learning took place.

"Nod your head when you see clearly a snapshot of yourself at a younger age. Remember to use these feelings of strength and competence as you watch that image."

3. *Float out behind, seeing you sitting here, watching the younger you.*

"Now I would like you to float up slowly, out of your body, so you can actually see yourself sitting here in comfort and strength holding my wrist. Take all the time you need. When you have succeeded in floating out of your body, nod that you have succeeded. [Anchor. This anchor may be required later if the person has difficulty dissociating and lapses into overwhelming phobic feelings.]

"Now, staying in this position, I want you to look past yourself, sitting here holding my wrist and feeling the feelings of adult resourcefulness."

4. *Turn the snapshot into a filmstrip: watch and listen in comfort and strength—watch and learn.*

"In a few minutes I'm going to ask you to turn the snapshot into a motion picture. With feelings of strength and comfort, I want you to watch and listen carefully to everything that happened to you way back then, so that you can make new understandings and learnings about what occurred and therefore have new choices.

"You can begin the movie now."

5. *Reintegration.*

"I want you to float down from the third position very slowly and step back in and reunite with your body sitting here with feelings of resourcefulness and strength.

"And now, I want you to do something very important. That younger person did something very powerful for you, that younger person went through all those feelings again for you, and let you watch and listen in comfort and strength to things that, in the past, have triggered overwhelming responses. I want you, in your mind's eye, to walk over to that younger you. I want you to reach out and use all the adult resources you have to comfort and reassure that younger person so that you will never have to go through that again. Thank that younger person for living through the old feelings for the last time for you. Explain that you guarantee the younger person lived through it, because you are from the future. And when you see on the face and in the posture and in the breathing of that younger you, now reassured that you will be there to take charge and care, I want you to reach out, take that younger you by the shoulders and actually feel that younger you enter your body. This part of you is a very energetic part, which is now freed from that phobic response. I want to invite your unconscious mind to select some pleasurable activity so that some of that energy can be used for yourself in the present and in the future."

Some severe cases may require a whole session to establish a strong, positive anchor. This is a necessity because if you do not have a powerful anchor, the person can slip into feelings. It is important to keep all consciousness with the positive anchor, comfort, and strength and to dissociate what the person is seeing and feeling.

Second Order Change—Reframing

Reframing, the transformation of meaning pattern, is one of the most useful and basic techniques of NLP. Reframing is used in instances of secondary gain, with psychosomatic conditions, and in dealing with interference or resistance. It transforms what formerly seemed like blocks to the operation of the system into valuable resources, given the appropriate context. Reframing is such a sophisticated process, that Bandler and Grinder have devoted an entire book to this technique alone. *

A great deal of what people are responding to is their own internal experience; that is, internally represented events that are often outside their own conscious awareness. One way of taking this human complexity into account, when helping a person to make some desired change, is by using the *six-step reframing pattern*. Reframing is a way of contacting the part of the person that is causing the behavior or preventing other behaviors from occurring. It allows us to find out what the secondary gain of the behavior is and to take care of it as an integral part of the change process.

Six-Step Reframing Pattern

1. *Identify the pattern to be changed.*

This step can be even more powerful if the pattern to be changed is given a code name; that is, a number, a letter, or a color to respect the integrity of the individual. It is important, in such an instance, for the client to select the code name, which often is quite revealing in itself. If the behavior the client wishes to stop is coded "Y," the programmer "P," and client "C," a reframing session might proceed as follows:

> P: I'm sure you have consciously decided to stop "Y"ing many times, only to find that you continue to "Y," and I'm convinced that the part of you responsible for pattern "Y" is your unconscious mind. Now, every part of you is endeavoring to achieve a positive outcome

*Richard Bandler and John Grinder, *Reframing, Neurolinguistic Programming and the Transformation of Meaning* (Moab, Utah: Real People Press, 1982).

and no part of you is trying to sabotage your attempt, not even pattern "Y," although, consciously, you may not realize this. It is your unconscious mind that has kept you alive this long and it's not going to let you down now. (Allying with the unconscious.)

2. *Establish communication channel with the part that generates the pattern.* Ask if it is willing to communicate with you in consciousness. Establish a yes/no signal.

P: Close your eyes, go inside yourself, and ask that part of your unconscious mind that makes you "Y" if it would be willing to communicate with you in conscious awareness, by giving you a nonverbal signal—a sound, an image, or any sensations or feelings of tension anywhere in your body. You don't have to try to make this happen. The part of you responsible for pattern "Y" will make its needs known through one of your sensory channels. You just have to be sensitive to detect the response. When you have a signal or a lack of signal, I want you to open your eyes and return to the room.
(Client opens eyes.)

P: Be alert and be here.

C: I experienced some tension in my neck.

P: Excellent, close your eyes and thank that part of your unconscious mind that makes you "Y" for giving you such a rapid and clear signal indicating that it is willing to communicate with you in conscious awareness. When you have thanked it and acknowledged it fully, I want you to open your eyes and return to the room.
(Client opens eyes.)

P: Close your eyes again. Go inside yourself and ask that part of your unconscious mind that makes you "Y" if it would agree to the following yes/no signal—an amplification of the tension in your neck will be a "yes" signal and a lessening or lack of sensation in your neck will be a "no" signal. When you have a signal or a lack of signal, I want you to open your eyes and return to the room.
(Client opens eyes.)

C: The tension in my neck got worse.

P: Excellent, close your eyes, go inside youself again, and thank that part of your unconscious mind that makes you "Y" for its excellent cooperation and for giving you such a clear and rapid signal "yes," it agrees to the proposed yes/no signal.
(If the signal had been a picture, the brightness and sharpness of focus would be the "yes" signal and a fading or dimming of the picture the "no" signal. If the signal had been a sound, an increase in volume would indicate "yes" and a decrease "no.")

3. *Go inside and ask part if it is willing to communicate its intentions to you in consciousness.* (This is separate from behaviors.)

P: This unconscious part that makes you "Y" has a positive *intention* that it's trying to accomplish for you. The manner in which it is going about it is not acceptable to you in conscious awareness. Can you think of any positive gains resulting from pattern "Y"?

C: Yes, it's trying to kill me.

P: That is a negative outcome. Are there any *positive* outcomes resulting from behavior "Y"?

C: Well, it gets me to reach out to my friends. I get my husband's attention and the children are more considerate when I am in behavior "Y."

P: It seems to me that behavior "Y" is one part that is very sensitive to your needs and is endeavoring to do its best to achieve positive outcomes for you. We are going to work with that part, to offer it better ways to accomplish what it's trying to do. When it has better ways, you can have what you want consciously and this part can continue to take care of you the way it wants to.

Close your eyes, go inside yourself, and ask that part of your unconscious mind that makes you "Y" if it has any understanding whatsoever of the positive *intent* and positive outcomes it is endeavoring to achieve for you when it makes you go into pattern "Y" and will it let you know in consciousness what it's trying to do for you. (Client opens eyes and smiles.)

C: Yes, the tension in my neck strengthened and I know what pattern "Y" is trying to do for me.

P: Excellent, close your eyes, go inside yourself, and thank that part for its cooperation.

(Client opens eyes upon completion of task.)

P: You may not like the *way* it goes about accomplishing pattern "Y," but do you agree that the *intention* is something you want to have the part do for you?

C: Yes.

(Now there is congruency between the intention of the unconscious part and recognition of this in consciousness.)

4. *Ask if part is willing to consider alternate, more powerful, satisfying ways, if available. Access creative part to generate at least three alternatives.*

P: I am going to ask you to go inside yourself and ask your creative unconscious part to generate three new powerful behaviors that will achieve the same positive outcomes and have the same positive *intent* as that part of your unconscious mind that makes you go into behavior "Y." These new behaviors should be immediate behaviors that you can put into operation almost anywhere, and they should achieve the positive outcomes *at least* as effectively as and hopefully *more* effectively than the pattern of behavior used until now to achieve that intention.

    Close your eyes, go inside yourself, and ask your creative part if it would be willing to do that.

C: Yes.

(Now there is congruency between the intention of the unconscious part and recognition of this in consciousness.)

    4. *Ask if part is willing to consider alternate, more powerful, satisfying ways, if available. Access creative part to generate at least three alternatives.*

P: I am going to ask you to go inside yourself and ask your creative unconscious part to generate three new powerful behaviors that will achieve the same positive outcomes and have the same positive *intent* as that part of your unconscious mind that makes you go into behavior "Y." These new behaviors should be immediate behaviors that you can put into operation almost anywhere, and they should achieve the positive outcomes *at least* as effectively as and hopefully *more* effectively than the pattern of behavior used until now to achieve that intention.

    Close your eyes, go inside yourself, and ask your creative part if it would be willing to do that.

C: Yes.

P: Tell it to go ahead and have the part that makes you "Y" signal, "yes," when it has accepted each of the three new choices. You may or may not be conscious of what the new alternatives are. As I'm talking to you, your creative part may be generating as many as a hundred alternate behaviors outside of your conscious awareness. I would like your creative part, in consultation with that part of your unconscious mind that makes you "Y," to select three new powerful behaviors tht will achieve the same intent and have the same positive outcomes, as that part of your unconscious mind that makes you "Y," is endeavoring to achieve for you.

C: The part that makes me "Y" has signaled "yes"; it accepts each of the three new choices generated by my creative part.

P: Excellent, close your eyes, go inside yourself, and thank that part for its cooperation.

    5. *Ask part if willing to accept responsibility for operationalizing new behaviors in the appropriate context.*

P: Close your eyes, go inside yourself, and ask that part of your unconscious mind that makes you "Y" if it is willing to take responsibility for putting into operation the three new powerful behaviors generated by your creative part.

C: Yes, the tension in my neck increased.

P: Go inside yourself and thank that part for its excellent cooperation.

6. *Ecological check—nothing will be put into effect until every part is satisfied.*

P: Close your eyes, go inside yourself, and ask your total unconscious mind if there is any part that has any objection whatsoever to putting into operation the three new powerful alternate behaviors generated by your creative part.

C: No objection, the tension in my neck diminished.

P: Close your eyes, go inside yourself, and thank your total unconscious mind for its excellent cooperation.

(Client opens eyes on completion of task.)

P: Since it takes three hours for the unconscious mind to integrate what we have just done, I do not want you to discuss this with anyone until three hours have elapsed.

C: Okay.

It is important to thank each part after the successful completion of a step in the reframing process. With reframing, you are giving requisite variety to the unconscious, which previously had only one choice about how to get what it wants. Eventually, people can use the reframe format by themselves to make any desired change in any area of their lives.

Reframing, strategies, and anchoring are the tools of NLP that allow you to do things formally and methodically. They are formal patterns of communication that are content free and can be used in any context of human communication and behavior. Following is a summary of the principal steps involved in the reframing procedure.

The Positive Outcome Frame

1. *Starting Point:* How did you get here? Was it easy or difficult for you to come to see me?

2. *Establish Rapport:* It is the programmer's task to go to the client's model of the world, rather than have the client come to the therapist's model.

3. *Gather High-Quality Information:* The highest-quality information is behavioral. Gathering sensory-grounded information is in itself a form of intervention.

4. *Present State:* What are you experiencing now? In what contexts do you experience it? Is there ever a time when you don't experience it? What positive gains does it get for you?

5. *Desired State or Positive Outcome:* This is eighty-five percent of the work. The client determines the desired state. What specifically do you want—(internal responses, external behaviors, or both? How will you know that you have it? In what contexts do you want it? What will happen if you get it? Are there any contexts in which you don't

want it? Has there ever been a time when you had it? How did you know you had it?

6. *Programmer's Flexibility:* This is very important because there are many ways of getting to the same outcome.

7. *Intervention/Technology*

8. Test: How do you know you have attained the desired outcome?

9. *Termination—Exit*

In NLP, change is not seen as a remedial phenomenon. Change is a generative or enrichment approach. NLP completely bypasses the whole phenomenon of working with problems because when the structure of subjective experience is changed, everything changes.

Counterindications for the Use of the Model

It has been my experience that the six-step reframe and anchoring are not effective if the client is on a high dosage of antidepressant or tranquilizing medication.

Family Therapy

A family consulting an NLP programmer need not have a problem. All that is required is that the members of the family have a goal they would like to achieve or something they would like to change in their lives. Once again, the purpose of NLP is to evolve people to where they would like to be.

While most family therapists are concerned with triangular interactions, the NLP programmer is more interested in dyadic patterns of communication within the family system. The metal model questions, representational systems, and polarities (5,6,12) remain the key principles, which are organized and used in a different way than in individual therapy. The family is perceived as a *system;* that is, as if it were a single organism with each member an essential part and therefore a resource to the satisfactory behavior of the organism as a whole. The assumption is that some portion of the family system's shared model of the world is impoverished and blocks the nurturing processes in the system.

It should be noted that one cannot establish rapport with a family as a whole. It is essential that the therapist establish rapport with each individual member of the family at both the conscious and unconscious levels.

The NLP programmer employs three steps to assist the family in the process of change:

1. Gathers information concerning what the family wants for itself as a unit and compares this with the present state of the family, including its resources.

2. In participation with the family, evolves the family system from its present state to the desired state, and
3. Through future-pacing, facilitates the integration of new choices and patterns of interaction created by the family and NLP programmer during interviews.

When working with a family, the therapist must pay careful attention to the ecological impact of any change or desired outcome on the interpersonal systems of which the client is a part; that is, the effect of any desired change on friends, neighbors, relatives, and employment, etc.

In the beginning stage, it is important to inquire how the family got to the therapist and to ask each family member directly what he or she wants from therapy. With regard to the latter, the following questions are particularly useful:

What are your hopes for yourself and your family in therapy?
How, specifically, would you like you and your family to change?
What do you want for yourself and your family?
How would you know, individually and as a family, if you had achieved these goals?
(The therapist may ask the family to act out their "desired state" in a role-play.)

In order to track and organize the communication patterns among family members, the neurolinguistic programmer would need to know the following regarding each family member: the representational system; the Satir category (Placater, Blamer, Computer, or Distractor); the recurrent patterns of communication incongruity; the primary sensory input channel for getting information; the primary output channel for self-expression; and the kind and extent of the semantic ill-formedness.

In addition, rules are considered constraints imposed by the family members upon themselves and each other. When one family member complains that she is not getting what she wants from another family member, the input channel being used for detection is usually not capable of picking up the messages in the output system the other family member is using to communicate. For example, one family member's output system may be giving positive verbal recognition with a smile, which another family member may attribute to be a form of ridiculing because his input system is limited to the visual channel, and so the auditory-digital message goes unheard. In many family systems, individuals are highly specialized in using one representational system. It is a particularly limiting kind of deletion when family rules restrict what input and output channels may be used to express certain kinds of messages.

To be effective, family therapy must produce some change in the way family members model or create representations as well as some change in the family rules so that the limits of the family system can be extended. Strategies for evolving a family system include relabeling, translating from one representational system to another, accessing of memories, employing the meta-model questions, in particular cause-effect and mind reading semantic ill-formedness; and educating members in more effective forms of communication.

In family therapy, the existing anchors that have produced unwanted responses are acted out in the therapist's presence. The technique of anchoring can be used to change these previously existing anchors.

Both *content* and *context reframing* are used in working with families. The purpose of reframing is to shift the perception of a family member with respect to another member's external behavior so that these perceptions may be dealt with in a more resourceful manner.

In a content reframe, the therapist attaches a positive intent to a family member's external behavior that elicits a negative response from another member. Thus, a client who recently complained to me about his "nagging wife" was told: "Do you realize that a nagging wife is trying to get close to her husband?" This statement was enough to shift the husband's objections from one of anger to one of appreciation. The validation of the wife's intent allowed her to shift her perception of her own role to one that was caring and supporting, rather than inhibitory.

In a context reframe, change in a family member's negative internal response to another family member's external behavior is accomplished by having the first family member realize the usefulness of the behavior in some other context. Thus, a father, complaining about his adolescent daughter's stubbornness, might be congratulated for teaching his daughter to be stubborn, as this behavior would serve her well in a situation where she was being taken advantage of.

In neurolinguistic programming, instead of making contracts between family members for agreed-upon changes in behavior, the responsibility for any behavioral change is put in the hands of the member who desires it. To set up a positive, self-reinforcing calibrated loop, the therapist assigns to each family member who desires a change in another family member the task of finding out what is needed in order to make the other member *want* to change her behavior.

The skilled family therapist acts as a role model and will make it a pleasant and rewarding experience for families to learn new ways of coping. The ideal outcome of family therapy is to create an open family system that will generate its own patterns of coping based upon sensory feedback. This is a difficult goal to achieve especially in the real world and with the time constraints on both the family and therapist. Homework is assigned to give family members practice in using new choices and patterns.

To prevent lapsing into former unwanted interactional patterns, a set of cues may be developed that will allow family members to detect and signal other family members that an old unsatisfactory pattern is beginning. Sculpturing can also be used as an effective signal.

Research

To date, there is little research that proves the validity or lack of validity of NLP, though practitioners who use it are impressed with its effectiveness.

The NLP model was developed originally by researching the behavior of people who were renowned for their ability to achieve outcomes in their chosen field. It is an outcome-oriented model and there is little interest in evaluating the truthfulness of the model's claims, but a great deal of interest in evaluating the *usefulness* of the model. NLP is concerned with identifying and utilizing behavioral patterns in ongoing interactions. Statistical quantities are considered of no value.

Gaps in Knowledge from a Social Work Perspective

NLP techniques are powerful and do work. Like all forms of intervention, from Freudian analysis to behavior modification, the neurolinguistic programming model attempts to manipulate the behavior of people. However, there are built-in safeguards. The *client* determines the positive outcome or desired state.

We are all manipulative a great deal of the time. Sometimes our manipulations work and at other times they do not. In our culture, as long as you are unaware of your manipulations, this is acceptable. It is important to remember that if you do something incongruent with the best interests of others, this will not serve you well in the long run.

At the very heart of the neurolinguistic programming model is a non-condemnatory, noncritical, totally accepting attitude. It respects each person's unique method of survival without blaming anyone.

When given the choice, a neurolinguistic programmer would choose the path that emphasizes internal personal control and empowerment over those involving external factors beyond our control. Because of this emphasis, not enough attention is given to external factors beyond the family and organization. A next step in NLP's continuing evolutionary process (the transformation of experiences previously regarded as environmental limitations into decision strategies in order to achieve desired outcomes) is to expand the concept of environmental limitations to include a sociopolitical and feminist analysis and address such issues as race and racism.

Case Vignettes

Neurolinguistic programming has changed my social work practice. I now see clients for shorter periods of time and there is greater client satisfaction as measured by the number of friends and relatives that clients refer to me. The techniques of mirroring and crossover mirroring allow me to establish rapport with clients who otherwise would be difficult to engage in a relationship process.

> In one recent incident, a middle-aged woman, who had lost interest in life, was referred to me by her family. She presented the usual signs of depression, her face and body drooped, she was untidy in her appearance, and she spoke in a flat monotone. She wanted relief from her "down" state but did not think anyone could help her. After making sure I had rapport, I applied the six-step reframe. At the end of the session, she was not sure that anything had changed but agreed to a second appointment in three weeks' time. There was a dramatic change in her appearance when she came for a second interview. She was neat and attractively groomed; she held her body erect and smiled. She wanted me to know that she had made changes in her life that thoroughly delighted both her and her family. Although she has the overall responsibility of running a hobby farm and caring for a number of children in late adolescence, she decided to take a part-time job in a local lawyer's office. She enjoys her new employment and feels that for the first time in many years she is doing something to please herself. I asked what she was doing in my office that evening. She claimed that her husband had asked the same question and had even advised her to cancel her appointment, since he was afraid I might do something to reverse her progress. I agreed with her husband that she was dealing effectively with her life and did not require a counseling session. I congratulated her for her creativity and excellent progress. I thanked her for letting me know that she had achieved her desired outcome and terminated the session, leaving the door open for her to return, if needed.

> A family physician referred a separated woman whose twenty-three-year-old daughter, the only girl in a family of three boys, had died sometime earlier in a tragic plane crash. The mother was unconsolable. The physician had spent hours with her in an attempt to help her complete the grief-work. Her rabbi had offered his comfort and support over an extended period, all to no avail. The mother continued to mourn and remained in a state of paralyzing grief with nothing being resolved. The family physician wondered if I could help.
> Fortunately, I recalled attending a workshop lead by John Grinder where he had mentioned that some people intuitively know how to deal with death and loss, while others need to be taught that pattern of modeling. He reminded us of a common phenomenon that frequently occurs when a couple has been together for many years. When one spouse dies, the other often dies shortly afterward. He gave the example of a peg-leg Irishman who swore like a drunken sailor and whose wife was a ladylike woman who never let a swear word cross her lips. Two weeks after the Irishman's death, his wife began swearing profusely. The fam-

ily laughed, as everyone knew that this was her way of coping, even although it lacked elegance.

I instructed the grief-stricken mother to find three characteristics that she had much admired in the deceased but had not developed fully in herself. By making a decision to acquire and develop these characteristics, she would not only make herself a survivor, but would honor the deceased in a more beautiful way than building an expensive monument to her memory. The woman immediately became more alert as I spoke, and stated that she had already begun to do this. Only yesterday her ex-husband had called and she had found herself talking to him in a very frank and direct manner, the way her deceased daughter would have done. I congratulated her for this discovery and instructed her to find two other characteristics of her daughter that she much admired and would want to develop in herself. Within two weeks this grieving mother had returned to work and resumed her life. She subsequently told me that this pattern of modeling was the only thing that helped her resolve her immobilizing grief.

References

1. Ard, B., and C. Ard. *Handbook of Marriage Counseling.* Palo Alto, Calif.: Science and Behavior Books, 1973.
2. Ashby, William Ross. *Design for a Brain: The Origin of Adaptive Behavior.* Science Paperbacks, 1965.
3. ———. *Introduction to Cybernetics.* London: London University, Paperbacks, 1964.
4. Bach, E. *Syntactic Theory.* New York: Holt, Rinehart and Winston, 1974.
5. Bandler, Richard, and John Grinder. *The Structure of Magic I.* Palo Alto, Calif.: Science and Behavior Books, 1975.
6. ———. *The Structure of Magic II.* Palo Alto, Calif.: Science and Behavior Books, 1976.
7. ———. *Patterns of the Hypnotic Techniques of Milton H. Erickson, M.D.,* Vol. 1. Cupertino, Calif.: Meta Publications, 1975.
8. ———. *Frogs into Princes.* Moab, Utah: Real People Press, 1979.
9. ———, and Judith DeLozier. *Patterns of the Hypnotic Techniques of Milton H. Erickson,* Vol. II. Cupertino, Calif.: Meta Publications, 1977.
10. Bateson, G. *Steps to an Ecology of Mind.* New York: Ballantine, 1972.
11. ———. *Mind and Nature.* New York: Dutton, 1979.
12. Callaway, E. "Schizophrenia and Interference," *Archives of General Psychiatry,* Vol. 22 (1970), pp. 193–208.
13. Cameron-Bandler, Leslie. *They Lived Happily Ever After.* Cupertino, Calif.: Meta Publications, 1978.
14. Dilts, Robert. *Roots of Neurolinguistic Programming.* Cupertino, Calif.: Meta Publications, 1976.

15. ———. *Applications of Neurolinguistic Programming.* Cupertino, Calif.: Meta Publications, 1983.

16. ———; John Grinder, Richard Bandler, Leslie C. Bandler, and Judith DeLozier. *Neurolinguistic Programming,* Vol. 1, Limited First Edition. Cupertino, Calif.: Meta Publications, 1980.

17. Dimond, S., and K. Beaumont. *Hemisphere Function in the Human Brain.* New York: Wiley, 1974.

18. Farrelly, Frank, and Jeff Brandsma. *Provocative Therapy.* Cupertino, Calif.: Meta Publications, 1978.

19. Gardner, H. *The Shattered Mind.* New York: Knopf, 1975.

20. Goleman, D. "People Who Read People," *Psychology Today,* July 1979.

21. Gordon, David. *Therapeutic Metaphors.* Cupertino, Calif.: Meta Publications, 1978.

22. Green, D. "Nominalization in Couple Counseling," *Journal for Specialists in Group Work.* Vol. 4, 2 (1979), pp. 75–79.

23. Grinder, John, and Richard Bandler. *Trance-Formations: Neurolinguistic Programming and the Structure of Hypnosis.* Moab, Utah: Real People Press, 1981.

24. ———. *Reframing: Neurolinguistic Programming and Transformation of Meaning.* Moab, Utah: Real People Press, 1982.

25. Grinder, John, Richard Bandler, and Virginia Satir. *Changing with Families.* Palo Alto, Calif.: Science and Behavior Books, 1976.

26. Haley, J. (ed.). *Advanced Techniques of Hypnosis and Therapy: Selected Papers of Milton H. Erickson, M.D.* New York: Grune and Stratton, 1967.

27. ———. *Uncommon therapy: The Psychiatric Techniques of Milton H. Erickson, M.D.* New York: Norton, 1973.

28. Hersen, M., and D. Barlow, *Single Case Experimental Designs.* New York: Pergamon Press, 1976.

29. John, E. R. "Switchboard vs. Statistical Theories of Learning and Memory," *Science,* Vol. 177, No. 8 (September 1972), pp. 850–864.

30. ———. "How the Brain Works—A New Theory," *Psychology Today,* May 1976, pp. 48–52.

31. Korzybski, A. *Science and Sanity,* 4th edition. Lakeville, Conn.: The International Non-Aristotelian Library Publishing Company, 1933.

32. Kuhn, T. S. *The Structure of Scientific Revolutions.* Chicago: University of Chicago Press, 1970.

33. Laborde, Genie. "Neuro-Linguistic Programming," *New Realities,* Vol. 4 (1981), pp. 8–14.

34. Laing, R. D. *The Politics of the Family.* New York: Vintage Press, 1969.

35. Laing, R. D., and A. Esterson. *Sanity, Madness and the Family.* London: Tavistock Publications, 1964.

36. Lankton, Steve. *ACSW,/Practical Magic, a Translation of Basic Neurolinguistic Programming into Clinical Psychotherapy.* Cupertino, Calif.: Meta Publications, 1980.

37. Maron, Davida. "Neurolinguistic Programming: The Answer to Change," *Training and Development Journal,* 1979, pp. 68–71.

38. McCormick, Donald William. "Neurolinguistic Programming: A Resource Guide and Review of the Research," *The 1984 Annual: Developing Human Resources.*

39. McMaster, M., and John Grinder. *Precision: A New Approach to Communication.* Los Angeles: Precision, 1980.

40. Miller, G. "The Magical Number Seven, Plus or Minus Two: Some Limits on Our Capacity for Processing Information," *Psychological Review*, Vol. 63 (March 1956).

41. Miller, G., Galanter, and K. Pribram. *Plans and the Structure of Behavior.* New York: Holt, 1960.

42. Pribram, K. *The Language of the Brain.* Englewood Ciffs, N.J.: Prentice-Hall, 1971.

43. ———. *The Holographic Hypothesis of Memory Structure in Brain Function and Perception.* Englewood Cliffs, N.J.: Prentice-Hall, 1974.

44. ———. "Problems Concerning the Structure of Consciousness," *Consciouness and the Brain.* Englewood Cliffs, N.J.: Prentice-Hall, 1976.

45. Satir, Virginia. *Peoplemaking.* Palo Alto, Calif.: Science and Behavior Books, 1972.

46. ———. *Conjoint Family therapy.* 3rd Edition, Palo Alto, Calif.: Science and Behavior Books, Inc., 1983.

47. Satir, Virginia, and Michele Baldwin. *Satir Step-by-Step, a Guide to Creating Change in Families.* Palo Alto, Calif.: Science and Behavior Books, Inc., 1983.

48. Schank, R., and K. Colby, *Computer Models of Thought and Language.* San Francisco: W. H. Freeman and Company, 1973.

49. Sheldon, W. H. *The Varieties of Human Physique: An Introduction to Constitutional Psychology.* Nafner, 1940.

50. ———. *Varieties of Human Temperament: A Psychology of Constitutional Differences.* New York: Harper, 1942.

51. ———. *Atlas of Men: A Guide for Somatyping the Adult Male at All Ages.* New York: Harper, 1954.

52. Vaihinger, H. *The Philosophy of "as If."* London: Routledge, Kegan Paul, 1924.

53. Watzlawick, Paul. *Pragmatics of Human Communication: A Study of Interactional Patterns, Pathologies and Paradoxes.* New York: Norton, 1967.

54. ———. *The Language of Change, Elements of Therapeutic Communication.* New York: Basic Books, 1978.

55. ———. *The Situation Is Hopeless But Not Serious, the Pursuit of Unhappiness.* New York: Norton, 1983.

56. Watzlawick, Paul, J. Weakland, and Richard Fisch. *CHANGE.* New York: Norton, 1974.

Annotated Listing of Key References

BANDLER, RICHARD, and JOHN GRINDER. *Patterns of the Hypnotic Techniques of Milton H. Erickson, M.D., Vol. I.* Cupertino, Calif.: Meta Publications, 1975.
This book provides an explicit model derived from Milton Erickson's work on the use of hypnotic language patterning in therapy—sometimes called the "Milton Model." Its usefulness is in increasing the therapist's flexibility and in reducing client resistance.

BANDLER, RICHARD, and JOHN GRINDER. *Frogs into Princes, Neurolinguistic Programming.* Moab, Utah: Real People Press, 1979.
Provides an excellent introduction to NLP and contains edited transcripts from a three-day introductory workshop presented by Richard Bandler and John Grinder. It is entertaining as well as informative and easy to read.

Bandler, Richard, John Grinder, and Virginia Satir. *Changing with Families, A Book About Further Education for Being Human.* Palo Alto, Calif.: Science and Behavior Books, 1976.
In this book, Bandler and Grinder present patterns and techniques derived from modeling Virginia Satir's renowned work with families. It forms the basis for the NLP family therapy model.

CAMERON-BANDLER, LESLIE. *They Lived Happily Ever After.* Cupertino, Calif.: Meta Publications, 1978.
This book is concerned with the application of the basic patterns of NLP to couple and sex therapy. Anchoring, change personal history, visual-kinesthetic dissociation, and six-step reframing are presented with case illustrations.

DILTS, ROBERT. *Applications of Neurolinguistic Programming.* Cupertino, Calif.: Meta Publications, 1983.
A book about the applications of neurolinguistic programming to business communication, in sales, in family therapy and interpersonal negotiation, in education, in creative writing, and health. There is also a chapter on the meta-model live and another on the application of the meta-model to the Socratic method of philosophical inquiry.

DILTS, ROBERT, JOHN GRINDER, RICHARD BANDLER, LESLIE C. BANDLER, JUDITH DELOZIER. *Neurolinguistic programming, VOL. I, The Study of the Structure of Subjective Experience.* Cupertino, Calif.: Meta Publications, 1980.
A highly academic treatise of the NLP model, which creates a new vocabulary, a new syntax, and a new way of thinking about the world rather than trying to make the NLP model fit existing ways of thinking. It is an invitation and challenge to the reader to think and process as neurolinguistic programmers do. It is the fundamental book on strategies.

CHAPTER 14

Ego Psychology

Eda Goldstein

What Is Ego Psychology?

When ego psychological concepts emerged in Europe and the United States in the late 1930s, they highlighted the importance of an individual's adaptive capacity and linked individuals to their social environment. "Here at last was the happy synthesis between the social order and the psychological depths— the ego, which bridged these two worlds" (13, p. 19).

Ego psychology comprises a related set of theoretical concepts about human behavior that focus on the origins, development, structure, and functioning of the executive arm of the personality—the ego—and its relationship to other aspects of the personality and to the external environment. The ego is considered to be a mental structure of the personality that is responsible for negotiating between the internal needs of the individual and the outside world.

The following seven propositions characterize ego psychology's view of human functioning.

1. Ego psychology views people as born with an innate capacity to function adaptively. Individuals engage in a lifelong biopsychosocial development process in which the ego is an active, dynamic force for coping with, adapting to, and shaping the external environment.

2. The ego is the part of the personality that contains the basic functions essential to the individual's successful adaptation to the environment. Ego functions are innate and develop through maturation and the interaction along biopsychosocial factors. Crucial among these are hereditary and constitutional endowment; the drives; the quality of interpersonal relationships, particularly in early childhood; and the impact of immediate environment, sociocultural values and mores, socioeconomic conditions, social and cultural change, and social institutions.

3. Ego development occurs sequentially as a result of the meeting of basic needs, identification with others, learning, mastery of developmental tasks, effective problem-solving, and successful coping with internal needs and environmental conditions, expectations, stresses, and crises.

4. While the ego has the capacity for functioning autonomously, it is only one part of the personality and must be understood in relation to internal needs and drives and to the internalized characteristics, expectations, mores, and values of others.

5. The ego not only mediates between the individual and the environment but also mediates internal conflict among various aspects of the personality. It can elicit defenses that protect the individual from anxiety and conflict and that serve adaptive or maladaptive purposes.

6. The social environment shapes the personality and provides the conditions that foster or obstruct successful coping. The nature of cultural, racial, and ethnic diversity as well as differences related to sex, age, and life-style must be understood in the assessment of ego functioning.

7. Problems in social functioning must be viewed in relation both to possible deficits in coping capacity and to the fit among needs, capacities, and environmental conditions and resources. (40, pp. xiv–xvi)

Historical Origins, Principal Proponents, and Theoretical Linkages

In the 1923 publication, *The Ego and the Id* (28), Freud presented a radical revision of his earlier topographic theory of mental functioning in which he described the unconscious, preconscious, and conscious regions of the mind (26). The view he proposed in 1923 and in later publications (27, 28, 29) became known as structural theory and marked the beginning of an ego psychology. Structural theory described the ego as one of three structures of the mental apparatus of the personality along with the id (the seat of the instincts) and the superego (the conscience and ego-ideal). Freud defined the ego by its functions: mediating between the drives (id) and external reality; moderating conflict between the drives (id) and the internalized prohibitions against their expression (superego); instituting mechanisms (defenses) to protect the ego from the painful experience of anxiety; and playing a crucial role in development through its capacity for identification with external objects.

Structural theory permitted greater understanding of the individual's negotiations with the external world and led to an appreciation of the impact of the environment and interpersonal relationships on behavior.

The first important extension of structural theory was initiated in Anna Freud's 1936 publication, *Ego and the Mechanisms of Defense* (24). She gave an expanded role to defense, identified a greater repertoire of defenses, and linked the origin of defenses to specific developmental phases. She also identified the importance of the adaptiveness of so-called defensive behavior.

A second important development in ego psychology was introduced by Heinz Hartmann in *Ego Psychology and the Problem of Adaptation* (46). Hartmann, both independently and then with his collaborators (47, 48) developed and refined the concept of the autonomy of the ego.

Hartmann proposed that both the ego and the id originate in an "undifferentiated matrix" at birth out of which each, having its own energy source, develop independently. The individual is born "preadapted" to an "average expectable environment" for the species, and the ego matures independently of the vicissitudes of the instincts and of conflict. Certain ego functions are "conflict-free" and have a "primary autonomy" from the drives.

A third crucial development in ego psychology is reflected in the work of Erik Erikson. In *Childhood and Society* (20) and "Identity and the Life Cycle" (21), Erikson described ego development as psychosocial in nature, involving progressive mastery of developmental tasks in each of eight successive stages of the human life cycle. He was the first to deal with adult growth and to see the importance of the ameliorating or compensatory effects of later crisis resolution. While adhering to the importance of biological factors in development, Erikson called attention to the influences of the interpersonal field, the environment, the society, and the culture on the child-rearing process and on ego development.

More recent contributions within psychoanalytic ego psychology stem from the work of those who have combined a theoretical and clinical perspective with observational studies of children. Grounded in classical psychoanalytic theory and ego psychology, Rene Spitz (90, 91, 92, 93) and Margaret Mahler (64, 65, 66, 67) generated crucial data and theory from their observational studies of children. Each has addressed the child's unique development as a function of his interactions with the caretaking environment. The stages by which the child's ego development evolves has been systematized. M. D. S. Ainsworth (1) and John Bowlby (12) have also been seminal in this area.

Unlike Erikson, Robert White (105, 106) broke away from the Freudian psychoanalytic tradition. He postulated that the individual is born with not only innate and autonomous ego functions that give pleasure in their own right, but also a drive toward mastery and competence. Thus, according to White, the ego actively seeks opportunities in the environment in which the individual can be "effective." In turn the ego is strengthened by successful transitions with the environment.

Many theorists—for example, White (108) have suggested that cognitive functioning is central to adaptive behavior, and Jean Piaget's theory of intelligence (75, 76, 77) offers concepts that complement those of ego psychology. Piaget evolved a general theory of intellectual development in which he identified a series of sequential stages. What is important is that the child's thinking, her view of the world, and her ability to assimilate and accommodate to it are shaped by the particular stage she is in.

Stress and crisis theory* also add to our understanding of ego functioning. There are numerous studies of how the ego copes under various types of biological, psychological, and environmental stress (42, 51, 59, 63, 87). A major contribution of crisis theory is the description of the ego's capacity to restore equilibrium through a characteristic use of coping mechanisms that lead to the mastery of stress and to crisis resolution.

While much of the crisis literature deals with the impact of life events on adults, research on child development has also contributed to the understanding of the interaction between innate personality features and the environmental conditions during early childhood that lead to the development of coping capacity on the one hand and to vulnerability on the other (22, 74).

Family systems theories, theories of small group behavior, and organizational theories all contribute to understanding the context in which individual development occurs all through the life cycle because individuals spend a large proportion of their time in families, small groups, and organizational structures. At the same time theories of family and group processes in particular have benefited from extensions of ego psychology. Concepts such as defense, adaptation and coping, the life cycle, identity, ego mastery and competence, coping with stress and crisis, problem-solving capacities, and person-environment mutuality have been useful in reconceptualizing the family as a dynamic system that changes over time in response to inner needs and outer demands and conditions.

Path into Social Work and Current Status

Important as was the contribution of psychoanalytic thinking to the development of the profession's knowledge base, many viewed it as turning the profession too far away from a concern with environment and social functioning. Even during the early days of psychoanalytic influence, another current also existed within the social work profession; it emphasized the social determinants of behavior and pointed to social treatment; that is, interventions directed at improving environmental conditions. Those who held this view, however, "were out of tune with the prevailing Freudian ethic and the preoccupation with personality change through psychological procedures" (89, p. 16).

Beginning in the late 1930s, though more significant in the post–World War II period, numerous individuals became associated with attempts to assimilate ego psychological concepts into social casework. Prominent among

*See Naomi Golan's chapter on crisis theory in this volume, pp. 296–340.

these were Lucille Austin (2, 3), Louise Bandler (5), Eleanor Cockerill and colleagues (16), Annette Garrett (31, 32), Gordon Hamilton (44, 45), Florence Hollis (52, 54), Isabell Stamm (96), and Charlotte Towle (100, 101).

Ego psychology embodies a more optimistic and humanistic view of human functioning and potential than that reflected in classical psychoanalytic theory. It views environmental and sociocultural factors as important in shaping behavior and in providing opportunities for the development, enhancement, and sustainment of ego functioning.

Ego psychological concepts were used to refocus the study and assessment process on (1) the client's person-environment transactions in the here and now, particularly the degree to which he is coping effectively with his major life roles and tasks; (2) the client's adaptive, autonomous, and conflict-free areas of ego functioning as well as his ego deficits and maladaptive defenses and patterns; (3) the key developmental issues affecting the client's current reactions; and (4) the degree to which the external environment is creating obstacles to successful coping.

Ego psychology provided the rationale for improving or sustaining adaptive ego functioning by means of work with both the individual and the environment. A repertoire of techniques for working with the ego was systematized. Ego psychological concepts recognized the reality of the client-worker relationship in contrast to an exclusive focus on its transference or distorted aspects and moved beyond an exclusive emphasis on insight as the mechanism for individual change.

Ego psychological concepts helped to transform the casework process from a never-ending, unfocused exploration of personality difficulties to a more deliberate and focused use of the phases of the casework process. Ego psychological concepts underscored the importance of the client's responsibility for directing her own treatment and life.

Despite ego psychology's potential to bridge person and environment in theory and practice, casework practice often was criticized for its focus on the inner life of the individual at the apparent expense of attention to the environmental component in intervention. As clients, who were "harder to reach" and "multiproblemed" appeared at the doors of social agencies and as economic pressures again began to plague all sectors of society, ego psychology and its related practices were criticized for being another form of blaming the individual and making her responsible for the social conditions that were causing her difficulties. Moreover, the concepts and associated practices stemming from ego psychology were not made operational and researched, so evidence supporting their efficacy was not forthcoming. This became increasingly important as the research that began to accumulate on casework effectiveness was negative or equivocal and as casework came under attack.

As attention has returned to carving out an important role for direct practice within the social work profession, ego psychology is enjoying a renaissance of interest. As a theory it has developed extensively since its emergence. It continues to provide the conceptual underpinnings to a variety to practice models, including the psychosocial, problem-solving, crisis intervention, and life models. It has important linkages to family and group theories and approaches as well as to the design of service delivery, large-scale social programs, and social policy.

More important, the ego psychological emphasis on normal coping strategies, adaptation, mastery, competence, cognitive processes, person-environment transactions, biopsychosocial factors in development, and the impact of life stresses and social change holds enormous promise as a unifying theoretical underpinning for a distinctive conception of social work practice. At the same time, refinements and extensions of psychoanalytic ego psychology that address the role of interpersonal relationships and internalized object-relations in normal and pathological ego development have provided an in-depth dimension to understanding human behavior.

Main Theoretical Concepts

Ego psychology is comprised of four main sets of concepts that encompass the structure and development of personality: ego functions, defenses, ego mastery and adaptation, and object relations.

Ego Functions

Ego functions are the means by which the individual adapts to the world. The most comprehensive effort to study ego functions can be found in the work of Leopold Bellak and his colleagues, Marvin Hurvich and Helen Gediman (7). They identified twelve major ego functions.

REALITY TESTING. This involves the accurate perception of the external environment, of one's internal world, and of the differences between them. The most severe manifestations of the failure of reality testing are seen in delusions and hallucinations (false beliefs and perceptions that cannot be objectively validated). Defenses, however, also distort reality to some extent.

JUDGMENT. This involves the capacity to identify certain possible courses of action and to anticipate and weigh the consequences of behavior in order to take action that achieves desired goals with minimal negative consequences.

SENSE OF REALITY OF THE WORLD AND OF THE SELF. It is possible to *perceive* inner and outer reality accurately but to *experience* the world and the self in distorted ways. A good sense of reality involves the ability to feel or to be aware of the world and one's connection to it as real, to experience one's own body as intact and belonging to oneself, to feel a sense of self, and to experience the separation or boundaries between oneself and others as distinct organisms. An individual may experience himself as estranged from the world around him (derealization), as if there were an invisible screen between him and others. In depersonalization, one feels estranged from one's own body as if one were apart from it and looking at it, as if it were a distinct object. Parts of one's body may seem disconnected. Certain distortions of body image also involve disturbances in the sense of reality. In a psychological sense, one may feel as if one has no identity of one's own, that parts of one's own inner experience are strange, or that one has an inner emptiness.

REGULATION AND CONTROL OF DRIVES, AFFECTS, AND IMPULSES.   This involves the ability to modulate, delay, inhibit, or control the expression of impulses and affects (feelings) in accord with reality. It also entails the ability to tolerate anxiety, frustration, and unpleasant emotions such as anger and depression without becoming overwhelmed, impulsive, or symptomatic.

OBJECT (OR INTERPERSONAL) RELATIONS.   This refers both to the quality of one's interpersonal relationships and to the level of development of one's internalized sense of self and others. Because of its importance it will be discussed in more detail later.

THOUGHT PROCESSES.   An important development in the maturation of thought processes is the individual's shift from primary process thinking to secondary process thinking. Primary process thinking follows the pleasure principle in that it is characterized by wish-fulfilling fantasies and the need for immediate instinctual discharge irrespective of its appropriateness. Wishes and thoughts are equated with action so that action upon the outside world is not necessary in order to obtain gratification in a psychological sense. In contrast, secondary process thinking follows the reality principle. It is characterized by the ability to postpone instinctual gratification or discharge until reality conditions are appropriate and available and replaces wish fulfillment with appropriate action upon the outside world. Wishes and thoughts alone are not sufficient in order to obtain gratification. Secondary process thinking is goal-directed, organized, and oriented to reality.

ADAPTIVE REGRESSION IN THE SERVICE OF THE EGO.   Adaptive regression in the service of the ego connotes an ability to permit oneself to relax the hold on, and relationship to, reality; to experience aspects of the self that are ordinarily inaccessible when one is engaged in concentrated attention to reality; and to emerge with increased adaptive capacity as a result of creative integrations.

DEFENSIVE FUNCTIONING.   The individual develops unconscious, internal mechanisms called defenses to protect himself from the painful experience of anxiety or from fear-inducing situations. Defenses can be adaptive or maladaptive. Adaptive defenses protect the individual from anxiety while simultaneously fostering optimal functioning. Maladaptive defenses also protect the individual from anxiety, but often at the expense of optimal functioning. This concept will be discussed in more detail later.

STIMULUS BARRIER. Each individual develops a mechanism by which it regulates the amount of stimulation received so that it is optimal—neither too little nor too great. Each individual appears to have a different threshold for stimulation. An important aspect of the stimulus barrier is the degree to which the individual is able to maintain her level of functioning or comfort amid increases or decreases in the level of stimulation to which she is exposed.

AUTONOMOUS FUNCTIONS. Certain ego functions—such as attention, concentration, memory, learning, perception, motor functions, and intention—have a primary autonomy from the drives and therefore are conflict-free; that is, they do not arise in response to frustration and conflict. They can lose their autonomy by becoming associated with conflict in the course of early childhood development. Other capacities of the individual that originally develop in association with frustration and conflict later undergo a "change of function" and acquire autonomy from the conflict with which they were associated. Thus, certain interests originally may develop as a way of coping with stress but later are pursued in their own right. The degree to which individuals are able to maintain and retain areas of primary and secondary autonomy is a crucial factor in assessment.

MASTERY-COMPETENCE. The organism experiences pleasure not merely through the reduction of tension or need but also through exercising autonomous ego apparatuses in the service of adaptaton. A mastery drive or instinct (49, 50, 105, 106) has been postulated by authors who believe there is an inborn, active striving toward interaction with the environment that leads to the individual's experiencing a sense of competence or effectiveness. This important concept will be discussed in more detail later.

SYNTHETIC/INTEGRATIVE FUNCTION. A primary feature of the ego is its capacity to "organize mental processes into a coherent form" (10, p. 23). The synthetic function is responsible for binding or fitting all the disparate aspects of the personality into a unified structure that acts upon the external world. The synthetic function is responsible for personality integration, the resolution of splits, fragmentations, and conflicting tendencies within the personality. In this respect there are individuals who may show good ego functioning on selected characteristics but whose overall personality integration is deficient.

Ego Strength

The term "ego strength" implies a composite picture of the internal psychological equipment or capacities that an individual brings to her interactions with others and with the social environment.

Important to the assessment of ego strength are the concepts of stability, regression, variability, and situational context. Within the same individual, certain ego functions may be better developed than others and may show more stability; that is, they tend to fluctuate less from situation to situation, or over time, and are less prone to regression or disorganization under stress. Further, even in individuals who manifest ego strength, regression in selected areas of ego functioning may be normal in certain types of situations—for example, illness, social upheavals, crises, and role transitions—and do not necessarily imply ego deficiencies. It is important to note that it is possible for the same individual to have highly variable ego functioning, although in cases of the most severe psychopathology, ego functions may be impaired generally. Finally, the situational context is a key variable in evaluating ego functioning because the social environment may evoke better or worse functioning.

The Concept of Defense

Defenses are part of the ego's repertoire of mechanisms for protecting the individual from anxiety by keeping intolerable or unacceptable impulses or threats from conscious awareness. Defenses operate unconsciously. All people use defenses, but their exact type and extent vary from individual to individual. All defenses falsify or distort reality to some extent, although in individuals who function more effectively such distortions are minimal or transient and do not impair the person's ability to test reality. To the degree that such defenses enable the person to function optimally without undue anxiety, they are said to be effective.

Efforts directed at modifying defenses create anxiety and are often unconsciously resisted by the individual. The person does not seek deliberately to maintain his defenses. This resistance, however, creates obstacles to achieving the very changes that the person says he would like. While it may seem desirable to try to lessen or modify certain maladaptive defenses in a given individual because they interfere with effective coping, such mechanisms also serve an important protective function for the person. In many cases they should be respected, approached with caution, and at times strengthened.

Under acute or unremitting stress, illness, or fatigue the ego's defenses, along with the other ego functions, may fail. When there is massive defensive failure the person becomes flooded with anxiety. This can result in a severe and rapid deterioration of ego functioning, and in some cases the personality becomes fragmented and chaotic, just as in psychotic episodes. When there is an extensive rigidification of defenses, an individual may appear exceedingly brittle, taut, and driven; his behavior may seem increasingly mechanical, withdrawn, or peculiar.

Common defenses can be described as follows (57):

REPRESSION. A crucial mechanism, repression involves keeping unwanted thoughts and feelings out of awareness, or unconscious. What is repressed once may have been conscious (secondary repression) or may never have reached awareness (primary repression). Repression may involve loss of memory for specific incidents, especially traumatic ones or those associated with painful emotions.

REACTION FORMATION. Like repression, reaction formation involves keeping certain impulses out of awareness. The way to ensure this, however, is to replace the impulse in consciousness with its opposite.

PROJECTION. When the individual attributes to others unacceptable thoughts and feelings that he himself has but is not conscious of, he is using projection.

ISOLATION. Sometimes the mechanism of isolation is referred to as isolation of affect, for there is a repression of the feelings associated with particular content or of the ideas connected with certain affects. Often this is accompanied by experiencing the feelings in relationship to a different situation.

UNDOING. This involves nullifying or voiding symbolically an unacceptable or guilt-provoking act, thought, or feeling.

REGRESSION. Regression involves the return to an earlier developmental phase, level of functioning, or type of behavior in order to avoid the anxieties of the present. Behavior that has been given up recurs.

INTROJECTION. Introjection involves taking another person into the self, psychologically speaking, in order to avoid the direct expression of powerful emotions such as love and hate. When the object (person) of the intense feelings is introjected, the feelings are experienced toward the self, which has now become associated with or a substitute for the object. Introjection is closely connected to three other mechanisms that are mentioned frequently: identification, internalization, and incorporation.

REVERSAL. Reversal involves the alteration of a feeling, attitude, trait, relation, direction, or what have you, into its opposite.

SUBLIMATION. Sublimation is considered to be the highest level or most mature defense. It involves converting an impulse from a socially objectionable aim to a socially acceptable one while still retaining the original goal of the impulse.

INTELLECTUALIZATION. The warding off of unacceptable affects and impulses by thinking about them rather than experiencing them directly is intellectualization. It is similar to isolation.

RATIONALIZATION. The mechanism of rationalization is the use of convincing reasons to justify certain ideas, feelings, or actions so as to avoid recognizing their true underlying motive, which is unacceptable.

DISPLACEMENT. Shifting feelings or conflicts about one person or situation onto another is called displacement.

DENIAL. The denial mechanism involves a negation or nonacceptance of important aspects of reality or of one's own experience that one may actually perceive.

SOMATIZATION. In somatization, intolerable impulses or conflicts are converted into physical symptoms.

IDEALIZATION. The overvaluing of another person, place, family, or activity, say, beyond what is realistic is idealization. To the degree that idealized figures inspire one or serve as possible models for identification, it can be an extremely useful mechanism in personality development and in the helping process. When used defensively, idealization protects the individual from anxiety associated with aggressive or competitive feelings toward a loved or feared person.

COMPENSATION. A person using compensation tries to make up for what he perceives as deficits or deficiencies.

ASCETICISM. This defense involves the moral renunciation of certain pleasure in order to avoid the anxiety and conflict associated with impulse gratification.

ALTRUISM. In altruism one obtains satisfaction through self-sacrificing service to others or through participation in causes. It is defensive when it serves as a way of dealing with unacceptable feelings and conflicts.

SPLITTING. This involves the keeping apart of two contradictory ego states such as love and hate. Thus, individuals who utilize splitting cannot integrate in consciousness contradictory aspects of their own feelings or identity or the contradictory characteristics of others. People are seen in "black or white" one-dimensional terms. This defense is said to be characteristic of borderline conditions.

Ego Mastery and Adaptation

White described the ego as having independent energies that propelled the individual to gain pleasure through manipulating, exploring, and acting upon the environment (105). He called these energies effectance and suggested that feelings of efficacy are the pleasures derived from each interaction with the environment. The individual's development of capacities to interact with the environment successfully is his actual competence. At the same time the individual has subjective feelings about such capacities, and this is termed his sense of competence.

In White's view, ego identity results from the degree to which one's effectance and feelings of efficacy have been nurtured. The degree to which competence and a sense of competence have developed are crucial components in the development and maintenance of self-esteem. Moreover, they affect present and future behavior because they reflect basic attitudes such as one's self-confidence, trust in one's own judgment, and belief in one's decision-making capacities, which shape the way people deal with the environment.

Erik Erikson viewed optimal ego development as a result of the mastery of stage-specific developmental tasks and crises. He argued that the successful resolution of each crisis from birth to death leads to a sense of ego identity and may be said to constitute the core of one's sense of self.

The term "crisis" reflects the idea that there is a state of tension or disequilibrium at the beginning of each new stage. Each crisis is described in terms of extreme positive and negative solutions, although in any individual the resolution of the core developmental crisis may lie anywhere on a continuum from best to worst outcome. Clearly, however, this developmental scheme implies that the ideal resolution of later phases will be dependent on early ones.

According to Erikson, resolution of each successive crisis depends as much on those with whom the individual interacts as on his own innate capacities. Similarly, crisis resolution is dependent upon the impact of culture and environment as it shapes child-rearing practices and provides opportunities or obstacles to optimal adaptation.

Erikson was among the first theorists to suggest that adulthood is a dynamic rather than static time and that ego development continues throughout adulthood. Others since have studied the evolution of the ego in the adult years more systematically.

There is mounting interest in, and evidence for, the idea that personality change occurs in adult life. Adulthood is seen to contain elements of the past as well as its own dynamic processes, which lead to such changes. Robert Butler (14), George Vaillant (104), Roger Gould (41), Daniel Levinson (62), Therese Benedek (8), and Calvin Colarusso and Robert Nemiroff (18) are among those authors who have made seminal contributions to understanding adult developmental processes.

Object Relations

While one usage of the term "object relations" refers to the quality of interpersonal relationships, a second usage refers to specific intrapsychic structures, an aspect of ego organization, and not to external interpersonal relationships (56, p. 3). In this view the infant is innately object-seeking from birth, the child develops her sense of self and of others as a result of her experiences with others. The inner representations of self and others, once developed, affect all subsequent interpersonal relations.

In contrast to viewing object relations as a single ego function, some authors view relations as providing the context in which all ego functions develop.

The separation-individuation process described by Margaret Mahler comprises a series of chronologically ordered phases, each of which leads to major achievements in the areas of separation, individuation, and internalized object relations (67).

THE AUTISTIC PHASE.   The newborn infant generally is unresponsive to external stimuli for a number of weeks and is dominated by physiological needs and processes. He sleeps most of the time and wakes when need states arouse tension. The infant's primary autonomous ego apparatuses are still somewhat undifferentiated and are not yet called into play to act upon the environment. The infant literally exists in his own world or in what has been termed an autistic state, although gradually he becomes responsive, if only fleetingly, to external stimuli. In terms of object relations the child is in a preattachment phase, which some have called a phase of primary narcissism.

THE SYMBIOTIC PHASE.   Gradually the protective shell around the child gives way, and he begins to perceive the "need-satisfying object," but this object is experienced within the infant's ego boundary and lacks a separate identity. In the symbiotic state the mother's ego functions for the infant, and it is the mother who mediates between the infant and the external world. The sensations the child experiences from the mother form the core of his sense of self, and this period marks the beginning of the capacity to invest in another person.

SEPARATION-INDIVIDUATION: THE DIFFERENTIATION SUBPHASE.   Differentiation begins at about four or five months. When the child is awake more often and for longer periods, her attention shifts from being inwardly directed or focused within the symbiosis to being more outwardly directed. The infant literally begins to separate her self-representation from the representation of her mother (the object).

Separation-individuation: the practicing subphase. The practicing subphase continues the process of separation of self and object representations and accelerates the individuation process, as the infant's own autonomous ego functions assume more importance. The first part of the practicing period, when the infant is approximately eight to ten or twelve months old, is characterized by the infant's attempts to move away from the mother physically, as, for example, through crawling. The infant thus expands his world and his capacity to maneuver in it autonomously, optimally always in close proximity to the maternal figure, who is there to provide support and encouragement.

In the early practicing subphase the child experiences the simultaneous pull of the outside world and of the mother, and separation anxiety may increase until the child becomes reassured that mother is still there despite his moving away from her. One can observe the repeated efforts initially on the part of the child to keep track of the mother even as he may crawl away from her and then his attempt to find her if she has been lost momentarily. Gradually the child is able to be on his own for longer periods of time.

During the second part of the practicing period, the child's ability to get around by himself seems to lead to "his love affair with the world." At times the child appears oblivious to his mother's temporary absence. The pleasure in his rapidly developing ego functions seems to enable the child to sustain the transient object losses inherent in his individuation.

The child consolidates his separateness during this period and acquires a more stable internal self-representation that is distinct from the object representation. At the same time the child's all-"good" self- and object experiences are separated from all-"bad" ones. Thus, when mother is frustrating she is experienced as all bad, although the child tries to rid himself of this feeling; when she is experienced as loving she is all good.

Separation-individuation: the rapprochement subphase. While in the practicing subphase the child is content to be away from mother for increasingly longer periods of time; in the rapprochement subphase he becomes more needful of her presence once again and appears to want his mother to share everything with him as well as to constantly reassure him of her love. This need for closeness while the child continues in his autonomous existence characterizes the rapprochement period.

During the rapprochment subphase, the child's belief in the mother's omnipotence is shed as the child realizes that he must stand on his own two feet. At the same time the child is frightened that now he will be completely alone and will lose the mother's love.

SEPARATION-INDIVIDUATION: ON THE ROAD TO OBJECT CONSTANCY. During this phase the child again seems able to be on his own to a greater degree than previously without undue concern about the mother's whereabouts. The child's internalization of the mother, which remains fluid for some time, begins to permit the child to pursue the full expression of his individuality and to function independently without experiencing or fearing separation, abandonment, or loss of love. The final achievement of object constancy implies the capacity to maintain a positive mental representation of the object in the object's absence or in the face of frustration. This normal phase of splitting is overcome in the later rapprochement subphase, when the good and bad self and good and bad object each begin to become integrated. Prior to this integration and to the development of object constancy, the self and the world are experienced in polar and fluctuating terms.

Blos has suggested a second separation-individuation phase occurring in adolescence (11). The healthy adolescent has an internalized sense of himself and others but now must disengage from the more infantile aspects of his self- and object representations in order to acquire a more realistically based sense of self and of his parents. This disengagement also requires the discovery of new love objects outside the orbit of the family. Those adults who show optimal functioning may relive separation-individuation themes throughout the life cycle, particularly at life transitional points or during more acute stresses. Nevertheless, the adult who has achieved a relatively stable (psychological) identity and who has an integrated and realistic conception of herself will have the capacity for mature and loving relations with others. Those who do not successfully complete this key developmental task will show serious interpersonal difficulties (9).

General Therapeutic Concepts

The Nature and Importance of Assessment

Ego assessment helps the practitioner determine whether interventive efforts should be directed at (1) nurturing, maintaining, enhancing, or modifying inner capacities; (2) mobilizing, improving, or changing environmental conditions; or (3) improving the fit between inner capacities and external circumstances.

The following questions are important guides to the practitioner in the assessment process:

1. To what extent is the client's problem a function of stresses imposed by his current life roles or developmental tasks?
2. To what extent is the client's problem a function of situational stress or of a traumatic event?
3. To what extent is the client's problem a function of impairments in his ego capacities or of developmental difficulties or dynamics?

4. To what extent is the client's problem a function of the lack of environmental resources or supports or of a lack of fit between his inner capacities and his external circumstances?
5. What inner capacities and environmental resources does the client have that can be mobilized to improve his functioning?

THE B. CASE

Mrs. B. was fifty-three when her mother, a self-sufficient seventy-three-year-old, went into heart failure in Mrs. B.'s presence. The paramedics arrived within minutes, revived the old woman, and transported her to a nearby hospital. For the next week Mrs. B. felt as though she was walking in a dream. When she spoke with doctors at the hospital, her voice and theirs seemed far away. She couldn't believe that her mother might die or become bedridden. A highly responsible and well-organized individual who had worked at the same position for eight years, she forgot to call her employer to tell him she would not be at work. When he needed information from her about specific tasks on which she was working, Mrs. B. could barely focus on remembering the essential details. While there were many questions she thought of asking the doctor, she was unable to do so. Mrs. B. felt immobilized, useless, helpless, and confused. She was fearful of going outside. With the support of solicitous friends and her thirty-year-old son, Mrs. B. began to cope somewhat better over the next few weeks and returned to work. Her employer was patient with Mrs. B.'s difficulty in concentrating. During this time she easily became overwhelmed and tearful. Her mother's condition did not improve, and Mrs. B. had trouble thinking about impending decisions that had to be made about where her mother should live and what additional assistance she would need. At the same time she could not consider the possibility that her mother might die or live on severely impaired. Soon afterward her mother died, and Mrs. B. felt devastated. Mrs. B. is an only child and has no living aunts or uncles on her mother's side. When Mrs. B.'s father died when she was eight, her mother went to work to support them both. Although poor before and after her father died, Mrs. B. remembers many good times and a close family life. Mrs. B. was a good student, had many friends, and was highly conscientious and responsible. Like her mother, she was cheerful and optimistic. Mr. and Mrs. B. raised one son, who is currently married, works as an accountant, and lives in the suburbs. Mrs. B. likes her daughter-in-law, sees her and her son once a month, and talks to her son weekly. She is looking forward to the birth of her first grandchild in several months. She has had a difficult time adjusting to three significant events in her life: her son's departure for the army and Vietnam in 1969, after which she returned to work; her husband's sudden death in 1974; and her mother's retirement to Florida in 1976. Nevertheless, she always has maintained "a stiff upper lip" and has looked on the brighter side of life.

Discussion: Mrs. B. is a woman whose ego appears to be overwhelmed by the acute stress of her mother's illness. This stress is accompanied by alterations in Mrs. B's autonomous functioning, thought processes, sense of self, synthetic functioning, and sense of competence. She also shows some regression (increased dependency needs and helplessness) and denial (inability to take in the implications of her mother's condition). There is no indication of difficulties related to life role, developmental tasks, or, more important, ego deficits or earlier developmental difficulties. We see an individual who has demonstrated reasonably good functioning in and received gratification from her major life roles, past and present, and whose ego functioning has enabled her to lead a life in keeping with her capacities. While she has shown some diminished functioning at points of stress involving separation and loss, Mrs. B. nevertheless has regained her equilibrium at these times with the help of her inner coping capacities and external supports, of which her mother has been quite important. The possible death or long-term disability of her mother was very threatening to Mrs. B. in the light of their close relationship and the role her mother has played in her life. She still has many external supports on which to draw (sympathetic employer, friends, son, daughter-in-law, and expected grandchild). While Mrs. B. may be able to undergo a successful mourning process without intervention, her pain may be eased and the length of the acute mourning shortened by a contact that would help her to ventilate, encourage her continued functioning, and decrease her sense of aloneness.

THE D. CASE

Mrs. D., a divorced fashion consultant, was forty-eight when a malignant tumor of the breast necessitated a radical mastectomy. Mrs. D.'s initial reactions to the surgery seemed good on the surface. When by herself, however, Mrs. D. would burst into tears and become inconsolable. She was irritable with her daughters, did not want other visitors, and did not cooperate with the nurses. When it was suggested that she attend a therapeutic self-help group for mastectomy patients, Mrs. D. refused. The doctor's attempts to discuss the need for preventive treatment as well as the devices that would improve her physical appearance were met with a nonchalant, almost blasé attitude. After such discussions Mrs. D. despaired or directed her anger at members of the nursing staff. As a child, Mrs. D. was told she was a beauty. The only memories she has of her mother's interest in her were related to the latter's buying her clothes. At night her mother would go out and leave Mrs. D. Mrs. D.'s father left home when she was five. Her mother describes him as a drunk and a womanizer, and he never made efforts to see Mrs. D. Mrs.

D. was an excellent student all through school. She was a self-reliant, conscientious, well-disciplined person with high standards for herself and others. Despite her popularity and beauty she felt alone, unattractive, and self-conscious about her appearance. Her relationships with friends were superficial and characterized by Mrs. D's inability to confide in anyone or to let people get close to her emotionally. Mrs. D. went to college on scholarship. After graduation she became a model. She married an exceptionally handsome, affluent, though irresponsible man whose alcoholism became more apparent after their marriage. Mrs. D. had two children in quick succession. Mr. D. ran away with his secretary after the birth of the second daughter. Mrs. D. feels that if she had been more attractive to Mr. D. he would not have left her. She entered the fashion field, worked her way up, and has been employed in a very responsible position for a number of years. Her daughters, ages twenty-one and nineteen, have had their share of difficulties. Mrs. D. dates but has refused many offers of marriage. She has not felt that any man has loved her for herself. Mrs. D. is able to take in the implications of her condition at times, but then she feels completely ugly, unworthy, estranged from her body, and guilty of misdeeds she cannot pinpoint. She feels as if she has no identity, present or future. She feels aware of her age, of her possible death, and of being unable to control her life.

Discussion: The disfiguring surgery that Mrs. D. has undergone and the diagnosis of cancer produced a massive crisis for Mrs. D. They mobilized denial, which has hampered her positive participation in her treatment and rehabilitation. It has been accompanied by efforts to control others, as manifested by her uncooperativeness and success in making others around her feel helpless. Her regression is evidenced by her withdrawal from others. She experiences an inner feeling of badness and ugliness. At the same time her anger is overwhelming her, and she strikes out at others. Her judgment is so impaired that she does not act on her own behalf. She feels a loss of a sense of self and feels hopeless. The acute stress has triggered a maladaptive response because it has disrupted the mainstays of Mrs. D's adaptation to the world—her physical appearance and her sense of control. It is doubtful that her emotional rehabilitation can be achieved without extensive help.

The Focus of Intervention

Generally, ego-oriented approaches can be grouped according to whether their goals are ego-supportive or ego-modifying (55, pp. 57–71). Ego-supportive intervention aims at restoring, maintaining, or enhancing the individual's adaptive functioning as well as strengthening or building ego where there are deficits or impairments. In contrast, ego-modifying intervention aims at changing basic personality patterns or structures.

Ego-restorative efforts help the individual regain her previous level of functioning and thus return to her previous equilibrium. Such efforts are important particularly with clients undergoing stress or crises that temporarily disrupt or overwhelm their usual ego functioning. Ego-restorative efforts also are important with clients who demonstrate marginal or poor functioning in normal conditions and who undergo a sudden disorganization or deterioration in their functioning.

Ego-maintaining efforts enable the individual to continue an optimal level of functioning within the constraints and resources of her particular capacities and life situation and thus maintain her equilibrium. Such efforts are important particularly with clients who show chronic difficulties in dealing with the stress of everyday life or with those whose social functioning is threatened by stressful circumstances. Often such individuals' functioning will worsen, or they will suffer greatly without intervention.

Ego-enhancing efforts enable the individual to achieve more optimal functioning in selected areas and thus to reach a new equilibrium based on a higher level of functioning. Ego building and ego strengthening efforts are variants of this type of intervention and are used with clients having ego deficits (9).

The Nature of Change

In an ego-supportive approach, change results from: (1) the exercise of autonomous ego functioning in the service of mastering new developmental, life transitional, crisis, or other stressful situations; (2) greater understanding of the impact of one's behavior on others; (3) learning and positive reinforcement of new behavior, skills, attitudes, problem-solving capacities, and coping strategies; (4) the utilization of conflict-free areas of ego functioning to neutralize conflict-laden areas; (5) the use of relationships and experiences to correct for previous difficulties and deprivations; and (6) the use of the environment to provide more opportunities and conditions for the use of one's capacities.

The Nature and Importance of the Helping Relationship

Ego-supportive intervention emphasizes the more realistic as well as the transferential aspects of the helping relationship. Consequently, the worker in an ego-supportive approach may encourage the client's accurate perception of the worker as a helping agent rather than as a transference figure. The worker provides a human and genuine experience in the helping relationship. In many instances, however, the worker uses the positive transference and becomes a benign authority or parental figure who fosters the client's phase-appropriate needs and development. In some instances the worker becomes a "corrective" figure to the client. A client may develop intense reactions to the worker of an unrealistic kind even in an ego-supportive approach. Such reactions do need to be worked with, but the aim, in most cases, is to restore the positive relationship rather than to trace the negative reactions back to their original sources in the client's past (55, pp. 228–246).

Another important aspect of the use of relationship in an ego-supportive approach is the worker's willingness to use himself outside of the client-worker relationship to function in a variety of roles on behalf of the client. It may be important for the worker to be an advocate or systems negotiator for the client, to meet with members of his family, and so on (43).

Specific Techniques

Among the psychological techniques used in ego-supportive intervention are those that are more sustaining, directive educative, and structured, in contrast to those that are more nondirective, reflective, confronting, and interpretive. Hollis described six main groups of psychological techniques that are important to ego psychological intervention: sustaining, direct influence; exploration, description, and ventilation; person-situation reflection; pattern-dynamic reflection; and developmental reflection (55, pp. 72–88). Other important techniques are education and structuring techniques.

Environmental intervention is critical to interventive efforts within an ego psychological perspective. For example, it may be important to mobilize resources and opportunities that will enable the individual to use her inner capacities or to restructure the environment so that it nurtures or fits better with the individual's needs and capacities. Environmental work also may be essential to modifying maladaptive patterns within an individual; for example, it may be utilized where the family system is perpetuating, reinforcing, or aggravating a family member's difficulties.

Appropriate Client Populations

Ego-supportive approaches generally are recommended for two large groups of clients: those whose characteristic ego functioning is disrupted by current stress, and those who show severe and chronic ego deficits. Ego-modifying approaches usually are recommended for those clients with reasonably good ego strength who show maladaptive patterns that interfere with the optimal use of their capacities, as well as for selected clients with severe and chronic maladaptive patterns who can tolerate or be helped to tolerate the anxiety associated with ego-modifying procedures. For this second group, interventive efforts often may include the use of hospitalization or other types of environmental structuring.

Duration of Intervention

Ego-supportive approaches may be crisis-oriented, short-term, or long-term. This is related to the fact that the individual may benefit from ego support in both acute and chronically stressful life circumstances and from long-term support of efforts aimed at improving selected areas of ego functioning. In contrast, ego-modifying efforts generally are long-term because of the difficulties involved in altering entrenched personality patterns or characteristics.

THE M. CASE

Ms. M. is a single, thirty-year-old, unemployed commercial artist who receives unemployment insurance. She has no close friends and spends every weekend visiting her parents. She would like to work in order to earn more money but is reluctant to seek full-time employment because of its demands. Recently she has been feeling desperate about her life and gets little pleasure from her solitary activities. Several months ago she became acutely psychotic and was briefly hospitalized. She recovered quickly, was discharged from the hospital, and began seeing a social worker at an outpatient clinic. Among Ms. M.'s major difficulties are her extreme suspiciousness and her tendency to merge with others in close relationships. On her last job she began to feel that her female employer wanted to have a sexual relationship with her merely because her employer was friendly and supportive. Ms. M. became fearful and withdrew from her to the point of being unable to work. At times she thinks others can read her mind and often attributes her own thoughts to others. While she tells herself that she is imagining these things, she is never fully convinced and expends a great deal of energy trying to contain her anxiety. She rarely asks people directly for reassurance, nor does she question them about what they mean when they say things she does not fully understand. The social worker experienced the struggle between Ms. M.'s observing ego and her irrational perceptions and fears within their own beginning relationship itself. When asked how she experienced her meeting with the worker, Ms. M. responded that she felt the worker was sympathetic but wondered if she was tape recording her. When asked what gave her that idea, Ms. M. pointed to a dictating machine that was on the worker's desk. The worker let Ms. M. check to see if the dictating machine was running, and Ms. M. seemed satisfied that it was not. Then she replied that she guessed it was a ridiculous idea but it just seemed to her for a moment that the worker might be recording the session. The worker commented that it was good that Ms. M. could ask her about the tape recording so that she could clear up her confusion. Ms. M. acknowledged that she lived in this kind of confusion most of the time and that this was a problem to her. They agreed that this was something they could work on together. The worker met with Ms. M. weekly, and they used the sessions to identify what Ms. M. was feeling, to help her sort out her feelings from the worker's , to help her expand her understanding of the possible motivations of the worker that did not relate to Ms. M. specifically, to help her find ways of recognizing when her perceptions might be distorted, and to find ways of correcting them before becoming overwhelmed by anxiety. Simultaneously the worker helped Ms. M. think through the ways she could pursue both work and interpersonal relationships gradually, not exposing herself to too much stress at once. They decided that free-lancing was a good option for Ms. M., since it permitted her to work by herself. The worker also suggested that Ms. M. attend a weekly discussion group at a local church. The group had a specific topic of interest each night and was followed by a coffee hour where people could socialize. Because of its structured nature, it seemed a less threatening way for Ms. M. to begin to involve herself in activities and meet others. Ms. M. and the worker discussed what happened at these meetings in order to help Ms. M. find new ways of coping with stressful situations and to reinforce her for her good handling of situations that arose. After a year Ms. M. felt much less fearful, seemed more related to the world around her and to herself, and was able to venture out to a somewhat greater extent. She was doing well in her free-lance work and felt some enhanced self-esteem.

Discussion: In this example the worker engaged in ego-building efforts with Ms. M., whose severe ego deficits were hampering her ability to use her capacities. The worker used the client-worker relationship as a testing ground in which Ms. M. could identify the difficulties she had in perceiving and communicating with others and could improve these important skills. The worker used Ms. M.'s observing ego in this process and tapped her motivation to improve herself. The worker helped Ms. M. understand her needs and capacities and structure her external life to meet these. The worker also provided a forum in which Ms. M. could discuss her current problems of everyday life and learn new ways of approaching these better. Part of this process was improving Ms. M.'s sensitivity to the motivations and needs of others. This work took a year and involved the techniques of sustainment, ventilation, direct influence, education, structuring, and person-in-situation reflection.

Application to Family and Group Intervention

Although family and group modalities generally draw on theoretical systems other than ego psychology and follow interventive principles different from those governing individual intervention, there are linkages between ego psychological concepts and group and family intervention.

While the family has its own life cycle (15) that is different from those of its individual members and can be characterized by unique internal processes (communication, roles, structure, and so on), it nevertheless is a potent force in personality development, is a crucial resource for the individual, reinforces adaptive or maladaptive patterns, and reacts to the problems encountered by individual members. Thus, intervention with the family does not always have to be thought of a systematic in nature. One can intervene to improve parent-child relationships or parenting skills (97), to enlist the family's positive participation in the treatment of a relative (37), to resolve marital conflict (6), or to help individual family members cope with the impact of illness or disability of a member (38).

Groups are a potent force in offering clients acceptance, reassurance, and encouragement; promoting problem-solving; enhancing and developing ego capacities; teaching skills and developing a sense of competence; providing information; promoting mastery; shaping or changing attitudes and behavior; and mobilizing people for collective action. Moreover, groups can be used to help individuals collaborate with helping agencies and personnel and to overcome their resistance to or discomfort with being a client (71, 61).

Implications for Community Intervention, Service Delivery, and Social Policy

Ego psychology's emphasis on the importance of developmental stages, role and life transitions, and stress and crisis to human functioning suggests the need for social work services to be positioned at places and times in peoples' lives where and when they are likely to need help (69, pp. 82–104; 70, pp. 42–88). Ego psychology alerts us to when and under what conditions during the human life cycle such help might be needed. Likewise, there are certain events and times in peoples' lives where help is needed or where the availability of help can prevent more serious breakdowns in social functioning. Separation, divorce, death, job loss, retirement, marriage, parenthood, and physical illness are examples.

Ego psychology can be particularly useful in directing service delivery toward primary prevention rather than only remediation (86, pp. 192–197). The understanding of what conditions or factors influence optimal development or promote effective coping is invaluable in establishing services that prevent problems from occurring or worsening. This approach leads to the identification of high-risk populations or individuals who can be reached before they encounter certain difficulties.

At the same time, ego psychology's view of the significance of chronic or stable impairments to the ego capacities that some individuals bring to their life transactions points to the need for a range of remedial, rehabilitative, or sustaining interventive services, many of which need to be offered on more than a short-term basis.

Ego psychology's appreciation of the significance of an individual's needs for mastery, decision-making, and autonomy suggests the importance of services that are structured to promote the client's active participation in matters affecting him.

Ego psychology's conception of the importance of social and environmental factors in promoting adaptive functioning points to the role of environmental intervention as part of direct practice efforts. Equally important, however, is the role of social workers in contributing to social policies more conducive to promoting human growth and preventng maladaptaton. Ego-oriented practice views the social and environmental context as a proper locus of interventive efforts if it is creating obstacles to the individual's growth and functioning. Clearly the goal of making the social environment and social policy more responsive to many client's needs requires that social workers actively engage in social and political action.

Current State of Research

In recent years, ego psychology as a body of theory has been enriched greatly by research (60, pp. 249–315). Greater sophistication in research methodology and design, more willingness on the part of theorists to subject their ideas to investigation, and expanded conceptions of the scope of ego psychology have led to more systematic study of child and adult development and the ways in which people cope with stress, crisis, and various types of life demands and events. Moreover, research from such other fields as sociology, social psychology, anthropology, and medicine has contributed to our understanding of human behavior. Tools for assessing normal and pathological ego functioning and adaptive and maladaptive coping also have evolved.

In contrast to these developments, systematic research on the nature and effectiveness of social work and psychotherapy based on ego psychological principles has been lacking. Social workers have been slow in integrating the findings that do exist into their practice.

When social casework and its ego psychological base came under attack in the 1960s, studies of social work intervention that were conducted were disheartening. They did not support the case for social casework (72). Upon closer analysis, however, the interventive goals, processes, and outcomes studied were not well selected in the research design. Thus it was not possible to understand why positive or negative results were obtained because the nature of intervention was not adequately defined, operationalized, and measured.

In the years since these studies, evaluation or outcome research has become increasingly important. Yet the problem of operationally defining psychodynamic and psychosocial variables and the interventions designed to affect these remains elusive to those engaged in practice.

It is critical that the rich knowledge base for social work practice provided by ego psychology receive more research attention from social work practitioners. Beginnings have been made in this area, and more is possible (30, 23). Outcome evaluation in itself, however, is not sufficient to advance the development and application of ego psychology to social work practice. More diverse research strategies that move us beyond the current preoccupation with large experimental or single case designs also are important.

Those involved in clinical practice must become involved in the formulation, design, and implementation of such studies either by acquiring clinical research expertise themselves or through collaboration with researchers interested in and challenged by the problems posed by clinical research.

The Future of Ego Psychology

While ego psychology plays an important role in the knowledge base of social work at present, it competes with other theoretical formulations. But ego psychology can regain its role as the unifying theory for social work practice. First, it is crucial that proponents of ego psychological theory not revert to an exclusive reliance on psychoanalytic ego psychological concepts on the one hand or attempt to divorce ego psychology from its psychoanalytic roots on the other. Second, it follows that social work practice or clinical social work should encompass a broad range of interventive strategies within a person-environment perspective.

A third determinant of the future of ego psychology as a unifying theory for social work practice will be its ability to generate a more comprehensive approach to work with the social environment.

Fourth, it is critical that more systematic efforts be made to integrate knowledge of racial, ethnic, social class, and life-style differences into our understanding of normal ego development and the processes of coping and adaptation.

Last, the practice implications of ego psychological concepts need more systematic study. This requires that research become an ally rather than an enemy of the social work practitioner and that both social work educational programs and social agencies develop more creative ways of involving practitioners in and equipping them with the skills for clinical research.

References

1. Ainsworth, M. D. S. "The Development of Mother-Infant Attachment," in B. Caldwell and H. Ricciuti (eds.), *Review of Child Development Research*, Vol. 3. Chicago: University of Chicago Press, 1973, pp. 1–94.
2. Austin, Lucille N. "Trends in Differential Treatment in Social Casework," *Social Casework*, Vol. 29 (June 1948), pp. 203–211.
3. ———. "Qualifications of Social Caseworkers for Psychotherapy," *Journal of Orthopsychiatry*, Vol. 26 (January 1956), pp. 47–57.

4. Bandler, Bernard. "The Concept of Ego-Supportive Therapy," in Howard J. Parad and Roger Miller (eds.), *Ego-Oriented Casework*. New York: Family Service Association of America, 1963, pp. 27–44.

5. Bandler, Louis. "Some Casework Aspects of Ego Growth Through Sublimation," in Howard J. Parad and Roger Miller (eds.), *Ego-Oriented Casework*. New York: Family Service Association of America, 1963, pp. 89–107.

6. Beck, Dorothy Fahs. "Marital Conflict: Its Course and Treatment as Seen by Caseworkers," *Social Casework*, Vol. 47 (September 1966), pp. 575–582.

7. Bellak, Leopold, Marvin Hurvich, and Helen Gediman (eds.). *Ego Functions in Schizophrenics, Neurotics, and Normals*. New York: Wiley, 1973.

8. Benedek, Therese. "Parenthood During the Life Cycle," in James Anthony and Therese Benedek (eds.), *Parenthood—Its Psychology and Psychopathology*. Boston: Little, Brown, 1970, pp. 185–208.

9. Blanck, Gertrude, and Rubin Blanck. *Ego Psychology in Theory and Practice*. New York: Columbia University Press, 1974.

10. ———. *Ego Psychology II: Psychoanalytic Developmental Psychology*. New York: Columbia University Press, 1979.

11. Blos, Peter. "The Second Individuation Process of Adolescence," in Aaron Esman (ed.), *The Psychology of Adolescence: Essential Readings*. New York: International Universities Press, 1975, pp. 156–177.

12. Bowlby, John. "The Nature of the Child's Tie to the Mother," *International Journal of Psychoanalysis*, Vol. 39 (1958), pp. 350–373.

13. Briar, Scott, and Henry Miller. *Problems and Issues in Social Casework*. New York: Columbia University Press, 1971.

14. Butler, Robert N. "The Life Review: An Interpretation of Reminiscence in the Aged," *Psychiatry*, Vol. 26 (January 1963), pp. 65–76.

15. Carter, Elizabeth A., and Monica McGoldrick (eds.). *The Family Life Cycle: A Framework for Family Therapy*. New York: Gardner Press, 1980.

16. Cockerill, Eleanor E., Lewis J. Lehrman, Patricia Sacks, and Isabel Stamm. *A Conceptual Framework of Social Casework*. Pittsburgh: University of Pittsburgh Press, 1953.

17. Coehlo, George V., David A. Hamburg, and John E. Adams (eds.). *Coping and Adaptation*. New York: Basic Books, 1974.

18. Colarusso, Calvin, and Robert A. Nemiroff. *Adult Development*. New York: Plenum Press, 1981.

19. Edward, Joyce, Nathene Ruskin, and Patsy Turrini. *Separation-Individuation: Theory and Application*. New York: Gardner Press, 1981.

20. Erikson, Erik. *Childhood and Society*. New York: Norton, 1950.

21. ———. "Identity and the Life Cycle," *Psychological Issues*, Vol. 1, No. 1 (1959), pp. 50–100.

22. Escalona, Sibylle K. *The Roots of Individuality: Normal Patterns of Development in Infancy*. Chicago: Aldine, 1968.

23. Fanshel, David. *The Future of Social Work Research*. Washington, D.C.: National Association of Social Workers, 1980.

24. Freud, Anna. *The Ego and the Mechanisms of Defense*. New York: International Universities Press, 1936.

25. Freud, Sigmund. *The Standard Edition of the Complete Psychological Works of Sigmund Freud*. 24 cols. Edited by James Strachey. London: Hogarth, 1953–66.

26. ———. *The Interpretation of Dreams* (1900), standard edition, Vols. 4 and 5. London: Hogarth, 1955.

27. ———. *Inhibitions, Symptoms, and Anxiety*. (1926), standard edition, Vol. 20. London: Hogarth, 1959.

28. ———. *The Ego and the Id*. (1923), standard edition, Vol. 19. London: Hogarth, 1961.

29. ———. *An Outline of Psychoanalysis*. (1940), standard edition, Vol. 23. London: Hogarth, 1964.

30. Garfield, Sol. L., and Alan E. Bergin. *Handbook of Psychotherapy and Behavioral Change*, 2nd edtition. New York: Wiley, 1978.

31. Garrett, Annette. "The Worker-Client Relationship," in Howard J. Parad (ed.), *Ego Psychology and Dynamic Casework*. New York: Family Service Association of America, 1958, pp. 53–72.

32. ———. "Modern Casework: The Contribution of Ego Psychology," in Howard J. Parad (ed.), *Ego Psychology and Dynamic Casework*. New York: Family Service Association of America, 1958, pp. 38–52.

33. Germain, Carel B. "An Ecological Perspective on Social Work Practice and Health Care," *Social Work in Health Care*, Vol. 3 (Fall 1977), pp. 67–76.

34. ———. *Social Work Practice: People and Environments*. New York: Columbia University Press, 1979.

35. ———. "The Physical Environment in Social Work Practice," in Anthony N. Maluccio (ed.), *Promoting Competence in Clients: A New/Old Approach to Social Work Practice*. New York: Free Press, 1981, pp. 103–124.

36. Golan, Naomi. *Treatment in Crisis Situations*. New York: Free Press, 1978.

37. Goldstein, Eda G. "Mothers of Psychiatric Patients Revisited," in Carel B. Germain (ed.), *Social Work Practice: People and Environments*. New York: Columbia University Press, 1979, pp. 150–173.

38. ———. "Promoting Competence in Families of Psychiatric Patients," in Anthony N. Maluccio (ed.), *Promoting Competence in Clients: A New/Old Approach to Social Work Practice*. New York: Free Press, 1981, pp. 317–342.

39. ———. "Issues in Developing Systematic Research and Theory," in Diana Waldfogel and Aaron Roseblatt (eds.), *Handbook of Clinical Social Work*. San Francisco: Jossey-Bass, 1983, pp. 5–25.

40. ———. *Ego Psychology and Social Work Practice*. New York: Free Press, 1984.

41. Gould, Roger L. *Transformations: Growth and Change in Adult Life*. New York: Simon and Schuster, 1978.

42. Grinker, Roy R., and John D. Spiegel. *Men Under Stress*. Philadelphia: Blakiston, 1945.

43. Grinnell, Richard M., Nancy S. Kyte, and Gerald J. Bostwick. "Environmental Modification," in Anthony N. Maluccio (ed.), *Promoting Competence in Clients: A New/Old Approach to Social Work Practice*. New York: Free Press, 1981, pp. 152–184.

44. Hamilton, Gordon. *Theory and Practice of Social Casework*. New York: Columbia University Press, 1940.

45. ———. *Theory and Practice of Social Casework*. 2nd edition. New York: Columbia University Press, 1951.

46. Hartmann, Heinz. *Ego Psychology and the Problem of Adaptation*. New York: International Universities Press, 1939.

47. ———, and Ernst Kris. "The Genetic Approach in Psychoanalysis," *Psychoanalytic Study of the Child*, Vol. 1 (1945), pp. 11–29.

48. ———, and Rudolph M. Lowenstein. "Comments on the Formation of Psychic Structures," *Psychoanalytic Study of the Child*, Vol. 2 (1946), pp. 11–38.

49. Hendrick, I. "Instinct and the Ego During Infancy," *Psychoanalytic Quarterly*, Vol. 11 (1942), pp. 33–58.

50. ———. "Work and the Pleasure Principle," *Psychoanalytic Quarterly*, Vol. 12 (1943), pp. 311–329.

51. Hill, Reuben. "Generic Features of Families Under Stress," *Social Casework*, Vol. 39 (February–March 1958), pp. 139–150.

52. Hollis, Florence. "Techniques of Casework," *Journal of Social Casework*, Vol. 30 (June 1949), pp. 235–244.

53. ———. "Contemporary Issues for Caseworkers," in Howard J. Parad and Roger Miller (eds.), *Ego-Oriented Casework*. New York: Family Service Association of America, 1963, pp. 7–26.

54. ———. *Casework: A Psychosocial Therapy*. New York: Random House, 1964.

55. ———. *Casework: A Psychosocial Therapy*. 2nd edition. New York: Random House, 1972.

56. Horner, Althea J. *Object Relations and the Developing Ego in Therapy*. New York: Aronson, 1979.

57. Laughlin, H. P. *The Ego and Its Defenses*, 2nd edition. New York: Aronson, 1979.

58. Lax, Ruth F., Sheldon Bach, and J. Alexis Burland. *Rapprochement*. New York: Aronson, 1980.

59. Lazarus, Richard S. *Psychological Stress and the Coping Process*. New York: McGraw-Hill, 1966.

60. ———, James R. Averill, and Edward M. Opton. "The Psychology of Coping: Issues of Research and Assessment," in George V. Coehlo, David Hamburg, and John E. Adams (eds.), *Coping and Adaptation*. New York: Basic Books, 1974, pp. 249–315.

61. Lee, Judith A. B. "Promoting Competence in Children and Youth," in Anthony N. Maluccio (ed.), *Promoting Competence in Clients: A New/Old Approach to Social Work Practice*. New York: Free Press, 1981, pp. 236–263.

62. Levinson, Daniel J. *The Season of a Man's Life*. New York: Knopf, 1978.

63. Lindemann, Erich. "Symptomatology and Management of Acute Grief," *American Journal of Psychiatry*, Vol. 101, No. 2 (September 1944), pp. 7–21.

64. Mahler, Margaret S. "On Child Psychosis and Schizophrenia: Autistic and Symbiotic Infantile Psychosis," in *The Psychoanalytic Study of the Child*, Vol. 7. New York: International Universities Press, 1951, pp. 286–305.

65. ———. *On Human Symbiosis and the Vicissitudes of Individuation*. New York: International Universities Press, 1968.

66. ———. "On the First Three Phases of the Separation-Individuation Process,"*International Journal of Psychoanalysis*, Vol. 53 (1972), pp. 333–338.

67. ———, Fred Pine, and Anni Bergman. *The Psychological Birth of the Human Infant*. New York: Basic Books, 1975.

68. Maluccio, Anthony N. (ed.). *Promoting Competence in Clients: A New/Old Approach to Social Work Practice*. New York: Free Press, 1981.

69. Meyer, Carol H. *Social Work Practice: A Response to the Urban Crisis*. New York: Free Press, 1970.

70. ———. *Social Work Practice: The Changing Landscape*. New York: Free Press, 1976.

71. Middleman, Ruth R. "The Pursuit of Competence Through Involvement in Structured Groups," in Anthony N. Maluccio (ed.), *Promoting Competence in Clients: A New/Old Approach to Social Work Practice*. New York: Free Press, 1981, pp. 185–212.

72. Mullen, Edward J., James R. Dumpson, and Associates. *Evaluation of Social Intervention*. San Francisco: Jossey-Bass, 1972.

73. Murphy, Lois Barclay. "The Problem of Defense and the Concept of Coping," in E. James Anthony and Cyrille Koupernik (eds.), *The Child and His Family*. New York: Wiley, 1970, pp. 66–86.

74. ———, and Alice E. Moriarity. *Vulnerability, Coping and Growth from Infancy to Adolescence*. New Haven: Yale University Press, 1976.

75. Piaget, Jean. *The Child's Conception of the World*. London: Routledge & Kegan Paul, 1951.

76. ———. *The Origin of Intelligence in Children*. New York: International Universities Press, 1952.

77. ———. *The Moral Judgment of the Child*. New York: Macmillan, 1955.

78. Rapaport, David. "The Autonomy of the Ego," *Bulletin of the Menninger Foundation*, Vol. 15 (1951), pp. 113–123.

79. ———. "The Theory of Ego Autonomy: A Generalization," *Bulletin of the Menninger Foundation*, Vol. 22 (1958), pp. 3–35.

80. ———. "A Historical Survey of Psychoanalytic Ego Psychology, *Introduction to Psychological Issues*, Vol. 1 (1959), pp. 5–17.

81. ———. "The Structure of Psychoanalytic Theory," *Psychological Issues*, Vol. 2 (1960), pp. 39–85.

82. Richmond, Mary L. *Social Diagnosis*. New York: Russell Sage Foundation, 1917.

83. Roberts, Robert W., and Robert H. Nee (eds.). *Theories of Social Casework*. Chicago: University of Chicago Press, 1970.

84. Robinson, Virginia P. *A Changing Psychology in Social Casework*. Chapel Hill: University of North Carolina Press, 1930.

85. ———. *The Dynamics of Supervision Under Functional Controls*. Philadelphia: University of Pennsylvania Press, 1950.

86. Roskin, Michael. "Integration of Primary Prevention in Social Work," *Social Work*, Vol. 25 (May 1980), pp. 192–197.

87. Selye, Hans. *The Stress of Life*. New York: McGraw-Hill, 1956.

88. Simon, Bernece K. "Social Casework Theory: An Overview," in Robert W. Roberts and Robert H. Nee (eds.), *Theories of Social Casework*. Chicago: University of Chicago Press, 1970, pp. 353–396.

89. Siporin, Max. "Social Treatment: A New-Old Method," *Social Casework*, Vol. 51 (July 1970), pp. 13–25.

90. Spitz, Rene. "Hospitalization: An Inquiry into the Genesis of Psychiatric Conditions in Early Childhood," in *The Psychoanalytic Study of the Child*, Vol. 1 (1945), 53–74.

91. ———. "Hospitalism: A Follow-up Report," *The Psychoanalytic Study of the Child*, Vol. 2 (1946), pp. 113–117.

92. ———. "Anaclitic Depression: An Inquiry into the Genesis of Psychiatric Conditions in Childhood," *The Psychoanalytic Study of the Child*, Vol. 2 (1946), pp. 313–342.

93. ———. *A Genetic Field Theory of Ego Formation: Its Implications for Pathology*. New York: International Universities Press, 1959.

94. ———. *The First Year of Life: A Psychoanalytic Study of Normal and Deviant Development of Object Relations*. New York: International Universities Press, 1965.

95. ———, with K. M. Wolf. "The Smiling Response: A Contribution to the Ontogenesis of Social Relations," *Genetic Psychology Monographs*, No. 34 (1946), 57–125.

96. Stamm, Isabel. "Ego Psychology in the Emerging Theoretical Base of Social Work," in Alfred J. Kahn (ed.), *Issues in American Social Work*. New York: Columbia University Press, 1959, pp. 80–109.

97. Strean, Herbert S. "Casework with Ego Fragmented Parents," *Social Casework*, Vol. 49 (April 1968), pp. 222–227.

98. Taft, Jessie. "A Conception of Growth Process Underlying Social Casework," *Social Casework*, Vol. 31 (October 1950).

99. ———. "The Relation of Function to Process in Social Casework," *Journal of Social Work Process*, Vol. 1, No. 1 (1937), pp. 1–18.

100. Towle, Charlotte. "Helping the Client to Use His Capacities and Resources," Proceedings of National Conference of Social Work, 1948. New York: Columbia U. Press, 1949, pp. 259–279.

101. ———. *The Learner in Education for the Professions*. Chicago: University of Chicago Press, 1954.

102. Turner, Francis J. (ed.). *Social Work Treatment*. New York: Free Press, 1976.

103. ——— (ed.). *Differential Diagnosis and Treatment in Social Work*, 2nd edition. New York: Free Press, 1976.

104. Vaillant, George E. *Adaptation to Life*. Boston: Little, Brown, 1977.

105. White, Robert F. "Motivation Reconsidered: The Concept of Competence," *Psychological Review*, Vol. 66 (1959), pp. 297–333.

106. ———. *Ego and Reality in Psychoanalytic Theory, (Psychological Issues)*, Vol. 2, No. 3. New York: International Universities Press, 1963.

107. ———. *Lives in Progress*. New York: Holt, Rinehart and Winston, 1966.

108. ———. "Strategies of Adaptation: An Attempt at Systematic Description," in George Coelho, David A. Hamburg, and John E. Adams (eds.), *Coping and Adaptation*. New York: Basic Books, 1974, pp. 47–68.

109. Wood, Katherine M. "The Contributions of Psychoanalysis and Ego Psychology to Social Casework," in Herbert Strean (ed.), *Social Casework: Theories in Action*. Metuchen, N.J.: Scarecrow Press, 1971, pp. 76–107.

110. Woodroofe, Kathleen. *From Charity to Social Work in England and the United States*. Toronto: University of Toronto Press, 1971.

Annotated List of Key References

BELLAK, LEOPOLD, MARVIN HURVICH, and HELEN K. GEDIMAN (eds.). *Ego Functions in Schizophrenics, Neurotics, and Normals*. New York: Wiley, 1973.
The most extensive, systematic, scholarly, and clinically relevant discussion of ego functions that exists in the literature.

COEHLO, GEORGE V., DAVID A. HAMBURG, and JOHN E. ADAMS (eds.). *Coping and Adaptation*. New York: Basic Books, 1974.
An excellent edited collection of papers that deals with how individuals cope with life situations. It also contains important theoretical and research-based discussions of the biopsychosocial nature of coping and adaptation.

ERIKSON, ERIK. "Identity and the Life Cycle," *Psychological Issues*, Vol. 1, No. 1 (1959), pp. 50–100.
This gives a systematic description of Erikson's eight life cycle stages and discusses their importance in personality development.

GOLDSTEIN, EDA G. *Ego Psychology and Social Work Practice*. New York: Free Press, 1984.
The first half of this volume discusses the history and main theoretical concepts of ego psychology. The second half traces the implications of these concepts for social work practice and includes numerous extensive case examples.

HARTMANN, HEINZ. *Ego Psychology and the Problem of Adaptation*. New York: International Universities Press, 1939.
This is a classic book that ushered in contemporary ego psychology. It discusses the concept of conflict-free ego functions and their role in adaptation.

MAHLER, MARGARET S., FRED PINE, and ANNI BERGMAN. *The Psychological Birth of the Human Infant*. New York: Basic Books, 1975.
This is the most comprehensive statement of Mahler's theory and research on separation-individuation. It is well-written and extremely useful in understanding her ideas.

WHITE, ROBERT F. *Ego and Reality in Psychoanalytic Theory (Psychological Issues)*, Vol. 2, No. 3. New York: International Universities Press, 1963.
This monograph considers the importance of mastery in early human development and is a reformulation of classical Freudian developmental theory.

CHAPTER 15

Client-Centered Theory

William Rowe

Introduction

Many of the tenets of client-centered theory have been hallmarks of the social work profession since its beginnings. The term "client" as opposed to "patient" was in popular use by social workers long before the field of psychology embraced client-centered theories. In addition, the values espoused by client-centered theorists were established and accepted by the earliest of workers, including Mary Richmond and Octavia Hill (37).

The fact that most of the theory and research in the client-centered approach has developed outside of the social work profession is somewhat of a historical anomaly. Carl Rogers developed many of the original principles of client-centered theory via the influence and observation of social work practitioners (53). The following pages present the historical origins and basic principles of client-centered theory and explore the confluence and divergence of client-centered theory with social work practice.

Historical Origins

Client-centered theory and Carl Rogers have been all but synonymous for over four decades. When an individual is so central to a thought system,

407

biographical data tend to illuminate the theory as well as the person. What is unique about Rogers's influence on client-centered theory is that even though he was its parent and chief proponent, his force was derived more from the integration and organization of existing concepts than from the generation of new ideas. This may account for the lack of authoritative rigidity and dogma that is characteristic of client-centered theory. Therefore, the persons and ideas that shaped Rogers's early development also influenced the formulation of client-centered theory.

Rogers's ideas were both an expression of and a reaction to the suburban upper-middle-class Protestant family to which he was born in 1902. His experience on the family farm, to which they moved when he was fourteen, led to an interest in agriculture and other scientific methodology and empiricism, which later became an important feature of client-centered theory (44). However, after studying agriculture at the University of Wisconsin, Rogers decided to pursue a career in the ministry and attended Union Theological Seminary in New York.

Rogers later applied the liberal religious outlook that he found at UTS to client-centered theory by stressing the importance of individuality, trust in feeling and intuition, and nonauthoritarian relationship (65). Even though Rogers was at UTS for a short time, he helped organize a study group that was reminiscent of later encounter groups.

After deciding that the ministry was too constrictive for his own professional growth and development, Rogers elected to pursue an M.A. in education and psychology at Columbia University. It was here that Rogers was significantly influenced by the pragmatic philosophy of Dewey and the educational wisdom of William Kilpatrick. Kilpatrick, as a leader of the progressive education movement, stressed learner-focused education and redefined education as a process of continuous growth (27). The connection between Kilpatrick's ideas and what was later articulated as client-centered theory is by no means coincidental.

Rogers began his professional career as a psychologist at the Rochester Child Guidance Clinic while continuing to work on his doctorate at Columbia. The academic and professional isolation he experienced in Rochester allowed him to develop his approach to working with clients in a relatively unencumbered manner. In this pragmatic creative environment, Rogers first became interested in effective therapeutic methods as preferable to psychological ideologies. After attending a two-day seminar led by Otto Rank, he found that his practice was similar to that of the Rankians. Rogers learned even more about Rank's theories from a social worker at the Rochester Clinic who had been trained at the Philadelphia School of Social Work (53).

In 1939, Rogers published *The Clinical Treatment of the Problem Child* (38), a book that drew heavily on the work of Jessie Taft and relationship therapy. Many aspects of Rankian-based relationship therapy, as expressed in this book, show up later as tenets of client-centered theory. Among these are emphasis on present experiences and circumstances, a positive valuation of the expression of feelings, a focus on individual growth and will, and a devaluation of the authority relationship in therapy. Relationship therapy continued to be developed in psychology by Rank, Taft, and C. H. Patterson and in social work by the functional school led by Taft, Virginia Robinson, and Ruth Smalley.

In "relationship therapy," Rogers found the practical affirmation of the progressive educational concepts that he had embraced earlier. There can be no mistaking the similarity between client-centered theory and the following description of therapist attitude by Taft:

> It is not so easy as it sounds to learn to ignore content and to go through it to the fundamental attitude and emotions behind it, but it is possible, if one has no need for the patient to be or feel one thing rather than another and then is free to perceive and accept what is happening even if it means rejection of the therapeutic goal. The analyst in this view has no goal, has no right to one. He is passive in the sense that he tries to keep his own ends out of the situation to the extent of being willing to leave even the "cure" so-called, to the will of the patient. (66, p. 108)

Rogers's definition and articulation of the essential elements of the counseling and psychotherapy he had practiced for a decade began at Ohio State University where he received an appointment in 1940. In the same year he attended a symposium at Teachers College at Columbia that was presided over by Goodwin Watson, who at the time was attempting to discover the essential elements of effective therapy. The model of therapy purported by Watson at this time was similar to the nondirective model that was to be the basis for Rogers's publication of *Counseling and Psychotherapy*. Rogers identified this as an emerging viewpoint for which there was a "sizable core of agreement" (39).

During his tenure at Ohio State University, Rogers reaffirmed his earlier commitment to empiricism. In his own work and that with his graduate students, he attempted to operationalize and study the process of psychotherapy. The recording and analysis of interviews and outcome research were significant innovations for the time. Those activities brought Rogers's ideas into the mainstream of psychology.

In 1945, Rogers accepted an invitation to head a new counseling center at the University of Chicago. The twelve years he spent there resulted in his wide recognition as a leading therapist, theorist, teacher, and researcher. This period also signaled the shift from the theoretical period described as nondirective to the period described as reflective or client-centered.

It was during this period that interest in Rogers's ideas developed in an ever-widening circle. "To me, as I try to understand the phenomenon, it seems that without knowing it I had expressed an idea whose time had come. It is as though a pond had become utterly still so that a pebble dropped into it sent ripples out farther and farther and farther having an influence that could not be understood by looking at the pebble" (53, p. 49). Theoreticians and practitioners from various fields, who gravitated to the principles that

Rogers espoused, advanced client-centered theories in their own disciplines. Rogers's flexibility and nonauthoritarian stance helped characterize him as the benign parent of client-centered theory in a variety of areas to be described later in this chapter.

In 1957, Rogers moved from the University of Chicago to the University of Wisconsin, where he received a joint appointment in psychiatry and psychology. In Wisconsin, Rogers attempted two monumental tasks. First, he attempted to move client-centered theory into the field of psychiatry, which to that point had maintained a stranglehold on the practice of psychotherapy. Second, he wanted to bridge the gap between clinical and experimental psychology. In the seven years he was in Wisconsin, he primarily succeeded in the first task in that he helped resolve the disciplinary jealousies and differences between psychiatry and psychology, a resolution that had ramifications far beyond Madison. Rogers's credibility in psychiatry increased at this time because of the completion of the work on schizophrenics that he, Eugene Gendlin, and others had begun in Chicago. He was frustrated by the second task, however, and resigned his appointment in psychology in 1963.

In 1964 a former student of Rogers convinced him to join the Western Behavioral Science Institute in California, where he was able to fully develop the work with encounter groups that he had begun in Chicago. Here Rogers turned his attention to "the facilitation of learning and the self-enhancement of the well functioning person" (50). In 1968 a change in leadership at the Institute brought about a change in working climate. As a result, Rogers and several staff members left to found the Center for Studies of the Person at La Jolla, California. Through the Center, which continues to operate today, Rogers has applied his approach to some perplexing problems. He has led a number of workshops on person-centered community building with diverse groups, such as Catholics and Protestants from Northern Ireland; multinational groups in Warsaw, Rome, and Venezuela; and numerous others.

Rogers continues to be an extraordinary philosopher and scientist. More than most, he lives what he professes. To date he has published more than a hundred articles and ten books that serve as a history and guide to client-centered theory. His last two books, *Carl Rogers on Personal Power* (52) and *A Way of Being* (53), move the basic nature of client-centered theory into the realm of politics and philosophy. The resulting impact of both of these ventures is, of course, yet to be tabulated.

Proponents of Client-Centered Theory

Social Work

Client-centered theory was highly acceptable to social workers from its inception. This is partly due to the fact that in its infancy, client-centered theory was more or less a conceptualization of many of the practices of "relationship therapy," which was the central force of the functional school of social casework. Many of the values that are expressed in client-centered theory are fundamental to social work practice. Rogers found himself closely aligned with the social work profession in the early part of his career and in fact held office in social work organizations at both the local and national levels while in Rochester (44). In the 1940s, Rogers and client-centered theory became identified with the field of psychology. Since social work had become entangled in the debate between the diagnostic and functional schools of casework, client-centered theory as a separate entity received less attention. Many of the principles of client-centered theory continued to be applied by social workers, but relatively little of this was reported or researched.

In the 1950s and 1960s the profession turned its attention to the development of a unified theory of social work based on the person-environment continuum. Client-centered theory to this point had appeared too person-centered to be of much use in this effort. Barrett-Lennard's description of client-centered theory and its usefulness in social work practice theory, as presented in the first two editions of *Social Work Treatment* (70, 72), was the first major reference in social work literature to Rogers's contribution (3).

In the 1970s an increased concern with effectiveness and accountability sent theorists and investigators in search of methods that could be demonstrated and evaluated. As a result there was a resurgence of interest in client-centered theory and its utility in social work since it was one of the few demonstrably effective treatment approaches. It was followed up by investigations into the value of client-centered principles in training social workers (26, 28, 57, 74). The recent applications of client-centered principles to the political process and community building may open new avenues for doing the same in social work practice.

Research

Investigators received a new impetus from the study of client-centered theory. Rogers's personal commitment to empiricism and to outcome-and-evaluation research opened new avenues in research that had previously not been considered. Rogers's objective observations of the subjective experience of counselors and clients through hypothesizing and testing were clearly innovative. While his initial interest was the systematic description of the process of psychotherapy, his attention then turned to effectiveness and outcome measures, and finally, attempts to substantiate his theoretical postulates.

John Shlien and Fred Zimring identified four stages in the development of research methods and directives in client-centered theory (60). In stage one the emphasis was on the client in the context of therapy. In stage two the emphasis expanded to cover the phenomenological aspects of perception and personality. In stage three the emphasis shifted to the study of the therapist, and in stage four all three elements merged to a focus on a process conception of psychotherapy. An extraordinary number of studies have been generated in all of these areas. Although many support the original claims, some challenge both the original assumptions and the external validity of some of the findings. Investigators such as Charles B. Truax and Robert Carkhuff, by their research, further refined, expanded, and substantiated the basic principles of client-centered theory.

The research on the core conditions of therapy is especially notable. There is considerable agreement across a number of professions, including psychology, psychiatry, social work, and nursing, that the core conditions are demonstrably linked with effective counseling practices. As such, the core conditions remain as one of the only substantive elements of effective counseling, and is supported by numerous studies.

With the possible exception of behavior therapy, no other approach has had such an intensive research orientation. This is in part attributable to the fact that, unlike most schools of therapy, client-centered theory was developed primarily in the university setting. This approach was expressed by Rogers in his statement that "client-centered therapy will at least be remembered for its willingness to take a square look at the facts" (42) and has been embraced by most of those associated with the client-centered orientation.

Counseling and Clinical Psychology

By far, client-centered theory has had its greatest impact on the field of counseling and clinical psychology. From the outset, it was clear that this approach represented a third force in American psychology. Many therapists embraced it as a desirable alternative to orthodox analysis or rigid behaviorism. The term "client" as opposed to "patient" or "subject" suggested the person's active voluntary and responsible participation. The process or "how to" of psychotherapy was described for the first time, allowing students to study and become proficient in observable counseling skills. A second attractive feature for counselors was the attention to the expression of positive humanistic values in a pragmatic approach to therapy. Finally, the continuing concern with effectiveness and outcome in the client-centered approach added to the credibility of the worker.

Many of the individuals who were influenced by Rogers and client-centered theory developed orientations of their own. Eugene Gendlin furthered the concept of "focusing" as a significant tool for change (17). Carkhuff, Bernard Berenson, and Truax (6, 11, 67) advanced the client-centered principles in greater depth and precision. Numerous others have incorporated the essential elements of client-centered theory, which will likely assure that it will continue to be a major component of the theory base of both counseling and clinical psychology.

Psychiatry

Rogers was for some time engaged in a struggle to get the field of psychiatry to recognize the value of client-centered theory to psychotherapy. Psychiatry to that point had retained a virtual stranglehold on the practice of psychotherapy. It was not until the results of his work with schizophrenics was published that psychiatry as a whole began to recognize the value of this approach (16, 43). Currently, client-centered theory is an accepted, if not widely practiced, orientation in psychiatry. It does not appear to have been developed or expanded, however, since Rogers turned his attention to working with nonpathological clients.

Some of the encounter group principles are still utilized in psychiatric settings in group psychotherapy and therapeutic communities. But, as psychiatry has increased its concern with the organic etiology of the more severe psychological impairments, there appears to be a diminishing interest in client-centered theory.

Administration and Leadership

The whole field of administration and leadership training has been noticeably affected by client-centered theory. Client-centered principles found easy application in conflict resolution, organizational behavior, and employer-employee relations. Many of the practices were utilized and expanded by those involved with National Training Laboratories in Bethel, Maine, and the numerous T-groups and sensitivity training sessions that were organized to help groups work more effectively and meaningfully (29, 36). Helen MacGregor's "Y theory" and Abraham Maslow's "Z theory" of management are both clearly reflective of the application of client-centered principles to this area (31).

Theoretical Perspectives and Basic Concepts

Theory Building

As noted earlier, Rogers was more a coordinator than a generator of the principles that are associated with client-centered theory. Because he essentially followed a deductive line of reasoning in his early investigations, his personality theory emerged ex post facto. Epistemologically, his work is best described by the term "humanistic phenomenology" (34). Rogers's "humanism" is related to his belief that humans are essentially growth-oriented, forward moving, and concerned with fulfilling their basic potentialities. He assumes that basic human nature is positive, and that if individuals are not forced into socially constructed molds, but are accepted for what they are, they will turn out "good" and live in ways that enhance both themselves and society.

Phenomenology is concerned with the individual's perceptions in determining reality. Rogers believes that knowledge of these perceptions of reality can help to explain human behavior. Objective reality is less important than our perception of reality, which is the main determinant of our behavior. The phenomenological approach has guided Rogers's approach to both therapy and research as he has struggled with the difficulty of perceiving reality through another person's eyes.

As a scientist, Rogers sees determinism as "the very foundation stone of science" (47), and hence is committed to objective study and evolution. He sees this approach as incomplete in fostering an understanding of the "inner human experience" and embraces the concept of freedom as critical to effective personal and interpersonal functioning.

Basic (Key) Concepts

Rogers gave a detailed presentation of his theories of therapy, personality, and interpersonal relationships in volume three of his *Psychology: A Study of a Science* (41). The following are nine propositions that outline the underlying personality theory for this approach.

1. "All individuals exist in a continually changing world of experience of which they are the center." The "phenomenal field," as it is sometimes called, includes all that the individual experiences. Only the individual can completely and genuinely perceive his experience of the world.
2. "Individuals react to their phenomenal field as they experience and perceive it." The perceptual field *is* reality for the individual. Individuals will react to reality as they perceive it, rather than as it may be perceived by others.
3. "The organism has one basic tendency and striving—to actualize, maintain and enhance the experiencing organism." Rogers suggests that all organic and psychological needs may be described as partial aspects of this one fundamental need.
4. "Behaviour is basically the goal-directed attempt of individuals to satisfy their needs as experienced in their phenomenal field as perceived." Reality for any given individual is that individual's perception of reality whether or not it has been confirmed. There is no absolute reality that takes precedence over an individual's perceptions.
5. "The best vantage point for understanding behaviour is from the internal frame of reference of the individual." This includes the full

range of sensations, perceptions, meanings, and memories available to the conscious mind. Accurate empathy is required to achieve this understanding.

6. "Most ways of behaving adopted by the individual are consistent with the individual's concept of self." The concept of self is basic to client-centered theory. Self-concept is an organized internal view consisting of the individual's perceptions of himself alone, himself in relation to others, himself in relation to his environment and the values attached to these perceptions. Self-concept is seen as an ever-evolving entity.

7. "The incongruence that often occurs between an individual's conscious wishes and his behaviour is the result of a split between the individual's self-concept and his experiences." As the individual gains an awareness of self, he develops a need for positive regard and positive self-regard. When the individual feels loved or not loved by significant others, he develops positive or negative self-regard.

8. "When there is incongruence between the individual's self-concept and experiences with others, a state of anxiety results." This anxiety is often the result of the incongruence between the ideal and real self. To lower an individual's anxiety the self-concept must become more congruent with the individual's actual experiences.

9. "The fully functioning individual is open to all experiences, exhibiting no defensiveness." Such a person fully accepts himself and can exhibit unconditional positive regard for others. The self-concept is congruent with the experiences and the individual is able to assert his basic actualizing tendency.

With regard to motivation, Rogers believes the organism is an active initiator that exhibits a directional tendency (52). He agrees with White's description of motivation as more than simple stasis: "Even when its primary needs are satisfied and its homeostatic chores are done, an organism is alive, active and up to something" (77). Rogers affirmed that there is a central source of energy in the organism that is concerned with enhancement as well as maintenance (52).

Some of the most significant features of Rogers's personality theory from the perspective of therapy are:

Assumption: We behave in accordance with our perception of reality. In light of this, in order to understand the client's problem, we must fully understand how she perceives it.

Assumption: We are motivated by an innate primary drive to self-actualization. The individual will automatically develop her potential under favorable conditions. These conditions can be established in therapy and the stance of the therapist must, as a result, be nondirective.

Assumption: The individual has a basic need for love and acceptance. This translates into a focus on relationship and the communication of empathy, respect, and authenticity by the therapist.

Assumption: The individual's self-concept is dependent upon the nature of the acceptance and respect she experiences from others. The client's self-concept can be changed by her experiencing unconditional positive regard in therapy.

Approach to Therapy

Goal

The basic goal of client-centered therapy is to release an already existing capacity for self-actualization in a potentially competent individual.

Underlying Assumptions

1. The individual has the capacity to guide, regulate, direct, and control himself providing certain conditions exist.
2. The individual has the potential to understand what is in his life that is related to his distress and anxiety.
3. The individual has the potential to reorganize himself in such a way as not only to eliminate his distress and anxiety, but also to experience self-fulfillment and happiness.

The Conditions of Therapy

In 1957, Rogers postulated what he believed to be the elements that were necessary and sufficient for a positive outcome in therapy. They were:

1. that the therapist be genuine and congruent in the relationship;
2. that the therapist be experiencing unconditional positive regard toward the client;
3. that the therapist be experiencing empathic understanding of the client's internal frame of reference; and
4. that the client perceive these conditions at least to a minimal degree.

These core conditions, as they came to be known, have been linked with positive outcome in therapy for a wide variety of clients in various settings (7, 11, 68). Additional dimensions of the therapist, such as concreteness, confrontation, self-disclosure, and immediacy, have been recognized as important (6). While these also appear to be important aspects of the helping process, there is not as yet the same degree of substantiation as there is for the core conditions.

Process of Therapy

The process of therapy and counseling in the client-centered approach is basically:

1. The therapist and client establish a mutual counseling contract.
2. The therapist presents an attitude in the relationship characterized by the core conditions.
3. The client's greatest capacity for problem-solving is released because he is free from the anxiety and doubts that were blocking his potential.

It is difficult to make a comprehensive statement about client-centered therapy because, true to its basic philosophy, it has been changing, evolving, and actualizing since its inception. Table 15–1, adapted from David Cole and J. T. Hart and T. M. Tomlinson (12, 24), illustrates some of the major points associated with those changes over the past forty years.

The person-centered developments referred to in the table are more indicative of Rogers's orientation since 1970. Some proponents of client-centered theory have continued to develop and refine the microlevel counseling aspects. Carkhuff and his associates have developed specific training programs where the novice counselor first learns how to discriminate between high-level responses (understanding and direction) and low-level responses (little understanding or direction). Second, the student counselor learns how to communicate high levels of accurate empathy, authenticity, and positive regard. Some examples of these are (8):

Client: I don't know if I'm right or wrong feeling the way I do, but I find myself withdrawing from people. I don't seem to socialize and play their stupid little games any more.

Counselor:

Low: Friendships like this are precarious at best.

Medium: You're really down because they won't let you be yourself.

High: You feel really bad because you can't be yourself and you want to be. The first thing you might do is spend a little time exploring who you are without them.

Client: Sometimes I question my adequacy of raising three boys, especially the baby. Well, I call him the baby because he's the last. I can't have any more, so I know I kept him a baby longer than the others. He won't let anyone else do things for him. Only Mommy!

Counselor:

Low: Could you tell me—have you talked with your husband about this?

Medium: You feel concern because your son is so demanding.

Table 15-1. The Development of Client-Centered Therapy

Therapy	Therapist Goals	Therapist Roles
Nondirective cognitive orientation (insight) 1940–1950	(1) Create an atmosphere of permission and acceptance (2) Help client clarify thoughts and feelings rather than interpret for him (3) Help client increase knowledge of self	(1) Passive, nonjudgmental listening (2) Empathic (3) Nonconfronting (4) Nonsharing of self (5) Feedback objective, rephrasing, repeating, clarifying
Client-centered or reflective emotional orientation (self-concept) 1950–1957	(1) Develop the conditions necessary for and sufficient for constructive personality change (2) Communicate to client •empathy •unconditional positive regard •genuineness	(1) Active listening (2) Accurate, empathic (3) Nonconfronting (4) Sharing of self (5) Noninterpretive (6) Feedback, subjective indicating how therapist believes client feels
Experiential existential/ encounter orientation (humanistic) 1957–1970	(1) Establishing therapeutic relationship (2) Reflecting client experiencing (3) Expressing therapist experiencing (4) Client growth as a unique individual and as a group member	(1) Active listening (2) Accurate empathy (3) Confronting (4) Sharing an authentic friendship (5) Interpreting if appropriate (6) Feedback is subjective prizing, loving, caring
Person-centered •community, •institution •political orientation (militant humanism) 1970 to present	Humanize and facilitate the actualization of communities, institutions, and political systems	(1) Apply effective components of person-centered approach to such organizations (2) Assert humanistic values (3) Quiet revolutionary

High: You're disappointed in yourself because you haven't helped him develop fully and you really want to. Now a first step might be to design a little program for you and for him.

Client-centered theory can no longer be described or evaluated in a singular fashion. So many individuals and groups have embraced the approach that the underlying philosophy and principles are evident even in approaches that are not specifically identified as client-centered. For the beginning counselor or therapist, client-centered theory still appears to offer a comprehensive approach. In a recent refinement of this approach, Angelo Boy and Gerald Pine offered the following reasons for utilizing client theory in counseling (5).

Client-centered counseling:

possesses a positive philosophy of the person
articulates propositions regarding human personality and behavior
possesses achievable human goals for the client
possesses a definition of the counselor's role within the counseling relationship
has research evidence supporting its effectiveness
is comprehensive and can be applied beyond the one-to-one counseling relationship
is clear and precise regarding application
has an expansive intellectual and attitudinal substance
focuses on the client as a person rather than on the client's problem
focuses on the attitudes of the counselor rather than on techniques
provides the counselor with a systematic response pattern
provides flexibility for the counselor to go beyond reflection of feelings
can be individualized to the particular needs of a client
enables client behavior to change in a natural sequence of events
can draw from the process components of other theories of counseling and human development

Application in Social Work

Person-Environment Continuum

Not surprisingly, client-centered theory is most often identified with the person end of the person-environment continuum. The concept of self is so important to Rogers's view of personality that it is often referred to as self-psychology or self-theory. Rogers views human nature as growth-oriented and positive and believes that maladaptation is generally more a problem in the environment than one in the person. In most cases client-centered therapy is predicated on the belief that the client's innate self-actualizing tendencies will flourish if the conditions are right. This view recognized the importance of the environment and places the locus of change in that area. Essentially, the environment should be altered or adjusted to suit humans, rather than the reverse.

This view has received limited acceptance in social work. Most social work approaches afford equal importance to both aspects of the person-environment continuum, at least in theory. In practice, a great deal of social work activity is directed toward helping the individual adjust to society. Client-centered theory is at odds with both of these points.

Values

The valuing process has been discussed at some length in client-centered theory and Rogers has hypothesized that "there is an organismic commonality of value directions" and "these common value directions are of such kinds as to enhance the development of the individual himself or others in his community and to make for the survival and evolution of his species" (45). This positive and hopeful view of human beings is by and large acceptable to a profession like social work that is dedicated to the enhancement of social relationships and functioning.

In addition to being concerned with the "organismic valuing process" client-centered theory professes both general and specific attitudinal values. In its early stages, client-centered theory was essentially neutral regarding values. Over the years it has progressed to the point where person-centered or humanistic values are asserted (11), such as the following (5, 45, 52):

1. The counselor who intends to be of service to a client must value the client's integral worth as a person.
2. Responsible action occurs within the context of a respect for the dignity and worth of others.
3. The counselor who values the client has a fundamental respect for the client's freedom to know, shape, and determine personal attitudes and behavior.
4. The client possesses free will; she can be the determiner of a personal destiny.
5. A person's free functioning not only tends toward a development of the self, but also includes one's responsibility to other persons.
6. The client enhances the self by fulfilling obligations to herself and others.
7. The client begins to relate to others with a sense of personal responsibility and ethical behavior.
8. Love and peace are basic strivings and must be advanced during one's lifetime.

These values are universally expressed and professed in social work. A belief in the fundamental dignity and worth of an individual is similar to 1 and 2. Social work's commitment to self-determination is captured in 3 and 4. The importance of social responsibility and reciprocity has also become a more broadly accepted value (13, 63) and is seen in 5, 6, and 7. Number 8 (a commitment to the advancement of love and peace) is a value that few social workers would reject, although as a value it is not articulated and asserted by the mainstream in the profession as yet.

The major values of the client-centered approach appear to be closely aligned with those expressed in social work. Some of this is based on the similarity of historical roots, but some is also due to the cross-cultural, time-tested effectiveness of these values. In other words, they appear to be functional as well as philosophical.

Social Work with Individuals

Client-centered theory has found both acceptance and expression in social work with individuals or "social casework." Client-centered theory is most closely aligned with the "functional" approach to social casework although there are areas of convergence and divergence with the other major approaches. This is understandable given Rogers's involvement with social work and the functional school in the 1930s.

PSYCHOSOCIAL HISTORY.   The place of a psychosocial history in casework, firmly established by Mary Richmond (37), for the most part has been broadly accepted by the profession. Client-centered theory has historically placed little emphasis on this aspect of the helping process. In applying the client-centered approach narrowly, workers would only concern themselves with history-taking to the degree to which the client was willing to present it. A broader interpretation of client-centered theory would also promote history-taking since a full appreciation and credible acceptance of the client can be better realized when the worker is cognizant of both the past and the present.

History-taking is one of the areas that must be reconsidered if client-centered theory is to find acceptance in social casework.

DIAGNOSIS.   Another area of divergence has been the place of diagnosis in casework. Client-centered theory has been fundamentally opposed to diagnostic classification. This theory's belief in the uniqueness of the person disallows the categorization, classification, and dehumanized labeling of individuals. Diagnosis has been and continues to be an important concept in social casework (25, 69, 71) where it is generally viewed as a dynamic and functional process. Smalley's approach, where the worker and client are both fully considered in the diagnosis, is most reminiscent of the client-centered approach.

Rogers has demonstrated that the client-centered approach is effective with a variety of diagnostic categories including schizophrenics and psychotics (53, 54). This research, coupled with the person-centered philosophy, has established some of the rationale for rejecting the concept of diagnosis.

The client-centered approach in social work need not reject this concept wholly, and may indeed discover that client-centered theory applied within the diagnostic framework can increase its effectiveness. This latter approach would undoubtedly be more acceptable to social caseworkers.

THE HELPING INTERVIEW.   By far the greatest contribution client-centered theory has made to social casework has been in the area of the helping interview. Most approaches to social casework recognize the utility of the "core conditions of helping." These conditions of communicating accurate empathy, authenticity, and positive regard in the helping interview have been demonstrated as effective by Truax, Carkhuff, and Sandra T. Mitchell. In the 1970s, social work educators introduced training in the core conditions to the social work curriculum (15, 23, 75). While these training procedures are not as yet widely accepted, they have generated a great deal of interest and experimentation (14, 28, 57, 58, 75).

The core conditions appear to be a good base from which to begin skill development in the helping interview. In order to be more broadly useful and acceptable to social caseworkers, they need to be expanded and adapted to fit the wide variety of casework situations and circumstances.

Social Work with Families

Client-centered principles have had a wide impact on the whole area of working with children and families. Rogers, in his doctoral dissertation and his first book, focused on therapy with children (38) and found it necessary to include the entire family. A few years, after Rogers published *Counseling and Psychotherapy* (39), Virginia Axline presented a work that drew from his nondirective principles and from the relationship therapy orientation of Taft (66) and Allen (1). Axline's approach to nondirective play therapy included the basic principles of acceptance, relationship, freedom of expression, and freedom of behavior (2). Others, like Clark Moustakas (33) expanded and developed these principles to help make the client-centered approach a significant force in child therapy.

By the late 1950s, therapists were increasingly including parents and family members in the counseling context and applying client-centered principles to working with families. Guerney described a process of filial therapy where parents were taught client-centered skills so they could deal with their children themselves (21, 22). Some explored the development of self-concept in families (73) while others used client-centered principles in working with couples (50).

While social workers have by and large found the client-centered applications to working with families useful and philosophically acceptable, they have essentially been overshadowed by the concurrent developments in the application of systems theory to both family work and social work. These two schools of thought appear to be fundamentally divergent in terms of basic assumptions, but may prove to be more compatible in actual practice than has been demonstrated to date.

Social Work with Groups

Group work, in the client-centered tradition, has received sporadic acceptance in social work circles. Social work had a rich history in group work long before client-centered principles were applied to this area. The major application of client-centered principles in group work has been through the encounter group or T-group, as developed by Rogers (48). The encounter group began in the 1940s with Rogers at the University of Chicago and Kurt Lewin in Bethel, Maine. Rogers viewed the intensive group experience as an important vehicle for therapeutic growth and attitudinal change, whereas Lewin focused on the improvement of human relations and interpersonal interaction.

Rogers noted the following as central to the process of change in intensive group experience (48):

climate of safety
expression of immediate feeling, reaction
mutual trust
change in attitudes and behavior
understanding and openness
feedback
innovation, change, and risk
transfer of learning to other situations

Many of the above are seen as essential elements of mutual aid in social group work (62). As well, the following description of the goals of the therapist-leader (4) are not incompatible with the orientation of many social group workers:

1. the facilitation of group members to take responsibility for themselves in whatever way is realistically possible;
2. the clarification and solution of problems and conflicts by a process of self-understanding and the development of an empathic understanding of others;
3. recognition of the client as she is and recognition of her reality as she sees it;
4. attempts to offer an attitude that is nonjudgmental in order to facilitate exploratory and self-reflective behavior in the client; and
5. recognition of the significance of maintaining as high a degree as possible of clarity about the leader's own views, feelings, and reactions while he is in the therapeutic relationship.

The expression of the core conditions by group leaders has been shown to have a positive impact on increasing client self-exploration (35).

Given the therapeutic aim of encounter groups, and their focus on the individual in group, they are most readily identified with the remedial model of social group work. Many of the underlying principles and some of the techniques are more reminiscent of the reciprocal model of social group work. Some aspects, such as adherence to democratic principles, are aligned with social group work in general.

Social Work with Communities

The more recent developments in client-centered theory have included an interest and involvement in the concept of community. Rogers has applied the fundamental principles of client-centered theory to both community concerns and community development. Much of this has been initiated from the Center for Studies of the Person through workshops and learning laboratories. Some concurrent efforts have continued at the University of Chicago, where Gendlin and others have established a therapeutic community called "Changes," which is based on client-centered principles (53). The experiments in community have included work with a wide variety of neighborhoods, cultures, religions, and political situations.

In the tradition of the client-centered orientation, writers have first concerned themselves with establishing propositions that describe the basic assumptions concerning communities. In his chapter on the client-centered system in the edition of this volume, Barrett-Lennard (3) postulated: "A well functioning community would be an open system in interface with other systems . . . continually in process . . . and characterized by an organismic egalitarianism." William Rogers suggests that, from the client-centered viewpoint, "individuals seek a community of belonging, understanding and mutual support that will enhance the actualization of life," and that "persons within a community are potentially better able to understand and articulate the identity and hopes of that community than are persons from outside" (56). William Rogers moves to the next phase by considering the necessary steps in the process of social change. Some of the client-centered principles highlighted in his approach are:

> the importance of listening deeply to the needs and concerns of individuals and groups within the constituent communities
> the facilitation of community self-perception
> the recognition and encouragement of indigenous leadership
> the facilitation of the communication among divergent groups
> the identification of community goals.

Among the approaches to social work with communities, client-centered theory is most clearly aligned with the principles of locality development. The client-centered approach to community development articulated by William Rogers is both astute and pragmatic. As such, it is generally more acceptable to social workers than the more esoteric, unstructured offerings that have developed out of such places as the Center for Studies of the Person and Changes. Many community workers in social work find the community-building techniques developed and experimented with in the person-centered approach to be useful in adjunct with their own theories. To this end, the person-centered approach affords an important laboratory for exploring different aspects of community building. Curiously, it is possible that the person-centered approach as it has evolved may be too value laden for most social work community organizers to embrace.

Social Work Research

Social work research has only recently begun to be viewed as critical to the advancement of the profession and its activities. The challenges of investigating and evaluating this multifaceted and loosely conceived profession have been many. The research methods employed in client-centered research appear to be particularly adaptable to the needs of social work research. The stages of development in client-centered research are closely aligned with social work concerns.

The first level of development in client-centered theory consisted of the recording of cases, the definition of concepts, the development of objective measures of the concepts, the application of the concepts, and the establishment of the relationships existing among the concepts. This approach has been useful in social work research when workers attempt to quantify and evaluate practice as seen in Larry Shulman's study on casework skill (61). It is recognized that much of what has been seen as practice wisdom in social work could be better understood and utilized if it were subjected to this kind of rigor (63).

Another stage of research in client-centered theory that is also directly useful to social work is the outcomes research. Through the use of creative investigative techniques, including the Q-sort, numerous effectiveness and outcome studies have been done. Social work researchers have become increasingly concerned with the same issues in light of increased demands for accountability. As social workers become increasingly able to define and operationalize their objectives, these research techniques will be useful.

Research in client-centered theory has developed along phenomenological lines and eventually evolved into a study of process. In social work, process is generally seen as equally important as goals or outcomes. For this reason it is likely that many of the research techniques developed in client-centered theory can be tailored to the needs of social work research. Progress has been rapid in client-centered theory because it has been well defined and conceptualized and there has been enormous commitment to empirical research and validation. As these efforts continue in social work, similar research techniques can be employed.

Social Work Administration

For many years, Rogers has viewed the tenets of client-centered theory as applicable to all human interaction. In *Carl Rogers on Personal Power* (52) he describes how these features have been successfully applied to agencies and organizations. Rogers provides examples of how person-centered approaches have resulted in greater productivity, as well as greater career and personal satisfaction. In this approach, leadership is characterized by influence and impact, rather than power and control. The person-centered administrator, where possible, gives autonomy to persons and groups, stimulates independence, facilitates learning, delegates responsibility, encourages self-evaluation, and finds rewards in the development and achievements of others (52).

Person-centered theories of administration did not originate with Rogers. A person-centered orientation has been expounded in administration circles since the early part of this century (59). The major contribution of Rogers has once again been the operationalization and application of the concepts within an organized framework.

Social workers have found many of the person-centered aspects of administration to be compatible with their values. There has been a great deal of interest in and experimentation with participatory management approaches (32, 59) and equality-based supervisory practices (30). Rogers's approach to administration, with its antiauthoritarianism, has limits in its broad application in social work. The principles as they are applied and refined, however, may mature into an acceptable, coherent, and functional administrative orientation.

Conclusions

There are numerous areas of convergence and compatibility between client-centered theory and social work practice, as has been born out by the material in the preceding pages. Given the simularity in philosophy and practice, it is in some ways curious that client-centered theory is not more accepted by the profession. For example, not long ago Howard Goldstein (18) published an article entitled "Starting Where the Client Is" in which he competently articulated the value of this long-time social work adage. It is odd that he made only passing reference to Rogers and client-centered theory considering the amount of theory and research available to support his thesis. The following points may help to illuminate this oddity.

Rogers presents what many believe is a naive and one-sided view of human nature. Many social workers support this positive view of humanity in theory, but decades of practice with some of the more disturbing problems in society (poverty, child abuse and neglect, wife battering) diminishes enthusiasm for such beliefs. Much of client-centered theory was developed in controlled university settings, whereas the social worker's environs are often far more problematic.

Second, most of the research validating the concepts has taken the expressions of the clients at face value and gives little attention to unconscious processes. Many social workers firmly believe in the importance of understanding unconscious motivations in clients and have experienced the usefulness of this understanding in both assessment and intervention phases of work.

Another area of divergence between client-centered theory and social work pertains to the concept of authority. Rogers takes an extreme position against authority and sees it as an essentially destructive component of relationships. While many social workers deemphasize authority, the major concern is more often how to make positive use of it, as opposed to simply denying its existence. Not all client-centered therapists are as adamant about this issue as Rogers, and some of the more recent contributors have included, rather than rejected, the concept of authority relationships (5).

The development of client-centered theory in many ways is a microcosm of the development of the social work profession. Both began with the worker-client interaction and progressed to include groups, families, organizations, communities, and political systems. The client-centered metaphor is highly appropriate for both theory and practice in a profession that has traditionally attempted to encompass both science and compassion. In essence, both the organizing metaphor and the research practices of client-centered theory are valuable to social work. It is essential that professional boundaries do not curtail that value, and that the recent movement toward reconsideration of the client-centered contribution in social work be expanded.

References

1. Allen, F. H. *Psychotherapy with Children*. New York: Norton, 1942.
2. Axline, Virginia M. *Play Therapy*. Boston. Houghton Mifflin, 1947.
3. Barrett-Lennard, G. T. "The Client-Centered System Unfolding," in Francis J. Turner (ed.), *Social Work Treatment*, 2nd edition. New York: Free Press, 1979.
4. Beck, A. M. "Phases in the Development of Structure in Therapy and Encounter Groups," in D. A. Wexler and L. M. Rice (eds.), *Innovations in Client-Centered Therapy*. New York: Wiley, 1974.
5. Boy, Angelo V., and Gerald J. Pine. *Client-Centered Counseling: A Renewal*. Boston: Allyn and Bacon, 1982.
6. Carkhuff, Robert R. *Helping and Human Relations*, Vols. 1 and 2. New York: Holt, Rinehart and Winston, 1969.
7. ———. *The Development of Human Resources*. New York: Holt, Rinehart and Winston, 1971.
8. ———. *Counselor-Counselee and Audio-Tape handbook*. Amherst, Mass.: Human Resource Development Press, 1976.
9. Carkhuff, Robert R., and Bernard G. Berenson. *Beyond Counseling and Therapy*. New York: Holt, Rinehart and Winston, 1967.
10. ———. *Teaching as Treatment*. Amherst, Mass.: Human Resource Development Press, 1976.
11. ———. *Beyond Counseling and Therapy*, 2nd edition. New York: Holt, Rinehart and Winston, 1977.
12. Cole, David R. *Helping*. Toronto: Butterworths, 1982.
13. Compton, B., and B. Gallaway. *Social Work Processes*, revised edition. Homewood, Ill.: Dorsey Press, 1979.
14. Fischer, J. "Training for Effective Therapeutic Practice," *Psychotherapy: Theory, Research, and Practice*, Vol. 12 (1974), pp. 118–123.

15. ——. *Effective Casework Practice*. New York: McGraw-Hill, 1978.

16. Gendlin, Eugene T. "Client-Centered Developments and Work with Schizophrenics," *Journal of Counseling Psychology*, Vol. 9, No. 3 (1962), pp. 205–211.

17. ——. *Focusing*. New York: Everest House, 1978.

18. Goldstein, Howard. "Starting Where the Client Is," *Social Casework*, Vol. 64 (May, 1983), pp. 267–275.

19. Gordon, T. *Parent Effectiveness Training*. New York: Wyden, 1970.

20. ——, and N. Burch. *T.E.T. Teacher Effectiveness Training*. New York: Wyden, 1974.

21. Guerney, B. G. "Filial Therapy: Description and Rationale," *Journal of Consulting Psychology*, Vol. 28 (1964), pp. 304–310.

22. ——, L. F. Guerney, and M. P. Andronico. "Filial Therapy," in J. T. Hart and T. M. Tomlinson (eds.), *New Directions in Client-Centered Therapy*. Boston: Houghton Mifflin, 1970, pp. 372–386.

23. Hammond, D. C., D. H. Hepworth, and V. G. Smith. *Improving Therapeutic Communication*. San Francisco: Jossey-Bass, 1978.

24. Hart, J. T. "The Development of Client-Centered Therapy" in J. T. Hart and T. M. Tomlinson (eds.), *New Directions in Client-Centered Therapy*. Boston: Houghton Mifflin, 1970.

25. Hollis, Florence. *Casework: A Psychosocial Therapy*, 2nd edition. New York: Random House, 1972.

26. Keefe, T. "Empathy: The Critical Skill," *Social Work*, Vol. 21 (1976), pp. 10–14.

27. Kilpatrick, W. H. *Foundation of Method*. New York: Macmillan, 1926.

28. Larsen, J. A. "A Comparative Study of Traditional and Competency-Based Methods of Teaching Interpersonal Skills in Social Work Education." Doctoral dissertation, University of Utah, 1975.

29. Lewin, K. *Field Theory in Social Science*. New York: Harper, 1951.

30. Mandell, B. "The Equality Revolution and Supervision," *Journal of Education for Social Work*, Winter 1973.

31. Maslow, Abraham. *The Farther Reaches of Human Nature*. New York: Viking, 1971.

32. McMahon, Peter C. *Management by Objectives in the Social Services*. Ottawa: Canadian Association of Social Workers, 1981.

33. Moustakas, Clark E. *Children in Play Therapy*. New York: McGraw-Hill, 1953.

34. Nye, Robert D. *Three Views of Man*. Monterey, Calif.: Brooks/Cole Publishing, 1975.

35. O'Hare, C. "Counseling Group Process: Relationship Between Counselor and Client Behaviours in the Helping Process," *The Journal for Specialists in Group Work*, 1979.

36. Pfeiffer, J., and J. A. Jones. *Handbook of Structured Experiences for Human Relations Training*. Iowa City, Iowa: University Assoc., 1971.

37. Richmond, Mary E. *Social Diagnosis*. New York: Russell Sage Foundation, 1917.

38. Rogers, Carl R. *The Clinical Treatment of the Problem Child*. Boston: Houghton Mifflin, 1939.

39. ———. *Counseling and Psychotherapy.* Boston: Houghton Mifflin, 1942.

40. ———. "The Necessary and Sufficient Conditions of Therapeutic Personality Change," *Journal of Counseling Psychology,* Vol. 21 (1957), pp. 95–103.

41. ———. "A Theory of Therapy, Personality and Interpersonal Relationships, as Developed in the Client-Centered Framework," in S. Koch (ed.), *Psychology: A Study of Science,* Vol. 3. New York: McGraw-Hill, 1959, pp. 184–256.

42. ———. "Significant Trends in the Client-Centered Orientation," *Progress in Clinical Psychology,* Vol. 4 (1960), pp. 85–99.

43. ———. "A Theory of Psychotherapy with Schizophrenics and a Proposal for Its Empirical Investigation," in J. G. Dawson, H. K. Stone, and N. P. Dellis (eds.), *Psychotherapy with Schizophrenics.* Baton Rouge: Louisiana State University Press, 1961, pp. 3–19.

44. ———. *On Becoming a Person.* Boston: Houghton Mifflin, 1961.

45. ———. "Toward a Modern Approach to Values: The Valuing Process in the Mature Person," *Journal of Abnormal and Social Psychology,* Vol. 68, No. 2 (1964), pp. 160–167.

46. ——— (ed.). *The Therapeutic Relationship and Its Impact: A Study of Psychotherapy with Schizophrenics.* Madison: University of Wisconsin Press, 1967.

47. ———. *Freedom to Learn.* Columbus, Ohio: Merrill, 1969.

48. ———. *Carl Rogers on Encounter Groups.* New York: Harper and Row, Inc., 1970.

49. ———. *Becoming Partners: Marriage and Its Alternatives.* New York: Delacorte, 1972.

50. ———. "My Personal Growth," in Arthur Burton et al. (eds.), *Twelve Therapists.* San Francisco: Jossey-Bass, 1972, pp. 28–77.

51. ———. "Client-Centered and Symbolic Perspectives on Social Change: A Schematic Model," in D. A. Wexler and L. M. Rice (eds.), *Innovations in Client-Centered Therapy.* New York: Wiley, 1974.

52. ———. *Carl Rogers on Personal Power.* New York: Dell, 1977.

53. ———. *A Way of Being.* Boston: Houghton Mifflin, 1980.

54. Rogers, Carl R., E. J. Gendlin, D. J. Kiesler, and C. B. Truax (eds.). *The Therapeutic Relationship and Its Impact: A Study of Psychotherapy with Schizophrenics.* Madison: University of Wisconsin Press, 1967.

55. Rogers, Carl R., and D. Stevens. *Person to Person.* New York: Pocket Books, 1975.

56. Rogers, William R. "Client-Centered and Symbolic Perspectives on Social Change: A Schematic Model," in D. A. Wexler and L. N. Rice (eds.), *Innovations in Client-Centered Therapy.* New York: Wiley, 1974.

57. Rowe, William. "Laboratory Training in the Baccalaureate Curriculum," *Canadian Journal of Social Work Education,* Vol. 7, No. 3 (1981), pp. 93–104.

58. ———. "An Integrated Skills Laboratory," *Review '83,* 1983, pp. 161–169.

59. Schatz, Harry A. "Staff Involvement in Agency Administration," in Harry A. Schatz (ed.), *Social Work Administration.* New York: Council on Social Work Education, 1970.

60. Shlien, John M., and Fred M. Zimring. "Research Directives and Methods in Client-Centered Therapy" in J. T. Hart and T. M. Tomlinson (eds.), *New Directions in Client-Centered Therapy.* Boston: Houghton Mifflin, 1970.

61. Shulman, Larry. "A Study of Practice Skills," *Social Work*, Vol. 23, No. 4 (July 1978), pp. 274–281.

62. ———. *The Skills of Helping.* Itasca, Ill.: Peacock, 1979.

63. Siporin, Max. *Introduction to Social Work Practice.* New York: Macmillan, 1975.

64. Smalley, Ruth E. *Theory for Social Work Practice.* New York: Columbia University Press, 1967.

65. Sollod, Robert N. "Carl Rogers and the Origins of Client-Centered Therapy," *Professional Psychology*, Vol. 4, No. 1 (1978), pp. 93–104.

66. Taft, Jessie. *The Dynamics of Therapy in a Controlled Relationship.* New York: Harper, 1951.

67. Truax, C. B., and Robert R. Carkhuff. *Toward Effective Counseling and Psychotherapy: Training and Practice.* Chicago: Aldine, 1967.

68. Truax, C. B., and K. M. Mitchell. "Research on Certain Therapist Interpersonal Skills in Relation to Process and Outcome," in A. E. Bergin and S. L. Garfield (eds.), *Handbook of Psychotherapy and Behavior Change: An Empirical Analysis.* New York: Wiley, 1971, pp. 299–344.

69. Turner, Francis J. *Differential Diagnosis and Treatment in Social Work.* New York: Free Press, 1968.

70. ——— (ed.). *Social Work Treatment.* New York: Free Press, 1974.

71. ———. *Differential Diagnosis and Treatment in Social Work*, 2nd edition. New York: Free Press, 1976.

72. ———(ed.). *Social Work Treatment*, 2nd edition. New York: Free Press, 1979.

73. Van der Veen, F., et al. "Relationships Between the Parents' Concept of the Family and Family Adjustment," *American Journal of Orthopsychiatry*, Vol. 34 (January 1964), pp. 45–55.

74. Wallman, G. "The Impact of the First Year of Social Work Education on Student Skill in Communication of Empathy and Discrimination of Effective Responses." Doctoral dissertation, Adelphi University, 1980.

75. Wells, R. A. "Training in Facilitative Skills," *Social Work*, Vol. 20 (1975), pp. 242–243.

76. Wexler, D. A., and L. M. Rice (eds.). *Innovations in Client-Centered Therapy.* New York: Wiley, 1974.

77. White, Robert W. "Motivation Reconsidered: The Concept of Competence," *Psychological Review*, Vol. 66 (1959), p. 315.

Annotated Listing of Key References

BOY, ANGELO V., and GERALD J. PINE. *Client-Centered Counseling: A Renewal.* Boston: Allyn and Bacon, 1982.
In this book, the authors focus on the current application of client-centered theory to individual and group counseling. Boy and Pine recognize the shift of most person-centered authors to applications in teaching, administration, community building, race relations, and conflict resolution. They offer a refinement of the original client-centered counseling principles and renewed possibilities for individual and group application. In addition, Boy and Pine critically discuss the counseling concerns of personality theory, values, accountability, evaluation, and counselor education.

CARKHUFF, ROBERT R., and BERNARD G. BERENSON. *Beyond Counseling and Therapy*, 2nd edition. New York: Holt, Rinehart and Winston, 1977.
Carkhuff and Berenson have significantly advanced client-centered theory through both clinical and research efforts. This book supplies a comprehensive statement of the research and clinical observations that support their view of the client-centered model of helping. The authors compare the client-centered approach with other major helping theories and show the rationale for their particular beliefs. In addition, the philosophy, values, and content of a training approach for counselors are outlined.

FISCHER, J. *Effective Casework Practice.* New York: McGraw-Hill, 1978.
In this book, Fischer presents an approach to casework that bridges the gap between research and practice. He describes an eclectic approach that consists of empirically validated helping models. Fischer's "integrative model" includes components of behavior modification, cognitive procedures, and the core conditions of helping. A model for training and learning the core conditions is presented. Fischer's book represents one of the few significant references to client-centered theory in social work literature.

ROGERS, CARL R. *On Becoming a Person.* Boston: Houghton Mifflin, 1961.
This is a classic publication that helped establish Rogers and client-centered theory as a major force in American psychology. Rogers articulates the culmination of three decades of theory development, clinical practice, and clinical research as a cohesive approach to helping and personal growth. As such, it is an excellent first reading for individuals interested in the client-centered approach.

ROGERS, CARL R. *Carl Rogers on Personal Power.* New York: Dell, 1977.
In this book Rogers describes the impact of the person-centered approach on relationships, education, administration, and political systems. He reiterates the theoretical foundation of this approach and shows how it translates into a base for political activity and what he terms the "quiet revolution." Rogers details the principles of the person-centered approach and describes a number of examples of these principles in practice, in the workplace and in the political arena. In conclusion, Rogers offers some humanistic alternatives to polarized conflict and entrenched political structures.

CHAPTER 16

Family Treatment

Sonya L. Rhodes

Introduction

Family therapy is a method of psychotherapy of considerable importance to current social work practice. It is based on a knowledge and understanding of the family as a social system in which family members relate to each other in patterned ways that can be observed and understood. In troubled and disturbed families such patterns are maintained at the expense of the growth and development of individual members. Thus, a troubled family member is viewed as a part of a family system, and his individual problems are best understood as a means of aiding the family to maintain its equilibrium at a manageable level.

A therapist must understand how the family functions as a system. Each individual member of the family, and each subsystem of the family, must be seen as a component of the entire family system. Families are viewed as open systems in which members enter and exit over the course of the life cycle, thereby altering the boundaries of the family. Experience has shown that most families are best understood from a three-generational perspective of interlocking reciprocal and repetitive relationships.

Understanding of how these members interact is used to shape inter-ventions that aim at influencing the functioning of the family as a group as well as each individual family member. The family may be treated as a whole group or as smaller subgroups (subsystems) with or without extended family. At times, grandparents or sibling systems are targeted in a designated phase of treatment. As well, individual family members may be the focal point of a family-oriented treatment as the reciprocal and interactive effect family members have on one another is addressed. Decisions about whom to include and when to include them are based on an understanding of family dynamics, a clarification of treatment focus, and long- and short-term goals.

Historical Origins

Family systems theory has not evolved from the contributions of any one major figure, but from efforts and experimentations, which occurred simultaneously in different parts of the country, out of which has emerged a body of knowledge founded on a unified system of principles. Family theory and therapy literature has proliferated and several schools of family therapy have emerged offering a variety of approaches to the treatment of dysfunctional units.

Family therapy began about thirty-five years ago when studies of severely disturbed children and adolescents raised the following questions: Why did disturbed adolescents who improved in the environment of a hospital revert to mental illness as soon as they returned home? When one child in a family improved, why did another child in the same family become ill? Why did some patients show only minimal progress after years of conventional individual psychiatric treatment? These questions challenged some researchers who looked for answers in family relationships, interactions, and patterns of communication. Research with the patients (children and adolescents) and their families resulted in new ideas about the nature and course of mental illness.

In the decade between 1950 and 1960, researchers in several different parts of the United States began to study family problems: Gregory Bateson, Don Jackson, Jay Haley, Virginia Satir, and John Weakland in California; Nathan Ackerman in New York; Murray Bowen in Kansas and then Washington; Theodore Lidz in New Haven; and Carl Whitaker in Atlanta. As their ideas emerged it could be seen that they were all exploring family variables and individual symptomatology within a systems perspective. (It is important to remember that in those days this focus on interpersonal forces— or transactional processes—was a radical departure from the dominant psychoanalytic approach to understanding and treating mental illness.)

An epistemological breakthrough occurred in behavioral sciences when the California team developed a theory about communication that included the double-bind theory of schizophrenia. The central idea of communication theory is that communication is processed at two levels: the logical level (content level), and the analogic level (communication about the communication, or meta communication). The analogic is the more powerful of these levels and includes nonverbal clues and a tone and quality of voice and body movement. The analogic level of communication is the key to understanding the rules by which family members cue each other and thereby create and sustain a pattern of interaction.

As a simple example, a mother beckons her three-year-old son to her lap. As he climbs up, she sighs under her breath and says, "You're ruining my dress." The two messages the child receives—"Climb on me" and "Don't ruin my dress"—are impossible to satisfy simultaneously. If the child responds to the message "Don't ruin my dress" and retreats, the mother further confuses him by saying "Don't you love your mother anymore?" If he stays on her lap, the mother fusses and blames him for ruining her outfit. The cumulative effect of a family that confuses its members by not acknowledging inherent contradictions in the messages—a process called double bind—results in a no-win position for the child as well as a lack of validation for his perceptions and thoughts. A more benign and less pathological mixed message is the parent who tells a child to do something—for example, "Clean your room!"—in a tone that disqualifies the parental authority (pleading tone of voice), leaving the child confused as to what the parent really expects.

The California group of researchers outlined a theory that emphasized the process by which family members share a secret network of rules that govern everyone's behavior (6, 7). Bateson et al. believed that his double-bind communication operated in the dysfunction that is called schizophrenia. The schizophrenic patient (often adolescent) is "chosen" by the family to bear the burden of the family's hidden tensions. The real disturbance was thought to be in the family members' relationships with one another, and the schizophrenic patient was a symptom of family dysfunction.

The status of communication theory's contribution to the etiology of schizophrenia is controversial today. Because of more recent biological and genetic research on schizophrenia, the schizophrenic family member would be viewed by most therapists as the constitutionally vulnerable member. Thus, schizophrenia is seen as a more complicated condition with family dynamics, biochemical factors, and stress factors operating. However, one cannot overestimate the impact of communication theory's introduction of a dramatic theoretical counterpoint to the psychoanalytic tradition that dominated the mental health field. Furthermore, the California group was research-oriented, and their prolific publications documented their findings and advanced their theories.

On the East Coast several other pioneers independently developed their own frameworks for family therapy. The late Dr. Nathan Ackerman is considered by many to be the father of family therapy. Ackerman was a psychoanalyst who broke with traditional child psychiatry by approaching a child's neurosis as part of an interlocking system of family conflicts. In his approach he applied and transposed individual psychodynamics to family dynamics across three generations (1). In addition to his theoretical contributions, he was famous for his controversial interviewing style in which he used free associations, provocative comments, flirtations, and interpretation to expose the unconscious level on which the family operated.

Another charismatic interviewer is Dr. Salvador Minuchin, the founder of the structural school of family therapy. Originally, Minuchin worked with delinquent boys in residential treatment, and he was one of the few family therapists to work with poor families. In order to understand their problems and prepare their families for discharge, Minuchin focused on family treatment (10). The structural approach to family therapy, which developed from his work with these families, emphasizes clear boundary definition, the development of functional alliances, the normalizing of the role of the parental child (the child who functions as a parental surrogate), and the development of tasks directly related to improve family functioning (9). Minuchin went on to the Philadelphia Child Guidance Clinic where he created new approaches for working with families where there is a life-threatening psychosomatic illness (11).

Dr. Murray Bowen, in Kansas and later in Washington, has created an approach to family treatment that places individual disturbance within the historical context of the three-generation family. His theory is based on the notion that individual and marital problems reflect a lack of differentiation from one's family of origin. Detriangling oneself from one's family origin is the key, and Bowen developed the role of therapist as "coach" to enable individual patients to return home in a series of planned visits to work on their basic relationships (2).

In Baltimore and New Haven, Dr. Theodore Lidz focused on the disturbed marital relationships in families with schizophrenic offspring. Lyman Wynne and his colleagues (20) studied families of schizophrenics. They identified the family style of "pseudo-mutuality" as one in which there is a false closeness, a family that emphasizes excessive harmony and avoids all conflict. These families participate in rituals that deflect anger and embrace peace at the cost of individual development. Cooperation is considered the ultimate family virtue. For the adolescent who needs to be able to express anger and experiment with nonfamily ideas, this family is toxic. The failure of such a family to embrace the individuation of its individual members contributes to the psychotic break of that family's adolescents.

Although not a theorizer, Dr. Carl Whitaker is one of the most intuitive and brilliant family therapists to watch in action. His approach is considered "experiential" because it depends on the therapist's ability to interact with the family spontaneously and authentically.

All these pioneers in family therapy broke away from traditional approaches to therapy and revolutionized the mental health professions. At this point there are many different approaches to family therapy; however, most of the differences are in style, technique, or emphasis of the therapy, rather than in family theory itself. All the different schools of family therapy originate from the theoretical position of one or more of the original founders.

All family therapists agree on these basic concepts: behavior of family members is interlocking, family problems repeat from one generation to the next; and an individual's symptoms reflect wider problems in the way family members relate to one another.

Family Treatment and Social Work: A Compatible Relationship

The history of the social work profession since the days of Mary Richmond has been shaped by the struggle to find a balanced perspective with respect to the interacting forces of the individual and her environment. Over the decades this perspective has vacillated between focus on the intrapsychic conflicts and personality deficits of the individual to the social and political activism of the community organizers who aim at changing social institutions within casework.

In the 1950s, social work practice in child guidance shifted to include mother-child dyads, heralding general developments in the field. However, it wasn't until the late fifties and sixties that families as a whole, or even mother-child dyads, were seen together. From then on, family treatment has burgeoned in social work settings, and social workers compose the largest single group of practitioners in family therapy (3).

Over the last fifteen years the legitimate focus of social casework has been defined, redefined, and refined as the person in transaction with his social environment. Since the family is the most potent social environment for the emotional, social, and intellectual growth of its members, there is a natural fit between one-to-one treatment and family therapy. Thus, family intervention as a treatment modality found within social work a compatible environment for its development, expansion, and experimentation. The application of family systems theory and therapy to medical, psychiatric, family service, and community health settings has had a dramatic effect on casework training and the kinds and nature of services delivered.

Family treatment is as much a way of thinking about behavior as it is a method of intervention. Since the family does not exist in a vacuum (any more than does the individual), family approaches are theoretically and practically linked to larger and smaller systems in the ecological environment. The interdependent systems of peer, neighborhood, and school environments interact with economic, political, and cultural systems. Thus, micro and macro systems exert dynamic forces on the individual members and the family as a group.

The multiple impact of these forces on the family unit can only be accounted for by a theory that is multicausal and interactional in its approach to understanding behavior in a contextual framework. A brief clinical example follows.

Mr. and Mrs. U. are referred by their physician to a clinic for counseling after the death of their oldest child in a car accident. The remaining nuclear family consists of Mr. and Mrs. U. and their nine-year-old son, Eddie. Eli, the child who died, was approaching his thirteenth birthday. During intake, the following facts are reviewed with respect to their bearing on the family crises: Mr. and Mrs. U. are a Jewish family who immigrated to this country from Russia seven years ago with the help of distant family members in the United States. No other members of their immediate family joined them, and they are relatively isolated in their Bronx apartment. Eddie, socialized in American schools, is both temperamentally and culturally Americanized in that he is less respect-ful, more peer-oriented, and less dependent on his parents than was Eli. He was and is unfavorably compared to his brother over and over. The parents, well-matched in Russia where they lived with Mrs. U.'s ex-tended family, had been having marital problems for the last few years. These problems, however, were tempered by Mrs. U.'s close relationship with her eldest son, whose poetic nature and introspective tendencies meshed with Mrs. U.'s need for a sympathetic relationship to compen-sate for her loss of extended family ties and poor marriage. Mr. U., a hard worker as a watch and jewelry repairman, is isolated and lonely, and suffers the criticism of his wife and American friends who are dis-appointed that he is not "more ambitious" and able to open his own jewelry store. Without going into a lengthy case discussion, the family, in the throes of mourning the tragedy of the death of a child, which requires major emotional shifts in every family, is also acculturating to a new way of life, relinquishing former values, confronting multiple losses, and adjusting to peer and work influences that are unfamiliar. They are isolated from extended family who are not available to aid the mourning process or help the family cope in parental and marital tasks. Intervention must address all these aspects.

The diagnosis of family functioning is based on general symptoms theory enriched with psychodynamic, small group, family, and organization theory to assess fully the impact of social forces on individual and family develop-ment. Within these orientations, family therapy targets on interrelationships between family members out of a conviction that such alterations will con-tribute to individual growth.

Life Cycle of the Family as a Framework for Family Therapy

In this framework the family is conceived of as a structure that changes in predictable ways over time. Rhona Rapoport's seminal writing represents a marked departure from demographic approaches to the life cycle of the family by identifying intrapsychic and interpersonal tasks that characterize the first phase of marriage (13). This conceptual approach is thematic in the writing of Frances H. Scherz, who sees family tasks as emerging in transitional stages (16). However, a systematic approach to processes of change in a family over time, consistent with the convergence of biopsychosocial forces affecting family members, has only recently been explicated in the literature (14).

Each stage in the life cycle of the family is characterized by an expectable family crisis. Such crises develop through a combination of the biological, psychological, and social factors to which each family member must respond. To resolve these crises, phase-specific family tasks must be confronted, undertaken, and completed. The way these family tasks are carried out depends upon the developmental tasks of individual family members. Thus, individual developmental needs influence family development and are as well influenced by family needs.

Implicit in a synthesis of developmental and systems thinking about the family is the assumption that the family is an adaptive unit with resources for the growth and maturation of its members. Transitional crises are predictable and necessary, in response both to the changing needs of family members and to pressures exerted from external systems. The family copes with maturational and social demands through task management involving shifts in internal organization as well as in transactions with outside social and cultural structures. The phase-specific family tasks have a cumulative effect; adequate task handling at early stages strengthens the family's ability to handle subsequent stages effectively. The family life cycle model begins arbitrarily, at the time at which two people join in a coupling process, through the stage of childbearing and rearing, the disengagement process in adolescence, followed by the empty nest, and ends with the death of one of the founding members. In reality, however, there is no beginning or end; the stages, artificially numbered for the purposes of explication, are in reality sequential and cyclical, and involve multigenerational processes.

Homeostasis and Change: Stability and Transformation

The application of general systems theory to family systems and to a therapeutic modality that aims to alter dysfunction in families focuses the attention of family therapists on how the family regulates and manages change. In the healthy family, there is a dialectic between the family's flexibility in response to the changing needs of its members and/or the impact of social and economic forces, and the family's stability created by the rules of their interaction. A family that does not change is dysfunctional because it is not adapting to new external inputs and internal differentiating forces. A family that is constantly changing is also dysfunctional because it is a chaotic and unpredictable environment for its members. Thus, the healthy family alters its patterns under the impact of change and stabilizes itself between transitional periods.

An example of how homeostatic versus change processes are addressed in family treatment follows:

Family "S" consists of Mr. and Mrs. S. and their adult children: Peter, David, Virginia, and the identified patient, Linda, age twenty-eight. Linda has been diagnosed as having bipolar illness for which she has had several hospitalizations, and she is presently under a psychiatrist's care. Lithium has been prescribed and although her condition has improved she is unable to make maximum use of the rehabilitation program to which she has been referred. A family consultation is held with an experienced family therapist. All family members are present. During this interview, a long-standing family pattern is revealed. Mr. and Mrs. S. have had severe but unacknowledged marital problems that have resulted in elaborate efforts by all the children to mediate the tensions between their mother and father. Mother and children have been very close, with Mrs. S. sacrificing her own needs on their behalf in exchange for their loyalty. Mr. S. has been devoted to his work.

The beginning of Linda's symptoms tied historically to the necessity for life cycle changes in the family that the family was unable to make. As the family approached the stage in the life cycle when each child struggled with separation from the family, family tensions increased. During the period in which the children were preparing to leave the family, Mr. S. retired from his job, forcing him to be home more than was usual and upsetting the balance in the marriage. Linda, as the youngest child, and always closest to the mother, developed a severe case of rheumatoid arthritis at age twenty, and then, about a year later, became agitated and depressed. Her first diagnosis was schizoaffective illness, and then, several hospitalizations later, a more precise diagnosis of bipolar illness was made. Her emotional difficulties, compounded by a biochemical condition, were used by the family as a way of hiding other problems. Her illness, now managed by lithium, continued to function as a family stabilizer, keeping the family united and close and helped it to deal with the impact of separating family members. It also justified Mrs. S.'s "inability" to travel with her retired husband (which is what the husband wanted to do), and allowed mother and daughter to be overinvolved with one another. Furthermore, all the other siblings are able to achieve a small degree of emotional distance from the family now that Linda is the focus of all family concern. The family has become a dysfunction-maintaining homeostatic system in that it preserves its organizations (that is, as an overclose family with a serious and chronic marital rift) through Linda's incapacitating symptoms. Treatment must address the family's difficulty with separation, the marital problems between Mr. and Mrs. S., and the impact of Mr. S.'s retirement.

Family Boundaries

The notion of boundaries is a central concept in family theory. The boundaries in a family define who participates in the family and how. A key to understanding families is to understand how boundaries define relationships within the family.

An *external* boundary distinguishes the family from the outside world. *Internal* boundaries define and separate the different relationships inside the family—parents, parent-child, and siblings. Both sets of boundaries can be open or closed, clear or murky, rigid or flexible.

All through the life cycle of the family the boundaries are expanding (birth, marriage, remarriage) or contracting (when children become adults, death). Entrance to and exits from the family necessitate changes in members' relationships with one another, and result in a reorganization of the family's internal and external boundaries.

All families fall somewhere along a continuum in which at one end, rigid and impenetrable boundaries within the family separate individuals in the disengaged family, and, at the other end, murky, weak boundaries fuse members in the enmeshed, overly close family. (The S. family in the previous case example is a typical enmeshed family.) Families with rigid internal boundaries are usually excessively open to the outside. And families with weak internal boundaries are usually closed to the outside world. In healthy families both inner and outer boundaries are clear and flexible.

Most families fall somewhere between these extremes, with some relationships too close and others overly distant. When family relationships consistently reflect either extreme, the family is considered dysfunctional. This dysfunction is often reflected by the existence of symptomatic family members.

The following are presented as "pure forms," sometimes found in clinical practice, for didactic purposes.

The Enmeshed Family

In this form, family members are poorly differentiated from one another, forming what Murray Bowen calls an "undifferentiated ego mass." Family members sometimes speak for one another, often use the pronoun "we," arduously avoid conflict, and rigidly adhere to rules emphasizing cooperation with and compliance to family dogma. The behavior of one family member speaks contagiously to every other member in the family rather than being confined in the subsystem where it began. The parents don't define a separate boundary around their relationship, and therefore obscure the necessary generational boundaries that characterize the healthy family. Parent-child coalitions exist that serve the purpose of obscuring marital tensions which go unresolved. The family is relatively closed to the outside world and efforts by the therapist to penetrate the inner circle of the family are foiled. The family sticks together like glue and all members are collusive in preserving family unity. Individual freedom is thwarted through guilt, and dependency is encouraged. Loyalty to the family is the family credo. Symptomatic family members often emerge in adolescence and have illnesses that keep them dependent on the family and justify family overinvolvement.

The therapist's task with the enmeshed family is to encourage individual subsystems and generational boundaries between members and between parents and children. The therapist fosters autonomy and independence, blocks intrusive family patterns, establishes parental boundaries, supports sibling subsystems, encourages the expression of conflict, and breaks up parent-child coalitions.

The Disengaged Family

In these families there is an "every man for himself" atmosphere. Family cohesion is lacking and strong alliances between family members are rare. Family members may appear "independent," but upon closer examination this independence proves to be superficial and represents the member's efforts to survive in a nonnurturing environment. Because there is a vacuum in parental leadership with no clear generational boundaries, caretaking functions are often carried by a parental child who functions as a surrogate parent. Disengaged families have been called "under organized" by Harry Aponte. Symptomatic family members often act out antisocially in the community and/or children are behavior problems at home or at school.

The therapeutic task is to help the family organize itself. Adult leadership has to be established as a first priority in these families. Such leadership needs to set limits and encourage functioning in individuals appropriate to age, ability, and developmental needs. Concurrently, appropriate boundaries between family and nonfamily worlds need to be established.

Triangles, Scapegoats, and Cross-Generational Coalitions

When a relationship between any two members of a family gets too intense for the members to resolve their problems between them, and a third member is then involved, a triangle is formed. The triangled family member acts as a go-between, mediator, confidant, or scapegoat. For example, every time Mr. and Mrs. Y. have an argument, Mrs. Y. goes to her mother's. There, with her sisters and her mother, they discuss her problems with her husband. All agree that he is "difficult."

The most serious triangle involves a stable cross-generational coalition between a parent and a child. This coalition functions to alleviate tensions between that parent and the spouse. The following example shows how triangles, scapegoating, and coalitions work to detour family and marital tensions.

> Mrs. B. waits for Mr. B., who is late for dinner. The children are hungry and anxious to do their homework and watch T.V. Mrs. B. thinks her husband's lateness is typical of his inconsiderate attitude toward her, and she thinks he takes her for granted. Finally, Mr. B. comes in the front door. He slams his lunch pail on the telephone desk in the front hall, a nonverbal announcement that he has had a tough day and doesn't want to be hassled. Mrs. B. makes no comment and calls everyone to the table. As they begin the evening meal, Evan, the youngest son, spills his milk. Mr. and Mrs. B. verbally pounce on him for being so careless. Mr. B. blames Mrs. B. for not being stricter with the children about table manners, and Mrs. B. retaliates by claiming that Mr. B. made the children edgy by being so late. Evan cries and leaves the table. Mrs. B. leaves also, to soothe Evan.

If such a pattern is repeated often, and if it takes the form of an approach to the child that brings the adults together in concern for or anger at the child, this pattern is called "scapegoating." The term "scapegoating" is used when the pattern of triangling worsens until the child's normal development is blocked, signified by the child's having a major symptom.

Parents and siblings attack or blame the scapegoat, who is perceived as "bad" or "sick." Everyone else in the family may appear normal and healthy because they detour all family conflict through one person. The elected family scapegoat is usually a child, although the family can also designate an adult as the problem. In one of the most common forms of family scapegoating one sibling becomes the "bad" or "sick" sibling while the other is almost perfect, the "good" sibling. These divergent roles, assigned and maintained by the family, represent the "good" and "bad" unintegrated aspects of the parents. They also can reflect family secrets in the parents' families of origin, as discussed below.

Family Schism

A schism in the family usually refers to a failure on the part of the marital pair to achieve a level of satisfaction in the relationship. This "emotional divorce" between the parents is obscured most often by the focus on children along with strong parent-child cross-generational coalitions. A child's symptomatic behavior stabilizes the family and prevents the surfacing of marital tensions that might result in the break up of the marriage. In this way, the symptomatic child protects and rescues the parents from their problems with each other.

Family Secrets and Myths

Every family has secrets that family members loyally guard. Some secrets are common—hostility disguised as affection, tyranny in the guise of benevolence, sexual infidelity, marital rifts. Others are more unusual—illegitimacy, mental illness in the family, alcoholism, incest, and suicide. The nature of the secret is not as important as how members perceive the secret, and how much they invest in protecting it.

To keep a secret many lies—or family myths—have to be made up. These myths often build like an inverse pyramid: a secret no bigger than a pea is on the bottom; the myths build up on top of it until the whole structure trembles with its own weight. Family history, reality, and family relationships become distorted by efforts to keep secrets through family myths. Children are especially burdened by such secrets because they sense the truth but feel bound to keep the secret from being exposed. They live in a shadow of partial truths, taboos, vague answers, and contradictions that don't make sense.

Most secrets are buried in the history of the family and sometimes family members don't even know exactly what this secret is. The myths surrounding the secret are passed from one generation to the next. Although family secrets can be protected from generation to generation, with each successive generation the recycled secret and its growing volume of myths distort family relationships more. Family secrets and myths are not passed on if they can be exposed, confronted, and dealt with.

In one family the disclosure of a family secret explained the sexual acting out of a sixteen-year-old girl. The secret was that an "uncle" was actually a half-brother. The parents had avoided dealing with the mother's premarital sexual experience and the circumstances of her having an out-of-wedlock child at sixteen (the designated "uncle") because of the implications for the marriage. The sexual acting out of the girl could be understood in the light of the family secret.

Diagnosis and Treatment Planning in Family Therapy

Family therapy, based on a systemic view of behavior, requires a complicated analysis on several different levels of diagnosis. On the broadest level the family is viewed as part of the subcultures and community to which it belongs. The values, expectations, and cultural practice of these societies orient the family therapist to the belief systems that shape family patterns and create dilemmas for families. On another level, the family is viewed as an internal organization with rules that define behavior within the family. But in addition, each family member, as well as being viewed as a part of the family system, must be understood as a discrete person with a unique internal life and developmental needs separate from his role in the family. The therapeutic task for the family therapist is to synthesize these levels of analysis into an integrated diagnostic picture of the family as a whole without losing sight of individual members. Because social and behavioral science theory has not caught up with the task of integrating individual and social systems theories, diagnosis often errs at one end of the continuum or the other. Symptomatic behavior of an individual may be seen as reflecting internal conflict or structural deficits within the individual with only a peripheral view of the family as a collaborative or ameliorating resource. Systemic thinking about the symptomatic family member as a family stabilizer may ignore constitutional variables, individual developmental histories, and internal psychological states that contribute to symptomatic vulnerability.

When the family therapist approaches the problems of an individual person, the therapeutic lens needs to be both telescopic and wide-angled. Family therapists in the mental health field should have exposure to psychodynamic, object relations, cognitive, and behavioral theories as well as to systems theories. Without an individual framework, the family therapist will tend to ignore individual variables and eliminate resources and modalities that will be helpful: multimodel (combined individual, group, conjoint, family treatment) approaches; psychoeducational approaches; pharmacologic interventions; and behavioral strategies.

On the other hand, clinical diagnosis and the application of *DSM* classification nomenclature can be controversial in settings where family therapy is the principle orientation. While many family therapists find descriptive diagnosis useful, others maintain that individual diagnosis confines the therapist to a one dimensional view of individual pathology, traps the therapist into a "medical model" of therapy, and fails to elaborate the contextual meaning of dysfunction. These family therapists refrain from individual diagnosis, maintaining that such an orientation constricts and narrows the therapist's view, eroding a systemic formulation of behavior. It is this author's opinion that a family orientation is not compromised by individual diagnosis when the individual assessment is considered together with family and cultural processes. However, a comprehensive theory that helps organize data toward this end is yet to be developed.

One of the most challenging tasks of the family therapist is to engage the family in treatment. Most often the family presents the symptomatic family member for treatment. It is essential that the therapist invite all members of the household in for the first consultation. Conceding to the family definition that "Susan's depression" or "Johnny's failure in school" is "the problem" puts the therapist at a disadvantage from the start by reinforcing the displacement of the family problem onto the symptomatic family member. Contrary to expectations of therapists unfamiliar with a family orientation, establishing a family format right from the start is not difficult to accomplish. A firm request followed by a brief explanation that the presence of family members will help you understand and evaluate "Susan's depression" or "Johnny's failure in school" is usually sufficient. If the family member calling objects, you can emphasize, very matter-of-factly, that this procedure enables you to get the most information about Susan's or Johnny's problems, which is affecting everyone in the household. It is not necessary to explain your family therapy orientation since your recommendations will flow from an assessment based on your experience with the family and their experience with you.

The therapeutic task of the first session is twofold: first, to clarify the nature of the problem (including the symptoms of the identified patient) and to begin to form a hypothesis about how family members are organized around the problem, and second, to help family members perceive that they are part of the problem.

The family therapist takes charge of the session from the beginning. Usually the session begins by the family being asked what they see as the problem. This often focuses on a particular family member. Some therapists begin with a genogram, a diagram of the family tree over three generations, which identifies family members and important dates that reflect stress points in the history of the family. The therapist, while active and empathic, searches for clues about underlying family problems, nodal points in the recent history of the family that often lead to an understanding of precipitants to the current stress in the family. During early sessions, the therapist will often permit situations to develop that manifest how the family functions. As the family situation emerges, the therapist consciously attempts to engage the most powerful family members in order to enlist their active participation in the treatment. This joining with key family members may be the most important task of the engagement process.

A contracting process flows out of a consultation process that includes from one to three sessions. The primary goal of this process is to establish a connection between the problem as the family sees it and relationships within the family and to help the family members become aware of the necessity for family involvement.

Specific Approaches to Treatment: Schools of Family Therapy

While the several major treatments differ in their approach, their views of the role of therapist, and their technique, they do *not* differ in their underlying assumptions about how families work. If you can imagine all the leaders of the different schools in one room, they would agree in the areas of assessment and diagnosis, but they would disagree about the best approach to address the problem. However, their therapeutic styles would, most likely, be complementary rather than contradictory. Each family might respond more positively to a single approach, or several different approaches could be combined to address the needs of any one family. A brief description of the several major schools of family therapy follows.

The structural school of family therapy is represented by the teachings, demonstrations, and writings of Salvador Minuchin, Harry Aponte, and Braulio Montalvo. The goal of this therapy is to restructure, or realign, family relationships. This is accomplished by changing the family organization by altering the boundaries, alignments, and power coalitions within the family. The therapist is purposeful and active; she joins (creates a therapeutic alliance) with key figures in family transactions, and with this alliance destabilizes family patterns to create newer, more functional alliances and boundaries. The structural therapist induces "enactments," which are specific interactions that the therapist promotes within a session. The therapist also assigns tasks to be done at home between therapy sessions.

An edited film of the treatment of a black, single mother and her four children demonstrates the treatment approach of the structural school. The film is called *A Family with a Little Fire.* The presenting problem is that the seven-year-old female child has started a fire in the house. Braulio Montalvo is the therapist. In the first phase of the therapy, Montalvo focuses on the circumstances of the symptomatic behavior (when, how, where) and then on the relationship sequences prompted by the symptomatic behavior (who did what to whom as a result of "the problem"; how did the relationship line members up; what was "accomplished" by the sequences). For instance, his line of questioning reveals that the eldest male child maintains a special, privileged relationship with the overburdened mother when he saves the day by putting out the fire. He ends up a hero, which elevates his status and reinforces his role as the "parentified" child—that is, the child who carries a parent-like role. The symptomatic child, the youngest of the two middle female children, is routinely dismissed by the mother as worthless and incompetent. Montalvo's interventions, which are described below, aim at realigning the family so that the mother is in more control, that the strong mother-son alliance is weakened while the mother-daughter alliance is strengthened, and both the mother and daughter are redefined as competent. The central intervention is the following task, which involves all the family members: the mother is to teach the daughter how to light matches so that she doesn't hurt herself or anyone else. The mother is to do this once or twice a day, for ten minutes only (using the stove timer), and if the daughter cries the mother is to stop. The task is cast as a pleasant activity only involving mother and daughter. Montalvo assigns the eldest male child the task of watching the other children during the period when mother and daughter are practicing lighting fires. In this way, the therapist gives this overburdened single mother a manageable and appropriate task that strengthens the mother-daughter relationship.

In the next phase of therapy, when the task has successfully been accomplished, the therapist focuses on the mother's social life, encouraging her to have more of a life outside the family. The metaphor of "lighting fires" is subtly used throughout the tape as a reference to the frustrated sexuality of the mother. The treatment is successful is and terminated after three sessions.

The psychodynamic model, as developed by Nathan Ackerman until his death in 1971, has incorporated object relations theory into an approach that is used with well-motivated families and couples in marital therapy. As practiced today, the therapy focuses on unconscious processes that dictate the relationships between family members. Key concepts in this model are the relationship of projective identification to family scapegoating, and complementarity between marital partners, which provides the basis for projection and collusion.

The role of the therapist employing a psychodynamic model is to uncover the unconscious forces that are distorting relationships. The therapist may utilize historical material from family members' past experiences, or may invite extended family (grandparents, aunts, uncles) into the sessions in order to rework conflicts in these primary relationships toward a more satisfactory resolution. The successful outcome of the therapy depends on understanding, insight, and the resolution of unresolved interpersonal-intrapsychic issues.

Carl Whitaker and his students Augustus Napier and David Keith are the leaders of the symbolic-experiential model of family therapy. The distinguishing feature of this approach is that the therapist's personality is a central feature of the dynamics of the therapy. The therapist, while skilled and disciplined as a family therapist, interacts with the family in a spontaneous, nondidactic nonhierarchal manner, providing an experience of authenticity for the family. Interpretations are not offered. Although insight is not sought it may be the result of the therapy. The focus of the therapy is in the here and now, and more specifically in the relationship between the therapist and family member(s). Since the family is expected to take the initiative for the session, Whitaker's families tend to be highly motivated. It is difficult to characterize this therapy because it tends to be so heavily influenced by the therapist's personality style, and the therapist's capacity to grow in his connection with the family. It is the intermeshing of the therapist's and the family's impetus for growth that results in successful treatment.

Murray Bowen has trained several generations of family therapists, including Tom Fogarty, Phil Guerin, and Betty Carter. Unlike the other schools of family therapy, which require the whole family to convene together, his can be done with one person *or* a whole group. The objective of the therapy is to help family members reduce their emotional reactivity and increase objectivity in their relationships with one another. Conceptually, the therapy is based on a three-generation model in which triangular relationships repeat themselves from generation to generation in a transmission process. All current problems (marital, parent-child, symptomatic child) are seen as reflecting back on problems with the parents' families of origin. Moreover, it is assumed that the parents are, to various degrees, undifferentiated from their families of origin and their siblings. Thus, the therapeutic task is to aid this differentiation process through coaching, based on a systematic analysis of the patterns in their family of origin. The object is to gain enough knowledge about oneself and the system to be able to change oneself in relationship to others.

In strategic therapy the clinician initiates a series of interventions to promote specific changes. The therapist takes control of the therapy and designs a particular approach for each problem. There are several different schools of strategic therapy: problem-solving therapy from Jay Haley and Cloe Madanes (5, 8); the Mental Research Institute therapy, which was developed by Paul Watzlawick, John Weakland, and Richard Fisch (19); and paradoxical therapy, which has several different advocates, including Mara Selvini-Palazzoli (17) in Italy and Peggy Papp (12) and Olga Silverstein in New York at the Ackerman Institute. Paradoxical therapy is usually employed with the most rigid and resistive families: those families who have long-standing chronically dysfunctional members, and those families who have not responded to more traditional family therapy approaches. But problem-solving therapy and MRI therapy are not restricted to rigid dysfunction-maintaining families.

Strategic therapists are concerned with the theory and means for inducing change. The therapist is not adverse to taking responsibility to initiate these changes, and plans a strategy, usually with the help of a co-therapist or consulting team, to maximize change in resistant families.

Pragmatism is an important characteristic of strategic therapies. Strategic therapists develop techniques that work no matter how illogical they might appear. Moreover, they are concerned with symptoms; the objective of the therapy is to eliminate the symptomatic behavior. Strategic interventions, though symptom-focused, are based on a hypothesis of how the symptom works as a dynamic of the family.

It is difficult to characterize treatment strategies as an amalgam of techniques because they are so varied. However, strategies include the techniques of prescribing, restraining, and reframing. These techniques are employed to encourage the family's homeostatic tendencies as a means of producing change. The following statement is offered as an example of a "paradoxical intervention" as practiced by Mara Silvini-Palazzoli and her team in Milan (17); it applies to the family described on p. 439. In the Palazzoli tradition this statement would be read to the family by one of the co-therapists at the closing of a session. It is also sent in written form to all family members, including those absent from the session, in the interim between the last and the next session.

> Your family impresses us as a very close family which is kept in a delicate balance by Linda's self-sacrifice. Actually, Mrs. S. sets the high standard for self-sacrifice through the devoted attention she bestows on all her children. Linda admires her mother and is doing her best to emulate her self-sacrifice. This allows Peter, David, and Virginia to create a comfortable degree of distance, yet closeness, with the family. Mr. S. waits patiently until the time when he and his wife can take a vacation together. We are very impressed with the delicate balance achieved in this family and realize that everyone is doing his or her part to keep it this way.

"Prescribing the symptom" as a technique refers to instructions to the family to engage in the very behavior the therapy aims to eliminate. In "restraining" strategies the therapist discourages change, or defines change as risky, dangerous, and undesirable because of the consequences that change would produce. "Reframing" refers to therapeutic efforts that define a symptom, or a person's behavior, or a series of behaviors in a favorable way, bringing to light the positive aspects of this behavior. "Reframing" is utilized in both nonparadoxical and paradoxical therapies and is referred to as "positive connotation."

It is important to remember that traditional therapy is based on an alliance between the prochange forces of the clients and the therapists who work together to counter the antichange forces (called "resistances" in traditional therapy). Strategic therapy developed out of an appreciation for the power of the antichange forces, which often defeat well-thought-out treatment and well-intentioned therapists. Strategic therapy calculates the strength of the antichange forces of the family and attempts to melt resistance through indirect means. Sometimes the expression "joining the resistance" is used to reflect how the therapy capitalizes on, and exaggerates, the resistive or homeostatic behavior as a means to eliminating it.

Divorce and Family Therapy

Since the late 1960s an extraordinary rise in the incidence of divorce has taken place in this country. Each year, from 1972 to the present, over a million children below the age of eighteen felt the impact of the divorce of their parents. It was estimated that thirty percent of all children growing up in the 1970s experiencd the divorce of their parents (18).

For both adults and children, divorce is a traumatic emotional experience. Since divorce requires the restructuring of all major relationships, many years of healing are required before the family stabilizes. The divorce process starts with marital tensions, escalates under the pressure of severe marital stress and frustration, and peaks with legal papers, battles, and encounters. From then on, the years of transition begin the shifts from nuclear family to single parenthood, shared or disputed custody arrangements, and the likelihood of remarriage with consequent blended-extended family structures.

Family therapists, with their expertise in family relationships, have played a major role in helping parents and children deal with these transitions, heal the hurts of failed relationships, cope with temporary instability, and rework relationships based on the realities of shared parenthood and stepparenting. Family therapists help families go through the emotional divorce—usually a two to three year process (17, 18): mourning the loss of the intact family, giving up fantasies of a reunion, giving up anger, and rebuilding relationships—long after the legal divorce has been completed.

Some family therapists specialize in divorce therapy, divorce mediation, remarriage, and stepparenting. Divorce therapy helps people who have decided to divorce deal with the issues and tensions between them in a therapeutic setting so as to minimize divorce trauma. Divorce mediation usually involves a collaboration between a family therapist and a lawyer who, in a nonadversarial atmosphere, helps a divorced couple draw up a legal document covering custody and financial arrangements. Emotional issues, which often enflame and generate legal battles, are defined and separated from the legal arrangements. Family therapists who specialize in the problems of divorced single parents and remarried families are acutely sensitive to the impact of unfinished business between divorced spouses on the children of divorced parents and remarried families.

Indications and Contraindications for Family Therapy: Research Findings

To date, there is some important research that is relevant to the question of how effective family therapy is in the treatment of individual, marital, and family problems. These findings cast some light on the difficult question of indications and contraindications for family therapy. Dr. Alan Gurman summarized his findings in an article entitled "Family Therapy, Research and the 'New Epistemology' " (4):

1. Family therapies are more effective than individual psychotherapy when family-related issues and problems are at the heart of the presenting problem.
2. In couples therapies, improved communication between the spouses is strongly associated with good outcome.
3. Conjoint couples therapy is clearly superior to individual therapy for marital problems; individual treatment for marital problems results in treatment failure twice as often as does joint treatment.

To conclude, the research on the effectiveness of family therapy, limited as it currently is, seems to bear out conventional wisdom: that family therapy works best when applied to parent-child, family, and marital problems. Clinical experimentation and refinement coupled with carefully designed research efforts will advance our expertise in matching specific "schools" of family therapy to specific kinds of family problems. This task remains the challenge of future generations of family therapists.

References

1. Ackerman, Nathan W. *The Psychodynamics of Family Life.* New York: Basic Books, 1958.

2. Bowen, Murray. "Theory in the Practice of Psychotherapy," in Philip J. Guerin (ed.), *Family Therapy: Theory and Practice.* New York: Gardner, Press, 1976.

3. Group for the Advancement of Psychiatry. *The Field of Family Therapy.* New York: GAP, 1970.

4. Gurman, Alan S. "Family Therapy, Research and the New Epistemology." *Journal of Marital and Family Therapy,* July 1983.

5. Haley, Jay. *Problem-Solving Therapy.* San Francisco: Jossey-Bass, 1976.

6. Jackson, Don D. (ed.). *Communication, Family and Marriage, Vol. 1.* Palo Alto, Calif.: Science and Behavior Books, 1968.

7. ———. *Theory, Communication and Change, Vol. 2.* Palo Alto, Calif.: Science and Behavior Books, 1968.

8. Madanes, Cloe. *Strategic Family Therapy.* San Francisco: Jossey-Bass, 1981.

9. Minuchin, Salvador. *Families and Family Therapy.* Cambridge, Mass.: Harvard University Press, 1974.

10. Minuchin, Salvador, Braulio Montalvo, B. G. Guerney Jr., B. L. Rosman, and F. Schumer. *Families of the Slums: An Exploration of Their Structure and Treatment.* New York: Basic Books, 1967.

11. Minuchin, Salvador, B. L. Rosman, and L. Baker. *Psychosomatic Families: Anorexia in Context.* Cambridge, Mass.: Harvard University Press, 1978.

12. Papp, Peggy. *Process of Change.* New York: Guilford Press, 1983.

13. Rapoport, Rhona. "Normal Crisis Family Structure and Mental Health," in Howard J. Parad (ed.), *Crisis Intervention: Selected Readings.* New York: Family Service Association of America, 1965.

14. Rhodes, Sonya. "A Developmental Approach to the Life Cycle of the Family," *Social Casework,* May 1977. Vol. 58, No. 5. pp. 301–311.

15. Satir, Virginia M. *Conjoint Family Therapy,* rev. ed. Palo Alto, Calif.: Science and Behavior Books, 1967.

16. Scherz, Frances H. "Theory and Practice of Family Therapy," in Robert W. Roberts and Robert H. Nee (eds.), *Theories of Social Casework.* Chicago: University of Chicago Press, 1970.

17. Selvini-Palazzoli, Mara, Luigi Boscolo, Gianfranco Cecchin, and Giuliana Prata. *Paradox and Counter Paradox*. New York: Aronson, 1978.

18. Wallerstein, Judith, and Joan Berlin Kelly. *Surviving the Breakup: How Children and Parents Cope with Divorce*. New York: Basic Books, 1980.

19. Watzlawick, Paul, John Weakland, and Richard Fisch. *Change: Principles of Problem Formation and Problem Resolution*. New York: Norton, 1974.

20. Wynne, Lyman, J. M. Rykoff, J. Day, and S. I. Hirsch. "Pseudo-Mutuality in the Family Relations of Schizophrenics," *Psychiatry*, May 1958.

Annotated Listing of Key References

ACKERMAN, NATHAN W. *The Psychodynamics of Family Life*. New York: Basic Books, 1958.
If there is a basic "text" on family therapy, in thoroughness and in its integration of contributions from the behavioral and social sciences, coming early in the development of family therapy, it is this book. Even today, most authors in this field define their thinking in terms of its borrowing as well as its differentiation from Ackerman's book.

BOSZORMENYI-NAGY, IVAN, and JAMES L. FRAMO (eds.). *Intensive Family Therapy*. New York: Harper and Row, 1965.
This compendium has a wealth of contributions from a variety of authors. It contains a historical view of the development of family therapy.

BOSZORMENYI-NAGY, IVAN, and GERALDINE M. SPARK. *Invisible Loyalties*. New York: Harper and Row, 1973.
This work comes closest to capturing that ineffable bond that makes families rather than mere groups of individuals—a bond a clinical lexicon does not touch.

LAIRD, JOAN, and JOANN ALLEN. "Family Theory and Practice," in Aaron Rosenblatt and Diana Waldfogel (eds.), *Handbook of Clinical Social Work*. San Francisco: Jossey-Bass, 1983.
An excellent up-to-date overview of the major concepts and trends in family therapy.

MINUCHIN, SALVADOR. *Families and Family Therapy*. Cambridge, Mass.: Harvard University Press, 1974.
Minuchin's ideas about structured family therapy are compelling, particularly for social workers whose training and experience focus on clients' social functioning.

SATIR, VIRGINIA M. *Conjoint Family Therapy*. Cambridge, Mass.: Harvard University Press, 1967.
Satir has been social work's most active expositor of family therapy concepts as well as a demonstrator of her methods to professional groups.

SHERMAN, SANFORD N. "Family Therapy," in Francis Turner (ed.), *Social Work Treatment*, 2nd edition. New York: Free Press, 1979.
A thorough review of the development of family therapy and its principal concepts by one of the early social work family therapists.

CHAPTER 17

Transactional Analysis: A Social Work Treatment Model

Denise Capps Coburn

A refreshing, optimistic theory of social treatment and change, Transactional Analysis brings strong support for the value of human beings. A primary assumption of this theory is that people are OK, which means that people can think, act spontaneously, and get close to other people in intimacy that is beneficial for all concerned. Further, the concepts of Transactional Analysis stress that people can and deserve to feel good both physically and mentally most of the time, and that we have awesome power to decide whether we will get this kind of life for ourselves and whether we have social systems that foster autonomy. These ideas are in close harmony with the ethics and values of professional social work.

Eric Berne, M.D., the founder of Transactional Analysis, lived from 1910 to 1970. He began his work constructing the concepts for his theory in the 1940s when he was training to become a psychoanalyst. Dr. Eugene Kahn, professor of psychiatry at the Yale School of Medicine, and Dr. Paul Federn of the New York Psychoanalytic Institute were Berne's intimate teachers, influencing much of his early thought and work. Particularly influential in Berne's developing theory was Federn's work on analysis and structure and function of multiple aspects of the ego and resulting human transactions. He was an analysand of Erik Erikson who, no doubt, also had a profound influence on his thinking.

Consideration of Erikson's theory on the importance of life's developmental stages (17) in determining specific individual responses to life experiences was a clear influence on Berne's theory; this focus on developmental factors in personality development has been expanded by Berne's followers, particularly Pam Levin Landheer (34).

Wilder Penfield's work with electrical stimulation of the brain produced evidence that memories of events, complete with color and smell, are recorded in the brain and are recallable. This discovery had a notable influence on Berne's work in constructing the three basic ego states of the personality, the beginnings of Transactional Analysis.

Sigmund Freud's work was also an important part of Berne's basic ideas. A. A. Brill, in the preface to Berne's first book, *The Mind in Action*, written in 1947 and revised in 1957, with a title change to *A Layman's Guide to Psychiatry and Psychoanalysis* (3), said:

> Berne is a young Freudian who like the new generation of Egyptians did not know Joseph and hence would follow a new path and expound the new psychology without the affectivity of the older Freudians. The psychoanalytic theories were well established when Dr. Berne mastered them; that is why he could complacently survey the whole field of psychoanalysis, the fons et origo, as well as all the deviations from it, and then easily separate the kernels from the sheaf.

Berne himself, in the Author's Foreword of the same book, said: "It is taken for granted that most of the ideas, like the ideas of every dynamic psychiatrist today, are based on the work of Sigmund Freud."

The San Francisco Social Psychiatry Seminars was a nonprofit educational corporation started by Berne in 1958. It was initially a small group of professionals interested in social treatment who met every Tuesday evening in San Francisco. The group included psychiatrists, social workers, psychologists, nurses, and other mental health professionals and students in these fields. Anyone with a degree in medicine or the social sciences engaged in work or enrolled in advance study at a recognized university, as well as certain well-qualified undergraduate students, were welcome. Various approaches to psychotherapy were discussed, including Berne's developing Transactional Analysis theory. Berne encouraged questions about theory and practice and presentations by seminar members about new ideas in treatment. Berne himself learned from these seminars, and included ideas from students in his own theory of treatment. The size of the seminars grew until it was not unusual to have people from all across the nation attending the Tuesday night meetings. In 1960 these seminars were granted a charter by the State of California. Also in 1960 the name was changed to San Francisco Transactional Analysis Seminars. Then, in 1970, the name was changed again to Eric Berne Seminars of San Francisco in honor of their founder.

In 1965 the International Transactional Analysis Association was founded to promote understanding and knowledge of Transactional Analysis and to provide training standards and appropriate training and certification of therapists. A training standards committee and an independently administered Board of Certification under the National Commission of Health Certifying Agencies direct the rigorous certification process. Over the years, membership has grown to nearly six thousand, with members in more than fifty countries.

Basic Assumptions of Transactional Analysis

1. People are born OK. I'm OK, you're OK position is a point of view about people that Berne says is not only good but true (50).

2. People in social/emotional difficulty are intelligent and capable of understanding their stress and the liberating process of change; they want, and need, to be part of the treatment process. If they are to solve their problems it is essential that they be involved in the healing process. Social work treatment supports client participation in an effective change process.

3. All social/emotional difficulties are curable, given adequate knowledge and a proper approach (50); but in some cases we haven't discovered how yet. People who may be called schizophrenics, alcoholic, delinquent, or deviant are basically good and capable of leading satisfying, healthy lives that do not interfere with the lives of others.

Theoretical Concepts of Transactional Analysis

Strokes

Strokes are defined as units of social recognition that are essential to survival. Berne based this idea on Rene Spitz's classic work with infants who were failing to thrive (47). Physical and social stimulation (strokes) brought remarkable improvement to the infants in a short time. Berne maintained, then, that stroking is necessary for human survival; he extended stroking to include verbal transactions.

People spend their lives seeking strokes, of which there are four kinds: negative, positive, conditional, and unconditional (49, 50). Negative strokes deny the reality of the spontaneity, rationality, and ability of people to be socially intimate. Positive strokes openly recognize the value, awareness, and spontaneity in people. If a person does not get positive strokes, he will settle for negative ones, since negative strokes are better than none at all. Conditional strokes must be earned; a person has to do something to get them—for example, "You did a good job!" Unconditional strokes do not require earning. You do not have to do anything special to get them; your existence is enough. An example of an unconditional positive stroke is, "I like to be with you."

Strokes can be given in three ways: verbally; nonverbally, such as by gestures, facial expression, and body movements—a wink, a smile, a frown; and physically, by body contact such as hugging, slapping, touching, or pushing.

Knowing your own and your client's stroke economy helps develop information on how you can problem-solve together (49). Knowing your own stroking patterns as a therapist will help develop your professional potency. Social work clients deserve positive verbal and nonverbal strokes for seeking help, for being willing to change, for changing, and for problem-solving for themselves. Modeling positive stroke-giving is an important and powerful part of effective social work practice. People can learn how to stroke freely and how to receive strokes that will help them find intimacy and avoid loneliness. One good approach to becoming stroke conscious is to use a stroke-awareness grid to record most liked and least liked strokes in all categories. Many people are taught not to stroke, especially not to stroke themselves positively. It is frequently thought of as "bragging" or "selfish." See Table 17–1.

In many families, children are taught to be critical of their own behavior and to give themselves internal negative strokes. A resulting inner dialogue may be: "You never do anything right," or "When are you going to get it together?" This is a good way to stay depressed, helpless, and passive. Positive internal stroking is a powerful way to maintain high self-esteem. In addition to family systems, welfare, health care, and educational systems are sometimes so rigid and inflexible that individuals do not have their needs met no matter what they do and, as Martin Seligman says, they learn helplessness, which fosters feelings of hopelessness, depression, and passivity (45).

Time Structure

Time structuring is defined by Berne in six ways (4), with accompanying advantages and disadvantages. They are listed in Table 17–2 (8).

In Transactional Analysis, the use of time is seen as important since ap-

TABLE 17–1. Stroke—Awareness Grid (with Examples Written in)

	Types of Strokes			
	Positive		Negative	
Methods of Stroking	*Conditional*	*Unconditional*	*Conditional*	*Unconditional*
1. Verbal	"You did a good job."	"I like you."	"I don't like your cooking"	"Drop dead."
2. Nonverbal	Smile when child obeys	Sitting with someone, feeling close and silent	Pointing finger and shaking it angrily	Turning away
3. Physical	Pat on back for job done	Backrub	A kick to stop daydreaming	Push downstairs Hitting to hurt Abuse-Rough pushing

TABLE 17–2. Modes of Time Structuring

	Social Advantage	Social Disadvantage
Withdrawal	Refreshment	Isolation
Ritual	Security	Social distance
Pastimes	Source of strokes	Avoidance of intimacy
Activities (includes daily work/job)	Creative self-fulfillment	Conditional strokes only based on doing something
Games	Structures time with some strokes	Avoids intimacy
Intimacy	Warmth and security; unconditional strokes from all categories; deep sense of well-being	Risk of loss

propriate time structuring is a way to stay socially healthy. The way a person structures time is a major factor in whether she is coping with life, problem-solving, and feeling as though there are good reasons to live. The individual has considerable control over how time is spent. Transactional Analysis encourages time spent for creative, spontaneous work and play.

Existential Positions

Transactional Analysis defines four basic life positions:

1. I'm OK—you're OK.
2. I'm OK—you're not OK.
3. I'm not OK—you're OK.
4. I'm not OK—you're not OK.

Franklin Ernst invented a diagram for gaining awareness of existential positions to lead to contracts for thought and behavioral changes to get to the OK-OK position (18), see Figure 17–1.

Structural Analysis

Structural analysis is defined by Berne as the first step in treatment (3). The personality is defined as being "made of three ego states each with a set of coherent systems of thought and feeling manifested by corresponding patterns of behavior." The three ego states are Parent, Adult, and Child; these make up the basic personality structure.

Berne's structural diagram of the ego states looks like Figure 17–2 (6, p. 12).

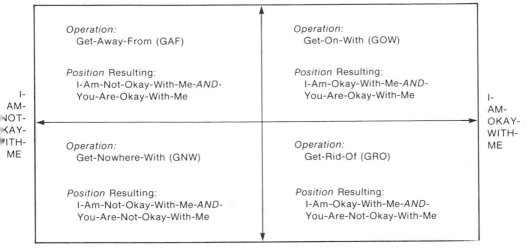

YOU-ARE-OKAY-WITH-ME

Operation: Get-Away-From (GAF) *Position* Resulting: I-Am-Not-Okay-With-Me-*AND*- You-Are-Okay-With-Me	*Operation:* Get-On-With (GOW) *Position* Resulting: I-Am-Okay-With-Me-*AND*- You-Are-Okay-With-Me
Operation: Get-Nowhere-With (GNW) *Position* Resulting: I-Am-Not-Okay-With-Me-*AND*- You-Are-Not-Okay-With-Me	*Operation:* Get-Rid-Of (GRO) *Position* Resulting: I-Am-Okay-With-Me-*AND*- You-Are-Not-Okay-With-Me

I-AM-NOT-OKAY-WITH-ME (left) I-AM-OKAY-WITH-ME (right)

YOU-ARE-NOT-OKAY-WITH-ME

Figure 17–1.

The Parent ego state is like a tape recorder containing recorded messages about how to get along in life—messages such as study, work, please others—from adults who tended us such as parents, teachers, friends, etc.

The Adult ego state is like a computer; it gathers facts and makes decisions based on information. There are no feelings manifested in this state.

The Child ego state contains natural feelings, sensations, and urges present since the beginning of life (archaic), and includes all of the body, skin, brain, lungs, heart, etc.

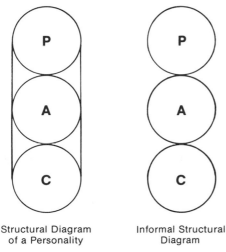

Structural Diagram
of a Personality

Informal Structural
Diagram

Figure 17–2.

An appropriate flow of energy from one ego state to another is essential to satisfying social interaction. The importance of structural analysis lies in the control and power involved in conscious, appropriate use of ego states. A winner is described as a person who maintains a basic self-confidence (27)—Berne said that between a tortoise and a hare it's better to be a winning hare (5, 29)—she uses her ego states consciously to get what she wants and needs. The Adult ego state can be in charge—asking questions, assessing, and making decisions that will allow the full development and expression of the Child ego state, which can be described as the center of creativity, joy, curiosity, and spontaneity, and thus the center of social being. The Parent ego state can also be used to assure protection and self-actualization for the Child and so a winner is further described as a person who keeps the appropriate ego state available and ready for use at all times. When a thinking, nonfeeling position is needed in a therapist, for instance, he can cathect (energize) his Adult ego state and figure out what is needed; he can consciously program himself: "Stay in your adult now. Keep strong control of your feelings right now. It is important for you to think clearly right now."

Berne gives four ways to identify or diagnose ego states: behavioral, social, phenomenological, and historical (4). Gesture, voice, and vocabulary are typical in each ego state for behavioral diagnosis. For instance, some Adult words are "how," "when," "where," "what"—words that assess and discover facts; feelings are not reflected behaviorally in the Adult ego state. A social diagnosis of an ego state involves how people react to you, a phenomenological diagnosis is experiencing in the present old feelings from the past—for instance, a person is probably in her Child ego state if she is crying as she did as a child when her dog died. Historically, diagnosing an ego state means looking at the past reflected in the present; for example, a person may be using a gesture typical of his father and will discover he is in his Parent ego state.

The process of deciding how one wants to be socially with others or internally with self at a particular time is an exciting and provocative approach to autonomous control of life. Social work theory and practice strongly support methods to gain autonomy.

The functional diagram further delineates the ego states as to function (see Figure 17–3). The Parent ego state functions in a nurturing or controlling manner, the Adult has no change from the way it is in the structural diagram, and the Child is divided into the Natural or Free Child and the Adapted Child. Berne describes the functional diagram as *descriptive* (6, p. 13). Stanley Woollams, Michael Brown, and Kristyn Huige note further delineation of the functions of the Parent and Child ego states as negative or positive (53). These are helpful theoretical refinements since it allows closer assessment of the quality of Parenting or the kind of adaption and free child function that is going on. For instance, a mother in a negative nurturing Parent ego state will overprotect her child and inhibit his growth, spontaneity, and

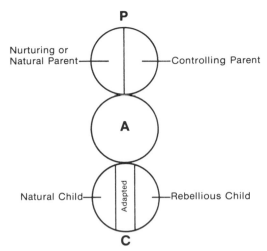

Figure 17-3. Descriptive aspects of the personality

social and intellectual development. This information will be helpful in assessment diagnosis and direction to effective treatment.

Second Order Structural and Functional Analysis

This more historical analysis of the evolution of the parts and functions of the personality can be most helpful in understanding behavior and attitudes and determining treatment goals. Second order analysis divides the Parent (P_2) and Child (C_2) ego states into further levels of structure and function. The Parent (P_2) structurally and functionally contains aspects of all three ego states of male and female caretakers.* In other words, P_2 is made up of Parent, Adult, and Child characteristics of parenting figures. This further breakdown of P_2 is shown in Figure 17-4.

The Adult, or A_2, stays the same, continuing to problem-solve and add new information gained from experience and development.

Figure 17-5 shows how C_2 is divided.

C_1, or the Child in the Child, is made up of feelings and needs and all body parts and physical systems that are present when a person is born. The body functions dictate the behavior—for example, the need for food produces hunger pangs and a call for food, a cry. Other needs for warmth, movement, and sensory stimulation also produce urges, discomfort, and behaviors to get the needs met—such as crying, fussing, wiggling, body stiffening, and relaxing. Everyone has these basic body needs from the beginning; they remain

*New blends of caretakers are emerging in modern families. Consideration of the impact of any significant caretaker is important.

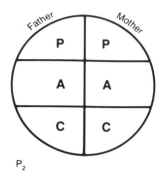

P_2

Figure 17-4. A second order diagram of P_2

and change through the various developmental stages of life, bringing different behavior and motivation based on varying developmental, physical, and social needs.

The Parent in the Child, P_1, is the part of the Child that behaves in a certain conditioned way to get parental approval, an attempt to ensure survival. In a certain family, the P_1 in the Child develops a specific pattern of behavior that over time becomes a "way to be" to get approval. P_1 will direct A_1 and C_1 to behave in this established way to get along and please the "big people." Sometimes P_1 will behave self-destructively if it seems that parental approval or attention will be gained through this type of behavior. Many body problems, such as asthma, anorexia nervosa, cardiovascular disease, and stomach and intestinal disorders, seem to have this element of P_1 behavior (11) as well as suicidal behavior (14). In such clients P_1 deems it a requirement for parental acceptance or recognition to be in pain, sick, or confused. P_1 is sometimes called the electrode because of the quick electriclike (conditioned) way it controls a person.

A_1 is the first Adult or the "Little Professor," the part of a person that is curious, creative, and intuitive, responsive and interested in what goes on around her from the beginning of life. Harsh, difficult, or gentle considerate birthing experiences seem to influence these early natural responses of the child, both physically and emotionally (9, 43). A_1 is interested in survival

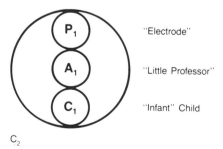

C_2

Figure 17-5.

and creatively observes and attempts to figure out early in life how to survive in her world.

Contaminations occur when the ego state boundaries of the Child and/or Parent permeate the Adult, and Child delusions or Parental bias are assumed to be fact; that is, Adult (6). This can be seen in Figure 17–6.

Exclusions occur when one or more ego states dominate a personality or when one ego state is not energized and functional. An unhealthy unresolved symbiosis may be present and two people may be interacting as though they have only three ego states between them; this interferes with the development of spontaneity, awareness, and intimacy (41, 42, 44)—see Figure 17–7.

John Dusay's Egogram, defined as a "bar graph showing the relationship of the parts of the personality to each other and the amount of energy emanating outward" (15, pp. 3 and 5) is an important diagram for diagnosis and treatment. A person's Egogram may vary in different social situations (15) and will provide information for needed changes in social interactions. See Figure 17–8.

Transactional Analysis Proper: Analysis of Interaction Between People

This part of Transactional Analysis theory describes a transaction as a unit of social interaction (6) made up of a stimulus and a response, the stimulus being sent from an ego state in one person to an ego state in another person. If the response to the stimulus comes from the expected ego state, the lines are parallel. This is called a *complementary transaction*, and the accompanying communication rule is that communication can go on indefinitely as long as the lines (vectors) are parallel. A *crossed transaction* occurs when the

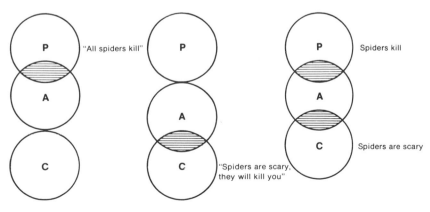

Parent Contamination:
A Bias or Prejudice

Child Contamination:
A Delusion or Phobia

Double Contamination:
High Confusion

Figure 17–6.

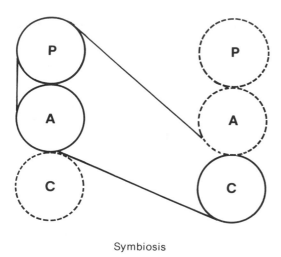

Symbiosis

= Energy not cathected
  in these ego states.

Figure 17–7.

response comes from an unexpected ego state and the lines (vectors) are crossed. Then the rule is that communication will stop abruptly; in order to resume, a switch in ego states will be necessary by one or both people (33). If the messages are sent both at a social level and at a psychological level, this transaction is called *ulterior transaction*. The psychological level is hidden, and the communication rule in this case is that the response given will be to the psychological message. This is adapted from Berne (6). See Figure 17–9.

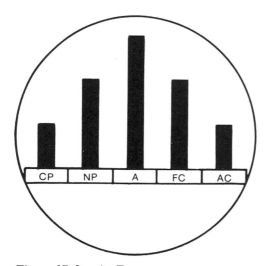

Figure 17–8. An Egogram

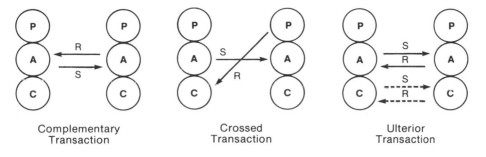

Complementary Transaction

Crossed Transaction

Ulterior Transaction

S = Stimulus
R = Response
———— = Hidden (not directly spoken—inferred)

Figure 17-9.

Script Analysis

A script is a life plan made in early childhood based on intuitive childhood decisions directed by parental programming and life experiences. Robert Goulding sees early childhood decisions as the child's idea of how to get strokes and how to survive (24). The child decides early, often before five years of age, how she will live her life, how she will use her time. She figures out intuitively how to survive in her family; she plans to succeed, die, get sick, fail, become insane, and often sets special times, such as "When I grow up I'll have fun," or "If things get bad enough I'll die or go crazy." She makes decisions or conclusions on the basis of parental messages and her own life experiences about her own OKness and the OKness of others. Parent values, rules, and slogans (counterscript messages) and negative "don't" messages (injunctions) from the unresolved problems in the Child ego state of the parent provide part of the base for a child's decision about how life will be for her. For instance, she may decide that to survive in her family she will have to "please mother," "stop thinking," or "never act like a child" with feelings such as sadness, guilt, anger, loneliness accompanying the decision. These feelings also become part of her personality (rackets) for the rest of her life unless she redecides about how she will feel and what she will do.

Claude Steiner developed a Script Matrix, which is a diagram showing the messages received by a child from parents or caretakers (50)—see Figures 17–10 and 17–11. Woollams suggests that the early parent messages all go to the Child ego state in a script diagram since the Parent and Adult are not developmentally available (51).

An important contribution to script theory is the concept of the *Miniscript* devised by Taibi Kahler and Hedges Capers (31), which is described as a second-by-second process by which a person lives out her script or maintains OKness. Miniscript theory identifies parental messages called "Drivers" that place conditions on OKness. The five Drivers are: Be Strong, Try Hard,

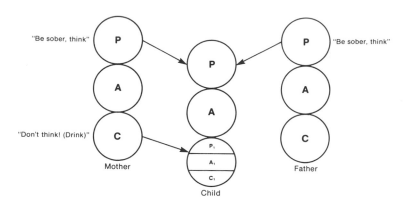

Figure 17-10. Script Matrix: an alcoholic

Hurry Up, Be Perfect, Please Me. They also identify four OK Miniscript positions: Allower, Goer, Be-er, and Wower positions (31).

Robert and Mary Goulding (21) have identified and named the following injunctions or parent messages that people may decide to live their lives by:

1. Don't Be—Don't Exist
2. Don't Be You
3. Don't Be a Child
4. Don't Grow
5. Don't Make It
6. Don't
7. Don't Be Important
8. Don't Belong
9. Don't Be Close or Don't Trust Anyone
10. Don't Be Well or Sane

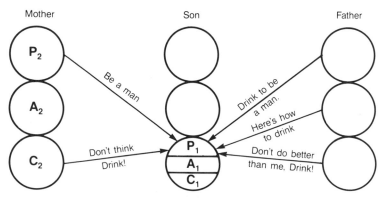

Figure 17-11. Revised Script Matrix

11. Don't Think
12. Don't Feel

Game Analysis and Racket Analysis

Games are defined by Berne as "an ongoing series of complementary ulterior transactions, progressing to a well-defined, predictable outcome" (6). They are repetitive in nature and both players have payoff feelings following the game transaction; these feelings verify that a game is being played. The feelings are uncomfortable and uniquely familiar to the person. Berne named these familiar bad feelings and their accompanying manipulative behaviors "rackets" because of their manipulative character.

Games and rackets are transactions that are out of awareness; people don't know they are using them. For instance, a person whose familiar bad feeling or racket is *guilt* may procrastinate and omit positive stroking of others, perform delinquent or criminal acts—all behaviors "designed" to keep his guilt racket active but out of conscious awareness. Another example of manipulative racket behavior can be seen in a child with a *rejection* racket. The child will emit negative, acting-out behavior resulting in rejection from those who care for him; in this way he maintains his racket feelings. A *lonely* husband may pout, clam-up, and behaviorally attempt to manipulate his wife into withdrawal with consequent loneliness for him. Both rackets and games are learned responses used by people who learned when they were young that straight asking and expression of real feelings didn't work and so they settled for whatever recognition they could get and discomfort from bad feelings. Underneath these rackets are real feelings, buried because they weren't permitted in childhood; racket feelings are substitute feelings that are "acceptable" in a particular family (16).

Describing racket feelings and their accompanying behavior patterns as "intrapsychic processes and associated behaviors related to script (life plan)," Richard Erskine and Marilyn Zalcman point out the value of knowing the client's racket system in order to develop effective assessment and treatment plans for stimulating client awareness and change. They present a method of racket analysis that is a significant addition to Bernian theory (19).

Games and rackets are played in three degrees, depending upon the intensity or the degree of discomfort in the payoff. First-degree games are mildly uncomfortable, often played at parties and other social gatherings; second-degree games bring more discomfort, and third-degree games result in tissue damage, injury, and death. Child/spouse abusers (30), criminals (12), alcoholics (50), many people with chronic illness (11), and others play third-degree games.

Stephen Karpman's Drama Triangle (32) identifies three primary game roles played by people to maintain their script: *Rescuer-Persecutor-Victim*.

His diagram of these roles is useful in client assessment and awareness of the roles they play and of options available for change.

Stamps

Some people collect bad feelings like trading stamps, and when they have saved enough, they trade their bad feelings or brown stamps in for a larger payoff. For instance, anger stamps are collected; when a person has enough, she can justify a drunken spree, a divorce, or an attempted suicide. Gold stamps are collected for good deeds. When a person saves enough gold stamps, she feels justified in taking a vacation.

Discounts

A discount is a denial of reality. Jacqui Schiff, social worker and founder of the Cathexic Institute in California, delineates three areas of discounting: self, others, and situation (41, 42, 44). Games start with a discount of at least one of these areas. A passive helpless-acting client is discounting herself and her ability unless she is in an immediate reality crisis (20). Becoming aware of bad feelings and the racket system, discounting, and transacting that keeps the bad feeling present is called game analysis and racket analysis. Winners do not play games or use rackets that interface with getting on with life.

Social Treatment with Transactional Analysis

Eric Berne was not interested in "making progress," he wanted cure, the sooner the better. Professional social workers are also interested in prompt relief of discomfort for clients—groups and communities. Establishing and maintaining a working bond with clients is essential to success and must be an immediate and continuing goal of an effective worker. Many people survive childhood, but in surviving they give up their spontaneity, rationality, and intuitive power (Child ego state).

Providing an Atmosphere for Change

The Child ego state of the client is made as comfortable as possible by offering snacks, pillows, warmth, humor, and time for physical activity (walking around) and relaxation (breaks) while receiving treatment. Goulding, at the Western Institute for Group and Family Therapy, says cookies in jars, delicious fruit, and relaxing meals provide an atmosphere for the Child in the client similar to what a loving grandmother would provide, encouraging change through an energized Child ego state. Social work theory and practice supports establishment of this caring position for developing the client/worker rapport necessary for problem-solving and change.

Initial Use of Positive Stroking

Asking for help is a sign of coping, an indication of client autonomy, a desire on the part of the client to take care of himself; often, however, asking for help is extremely difficult. Some people are trained from childhood not to ask and/or reveal feelings: "Speak only when spoken to"; "Don't interrupt"; "You shouldn't feel bad"; "Don't think about it or talk about it"; "Don't tell the family secrets, Dad might lose his job or get drunk, or Mom will get sick or crazy"; "I'll tell you how to feel and what to think"; "Run outside and play"; on and on. Considering all these possibilities, it is remarkable that some people ever ask for help. So when they do, it is vital to effective treatment that this initial demonstration of ego strength be recognized and stroked; stroke the client for coming, it is a good beginning for problem-solving. Powerful stroking transactions from the social worker to reinforce client autonomy in the beginning could be: "Good for you for coming in"; "I see you mean business about getting some solutions for your problem"; "Boy, getting a sitter, riding a bus, and getting here on time is a winning, I-mean-business position!" Other methods of stroking clients nonverbally and physically are: a warm or cool drink; snacks; a smile; involved listening; touching, such as hand shakes; supportive shoulder touching; natural small talk. A comfortable physical setting for group, individual, or family theory adds to a relaxed, natural, change-inducing atmosphere. Acceptance, understanding, and warmth from the therapist expressed by listening with attention, giving Adult feedback, and displaying optimism about change are expressions of caring that are essential to effective therapy and much appreciated by clients. Clinical experience and research support the effectiveness of a therapist's demonstrated caring and humanness on successful outcome of treatment (54).

Provision of Protection Through Clear Rules

It is a relief for a client whether in group, conjoint individual, or family therapy to know the *rules of the therapist*.* The rules should come from the Adult, Positive Nurturing Parent, and Positive Controlling Parent of the therapist (see Figure 17-3). They should be few and protective so that the Child in the client feels secure yet free to grow and change. Some effective protective rules are:

---

*"Therapist" applies to interveners instigating policy change for groups of clients in communities as well as smaller systems such as the individual or family.

1. Come to therapy clearheaded and ready to think—no alcohol or drugs;
2. Respect confidentiality of work done in therapy—no discussion of specific names and experiences outside of therapy;
3. Control violent, physical acting out—no hurting of self or others;
4. No sexual acting out in therapy sessions;
5. The therapist will be in charge of the decisions about use of therapy time—clients do not need to feel they are "taking up too much time," or that they "should not interrupt," etc., but respect the "use of time" decisions of the therapist as in the best interest of change and contract fullfillment.

Self-Awareness of Therapist and Meeting Self Needs Outside the Helping Relationship

Awareness of his own possible script issues, games, rackets, and contaminations (bias) is essential for effective use of therapy time by the therapist. This avoids negative responses to clients (countertransference) and can be done primarily by conscious, purposeful use of the three ego states while working. Respecting his own Child needs and wants and getting them met through friends and intimate relationships, not through clients, is also essential for the effective therapist. This provides the client with a strong therapist ready to think, feel, and solve problems; also *self-caring by the human service worker provides a living model* for clients to follow. The Child of the client can be very encouraged by exposure to this winning position in the professional.

Concentrate on Gains—Encourage Joy and Satisfaction Over Any Accomplishments

Celebration of accomplishments as they are made laces day-to-day existence and work with a sense of well-being for the client.

Deal with Obstacles to Client Joy and Autonomy from the Beginning

Concentration from the first on "what's in the way" will lead to change and comfort for the client and excitement, pleasure, and potency in work for the human service worker that can avoid "burnout." This stance is based on the optimistic, enthusiastic view that problems can be solved—the challenge of solution can be an adventure, "Let's find the answer together."

Structural Analysis

Identification of ego states and their appropriate use brings awareness and coping power to clients. For instance, some clients worry (Adapted Child) instead of enjoy (Free Child).

> A woman with a worry racket (pattern) from childhood became aware that when she had nothing to worry about in her own life, she worried about other people's problems or world problems. One day while going to work on a bus, she saw a woman and her little boy who looked "poor and unhappy"; she "couldn't forget them." On the bus, she thought of their problems, what they might be and on and on. She spent about two hours thinking. When she realized the time she spent doing this she said, "I can't believe I did that; I will probably never see them again."

Her awareness through treatment continued, and she contracted to stay in her Free Child more and away from the nonproductive worry or adaptation that she learned as a little girl.

Decontaminating and Degaming

Awareness of parental bias and childish fears that interfere with clear thinking is encouraged through expression of thoughts and feelings, social discomfort, confrontation by the therapist, and contracting for a well-thought-out change to allow the Adult, Positive Free Child, and Positive Nurturing and Controlling Parent ego states to control social functioning. Awareness of bad feelings and support of bad feelings by games can be gained through game, racket, and script analysis.

Script Analysis

Script Analysis consists of learning specifically what early messages were received by the Child ego state and what decisions about feelings, behaviors, and quality of life were made by the client during childhood.

> A thirty-year-old man whose father had died suddenly and unexpectedly when the man was 10 years old decided never to be commited to anyone again. When he became aware of his decision using a script matrix to diagram his messages, decisions, bad feelings, games, time structuring patterns, and existential position, he contracted to start commitment again by expressing his feelings openly and enjoying others. This was the beginning of change and new joy for him.

The use of racket confrontation, script questionnaire, and manifestations of caring helps the therapist encourage client autonomy and aids the client in giving up old destructive feelings and behaviors.

Racket Analysis

Racket Analysis can give the client and therapist important information about how the client keeps her racket system that supports her script going. Erskine and Zalcman define the racket system as "a self-reinforcing, distorted system of feelings and thoughts and actions maintained by script-bound individuals" (19); they further describe the racket system as having three components: script beliefs and feelings, racket displays, and reinforcing memories. Any intervention that stops the functioning of the racket system can stop the script and lead to awareness of new options for thinking and feeling. For instance, a shy, quiet retiring woman with a Don't Be Important script keeps the script activated by her behavior and the responses (memories) to her peasantlike, nonassertive position. Confrontation of her behavior and analysis of her intent and the results can lead to change to try friendly outgoing behavior that brings responses from others that let her feel important and script free.

Contracting

Transactional Analysis is a contractual and decisional model for change. The treatment contract is based on awareness and decision to change. The Adult ego state contracts for a change that makes sense and a change that the Child in the client wants; it is important in contracting to bring the Child of the client into the treatment plan, otherwise the plans may be sabotaged. Contracting entails work by the therapist and work by the client and considerations of time competency by the therapist and time commitment to treatment and change by the client.

Growing knowledge of the awesome connections between the mind and the body has stimulated some transactional analysts to take a holistic approach to contracting by taking double interrelated contracts, one contract for physical care and one for social/emotional change. For example, encouraging regular exercise, massage, good food, and rest can be vital to feeling changes in both mind and body. In cases where body constriction and tension is high, biofeedback and relaxation training may be valuable additions to treatment.

The following are contracts based on awareness gained through structural analysis, script analysis, time structuring consideration, decontaminating, and analysis of stroke economy.

My Child [ego state] isn't dead; for a while I thought he was, but now I can feel him moving way down under everything, and I'm gonna dig him out [burst of energy with awareness].

Contracts involving explicit new behaviors to gain control of life and find social fulfillment or contracts to thrill a therapist include:

I'm going to start brushing my teeth.
I'm going to live [not kill self].
I'm going to stay sober.
I'm going to spend more time with Janie [wife].
I'm going to tell Jim how I feel.
I'm going to smile more.
I'm going to dance more and eat less.
I'm going to exercise every day.

Change is exciting, scary, and sometimes painful.

Tim, who had been in weekly group treatment for about three months, decided one evening (after analyzing his script) to contract to smile more. His background was Mennonite and he had learned at home to "mask" (not to trust or get close to outsiders) his feelings and to keep them from showing in his face. He was actually (underneath) a warm, sensitive, responsive man who felt sad, socially alienated, and lonely, so he decided to show his warmth by smiling and not to follow his parental directive of "Don't Belong" when it fit his feelings (Child ego state). This, of course, was risky to him since it meant going against his learned family "protective" behavior; he did it anyway. When he returned to the group the following week, he reported with a big smile that he fulfilled his contract, but for the first three days his face was so sore that it hurt to touch it. "Talk about rusty, those muscles were really out of shape," he said. "Now I feel a lot happier and like I belong in my world!"

Redecision Therapy

Familiar bad feelings, behavior, and attitudes (rackets) such as guilt, fear, sadness, anger, pouting, yelling, discounting, cruelty, and dependency are brought to awareness by the combined use of Transactional Analysis, Gestalt, and behavioral techniques, discussion, and/or group interaction (21, 22). Since decisions are made in the Child early in life, redecision work done by the Child ego state in the client is more likely to be lasting than that done from the Adult ego state (24).

A forty-eight-year-old woman whose husband died nine years previous to treatment was still talking about her husband as though he were alive: "George always does that" and "I'm used to asking George." She remained in a depressed, stuck position. She had not separated herself from him. Working back with her sadness to early childhood allowed her to break her early symbiosis with her father, then say good-bye to her husband and begin to live again, probably for the first time fully. This woman became aware through script, racket, and structural analysis of her father's message to her: "Don't grow up"; she became aware that she had decided when she was little, not to leave her dad (to take care of him), and she was now stuck in not leaving her dead husband. In a piece of Gestalt double-chair work, she talked with her dad from her Child ego state and redecided to grow up and say good-bye to him. She also said good-bye to her husband, and decided to begin to live fully and autonomously for the first time in her life. She experienced significant relief and liberation (Child ego state).

Checking out time structuring using the six time structures often brings important awareness to a client of opportunities for needed behavior changes for fulfillment in social functioning.

Permission and protection (13) are treatment techniques that encourage and facilitate change. A therapist can give permission from all three ego states, such as giving a depressed suicidal client permission to live:

> Therapist:
> Nurturing Parent: You deserve to live and enjoy yourself.
> Adult: It makes sense that you stay alive; you can make the changes you need.
> Child: I want you around.

Steve Karpman would call this a bull's-eye because it reaches the client's three ego states all at once (33).

A client's redecision to live or express feelings or take care of himself requires that the therapist offer protection for the client's Child ego state while the change is being made. This is essential because early script decisions are made by children with survival as the intent. The Child fear (contamination) may be that to give up the script position may have disastrous consequences that interfere with survival. Special permissions are appropriate for each childhood decision and redecision. For instance:

Decision	Permission Needed to Redecide
Don't think	OK to think
Don't feel	OK to feel
Don't get close	OK to enjoy others

Versatility of Transactional Analysis as a Social Treatment Method

Since one of the impressive characteristics of Transactional Analysis is its flexibility, the concepts and treatment strategies can be effectively applied in individual, conjoint, family, group, and community intervention. Berne's early observations upon which he based his theory were made with individual clients in treatment and groups of clients in psychiatric hospital settings and in the army. Since then, many more uses have evolved and are applied by followers of Berne, in schools, hospitals, institutions, and workplaces, including working for peaceful international transactions around the world.

Limitation of the approach are not clear. Because of the cognitive aspects of this treatment, some practitioners question its use with mentally confused or severely deprived clients. However, Jacqui Schiff and other's work with schizophrenic clients, (44) work with abusing and neglectful parents (46) and criminals (12) has been productive and with some positive results. This success of the approach seems to hinge on the positive optimistic quality of the client/therapist relationship, which may bring some limitation for certain clients; however, there is no clear evidence yet to support this assumption. Otherwise, the wide applicability and influence of the theory on the therapeutic stance seems to open more and more use of the concepts in clinical practice, system changes, and research.

Group Therapy

Transactional Analysis is often used in groups with a "one-on-one" in-group approach. Each person in the group decides what she wants to get for herself in the group experience and agrees (contracts) to certain behaviors that will help her gain what she wants; these behaviors will be defined by the client with direction from the therapist, emitted in group, and will be observable by all and measurable. Members of Transactional Analysis groups often comment that while one person is working on change with the therapist they are also working on their scripts and redecisions; they often report seeing themselves with similar problems and making important changes for themselves through "being there" when someone else changes.

Couples Therapy

Transactional Analysis is being used in conjoint therapy where two people who are having difficulty getting along together come for change. This is often with married couples or other intimately involved pairs who are experiencing poor communication, sexual problems, and/or lack of intimacy.

Often, changes in the use of ego states will break up a destructive symbiosis in which the two are locked in a dependent relationship; for example, the wife may be acting childish and the husband like a parent, and then they switch to the husband being the childish one and the wife the parent—there is a shifting symbiosis with a continuous fight for the Child position in the relationship. Rita and Blair Justice found this "a consistent dynamic in abusive parents" (30).

Combining group therapy and couples therapy is one of the most exciting, challenging, and effective modalities. Treating four or five couples in a therapy group provides a fertile atmosphere for change. The following case illustrates this combination:

> Mary and Al had been married for twenty years. They were both depressed and confused over their lack of satisfaction in the marriage. As they worked on defining what needed to be changed it was clear that Mary was overtending Al. In talking about this Mary described a typical scene: she made coffee and set out a cup, cream, and sugar in the kitchen for when Al would arrive home from work or come in from outside. Then Mary went upstairs to sew. When Al came in, he called to Mary who left her sewing, came downstairs, poured Al's coffee, and went back to her work upstairs. As Al and Mary talked about this behavior group members listened and then expressed disbelief and humorous comments about Al's power over Mary and Mary's assumed peasant position. Al and Mary both saw the need for change in the behavior, and they did change it with resulting loss of resentment on Mary's part and development of warmth and closeness between them. Al and Mary were not aware of this behavior previous to group. Other group members saw these kinds of assumed roles in their relationships also and decided to change based on the new awareness.

The contagion for change in this modality is high and exhilarating for both clients and therapist.

Family Therapy

Many therapists are using Transactional Analysis with families to establish intimacy and joy in interaction and communication. Children in family therapy often are very helpful in the assessment period because observing their behavior and listening to their comments often immediately points out the family interactions as in the Jones family:

> Marie and Tom Jones, both twenty-eight years old, married, and with a sixteen-month-old daughter, Elizabeth, came into family treatment. Marie had been identified as an abusing mother during a recent report

from a day care center; she wanted help and willingly came to the family agency. During the initial interview it was clear that sixteen-month-old Elizabeth had a job: taking care of Mom. Elizabeth laid on the floor enjoying a bottle, kicking her feet slowly in the air and sucking. Marie began to cry. Elizabeth immediately threw down her bottle, rolled to her feet, toddled quickly over to her mother, put her cheek on her mother's cheek and patted her mother's chest, rocking back and forth until Mom stopped crying. As abruptly as she came she left—threw herself down again—jammed the bottle in her mouth and began to suck. Her father sat rigidly and watched with a stern face.

It was clear that Elizabeth decided early that in order to get along in that family she would have to keep mother soothed. Her script decision "Take care of mother—her needs are first—yours are second" is the behavioral message. "Don't count on Dad" is another clear message; it also makes sense that at one level Elizabeth would be resentful of interruptions by her mother and weakness in her father.

Ruth McClendon has done outstanding work with families using Transactional Analysis and System Approaches (2, 38). Parents and children are encouraged to be responsible for their own feelings in McClendon's work; children can observe their parents expressing old feelings of their childhood, working out decisions, becoming aware, and changing in the present family. This then frees the children to make changes and become children with responsive parents to take care of them; then the children will not be given negative messages from which to make tragic, getting-no-where scripts. With new transactions and positions, each family member can be autonomous and work out and practice new interactions before therapy is terminated.

Individual Therapy

Individual therapy with Transactional Analysis is very effective, particularly with confused or physically ill clients who have been heavily discounted when they were little. Persons who give up childlike qualities of spontaneity, curiosity, rationality and creativity benefit greatly from permission to be, to think, and to feel, and then learning ways to do that in therapy. These clients, who were severely discounted and stroke deprived as children, don't need script analysis. They know it was bad and the therapist agrees. Other individual work does involve script and change through awareness. The relationship between the therapist and the client is a most important aspect of individual treatment (54). If the client accepts support, direction, and caring he can gain the strength and energy needed for control of his life. Those clients need to know that "the light is on" for checking back to maintain gains after termination.

The following is a note from a client describing maintaining gains after successful individual therapy:

> I've been thinking how much I enjoy knowing a person like you. And I have come up with a short phrase that best describes it and that is: "You are the jumper cables for my Adult"—which every so often I have to use.
>
> Thank you
Matt.

Matt cured himself of serious colitis with individual followed by group therapy.

Research and Transactional Analysis

Many of Berne's theories have been supported by his respect for man's hungers, stimuli, structure, recognition, contact or touching (7, 9), a time structure, and incidents as reasons for motivation—and this is being reinforced by research. Studies on early infant bonding (43) indicate baby's readiness for assuming the "I'm OK" position, the natural position at birth, as well as showing positive responses to touching, breast-feeding, warm bath, voices of parents, and massaging immediately after birth (35). These responses are reported as smiling, relaxed "settling in" to the breast, vigorous and proficient sucking, "singing," head turning, and "looking" at the parent who speaks, almost as if he recognizes the parent's voice (9). Gentle birthing methods with loving persons—parents, physician, midwife, and important others—present receiving a child with joy and awe; touching and stimulating him as beautiful and important seems to be making a difference in the early response to life and may affect the child's human intimacy and ability to love as well as foster his physical development.

Social researchers are calling for more and careful studies of TA concepts (25) and prediction of outcome based on therapeutic stance. Research using script analysis and other Transactional Analysis concepts is creating knowledge about profiles of correctional community residents (12), seriously ill people (11), and abusing parents (28, 30) that can be used to predict, assess, and treat.

Treatment outcome research (1, 40) is also increasing with the suggestion for more follow-up study and more validation of high client reported satisfaction with Transactional Analysis treatment. Much of this research is being reported in the Transactional Analysis Research Index for support of ongoing study and evaluation (39). Many clients claim, "I changed my life using Transactional Analysis." It is an ongoing challenge to research to further clarify how this occurs and how long it lasts.

References

1. Bader, Elen. "Redecisions in Family Therapy: A Study of Change in an Intensive Family Therapy Workshop," *Transactional Analysis Journal*, Vol. 12, No. 1 (January 1982), pp. 27–39.

2. Barnes, Graham (ed.). *Transactional Analysis After Eric Berne.* New York: Harper's College Press, 1977.

3. Berne, Eric. *A Layman's Guide to Psychiatry and Psychoanalysis.* New York: Ballantine, 1947–1957.

4. ———. *The Structure and Dynamics of Organizations and Groups.* New York: Grove Press, 1963.

5. ———. *Sex in Human Loving.* New York: Simon and Schuster, 1970.

6. ———. *What Do You Say After You Say Hello?* New York: Grove Press, 1972.

7. Childs-Gowell, Elaine, and Phill Kinnaman. *Bodyscript Blockbusting: A Treatment Approach to Body Awareness.* Seattle: published by the authors, 1978.

8. Clayton, S. H., and R. L. M. Dunbar. "Transactional Analysis in an Alcohol Safety Program," *Social Work*, Vol. 22, No. 3 (May 1977), pp. 209–213.

9. Coburn, Denise. *Gentle Birth and Origins of Social Satisfaction.* Unpublished monogram on an exploratory study of twenty-five children birthed using gentle birth methods. Michigan State University, School of Social Work, 1977.

10. ———. *A Preventive Project Report: Elevating Self-Esteem of Mothers of Sexually Exploited Children Using a Transactional Analysis Treatment Model.* Presented at the Fifth International Congress on Child Abuse and Neglect. Montreal, Quebec, September 1984.

11. Coburn, Denise, and Christopher Coburn. *Bio-Psychosocial Factors in Pathogenesis and Treatment of Cardiovascular Disease: Emphasis on Coronary Heart Disease—A Team Approach.* Presented at the Annual Summer Conference of the International Transactional Analysis Association, Oakland, California, 1983.

12. Corsover, Harry. *Life Scripts of a Correctional Therapeutic Community.* Unpublished doctoral dissertation, University of Illinois at Urbana-Champaign, 1977.

13. Crossman, Patricia. "Permission and Protection," *Transactional Analysis Bulletin*, Vol. 5, No. 19 (July 1966), pp. 152–154.

14. Drye, Robert, Robert Goulding, and Mary E. Goulding. "No Suicide Decisions: Patient Monitoring of Suicidal Risk," *American Journal of Psychiatry*, Vol. 130, No. 2 (February 1973), pp. 171–175.

15. Dusay, John M. *Egograms—How I See You and You See Me.* New York: Harper and Row, 1977.

16. English, Fanita. "The Substitution Factor: Rackets and Real Feelings, Part I," *Transactional Analysis Journal*, Vol. 1, No. 4 (October 1971), pp. 27–33. "Rackets and Real Feelings, Part II," *Transactional Analysis Journal*, Vol. 2, No. 1 (January 1972), pp. 23–27.

17. Erikson, Erik H. *Childhood and Society.* New York: Norton, 1950.

18. Ernst, Franklin. "The O.K. Corral," *Transactional Analysis Journal*, Vol. 1, No. 4 (October 1971), pp. 33–41.

19. Erskine, Richard, and Marilyn Zalcman. "The Racket System: A Model for Racket Analysis," *Transactional Analysis Journal*, Vol. 9, No. 1 (January 1979), p. 51.

20. Golan, Namoi. *Treatment in Crisis Situations*. New York: Free Press, 1978.

21. Goulding, Mary McClure, and Robert Goulding. *Changing Lives Through Redecision Therapy*. New York: Brunner/Mazel, 1979.

22. Goulding, Robert L. "New Directions in Transactional Analysis, Creating an Environment for Change," in Sager and Kaplan (eds.), *Progress in Group and Family Therapy*, New York: Brunner/Mazel, 1972, pp. 105–134.

23. ———. "Thinking and Feeling in Transactional Analysis: Three Empasses," *Voices: The Art and Science of Psychotherapy*, Vol. 2, No. 1 (1975), issue 39.

24. ———, and Mary E. Goulding, "Injunctions, Decisions, and Redecisions," *Transactional Analysis Journal*, Vol. 6, No. 1 (January 1976), pp. 41–48.

25. Hurley, John R. "Ego State Identifiability: Toward Better Research," *Transactional Analysis Journal*, Vol. 3, No. 3 (July 1973), pp. 164–165.

26. James, Muriel. "Self Reparenting: Theory and Process," *Transactional Analysis Journal*, Vol. 4, No. 3 (July 1974), p. 32.

27. ———, and Dorothy Jongeward. *Born to Win*. Reading, Mass.: Addison-Wesley, 1971.

28. Johnson, Diane. *Abusive vs. Competent Mother: Prediction of Parenting Behaviors from Self-Reported Life History Variables*. Unpublished doctoral dissertation, Michigan State University, Department of Psychology, East Lansing, Michigan, 1979.

29. Jorgensen, Elizabeth W., and Henry I. Jorgensen. *Eric Berne: Master Gamesman*. New York: Grove Press, 1984.

30. Justice, Blair, and Rita Justice. *The Abusing Family*. New York: Human Services Press, 1976.

31. Kahler, Talbi, and Hedges Capers. "The Miniscript," *Transactional Analysis Journal*, Vol. 4, No. 1 (January 1974), pp. 26–42.

32. Karpman, Stephen. "Fairy Tales and Script Drama Analysis," *Transactional Analysis Journal*, Vol. 7, No. 26 (April 1968), pp. 39–44.

33. ———. "Options," *Transactional Analysis Journal*, Vol. 1, No. 1 (January 1971), pp. 79–87.

34. Landheer, Pam Levin. *Cycles of Power*. Published by the author, 1980.

35. LeBoyer, Frederick. *Birth Without Violence*. New York: Knopf, 1974.

36. Levin, Pam. *Becoming the Way We Are: A Treatment Guide to Personal Development*. Berkeley, Calif.: Published by the author, 1974; 3rd printing, 1979.

37. Lynch, James J. *The Broken Heart*. New York: Basic Books, 1977.

38. McClendon, Ruth, and Leslie B. Kadis. *Chocolate Pudding and Other Approaches to Intensive Multiple-Family Therapy*. Palo Alto, Calif.: Science and Behavior Books, 1983.

39. McGahey, Cheryl C., and Maudine Blair. *The Transactional Analysis Research Index: An International Reference Book* (updated yearly). Tallahasee, Fla.: Florida Institute for Transactional Analysis, 1976.

40. McNeel, John R. "Redecisions in Psychotherapy: A Study of the Effects of an

Intensive Weekend Group Workshop," *Transactional Analysis Journal*, Vol. 12, No. 1 (January 1982).

41. Mellow, Ken, and Eric Schiff. "Redefining," *Transactional Analysis Journal*, Vol. 5, No. 3 (July 1975), p. 303.

42. ———. "Discounting," *Transactional Analysis Journal*, Vol. 5, No. 3 (July 1975), p. 295.

43. Prescott, James. *The Humanist Alternative*. Keynote Address at the Fifteenth Annual International Transactional Analysis Summer Conference, Montreal, Quebec, 1977. (To inquire about copies, write ITAA, 1772 Vallejo St., San Francisco, CA 94123.)

44. Schiff, Jacqui. *Cathexis Reader*. New York: Harper and Row, 1975.

45. Seligman, Martin (ed.). *Helplessness—On Depression, Development and Death*. San Francisco: Freeman, 1975.

46. Sinclair Brown, Wendy. "A TA Redecision Group Psychotherapy Treatment Program for Mothers who Physically Abuse and/or Seriously Neglect Their Children." *Transactional Analysis Journal*, Vol. 12, No. 1 (January 1982), pp. 39–46.

47. Spitz, Rene. "Hospitalism, Genesis of Psychiatric Conditions in Early Childhood," *Psychoanalytic Study of the Child*. New York: International Universities Press, Inc., 1945, pp. 53–74.

48. Steiner, Claude. "A Little Boy's Dream," *Transactional Analysis Journal*, Vol. 1, No. 1 (January 1971), pp. 49–60.

49. ———. "The Stroke Economy," *Transactional Analysis Journal*, Vol. 1, No. 3 (July 1971), pp. 9–15.

50. ———. *Scripts People Live*. New York: Grove Press, 1974.

51. Woollams, Stanley J. "Formation of the Script," *Transactional Analysis Journal*, Vol. 3, No. 1 (January 1973).

52. ———, and Michael Brown. *Transactional Analysis: A Modern and Comprehensive Text of Transactional Analysis Theory and Practice*. Dexter, Mich.: Huron Valley Institute Press, 1978.

53. Woollams, Stanley, Michael Brown, and Kristyn Huige. *Transactional Analysis in Brief*. Ann Arbor, Mich.: Huron Valley Institute Press, 1974.

54. Yalom, Irvin, Morton Lieberman, and Matthew B. Miles. *Encounter Groups: First Facts*. New York: Basic Books, 1973.

Annotated Listing of Key References

BERNE, ERIC. *What Do You Say After You Say Hello?* New York: Grove Press, 1972.
This is an exciting, intellectually provocative presentation of Berne's major Transactional Analysis concepts—games, rackets, strokes, time structuring. He discusses the beginnings of games when children are young and formulating their script and life plan. Considerable material is presented on scripts.

BERNE, ERIC. *The Structure and Dynamics of Organizations and Groups.* New York: Grove Press, 1963.
This book contains extensive information on Berne's game theory, time structuring in groups related to games and rackets, and early life scripts reflected in behavior attitude and feelings of members of treatment groups. He presents diagrams of groups: seating, authority, organizational, group process diagnosis, and transactional diagrams.

GOULDING, MARY McCLURE, and ROBERT GOULDING. *Changing Lives Through Redecision Therapy.* New York: Brunner/Mazel, 1979.
This book by the founders and leaders of the First Training Institute in Transactional Analysis is a major contribution to the field of psychotherapy and, particularly, to the expansion and application of Transactional Analysis theory. The primary thrust of the book is to teach methods of change that lead to an autonomous and self-fulfilling life.

JAMES, MURIEL, and DOROTHY JONGEWARD. *Born to Win.* Reading, Mass.: Addison-Wesley, 1971.
This is a warm, sensitive, positive, and optimistic book about many social truths that Transactional Analysis supports, such as that persons are OK and that awareness can lead to change. Information about stroking, scripts, structural analysis, games, and all significant concepts are presented with exercises for experiential experiments on application of the theory. A very popular and well-received introduction to Transactional Analysis.

McCLENDON, RUTH, and LESLIE B. KADIS. *Chocolate Pudding and Other Approaches to Intensive Multiple-Family Therapy.* Palo Alto, Calif.: Science and Behavior Books, 1983.
This book is a landmark in family therapy, presenting impressive changes in family transactional patterns leading to achievement of satisfying family life goals. The intensive, interactional approaches combine Transactional Analysis, Gestalt, and family system strategies that result in awareness of unsatisfactory behavior and learning and integration of new behaviors. The material is presented as a set of four families in a week of intensive social treatment.

STEINER, CLAUDE. *Scripts People Live.* New York: Grove Press, 1974.
This popular book presents further developments of Berne's concept of life script or life plan chosen at an early age and followed throughout life unless changed through developmental experience or awareness leading to change. He includes methods to analyze and methods of therapy to change these scripts to winning life plans of love, thought, and joy.

WOOLLAMS, STANLEY, and MICHAEL BROWN. *Transactional Analysis: A Modern and Comprehensive Text of Transactional Analysis Theory and Practice.* Dexter, Mich.: Huron Valley Institute Press, 1978.
The major and solid theory of Berne's Transactional Analysis is presented with

new additions and expansions of theory by others who studied with and followed Berne. The book is rich with examples, diagrams, and case stories from years of varied and successful clinical practice. Paths to effective communication and personal change with Transactional Analysis leading to satisfying human interaction are clearly mapped, described, and defined by the authors.

CHAPTER 18

Psychosocial Theory

Francis J. Turner

Introduction

The term "psychosocial" has deep, strong roots in the history of social work. Although originally a generic term, used as a bridging concept between psychological and sociological thinking, it later became attached to a particular approach to social work practice. In addition to this proper designation as a social work thought system, it has once again taken on a more general usage among the helping professions to reflect a commitment to a broad perspective of human functioning. It is a term that fully belongs in the domain of social work. If there is a concept that clearly sets out a function of social work treatment different from the focus of other professions it is this one.

It is a concept that serves to prevent overemphasis on either the inner life of persons or our relationships with society. When applied to a system of clinical practice, it refers to the body of theory that stresses the need for an integrated focus on psychological and sociological functioning; that is, on our intrapersonal, interpersonal, and intersystemic behavior.

Psychosocial practice is a thought system that stresses healthy development. It has the interventive objective of establishing optimal conditions for human growth and development. "It is . . . an attempt to mobilize the strengths of the personality and the resources of the environment at strategic

484

points to improve the opportunities available to the individual and to develop more effective personal and interpersonal functioning" (35).

It is also an essentially optimistic approach to the human condition. This optimism stems from an increasing understanding of, and wonderment at, the potential of the human being to recover from serious deprivation and, in the face of overwhelmingly rejecting situations, continue to progress and develop.

In this chapter we will present an overview of this theory rather than a detailed examination of each of its component parts, relying on the bibliography to assist the reader who wishes to pursue this material more deeply.

Historical Origins

Civilized groups, whatever their origins, have always known that to survive and prosper a balance of physical, emotional, human, and spiritual nurture is needed. Over the centuries knowledge of this needed balance has not been fully utilized. Social work, with its formal origins in the traditions of the Charity Organization Society movement, is one channel through which society has attempted to formalize and use this awareness. Psychosocial practice as it exists today reflects these early roots and the subsequent development and refinement of ideas through the thinking of such social workers as Mary Richmond, Gordon Hamilton, Betsy Libby, Bertha Reynolds, Annette Garrett, Lucille Austin, and most recently Florence Hollis, as well as many others. The term itself seems to have been used first by Frank Hankins, a faculty member at Smith College, in 1930 (29). It was then picked up in Gordon Hamilton's early writings (27) and developed in the writings of Florence Hollis (33, 34, 35, 36). The term "psychosocial" can also be found in the writings of a wide range of other social scientists and practitioners as an important bridging concept. To date, however, it is only social work literature that has developed it into a distinct thought system.

This theory also reflects the tradition in social work of seeking knowledge from all relevant sources. Undoubtedly, the impact of psychoanalytic theory has been strong and lasting. For some this strong influence is seen as a weakness, while for others it gives the approach legitimacy. Other important sources have been the later ego psychology thinking of psychoanalysts such as Erik Erikson, Heinz Hartmann (32), and others, as well as the theories of sociologists Talcott Parsons and Robert Merton and anthropologists Clyde and Florence Kluckholn, to name only a few. More recently, psychosocial thinking has incorporated many of the concepts of learning theory, family theory, role theory, systems theory, and crisis theory that are so prevalent in today's practice. Further, psychosocial thinking has incorporated many concepts from the social sciences, such as class, ethnicity, race, religion, minority groups, values, and power. Thus, one of the distinguishing characteristics of the psychosocial approach is its openness to development and change. This in turn makes it considerably broader than its origins would indicate and vastly richer and more flexible than its critics would acknowledge.

Theoretical Base

Overview

The psychosocial system of therapeutic help builds from an understanding of biopsycho development, interpersonal influence, the influence of significant others, and the influence of significant environments and systems as essential characteristics in the development and maintenance of healthy and fulfilling human living. From this it follows that the knowledge bases of practice are drawn from the biological, psychological, and social components of human growth and development and their interaction. To these components are joined an understanding of the interrelatedness of the spectrum of systems in which persons function, their strengths and weaknesses, their potentials and limitations. On this knowledge base are developed skills in engaging responsibly and effectively in therapeutic and helping relationships with individuals, families, groups, and significant environments to bring about planned change in human functioning. Specifically, it seeks to understand persons in the context of their current reality and to use this understanding in a therapeutic way in the treatment of psychological, personal, interpersonal, and social problems and their relationships.

As mentioned earlier, the psychosocial approach holds an optimistic view of human potential. But this optimism is not a blindly naive one; our experience has all too clearly helped us to understand the complex and manifold ways in which human development may be curtailed, warped, damaged, and distorted by numerous, historical, intrapsychic, interpersonal, and environmental influences.

The general objective of psychosocial practice is the fostering of healthy growth patterns. It is understood that the structure and content of healthy psychosocial growth are complex; growth is developed, or hindered, through a combination of biological, material, physical, personal, and interpersonal factors in interaction with a wide range of significant environments. Because of this, psychosocial practice is strongly committed to an ongoing search for a fuller understanding of individuals, families, and groups in their psychosocial realities to better help them achieve their potential in a satisfying, fulfilling way.

Value Bases

One of the interesting phenomena of contemporary practice is the widespread interest in values and value orientations and their influence and importance in the therapeutic process. No longer are therapy and the therapist held to be value-free, nor is discussion of values with the client to be avoided. Thus any approach to practice must be aware of the values, implicit and explicit, of each thought system.

Psychosocial therapy is based on the general social work commitment to the importance and worth of each individual human person. Flowing from this is the related commitment to the goal of individual and social betterment, both materially and emotionally, and to the development of human potential. Because each person is considered to be important and of inestimable value, there is a strong belief in individual responsibility and the related concept of the importance of the individual's participation in his or her destiny. Since we as humans are social animals who fully reach our potential through relationships and identifications with family, friends, small groups, and communities, the concepts related to individual responsibility and participation are also transferable to family, group, community, and society.

Such value orientations are the content and product of millennia of theological, philosophical, and sociological thought. People can come to accept them through many pathways; regardless of their origin, they serve as the essential value orientation of psychosocial therapy.

Following on these is another set of commitments that rest somewhere between value orientations and the pragmatic outcome of experience. Included in this category are the familiar ideas of acceptance, permissiveness, uncondemning attitudes, congruence, confidentiality, competence, respect, and controlled emotional response as necessary components of helping relationships (8, 65). Originally, these qualities of practice emerged from our basic respect and commitment to individuals. Additional support for them came from experience. Thus we know from practice that work with an individual or a group more readily and effectively achieves its goal if a commitment to these qualities is demonstrated; that is, they are both philosophically and pragmatically sound.

Basic Assumptions About Human Behavior

Psychosocial therapy is also established on a series of assumptions about human behavior. It begins with the assumption that basic human nature is good. Human nature is also free, but not in an absolute way, for people are greatly affected by their histories. Yet, even though free, within limitation human behavior can be understood and predicted. Even though we are all individuals, there is much about us that is common, knowable, and predictable. Individuals are seen, therefore, as being somewhere between the "invincible masters of their fates" and the "powerless pawns of destiny."

It is assumed that human behavior cannot just be understood (this, of course, in a relative and developing way), it can also be influenced and changed in a predictable manner. In addition, available knowledge of human behavior can be transmitted through cognitive methods; that is, other people can be taught to understand and influence behavior. From this it follows that it is possible to hold individuals—for example, professionals—accountable for the misuse or nonuse of knowledge when there is community-sanctioned responsibility to use it.

As well, psychosocial therapy is strongly committed to a scientifically built and tested body of knowledge. It does not claim that all of its present concepts are of this nature, but it is committed to the pursuit of such a foundation. Related to this idea is a conviction that a structured approach to theory building is fully compatible with a humanitarian concern for the people we serve.

In seeking to influence and change behavior it is understood that physical, human, and situational agents have differential impact on individuals, groups, and communities. These influences are intersystemic, so that changes in one aspect of a person's functioning or reality has reverberating influences on other segments of their psychosocial condition. In our present state of knowledge, the extent or limitations of this intersystemic influence is not fully known.

A further assumption of this theory is that a person's past is important. Thus, in seeking to understand a person's current behavior, the important though nondetermining influence of earlier history must be acknowledged. Just as a person's ability to function adequately and successfully in a current situation results from skills, knowledge, attitudes, reflexes, perceptions, and experiences from the past, so can unsuccessful and stress-producing problem behavior be similarly influenced. But the interest in our clients' pasts is to help them understand and cope effectively with the present and thus with the future. Understanding past influences can bring about restored balance to current behavior. When either by chance or direction new and successful patterns of coping are acquired, future behavior will be influenced. A person who is helped to cope more effectively with a current situation can learn to use this experience to deal with future situations that only remotely resemble the original.

This historical component of human functioning and its importance in psychotherapeutic endeavors has been the source of considerable professional dispute. Positions have been taken ranging from an almost total dependence on understanding the past to its almost total disregard.

Surely the most elementary observation of non-therapy-based human interaction clearly indicates the importance of talking out, talking about, and reflecting on the past as an aid to current functioning, whether this be the sharing of a guilty secret with a close friend or a detailed examination of a prior experience with a knowledgeable associate to try to understand and learn from it.

The moving away from interest in a detailed process of history-taking emerged from two sources. On the one hand there was a valid concern that in some instances the gathering of history had become an end in itself, with little relevance to the subsequent intervention. On the other hand, as skill developed in short-term, present-centered treatment, there was no longer interest in long, detailed histories. Psychosocial thinking holds this should not be an either/or situation. The concept of relevency is the key issue requiring a professional judgment in each instance as to what knowledge of the past is required and, just as importantly, when in the process of a case is it required. In an interesting way, the growing body of knowledge of the long-term and long-delayed effects on current problems of many war-time experiences such as the holocaust has revived interest in the importance of a historical perspective in practice.

An additional essential assumption of this theory relates to nonconscious phenomena; that is, an individual is not fully aware of all the historical intrapersonal influences on her current functioning. Awareness of some experiences, attitudes, emotions, and memories is only partial, except in special circumstances or through the agency of specialized techniques. These unconscious components of a person's experience influence but do not determine behavior.

This question of the impact of the unconscious and preconscious on current behavior and its relative importance for psychotherapy is variously accepted in the spectrum of current clinical social work. This topic has been fully and masterfully dealt with by Hollis (33) and by Herbert Strean in his Chapter 2 of this book. Undoubtedly, one of the trends in psychosocial therapy has been a reassessment of the significance of the unconscious in practice. In this reassessment there has been no deemphasis on the importance of understanding the potential influence of unconscious and preconscious material on behavior. There has, however, been growing appreciation of the fact that considerable growth and healthy functioning can and does take place without direct use being made of this material. Undoubtedly, many clients are helped by social workers who have little sympathy with the concept of unconscious mental mechanisms. But we also know that clients can withdraw and treatment can be rendered ineffectual because the unconscious, preconscious, and historical components of the clients' reality are not considered, understood, or permitted to enter the purview of treatment in situations in which these influences have been a significant part of the problem.

Early on, psychosocial practice found in psychoanalytic theory its major source for understanding the individual and his relationship with society. This theory was modified and greatly strengthened by the developments of ego psychology, considerably enriched by the improved understanding of genetic endowment and by current sociology and psychology. All this has been integrated with the valuable insights and understandings derived from practitioners' practice wisdom and formal research.

But individuals are not only rational, psychodynamic, and interacting persons, they are also physical entities. Hence, some understanding of our biological nature is stressed in this practice theory. All of us are aware of how great can be the influence on our functioning of even as simple a thing as the common cold. Thus in practice we must always have some understanding of our clients' physical state, both chronic and transitory. In recent years we have become aware of a much closer connection between our emotional state and our somatic functioning. This further emphasizes the need to be closely attuned to our clients' physical well-being. There is a growing appreciation that this aspect of our clients' reality needs to be given more attention than it has been receiving in most schools of social work (41).

In applying these understandings of persons in interaction with their situations, psychosocial therapy has developed the following structure of intervention. These interventive resources are most easily dichotomized into those elements of treatment that consist of direct contact with the client and those elements consisting of activities by the social worker with other components of the client's life. The latter include such things as significant individuals and groups, environments, or material realities that are variously manipulated to bring about sought-after change. Useful as it has been to divide treatment into direct and indirect, an unfortunate tradition has developed of giving the direct work with clients more status than the indirect or environmental work. As treatment becomes more complex, this sharp division is hopefully becoming less relevant. All interventive resources are essentially neutral and become valued in individual cases to the extent that they are appropriately used in individual situations.

Direct Methods

Relationship

The essential component of direct work with the client has always been identified as the professional relationship that is fostered between the client and/or clients and the social worker. To such an extent has this been considered the pivotal point of treatment that, for some, the effectiveness of treatment has tended to be measured by the intensity of the relationship.

Social workers frequently forget the power of concerned, knowledgeable, trustworthy reaching out to clients, which becomes almost automatic to experienced practitioners. Over and over again we meet persons in our practice who have rarely had an opportunity in their lives to sit down and talk freely about themselves to someone who in a sincerely concerned way can hear, understand, and respond from a background of learning and experience that encompasses the combined history of many experiences. Too often we forget how helpful even a single such experience can be in a person's life. Most of us on reflection can recall occasions when an hour with a person significant to us has dramatically affected us and our subsequent life choices.

The potential positive effects of relationships are such that many persons can be helped by individuals not trained or consciously skilled in formal psychotherapeutic processes. This phenomenon unfortunately gives weight to those who argue against intensive and lengthy training for practice.

But as important as the formal helping relationship is, it is not in itself sufficient for practice. It is the skillful and understanding way in which this phenomenon is used and the length, intensity, frequency, content, and forms of interaction that are added to it that result in responsible, effective treatment.

Several years ago, the author was involved in a project with a family agency that had developed a long waiting list of people, each of whom had been seen once at intake. Our task was to reestablish contact with these people and offer them a brief service. On recontact, many of these persons indicated there was no longer a need for service, describing changes in attitude, perception, or behavior that had taken place from their one contact with the intake worker. These contacts were described with quotations, examples, and a sincerity that were certainly different from the responses of clients we meet in practice who did not wish to involve themselves in treatment after an initial contact.

Transference

One specific relationship component of interest in the psychosocial tradition is that of transference and countertransference (22). This concept is not currently being given the focused attention it received in the 1940s and early 1950s; nevertheless, it is still important. Transference reactions, if ignored, can create difficulties and problems in the course of treatment. Certainly our understanding of this phenomenon has expanded, and some components of relationship previously interpreted as transference reactions can be better explained in terms of values or ethnic differences and other life experiences. All transference reactions that take place need not be identified for the client or examined in treatment; what is important is that when this phenomenon is present its occurrence and strength be recognized, controlled if necessary, utilized when appropriate, and worked out if required.

Since each person, including the therapist, brings to new relationships the experiences of his own relationship history, it is essential in psychosocial practice for therapists to be aware of themselves and their own reactions as well as to try to understand those of their clients. We know that we do not all relate identically to all people, we know that there are kinds of people and situations that make us uncomfortable, anxious, guarded, or defensive. We need to be aware of our own responses to clients to ensure objectivity in assessing the nature of the relationship and the strength and relevance of material from earlier relationships that may be operating. It is hoped that training and experience teach us to understand and appropriately adjust.

It is because of this awareness of the influence of one's relationship history on all new relationships that psychosocial thinking stresses the need for a high degree of self-awareness on the part of the therapist. Hence it gives a particular emphasis to the need for supervision, consultation, and indeed at times one's own therapy to meet the need for objectivity in relationships.

Direct Treatment Procedures

In the past decades considerable attention has been given to identifying and classifying the range of procedures and techniques that describe the interactions that take place between social workers and clients. The work of Hollis and her associates has greatly assisted progress in understanding the specifics of these interactions (38). This development, and the content-analysis techniques that are a part of it, provide rich potential both for more precise understanding of this system and for comparison of various approaches to practice.

In the Hollis schema, emphasis is put on the twofold necessity of having the client look both inward and outward and reflect on the interconnection of these two components of reality. In doing this, six major forms of interaction are identified as taking place between clients and their social workers. Since these have been fully described in recent literature it will suffice simply to list them without description or comment.

The six major headings of worker-client interaction are:

1. Sustaining Procedures
2. Procedures of Direct Influence
3. Procedures of Ventilation, Description, and Exploration
4. Procedures that Encompass Reflective Consideration of the Current Person-Situation
5. Procedures that Encompass Reflective Consideration of Patterns of Personality and Behavior and Their Dynamics
6. Procedures that Encompass Reflective Consideration of the Past and Its Effect on Current Functioning

Each of these categories has specified subdivisions that permit precise quantification of the client and worker verbal content in interviews.

An important component of this classification system and its subdivisions is the way in which it draws attention to the twofold use of reflection on the intra and extra components of a situation. Examination of practice has shown the importance of helping a client focus on selected aspects of a situation to understand his own contribution to the situation and the related problem-solving and decision-making work. No one of the various items is considered to be of any more importance or value than another. Each has its place in practice. The challenge and responsibility for each practitioner in relation to particular cases, and for the field in relation to its body of knowledge, are to search for the optimum combination and blend of these procedures suitable for the treatment objectives established for individual cases or groups of cases.

Using this schema, research has demonstrated that patterns can be identified that indicate commonalities in practice (12, 36, 37, 52). A brief overview of these findings indicates that the greater part of interview content revolves around a combination of ventilative material and reflective consideration of the current situation, with important but limited use of the other procedures. Further, it has been found that sustaining, ventilation, and description are important in early interviews. Use of past-focused material and efforts to elicit such material are not nearly so extensive as some practitioners have thought. It has also been clearly demonstrated that in spite of our traditional discomfort about the use of direct influence with clients, we do use such procedures. When this is done effectively it is in a highly selected manner and in company with considerable sustaining material. Other research has demonstrated that clear and patterned differences can be observed in examining the interview content of situations where clients and workers are from different value orientations or from different ethnic groups (76).

Not as much precision is available in psychosocial therapy about other components of direct work. We know, of course, that factors such as the timing, length, and frequency of interviews, the setting of interviews, and the physical surroundings in which interviews take place all differentially affect interviews and their outcome. The locale of interviews is also an important variable in treatment—the use of office interviews, both formal and informal, home visits, and informal settings such as restaurants, cars, street corners, and park benches. Frequently, the decisions about use of these variations are made on the basis of pragmatics, agency policy, or at times on the basis of preference or desire to be nontraditional rather than on the exigencies of the case. Thus, we find colleagues who will interview only in a formal cross-the-desk situation while others will never interview in such a setting, insisting on a highly informal situation. Clearly, both have their place but this should be decided on the basis of case-related objectives rather than value preferences. As our knowledge of the multiinfluences on clients expands, more attention is being given to the differntial effects of the setting on client behavior and attitude. This interest is helping us to understand better the importance of physical surroundings, the location, the name, the auspices, and the policies of an agency (79).

Technical Aids

Another set of resources that is beginning to find its way into direct psychosocial treatment is the use of technical equipment as aids to treatment (4). Considerable progress has been made in understanding how equipment such as tape recorders and closed-circuit television can be used in observing, teaching, research, and the recording of practice. Less attention has been given to the ways in which these resources can be used as adjuncts to treatment itself. Some work has been done on letting clients in marital situations listen to themselves on audiotape. Some therapists have had families watch themselves on videotape and use the reactions of the various family members to this self-observation as the content of subsequent interviews. It has been found that in many instances these technical resources help the client in his reflective consideration of various aspects of the present-person-in-interaction-with-situation. Having the opportunity to observe himself and significant others in interaction through the medium of these resources provides the client with a rich opportunity for this type of process. There is also some experimenting going on with the use of two-way television as a means of providing direct service to clients unable to be present at a particular situation, such as members of an isolated community. Rather than rejecting these efforts as dehumanizing the relationship, we need to assess carefully their potential for providing services.

In addition to these recording procedures, there are other types of equipment beginning to be seen as adjuncts to therapy. It is clear that increasing use is going to be made of computers, not only as a way of storing and retrieving large amounts of data about clients and groups of clients, but also as direct aids to practice. For example, it is already possible to build programs that permit clients to give a great deal of their history through interaction with a computer. This might be particularly useful for very withdrawn or hostile clients. Use is also being made of various forms of stress measures, relaxation aids, and apparatus to assist in biofeedback procedures.

Although traditionally social workers have not made use of technical equipment in treatment, there is no reason why they shouldn't. A psychosocial orientation, with its commitment to openness, stresses that anything that will help a client should be used. Clearly, clients can be helped in this manner, and it follows that workers should be more attentive to this type of resource.

Work with Significant Others and Environments

Although an essential and significant aspect of psychosocial therapy involves direct contact with clients, an equally essential and significant component includes work with significant others, systems, and material aspects of a client's life. As mentioned, this direct involvement in the client's outer reality in conjunction with work with the personality is the distinguishing mark of this school, and indeed gives it its name.

Although always essential to psychosocial thinking, work in the client's environment has tended to be given secondary importance in practice. Two factors seem to have contributed to this. The first is sociological in that our society gives high status to the model of psychotherapy that uses the format of the intense clinical office-based type of interpersonal contact. Accompanying this valuation has been a related idea that this form of interpersonal helping requires skills and training at a level beyond environmental work.

The second factor stems partially from the first and is more a semantic one. In our tradition we have tended to collapse the complex, multifaceted external environment of the client into single terms, such as "milieu," "environment," or "external reality." This has resulted in a tendency to oversimplify these components of reality.

A result of this two-faceted underestimation of the importance and status of environmental work has been a corresponding underuse of these components of treatment, a tendency to take understanding of their dimensions for granted, and a failure to give them the same detailed study that is given to direct client contacts.

There has been some increased interest in this aspect of treatment stemming from the recent renewal of concern for clients' rights, advocacy, and the damaging effects of some components of established systems on people. Even here, though, only partial components of the client's environment have been stressed, rather than the total spectrum. Thus, for some colleagues, all work in the environment must be carried out in a stance of advocacy or confrontation. Important as these strategies are, they do not have an inherent preferential place. They are valuable only when they are appropriate for the situation and goals of treatment. Just as inappropriate use of sustaining techniques can be detrimental to a client, so can an inappropriate use of any of the skills in environmental intervention.

The knowledge of human behavior, social systems, and their interaction required to intervene efficiently and effectively in the client's external reality is just as demanding as that required in direct work. Not only is this aspect of treatment just as demanding, it can also be just as effective. For example, highly developed skills are required to involve effectively an employer already overburdened with his own problems to work with a troubled adolescent trying to find his way in a first employment situation. Such an intervention can have healing and growth potential for the young man as significant and long-lasting as many weeks of one-to-one treatment. (As a side effect, such intervention may have positive results for the employer as well.)

A particularly useful and indeed powerful component of indirect help consists in work with significant others in a client's life—such as friends, family, and close associates and peers. Sometimes this is done on a case-by-case basis, although there is increasing awareness of the benefit of utilizing the potential of friends, volunteers, and indigenous workers on a regular basis.

An excellent formulation of the functions and roles in this external component of treatment is presented by Hollis (39). She discusses this material from a threefold approach: the types of communications used, the range of resources that are called upon, and, most importantly, the range of roles that can be employed. It is this last component that has been given the least critical attention in practice. We have frequently and variously identified the range of resources used in practice, but we have tended to underestimate the range of roles we have used by a failure to identify them specifically. The roles identified by Hollis are those of provider, locator, creator, interpreter, mediator, and aggressive intervener (39, p. 155). To this list can be added the role of broker, which describes that cluster of activities in which the social worker serves as coordinator and manager of various services and resources in which the client is involved, a most essential role in today's multiservice practice.

The challenge for the therapist related to the indirect methods of practice is to identify the various components of environmental treatment, understand their interconnectedness, and collate knowledge of the differential use of these roles for specific clients and clusters of clients.

There is also the additional challenge of further developing an understanding of the balance between direct and environmental procedures best suited for individual cases. Finally, there is the challenge of ensuring that these facets of practice are given proper weighting as effective therapeutic resources. The persistence of a pattern of thinking that differentially values environmental work with the concomitant tendency to relegate responsibility for it to nonprofessionals is a disservice to our clients. As mentioned earlier, it is hoped that this dichotomization of intervention will disappear and be replaced with the concept of a spectrum with intensive psychotherapy at one end and the provision of material assistance at the other and efforts made to understand the strengths and limitations of all steps on the spectrum for particular situations.

Psychosocial History and Diagnosis

The foregoing pages have presented a highly condensed summary of the range of resources and roles available to the psychosocial practitioner. The task for today's practitioner is to appreciate the component parts of this range, to understand their potential and limitations and the exigencies of the situation, and from this to structure, with the client, a pattern of interaction that will best achieve the case goals.

To make most efficient use of this spectrum of psychological, societal, and material resources, psychosocial therapy emphasizes the necessity for understanding each treated situation as completely as is appropriate; that is, for a full assessment and diagnosis. It is this aspect of treatment that causes some to designate this school the "diagnostic school." Also, it is this component of practice, or rather a misunderstanding of it, that has been the focus of criticism. For some the term "diagnosis" as applied to social work practice is pejorative. This negative approach has been strengthened by the current reaction against classifying human behavior and the misuses to which classifications can and have been put. In a related way, but not as extensively, the emphasis that psychosocial treatment has put on the psychosocial study, or history, is also under criticism.

Focus on these two components of practice is based on the premise that the decision as to which of the many available components and procedures are to be used in a particular situation must be based on adequate knowledge and understanding of the person and situation. This in no way implies that the client is excluded from such decisions, or that treatment is chosen categorically. It does mean that for the social worker to make most effective use of the available knowledge and skills to achieve the goals mutually arrived at, decisions need to be made as to who the client is, what are the needs and wants, what are the strengths and limitations of the person and situation that can help or hinder, what resources are available, and what knowledge can be brought to this situation from other similar or dissimilar experiences. The purpose of the psychosocial study and diagnosis is to bring together the available components of the situation in an orderly, economic manner that permits adequate assessment and responsible decisions to be made.

But, like all components of practice, diagnosis must be related to the nature of the case and setting. Thus its nature, content, and detail will vary according to the time available, the type of problem, the nature of the request, the services available, the setting, and the skill of the worker.

Diagnosis, as both a process and a fact, is not by definition a voluminous enterprise. In both psychosocial study and diagnosis the law of parsimony applies. Only that amount of information is required which is necessary to reach the conclusions demanded by the situation. Thus, a person inquiring of an agency about available resources for institutional care of an aged relative need not be expected to give a complete history of all components of her history nor need the social worker involved prepare a lengthy detailed diagnosis. This doesn't imply that the worker ignores other questions the client may wish to ask, other potential areas of difficulty related to the request, other aspects of the client's life that may be affected by the request, other needs the client may have, other services the client might be able to use or the possibility that the original request is a hidden call for help for some other problem. These areas will be thought of against the worker's experience in similar situations, the assessment of the client's wishes and the perceived adequacy of the client's functioning out of which decisions are made as to planned procedures.

Thus a twenty-minute interview skillfully conducted usually represents a bewilderingly complex array of assessments, judgments, categorizations, and decisions by the social worker, many of which are almost intuitive; that is, the worker is constantly engaged in a diagnostic process.

Social workers are often accused of making things too complex, of looking for pathology when it isn't there, of involving clients in complex processes when simple ones would suffice. Such criticisms are not to be automatically disregarded, but neither should they be unquestioningly accepted. Life is complex; problems do have multiple and differential impacts; individuals do vary in their ability to cope with situations; people do disguise requests in a variety of ways. I shall never forget a client I saw at intake a few years ago who, in a quiet, controlled way, was inquiring about getting help for his wife whom he described as depressed, worried, and acting strangely. Following this interview, in which the situation was clarified, alternatives considered, help offered, and a plan made to see the wife, the man went home and a short time later committed suicide. His last unrecognized appeal for help had been disguised in a request for help for his wife.

Frequently, the criticisms of the diagnostic component of psychosocial therapy are in reality legitimate criticisms of the misuse of diagnosis; that is, of the process of diagnosis, not the diagnosis itself. One still meets colleagues for whom diagnosis seems to be identified with assigning a single-term label. The responsibility of arriving at a clear and precise assessment of clients-in-situations is misunderstood to mean narrow categorization. Clearly, this is not possible; if attempted it is irresponsible practice. But this type of criticism of diagnosis has by now been overstated and too often repeated. It seems to be more and more a rationale for avoiding the highly complex and awesome responsibility of reaching decisions about other human beings, the inescapable responsibility of anyone in a helping profession.

Settings

Psychosocial treatment is not restricted as to the settings in which it is best used. Although the early development of this thought system emerged principally from practice as observed in traditional agencies such as child welfare, family agencies, and private practice, the literature of the last few years reflects a widening application. For example, there is a notable expansion of interest in the health field as health becomes more responsive to the critical role of personality and reality issues. Another area where a psychosocial orientation, including a strong commitment to physical issues, is important, is that of child-abuse. In these matters, as in situations around suicide and homicide, the decisions and judgments by social workers have life and death implications.

Assuredly, there are settings that offer more opportunity to use the entire spectrum of attitudes, knowledge, and skills than others, but any setting committed to the improved psychosocial functioning of individuals, groups, and families, permits the application of this method. Some settings with a strong, controlling, authoritarian commitment create difficulties in the nature of client involvement, the setting of goals and objectives, and the range and kind of resources available to the social worker. Similarly, in some settings the worker may seriously question policies and practice or feel constrained by the limitations in resources that restrict the scope of intervention. But commitment to an open approach, as in this orientation, implies commitment to an ongoing search for ways of making more effective use of the settings in which psychosocial therapy is practiced, as well as a search for making the settings more useful for treatment.

Methods of Psychosocial Practice

Psychosocial practice has a strong historical connection to the casework tradition, thus its earlier emphasis on one-to-one treatment. As an open system it strongly supports the readiness of social workers to use a wider range of treatment modalities and to move comfortably from individual to joint, family, group, and community-based practice. The theories and methods of psychosocial therapy are not restricted to one-to-one practice, but are fully applicable to practice that utilizes joint interviewing as well as family and group methods. The knowledge required to understand clients in interaction with others and their situations includes by definition the spheres of dyads, familial and group dynamics, and their interactions. The goals of much of group and all family practice are fully consonant with the goals of psychosocial treatment. This is not to imply that psychosocial theory encompasses all forms of group and family treatment, but that this theory and practice base are sufficient and adequate preparation for a practitioner wishing to utilize a group and family modality of practice. If one's training and experience have been directed to a single form of practice, then additional supervised experience is required to develop other methodologies. But if an individual's training has been based on psychosocial theory and has included experience in a range of treatment modalities, the person is then well equipped for the multimethod demands of current practice. The profile of direct and indirect interventive methods, the understanding of relationship and its multiple manifestations, and the emphasis on use of self in treatment are all applicable and essential to a multimethod approach.

It is not being suggested that individual, joint, family, and group practice are identical. A minimum of experience quickly will show how different are the demands put on a practitioner in a family interview as compared to an interview with a single member of that family. The psychosocial approach differs from a generalist approach in that it holds that although there is a common core of the therapeutic concepts in all methods there are, however, differences between methods, just as there are vast differences between cases treated on a one-to-one basis. Each modality creates specific demands and patterns related to the use of time, content, and focus of interviews or sessions, relationship patterns and difficulties, transference manifestations, use of resources, contract, setting objectives, and goals and termination. These differences need to be learned, but all are within the present perspectives of psychosocial treatment. Every worker, if not skilled in all methods, has a responsibility to understand the potentials and limitations of all methods and how they apply to the needs, values, wishes, and abilities of particular client or client groups.

Clearly, in multiple client interviews complex communications, relationship and transference alignments occur and differential use is made of the procedures used in one-to-one as well as others specific to the modality. But it is important to see that these are not totally different treatment methods requiring differential theoretical bases. As mentioned earlier, a person who has limited his experience and practice to a single mode of treatment might well be weak in some elements of theory as well as skill, but these are individual limitations, not limitations in the system itself.

These ideas are not fully accepted by everyone; in many ways they go against our strongly established traditional terminology of casework and group work. In this age of terminological confusion one hesitates to suggest new terminology, especially if it deemphasizes already well-established terms. Certainly we should never lose the rich and separate traditions from which casework and the clinical elements of group work emerged. What is suggested is that the term "psychosocial" does contain all the elements of the demands of today's clinical practice in social work and overcomes the difficulties arising from a separate tradition of casework and group work and the more recent one of family therapy. There are, of course, many theoretical differences among group workers and among family therapists, but those who find value in the psychodynamic theory are close to psychosocial thinking.

In advocating a common base for all methods of clinical social work practice, it is not being argued that all practitioners need to be equally skilled in all methods. Just as some social workers are more interested, comfortable, and competent in working with specified kinds of clients and situations, so some will use different patterns of treatment. But we do a disservice to our clients if we restrict ourselves exclusively to a single modality, be this individual, family, or group. We can greatly extend our skills and make ourselves more helpful to clients by introducing a range of treatment alternatives into our practice. In those instances where practitioners prefer to concentrate on one mode of practice, they need to associate themselves with colleagues who can supplement with other modes when needed.

Community

These ideas about clinical intervention do not apply as clearly to work with communities as with dyads, groups, and families. There still is a clear division between practice with individuals, families, and groups seeking to achieve improved psychosocial functioning for themselves and their families, and practice aimed at helping sections of the community or the entire community to organize and develop resources needed to achieve community goals and aspirations, although there is a common value base.

Since these areas are all a part of social work, we should not be surprised that the distinction between these two streams of practice is not a precise one. Although in the heat of battle between clinical social workers and resource-development social workers there seems to be little in common, the psychosocial tradition strongly associates itself with community organization and development, social action, and social change. This has been especially true in the family agency field. There are few experienced practitioners in this field who have not committed much of their professional and personal time and resources to this broad area of concern.

In the psychosocial tradition there is a clear commitment to concern for and at times direct work with communities. Certainly, in our diagnostic activities, it is essential that we seek to understand the reality and impact of the various systems and subsystems both as they exist and as they are perceived by the client. To make these assessments requires knowledge of community structure, power, systems, history, tradition, and values. Beyond assessment and diagnosis, in moving into environmental work, the same knowledge helps us to evaluate the potential and limitations of the components of the client's significant others. Only with this knowledge can we plan realistic goals with the client.

It is easy to underestimate how crucial such knowledge can be for clients. Tremendous relief and security can be provided clients by our knowledge of a community, its exigencies and foibles, its strengths and resources.

But more than just knowledge about communities is involved; frequently it is necessary to intervene actively in these communities. To be effective in such endeavors necessitates knowledge of systems, their functioning, ways in which they can be altered, an accurate diagnosis and assessment of each specific situation, and skills in taking appropriate action.

One of the roles earlier identified in environmental work with clients was that of creator of resources. In our practice we frequently involve ourselves or our agencies in efforts aimed at meeting identified gaps in resources needed by our clients; when successful in these efforts we have also contributed to the needs of the entire community. A particular facet of this resource-development role that is being given particular attention in current practice is work with groups of clients who themselves have identified a community need and set out to meet it. A recent example was seen in a family agency where the social workers became aware from their caseloads of serious gaps in community services for single-parent families. Out of this awareness developed a project conducted by the single parents themselves aimed at both improving services and changing community attitudes.

Thus the psychosocial practitioner has a responsibility for understanding community functioning, for being aware of the potential of community organization and development skills, and for achieving some competence in skills related to the needs of the clients for which responsibility has been taken.

Relationship to Other Thought Systems

Because of the aforementioned interest in other theoretical orientations, psychosocial treatment has been open to and positively influenced by many of the systems considered in this book; this point is clearly indicated in the third edition of Hollis's classic book on casework (33). In the intervals between the three editions of this work, the influence of systems theory, role theory, communications concepts, family theory, learning theory, and crisis theory can be observed as well as developments internal to the system, resulting from increased experience, research, and reconceptualization. These influences do not represent radical changes in the system; they do indicate an enriched understanding, a realigning of concepts, clearer systematization of ideas, more precise categorization of methodology, and a clearer awareness of interrelatedness of concepts. These developments are the sought-after signs of any healthy developing system. It is presumed that as efforts at reconceptualizing the psychosocial model continue, more precise integration from other schools of thought will take place.

Present Status

Psychosocial thinking takes a similar approach to this range of thought systems currently influencing social work practice as it does to a multi-method-based practice orientation. Although this system strongly reflects a continuing influence of psychodynamic thinking, it is open to new ideas and recognizes that each of the other systems represents an important contribution to practice. Again, rather than suggesting that all practitioners need to be competent in all systems, it is necessary that we be aware of the potential of each system to help some clients and to strive to ensure that the best combination of theory setting, timing service, and skill are available.

It is difficult to identify any component of current social work practice that is not and has not been influenced by psychosocial thinking. Both the intensity of this influence and the extent to which individuals acknowledge it vary, but to a continuing degree the generic concepts of psychosocial thinking form the base for much of current clinical social work practice. This strong influence of psychosocial thinking is a long-standing one. What is different is the nature of its influence. Within the profession it describes a practice position not always acceptable to all. In past years, when the psychological components of human behavior were being stressed and interest in the psyche, psychodynamics, and psychotherapy were to the fore, this term helped workers keep a balanced focus. Now that the pendulum has swung back and the social components of behavior and its influences are in the limelight it serves the opposite role of keeping persons' inner functions in perspective.

For some, retaining an interest in, concern for, and declared competency in the understanding and management of psychological issues is said to be an immature holding on to a relationship with psychiatry and a medical model of psychopathology. This approach would have our profession identify only with the social concept. Within this purview the principal concern of social work is the clients' social condition, including the people, systems, and resources that variously influence it. These areas are and always have been an essential part of the warp and woof of social work. What is dangerous about the stress on the term "social" in an exclusive way is the concomitant conclusion that clients' psychological life and functioning are not directly included in the scope of professional activity and intervention. Few, of course, would deny an interest and concern in these areas, only that we have a direct responsibility.

Another aspect of the current status of this theory is a tendency to see it in a narrow deterministic sense that interprets all current functioning in terms of early developmental influences. Undoubtedly, there was a time when considerably more emphasis was put on the influence of past experiences on present behavior, but the extent to which this took place in practice has been greatly exaggerated. Practitioners of this persuasion have long known that overemphasis on the influence of early years creates too narrow an expectation for people and a sense of finality about a person's potential.

As essential as an understanding of the early years of development is, we know that this is not the only period of growth. The maturation process continues all through life. Some of the effects of this increased understanding of human potential can be seen in recent work with groups of retarded persons, with highly deprived families, and with aged individuals.

Related to this is a continuing tendency to see this approach to practice as based on a single theoretical orientation to the exclusion of other theories. As discussed earlier, this viewpoint overlooks the richness of psychosocial thinking. In fact, one of the current weaknesses of this approach is that at this point in history the system is so strongly influenced by such a wide range of thought systems that it is difficult to give precise boundaries to the term "psychosocial." Rather than call this a current weakness, perhaps it is better expressed as a possible area of criticism. For being open to many sources of influence is this school's greatest strength and potential. A commitment to openness, of course, creates a gigantic challenge of assimilation, integration, synthesizing, and reformulation.

A related type of criticism is the suggestion that present psychosocial thinking is really only a collection of borrowed concepts and techniques and, in fact, has contributed little of its own. Such an attitude underestimates the tremendously rich contribution this approach to social work practice has made in the skillful management of individual, family, and group relationships; the enlargement of our understanding of the human potential; the lifelong process of growth and development; an increased perception of the dimensions of interaction of person and person, and person and situation; and the intersystemic interaction of significant environments. In addition, there have developed enlarged knowledge and skill in making maximum effective use of society's resources, both material and personal. A further contribution that must be noted is the importance that has been placed on understanding and focusing on the here and now in the client's life. Finally, and perhaps most importantly, credit must be given to the great progress that has been and is being made in the classification and categorization of patterns of psychosocial problems and methods of intervention and their interconnectedness. It is out of these developments that new theoretical formulations can be made and tested.

Because of its long tradition, a tradition that is longer than that of most of the other approaches discussed in this volume, there is a tendency in current discussions to refer to psychosocial theory as "traditional casework thinking." Since it is currently fashionable to disparage things traditional, frequently psychosocial therapy is used as a point of departure for new ideas grounded on other theoretical bases. Too often in such comparisons differences are overstated, particular concepts are overstressed, similarities are ignored or underemphasized, and, even more serious, it is not acknowledged that many of the newer developments are actually further elaborations of a psychosocial base.

One point that must be emphasized in this discussion of current influences stems from the traditional association of this approach with casework and the casework tradition mentioned earlier. This, in turn, has also tended to be identified principally with one-to-one intervention (33). One of the unfortunate consequences of this mistaken view is that colleagues with an individual orientation to practice who wish to expand their treatment armamentarium to include modalities of joint, group, family, and community work sometimes think they must turn to other theoretical approaches and other schools of practice for their orientation to these additional interventive modalities, failing to appreciate the fact that these modalities are now available in the psychosocial approach itself.

It is, of course, appropriate to turn to other thought systems available in both theory and practice, as the various chapters of this book indicate. What creates problems for the practitioner is the persistent misconception that other treatment styles are totally separate; that is, once again the emphasis is on differences rather than similarities. This tendency to encapsulate treatment modalities is further reinforced by our tradition of personifying practice methods. Thus we still refer to caseworkers, group workers, and family therapists rather than to social workers, who utilize these methodologies in practice.

Fortunately, this tendency has not taken place to the same extent when theory is being considered. We tend to be much more comfortable in incorporating bodies of theory even though we may continue to use a particular practice form. Thus, even the most committed one-to-one therapist will agree that knowledge of group theory and family dynamics, communication concepts and social systems, to name but a few, are essential to work effectively with a client even though the process being used is one-to-one.

As has been said, this system is an open one, committed to an ongoing search for more sensitive ways of understanding people in interaction with situations and, equally important, to a search for more effective ways of achieving the goals of intervention. As an open-thought system it has to be prepared to alter and modify ideas, beliefs, and techniques, cherished though they may be, when others are found to be more relevant, productive, or economical and effective. It follows that this approach to practice needs to be committed to an ongoing and active research thrust, including responsible experimentation with and evaluation of approaches and techniques both new and traditional.

In examining the present status of psychosocial therapy, the risk of becoming conceptually overextended must be kept in mind. To be equipped to practice in this framework in its fullest context requires knowledge and skill in a wide range of areas. It is this necessary dependency on a multiple skill and knowledge base that creates the great contemporary challenge for social work practitioners and educators.

A particular strength of psychosocial practice is its ability to accommodate to multidisciplined settings. As society and its professions become more knowledgeable about the multicausation of problems, and the need for multifaceted interventions, the reality of multidisciplined practice expands. Such practice requires particular skills in interpersonal relationships, an openness to new ideas, and a strong sense of autonomy. Such practice situations are frequently found in the health field, and here a psychosocial formulation of the situation is frequently the intervention of choice with the social worker as prime therapist in partnership with colleagues from medicine. This cooperative activity is especially important in cases involving such diagnostic variables as depression, schizophrenia, anorexia nervosa and bulimia, and psychogenic illnesses.

This approach to practice must seek to find a balance between several choices or directions. One is to focus on a broad knowledge of many fields, theories, techniques, and viewpoints and how they are interconnected. A second is to follow a narrow monolithic commitment to method and theory. A third is an even more dangerous alternative; to develop a cynical antiintellectual stance that professes there is no certitude and no available useful tested knowledge upon which one can draw. If this third option is elected, the only recourse in practice is to a present-oriented, impressionistic reliance on the outcome of a spontaneous, concerned human encounter. There is, in addition, a fourth option; this one consists of oversimplifying practice. Since psychosocial therapy is strongly committed to making use of all aspects of a client's life, many of which are the mundane factors of daily living, there is a risk of seeing such activities as being uncomplicated and requiring little more than goodwill and human concern. Because these facets of treatment are indeed commonplace, they create a particular challenge to the therapist seeking to use them in a planned effective way.

Overall Assessment

A responsibility of any approach is to examine its own weaknesses and strengths. Thus, although psychosocial therapy is committed to an open approach to knowledge, this does not imply that the system has no boundaries.

It would be presumptuous to claim for psychosocial therapy all knowledge and all skill in human behavior.

One of the risks in a volume seeking to present a spectrum of approaches to social work practice is that of overstating or overselling one's own viewpoint. This is a particular risk for the psychosocial approach since it is established on a broad and developing base. It can easily aspire to become all things to all people or to present an approach implying all that is worth knowing is contained within this framework.

To date, this approach has tended to understress the physical functioning of clients except in settings directly related to health. However, as indicated earlier, this is changing, and with growing understanding of intersystemic functioning will change still further. Similarly, in direct work with clients, the psychosocial therapist does not seek to examine extensively the unconscious components of personality structure. Thus it follows that this theory of practice does not use the full range of psychoanalytic techniques. Neither does it use hypnosis as a part of its range of treatment procedures.

Nor has this approach to practice made direct use of the resources of psychometrics, except in a highly limited way. Although we have always worked closely with psychologists and their psychometric skills, we have not considered it necessary to equip ourselves with these competences.

In a similar way, psychosocial treatment is limited by the scope of its interventive targets. Vast and rich as has been the experience of this school of practice, it in no way claims to be competent in dealing with all existing psychosocial difficulties. Clearly this type of treatment cannot cure many of the serious physical, emotional, mental, and social handicaps of people. Frequently, it is able to help persons function more comfortably and satisfyingly within such limitations without undoing them. In a more specific area, psychosocial therapy does not claim to treat more serious forms of mental illness, although, again, it does contribute to the alleviation of aggravating circumstances, frequently with dramatic results.

This system of therapy, to date, has not been dramatically effective in dealing with family systems that are marked with multifaceted long-term serious problem functioning, although some progress has been made with this challenging group. Nor does it pretend to address the crippling societal situations which many of our clients face on a day-to-day basis. For these we must be careful that we do not offer therapy when what they need is a safe home.

For a long time psychosocial practice seemed to have avoided intensive concern with the many sexual problems, concerns, and difficulties experienced by large numbers of our clients. Frequently we avoided sexual issues, and when we did address them we tended to see such problems as symptomatic rather than as areas for direct intervention. Happily, this is changing rapidly and to an increasing extent therapists can be found who are highly skilled in assisting persons with a wide range of sexual difficulties (24).

On the positive side, psychosocial therapy has shown itself to be highly effective with most emotional, personal, interpersonal, situational, and intersituational problems. Although there has been a tradition to see this approach as highly problem- and pathology-focused, in current practice a growing emphasis can be observed on strengths, potential, and healthy functioning.

Another of the strengths of this theory lies in its tradition of borrowing, incorporating, rethinking, and reformulating knowledge from without and adding to these its own insights, experiences, and tested concepts. But this is also its vulnerability, in that it is continually being tempted by new perceptions and formulations, even before we have fully integrated and understood what we know about psychosocial functioning from our own knowledge and experience. Among our colleagues who would identify themselves with this school would be found a wide range of theoretical and conceptual viewpoints. These viewpoints are frequently not contradictory or mutually exclusive but, rather, represent emphases on different components of this theory. This does not imply in any way that these are negligent or biased practitioners. These are colleagues who are strongly committed to ethical, responsible practice and achieve commendable results in practice. It does imply, though, that all of us can enrich our practices to the extent that we can fully appreciate the implications and resources of this practice system.

From without, the systems' greatest challenge is to demonstrate in a scientifically acceptable way the differential results of our activities. By now enough has been made of the apparently disappointing results of some well-known evaluative projects of recent years. It is essential that we continue to focus on well-designed, thoroughly conducted outcome studies. We must continue to improve the whole structure of available research methodologies and experiment with ways of adapting them to our practice. We have been remiss in describing what we do in precise and accurate terms. We have not as yet made sufficient use of available audiovisual technology to record our contacts with clients. These processes give us rich opportunities to develop and test paradigms of interventive activities.

We have been particularly remiss in declaring the goals we establish with our clients in a format that permits examination and comparisons with outcome and patterns of intervention. As has been pointed out by others, when we do not do this, others do it for us and often in an inappropriate way. Thus, an overall goal for practitioners in this school should be to put heavy stress on documenting practice more specifically. This can be accomplished in two ways: presenting clearer formulations of our diagnostic thinking and its development through the life of the case, and specifying goals for treatment. We must also begin to make more ante-factum statements about our choice of treatment emphases and resources related to our diagnosis and goals.

The prior points have been made before, as has the appeal for continuing and expanded research of high quality. In the past two decades we have trained a large number of skilled researchers. We still seem to be expending considerable energy on exhortations about our shortcomings rather than on hard clinical research. We cannot be dissuaded because of the unfavorable results of some projects. As committed researchers we have to be ready to accept findings, whether favorable or unfavorable. Only by continually and directly studying our therapeutic activities will we better understand when and why we are effective and when and why we are not. Happily there has been a marked improvement in the more detailed type of research, as for example in the work of Ellison (13), Gibbs (23), Gomez (25), Harel (31), and Williams (81).

One of the pressing difficulties in current research is the lack of a system of describing and classifying cases into groupings that permit more accurate comparison of input and outcome and thus specify the differential effectiveness of various clusters and emphases of intervention (77). This has become more of a challenge to us as we broaden the spectrum of significant environments included in assessments. In turn, this necessitates different kinds of classifications and interclassifications of persons, problems, resources, symptoms, behavior patterns, and treatment goals. Thus, our overall research challenge is to bring to the fore the strengths of the system by improving and testing our conceptual framework. The increased availability, sophistication, and comfort with computers will help greatly in this regard.

Psychosocial therapy is and has been a significant component of the history of social work. At its present stage of development, it both reflects the tradition of the profession and responds to the demands of current practice in terms of available conceptual and practice resources. It is committed to modify and improve its effectiveness and scope, the soundness of its theoretical base, and the communicability of its knowledge and skills. It is an orientation to practice that can be proud of its achievements to date yet should be fully aware of its limitations and the vast array of conceptual and research tasks still to be accomplished.

References

1. Ackerman, N. W., F. L. Beatman, and S. N. Sherman (eds.). *Expanding Theory and Practice in Family Therapy.* New York: Family Service Association of America, 1967, pp. 109–124.
2. ———. *The Psychodynamics of Family Life: Diagnosis and Treatment of Family Relationships.* New York: Basic Books, 1958.
3. Agger, Eloise M. "Psychosocial Determinants of Unwanted Pregnancy: A Neurobehavioral Research Study on Pre-disposing Stress, Relationship, Self-Orientation, and Personality Factors." Catholic University, D.S.W., 1983.
4. Alger, Ian, and Peter Hogan. "Enduring Effects of Videotape Playback Experience on Family and Marital Relationships," *American Journal of Orthopsychiatry,* Vol. 39, No. 1 (January 1969), pp. 88–94.

5. Bahn, Anita K. "A Multi-Disciplinary Psychosocial Classification Scheme," *American Journal of Orthopsychiatry*, Vol. 41 (October 1971), pp. 830–845.

6. Bakalar, H. R., J. D. Moore, and D. W. Hight. "Psychosocial Dynamics of Pediatric Burn Abuse," *Health and Social Work*, Vol. 6, No. 4 (1981), pp. 27–32.

7. Barrett-Lennard, G. T. "Significant Aspects of a Helping Relationship," *Canada's Mental Health, Supplement 47*. Ottawa: Department of National Health and Welfare, July–August 1965.

8. Biestek, Felix B. *The Casework Relationship*. Chicago: Loyola University, 1957.

9. Caplan, G. "Mastery of Stress: Psychosocial Aspects," *American Journal of Psychiatry*, Vol. 138, No. 4 (1981), pp. 413–420.

10. Christ, G. H. "A Psychosocial Assessment Framework for Cancer Patients and Their Families," *Health and Social Work*, Vol. 8, No. 1 (1983), pp. 57–64.

11. Cohen, M. M., and D. K. Wellisch, "Living in Limbo: Psychosocial Intervention in Families with a Cancer Patient," *American Journal of Psychotherapy*, Vol. 32, No. 4 (1978), pp. 561–571.

12. Ehrenkranz, Shirley M. "A Study of the Techniques and Procedures Used in Joint Interviewing in the Treatment of Marital Problems." Doctoral dissertation, Columbia University, School of Social Work, New York, 1967.

13. Ellison, E. S. "Issues Concerning Parental Harmony and Children's Psychosocial Adjustment," *American Journal of Orthopsychiatry*, Vol. 53, No. 1 (1983), pp. 73–80.

14. Evans, Ron L., and Robert M. Miller. "Psychosocial Implications and Treatment of Stroke," *Social Casework*, Vol. 65, No. 4 (1984), pp. 242–247.

15. Finley, B. S., C. S. Crouthamel, and R. A. Richman. "A Psychosocial Intervention Program for Children with Short Stature and Their Families," *Social Work in Health Care*, Vol. 7, No. 1 (1981), pp. 27–34.

16. Frank, R. A., and D. J. Cohen. "Psychosocial Concommitants of Biological Maturation in Preadolescence," *American Journal of Psychiatry*, Vol. 136-2, No. 12 (1979), pp. 1518–1524.

17. Freud, Anna. *The Ego and the Mechanisms of Defense*. New York: International Universities Press, 1946.

18. Freud, Sigmund. "The Unconscious" (1915), in Ernest Jones (ed.), *Collected Papers, Vol. 4*. London: Hogarth, 1949, pp. 98–136.

19. Gallagher, D. E., L. W. Thompson, and J. A. Peterson. "Psychosocial Factors Affecting Adaptation to Bereavement in the Elderly," *International Journal of Aging and Human Development*, Vol. 14, No. 2 (1981–1982), pp. 79–95.

20. Garrett, Annette. *Interviewing, Its Principles and Methods*, 3rd edition. New York: Family Service Association of America, 1982.

21. ———. "Modern Casework: The Contributions of Ego Psychology," in Howard J. Parad (ed.), *Ego Psychology and Dynamic Casework*. New York: Family Service Association of America, 1958, pp. 38–52.

22. ———. "The Worker-Client Relationship," in Howard J. Parad (ed.), *Ego Psychology and Dynamic Casework*. New York: Family Service Association of America, 1958, pp. 53–72.

23. Gibbs, J. T. "Psychosocial Factors Related to Substance Abuse Among Delin-

quent Females: Implications for Prevention and Treatment," *American Journal of Orthopsychiatry*, Vol. 52, No. 2 (1982), pp. 261–271.

24. Gochros, Harvey S. "Sexual Problems in Social Work Practice," *Social Work*, Vol. 16 (January 1971), pp. 3–5.

25. Gomez, Ernesto A. "The Evaluation of Psychosocial Casework Services to Chicanos: A Study of Process and Outcome." Doctoral dissertation. Austin, Tex.: R.L.D., 1982.

26. Guida Brown, D., et al. "Group Intervention: A Psychosocial and Educational Approach to Open Heart Surgery Patients and Their Families," *Social Work in Health Care*, Vol. 9, No. 2 (1982), p. 47.

27. Hamilton, Gordon. *Theory and Practice of Social Casework*, 2nd edition. New York: Columbia University Press, 1951.

28. Handel, Gerald (ed.). *The Psychosocial Interior of the Family: A Sourcebook for the Study of Whole Families*, 3rd edition. New York: Aldine, 1985.

29. Hankins, Frank. "The Contributions of Sociology to the Practice of Social Work," in *Proceedings of the National Conference of Social Work, 1930*. Chicago: University of Chicago Press, 1931, pp. 528–535.

30. Hanna, E. A., and J. G. Schachter. "An Integration of Psychosocial Concepts into the Education of General Practitioners," *Social Work in Health Care*, Vol. 4, No. 4 (1979), pp. 393–408.

31. Harel, Z., and L. Noelker. "Sector-related Variation on Psychosocial Dimensions in Long-Term Care for the Aged," *Social Work in Health Care*, Vol. 4, No. 2 (1978), pp. 199–208.

32. Hartmann, Heinz. *Ego Psychology and the Problem of Adaptation*. New York: International Universities Press, 1958.

33. Hollis, Florence. *Casework: A Psychosocial Therapy*, 1st edition. New York: Random House, 1964.

34. ———, and Mary E. Woods. *Social Casework: A Psychosocial Therapy*, 3rd edition. New York: Random House, 1981.

35. ———. *Encyclopedia of Social Work*, Vol. 11. Washington, D.C.: National Association of Social Workers, Inc., 1977, pp. 1300–1307.

36. ———. "The Psychosocial Approach to the Practice of Casework," in Robert Roberts and Robert Nee (eds.), *Theories of Social Casework*. Chicago: University of Chicago Press, 1970, pp. 33–75.

37. ———. "A Profile of Early Interviews in Marital Counseling," *Social Casework*, Vol. 49 (January 1968), pp. 35–41.

38. ———. *A Typology of Casework Treatment*. New York: Family Service Association of America, 1968.

39. ———. "Personality Diagnosis in Casework," in Howard J. Parad (ed.), *Ego Psychology and Dynamic Casework*. New York: Family Service Association of America, 1958, pp. 83–96.

40. Jamison, K. R., D. K. Wellisch, and R. O. Pasnau. "Psychosocial Aspects of Mastectomy 1: The Woman's Perspective," *American Journal of Psychiatry*, Vol. 135, No. 4 (1978), pp. 432–436.

41. Johnson, Harriette C. "The Biological Bases of Psychopathology," in Francis Turner (ed.), *Adult Psychopathology*. New York: Free Press, 1984, pp. 6–72.

42. Kendall, Katherine A. (ed.). *Social Work Values in an Age of Discontent.* New York: Council on Social Work Education, 1970.

43. Kluckhohn, F., and J. P. Spiegel. "Integration and Conflict in Family Behaviour," *Group for the Advancement of Psychiatry Report, No. 27.* New York: G.A.P., 1957.

44. Lewan, M. R. "The Psychosocial Effects of Bulimia on Women's Lives," *Smith College Abstracts of Master's Theses,* Vol. 54, No. 1 (1983), p. 31.

45. Littner, Ner. "The Impact of the Client's Unconscious on the Caseworker's Reactions," in Howard J. Parad (ed.), *Ego Psychology and Dynamic Casework.* New York: Family Service Association of America, 1958, pp. 73–87.

46. Lusk, M. W. "The Psychosocial Evaluation of the Hospice Patient," *Health and Social Work,* Vol. 8, No. 3 (1983), pp. 210–218.

47. Lutz, Werner A. *Concepts and Principles Underlying Social Casework Practice.* Washington, D.C.: National Association of Social Workers, 1956.

48. Merton, Robert K. *Social Theory and Social Structure.* Glencoe, Ill.: Free Press, 1957.

49. Meyer, Carol H. *Social Work Practice: A Response to the Urban Crisis.* New York: Free Press, 1970.

50. Monsour, N., and S. S. Robb. "Wandering Behavior in Old Age: A Psychosocial Study," *Social Work,* Vol. 27, No. 5 (1982), pp. 411–416.

51. Mosher, L. R., and S. J. Keith. "Research on the Psychosocial Treatment of Schizophrenia: A Summary Report," *American Journal of Psychiatry,* Vol. 136, No. 5 (1979), pp. 623–631.

52. Mullen, Edward J. "The Relation Between Diagnosis and Treatment in Casework," *Social Casework,* Vol. 50 (April 1969), pp. 218–226.

53. Northen, Helen. *Clinical Social Work.* New York: Columbia University Press, 1982.

54. O'Neil, Mary Kay. "Affective Disorders," in Francis Turner (ed.), *Adult Psychopathology.* New York: Free Press, 1984, pp. 148–180.

55. Parad, Howard J. (ed.). *Crisis Intervention: Selected Readings.* New York: Family Service Association of America, 1965.

56. ———. *Ego Psychology and Dynamic Casework.* New York: Family Service Association of America, 1958.

57. Polansky, Norman A. *Ego Psychology and Communication.* New York: Atherton Press, 1971.

58. ———, and J. Kounin. "Clients' Reactions to Initial Interviews: A Field Study," in *Human Relations,* Vol. 9 (1956), pp. 237–264.

59. Pollak, Otto, Hazel M. Young, and Helen Leach. "Differential Diagnosis and Treatment of Character Disturbances," *Social Casework,* Vol. 41 (December 1960), pp. 512–517.

60. Pollitt, Ernesto, Aviva Eichler, and Cee-Khoon Chan. "Psychosocial Development and Behavior of Mothers of Failure-to-Thrive Children," *American Journal of Orthopsychiatry,* Vol. 45 (July 1975), pp. 525–537.

61. Rafuls, Silvia. "Psychosocial Implications of Neonatal Transports." Unpublished paper, Third National Conference on Pediatric Social Work, Miami, Florida, 1984.

62. Reid, William J., and Ann W. Shyne. *Brief and Extended Casework*. New York: Columbia University Press, 1969.

63. Richmond, Mary E. *What Is Social Casework?* New York: Russell Sage Foundation, 1922.

64. Roberts, Robert W., and Robert H. Nee (eds.). *Theories of Social Casework*. Chicago: University of Chicago Press, 1970.

65. Rogers, Carl R. "Characteristics of a Helping Relationship," *Canada's Mental Health, Supplement 27*. Ottawa: Department of National Health and Welfare, March 1962.

66. Russell, A. "Late Psychosocial Consequences in Concentration Camp Survivor Families," *American Journal of Orthopsychiatry*, Vol. 44 (July 1974), pp. 611–619.

67. Salomon, Elizabeth L. "Humanistic Values and Social Casework," *Social Casework*, Vol. 48 (January 1967), pp. 26–39.

68. Silberfarb, P. M., L. H. Maurer, C. S. Crouthamed. "Psychosocial Aspects of Neoplastic Disease: I. Functional Status of Breast Cancer Patients During Different Treatment Regimens," *American Journal of Psychiatry*, Vol. 137-1, No. 4 (1980), pp. 450–455.

69. Starr, S. "Social Work and Liaison Psychiatry: A Psychosocial Team Approach to Patient and Staff Needs in a Hemodialysis Unit," *Social Work in Health Care*, Vol. 7, No. 3 (1982), 77–82.

70. Thompson, R. W. "A Conceptual Framework for Psychosocial Rehabilitation," *American Journal of Orthopsychiatry*, Vol. 51, No. 2 (1981), pp. 317–326.

71. Timberlake, E. M. "Psychosocial Functioning of School Phobics at Follow-Up," *Social Work Research and Abstracts*, Vol. 20, No. 1 (1984), pp. 13–18.

72. Turner, Francis J. *Adult Psychopathology*. New York: Free Press, 1984.

73. ———. *Differential Diagnosis and Treatment in Social Work*, 3rd edition. New York: Free Press, 1983.

74. ———. *Social Work Treatment*, 2nd edition. New York: Free Press, 1979.

75. ———. *Psychosocial Therapy*. New York: Free Press, 1978.

76. ———. "Ethnic Difference and Client Performance," *Social Service Review*, Vol. 44 (March 1970), pp. 1–10.

77. ———. "The Search for Diagnostic Classifications." Unpublished paper. The Learned Societies, University of York, 1969.

78. Weiss, J. O. "Psychosocial Stress in Genetic Disorders: A Guide for Social Workers," *Social Work in Health Care*, Vol. 6, No. 4 (1981), pp. 17–32.

79. Weissman, H., I. Epstein, and A. Savage. *Agency-Based Social Work*. Philadelphia: Temple University Press, 1984.

80. Wellisch, D. K., K. R. Jamison, and R. O. Pasnau. "Psychosocial Aspects of Mastectomy II: The Man's Perspective," *American Journal of Psychiatry*, Vol. 135, No. 5 (1978), pp. 543–546.

81. Williams, Janet B. W. "Psychosocial Stressors and Major Depression, Schizophrenia and Schizophreniform Disorder." Columbia D.S.W., 1981.

Annotated Listing of Key References

HAMILTON, GORDON. *Theory and Practice of Social Casework*, 2nd edition. New York: Columbia University Press, 1951.

This book, now a classic in the casework field, brings together both a theoretical base for psychosocial practice as well as a specification of the major components of such practice. It was written during the period when psychodynamic theory was the principal theoretical base underlying clinical social work practice.

HANDEL, GERALD (ed.). *The Psychosocial Interior of the Family: A Sourcebook for the Study of Whole Families*, 3rd edition. New York: Aldine, 1985.

An excellent compendium of a psychosocial perspective of the family from a rich and diverse number of viewpoints. It reflects well the broad scope of psychosocial thinking.

HOLLIS, FLORENCE, and MARY E. WOODS. *Casework: A Psychosocial Therapy*, 3rd edition. New York: Random House, 1981.

This third edition of the key text in psychosocial thinking reflects the openness of the system to new ideas yet retains the basic traditional concepts. Mary Woods' contributions to this important work bring an expanded dimension to the significance of this sytem.

RICHMOND, MARY E. *What Is Social Casework?* New York: Russell Sage Foundation, 1922.

An important historical sourcebook for psychosocial therapy. In this short, well-written book can be found the broad outline of current practice within this tradition. Much of what is said is still relevant today, and many of the trends in current psychosocial practice are anticipated, although expressed in different terminology.

TURNER, FRANCIS J. *Differential Diagnosis and Treatment in Social Work*, 3rd edition. New York: Free Press, 1983.

This book contains a collection of over eighty articles, each of which deals with a specific client type or problem, principally within a psychosocial framework. The unifying concept in the book is that effective treatment necessitates diagnostic understanding of the client and a specific selection of a profile of procedures and resources to achieve the identified goals of treatment within the client's strengths and limitations.

TURNER, FRANCIS J. *Psychosocial Therapy*. New York: Free Press, 1978.

The principal thrust of this book is to show how the open quality of psychosocial treatment expands the range of therapeutic resources and applications.

CHAPTER 19

Systems Theory

Margaret R. Rodway

Introduction and Summary of Systems Theory

Systems theory is a large domain that has had a major impact on the theory and practice of social work. It was developed largely in response to the needs of a number of different disciplines in order to analyze complex interactive situations in which the whole is more than the sum of the parts. "Systems theory is a framework, a metatheory, a model in the broadest sense of that over-abused term. It is a model available to any dynamic, recurring process of events" (51, p. 12) and helps us to understand people, both individually and collectively in terms of concepts such as structure, boundary, equilibrium, entropy, equifinality, interaction, and dependence of parts, conflict, and input and output of resources (13, 60).

The person-in-situation concept has long been identified as the crucial base from which the social work profession has developed (23, 53) and the systems model has contributed immeasurably to the conceptualization of this person-in-situation concept (51).

Historical Perspectives

Von Bertalanffy is usually credited as the originator of general systems theory. His scientific endeavors in the physical sciences, which began in the 1920s, resulted finally in a proposal of general systems theory in 1956 that he described as "the formulation and derivation of those principles which are valid for 'systems' in general" (7). In the development of his theory, Von Bertalanffy had synthesized concepts gained from a variety of disciplines, such as philosophy, psychology, and neurophysiology.

The introduction of social systems ideas to social work is credited to Lutz (41) in the 1940s and the introduction of general systems ideas to Hearn (29) in the late 1950s. The relationship of general systems theory to social work has occupied an important position ever since. During the 1960s a number of papers were presented on general systems theory by social work educators and engendered further interest (30, 37, 51, 57, 62).

During the 1970s there was a marked increase in the application of systems theory to social work (22, 45, 50, 60) in terms of development of practice approaches that relied heavily on systems theory. The late 1970s and early 1980s has seen the development of the ecological, life model, and competence approaches to practice; all of which utilize systems ideas (3, 21, 26, 43). It should be noted, however, that the ecological approach derived more from the biological sciences than the physical sciences, from which general systems theory was primarily developed.

Current Status

While systems theory has been in prominent usage in social work since the 1960s, there have been many modifications, adaptations, and revisions. Indeed, it has been suggested that it has moved away from a well-defined theoretical framework to a rationale, a context, or an operational style (63). Meyer (45) was identified previously as one of the early developers of an approach to practice based on systems theory. It is noted that her use of the theory was interwoven with a transactional framework. Crisis theory is often elucidated by systems terms to explain or clarify concepts. The synthesis of systems and communication theory has become an important aspect of social work practice. While the ecological and family-centered approaches put forward by Hartman (27), Aponte (4), and Hoffman (32) parallel systems ideas, they have been eclectic in their incorporation of other frameworks. For example, Hartman draws heavily on Bowen's conceptions in addition to communication theory (10). Similarly, Germain and Gitterman's life model approach builds on the ideas of Bandler (5) as well as other theoretical concepts.

Within the past two decades, systems theory has become a theoretical framework for an increasing number of social workers. Indeed, it has been observed that it is the most popular theory used in contemporary social work (64). Certainly it represents a revitalized interest in social aspects of problems and is seen as an alternative to the medical model of social work practice (33, 46). It also offers a tool for relating micro-macrosocial events. As well, it has provided a larger perspective on the interaction between the individual and the environment and has been affirmed as providing a more useful account of social change than other current frameworks.

Earlier mention was made of the contribution that systems theory has made in the profession toward reducing the tension between the two perspectives of individual development and environmental factors. The use of systems concepts has assisted social workers in taking a broader view of their role and function, which includes the two perspectives.

The "essential" nature of social work practice has been identified by a number of writers as the dual emphasis on the individual and his environment. In essence, social work is about "an interactional field in which transactions occur between environmental demands on the one hand and people's coping capacities on the other" (6). Similarly, "the central social work focus is placed at the interface between or the meeting place of person and environment" (23, 30). Systems theory is clearly a current orientation to practice that focuses attention to "the point where it belongs, the transactions that occur between individuals and their environments and the potential of the transactions for enhancing or diminishing the capacity of individuals to gain satisfaction from life and to promote the satisfaction of others" (66, p. 392).

Concepts and Dimensions

While many concepts have been identified in the large domain occupied by systems theory, only those of particular relevance to social work practice will be reviewed.

The central concept is the *system*, "a set of objects, together with relationships between the objects and between their attributes" (31, p. 335). There are three types of systems: conceptual, real, and abstracted. The latter two have the greatest relevance for social work since real systems are living and can be observed while abstracted systems are classes of behavior and relationships that can be inferred from real systems.

From this central concept, a number of characteristics or constructs emerge. First is the specification of *open versus closed systems.* The latter are self-contained and do not depend on the environment while the former are characterized by an active exchange with the environment. Human growth and development is an example of this active exchange of energy with the environment. Systems vary in terms of their openness and closedness so that "much of social work is devoted to helping the client achieve an optimum degree of openness for the conditions of the moment and the capacity to change this state as conditions change" (39).

Boundary is a construct that specifies what is inside or outside the system. It is defined as the line forming a closed circle around selected variables, where there is less interchange of energy across the line of the circle than within the delimiting circle.

The property of permeable boundaries defines what is inside and what is outside the system. The boundaries are defined by the criteria used by an observer.

The *importation of energy* of the open system is seen as a crucial aspect of systems theory. Through-put is used to denote the process by which the system acts upon the energy imported. Output or "the product exported into the environment, furnishes the sources of energy for the repetition of the cycle of activities. The energy reinforcing the cycle of activities can derive from some exchange of the product in the external world or from the activity itself" (35).

A characteristic of open and closed systems is that of *entropy/negentropy*, which is viewed as a universal principle affecting all systems. Negentropy is seen as the tendency of living systems to import more energy than they export. If the living system maintains a higher level of energy than it loses, it is able to grow and develop. If, however, the living system exports more energy than it maintains, this is referred to as entropy and as a result the system begins to lose its vitality and decays. As an illustration of entropy/negentropy, in the early stages of the life cycle when growth is rapid, negative entropy far outweighs positive entropy and in old age entropy has the balance of power (31, p. 346).

A second characteristic of open and closed systems is that they attain *stationary states.* "In closed systems, it is a state of equilibrium or rest while in open systems, it is a dynamic interplay of forces giving the appearance of rest but being in reality a dynamic steady state" (31, p. 346). This characteristic is illustrated by the use of a family system: "It is never in a state of total equilibrium. Each member within the family has his own dynamic equilibrium level. . . . When these equilibrium states come together in some unitary whole (the family group) a homeostatic balance is achieved. However, this homeostatic balance is neither static nor stable but forever changing" (19). Any disturbing external condition may cause the family to reestablish the homeostatic balance, which is referred to as the property of *self-regulation.*

Another closely related concept to steady state is *equifinality*, which indicates that a particular final state can be reached from different initial conditions and by a variety of paths. However, an opposite principle to equifinality has been proposed called multifinality, which suggests that similar initial conditions may lead to dissimilar end-states (44).

Feedback is a property of open systems that has been described as systems "gathering information about how they are doing. Such information is then fed back into the system as input to guide and steer its operation" (13, p. 303). Systems also affect the environment. The overall process of affecting the environment and being affected by the environment is feedback. Improving the feedback process of a client can greatly enhance corrective action to be taken. A further dimension has been added to feedback in the concepts of *morphostasis* and *morphogenesis* (44). Morphostasis processes tend to return the system to the state from which it deviated while morphogenic processes lead to change in the system.

Every system contains *subsystems*, all of which are part of a suprasystem, or the subsystem in its environment. There are two types of subsystems: a general purpose subsystem that doesn't play a specialized role in the larger system, and a special purpose subsystem that does play a specialized role (31, p. 346).

A closely related concept is that of the *holon*, an entity that is simultaneously both a part and a whole (36). The notion of focal system has been added to the holon; the former becomes the system of primary attention at any point. To illustrate the mutuality of the holon-focal system concept, a family may be viewed as a holon or as a focal system. When viewed as a holon, all aspects of the family's environment must be taken into account: the neighborhood, community, and other aspects of its particular setting (2).

Finally, *differentiation* is a construct that explains the developmental sequences and changes over time within systems or the movement from undifferentiated wholeness to differentiated parts. A family may be viewed as a prime example of this process. "Parental roles become differentiated as the child grows, shifting from protective actions in the child's infancy to the intent to foster independence in the later teens" (22).

Many in the profession have examined, tested, and applied systems concepts to social work practice. Traditional social work concepts have been converted into systems concepts, and systems theory has given social work the conceptual tools to explain long-standing notions and to guide and give direction to social work practice (63). Hearn's publication on theory building (29) began a search for a basic and holistic conception of social work that is current today.

A systemic framework expands the conceptual and actual boundaries within which the social worker employs his knowledge and skills. The use of a systemic boundary includes the significant inputs into the lives of the unit of attention. The worker is concerned with the total environment at all times, although she may be immediately concerned only with a particular part of the system. Targets of intervention are located within all categories of human organization: individual, dyad, family, group, organization, or society (29, 66). The application of systems concepts to practice will be examined in more detail in a succeeding section.

System-Centered Treatment

Perhaps the most salient feature of the systemic framework for practice is that it allows for different modes of intervention so that clients are not faced with a single approach. This capacity is based on the concept of equifinality and enables the social worker to use the breadth of her interventive knowl-

edge while providing for alternatives in the use of a range of helping modalities. Allowance for such eclecticism could be viewed as true
individualization of the complexities of problems that client groups present.
This process is described as individualizing the person-situation complex in
order to achieve the best match between each person and his environment
(23). In addition to individualizing the approach, systems as a conceptual
framework "enables us to bring order into the massive amount of data from
all of the different frames of reference or fields of knowledge that provide
the base for social work practice" (25, p. 468).

A systems approach also shifts attention from the individual to interaction and hence the onus for change is not the client systems alone (25).
There are three attributes that distinguishes systems approaches from others:
(1) the unit of client-worker attention is expanded to include the life space
or the field of relevant systems; (2) individuals are viewed as active, purposeful, and goal seeking; their development and functioning are outcomes
of transactions between their genetic potential and their environment; and
(3) a reorienting of interventive procedures toward releasing growth, adoptive transactions, and improved environments (20).

Hearn describes the process of intervention from a systems theory perspective as one that aims at helping the target system establish and maintain
a steady state representing the best fit between system and environment. This
is done by seeking to alter both the environment and aspects of the selected
system through a variety of methods. At times the goal will be to strengthen
the influence of selected aspects of the environment on the client system, in
other instances it is to lessen these same influences to permit the client to
function more independently (29, p. 51).

Theorists who have developed a model of practice primarily based on
systems theory—such as Goldstein (22), Pincus and Minahan (50), and Siporin (60)—view the activity of the social worker in relation to such different
types of subsystems as change system, change agent system, personality and
social system, client system, target system, and action/intervention system.
These frameworks help the social worker analyze the variety of change efforts
involved, identify tasks and targets to be focused, determine which method
is most appropriate to the problem, and focus on the variety of other systems
involved in the change process (50).

Figure 19–1 (p. 520) shows the process of system-centered intervention.

Phases of Treatment

Generally, stages of social work treatment have been viewed as a successive,
linear process while system-centered treatment would view such stages as
a cyclical process. Both Goldstein (22) and Lippitt, Watson, and Westley (40)
have formulated their stages of the change process on a cyclical basis. The

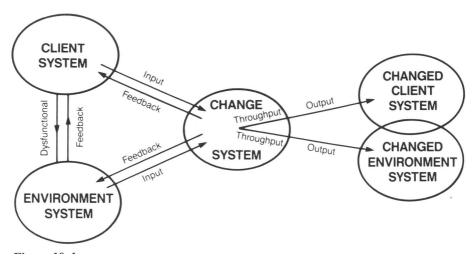

Figure 19-1

(Adapted from A. Vickery, "A Systems Approach to Social Work Intervention: Its Uses for Work with Individuals and Families," *British Journal of Social Work*, Vol. 4, No. 4 (1974), pp. 389–404)

seven stages proposed by the latter writers provide a comprehensive format from which to review the treatment process: development of a need for change; establishment of a change relationship; clarification or diagnosis of the client system's problem; examination of alternative routes and goals—establishing goals and intentions of action; transformation of plans into actual change efforts; generalization and stabilization of change; and achievement of a terminal relationship.

While this delineation of stages may appear to be linear in nature, they add that "most change processes start over and over again as one set of problems is solved and a new set is encountered," hence the work of each phase become mixed up and the final objective may be achieved by a process that seems rather complex to the observer who is looking for a clear-cut developmental sequence.

Development of a Need for Change

This first stage is described as follows:

> The social work practitioner employs the working model of the system with which he is working even as he constructs it. Indeed, he could not build it if he did not simultaneously employ his developing model of the concrete situation to test out insights, hypotheses, and dimly felt formulations; to refine his understandings; and to guide his earliest, as well as his continuing, interventionary efforts.

While he reaches no hasty intial conclusions, it is obvious that he has to start actively employing his knowledge and skill in a tentative way immediately upon initial contact with the system. And his first moves—if they are not to be mere fencing, maneuvering for position, masking, or dissembling—must consist of the search for common ground and of active engagement with the individual's problem, the group's concerns, or the organization's functions. (37)

The identification of the need for change with the system that initiated contact, and the system's willingness to change, is a crucial first step in this stage. In order to help that system, the social worker may have to reach out to make contact with other systems involved in the change process (60, p. 213).

Establishment of the Change Relationship

Within social work, there has traditionally existed a unanimity about the importance of this relationship. While relationship has generally been conceptualized as referring to interactions between two persons, system-centered practice involved relating to larger units such as couples, families, groups, organizations, or community subgroups (22, p. 138).

The social worker, because she is working with different systems, may have different relationships with each part of the various sytems. Each of these relationships may have elements of collaboration, bargaining, and conflict depending on the system with which she is working (50).

A number of the concepts of system theory have relevance to the worker-client relationship (64, p. 273). The principle of steady state referred to earlier needs to be considered whenever the change efforts are effective because significant others in the client's environment may be upset with or resent such changes. This, in turn, may affect the client's motivation to continue in treatment.

Feedback and the process of information gathering and dissemination by the system has crucial implications for the relationship between worker and client. The communicational feedback system is seen as crucial in explaining the circular change of events that result from an ongoing exchange of information.

Enhancing functional communication patterns points first to the selective use of language that is free of ambiguity and geared to the client system's maximum level of comprehension. Talking down is not implied here; instead, the aim is to meet the client system on some ground of mutual understanding. The second element is the practitioner's responsiveness to and use of latent levels of communication. (22, p. 224)

Finally, the hierarchical concept in systems theory has implications and consequences for communication if the worker creates or maintains status differences between himself and the client (64).

Clarification or Diagnosis
of the Client Systems Problem

The client system is defined as the specific system that is being helped (40). A systemic framework provides a conceptual structure that ensures a transactional understanding of the client system in its relationships with other systems:

> The purpose of the worker's problem assessment is to help him understand and individualize the situation he is dealing with and to identify and analyze the relevant factors in a particular situation. Based on this understanding he will make decisions on which aspects of the situation he will deal with, goals for the change effort, and means of achieving these goals. The problem assessment is never an end in itself. Its purpose is not to classify, categorize, or assign diagnostic labels to a person or situation. Rather, the decisions about the future course of the planned change effort are the products of the assessment process. (50, p. 102)

A number of factors are addressed in such a formulation of a problem assessment. The first of these is identifying and stating the problem (the social situation or condition evaluated as undesirable). To provide a complete statement of the problem, the social worker must identify "the behaviors or social conditions in question, the people who are evaluating it and the reasons for their evaluation" (50, p. 105). Problems are seen not as the property of a particular individual, but as a description of their interactions.

A second major focus of her assessment is a detailed analysis of the problem in terms of the dynamics of the social situation that is of concern. There is not an emphasis on identifying a single causal factor but rather looking at all the elements of the situation (environment) that may be producing or maintaining the problem.

In order to achieve a comprehensive understanding and reporting of assessment, the use of a checklist-matrix outline could be utilized that would examine the client, family, primary institution, and socioeconomic environment in terms of observed problems and possible causes, as well as ideal interventive, action plans, intended consequences, and possible unintended consequences (34). Such an outline could provide a more efficient comprehensive and systematic evaluation than the traditional interview method and could help the social worker recognize the interactive effects of all the components of the matrix. Considerable efforts are being made to "describe dynamically more and more complex interactions with or between more and more complex systems . . . and diagnostic terms that describe interactional relationships are being developed" (25, p. 468).

It should be noted that assessment is an ongoing and cyclical aspect of the entire treatment process. In the stages following the "formal" assessment phase, assessment aims at more precise and purposeful understanding (22, p. 232).

Examination of Alternative Routes and Goals

A systems perspective "encourages a comprehensive, multidimensional effort; the use of a set of helping objectives and . . . provides some greater assurance that services probably will have more constructive than disserving consequences in these respects" (60, p. 259). The helping objectives include problem, person, and situation elements. The translation of the client's needs into specific goals and subgoals is a crucial aspect of this process (50). An examination of the feasibility of these goals, establishing their priority, and exploring alternate routes are all important aspects of goal and objective setting. In addition, the social worker generally, in collaboration with the client system, identifies the specific people or targets (the target system) that will also have to change or be changed if client goals are to be reached. The client and target system may be the same, partially overlap, or be completely separate.

A systems perspective encourages the formulation of a helping plan to effect change.

> Like the assessment process, planning is a shared enterprise with the client, and in part, with the helping work group. Effective objectives and tasks show certain common characteristics: they need to be understandable to the client; specify terminal behaviors; relate directly to the concerns and capacities of the client; be attainable through the client's activity and participation and through legitimate means; be time-limited and periodic. They should refer to an improved state of social functioning for the client and indicate also the standards for judging outcomes as acceptable.
>
> The development of a helping plan should emphasize short-term objectives and limited tasks, with priority given to the subtasks and conditions for the client's achievement. The planning process itself should be a learning and growth experience for the client. (60, p. 287)

Following the development of the helping or intervention plan, the need for selecting specific intervention procedures and developing a method for evaluating the impact of the program is identified (18). The selection of specific intervention procedures is based on the type of behavior change that is desired or necessary.

The organization of an intervention or action system is a major task in the planning process:

> Its structure and functioning processes, as well as the selection of the members, are influenced by their common purposes and interests, by the need to meet helping task requirements and responsibilities and to facilitate harmony, productivity and a supportive constituency. This intervention system should be an informal, flexible work and reference group, guided in its development by the social worker (and social work staff team). This helping work group needs to develop so that it can be functionally related to the wider community and is capable of becoming a strengthening aspect of the community's natural helping network or formal welfare system. (60, p. 287).

Transformation of Plans into Actual Change Efforts

> The participants in the helping situation consist of the client, social worker, social agency, staff team, and intervention system. Each plays its part in terms of certain role expectations, of rights and obligations, which govern and limit the conditions for the action. The performers themselves take their places in the intervention system, or helping work group, which represents the ecological system of the case or program of service. This group includes the client and his social network and situation, as represented by his "significant others," who are recruited for contributions to needed helping tasks. The client has a central place in this group, though there is some question as to the extent to which the client or client representatives can become participatory members of social agencies. The social worker and other members of the staff team lead the work group and also serve as helping models for its members. They take responsibility for helping the work group to expand and contract as needed, and then to dissolve or transform itself into an ongoing helping organization. (60, p. 190)

The negotiating of contracts is a crucial aspect of the transformation of plans into change efforts that should not be imposed by the worker on another system. "Rather, it is the deliberate and conscious articulation and shaping of the informal working agreements that are inherent in all relationships into a form that will facilitate the planned change process" (50, p. 163). Contracts may be between the worker and client system (primary) or between the worker and other systems related to the change effort (secondary).

A number of interactional activities are involved in this phase of system-centered intervention. The social worker's use of influence is seen as underlying most of these activities. Such influence is used to change behavior, attitudes, and belief. Four major means of influence processes are identified in the change effort. The first of these is the use of positive inducement for compliance (rewards) or negative inducement for not complying (punishment). The second means of influence is persuasion, which is aimed at the client system's willingness to accept the social worker's requests for information. Professional knowledge, expertise, and the use of communications skills are all facets of the persuasive process. Helping the client system view significant others in their social situation in a new way (58) and identifying "systems of events" through the use of interactive and overlapping questions (9) are examples of the use of persuasion.

The use of the change relationship is the third means of influencing the client system, while change of the client system's immediate and social environment is the fourth. Appropriate change in the client system's environment depends largely on the social worker's ability to assess the impact on both aspects of the environment. In addition to this indirect use of influence, a more direct skill that may be used is that of helping client systems negotiate change in the other systems in which they are involved (58).

The interactional activites and skills that are part of this stage are many and diverse. A set of skill dimensions has been identified that is useful in terms of summarizing: intellectual and analytical; expressive; cognitive and behavioral; technical; ethical; and style (52).

A final aspect of transforming plans into actual change efforts is the development of an intervention or action system within which the social worker integrates herself with the client system (60, p. 278). Such a system may involve several persons, including other helpers, agencies, and persons from the client's significant others. Some intervention systems may already exist while in other situations it may be necessary to create a new intervention system in order to accomplish the necessary change.

Generalization and Stabilization of Change

Coordination and maintenance of the change efforts are a crucial aspect of this phase. A number of problems may occur at this point that will require interactional interventions by the worker. These may be problems within any of the systems; that is, client, changes, action intervention, and environmental. Problems in internal functioning may also develop at any point. As well, the relationship between action interventive systems may exhibit difficulties. Problems within systems and in internal functioning often occur when roles, norms, and contracts are unclear and poorly developed. However, when they are in well-defined active forms, roles, norms, and contracts are the forces within systems that ensure maintenance and continuity of the change efforts. Interorganizational boundaries between subsystems may create relationship difficulties (21). In terms of relationship, problems between action systems, operating procedures, communication channels, and membership components all need to be carefully delineated and monitored. Spontaneous, creative activity guided by professional practice principles and a commitment to achieving tasks and objectives are viewed as crucial to the smooth functioning of interventive systems (60). Finally, the coordination of action systems in terms of consistency of task and purpose is essential to this phase.

With regard to stabilization and generalization of change, it is necessary for the social worker to determine the steps to be undertaken which will ensure that the changes and gains will be maintained. In addtion, he must assess what factors may impede the change effort and take steps to prevent such impediments. The social worker may also use interventions that will enable the client system to practice what has been gained, such as reenactment and identifying and clarifying other situations related to the newly found problem-solving skills.

Achievement of a Terminal Relationship

The concept of termination may not be viable in a system-centered approach to treatment because it infers a linear and final aspect to a cyclical process.

Indeed, ending also denotes the beginning of a new stage for the client system. This poses specific tasks and activities for the client and interventive systems that include: dealing with the feelings and issues of separation (disengagement); planning and preparation for the next steps in terms of the situations' needs; and finally, evaluation of the change efforts. The interventive system itself may influence the process of termination, particularly with respect to how it structures and uses time. The foregoing phases and principles of treatment will be illustrated in detail in a case example that is included in a later section.

System-Centered Intervention
with Specific Client Groups

Systems principles provide a common framework for viewing individuals, groups, organizations, and communities as "clients" or as the means by which service is rendered to "clients" (30). In terms of application to differing client systems, the foregoing description of system-centered treatment is directly relevant, particularly with individuals. There are, however, some particular aspects of treatment unique to practice with couples, families, and groups that will be addressed.

Application to Couples and Families

Systems concepts underlie a number of recently developed approaches to working with couples and families: for example, structural (47); strategic (42); systemic (56); problem-centered therapies (16); and family-centered social work practice (28). The more general features of a system-centered framework will be addressed in this section.

Intervention with couples and families relies heavily on the utilization of relational and transactional concepts as well as on functional and structural aspects. A systems orientation can, therefore, play an essential role in effectively intervening. The marital or family system itself, including the subsystems operating within the family as well as its relationship to contiguous systems, all must be taken into account. To understand the total family system, it is necessary to understand the nature and degree of disturbance in the subsystems; that is, the marital, parent-child, and sibling relationship (54). The use of transactions between family members or between a couple rather than the characteristics of each individual would be used as the primary data (61).

Rodway has observed that couple and family relationships take the form of a highly complex interpersonal system (55). Contiguous systems may include the natural systems in the family's life or they may be systems that enter the family life when a particular problem or event occurs. It is important for the social worker to understand the position of the couple or family within the contiguous systems. A central skill for the social worker is to be able to focus on the whole system of the family, which is both the sum of its parts and their goal-directed organization.

The concept of circular causality is an important theme in understanding the family system. It highlights the fact that the family members' behavior both affects and is affected by the behavior of the other. Any particular behavior, emotion, or symptom is seen as only a part of the circular causal sequence and the relationships are assessed in terms of circular maintenance, which are important in understanding the system. These can be diagrammed to facilitate the social worker's and family's understanding of the behavior and to encourage an explicit awareness of the maladaptive patterns (65).

Feedback is a useful aspect of systems theory for identifying patterns of communication, both functional and dysfunctional, and helping the family deal with those that are dysfunctional. For example, a family may pay little attention to new incoming information that cuts it off from opportunities for growth and development (19). The social worker then provides the necessary support and encouragement so that family members can be more open to new input.

Boundaries have a particular relevance for work with families. When the boundaries of the subsystem are neither firm nor clear, they can be sources of maladaptive relationship and communication patterns. At the same time, the boundary must be permeable in order to enhance the need for mutuality and nurturance between the subsystems. The social worker then aims to open the family boundary to permit new information to enter.

The concept of equilibrium or steady state is an important consideration. The family as a group is composed of all the different levels of each member's equilibrium, which come together in a unitary whole or homeostatic balance. Rodway suggests that there is, in fact, an intermeshing of individual and family homeostasis that occurs in interaction among family members, and it is at a level of directly observable behavior (54). It is crucial for the social worker to understand how this balance is maintained so that one or more member's adjustment is not sacrificed to maintain a destructive balance.

Morphogenic and morphostatic tendencies of family systems are significant areas for assessment and intervention. These coexisting tendencies toward change and to resist change must be carefully examined since families with morphostatic tendencies will resist change efforts by the social worker and strive to maintain a dysfunctional systemic balance (19).

Case Example

In order to illustrate the relevance of systems concepts to actual practice, work with a couple will be described and analyzed (24). The case to be discussed was seen in a hospital setting that offered social work treatment through a variety of clinics.

> Mr. and Mrs. C. were referred for marital therapy by a child protection worker following the apprehension of their ten-month-old daughter, Julia. The child was taken into custody with the agreement of the parents following a report expressing concern about the present parenting and caretaking practices of the parents and indicating that the child had received a burn caused by a cigarette.
>
> When the child protection worker contacted Mrs. C. she expressed a great deal of ambivalence in regard to her feelings toward her husband. Mrs. C. noted much dissatisfaction and unhappiness with the present marital relationship. With the agreement of the parents, the child protection worker recommended that because of the expressed concerns regarding appropriate care and parenting and also the indicated marital problems, Julia should be taken into the custody of the Department of Social Services. The latter has legal responsibility for all children deemed to be inadequately cared for.
>
> When seen by the social worker assigned to the case, Mr. and Mrs. C. indicated the burn received by Julia had actually resulted from the child touching a hot iron while in the care of her father. The father had sought immediate medical attention and the subsequent burn was described as superficial. The marital relationship was described as somewhat tense in that Mrs. C. was expressing a great deal of ambivalence with regards to her commitment to the relationship. Both she and her husband indicated that since the birth of Julia, they have been experiencing more and more difficulty in the areas of communication and their sexual relationship. According to both, Mrs. C. was the most dissatisfied with the relationship, not only questioning her sense of self as an individual and as a mother, but also questioning her relationship to her husband regarding her feelings as to whether or not she loved him. Mr. C., on the other hand, expressed that he was generally satisfied with the marriage and did not want a separation.
>
> Mrs. C. indicated that she had been in foster care for most of her childhood, had been sexually abused by cousins, and had no contact with her family located in another part of the country. Her relationships with men prior to her marriage had also been abusive.

ASSESSMENT AND TREATMENT APPROACH. An assessment of the total structure in which the problem is lodged, or the social context, would be an important first step in this case. This analysis would then generate the appropriate strategies and interventions for problem resolution. Figure 19–2 illustrates the variety of systems involved with this couple and the process of intervention.

For the system-centered social worker, in terms of the request for marital

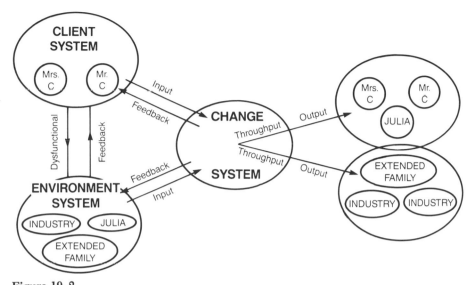

Figure 19-2

(Adapted from A. Vickery, "A Systems Approach to Social Work Intervention: Its Uses for Work with Individuals and Families," *British Journal of Social Work*, Vol. 4, No. 4 (1974), pp. 389–404)

therapy, the issue of Mrs. C.'s traumatic past held little relevance for his assessment of the marital conflicts. His focus was on the "here and now" and his task was to attempt to understand the typical patterns of interaction of the couple. This led to an intervention where some change was effected in their typical and predictable manner of interacting.

Their relationship was classified as complementary where their behaviors were different but at the same time mutually fitted together. It was noted that they habitually exchanged opposite behaviors according to a fixed formula. In systems terms, all couples have the task of establishing a satisfactory balance in the closeness-distance dimension of their relationship. Initial assessment was concerned with understanding the function of Mrs. C.'s ambivalence regarding her commitment to the marriage. The social worker then explored the existing process of negotiation of the couple between their marital and personal boundaries that would enable them to experience both a "separateness" and "belongingness." It emerged that there had been long-standing problems with intimacy on the part of both partners. There was a process where when one of the partners withdrew (Mrs. C.), the other partner pursued (Mr. C.). This, in turn, caused Mrs. C. to become even more emotionally withdrawn, and as a result both were expressing anxiety in relation to the threat of a possible separation.

The assessment further revealed that the marital relationship had incorporated Julia as a restraint that allowed the couple to join together in concern as parents, thus diminishing the threat of disengagement. At the same time, the inclusion of Julia in the marital system allowed them to enter into conflict, usually around the issues of parenting, thus allowing them to become more distant. Julia was then acting as a marital distance regulator to continually monitor and control the delicate balance between the closeness-distance and separation-belong pattern that this complementary couple had established.

Both Mr. and Mrs. C. held the other responsible for their present distress in the marital relationship, with Mr. C. indicating that it was his wife's aloof, withdrawn nature that was responsible and Mrs. C. indicating that it was her husband's intrusive-nagging behavior about her feelings and his persistent sexual advances that created problems. Their attempted solutions prior to their engagement in treatment were to expect that the problem would be solved if the other would change. These attempts only served to reinforce their complementary interchanges and, as such, perpetuated "the mess," the term they used to describe the marriage.

It was important for the social worker to avoid the couple's prescription for his involvement by not replacing Julia as the marital distance regulator. His goal was to participate in the newly formed triadic therapeutic system in a neutral way. This, in turn, helped the couple monitor and change the closeness-distance balance in their relationship. Rebalancing was the specific intervention that was applied to the distance-pursuit pattern. The therapeutic task was to stabilize the marriage by providing the information that would both hold the couple together as well as allow them to achieve an acceptable distance. The couple's accepted construction of events surrounding the problem was continually challenged. Their attempts to locate the "mess" in each other was relocated in the relationship. Finally, the social worker also focused attention on improvement in the couple's parenting skills, which had been raised initially.

By the end of the treatment process, both partners indicated that there had been a significant improvement in their relationship. More specifically, Mrs. C. was feeling much better about herself and had obtained a job. This time away from her husband and child provided the necessary distance needed both by her and by the relationship. Her job performance also increased her sense of self-worth. As she felt better about herself, she felt better about the relationship, and there was a substantial improvement in their sexual relationship. The couple's confidence and ability in parenting and child management had also improved greatly. Both partners were optimistic that their observed changes in behavior would continue to change in a positive direction.

Application to Groups

A small group is defined as a dynamic system whose members must be understood in terms of their relation to each other rather than as discrete entities. In systems terms, it exchanges material with its environment and endeavors to maintain a steady state. It forms subsystems whose functions are necessary for its survival. The subsystems tend to achieve a functional unity (29).

The boundary of the group is always determined arbitrarily based on the amount and intensity of interaction among its members. The group's environment consists of everything that is outside its boundary; that is, all factors affecting the group, from its point of view, in a significant way. To maintain the group in a steady state, a structure is needed for the various subsystems so that they may function in an interrelated manner. In turn, the structure is constituted by states, role, and relationship factors. In the process of maintaining a steady state, energy operates through the group's members and is exchanged with its environment. Steady state is also dependent on the information carried by and expressed through members. The concept of a communicational feedback system is useful in explaining the circular change of events that result from an ongoing exchange of information. Such exchange also defines the relationships among group members. Although difficult to achieve, open communication is essential.

All of these systems parameters have implications for practice with groups. The need for and purpose of the group must be clearly understood and articulated by the social worker. This in turn determines group composition and its inherent factors of selection. Each potential member must be assessed in terms of how she will contribute to the internal functioning of the system; for example, selecting members on a continuum that avoids extremes of behavior may prevent the formation of homogeneous subgroups who could undermine the function of the group (22).

The group setting is an important consideration; for example, when working with groups on their "homeground," rather than in the agency, it is possible to obtain a more accurate assessment of the larger systems that are impacting the group. Use of a homeground setting also facilitates the more accurate determination of targets of change and whether they are within or outside the group itself.

The composition and nature of the relationships that comprise the subgroups must be closely examined by the social worker. Problems may result when subgroups become isolated or are in conflict.

The social worker's judgments, based on appraisal of events, determine what she does next, which in turn evokes another response from the group. The degree to which group members respond to such feedback accurately and openly enhances stability and continuity. The size of the group is an important factor in determining how the group members and subgroups relate and is determined according to the group purpose.

Types of Clients, Problems, and Settings
Most Appropriate for a Systems Approach

The literature reveals a number of applications of systems theory to varying clients, problems, and settings. Systems theory provides more useful guidelines for assessment and treatment of alcohol dependent individuals than does the traditional illness conception of this problem (17). In viewing alcohol dependent persons from a systems perspective, two groups are identified: those who are not fundamentally in a social system—that is, isolates without significant others—and those who are in a social system. The latter group constitutes the majority of alcohol dependents. For the group who are socially isolated, the need for the social worker to pursue the establishment of connections with others is important. For those who are part of a social system, the social worker focuses on the subsystems to which an alcoholic is connected in order to exert social system pressure that will lead to a creative crisis state in the alcoholic.

The use of systems theory in foster home studies has also been documented (1). Drawing from family system and communication theory, a study process for foster parents was designed that encompassed the following dimensions of the family within the system: nuclear family emotional system; triangles in the system; transgenerational themes; family projection process; history of losses to the family; and communication patterns. Based on a three-year study, it was concluded that the use of a systems theory brought order and specificity to the selection of foster homes.

A marriage enrichment program based on systems theory is proposed as an alternate to the variety of programs that have been developed in this area (15). It was formulated from the systems concepts of circular causality, the identification of predictable interaction patterns, and the adoptive and homeostatic mechanisms. Based on experience with the five-phase model, it was concluded that marriage enrichment programs would benefit when systems concepts are used in such applied programs for couples.

A systems approach to the provision of social work services in health settings was utilized to project the role of the social worker in such agencies (49). Within this theoretical framework, both the social worker and the patient were viewed as being influenced by powerful forces within and outside the health setting. To a much lesser degree, the patient and social worker's ability to influence the organization was also a component to be considered. The framework enabled the identification of impediments and barriers to effective social work in hospitals as well as the discovery of alternative directions and solutions to some of the impediments. Further, it was concluded that the most effective provision of social work services in these organizations must be combined with organizational change and social action programs.

There are a range of problems that may require a systems approach:

> When the client or significant other (e.g., employer) has an unclear or inadequate perception of the client's role; when roles seem to merge inappropriately (problem of role separation); when the problem involves inability of significant others to handle a problematic situation; when the worker's own agency or another agency needs help in providing services; when a gap in services is identified; when the prevailing community attitudes regarding the client and/or his or her problem need modifying; when the client is having problems with formal

organizations; when clients need help in preparing for recurrent life problems and tasks and to make transitions in roles and stages in the life cycle. (This latter situation is of particular importance for a variety of preventive measures such as those in programs for family life and sex education and programs providing anticipatory guidance and special care for individuals at risk or in high-stress situations.) (18, p. 110)

Implications of Systems Theory for Social Work Research

A critical need in social work is more research and the development of a social work science. Studies of the interactions between individuals and their environment and of the particular methodologies applied to the variety of problems and populations are but a few examples of much needed research.

Systems theory has potential in this regard. There is promise in the use of this perspective for "organizing these valuable insights of the past and present, because it embraces a holistic conception of complex adaptive systems viewed centrally in terms of information and communication process and the significance of the way these are structured for self-regulation and self-direction" (12, p. 508). It has considerable capacity for relating process to outcome that could provide predictive ability for specific interventions.

At the present time, systems theory provides a descriptive model rather than a research model that could furnish guidance for both research and action. A current difficulty in utilizing systems theory in research has been the specification and naming of the linkages between systems and subsystems (59). What is beginning to be developed are process terms such as input-output and through-put. In addition, validation and refinement of propositions related to systems theory is underway. However, until theorists can inform researchers of these critical linkages, scientific study is greatly deterred and the profession must move with caution in adopting theoretical structures that are not adequately established.

Summary and Conclusions

This final section outlines the major contributions of systems theory to social work, identifies the present gaps in knowledge and limitations of this perspective, and describes some specific directions to be followed in the future.

Perhaps the major contribution of systems theory has been again placing the environment in the forefront of practice rather than viewing it as a background to the focus of attention; e.g., the person. It has also brought clearly into focus the complex interactive nature of the environment and its multi-faceted relationship to human development and functioning.

Systems theory has highlighted the existential dilemma in the individual's becoming a part system in the collective human system. More specifically, the conflict exists between being a whole person and becoming a subsystem that may involve subordinating one's integrity (51).

It has provided our profession with guidelines and direction for broader work with clients and the organizations that impact on their lives. Organizations may become more responsive to client needs because of the increased emphasis on advocacy and mediation that is inherent in systems theory (48).

A systems perspective has contributed to more imaginative use and deployment of manpower. The concept of equifinality suggests that different approaches to intervention will achieve a similar outcome since each action taken will affect another that will, in turn, activate other impetus for change. This perspective suggests that specific aspects of intervention with clients may be more effectively undertaken by workers with differing levels of education and experience; that is, diploma, bachelor's or master's degrees. It may also be most appropriate to involve a member of the system being serviced or to include the services of a self-help group. Systems theory has also brought into prominence the concept of the action system and the social work team or interdisciplinary team.

Systems theory offers the alternative of less emphasis on pathology and more emphasis on the interaction of the client with the variety of systems in his environment. It directs the social worker's attention to the study of behavior and its consequences in all the subsystems rather than looking for the origin of the problem in the individual or client system. Within this viewpoint, symptoms are seen in terms of function for and across systems (48).

Finally, this perspective has a particular relevance for intervention in crisis situations because of its emphasis on an assessment that takes into account the variety of aspects of the person-in-situation. It also provides a framework for determining those elements that are rigid (morphostatic) and those that are accessible to change (morphogenic) (48).

Reactions to systems theory within the profession have varied from caution to resistance to enthusiasm to acceptance and utilization. It will be recalled that systems theory has been described as a "metatheory" or "theory about theories" which describes how systems function. Critics support the concept that it fails to look at the why or the causative nature of problems.

Another difficulty with the use of this theory is its high level of abstraction, which makes its translation into practice difficult: "this high level of abstraction becomes an impediment only if the theory building process stops at the conceptualizing phase. One need only take the next step which is to concretize or elaborate the practical implication of the theory derived from the abstract construct, to overcome this process (29, p. 54). Much has been done in this regard but this important task still requires considerable effort. Additionally, the nature of the systems language itself—e.g., entropy, through-put—can be alienating and confusing.

The concept of homeostatis has been problematic in this theory throughout its development. Systems theory must avoid the homeostatic or any other equilibrium concept when working with social systems (11). For this concept to be useful then, social workers must have a clear idea of the nature of healthy growth, development, and functioning. In addition, "accepted" becomes a key phrase in terms of established social norms since any problematic behavior is a deviance from such norms and creates a disturbance in the state of equilibrium (14). Homeostatis suggests that the process of internally generated social change is so subtle as to often be unnoticeable. This could lead social workers to conclude that social change takes care of itself and that they do not need to look within the system for sources of change (38).

Leighninger has perhaps provided the most critical analysis of systems theory (38). He suggests firstly that many social workers in their use of systems theory take similarities among systems for granted, rather than looking at structural similarities and differences. To address this difficulty, Leighninger proposes that professionals must test, not assume, the similarities in systems properties. He notes additionally that the holistic promise of systems theory for social work has been its most appealing aspect, yet the contribution of the theory to this promise remains to be fully established.

In terms of future directions for the use of systems theory in social work, the need for research in a variety of directions has already been commented on but should be reinforced.

Currently there are two main trends in the systems approach termed "mechanistic" and "organismic humanistic" (8). The mechanistic trend refers to cybernetics, regulation by feedback, computerization, and the methods of systems engineering. The organismic humanistic trend emphasizes: the wholeness of the organism and its accessibility to scientific research; the active nature of the organism; the specificities of the human; the trend toward higher order and organization; and the trend's manifestation in human creativity and the introduction of specifically human values into the scientific worldview. The latter trend has much more relevance for the human services if they are to avoid depersonalization and dehumanization.

A new way of conceiving living systems needs to be developed. While initial attempts have been made in this regard, more remains to be accomplished. A second perspective for the future is a much more in-depth exploration of the environment, particularly the turbulent type of environment that is often encountered in social work (30).

In conclusion, it can be stated that "the systems approach in its various aspects will be indispensable if better solutions of pressing problems are to be arrived at. In its humanistic trend, it may contribute toward a reorientation of thought and attitude" (8). This captures the essence of the contribution that systems theory may ultimately make to social work.

References

1. Anderson, L. "A Systems Theory Model for Foster Home Studies," *Child Welfare*, Vol. 61, No. 1 (1982), pp. 37–47.

2. Anderson, R., and I. Carter. *Human Behavior in the Social Environment.* Chicago: Aldine, 1974.

3. Aponte, H. "The Family-School Interview: An Eco-Structural Approach," *Family Process*, Vol. 15 (1976), pp. 303–312.

4. ———. "Diagnosis in Family Therapy," in C. Germain (ed.), *Social Work Practice: People and Environments.* New York: Columbia University Press, 1979.

5. Bandler, Bernard. "The Concept of Ego-Supportive Psychotherapy," in Howard J. Parad and Roger R. Miller (eds.), *Ego-Oriented Casework: Problems and Perspectives.* New York: Family Service Association of America, 1963.

6. Bartlett, H. *The Common Base of Social Work Practice.* New York: National Association of Social Workers, 1970.

7. Bertalanffy, L. V. "General Systems Theory," *General Systems Yearbook*, Vol. 1, No. 4 (1956).

8. ———. "Introduction" in H. Werley, A. Zuzick, and M. Zagkowski (eds.), *Health Research: The Systems Approach.* New York: Springer, 1976.

9. Bloom, M. *The Paradox of Helping.* New York: Wiley, 1975.

10. Bowen, Murray. "Theory in the Practice of Psychotherapy," in Philip J. Guerin (ed.), *Family Therapy: Theory and Practice.* New York: Gardner Press, 1976.

11. Buckley, W. *Sociology and Modern Systems Theory.* Englewood Cliffs, N.J.: Prentice-Hall, 1967.

12. ———. *Modern Systems Research for the Behavioral Scientist.* Chicago: Aldine, 1968, p. 508.

13. Chin, R. "The Utility of Systems Models and Developmental Models for Practitioners," in W. G. Bennis, K. D. Berne, and R. Chin (eds.), *The Planning of Change.* New York: Holt, Rinehart and Winston, 1961.

14. Decker, J., and J. Redhorse. "The Principles of General Systems Theory Applied to the Medical Model: Who Benefits," *Journal of Sociology and Social Welfare*, Vol. 6, No. 2 (1979), pp. 144–153.

15. Elliott, S., and B. Saunders. "The Systems Marriage Enrichment Program: An Alternative Model Based on Systems Theory," *Family Relations*, Vol. 31 (1982), pp. 53–60.

16. Epstein, N., and D. Bishop. "Problem Centered Systems Therapy of the Family," *Journal of Marital and Family Therapy* (1981), pp. 23–31.

17. Finlay, D. "Alcoholism and Systems Theory: Building a Better Mousetrap," *Psychiatry*, Vol. 41 (1978), pp. 272–278.

18. Fischer, J. *Effective Casework Practice: An Eclectic Approach.* New York: McGraw-Hill, 1978, pp. 110–116.

19. Freeman, D. "A Systems Approach to Family Therapy," *Family Therapy*, Vol. 3, No. 1 (1976).

20. Germain, Carol B. "Knowledge Base of Clinical Social Work," in A. Rosenblatt and D. Waldfogel (eds.), *Handbook of Clinical Social Work.* San Francisco Jossey-Bass, 1983.

21. ———, and Alex Gitterman. *The Life Model of Social Work Practice.* New York: Columbia University Press, 1980.

22. Goldstein, H. *Social Work Practice: A Unitary Approach.* Columbia: University of South Carolina Press, 1973.

23. Gordon, W. "Basic Constructs for an Integrative and Generative Conception of Social Work," in G. Hearn (ed.), *The General Systems Approach: Contributions Toward an Holistic Conception of Social Work.* New York: Council on Social Work Education, 1969.

24. Guthrie, B. "A Case Presentation from Two Perspectives of Psychotherapy: A Psychoanalytic Approach and a Systems Approach." Unpublished paper. Calgary: University of Calgary, 1985.

25. Hartman, A. "To Think About the Unthinkable," *Social Casework*, Vol. 51, No. 8 (October 1970), pp. 467–474.

26. ———. "Diagrammatic Assessment of Family Relationships," *Social Casework*, Vol. 59 (1978), pp. 464–476.

27. ———. "The Extended Family as a Resource for Change: An Ecological Approach to Family Centered Practice," in C. Germain (ed.), *Social Work Practice: People and Environments.* New York: Columbia University Press, 1979.

28. ———, and J. Laird. *Family Centered Social Work Practice.* New York: Free Press, 1983.

29. Hearn, Gordon. *Theory Building in Social Work.* Toronto: University of Toronto Press, 1958.

30. ———. *The General Systems Approach: Contributions Toward an Holistic Conception of Social Work.* New York: Council on Social Work Education, 1969.

31. ———. "General Systems Theory and Social Work," in Francis J. Turner (ed.), *Social Work Treatment.* New York: Free Press, 1979.

32. Hoffman, L. "Breaking the Homeostatic Cycle," in Philip J. Guerin (ed.), *Family Therapy: Theory and Practice.* New York: Gardner Press, 1976.

33. Janchill, M. "Systems Concepts in Casework Theory and Practice," *Social Casework*, Vol. 5 (1969), pp. 74–82.

34. Johnson, H. "Integrating the Problem-Oriented Record with a Systems Approach to Case Assessments," *Journal of Education for Social Work*, Vol. 14, No. 3 (1978), pp. 71–77.

35. Katz, D., and R. Kahn. *The Social Psychology of Organizations.* New York: Wiley, 1966.

36. Koestler, A. *The Ghost in the Machine.* London: Hutchison, 1967.

37. Lathrope, D. "The General Systems Approach in Social Work Practice," in G. Hearn (ed.), *The General Systems Approach: Contributions Toward an Holistic Conception of Social Work.* New York: Council on Social Work Education, 1969.

38. Leighninger, R. "Systems Theory and Social Work," *Journal of Education for Social Work*, Vol. 13, No. 3 (1977), pp. 44–49.

39. Lennard, H., and A. Bernstein. *Patterns in Human Interaction.* San Francisco: Jossey-Bass, 1969.

40. Lippitt, R., J. Watson, and B. Westley. *The Dynamics of Planned Change.* New York: Harcourt, Brace, 1958.

41. Lutz, J. *Concepts and Principles Underlying Social Casework Practice.* New York: National Association of Social Workers, 1956.

42. Madanes, Cloe. *Strategic Family Therapy.* San Francisco: Jossey-Bass, 1981.

43. Maluccio, Anthony. *Promoting Competence in Clients: A New/Old Approach to Social Work Practice.* New York: Free Press, 1981.

44. Maruyama, M. "The Second Cybernetics: Deviation Amplifying Mutual Causal Processes," *American Scientist*, Vol. 51 (1963).

45. Meyer, Carol. *Social Work Practice: A Response to the Urban Crisis*. New York: Free Press, 1970.

46. ———. "Direct Services in New and Old Contexts," in A. Kahn (ed.), *Shaping the New Social Work*. New York: Columbia University Press, 1973.

47. Minuchin, Salvador. *Families and Family Therapy*. Cambridge, Mass.: Harvard University Press, 1974.

48. Mishne, J. "The Missing System in Social Work's Application of Systems Theory," *Social Casework*, Vol. 3, No. 9 (1982), pp. 547–553.

49. Nacman, M. "A Systems Approach to the Provision of Social Work Services in Health Settings," *Social Work in Health Care*, Part 1. Vol. 1, No. 1 (1975), pp. 47–53; Part 2, Vol. 1, No. 2 (1975), pp. 133–143.

50. Pincus, A., and A. Minahan. *Social Work Practice: Model and Method*. Itasca, Ill.: Peacock, 1973.

51. Polsky, N. "System as Patient: Client Needs and System Function," in G. Hearn (ed.), *The General Systems Approach: Toward an Holistic Conception of Social Work*. New York: Council on Social Work Education, 1969.

52. Ramsay, R. "The Use of a Geometric Systems Approach to Establish a Model and Method of Social Work," in M. R. Rodway (ed.), *Teaching Social Work Methods: Perspectives and Dimensions*. Calgary: Faculty of Social Welfare, University of Calgary, 1985 (in press).

53. Richmond, Mary. *Social Diagnosis*. New York: Russell Sage Foundation, 1920.

54. Rodway, M. R. "Family Human Social Functioning: An Integrative Approach to Family Practice," in D. Freeman (ed.), *Perspectives on Family Therapy*. Vancouver: Butterworth and Co., 1980.

55. ———. "Couple Growth Counselling," *Social Work Review*, inaugural issue (December 1983), pp. 201–214.

56. Selvini-Palazzoli, Mara, Luigi Boscolo, Gianfranco Cecchin, and Giuliana Prota. *Paradox and Counter-Paradox*. New York: Aronson, 1978.

57. Shulman, L. "Social Systems Theory in Field Instruction: A Case Example," in G. Hearn (ed.), *The General Systems Approach: Contributions Toward an Holistic Conception of Social Work*. New York: Council on Social Work Education, 1969.

58. ———. *The Skills of Helping Individuals and Groups*. Itasca, Ill.: Peacock, 1979.

59. Sills, G. "Bridging the Gap Between Systems Theory and Research," in H. Wesley, A. Zuzick, and A. Zagarnick (eds.), *Health Research: The Systems Approach*. New York: Springer, 1976.

60. Siporin, M. *Introduction to Social Work Practice*. New York: Macmillan, 1975.

61. Sluzki, C. "Marital Therapy from a Systems Theory Perspective," in T. Paolino and S. McCrady (eds.), *Marriage and Marital Therapy*. New York: Brunner/Mazel, 1978.

62. Stein, Irma L. "The Application of Systems Theory to Social Work Practice and Education." Paper presented at the Annual Program Meeting of the Council on Social Work Education, New York, January 1966.

63. ———. *Systems Theory, Science and Social Work.* Metuchen, N.J.: Scarecrow Press, 1974.

64. Strean. Herbert. "Worker-Client Relationships," in A. Rosenblatt and D. Wald-fogel (eds.), *Handbook of Clinical Social Work.* San Francisco: Jossey-Bass, 1983.

65. Tomm, K. "Towards a Cybernetic Systems Approach to Family Therapy at the University of Calgary," in D. Freeman (ed.), *Perspectives on Family Therapy.* Vancouver: Butterworth and Co., 1980.

66. Vickery, A. "A Systems Approach to Social Work Intervention: Its Uses for Work with Individuals and Families," *British Journal of Social Work,* Vol. 4, No. 4 (1974), pp. 389–404.

Annotated Listing of Key References

FORDER, A. "Social Work and System Theory," *British Journal of Social Work*, Vol. 6, No. 1 (1976), pp. 23–34.

The contribution of general systems theory to an understanding of social work method is considered in this article. After reviewing the implications of system theory for social work more generally, the author concludes that its contribution to practice in terms of being a guide to appraisal and intervention is its most noteworthy aspect.

HARTMAN, A., and J. LAIRD. *Family Centered Social Work Practice.* New York: Free Press, 1968.

A conceptualization of social work family practice is presented that is based on three frameworks for intervention, one of which is systems theory. The systems framework is utilized for understanding and intervening in the relationship between the family system and its subsystems and individual members. The authors have carefully reinterpreted in a systems/cybernetic process, the various concepts of practice such as contracting, assessment, and intervention.

HEARN, GORDON. "General Systems Theory and Social Work," in Francis Turner (ed.), *Social Work Treatment*, 2nd edition. New York: Free Press, 1979, pp. 333–359.

Gordon Hearn has been recognized as the leading social work system theorist. This chapter addresses a number of issues that emerge when considering the relationship of systems theory to social work: theory building; model building; conceiving social work holistically; the social work domain; and, finally, systems theory and a new world view.

PINCUS, A., and A. MINAHAN. *Social Work Practice: Model and Method.* Itasca, Ill.: Peacock, 1973.

Although written from the perspective of a common core base of knowledge for social work practice, the authors rely heavily on systems concepts in their formulation of a model. Of particular interest is their conceptualization of the activities of the social worker in relation to four types of systems: change agent, client, target, and action.

STEIN, IRMA L. *Systems Theory, Science and Social Work.* Metuchen, N.J.: Scarecrow Press, 1974.

Irma Stein provides a scholarly survey of the literature in general systems theory and of social work literature that has utilized general systems constructs. The historical development of the major concepts of general systems theory, along with their present status is presented. Her focus is on how such concepts are being applied in the literature rather than their application to social work practice. This text will interest those practitioners who wish to gain a more in-depth understanding of systems theory as it relates to social work.

CHAPTER 20

Role Theory

Liane Vida Davis

Introduction

In what may be the most widely referenced book on role theory within social work, Bruce Biddle and Edwin Thomas observed almost twenty years ago that "Role theory is a new field of inquiry. . . . Indeed, with the exception of fragmented commentary, the scholars of role have not identified, articulated, and analyzed the component aspects of role theory: namely its domain of study, perspective, language, body of knowledge, theory, and method of inquiry" (6, p. 3).

Close to fifteen years later Biddle observed that the failure of the scholars of role theory to generate an integrative theoretical statement had resulted in considerable ambiguity about its central assumptions and domain of study (5). Perhaps role theory has failed to generate an integrative theoretical statement because, as Marvin Shaw and Phillip Costanzo have suggested, it is not a theory. For them "(r)ole theory is a body of knowledge and principles that at one and the same time constitutes an orientation, a group of theories, loosely linked networks of hypotheses, isolated constructs about human functioning in a social context, and a language system which pervades nearly every social scientist's vocabulary" (51, p. 295).

Despite this confusion as to its domain, there is little doubt that "the constructs of role theory are exceptionally rich in their empirical referents and provide an approach to the analysis of social behavior which is missing from many other theories" (14, p. 244). Furthermore, because role theory seeks to explain the ways in which the behavior of the individual is directly and indirectly influenced by the social environment, it is a system that is both congruent with and can provide theoretical and empirical support for social work's historical emphasis on person-environment transactions. As Herbert Strean observed in the earlier editions of this book, "role carries a considerable freightage of meaning in social work because it implies a means of individual expression as well as dimension of social behavior" (54, p. 387).

Historical Origins

Role theory has roots within both academic and nonacademic institutions. The concept of role itself is drawn from the theater and has been passed down through the centuries to characterize the observable behaviors that persons enact in their patterned interactions with others (46). It captures the central view of role theory that we play many parts in our lives whose basic scripts are provided by others yet whose enactment is uniquely our own.

Other role theory constructs are rooted within the many disciplines of formal social science. This interdisciplinary perspective on human conduct is, for many, its major strength (2, 5, 44, 46). There is only space to mention a few of the historic luminaries whose contributions on role have had a significant influence on the ways in which we as social workers practice. George Herbert Mead, the sociologist, introduced the concept of *role taking* and focused on its significance in the development of an individual's self-concept (33). We lay the foundation for a sense of who we are by identifying with significant others, internalizing their attitudes as our own, and seeing ourselves as others see us. Joseph L. Moreno introduced the use of *role playing* as a therapeutic technique to be used for both the learning of new behaviors and to facilitate clients' ability to understand another's perspective (38). Ralph Linton, the anthropologist, and Robert K. Merton, the sociologist, were more concerned about the relationship between the social structure itself and the ways in which persons fulfilled their socially designated obligations (27, 36). Linton distinguished between the static aspects of role behavior—that is, the positions or statuses designated by social systems—and their dynamic aspects—that is, the patterned behaviors, or roles, expected of and enacted by those who occupied them. Linton conceived of persons as enacting one role for each of the many statuses they occupied. Merton observed that there were actually a set of different roles—that is, a role-set—potentially associated with each status. Together, their contributions make us aware of the myriad ways in which the behaviors we enact in interaction with others are influenced by the positions we occupy in society and vary as we interact with different persons.

Role Theory: What Is It?

My failure to define the subject matter of role theory thus far has not been an oversight. In part it has been to demonstrate that many of its concepts are accessible to persons with little formal education in the theory itself. This has been both a strength and a weakness for its theoretical development and utilization. It has resulted, on the one hand, in the widespread application of its central concepts across a broad array of situations by both lay persons and professionals. On the other hand, this utilization has occurred with a rather broad disregard for the carefully operationalized definitions of central constructs offered by the theorists. This rather liberal, if inexact, incorporation of role theoretic constructs into common usage has been aided by the wide diversity of definitions and usages offered by the theorists themselves.

One of the major reasons the domain of role theory is so difficult to define is that it takes on different identities depending in large part on the discipline of the writer. It is, for example, somewhat different for psychologists than it is for sociologists. Social psychologists are primarily concerned with the ways in which socially prescribed roles influence the behavior of persons. They focus their attention on such issues as: the processes by which individuals are socialized into role behavior; the stresses placed on the individual by the necessity to perform multiple roles; the impact on the individual of the sanctions imposed for violation of normative role behavior; the ways in which the interaction between persons is structured by their role expectations of one another and of themselves in their complementary positions; the ways in which an individual's sense of self is influenced by the various positions she occupies and the effectiveness with which she plays her roles. Most recently, concern for role within social psychology has been focused on the myriad ways in which persons' public selves—that is, their public role behavior—and their private selves diverge from one another, as well as the reasons for and the consequences of such discrepancies (51).

Sociologists are more concerned with the macro issue of how the system of role behaviors help maintain the social structure itself. Since the stability of the social structure depends in part on the extent to which individuals enact normative role behaviors, concern is focused on such issues as: the mechanisms used to assure conformity to socially normative behaviors; the impact of engaging in deviant behaviors; the relationship between those in positions of social control and those in positions to have their behavior controlled; as well as the myriad ways in which the behavior of individuals in their daily interactions reflects social rather than psychological forces.

Central Terms

As indicated earlier, one of the major sources of confusion for the student of role theory has been the myriad ways in which central terms have been defined. In selecting the central terms I have chosen to provide the most commonsensical definitions, high-lighting those instances in which the differences appear to be qualitatively significant.

Social position and *social status* are often used interchangeably in the literature to refer to a "socially recognized category of actors" (56, p. 439). While *status* seems to be more frequently used than *position,* I prefer to use *position* because it is less value-laden. Positions are classifications of persons (6). Among common positions are teachers, social workers, women, children, fathers. The major confusion in the literature is whether position refers solely to the identity or carries other meaning. Some include the associated behavioral expectations within the definition of position (46), others include the placement of the position within the social structure itself (50).

Ascribed positions are those that are independent of the qualities of the individual and depend instead on accidents of birth, social experience, or maturity. Common ascribed positions are woman, man, child, adult, black, handicapped person. Kingsley Davis has observed that ascribed positions have primacy over those achieved since they are often based on characteristics present at birth and, as a result, lay the foundation for subsequent socialization (13).

Achieved positions are those that are attained through skill or effort. Common achieved positions are social worker, musician, politician. It has been observed by many that the distinction between ascribed and achieved positions is not as clear in reality as it is in theory (5, 13). One enters most positions through a combination of ascription and achievement. Hard work and intelligence are certainly requisites for becoming a college professor. There is little doubt, however, that entry into the position of college professor is facilitated by having been born a white male in a family that has both an adequate income and a set of values that places a high priority on education. Knowing that there is a mechanism to change one's position serves to motivate persons toward social ends (13).

Status refers to the value of the position (5). Among the most common criteria used to determine status are: prestige, wealth, and authority. A position has a higher status if its occupants have more prestige, are wealthier, and are able to wield authority.

The relationship between status and position is well illustrated with reference to the differential status of the ascribed positions of men and women. Almost twenty years ago, Kingsley Davis commented on the fact that in every society sex difference is used as a way of assigning and giving a monopoly to different statuses which in turn results in one sex receiving more status than another, causing tension between such ascriptions.

Role refers to the characteristic behaviors enacted by persons occupying social positions. A role is "a patterned sequence of learned *actions* or deeds performed by a person *in an interaction situation* [emphasis added]" (46, p. 225). The concept of role serves as a metaphor to denote that "conduct adheres to certain 'parts' or statuses rather than to players who recite or read their 'parts' " (45, p. 101). Roles are classifications of behaviors (6). They do not exist in isolation but are designed to "fit in with the reciprocal functions of a partner in a relationship" (30, p. 9).

The concept of *role partner* has been introduced to capture this socially interactive, reciprocal, nature of role behavior (51). The role of mother is enacted vis-à-vis the role of child or the role of father; the role of social worker is enacted vis-à-vis the role of client or the role of psychologist.

Role-set refers to the varied roles potentially associated with any single position. Social workers, for example, enact one set of behaviors for clients, another set of behaviors for supervisors, another set of behaviors for the agency administrator, and yet another set of behaviors for their peers.

Role expectations are the set of expectations for the behaviors of a person or a position held by a particular person or by a generalized other. Since roles are enacted in interaction with another, there are both role expectations held by the actor (also referred to as ego) and reciprocal role expectations of the other (also referred to as alter.) Expectations include both *rights* and *obligations* (36, 46). In common parlance many of the "oughts" and the "shoulds" to which persons are subjected derive from role expectations.

Role expectations vary in the generality with which they are held by others. Some are held by society in general, others are group specific, still others are more idiosyncratic. Society, for example, holds certain expectations of mothers; however these differ as a function of ethnicity or socioeconomic class. A specific child may, furthermore, have his own expectations of how his mother should behave.

Role complementarity exists when the role behavior and role expectations of persons in an interpersonal system are harmonious. "The *principle of role complementarity* . . . states that role definitions, expectations, and enactive behaviors of people should fit together and mutually complete each other's needs" (52, p. 106). Lack of complementarity may result from: lack of knowledge of the role system; discrepant goals on the part of the role partners; disagreement as to the right of one of the partners to occupy the role; and absence of appropriate resources to facilitate role performance (30). Role complementarity results in satisfactory role relationships; lack of complementarity results in dissatisfactory relationships as well as individual and interpersonal stress.

Norms are role expectations that serve to prescribe behaviors that *ought* to be performed by the person holding a given position. "[I]t is largely through . . . (norms) . . . that . . . (a person's) . . . conduct is regulated and integrated with the conduct of his fellows" (12, p. 110).

While norms and expectations have frequently been used interchangeably in the literature, Shaw and Costanzo suggest that it is more useful to reserve the term "norm" for role expectations that are socially prescribed (51). Other expectations, more idiosyncratic in nature, assist us in anticipating the behavior of specific others enacting their roles. While not necessary for society in general, these expectations facilitate interpersonal behavior as they enable persons to predict the behavior of those with whom they regularly interact.

It is a norm for fathers to financially support their families. While it is not normative as yet, there are an increasing number of fathers who are also engaging in extensive child care behaviors vis-à-vis their children. Thus, a specific mother may expect a specific father to bathe, feed, clothe, and engage in other care-taking activities for his own child.

Social identity is the sense of ourselves that we derive from the positions we occupy and the adequacy with which we and significant others judge our role performance. It is through the reciprocal interactions one has with others, the repeated experience of describing who we are, that we develop and internalize our social identity (45). At one and the same time we may be mothers in relation to children, children in relation to mothers, students in relation to teachers, and teachers in relation to students. Our social identity reflects the complexity of these myriad role relationships. The concept of social identity implies, furthermore, that a part of our self-identity changes along with the changes in the roles we enact.

Concepts That Describe Role-Related Difficulties

There are a number of constructs in the role literature that describe role situations that are likely to result in the experiencing of intrapersonal stress and/or interpersonal difficulties. These constructs are especially useful for the social worker interested in accurately utilizing role theory terminology for understanding impediments to, and intervening to facilitate, effective role performance.

Role conflict is generically used by some theorists to refer to difficulties that persons experience in the performance of their roles. More exactly, role conflict occurs when a person experiences incompatible demands in the performance of his designated roles. Role conflict may be experienced only internally or may be expressed interpersonally (52). Two subtypes of role conflict have been identified in the literature:

Interrole or interposition conflict occurs when the role expectations associated with various positions held by an individual are incompatible with one another (51, 57). For example, many women in contemporary society experience interrole conflict in attempting to adequately fulfill their roles as worker, wife, and mother.

Intrarole or intraposition conflict occurs when the expectations associated with a single position are incompatible with one another (51, 57). This is likely to occur when there is lack of consensus about role expectations. For example, a woman may experience intrarole conflict when the expectations of the role of mother held by her own mother, her husband, and herself are incongruent with one another.

Role ambiguity occurs when the expectations for adequate role performance for a given position are unclear or incomplete (5, 57). It has also been used to refer to roles for "which no place has been made in the social system" (42, p. 151). There are many persons who, upon entering positions, need to learn appropriate role expectations; that is, be socialized. This is not in itself role ambiguity, it is only such if the role expectations themselves are unclearly defined. Role ambiguity will be expected when new roles are developing or old roles are in the process of being redefined. For example, one would expect a substantial amount of role ambiguity to exist for those persons trying nontraditional couple relationships, such as egalitarian marriages and lesbian and gay couples.

Role overload occurs when a person is faced with a set of roles that are too complex. There is no simple relationship between the number of roles that a person can handle and the amount of role overload experienced. Some persons thrive on multiple roles, others are stressed by only a few (5). Some women, for example, thrive in balancing family and work obligations, others experience considerable stress.

Role discontinuity refers to the lack of similarity between the roles an individual is expected to perform at various stages of the life cycle or at sequential points in time. This term, first introduced by Ruth Benedict, is usefully applied to understanding the stresses that a person experiences and the supports that are required to facilitate the transition from a familiar role to a dissimilar one (5). Common instances of role discontinuity occur in the transition from worker to retired person, from married person to single person, from alcholic to recovering alcoholic.

Deviant and Variant Roles

Society creates norms largely to regulate and integrate the behavior of persons, thereby ensuring a stable social structure. While there is considerable disagreement about the causes of deviant behavior, the development of deviant identities, and the subsequent enactment of deviant roles, there is substantial agreement about those roles that are considered to be deviant (20, 47, 48). Among the more commonly discussed roles are those of mental patient, alcoholic, prisoner, delinquent, gay, and lesbian. Furthermore, there is agreement that society systematically "punishes" those who engage in deviant behaviors in order to force their conformity and/or to assure the continued conformity of others.

Persons may learn to enact deviant roles through modeling, as in the case of the alcoholic; they may enact them because they have been denied access to normative roles, as in the case of the delinquent (11, 45); or they may enact them because society is intolerant of behavior that is different, as in the case of the gay or lesbian. Regardless, deviant roles are stigmatized by society, and, as a result, persons who enact them may internalize a degraded social identity (45).

Role Theory and Its Relationship to Other Theories

Because of its interdisciplinary nature and the generality with which social scientists have used the language of role, role theory at times seems to both incorporate and to be incorporated into many other theoretical perspectives. There are few theories with which it comes into critical conflict. The major issues are those of differential emphasis.

Role theory does differ substantially from psychoanalytic theory, for example, by emphasizing the social determinants of behavior, by focusing on contemporaneous conflicting role expectations and role performance as major sources of psychological distress, and by emphasizing the primarily conscious facets of social relationships.

Because role behavior is learned through such processes as modeling, identification, and reinforcement, it draws directly on, and is therefore congruent with, a social learning approach to both understanding human behavior and social work intervention. However, it differs from a social learning theory perspective in the holistic quality of what is learned. Role theory is less concerned with how persons learn the specific behaviors they enact in their myriad roles and more concerned with how they learn and enact "the generic quality of the behavior and the goals and motives of that behavior" (51, p. 300).

In this sense it is similar to theories of behavior that focus on the organizing influence of cognitions on behavior and feelings (22, 29, 34, 35). It is also congruent with a symbolic interactionist perspective within sociology that focuses attention on the ways in which behavior and thoughts are created in the process of interacting with others (4).

Role Theory's Entry into Social Work

Because of social work's historical emphasis on the person-environment configuration, role concepts have found a comfortable home within social work. Florence Hollis, in her psychosocial approach to casework, emphasized the utility for diagnosis of understanding the ways in which normative expectations are dependent on gender, age, and class as well as the ways in which they can help locate "the spots at which external pressures are strong and the ways in which the individual is reacting in an unhealthy fashion" (25, p. 187). As with many subsequent social work theoreticians, she also used role theory to conceptualize the client-worker relationship and the ways in which the client's initial expectations regarding the role of the social worker influence the subsequent course of treatment.

There is perhaps no book in the social work practice literature that better captures the broad perspective that role theory has to offer than Helen Harris Perlman's *Persona: Social Role and Personality*. "Persona," the Latin word for the masks used in Greek dramas, is used to capture the notion that we know others through the varied masks we don in our interactions with others. Perlman's major thesis throughout this book is that the transactions between individuals and their environments are, for the most part, "contained and aligned by socially defined position and their functions—by roles" (42, p. 3).

She emphasizes the fact that society merely provides the basic script for behavior. It is within the ongoing transactions between persons that the scripts are acted out, the role behaviors finely tuned.

The importance of role theory for Perlman is best expressed in her belief that change in adulthood occurs through the roles we play.

> Personal change in adulthood, then, in large or small degree, of one or more dimensions, may be given thrust, undergirding, direction, and shaping by the person's experience of action, of making things happen, in the adult roles he undertakes to carry. The tensions generated within transactions between persons bound in role relationships, the emotional involvement of mutuality or conflict, the investment of self—of anxieties, hopes, fears, wishes—in the struggle for gratification and rewarding outcomes, the discharge of tension in the "doing" of a role, the feedback from other persons or from circumstances that give evidence of competence and "payoff"—all these moving forces are involved in active performance of vital roles (42, p. 36)

Perlman also understands the value of role prescriptions for facilitating the daily interactions between persons, freeing up energies for the more important decisions of life. And she, too, focuses attention on the use of role theoretic concepts for understanding early client-worker relationships (42, p. 166).

Contemporary Applications of Role Theory Within Social Work

Contemporary social work texts are replete with references to role theory. The concepts of role provide a language congruent with social work's historical focus on transactions between persons and their environment. It can be used to talk about the distress that persons experience when they and their environments are ill-matched; it also can facilitate talking about many of the interventions that social workers use to restore a balance between persons and their environments.

The application to social work practice can best be divided into three major areas: intake; assessment and diagnosis; and intervention strategies and techniques for various units of practice.

The Use of Role Theory Concepts at Intake

There is ample evidence that clients and workers differ in their expectations of what both "good" clients and "good" social workers do (30, 32, 40). This lack of clarity about client and worker role behavior is understandable given that many persons seeking social work intervention have had little prior direct experience with social workers and have derived their knowledge from the too-frequently inaccurate stereotypes perpetuated by the media or from secondhand knowledge of the behaviors of many persons who, while carrying the label social worker, are often not professionally educated.

The misunderstanding of appropriate client and social worker roles has a number of implications for the social work treatment process. There is, for example, evidence that lack of congruence between client and social worker as to their respective roles is a significant factor in premature termination from treatment (9, 30, 40). Furthermore, there is ample evidence that "continuance can be increased, and/or positive outcomes enhanced, when the initial contacts with the client are devoted to structuring the mutual expectations of client and practitioner" (15, p. 140). From this perspective, therefore, effective social work practice can be enhanced by educating clients as to "helpful client behaviors" (17, p. 73).

As noted earlier, social workers have historically recognized the importance of clarifying role expectations during the initial stages of the treatment process (19, 33). Recent practice literature has focused on identifying a set of practice skills, referred to as *role induction procedures*, that can effectively accomplish what is primarily an educative function.

Role induction begins by "starting where the client is" and exploring the expectations that the client holds when he enters the social work agency. As Dean Hepworth and JoAnn Larsen note, sometimes clients convey these expectations with little prompting from the social worker: "A woman dragging her reluctant husband to a family service agency for marital therapy began the initial interview by telling me: 'I'm frustrated because he won't listen to me. I was hoping that you could tell him how to behave and that, if he heard it from somebody other than me, he would listen and change' " (24, p. 272).

Only after the clients have been helped in verbalizing the expectations they hold both of the role of social worker and of the role of client, should the social worker *educate* the client as to more appropriate role behaviors that will better achieve the client's goals and also respect basic social work values. Establishing formal contracts with clients has been suggested as one way to ensure that both client and worker are in agreement as to their respective roles (15, 24, 31, 49).

Regardless of the direction of change that is in the client or the worker, there is little doubt that clarification of social worker and client roles early in the treatment process can enhance the likelihood that treatment will be effective as well as resulting in increased congruence between worker and client as to their satisfaction with the treatment outcome.

Assessment

During assessment, role theory is valuable in focusing our attention on: (1) the ways in which clients' problems are created out of their incomplete and inadequate socialization into the myriad roles they are expected to enact in their daily lives; (2) the ways in which their difficulties stem from insufficient contemporary support for the roles that are expected of them; as well as (3) the inherently interactive nature of many of the problems that individuals think are their own. Because it emphasizes the social determinants of human behavior and human interaction, it serves to embed the assessment of persons and the problems they are experiencing within an ongoing interpersonal and societal context.

Carel Germain and Alex Gitterman's ecological systems* theory approach to practice easily incorporates the language of role to identify ways in which status and role influence both the practice of social work and the problems that social work clients experience (19).

Concepts of role also help focus our attention on the relationship between positions, status, and access to resources and power. At this time in our profession, when there seems to be considerable emphasis on treating the person (or persons), it is all too easy to forget the extent to which the problems of social work clients are due to the positions they have been born into, or otherwise achieved through no choice of their own, that have denied them access to the resources others more fortunate have in abundance. The use of role theory directs us away from excessive concern with individual psychopathology and toward an understanding of the social determinants of such behavior. The following case vignette provides a good example of a situation where role concepts such as role overload, role conflict, and role ambiguity are important to gain a full picture of the presenting situation.

> Beth, a thirty-four-year-old single parent, sought services at a family services agency. She talked almost obsessively about her ex-husband, his wealthy girlfriend, and how she was struggling financially while they led an easy life. During the initial interview she kept secret the fact that she had recently been convicted of embezzling funds from her former employer and was facing court sentencing in a few weeks. She did talk of her lengthy history as an abused wife, of having been placed in a mental hospital by her ex-husband early in their marriage. She cried easily, seemed to see herself as totally unable to care for herself or her two children, talked freely of the need for a man to help her.
>
> It would have been easy, early in the assessment, to focus on her "dependent personality," on her "learned helplessness," yet that would have missed an essential component of the problem. She was a newly singled parent. She was cut off abruptly from financial resources that she and her children needed to live adequately. Because of her job, low-paying as it was, she was denied access to many of the services that she might have received had she been unemployed. And, furthermore, the system could not protect her from a husband who only erratically chose

*See Chapter 23.

to provide his court-mandated support payments. Thus, she had few supports for the multiple roles she was playing.

Role theory helps us identify the status-role demands that are likely to be significant sources of stress for people. This is especially important today given the many changes that are currently occurring in society that influence role behaviors. For this reason, role theory provides an especially useful perspective for understanding many of the stresses that individuals, couples, and families are experiencing today that bring them to seek social work assistance.

INDIVIDUAL ASSESSMENT.   At the individual level, there has been a noticeable increase in the numbers of persons who are experiencing distress from role changes engendered by marital dissolution. Wives become single persons and single parents; they lose the high status that had previously accrued to them through their role as wife to a successful husband and, as a result, feel a devalued self-identity. Husbands become single persons, part-time fathers, or, sometimes, nonparents.

An increasing number of persons are choosing to adopt openly what are considered, by many, to be deviant, generally stigmatized, roles. For example, as men and women are more openly enacting gay and lesbian roles they may present themselves at a family service agency for help in coping with family pressures to adopt more conforming roles.

Policy decisions have brought others in deviant roles into greater contact with the larger society. The various deinstitutionalization policies of the last two decades have increased the visibility of the mentally ill, the mentally retarded, and the physically handicapped, while not simultaneously significantly influencing social attitudes regarding their deviant identities. They, too, may require social work intervention to moderate the impact of the social stigmatization.

COUPLE ASSESSMENT.   At the couple level, social workers are increasingly confronted with persons who, while intellectually committed to enacting their couple roles in nontraditional ways, often discover a lack of support for their behaviors and, as a result, experience psychological conflict in their enactment (43). While especially true among young couples, there are also an increasing number of older persons who may seek counseling to assist in the renegotiation of their roles vis-à-vis their marital partner when the woman decides to reenter the labor market. While still a relatively small group, gay and lesbian couples are also beginning to see social workers for their relationship difficulties, which often center around the absence of role models and the need to invent new roles for themselves.

FAMILY ASSESSMENT.   At the family level, social changes are reflected in the large number and varieties of nontraditional families. By the standards of the 1950s or 1960s, there are presently more deviant family types than there are normative family types. There are both dual-work and dual-career families; there are single-parent families; there are blended, reconstituted, stepparent families; there are gay and lesbian families. Each of these family forms requires that new role behaviors be learned, new role expectations internalized, new social supports provided. Not surprisingly, social workers are often turned to for assistance in this process.

Role theory offers a non-pathology-oriented perspective from which to assess clients and the problems they present. During the assessment process it directs us to consider: first, conditions that are facilitating or inhibiting the learning or performance of desired role behavior; and second, the contributions of role conflict, in the broadest sense, to intrapersonal and interpersonal stress. For example, in assessing a single parent who has been referred to the Child Abuse Hotline, a social worker using role theory would be concerned about (1) the availability and accessibility of social supports for effective parenting behavior (daycare, supportive adults, financial resources); (2) opportunities for the single parent to have learned parenting behavior (that is, who were the role models and how effective were they in their parenting behavior?); and (3) present-day conflicts that may exist in carrying out parental, occupational, and social roles. Even when assessing personal capacities in this case, a role theory perspective would look at them in terms of their impact on the learning and/or performance of role behaviors. In what ways, for example, does having a specific handicapping condition influence the learning and/or performance of parenting behaviors? How does this person's difficulty establishing intimacy interfere with her ability to parent effectively?

The message that is communicated throughout the assessment process is that the problem does not reside within the individual, but is instead located in the transaction between the individual and society. In some instances the individual may, for a variety of reasons, be failing to perform adequately socially expected roles; in other instances, the individual may be choosing to enact socially deviant roles. Interventions may include providing appropriate role models for the learning of new behaviors, advocating for services to support the performance of role behavior, facilitating a support group for persons choosing to openly enact deviant role behaviors, and lobbying for antidiscriminatory legislation for socially stigmatized persons.

Implications for Social Work Treatment

Individual Treatment

Role theory's application to individual treatment follows directly from the previous discussion. Many persons who are seen by social workers come or are referred because they are having difficulty adequately fulfilling the various roles that they are "supposed" to be playing. Young persons may have difficulty performing such socially expected roles as student, boyfriend or girlfriend, or even parent. Older persons may have difficulties enacting their roles as worker, parent, spouse, child. As has been suggested, many of the interventions are aimed at providing an environment that is facilitative of adequate role performance. That may mean advocating within a school setting for a teenager; it may mean advocating at the local social services department for a teenage mother. Sometimes, however, the inability to perform adequately in expected roles is due to lack of knowledge of role expectations and lack of skills in the performance of role behaviors. When this is the case, social work interventions can be directed toward teaching the appropriate role behaviors either in individual or in group treatment.

While there are many ways for learning appropriate role behavior, perhaps the most promising contemporary one involves a variety of cognitive behavioral techniques. Cognitive behavioral theory has taught us the importance of breaking down what is taught into teachable components. There have been, for example, a plethora of training models for the teaching of assertion skills held to be important for the performance of a wide variety of roles. Recently, Richard Barth and Steven Schinke have extended this perspective to showing adolescent parents a set of skills to facilitate their utilization of social supports by teaching them to reach out to others, to request help from others, and to seek help appropriately (3, p. 531). Their training program, an exemplar of the many that have come into widespread use in recent years, teaches a variety of interpersonal and cognitive skills by describing them, providing examples, demonstrating their use in role plays, practicing their use through role play, and providing feedback. While the training program itself may seem highly specific, their overall approach recognizes the importance of skills to the wide variety of roles that persons play in their lives.

Individual treatment can go beyond the educative function in assisting persons with role difficulties. Many persons seek counseling because of the guilt (or other negative emotions) they experience when they feel they are not carrying out their socially expected roles in an acceptable manner. Certainly an appropriate social work intervention is to explore clients' feelings about their inadequate role performance as well as to help them more realistically appraise their role performance.

> Beth, whom we met before, felt a failure as a mother. Unable to provide her children with the tangible comforts that her ex-husband lavished on them during their infrequent visits, she seriously questioned whether she should relinquish her children to him. She felt inadequate as a mother, as a provider for her children's needs. Counseling focused on helping her define for herself what good mothering was (something that she herself had lacked in her own childhood) and in reevaluating her own competencies as a mother.

There has recently been a wealth of literature on the predictable changes that persons go through in adulthood as they evaluate and reevaluate their performance in the central roles in their lives (26, 59). While many persons go through these changes with minimal stress, others turn to social workers when they experience extreme dissatisfaction with the ways in which their lives have developed, yet are unable to envisage the possibility of change. By the time they come for counseling they may have had their self-esteem seriously undermined and present with symptoms of clinical depression as in the following case.

Paul, a civil servant, came in for counseling six months before his fiftieth birthday presenting as major problems the tremendous unhappiness he felt in his job, his sense of worthlessness at having failed to fulfill his parents' (and his own) expectations, and a strong desire to do something more meaningful with his life yet with a total inability to see any feasible alternatives. While assessment suggested the presence of some personality traits that had probably served to impede his job advancement, Paul was an exceptionally bright and able man whose abilities had not been utilized by an occupational system that oftentimes failed to reward accomplishment. Treatment was multipronged: (1) he was referred for career counseling to explore alternative options; (2) the salience of other roles, from which he obtained far more positive feedback and in which he felt successful, were heightened so that they became more significant contributors to his social identity and his sense of self-worth; (3) he learned to invest less energy and less of his self-esteem in his work role; and (4) his wife's assistance was enlisted to provide additional support in decreasing the value of his work role and increasing the value of his spousal role to his sense of worth.

Many of the roles we take on in life are those we are taught we must play. Persons often come into counseling because they are caught in conflicts between the oughts and the wants. Often, prior socialization is so strong that the clients do not see the possibility of alternative roles or are fearful of admitting the possibility they do see to themselves or to significant others. Individual counseling can provide them with a safe and supportive environment in which to evaluate major life decisions.

Donald, doing poorly in college, used social work counseling to explore joining the army. Because he was facing this decision in the post-Vietnam era, he had little social support for his decision to give up a highly valued position, that of college student and eventually of professional, to take on a recently devalued position, that of soldier. The supportive, nonjudgmental atmosphere of the therapeutic relationship allowed him to decide to quit school and pursue an army career.

Group Treatment

Oftentimes the role problems people experience can best be treated within a group setting. This is especially appropriate when the difficulties that are experienced are due to lack of social support for role behavior. The popularity and diversity of self-help groups organized around themes of role attests to the importance of group support for coping with a variety of role difficulties. Some revolve around themes of role transition: Children of Separated and Divorced Parents; Post-Stroke Association; Sharing and Caring for Post-Cardiac Patients; Stepfamilies; Equal Rights for Fathers; Parents Without Partners. Others offer support to persons with socially deviant identities: Alcoholics Anonymous; Gambler's Anonymous; Parents Without Partners; Adult Children of Alcoholics; Recovery for Persons with Nervous Symptoms.

Social workers have long recognized the value of professionally led support groups for persons experiencing role transitions. It is not uncommon for family service agencies to run ongoing groups for separated and divorced persons, for retiring persons, for single parents. Although less common, because less socially sanctioned, there are also professionally led support groups for persons experiencing the social strain of having chosen to enact a deviant or variant life-style.

Social group work is especially useful for resocializing persons into normative role behavior. Charles Garvin has noted that social group work can be used both to bring about the resocialization of persons "who have not yet determined that they wish to fulfill a nondeviant, socially acceptable role" as well as for persons who voluntarily elect to attain new role behaviors. In this way, social group work performs both a social control and an educative function for society (18, p. 49).

One of the primary group techniques for teaching new role behaviors is that of role playing. Ronald Toseland and Robert Rivas have identified nine structured and unstructured role playing procedures (58). They include:

Own role: In this, a member plays the protagonist out of his own experience, while other group members enact reciprocal roles. This is useful for both assessing a person's interpersonal skills and for learning new behaviors.

Role reversal: In this, the member takes on the role of another person. This enables her to see the situation from another's perspective, thus enhancing empathy.

Autodrama, monodrama, and *chairing:* In this, the member, while moving from chair to chair, plays the multiple roles that represent the different ways he sees himself. This is especially useful for helping a person become aware of the interrelationships among the myriad roles enacted in his life.

Sculpting and *choreography:* In this, the member uses the group to choreograph a dramatic reenactment of a real or symbolic situation in her life. The emotional involvement of the participants in the process makes it useful both for assessing and for gaining new perspectives on conflictual experiences.

Toseland and Rivas identify five additional procedures that can be used as adjuncts to supplement the impact of those discussed above. They include "on-the-spot interview," "soliloquy," "doubling," "mirror," and "sharing."

Family Treatment

Because of its focus on the transactional nature of human dysfunction, family treatment easily incorporates role terminology, albeit on its own terms. Family therapists have, for example, been far less concerned with the socially prescribed roles that persons generally enact in their families—that is, mother, father, daughter, son—and far more concerned with what have been referred to as "irrational role assignments" by which family members explicitly or implicitly are assigned roles that are reflections of unconscious attempts to act out conflicts originating in early family experiences (16, p. 274).

Among the classic roles of concern to family therapists has been that of the "scapegoat" (the "crazy person," the "sick one") who acts as the safety valve to defuse potentially destructive family disharmony (1, 21). A more elaborate view of the family system as it enacts roles is the "drama triangle," in which the roles of Persecutor, Victim, and Rescuer are alternately enacted by different family members.

Family therapists agree on the necessity to disrupt the nature of the family role relationships in dysfunctional family systems whose stability is achieved at the expense of its individual members through a range of strategies.

Community Practice

One of the central aims of community practice is to enhance the effectiveness with which persons receive services from social welfare institutions. While a caseworker advocates for the individual client, the community worker's concern is with effecting change in the institutions themselves or in the transactions between the institutions and the service recipients. It has been suggested that role concepts are, therefore, especially relevant to help the community worker understand and assess the relationship between the individual and the social structure. They focus the worker's attention on "the role relationships of the actors in agency and institutional systems—the clients, agency personnel, policymakers, and community reference groups" (7, p. 30).

Role concepts are also useful for understanding the ways in which the community worker functions to effect such changes. Social planner, grassroots organizer, interagency policymaker, administrator, program director, social reformer, social engineer, as well as the more generic community organizer, have all been identified as relevant community worker roles (7, 52). The social planner may formulate social policy or develop and improve existing services and the manner in which they are delivered to the clients. The community organizer may establish linkages between community members and groups in order to foster social integration and facilitate the identification and development of necessary services within the community.

The social worker often functions in these roles because there is an absence of other persons within the community to carry them out. Sometimes it is necessary for the social worker to enact the role in order that a task may be accomplished; at other times it may be more appropriate for the social worker to teach community persons to fulfill the needed roles. George Brager and Harry Specht have suggested that the unique contribution of the social worker within the community is his "knowledge of the requisite roles to be filled and his skill in helping constituencies to fill them" (7, p. 85).

Research Implications for Social Work

As this article suggests, the perspective of role theory offers a number of opportunities for social work researchers. Despite this, there is little new literature that draws upon its perspective. A few suggestions as to ways to apply role theory to social work research are presented below.

Many of the clients that social workers see are involved in role transitions. It would certainly be beneficial to clients and practitioners to examine the impact of different treatment modalities on the stress experienced from such role transitions. Under what conditions is group treatment more effective at facilitating role transitions than is individual treatment? For what types of clients and what kinds of role transitions? Since many of the role transitions occur within families, when should family treatment be the preferred model of intervention?

Clients of social workers are often enacting deviant and/or stigmatized roles. While there has been research on treatment models for resocializing abusive parents (8), there is a need for similar research on intervention models to prevent socialization into dysfunctional parental role behavior.

Social workers have had a historic concern with delinquency prevention. One of the more recent trends in delinquency programs has been the widespread development of diversionary programs designed to prevent predelinquents from the further learning of delinquent behaviors and the subsequent stabilization of a delinquent self-identity. There has been criticism of both the effectiveness with which diversionary programs can prevent adolescents from being stigmatized (10) and of the weak relationship between causal theories of delinquency and intervention strategies used in such programs (23). Social work researchers can certainly utilize a role theoretic perspective to facilitate the development and evaluation of such programs.

Conclusion

Despite the many references to role constructs within social work literature, it has been only peripheral in the development of our knowledge base. This is ironic given the congruence of its central tenets with social work's emphasis on the person as she transacts with her environment.

Role theory offers one perspective to help free social workers from excessive concern with the "inner space" of the client and direct their attention to the myriad ways in which the behavior of clients is influenced by their contemporary interpersonal relationships as well as the society that both defines and enforces conformity to appropriate role behavior.

As social workers we also must be continuously aware that it is the majority society, to which most of us belong and whose values we have internalized, that defines normative role behavior. Helen Harris Perlman reflects this sensitivity to cultural differences when she writes:

> Nowhere within the thought-action perspectives that social role provides is there prescription for imposing the helper's norms upon the helped, nor for imprisoning the helped person in the mores and standards, middle class or other, of the helper. Nothing in the role concept bespeaks rigidity or authoritarianism. . . . The *client's* role affects and ideas are brought to the forefront, not the helper's; the demands and requirements lie in his reality, in his transactions with people and tasks, not in some prestructured imposition by his helper. (42, pp. 223–224)

Thus, social work from a role theory perspective understands the influence of the social structure but protects the individual's right to self-determination.

References

1. Ackerman, Nathan. "Prejudicial Scapegoating and Neutralizing Forces in the Family Group, with Special Reference to the Role of 'Family Healer,' " in J. Howells (ed.), *Theory and Practice of Family Psychiatry.* New York: Brunner/Mazel, 1968.
2. ———. *The Psychodynamics of Family Life.* New York: Basic Books, 1954.
3. Barth, Richard P., and Steven P. Schinke. "Enhancing the Social Supports of Teenage Mothers," *Social Casework*, Vol. 65 (1984), pp. 523–531.
4. Berger, Peter L., and Thomas Luckmann. *The Social Construction of Reality.* New York: Anchor Doubleday, 1967.
5. Biddle, Bruce J. *Role Theory: Expectations, Identities, and Behaviors.* New York: Academic Press, 1979.
6. ———, and Edwin Thomas (eds.). *Role Theory: Concepts and Research.* New York: Wiley, 1966.
7. Brager, George, and Harry Specht. *Community Organizing.* New York: Columbia University Press, 1973.

8. Breton, Margot. "Resocialization of Abusive Parents," *Social Work*, Vol. 26 (1981), pp. 119–122.

9. Briar, Scott. "Family Services," in H. S. Maas (ed.), *Five Fields of Social Service: Reviews of Research*. New York: National Association of Social Workers, 1966.

10. Bullington, Bruce, James Sprowls, Daniel Katkin, and Mark Phillips. "A Critique of Diversionary Juvenile Justice," *Crime and Delinquency*, Vol. 24 (1978), pp. 59–71.

11. Cloward, Richard, and Lloyd Ohlin. *Delinquency and Opportunity: A Theory of Delinquent Gangs*. New York: Free Press, 1960.

12. Davis, Kingsley. "Social Norms," in Bruce J. Biddle and Edwin Thomas (eds.), *Role Theory: Concepts and Research*. New York: Wiley, 1966.

13. ———. "Status and Related Concepts," in Bruce J. Biddle and Edwin Thomas (eds.), *Role Theory: Concepts and Research*. New York: Wiley, 1966.

14. Deutsch, Morton, and Robert H. Krauss. *Theories in Social Psychology*. New York: Basic Books, 1965.

15. Fischer, Joel. *Effective Casework Practice: An Eclectic Approach*. New York: McGraw-Hill, 1978.

16. Framo, James L. "Symptoms from a Family Transactional Viewpoint," in C. J. Sager and H. S. Kaplan (eds.), *Progress in Group and Family Therapy*. New York: Brunner/Mazel, 1972.

17. Gambrill, Eileen. *Casework: A Competency-Based Approach*. Englewood Cliffs, N.J.: Prentice-Hall, 1983.

18. Garvin, Charles. *Contemporary Group Work*. Englewood Cliffs, N.J.: Prentice-Hall, 1981.

19. Germain, Carel B., and Alex Gitterman. *The Life Model of Social Work Practice*. New York: Columbia University Press, 1980.

20. Gove, Walter R. *The Labeling of Deviance: Evaluating a Perspective*. New York: Wiley, 1975.

21. Haley, Jay. *Strategies of Psychotherapy*. New York: Grune and Stratton, 1963.

22. Harris, Ben, and John Harvey. "Attribution Theory: From Phenomenological Causality to the Intuitive Social Scientist and Beyond," in Charles Antaki (ed.), *The Psychology of Ordinary Explanations of Social Behaviour*. London: Academic Press, 1981.

23. Hawkins, J. David, and Mark W. Fraser. "Theory and Practice in Delinquency Prevention," *Social Work Research and Abstracts*, Vol. 7 (1981), pp. 3–13.

24. Hepworth, Dean H., and JoAnn Larsen. *Direct Social Work Practice*. Homewood, Ill.: Dorsey Press, 1982.

25. Hollis, Florence. *Casework: A Psychosocial Therapy*. New York: Random House, 1964.

26. Levinson, Daniel J. *The Seasons of a Man's Life*. New York: Ballantine, 1979.

27. Linton, Ralph. *The Study of Man*. New York: Appleton-Century, 1936.

28. Loewenstein, Sophie Freud. "Inner and Outer Space in Social Casework," *Social Casework*, Vol. 59 (1979), pp. 19–28.

29. Mahoney, Michael J. *Cognition and Behavior Modification*. Cambridge, Mass.: Ballinger, 1974.

30. Maluccio, Anthony N. *Learning from Clients*. New York: Free Press, 1979.

31. ———, and Wilma D. Marlow. "The Case for the Contract," *Social Casework*, Vol. 19 (1974), pp. 28–36.

32. Mayer, John E., and Noel Timm. *The Client Speaks: Working Class Impressions of Casework*. London: Routledge, 1969.

33. Mead, George Herbert. *Mind, Self and Society*. Edited by Charles W. Morris. Chicago: University of Chicago Press, 1934.

34. Meichenbaum, Donald. *Cognitive-Behavior Modification*. New York: Plenum Press, 1977.

35. Merluzzi, Thomas V., Thomas E. Rudy, and Carol R. Glass. "The Information-Processing Paradigm: Implications for Clinical Science," in Thomas V. Merluzzi, Carol R. Glass, and M. Genest (eds.), *Cognitive Assessment*. New York: Guilford Press, 1981.

36. Merton, Robert K. *Social Theory and Social Structure*. Glencoe, Ill.: Free Press, 1957.

37. Minuchin, Salvador. *Families and Family Therapy*. Cambridge, Mass.: Harvard University Press, 1974.

38. Moreno, Joseph L. *Who Shall Survive?* Washington, D.C.: Nervous and Mental Diseases Publishing Co., 1934.

39. Nisbett, Richard, and Lee Ross. *Human Inference: Strategies and Shortcomings of Social Judgment*. Englewood Cliffs, N.J.: Prentice-Hall, 1980.

40. Overall, Betty, and Harriet Aronson. "Expectations of Psychotherapy in Patients of Lower Socioeconomic Class," *American Journal of Orthopsychiatry*, Vol. 31 (1963), pp. 421–430.

41. Parsons, Talcott. *The Social System*. New York: Free Press, 1951.

42. Perlman, Helen Harris. *Persona: Social Role and Personality*. Chicago: University of Chicago Press, 1968.

43. Rice, David G. *Dual-Career Marriage: Conflict and Treatment*. New York: Free Press, 1979.

44. Rommetveit, R. *Social Norms and Roles*. Minneapolis: University of Minnesota Press, 1954.

45. Sarbin, Theodore R. "Notes on the Transformation of Social Identity," in L. M. Roberts, N. S. Greenfield, and M. H. Miller (eds.), *Comprehensive Mental Health: The Challenge of Evaluation*. Madison: University of Wisconsin Press, 1968.

46. ———. "Role Theory," in G. Lindzey (ed.), *Handbook of Social Psychology*, Vol. 1, Cambridge, Mass.: Addison-Wesley, 1954, pp. 223–258.

47. Schur, Edwin M. *Interpreting Deviance*. New York: Harper and Row, 1979.

48. ———. *Labeling Deviant Behavior*. New York: Harper and Row, 1971.

49. Seabury, Brett A. "The Contract: Uses, Abuses, and Limitations," *Social Work*, Vol. 21 (1976), pp. 16–23.

50. Secord, Paul, and Carl Backman. "Personality Theory and the Problem of Stability and Change in Individual Behavior," *Psychological Review*, Vol. 68 (1961), pp. 21–32.

51. Shaw, Marvin R., and Phillip R. Costanzo. *Theories of Social Psychology*, 2nd edition. New York: McGraw-Hill, 1982.

52. Siporin, Max. *Introduction to Social Work Practice*. New York: Macmillan, 1975.

53. Stierlin, Helm. *Psychoanalysis and Family Therapy*. New York: Aronson, 1977.
54. Strean, Herbert S. "Role Theory," in Francis J. Turner (ed.), *Social Work Treatment*, 2nd edition. New York: Free Press, 1979.
55. ———. "The Application of Role Theory to Social Casework," in Herbert Strean (ed.), *Social Casework: Theories in Action*. Metuchen, N.J.: Scarecrow Press, 1971.
56. Stryker, Sheldon. "Symbolic Interaction as an Approach to Family Research," in J. G. Manis and B. N. Meltzer (eds.), *Symbolic Interaction: A Reader in Social Psychology*, 2nd edition. Boston: Allyn and Bacon, 1972.
57. Thomas, Edwin J., Ronald A. Feldman, with Jane Kamm. "Concepts of Role Theory," in Edwin J. Thomas (ed.), *Behavioral Science for Social Workers*. New York: Free Press, 1967.
58. Toseland, Ronald W., and Robert F. Rivas. *An Introduction to Group Work Practice*. New York: Macmillan, 1984.
59. Vaillant, George. *Adaptation to Life*. Boston: Little Brown, 1977.
60. Watzlawick, Paul, John Weakland, and Richard Fisch. *Change: Principles of Problem Formation and Problem Resolution*. New York: Norton, 1974.
61. Weeks, Gerald R., and Luciano L'Abate. *Paradoxical Psychotherapy: Theory and Practice with Individuals, Couples, and Families*. New York: Brunner/Mazel, 1982.

Annotated Listing of Key References

BIDDLE, BRUCE J. *Role Theory: Expectations, Identities, and Behaviors.* New York: Academic Press, 1979.

In this book, Biddle presents an integrated theoretical approach to role theory. It will be most useful to the social work researcher seeking clarity about ways to operationalize central role terminology.

BIDDLE, BRUCE J., and EDWIN THOMAS (eds.). *Role Theory: Concepts and Research.* New York: Wiley, 1966.

This book remains the most comprehensive book on role theory for a social work audience as it provides numerous brief chapters in which roles concepts are applied to issues of concern to social workers.

PERLMAN, HELEN HARRIS. *Persona: Social Role and Personality.* Chicago: University of Chicago Press, 1968.

This book still provides an excellent example of the varied ways in which role theory can be fruitfully applied to understanding a variety of individual and family problems confronting social work clients.

RICE, DAVID. *Dual-Career Marriage: Conflict and Treatment.* New York: Free Press, 1979.

This is but one of the recent books that focuses attention on the role conflicts engendered by changing social norms vis-à-vis the roles of men and women in marriages. It is unique in that Rice relates the role conflicts to issues in marital counseling.

CHAPTER 21

Feminism and Social Work Practice

Mary Valentich

In 1971 this author presented a lecture to social work students on the changing roles of women. My enthusiasm for the ideas of Betty Friedan (29) and Germaine Greer (35) was evident, the students were responsive, and we reflected on the possibility of equality between women and men. In the 1980s we are still debating the rights, responsibilities, and rewards of men and women, their opportunities for personal and professional growth, and how social institutions support or constrain such opportunities. As a social movement, feminism has heightened our awareness of societal injustice to women, and social work and other helping professions have challenged the sexist foundations of professional education and practice (6, 25, 36, 50, 82, 84, 94).

This chapter examines the impact of feminism on social work practice, particularly through the development of feminist therapy or feminist counseling. There are a few references in recent social work literature to feminist social work practice (7, 26, 57), but this designation may be premature. Our knowledge of what social workers who label themselves as feminists actually do in practice is very limited (7). It may even be unwise to designate yet one more approach to "be accorded a place, along with the several hundred other different types of therapy, and viewed as a technique that can be learned, perhaps in a weekend workshop" (69, pp. 211–212).

Controversy exists about the nature of feminist practice. While Susan

Penfold and Gillian Walker contend that "feminist therapy must be viewed as a perspective, not as a technique; a way of seeing, understanding and making connections" (69, p. 212), Mary Russell proposes that "feminist counseling be viewed as a distinctive counseling method that has grown out of a nucleus of discrete and specifiable skills" (79, pp. 3–4). Russell defines feminist counseling as: "A collaborative process between counselor and client in which both identify, analyze, and attempt to remediate the social, cultural, and psychological barriers to women's optimal functioning, setting as the immediate goal the alleviation of the client's personal distress and as the long-term goal the effecting of social change" (79, p. 15).

Clearly a phenomenon of significance has emerged, be it a thought system, a value orientation, a set of skills, or some constellation of these. Whether we call it feminist counseling, feminist therapy, or feminist social work practice, this evolving way of helping, offered primarily by women to women, should be understood in the context of contemporary feminism.

The Second Wave of Feminism

The first wave of feminism in North America occurred around the turn of the century when women fought for the right to vote (90). Contemporary feminism was heralded by the publication of Friedan's *The Feminine Mystique* (29), which attacked the myth that women's happiness rested in their fulfillment of the roles of wife and mother. The origins of the Women's Liberation Movement and its diversity of expression have been documented (28). Feminism represents a mix of ideological positions, and these have been characterized in terms of the political philosophies from which they derive (24). Numerous typologies of feminism have been developed (87), although these may be far removed from the complexities of feminists' lives. Three prominent categories in the feminist literature are liberal feminism, socialist feminism, and radical feminism.

Liberal or "mainstream" feminism as espoused by Friedan and members of the National Organization of Women (NOW), which was formed in 1966, focuses on freedom of choice, individualism, and equality of opportunity. Liberal feminists vary, however, in the degree to which they acknowledge the patriarchal, economic, and racial biases of these ideas (24). Socialist feminism emphasizes class analysis and argues that women's liberation will require structural changes in the economy and the family (58). Radical feminism emphasizes individual autonomy, mistrusts authority and bureaucracy, and views women's reproductive freedom as critical to their liberation. Zillah Eisenstein argues, however, that feminism incorporates both liberal and radical ideas in that it views women both as independent beings as well as members of an oppressed sexual class (24).

Despite the diversity of ideological strands within feminism, there are commonalities (40, 90). Most importantly, feminism aims for equality of men and women. There is a high valuation of women, and their experience is seen as the basis for theory and action (14, 87). Feminism holds that social roles should not be assigned solely in terms of sex, and that each person has the right to strive for self-fulfillment in keeping with the rights of others. While some feminists may strive for personal goals, others will emphasize collective action in all spheres. Feminism believes that change for the better is possible primarily through the efforts of women, although men are not excluded from contributing to the change process.

These beliefs about women and the possibility of improving their condition have influenced the development of alternative services for women who have been victims of violence, and new forms of practice designed to help women move from victim to survivor and even to warrior status (14).

Historical Origins of Feminist Therapy

As feminists in the 1960s identified women's vulnerability in the workplace, at home, and in the street (32), they began to scrutinize the institutions offering help to women. Psychiatry and mental health services came under fire: oppressive conditions in families and communities were not recognized as contributing to women's private troubles; different standards of mental health prevailed for men and women (12); treatment approaches emphasized adjustment to traditional gender roles; and medication was overprescribed (15, 85). Criticism of psychiatry has persisted into the 1980s (65, 69, 98), but in the meantime feminists have taken several major initiatives to help women (61).

First, women developed their own support system: consciousness-raising groups proliferated in the 1970s to help women understand that "the personal is the political" (39, 51, 90). These leaderless groups of women were not therapy groups, but they gave women a chance to deal with a range of problematic personal issues, as well as take social or political action if the group desired (53).

Second, grass-roots organizations emerged during the 1970s to offer distress lines and crisis intervention services to women who had been battered or sexually assaulted (19, 61). These women's centers were usually organized as collectives. Professionals were not prominent in their formation, and activities included counseling by lay persons, community education, and social action. While many of these organizations evolved into more traditional community agencies with a professional staff, more secure funding, and a hierarchical structure, initially they were designed by women for women and as alternatives to existing services (2, 71, 95).

Third, a women's health movement emerged as a response to medical control of women's bodies (70, 80). The publication of *Our Bodies, Ourselves* (5) inspired women to regain power over their own bodies by participating in decisions about medication, surgery, and practices related to pregnancy, childbirth, and abortion.

Finally, feminists recognized a need for therapeutic intervention beyond the purview of consciousness-raising groups and crisis intervention services. Women continued to seek help from professionals, and increasingly they requested a woman who would *understand.* In the early 1970s, in both the feminist and professional literature, there were calls by feminists, including psychologists and social workers, for a feminist approach to practice (52, 89, 102). In her book *Therapy with Women* (90) Susan Sturdivant presents a detailed account of the emergence of feminist therapy, identifying early proponents and describing the development of collectives offering feminist therapy, the appearance of articles on women's issues in psychology and social work journals, and the growing concern of the helping professions about sexist practices.

Although several professions, in particular psychology and social work, have figured prominently in the development of feminist therapy, the remainder of this chapter will focus on social work and feminist practice.

The First Decade: 1970–1980

Barbara Stevens's article (89), published in 1971, presented an early challenge to social work to examine the implications of women's liberation for practice. In particular, Stevens highlighted the importance of the therapist's ability to empathize with a woman's desire to act assertively and to develop herself socially and intellectually.

By the mid-1970s, social workers were more definitive in criticizing the profession for its lack of attention to the sex of the worker and client (83), and in urging it to review its neo-Freudian theoretical base and develop approaches to practice that would not rely on "medical model" thinking (55, 100). Assertiveness training—which includes behavioral techniques such as modeling, reinforcement, rehearsal, and feedback—was seen as helpful to women in claiming their rights. By this time, collectives of female practitioners had established themselves for the purpose of developing a feminist approach to practice (73), and there was an awareness that new types of services were necessary in relation to women's issues. Thus Janet Rosenberg described a six-week educational program for women wishing to understand role conflicts generated by the women's movement (77). Caree Brown and Marilyn Hellinger's research on therapists' attitudes to women demonstrated continuing concern about sexist attitudes interfering with effective practice with women (13).

Susan Thomas's research, reported in 1977 (92), reflected a coming-of-age for feminist therapy as well as for social work involvement in this arena. Feminist therapy had become visible: by 1976 half of the advertisements in

Ms. magazine referred to feminist therapy; in major centers feminist therapy collectives existed; and referral lists of feminist therapists were compiled. Thomas's survey of 175 feminist therapists in the West Coast region of the United States identified the typical feminist therapist as a woman with an M.S.W., in practice for five years, working full or part-time in private practice or a public agency, seeing primarily women as clients, both individually and in groups, and basing her work on an eclectic or Gestalt theoretical orientation.

Despite the ferment of the women's movement in the 1970s and the increasing attention by the profession to women's issues, it is important to maintain an overall perspective on social work's commitment to improving women's social conditions. Jean Quam and Carol Austin's (72) impressive review of the coverage of women's issues in eight social work journals between 1970 and 1981 revealed only a slight increase in the profession's attention to questions concerning women (72).

An important distinction was made during this period between nonsexist and feminist therapy (61, 74). Essentially, any therapy, except Freudian analysis, could be nonsexist; that is, value women and keep all possibilities open for personal and professional growth. Feminist therapy, however, held that social change was essential to eradicate sexism and that female clients should have opportunities to collaborate with other women in the attainment of personal and social goals.

By 1980 the first serious reservations about feminist therapy were being expressed. Thomas had concluded that "Feminist therapy must be understood more as a part of a social movement than as a type of psychotherapy and less as a theoretical orientation in the traditional sense than as a belief system and a number of ways in which that system is put into practice" (92, p. 452). Mary Russell maintained that feminist therapy was still in an early evolutionary state, reacting to traditional therapeutic modes and not yet developing its own theoretical formulations (78). She considered the development of feminist therapy to be justified only as it demonstrated a more adequate theoretical base, received empirical validation of its effectiveness, and offered a significantly different contribution than other approaches.

From 1980 to 1985

The maturing of feminist practice in social work became evident during this period. The first book on women's issues and social work practice was published in 1980 (67). Its editors, Elaine Norman and Arlene Mancuso, advanced the feminist assumption that women everywhere are systematically discriminated against. The authors examined the experiences of women who were poor or working class, elderly, black, battered, alcoholic, lesbian mothers, social work administrators, and women in need of physical and mental health services. Practice questions were discussed in relation to micro, mezzo, and macro levels of intervention. Gloria Donadello's chapter on women and mental health dealt briefly with feminist therapy, noting its dual focus on self-actualization and social action: "to change society's commitment to a patriarchal system for a healthier commitment to an equalitarian system providing the potential and opportunity for self-actualization for everyone" (20, p. 214).

In 1981, NASW sponsored a Conference on Social Work Practice in a Sexist Society, and *Social Work* published a special issue on women. Sharon Berlin and Diane Kravetz, the editors, noted the contribution of feminists in identifying and documenting the victimization of women and called for an alliance between feminism and social work in order to work toward provision of better social resources, reform of policies and programs, development of direct services to women, and a practice-oriented scholarship about women (3).

Berlin and Kravetz reflect the liberal reform tradition of social work and endorse a liberal feminist approach to practice (95). This involves an understanding of the sexist oppression of women (81), and of the need to change the patriarchical system. Practitioners vary, however, in their beliefs about how much change, how to effect the changes, and who should take the initiative. The articles in the issue address wife-abuse, incest, prostitution, and depression in housewives. They present a range of interventive strategies that include individual counseling; hotlines; information and referral services; emergency shelters; kinship, friendship, and patient support networks; self-help groups; neighborhood and community organization; participation in policy development and planning; advocacy; allocation of resources to women; and development of coalitions. Feminism has challenged social work to reexamine its commitment to social change as well as available strategies for such change. One may conclude with Helen Levine that feminist counseling is "a way of linking women's personal struggles with the political context of our lives as both providers and consumers of services, and working toward change together" (56, p. 87).

In this same period, Helen Collier (17), a psychologist, and Mary Russell (79), a social worker, presented models of feminist counseling. While client involvement in groups and advocacy are not excluded, Collier and Russell emphasize intervention with the individual.

Collier's change model is based on Virginia Satir's work and is directed to all mental health professionals working with women. Proposing a sex-fair therapy—that is, one free of sex-biased values—she identifies three important sets of actions by therapists: counteracting the negative consequences of socialization in the client's life; providing the client with whatever she is unlikely to get in her own environment; and working openly with any crisis or problem in any aspect of a woman's life.

Russell describes those skills most relevant in a feminist approach to counseling women and provides information about their effectiveness and a format for learning them. The skills include: positive evaluation of women;

social analysis; encouragement of total development; behavior feedback; and self-disclosure.

Feminist practice in social work likely reflects the diversity of feminist expression, but with some commonalities. In an attempt to identify, describe, and analyze the key dimensions of feminist social work practice, NASW sponsored the Feminist Practice Project (7, 8). Its purpose was to improve practice with and for women by fostering the development of social work practice models based on feminist theory and commitments. The pretest findings of the Feminist Practice Project suggest that there are two major groups of feminist practitioners: the liberal reformist, and the radical (7). Both groups agree that women have been systematically denied opportunities and choice, particularly in the family and workplace. The liberal reformists view this as the result of sexist socialization and acculturation patterns, and practice emphasizes resocialization and reeducation, with reform occurring in the context of the current, albeit modified, social order. The radicals seek a more fundamental change in the social order, with practice directed to the control of resources, creating opportunities for choice, and emphasizing political action and organizing to achieve goals.

While an increasing number of social workers in the 1980s are calling themselves feminists, there appears to be an avoidance of the term "feminist therapy." Russell's rationale for using "counseling" is pertinent in this regard: "Psychotherapy is an intensive process of remediation of psychological dysfunction or adjustment to psychic stressors. Counseling, in contrast is a more developmental, educative, or preventive process. . . . The goal of feminist counseling is remediation on both the psychological and social levels" (79, p. 14). The beginning use of the designation "feminist social work practice" (7, 26, 57) suggests that social work may be integrating perspectives and interventions that in the 1970s seemed unfamiliar, radical, and reserved for a small number of practitioners with a special interest in women.

The remainder of the chapter examines feminist social work practice in terms of its theoretical orientations, major concepts, interventions, and application to individuals; families and groups; and communities. The chapter concludes by reviewing issues related to feminist practices in social work.

A Conceptual Base for Practice

The cultural context for the development of a conceptual base for feminist practice includes: the literature on women's oppression by Friedan, Greer, Steinem, Firestone, Millet, Morgan, Brownmiller, and Dworkin (87); feminist music and poetry; art, such as Judy Chicago's Dinner Party; and films, such as *Not a Love Story*. Within this context, and subject to a myriad of personal experiences that have influenced their development as feminists, women have challenged traditional psychotherapeutic theories and practices and have begun to evolve a theoretical framework that gives women a central place (34, 48).

The theoretical foundation for much traditional psychotherapy has been Freudian theory (61, 78). Since the 1970s, feminist scholarship has given substantial attention to a critique of Freudian formulations about woman as passive and, essentially, inferior to men (27, 40, 50, 65, 74). Feminists are aware of the reformulations of Freudian theory by Horney and Thompson who posited sociocultural factors as explanatory of women's emotional problems (74). While psychoanalysis has generally been excluded as a treatment approach, some feminists base their practice on psychoanalytic theory (23). Of particular note is Susie Orbach's *Fat Is a Feminist Issue* (68), a liberating treatise for women suffering from a societally induced obsession with being slim.

Feminists have generally been skeptical about much of the past psychological theorizing about women (60), believing that theorists such as Sullivan, Erikson, Maslow, and Kohlberg have not perceived and valued women as independent beings (31, 63). Their theories were formulated with predominant reference to male psychological development and experience. The psychology of women not only received secondary consideration, but women's psychological development was seen as circumscribed by traditional gender roles. Such psychological attributes as emotionality, passivity, and dependence were viewed pejoratively and ascribed to women. Erikson and Lidz have received particular criticism from social work (82) that relied so heavily on their work during the 1960s and 1970s.

Feminism theory has not yet developed a personality theory of woman as flexible, adaptive, and capable of change. Lerman has suggested a starting point: the concept "the personal is the political"; that is, that women's mental health is directly related to the degree women are valued in their culture for their personal attributes and social role performance (54). Individuals are to be understood in terms of environmental forces impinging on them, and women's "craziness" or "deviance" is seen as resulting from oppressive social structures (88). Jean Miller (63), Carol Gilligan (31), and Alexandra Kaplan (48) have been active in the development of new ways of understanding women.

Theoretical perspectives congruent with feminism are social psychological and sociological. Thus, learning theory that focuses on the socialization of women with respect to gender identity and gender roles (16, 40) provides an important foundation for a feminist practice. Sturdivant (90) offers an interactional model of behavior that is compatible with feminist perspectives and social work's traditional emphasis on the person-in-situation. For her the individual, social situation and culture are seen to be interrelated through role (see Chapter 20). This presumes functioning at three levels, viz, emotional, cognitive, and social, which together produce personality. The emotional level consists of feelings, impulses, drives, needs, motives, and value-conclusions; the cognitive level of thoughts, ideas, and basic premises about people and life. These two factors interact with the current social context, previous social conditioning, and cultural norms to determine behavior (90, p. 133).

Evidence of conceptual development by feminists includes the distinction between sex and gender (34, 58), with the former referring to physiological differences between women and men, and the latter to sociocultural elaborations of these differences. The concept of gender refers to one's status as feminine, masculine, or androgynous, while gender role includes the prescribed behaviors, attitudes, and characteristics associated with gender status. Androgyny, which refers to possession of both masculine and feminine traits, was initially hailed as a model of optimal functioning (49), but reservations have been expressed about the desirability of classifying traits as either masculine or feminine (40). "Woman as victim" is another concept that earlier enjoyed much greater prominence. Because of the connotations of victim as helpless and in need of protection, and its association with theories of victim-precipitation that seem to "blame the victim" (95), the term "victim" has given way to "survivor."

The Interventive Process

In feminist practice, the three phases of exploration, action, and termination characterize the interventive process, but the activity of practitioners varies. Thus Levine states that there is no formal assessment, diagnosis, or treatment—processes she perceives as equating individual problems with pathology (56). On the other hand, Russell (79) identifies the primary task of the beginning phase of counseling as the development of a thorough assessment of the presenting problem. Feminist practitioners would, however, avoid the use of diagnostic labels, emphasize present concerns, and use historical material to facilitate the client's understanding of her oppression.

Feminist practitioners would also agree on the importance of a helping relationship involving two equals (7, 55). The expert role for the practitioner is seen as detrimental to the woman's growth because dependence on authority might be reinforced. A variety of means have been used to demystify the helping process, equalize the relationship, and bring the social worker and client or consumer together as individuals: the use of first names; self-disclosure by the worker not only of her feminist values but also personal experience; an informal and comfortable setting for the interview; a sliding scale of fees; no or minimal record-keeping; permitting clients access to their records; development of contracts; providing the client with the rationale for and explanation of interventions; and involving the client in decision-making about interventions.

The nature of an egalitarian relationship between worker and client has received clarification. In Russell's view there are inevitably inequities among people, and it is misleading to overlook these differences when emphasizing equality (78). Equality between worker and client means that both should be treated with dignity and respect, and as equally human. The worker's expertise is shared with the client, so that the client can take charge of her own life and become her own therapist (17, 92).

With respect to the action phase, Thomas's survey of feminist social workers is instructive (92). Although the respondents had difficulty in specifying what they did, Thomas categorized their activities into five components that, in her view, characterized feminist therapy: feminist humanism; feminist consciousness; changes in the traditional relationship between therapist and client; consciousness-raising; and emphasis on the commonality of women's experiences. Most prominent among the skills identified were giving permission to clients to act in nontraditional ways; modeling such behavior; validating clients' perceptions; self-disclosure; developing clients' awareness of a sexist social structure, and offering a social structural explanation of their distress; encouraging the development of support groups; and providing opportunities for group therapy and collective action to achieve social goals. Throughout the encounter, therapists employed various means, such as those noted above, to avoid an abuse of their power.

Thomas's work may have facilitated the examination of skills that has occurred in the 1980s. Thus, Sturdivant describes sex-role analysis and differential power analysis and their use in cognitive-restructuring with women (90). After the client develops an expanded awareness of her situation, she then is responsible for taking charge of her own life, and may also participate in social action. The process for these changes is resocialization, a reshaping of one's self-definition best accomplished through an all-female therapy group that "provides positive role models, affords opportunities for experiential learning and practice of new behaviors, and gives validation of feelings and perceptions by other women" (90, p. 148).

Collier suggests that change may occur in self-esteem, communication, taking risks, and rules (17). The therapist helps a woman develop her own skills to remove external and internal manifestations of sex inequality by demonstrating and encouraging sex-fair attitudes. The therapist is a catalyst for the client's growth and provides a supportive environment where the client is met on her own terms; she is helped to discard restrictive ideas and behaviors; and new information, skills, and other resources are provided so that she can consider alternatives.

Russell believes none of the skills she describes in themselves define feminist counseling, nor are the skills necessarily unique to feminist counseling: "What is unique is the constellation of skills, their avowed feminist purpose, and their interaction in the counseling encounter, which gives feminist counseling its special character. The net result of skill interactions is a counseling mode that is active, direct, externally oriented, present focused, behaviorally oriented, and egalitarian" (79, p. 53). Most of the skills she presents involve several levels, ranging from a straightforward to a complex application. Few of them have been systematically investigated in their application to feminist counseling, but there is empirical support for their effectiveness when used in other contexts. Thus, Russell suggests that behavior feedback and self-disclosure are effective in working with women. She also presents indirect evidence for the effectiveness of positive evaluation of women; social analysis (like sex role analysis); and encouragement of total development. Her discussion of skills focuses on work with the individual client, with collective action a possibility in the termination phase of counseling.

Finally, the pretest data from the Feminist Practice Project (7) suggest that feminist practitioners focus on personal and social goals, the latter very broadly defined, and emphasize empowerment of women through teaching problem-solving, interpersonal and life-management skills, and through their participation in collective action. There is widespread use of consciousness-raising techniques, which result in women becoming aware of oppressive social conditions. This awareness leads to collective actions, which often include building and engaging in coalitions—associations of women's groups that share some objectives. These feminist practitioners also made use of networking, support, and self-help groups.

Some feminist practitioners include techniques that are not widely used in counseling. They adopt a holistic perspective that seeks to integrate spiritual and physical dimensions in their social work practice. In addition to using relaxation or self-examination exercises that are fairly widely practiced, this group gives prominence to such techniques as psychic healing, meditation, massage, dance, and art. Mary Bricker-Jenkins and Nancy Hooyman refer to this variation as the psychic/leveler perspective (7).

Thus far, the ending phase has received little attention. This may be because feminist practice includes personal and social change goals. The latter are not easy to specify, and it may be difficult to know when intervention ends. On the other hand, for practitioners such as Russell (79), or some of those studied by Thomas (92), therapy ends when client goals are achieved or the client wishes to stop. Group involvement occurs outside therapy or after the termination of counseling.

The duration of the interventive process also receives little attention, again perhaps because of the diversity of goals. With respect to the attainment of personal goals, Thomas notes that feminist therapy with its emphasis on action should be shorter than other approaches (92).

Individual and Group Intervention

A feminist approach to practice involves individual change through engagement of an individual client in a one-to-one situation or a group experience. The latter may be a therapy, self-help, or support group that occurs outside the individual counseling and, possibly, as the individual counseling nears an end. Individual change is often the prelude to collective action toward social goals. While much feminist practice literature focuses on intervention with individual clients, work with groups is a hallmark of a feminist approach to practice.

Consciousness-raising groups have been a prominent feature of the women's movement (39, 51), but these have been seen as alternative mental health resources rather than as an integral component of a feminist approach to practice. Their techniques have, however, been incorporated in feminist practice with groups. Excellent examples of the use of groups for personal and social change purposes may be found in work with sexual assault survivors and battered women. Thus, Ginny NiCarthy, Karen Merriam, and Sandra Coffman consider their mutual help groups for battered women to be a part of feminist practice (66). They discuss issues of location, confidentiality, leadership techniques, and group exercises. They also describe second phase groups that follow crisis intervention and groups for specific populations, such as women of a particular ethnic group or religious faith; women with physical disabilities; teenagers; recovering alcoholic women; and lesbians.

Another prominent group intervention employed in practice with women has been assertiveness training. The literature on this is considerable (41), and the techniques can be employed successfully in relation to a host of problems. It is important for the leader to be appreciative of the client's social context and not hold the individual responsible when desired results are not achieved. For example, in helping women to act more assertively at work, it is important to establish what rights are secure in their place of employment, and to identify those goals that may be attainable by individual assertive effort and those that require group action. Further, the possible consequences of assertiveness efforts should be assessed.

Thus far, feminist practice has been discussed only with reference to women as clients. This focus is understandable because feminist practice derives primarily from the efforts of lay persons and professionals who have provided services for women who were sexually abused, battered, and in need of contraceptive and abortion services. While some radical feminists may wish to concentrate their change efforts on women to the exclusion of men, the realities of social work practice include female clients with significant involvement with men as well as male clients. Generally, the feminist practice literature does not consider the situation of feminist practitioners who work with male clients.

Russell, who defines feminist counseling as counseling of women by women, does, however, make reference to relationship counseling: "Women must first clarify what they want and need from their relationships with men, as opposed to what they have been socialized to expect. . . . Individual counseling with women may need to precede relationship counseling, even when the distress relates particularly to the relationship" (78, p. 23). She does not, however, elaborate the nature of relationship counseling by a feminist. Jean Robbins (76), a psychologist and feminist therapist who practices with women, men, and couples, does discuss the pitfalls in relationship counseling: placing more value on male rather than female participation; engaging in rivalry with the female client for the male client's attention; and giving undue attention to the male's work. Eveline Milliken's (64) exploration of the applicability of feminist practice to men as members of couples or as individual clients is an initial step in still uncharted territory.

The issue of feminist practitioners working with male clients may receive more attention as feminist practice in family therapy develops. Feminist thought has not been prominent in family therapy (42), but there are signs of activity, such as meetings of feminist family therapy practitioners, the development of a newsletter, and criticism of the sexist stance of some family therapy models—for example, in the treatment of sexual issues (59).

While advocates for battered women and sexually assaulted children have been skeptical about family therapy approaches that emphasize the system as dysfunctional and lessen the responsibility of the male offender, feminist practice can include work with families. Thus, in situations where girls have been sexually abused, work with individuals will likely precede work with the family as a unit and/or participation of family members in groups of survivors or parents.

Families could also become members of social action groups. Just as families in the 1950s banded together to secure rights for developmentally disabled children, comparable actions might be taken by coalitions of families working to improve day care or after-school services, sex education opportunities, or services to families-at-risk, such as those headed by adolescent single mothers.

Community Intervention

While feminist practice is concerned with political action and strategies to change institutional structures and practices (74), social work has been more successful in explicating those change activities related to micro rather than mezzo or macro levels of intervention. An exception is the book edited by Norman and Mancuso (67). At the mezzo level, it proposes that neighborhood groups of women may organize for change, alternative mental health care systems may be developed, and advocacy on behalf of women may occur. At the macro level, feminist practitioners and clients may engage in developing coalitions to work toward common goals, as well as collaborate in lobbying and other efforts to effect legislative changes and the allocation of resources to women.

One feature of community intervention by feminists is its collaborative nature. Although social workers and other professionals were initially viewed with suspicion by grass-roots organizations of women, collaborative efforts are not unusual in such agencies. Community education is a major intervention designed to change knowledge and social attitudes about problems such as sexual assault and sexual abuse of children. Collective actions may include political lobbying, demonstrations, presenting proposals for legislative changes, and building coalitions. Social work's contribution may not always be evident because of the collective nature of these efforts, which also include the consumers of services.

Issues in Feminist Social Work Practice

Women as Clients

It has been suggested that feminist practice is more effective with younger, better-educated, verbally fluent, middle-class women (62, 78), and possibly those receptive to feminist values (21). Yet the ideal is a feminist practice available to all women, of any sexual orientation, life-style, color, or class. Quam and Austin's review of the social work literature (72) on women's issues demonstrates, however, that minimal consideration was given to minority group women, single mothers, and lesbians. It is, however, important for social work to demonstrate a commitment to all women who are oppressed. Thus, increasing attention to women in poverty is a hopeful sign (101). Further, while the literature focuses on adult women, feminist social workers do practice with girls and female adolescents—for example, in sexual abuse situations, and with adolescents in need of contraceptive information, pre- and postpregnancy and abortion services.

The ongoing concern of feminist practice with women and their sexuality—be it in their reproductive role, as targets for sexual abuse, or as assertive partners in sexual relationships with women and men—suggests that control of women's sexuality remains a cornerstone of North American society. Despite the greater freedom of contemporary women to express their sexuality as they see fit (38), the fundamental task of liberating women as sexual persons remains. Feminist social work practice can make an important contribution in this arena.

Men as Clients

The focus of feminist practice on women's concerns has meant that the literature on feminist counseling gives little guidance to social workers who have male clients. For example, feminist practitioners, working with families in which the father has sexually abused his daughter, may find their reserves of tolerance and empathy quickly drained. Application of social analysis, for example, is not likely to be effective with these men who are usually involuntary clients with little desire to change. The challenge for feminist practitioners is to remain cognizant of the trauma suffered by their female clients, assign responsibility for the abuse to the male, and still remain open in promoting appropriate behavior.

Conflicts for the social worker may occur in any couple counseling situation where traditional gender role expectations interfere with the personal growth of the female partner. Thus, in sexual counseling, a delicate balance is to be maintained in supporting the woman's developing assertiveness in her sexual expression, challenging attempts by her partner to thwart her growing confidence, and facilitating the couple's discovery of new ways to resolve problems. Further, the practitioner is expected at some point to make explicit the feminist values that underpin counseling.

While some might argue on ideological grounds that feminist practitioners should focus their efforts on women, there may be no reason at the level of technique to exclude men. As Sophie Loewenstein notes, "many of the creative techniques embodying feminist princinples will be equally useful for casework for men" (57, p. 532).

Men as Feminist Practitioners

While most of the feminist practice literature assumes that women are the practitioners, male social workers with feminist perspectives do exist. Some refer to them as pro-feminist to recognize their support for feminist ideals and yet reserve the term "feminist" for women (93). Loewenstein (57), echoing numerous other feminist practitioners, has expressed her profound doubts about the possibility of a creative encounter between a male professional and a female client. Her reservations include the possibility that some male workers will expect women to conform with traditional role expectations, the fact that some males have engaged in sexual activity with their clients, and the risk that female clients may fall into familiar and unproductive dependence patterns with male counselors. Further, women have been socialized to hide their "negative" feelings and, in particular, their anger from men (47).

Loewenstein proposes that female caseworkers work with women, and that males work with men who oppress women—for example, with adolescent fathers, men who rape, husbands who beat their wives, and fathers who sexually abuse their daughters. Loewenstein also sees a role for male social workers in working for social change through advocacy and efforts to change legislation. Her stance may reflect a middle position between the extremes of "no role for men" and no differentiation of interventive activity by gender of the worker.

Another argument is that male feminist social workers have not been given much opportunity or support of practice utilizing a feminist approach. As more is learned about these social workers and their clients, and the effectiveness of their practice, there may be a basis for reducing the gap between men and women in social work that is now evident. Some feminists may view this position as inviting another takeover by males of female terrain (36). On the other hand, to limit the opportunities of male feminist practitioners to work toward sex equality, and, in particular, to influence other men in the profession and beyond, seems short-sighted.

There is considerable literature on the effects of practice of the gender of the counselor (46, 91). Generally, the findings are inconclusive, but further investigation may clarify this issue. In the meantime, it is desirable that all clients, men and women, be able to exercise their preference for the gender of their counselor.

Boundaries of Feminist Social Work Practice

A major issue relates to the boundaries of feminist social work practice, albeit, primarily practice with women: Is it so encompassing that all social work practice informed by a feminist perspective should be included? Audrey Faulkner reaches this conclusion in her analysis of the aging of women:

> While social work's interventions include those directed toward an individual's intrapsychic and emotional adjustment, they also encompass preventive and remedial measures aimed at altering the family, community, and societal context of the individual. Social action, community organization, and impacting public policy are imbedded in the history and philosophy of social work, as much as is direct mental health. Feminist social work, it would follow, must bring to bear on the problems of women the skilled application of the range of knowledge and strategies developed within each of the profession's subareas. (26, p. 71)

Perhaps feminist social work is simply an expression of quality social work practice. Such a conclusion would be erroneous: witness Faulkner's identification of twelve goals in social work and social work education's involvement with older women. These include major allocations of resources to older women; major attention in education curricula; high status for professionals working with elderly women; development of new theories about older women; and professional activities by researchers, planners, social activists, and clinicians, all designed to enhance the social conditions and social role functioning of elderly women. Some progress has been made since 1980, but the plight of elderly women is still a feminist concern.

It is neither timely nor appropriate to abandon the feminist label. While feminism and humanism share similar values about the worth of individuals, feminist analysis continues to reveal pervasive problematic experiences of women, and to explain them in terms of social structural factors. Further, feminist practitioners provide a critical monitoring of new theories and methodologies for sexist bias.

Research in Feminist Social Work Practice

There is considerable literature on feminist concerns about social and psychological research (75, 87, 97). The major criticism is that, by and large, such research has omitted or distorted the experience of women. Some feminists have responded by repudiating research, others have promoted the development of a feminist social science. One view, the "theory from experience" position, is that feminist research should be grounded in women's experience of women's reality (87). This phenomenological orientation has led some feminists to favor qualitative methodologies as the appropriate investigative procedures for such research. Further, the customary superior-inferior status difference between investigator and subject has been redefined as an egalitarian relationship of two co-researchers and the investigator's detachment from the subject replaced by a relationship in which co-researchers share with each other their motivations for participating in the research and personal experiences that are relevant to the investigation (4).

It would, however, be unfortunate to link feminist research only with qualitative methodologies. As Joan Cummerton states, "Feminist research is research guided by feminist values and theory and *not* a prescriptive or necessarily unique set of methodological tools" (18, p. 1). She also contends that "Feminist research *always* has a political focus. It is designed with social change in mind—to further the interests of the participants and the population to which they belong" (18, p. 3). It should be recognized that research on feminist social work practice will be conducted within the context of the evolving feminist research movement described above.

Much of the research on feminist counseling has been conducted by psychologists and meets what Clara Hill has described as the "traditional criteria of psychotherapy research . . . client variables, counselor variables, independent or treatment variables, and dependent or criterion variables" (37, p. 53). A major thrust of this research during the 1970s was to demonstrate empirically the relationship of the gender of the counselor to the effectiveness of counseling with women clients (45). The findings from this substantial effort are inconclusive (10, 46), perhaps partly because many of these studies have suffered from inadequate designs or have failed to overcome the vexing methodological and operational problems that plague all psychotherapy outcome research. Nevertheless, it must be acknowledged that a major hypothesis of feminist practice has received little support. It has not been demonstrated that female counselors are more effective with female clients than male counselors.

There is little current research on gender, perhaps because psychotherapy researchers are pursuing other objectives. Marilyn Johnson and Arthur Auerbach have recommended that the search for main effects in gender be abandoned, and that consideration of gender effects become a routine component of all psychotherapy research (44). While Brodsky and Hare-Mustin have developed a comprehensive list of priorities for research on women and psychotherapy (10), it should be noted that feminist practice includes work toward social goals, and this activity warrants study.

Social workers have yet to make a significant contribution to research on feminist practice. Russell's challenge to feminist social workers to strive for empirical validation of their work has yet to be taken up in any comprehensive way (78). There are a number of psychosocial problems particularly salient to women that have received scant or fragmented research attention. These include depression, agoraphobia, eating disorders, and marital and family conflict. Little research attention has been given to studying the availability, coverage, and effectiveness of many services designed for women or used predominantly by women—perinatal services, sexual assault services, services for battered women, and marital transition services.

One important social work study, Thomas's survey of social workers who identified themselves as feminist practitioners, has already been described (92). Another significant study in progress at the time of writing is the Feminist Practice Project sponsored by NASW. Its purpose is "to identify, analyze and describe politically oriented models of social work practice with and for women which are based on feminist theory" (7, p. 4). It is to be hoped that this project will give stimulus and direction to future feminist-oriented social work research.

Concluding Note and Vignettes

It may be, as Donadello states, that feminism is "a bright ray of hope" (20, p. 215) that will serve to inform social work practice in ways that are liberating for clients as well as practitioners. Not only do we seek new strategies and techniques to achieve goals, but new visions.

The following three vignettes illustrate the author's style in feminist practice involving work with individuals and couples.

CASE A

Ms. X. initially sought help for a career decision. She was thirty, single, and discouraged about her dependence on her parents and her inability to develop a "permanent" relationship with a man. Over the next five years, employing a periodic case strategy (96)—that is, engaging in sequences of intervention—we focused on the following goals: making several leisure and career decisions; becoming more sexually responsive; developing more gratifying intimate relationships with men; dealing with a beating she received from a boyfriend; becoming more independent of her parents; developing more comfort with her unmarried state; and becoming more assertive in personal and professional situations.

Throughout the contact, I encouraged her to pursue nontraditional gender role goals if she desired; offered her a social structural perspective in relation to various problems she encountered; used cognitive-restructuring to help her to stop negating herself; taught her assertiveness skills to use personally and professionally; and finally, encouraged her to become involved in a women's center where she could receive support for her new ways of thinking and acting. A personal and professional relationship coexist, and progress has been made in relation to all goals.

CASE B

Ms. Y. was referred to me after she was sexually molested at work by a fellow worker. Thanks to the advocacy efforts of a female colleague, the company was prepared to pay for a limited number of sessions. I agreed to this arrangement, but indicated my willingness to continue if need be. The initial focus was the alleviation of anxiety and guilt related to the molestation. Then, problem-solving began in relation to changes in her relationship with her boyfriend, job plans, and dealing with ongoing harassment from male workers regarding her complaining about the molestation. In addition, there was a careful review of the extent to which she wished to participate in a work group that had formed to seek a company policy and set of procedures related to sexual harassment on the job. Cognitive restructuring and assertiveness training were major techniques employed.

As she regained her confidence in the work situation, which included encountering the offender, she conveyed her anger to him and male colleagues who had made light of the situation. She identified a level of modest activity in the lobbying group that was comfortable for her, and she took initial steps to find more satisfying employment within the same company.

CASE C

Ms. Z. sought help because she was sexually disinterested in her partner and feared the marriage would break down. She presented herself as given to hysterical outbursts that would provoke a review of the situation, but no long-term change. After several sessions in which I emphasized her right to her feelings and her observations about the relationship, and her freedom to choose her level of sexual involvement, she asked to bring her partner for sexual counseling. For several months I saw them as a couple with goals of improving their communication about problematic issues and their sexual relationship.

A persistent conflict pertained to her views on how he should manage his job. When I presented options to Ms. Z. about utilizing her abundant energy and organizational ability in work outside the home, she was not receptive. She believed she should be taken care of financially by her husband and preferred being at home looking after their child. There was improvement both in their communication and their sexual relationship, and a recommitment to the relationship. After a year she came to see me regarding a decision to have a second child; two years later she returned to consider job and school options that would enable her to work full time within two years, while her husband became a full-time househusband.

References

1. Adams, Margaret. "The Single Woman in Today's Society: A Reappraisal," *American Journal of Orthopsychiatry*, Vol. 41, No. 5 (1971), pp. 776–786.

2. Ahrens, Lois. "Battered Women's Refuges," in Frederique Delacoste and Felice Newman (eds.), *Fight Back! Feminist Resistance to Male Violence*. Minneapolis: Cleis Press, 1981, pp. 104–109.

3. Berlin, Sharon, and Diane Kravetz. "Women as Victims: A Feminist Social Work Perspective," *Social Work*, Vol. 26, No. 6 (1981), pp. 447–449.

4. Bombyk, Marti, Mary Bricker-Jennings, and Marilyn Wedenoja. "Reclaiming Our Profession Through Feminist Research: Some Methodological Issues in the Feminist Practice Project." Paper presented at Symposium on the Status of Women in Social Work Education. Council on Social Work Education, Washington, D.C., February 17, 1985.

5. Boston Women's Health Collective. *Our Bodies, Ourselves—A Book by and for Women*. New York: Simon and Schuster, 1984.

6. Brandwein, Ruth A., and Anne E. Wheelock. "A New Course Model for Content on Women's Issues in Social Work Education," *Journal of Education for Social Work*, Vol. 14, No. 3 (1978), pp. 20–26.

7. Bricker-Jenkins, Mary, and Nancy R. Hooyman. "Feminist Practice Project," *Womanpower*, Summer 1984, pp. 4–6.

8. ———. *Not for Women Only: Social Work Practice for a Feminist Future*. New York: NASW Publications, in press.

9. Brodsky, Annette M. "A Decade of Feminist Influence on Psychotherapy," *Psychology of Women Quarterly*, Vol. 4, No. 3 (1980), pp. 331–340.

10. ——— and Rachel T. Hare-Mustin. "Psychotherapy and Women: Priorities for Research," in Annette M. Brodsky and Rachel T. Hare-Mustin (eds.), *Women and Psychotherapy—An Assessment of Research and Practice*. New York: Guilford Press, 1980, pp. 385–410.

11. ——— (eds.). *Women and Psychotherapy—An Assessment of Research and Practice*. New York: Guilford Press, 1980.

12. Broverman, I. K., D. M. Broverman, F. E. Clarkson, P. Rosenkrantz, and S. R. Vogel. "Sex-Role Stereotypes and Clinical Judgments of Mental Health," *Journal of Consulting Psychology*, Vol. 34, pp. 1–7.

13. Brown, Caree R., and Marilyn Levitt Hellinger, "Therapists' Attitudes Toward Women," *Social Work*, Vol. 20, No. 4 (1975), pp. 266–270.

14. Butler, Sandra. "Treatment Perspectives—A Feminist View." Paper presented at Counselling the Sexual Abuse Survivor: a Conference on Clinical and Social Issues. Winnipeg, Manitoba, February 19, 1985.

15. Chesler, Phyllis. *Women and Madness*. New York: Avon Books, 1972.

16. Chetwynd, Janet, and Oonagh Hartnett (eds.). *The Sex Role System*. London: Routledge and Kegan Paul, 1978.

17. Collier, Helen V. *Counseling Women—A Guide for Therapists*. New York: Free Press, 1982.

18. Cummerton, Joan M. "Women and Feminist Research: Commonalities, Issues, Implications." Paper presented at Symposium on the Status of Women in Social Work Education. Council on Social Work Education, Washington, D.C., February 17, 1985.

19. Delacoste, Frederique, and Felice Newman (eds.). *Fight Back! Feminist Resistance to Male Violence*. Minneapolis: Cleis Press, 1981.

20. Donadello, Gloria. "Women and the Mental Health System," in Elaine Norman and Arlene Mancuso (eds.), *Women's Issues and Social Work Practice*. Itasca, Ill.: Peacock, 1980, pp. 201–217.

21. Dworkin, Sari. "Traditionally Defined Client, Meet Feminist Therapist: Feminist Therapy as Attitude Change," *Personnel and Guidance Journal*, Vol. 61, No. 5 (1984), pp. 301–305.

22. Editorial Committee. *'76 and Beyond*. Special issue of *The Social Worker*, 1976.

23. Eichenbaum, Luise, and Susie Orbach. *Understanding Women—A Feminist Psychoanalytic Approach*. New York: Basic Books, 1983.

24. Eisenstein, Zillah. *The Radical Future of Liberal Feminism*. New York: Longman, 1981.

25. Fanshel, David. "Status Differentials: Men and Women in Social Work," *Social Work*, Vol. 21 (1976), pp. 421–426.

26. Faulkner, Audrey. "Aging and Old Age: The Last Sexist Rip-Off," in Elaine Norman and Arlene Mancuso (eds.), *Women's Issues and Social Work Practice*. Itasca, Ill.: Peacock, 1980, pp. 57–89.

27. Feminist Therapy Support Group. "The Roots of Feminist Therapy," *Healthsharing*, Winter 1982, pp. 12–18.

28. Freeman, Jo. "The Origins of the Women's Liberation Movement," *American Journal of Sociology*, Vol. 78, No. 4 (1973), pp. 792–811.

29. Friedan, Betty. *The Feminine Mystique*. New York: Dell, 1974.

30. Gilbert, Lucia A. "Feminist Therapy," in Annette M. Brodsky and Rachel T. Hare-Mustin (eds.), *Women and Psychotherapy—An Assessment of Research and Practice*. New York: Guilford Press, 1980, pp. 245–266.

31. Gilligan, Carol. *In a Different Voice*. Cambridge, Mass.: Harvard University Press, 1982.

32. Gornick, Vivian, and Barbara K. Moran (eds.). *Woman in Sexist Society*. Scarborough, Ontario: Basic Books, 1971.

33. Greenglass, Esther R. *A World of Difference—Gender Roles in Perspective*. New York: Wiley, 1982.

34. Greenspan, Miriam. *A New Approach to Women and Therapy*. New York: McGraw-Hill, 1983.

35. Greer, Germaine. *The Female Eunuch*. London: Granada, 1970.

36. Gripton, James. "Sexism in Social Work: Male Takeover of a Female Profession," *The Social Worker*, Vol. 42, pp. 78–89.

37. Hill, Clara E. "A Research Perspective on Counseling Women," *The Counseling Psychologist*, Vol. 6, No. 2 (1976), pp. 53–55.

38. Holroyd, Jean. "Psychotherapy and Women's Liberation," *The Counseling Psychologist*, Vol. 6, No. 2 (1976), pp. 22–28.

39. Home, Alice. "A Study of Change in Women's Consciousness-Raising Groups," *Canadian Journal of Social Work Education*, Vol. 6, Nos. 2 and 3 (1980), pp. 7–24.

40. Hunter College Women's Studies Collective. *Women's Realities, Women's Choices*. New York: Oxford University Press, 1983.

41. Jakubowski, Patricia Ann. "Self-Assertion Training Procedures for Women," in Edna I. Rawlings and Dianne K. Carter (eds.), *Psychotherapy for Women— Treatment Toward Equality*. Springfield, Ill.: Charles C. Thomas, 1977, pp. 168–190.

42. James, Kerrie, and Deborah McIntyre, "The Reproduction of Families: The Social Role of Family Therapy?" *Journal of Marital and Family Therapy*, Vol. 9, No. 2 (1983), pp. 119–129.

43. Jehu, Derek, Carol Klassen, and Marjorie Gazan. "Cognitive Restructuring of Distorted Beliefs Associated with Childhood Sexual Abuse," in James Gripton and Mary Valentich (eds.), *Social Work Practice in Sexual Problems*. New York: Haworth Press, in press.

44. Johnson, Marilyn, and Arthur H. Auerbach. "Women and Psychotherapy Research," in Lenore E. Walker (ed.), *Women and Mental Health Policy*. London: Sage, 1984, pp. 59–77.

45. Kaplan, Alexandra G. "Toward an Analysis of Sex-Role Related Issues in the Therapeutic Relationship," *Psychiatry*, Vol. 42 (1979), pp. 112–120.

46. ———. "Female or Male Psychotherapists for Women: New Formulations," *Psychotherapists for Women*, Vol. 82, No. 2 (1984), pp. 1–9.

47. ———, Barbara Brooks, Anne L. McComb, Ester R. Shapiro, and Andrea Sodano. "Women and Anger in Psychotherapy," in Jean H. Robbins and Rachel J. Siegel (eds.), *Women Changing Therapy—New Assessments, Values and Strategies in Feminist Therapy*. New York: Haworth Press, 1983, pp. 29–40.

48. Kaplan, Alexandra G., and Janet L. Surrey. "The Relational Self in Women: Developmental Theory and Public Policy," in Lenore E. Walker (ed.), *Women and Mental Health Policy*. London: Sage, 1984, pp, 79–94.

49. Kenworthy, Joy Anne. "Androgyny in Psychotherapy: But Will It Sell in Peoria?" *Psychology of Women Quarterly*, Vol. 3, No. 3 (1979), pp. 231–240.

50. Kravetz, Diane. "Sexism in a Woman's Profession," *Social Work*, Vol. 21 (1976), pp. 448–454.

51. ———. "Consciousness-Raising Groups in the 1970s," *Psychology of Women Quarterly*, Vol. 3, No. 2 (1978), pp. 168–186.

52. Kronsky, Betty J. "Feminism and Psychotherapy," *Journal of Contemporary Psychotherapy*, Vol. 3, No. 2 (1971), pp. 89–98.

53. Lacerte, Judith. "If Only Jane Addams Had Been a Feminist," *Social Casework*, Vol. 57, No. 10 (December 1976), pp. 656–660.

54. Lerman, H. "Some Barriers to the Development of a Feminist Theory of Personality," in L. B. Rosewater and Lenore E. Walker (eds.), *A Handbook of Feminist Therapy*. New York: Springer, in press. Cited by L. B. Rosewater, "Feminist Therapy: Implications for Practitioners," in Lenore E. Walker (ed.), *Women and Mental Health Policy*. London: Sage, 1984, pp. 267–279.

55. Levine, Helen. "Feminist Counselling—A Look at New Possibilities," *'76 and Beyond*. Special issue of *The Social Worker*, 1976, pp. 12–15.

56. ———. "Feminist Counseling: Approach or Technique?" in Joan Turner and Las Emery (eds.), *Perspectives on Women in the 1980s*. Winnipeg: University of Manitoba Press, 1983, pp. 74–87.

57. Loewenstein, Sophie Freud. "A Feminist Perspective," in Aaron Rosenblatt and Dianna Waldfogel (eds.), *Handbook of Clinical Social Work*. San Francisco: Jossey-Bass, 1983, pp. 518–598.

58. Mackie, Marlene. *Exploring Gender Relations—A Canadian Perspective*. Toronto: Butterworths 1983.

59. Mackinnon, Laurie, and Dusty Miller. "The Sexual Component in Family Therapy: A Feminist Critique," in Mary Valentich and James Gripton (eds.), *Feminist Perspectives in Social Work and Human Sexuality*. New York: Haworth Press, in press.

60. Malmo, Cheryl. "Sexism in Psychological Research," in Jill M. Vickers (ed.), *Taking Sex into Account: The Policy Consequences of Sexist Research*. Ottawa: Carleton University Press, 1984.

61. Maracek, Jeanne, and Diane Kravetz. "Women and Mental Health: A Review of Feminist Change Efforts," *Psychiatry*, Vol. 40 (1977), pp. 323–329.

62. Maracek, Jeanne, Diane Kravetz, and Stephen Finn. "Comparison of Women Who Enter Feminist Therapy and Women Who Enter Traditional Therapy," *Journal of Consulting and Clinical Psychology*, Vol. 47, No. 4 (1979), pp. 734–742.

63. Miller, Jean Baker. *Toward a New Psychology of Women*. Boston: Beacon Press, 1976.

64. Milliken, Eveline. *New Directions in Social Work: Feminist Counselling With Male Clients*. Unpublished master's project, University of Calgary, 1985.

65. Mowbray, Carol T., Susan Lanir, and Marilyn Hulce (eds.). *Women and Mental Health—New Directions for Change*. New York: Haworth Press, 1984.

66. NiCarthy, Ginny, Karen Merriam, and Sandra Coffman. *Talking It Out—A Guide to Groups for Abused Women*. Washington, D.C.: Seal Press, 1984.

67. Norman, Elaine, and Arlene Mancuso (eds.). *Women's Issues and Social Work Practice*. Itasca, Ill.: Peacock, 1980.

68. Orbach, Susie. *Fat Is a Feminist Issue*. New York: Berkley Books, 1984.

69. Penfold, P. Susan, and Gillian A. Walker. *Women and the Psychiatric Paradox*. Montreal: Eden Press, 1983.

70. Polansky, Elinor. "Women and the Health Care System," in Elaine Norman and Arlene Mancuso (eds.), *Women's Issues and Social Work Practice*. Itasca, Ill.: Peacock, 1980, pp. 183–199.

71. Pride, Anne. "To Respectability and Back: A Ten-Year View of the Anti-Rape Movement," in Frederique Delacoste and Felice Newman (eds.), *Fight Back!*

Feminist Resistance to Male Violence. Minneapolis: Cleis Press, 1981, pp. 114–119.

72. Quam, Jean K., and Carol D. Austin. "Coverage of Women's Issues in Eight Social Work Journals, 1970–81," *Social Work*, Vol. 29, No. 4 (1984), pp. 360–365.

73. Radov, Carol. G., Barbara R. Masnick, and Barbara B. Hauser. "Issues in Feminist Therapy: The Work of a Women's Study Group," *Social Work*, Vol. 22, No. 6 (1977), pp. 507–509.

74. Rawlings, Edna I., and Dianne K. Carter (eds.). Psychotherapy For Women Treatment Toward Equality. Springfield, Ill.: Charles C. Thomas, 1977.

75. Reinharz, Shulamit, Marti Bombyk, and Janet Wright. "Methodological Issues in Feminist Research: A Bibliography of Literature in Women's Studies. Sociology and Psychology," *Women's Studies International Forum*, Vol. 6, No. 4 (1983), pp. 437–454.

76. Robbins, Jean Hammerman. "Complex Triangles: Uncovering Sexist Bias in Relationship Counseling," in Jean H. Robbins and Rachel J. Siegel, *Women Changing Therapy—New Assessments, Values and Strategies in Feminist Therapy.* New York: Haworth Press, 1983, pp. 159–169.

77. Rosenberg, Janet. "Women in the Mirror," *Social Work*, Vol. 21, No. 6 (1976), pp. 528–530.

78. Russell, Mary. "Feminist Therapy: A Critical Examination," *The Social Worker*, Vol. 47, Nos. 2 and 3 (1979), pp. 61–65.

79. ———. *Skills in Counseling Women—The Feminist Approach.* Springfield, Ill.: Charles C. Thomas, 1984.

80. Ruzek, Sheryl Burt. *The Women's Health Movement—Feminist Alternatives to Medical Control.* New York: Praeger, 1978.

81. Schaef, Anne Wilson. *Women's Reality—An Emerging Female System in the White Male Society.* Minneapolis: Winston Press, 1981.

82. Schwartz, Mary C. "Sexism in the Social Work Curriculum," *Journal of Education for Social Work*, Vol. 9, No. 3 (1973), pp. 65–70.

83. ———. "Importance of the Sex of Worker and Client," *Social Work*, Vol. 19, No. 2 (1974), pp. 177–185.

84. Scotch, C. Bernard. "Sex Status in Social Work," *Social Work*, Vol. 6 (1971), pp. 5–11.

85. Smith, Dorothy E., and Sara J. David (eds.). *Women Look at Psychiatry.* Vancouver: Press Gang Publishers, 1975.

86. Spender, Dale (ed.). *Feminist Theorists—Three Centuries of Key Women Thinkers.* New York: Pantheon, 1983.

87. Stanley, Liz, and Sue Wise. *Breaking Out: Feminist Consciousness and Feminist Research.* London: Routledge and Kegan Paul, 1983.

88. *Stephens, M. K. "One Woman Among Many: A Structural Approach to Social Work," Canadian Journal of Social Work Education*, Vol. 6, Nos. 2 and 3 (1980), pp. 45–58.

89. Stevens, Barbara. "The Psychotherapist and Women's Liberation," *Social Work*, Vol. 16, No. 3 (1971), pp. 12–18.

90. Sturdivant, Susan. *Therapy with Women—A Feminist Philosophy of Treatment.* New York: Springer, 1980.

91. Tanney, Mary Faith, and Janice M. Birk. "Women Counselors for Women Clients? A Review of the Research," *The Counseling Psychologist,* Vol. 6, No. 2 (1976), pp. 28–32.

92. Thomas, Susan Amelia. "Theory and Practice in Feminist Therapy," *Social Work,* Vol. 22, No. 6 (1977), pp. 447–454.

93. Tolman, Richard M., Donald D. Mowry, Linda E. Jones, and John Brekke. "Developing a Profeminist Commitment." Paper presented at the Annual Program Meeting, Council on Social Work Education, Washington, D.C., February 19, 1985.

94. Turner, Joan, and Lois Emery (eds.). *Perspectives on Women in the 1980s.* Winnipeg: University of Manitoba Press, 1983.

95. Valentich, Mary, and James Gripton. "Ideological Perspectives on the Sexual Assault of Women," *Social Service Review,* Vol. 58, No. 3 (1984), pp. 448–461.

96. ———. "Helping People with Sexual Problems: A Periodic Case Strategy," *Journal of Sex Education and Therapy,* in press.

97. Vickers, Jill McAlla (ed.). *Taking Sex into Account: The Policy Consequences of Sexist Research.* Ottawa: Carleton University Press, 1984.

98. Walker, Lenore E. (ed.). *Women and Mental Health Policy.* London: Sage, 1984.

99. Weissman, Myrna, Cynthia Pincus, Natalie Radding, Roberta Lawrence, and Rise Siegel. "The Educated Housewife: Mild Depression and the Search for Work," *American Journal of Orthopsychiatry,* Vol. 43, No. 4 (1973), pp. 565–573.

100. Wesley, Carol. "The Women's Movement and Psychotherapy," *Social Work,* Vol. 20, No. 2 (1975), pp. 120–124.

101. "Women and Poverty," *Signs,* Vol. 10, No. 2 (1984).

102. Wyckoff, Hogie. "Radical Psychiatry for Women," in Edna Rawlings and Dianne K. Carter (eds.), *Psychotherapy for Women—Treatment Toward Equality.* Springfield: Charles C. Thomas, 1977, pp. 370–392.

103. Yurmark, Judith L. "The Role of Women in Social Casework Literature and Its Relation to Psychoanalytic Theories of Female Psychology," in "Abstracts of Master's Theses," *Smith College Studies in Social Work,* Vol. 43 (1972–73), pp. 83–84.

Annotated Listing of Key References

BOSTON WOMEN'S HEALTH COLLECTIVE. *Our Bodies, Ourselves: A Book by and for Women.* New York: Simon and Schuster, 1984.
This new edition is a further milestone in the women's health movement. It represents an informative and inspiring compilation of "everything you wanted to know about pregnancy, childbirth, and contraception." It has been widely translated and serves as a professional manual for female clients.

SCHWARTZ, MARY C. "Importance of the Sex of Worker and Client," *Social Work,* Vol. 19, No. 2 (1974), pp. 177–185.
An article that continues to be a useful introduction of the significant psychosocial implications of the worker's sex.

STEVENS, BARBARA. "The Psychotherapist and Women's Liberation," *Social Work,* Vol. 16, No. 3 (1971), pp. 12–18.
This is one of the first attempts to examine stereotypical expectations of therapists treating women. Particular emphasis is put on the positive use of women's assertiveness.

THOMAS, SUSAN AMELIA. "Theory and Practice in Feminist Therapy," *Social Work,* Vol. 22, No. 6 (1977), pp. 447–454.
A research-based article that identifies the important contribution of social work to feminine therapy.

VICKERS, JILL MCALLA (ed.). *Taking Sex into Account: The Policy Consequences of Sexist Research.* Ottawa: Carleton University Press, 1984.
A helpful critique of research that fails to depict clearly the feminine reality.

CHAPTER 22

Marxist Theory
and Social Work

Steve Burghardt

In 1934, Joan Price, a recent college graduate in education, took a job in a new public relief office located in an old warehouse on the Lower East Side of New York City. Her first desk was a crate she shared with two other workers. Her investigation time in the nearby community took twenty hours a week; paperwork took fourteen. She did not have an M.S.W., and her working conditions made recent unionization appeals by the insurgent Rank and File clubs sound exciting. Her salary was $1,300 a year, about one-third less than her professional supervisor. And the federal government was spending the unheard of amount of $4 billion a year for relief.

In 1984, Joan Price's granddaughter, a recent M.S.W., held a job in a social service department of a major voluntary hospital and worked primarily on discharge planning. She had her own office, but secretarial help had been lost in a recent budget crunch. Her functional responsibilities left her little time to visit the ward, let alone any community; besides, her clients were located throughout the city. Not only were all her forms in triplicate; her productivity was measured in monthly printouts that forced her and co-workers to maintain an active pace. Unionization had been mentioned, but she wondered if that ran counter to professional values. Her salary was $17,300 a year, but had been frozen for two years. The freeze hurt because her expenses for advanced clinical training had just gone up. And welfare state costs were running about $468 billion a year, a 120 percent increase in eight years.

These two vignettes, drawn from actual social work experience, describe how social work in North America has changed over the years. But why has so much changed? How could it be that the welfare state would be so much larger than in the past and yet a social worker's distance from clients so much greater? Why was "private practice" unheard of in social work circles in the 1930s but is the common echo in every social work school's corridors? How could it evolve that Joan Price's grandaughter can have her professional M.S.W. degree and her own office and yet have less job autonomy than her unlicensed predecessor?

The answers to these questions, as contradictory and puzzling as they seem, remain in a jumble without a clear analytical framework that roots the conditions of social work in some clear fashion while exploring the twists and turns of daily practice experience. Without seeing how changes in the size and direction of the welfare state affect how a social worker practices, a practitioner is too often left with the fear that "I'm not doing enough" when particular individual problems continue. Likewise, without being able to see how one's practice experience does affect larger social forces, social workers come to believe that "social change" occurs only through community organization.

I believe that Marxist theory most lucidly places the changing conditions of social work in a framework that holds out continuous possibility for on-going politicized activity for social workers from every method—case, group, and community work. Of course, to write about the influence of Marxist theory on social work is more than a little intimidating. After all, there is more to Marxism than just Marx. Indeed, there have been so many different kinds of Marxists that Marx himself once declared that he probably wasn't one![1]

Anyone wishing to read about (or, alas, write about!) a synthesis of Marxist theory faces the daunting reality of how profound and widespread the influence of Marxism is throughout the world.[2] No other singular system of thought has so influenced the direction of so much activity and so much discourse; certainly no other work other than the Bible has generated so much debate and so much enlightenment as Marx's *Capital*. As Robert Heilbroner noted, that its insights continue to cause so much controversy and seem so germane to modern life in ways that Adam Smith's *A Wealth of Nations* does not, can be traced to the magnitude of its objectives: not simply an understanding of capitalism itself, but a systematic inquiry into the very processes of our social existence that lurk beneath the trappings of everyday life.[3]

To my mind, these very concerns lie at the heart of social work, although the vehicles for exploring them have often been quite, quite different.

That noted, a work of this kind must place tremendous restrictions on what it can and cannot do. It cannot elucidate all the variations on Marxist theory that exist on even one subject, be it political economy, alienation and class consciousness, the nature and direction of class struggle, or what have you. At the same time, it cannot be a singular presentation of my own Marxist beliefs, although undoubtedly whatever synthesis I attempt will have its particular biases. What I can do is make my approach, assumptions, and objectives clear from the outset. First, I assume that most readers of this anthology will be unfamiliar with and perhaps a little nervous about Marxist theory. That means I must begin with an explanation of what are generally agreed to be the basic outlines of Marxist thought, clarifying the most popular misunderstandings. Second, I believe there is a frightening ignorance of the Old Master's actual writings by both the left and the right, especially in the United States. I will therefore seek to clarify what Marx and Engels actually said on subjects germane to either our understanding of Marxism or its impact on social work itself, differentiating their work from others.* Third, while Marx was a genius and Engels certainly brilliant, neither deserve (nor sought) to be perceived as transcendent gods writing untarnished parables of truth. They were European men of the nineteenth century, and a lot has happened over the last one hundred years or so to reveal their limitations as well as their strengths. In that time, other Marxists, as well as feminists, black nationalists, and (yes!) Freudians have made significant contributions and revisions in their original works. This is especially true in areas related to the growth of the welfare state and the tremendous insights of Freud and other clinical theorists, including the work of many feminists.[4] I plan to address these shortcomings in the work. Finally, my primary objective here is not to turn readers into Marxists right away, as nice and as grandiose as I might think that to be. It is to show that Marxism, as a method of thought and action, is an invaluable tool in the development of one's social work practice that simultaneously liberates social workers from their often self-perceived roles as co-optive agents of social control while making them, in action with their clients, more effective activists in the struggle for major social change.

I plan to return to the case vignettes presented at the start of this chapter to help explain concretely what Marxism means for the individual social worker. As you read through the more theoretical sections of this work you can know that eventually the practice implications will be made through the prism of these vignettes. By the end, for example, one hopefully can see that the push toward private practice is connected to the pull toward a more centralized, less flexible welfare state that is now required under the crisis-ridden economic conditions of late-twentieth-century capitalism. Through such awareness, of course, comes the increased ability to act in a clearer, more politically conscious way.

*In this task I have been aided tremendously by the works of Hal Draper and Robert Heilbroner, whose respective work as Marxologists has been invaluable to me and others seeking demystification. Their most important works regarding this task of demystification are part of the reference material.

A Brief Outline of Marxist Theory

This ongoing attempt to see theoretical insight as immediately connected to potential political change quickly distinguishes Marxist theory from other systems of thought. Most modern North American social science creates dichotomies between "thought" and "action." However, Marx, in his earliest writings, always believed there was a necessary unity between thought and action. This connection between apparent opposites is the first of four distinctive elements to Marxist theory: *the use of a dialectical approach to knowledge and practice.* *

As soon as most people hear the word *dialectics* they either go blank or turn numb, or both. I know I certainly did, seeing dialectics in foreboding, Germanic tones of abstruse reasoning designed to scare activists from understanding. But Marx, from his earliest writings on Feuerbach, was always in search of the essence of things that lay beneath the surface appearance, an essence he identified as dynamic and conflictual, one that necessarily has contradictory elements that over time must foster change. I will explore this concept later in greater detail, especially when I look at social work practice.

The second unifying element of Marxism is its materialist approach to history. This approach emphasizes (but does not make all-inclusive) the central role played in history by the productive (economic) forces in a particular epoch. As will be seen later, a materialist approach therefore focuses on the class and social struggles over how and what those productive forces make (be it feudal grains or capitalism's cars, but especially the level of surplus value),† seeing such struggle as the primary motor for change in society. As will be seen, the rise of social work as a profession is tied to this materialistic analysis.

A third common element is a critique of capitalism. This is perhaps the most well-understood element of Marxist thought. Almost everyone notes Marx's analysis and condemnation of what capitalism "is," and all Marxists use his original conceptions as a basis for their own work in exploring capitalism. At the same time, recent Marxist writings help explain how dynamic and changing are the functions of the welfare state under capitalism—functions not as irrelevant to progressive social change as was once argued by the left.

Finally, of course, is the Marxist commitment to socialism. While perhaps most people would readily identify this part of Marxist thought, the discussion on both how one arrives at and what socialism is have meant very

---

*I again wish to acknowledge my debt to Heilbroner here, whose more general framework greatly expedited the more specific focus of this work.

†Briefly, surplus value's source lies in the capitalist labor process. Here the worker exchanges his labor with capital to produce a value greater than the value of his labor power. This difference (usually seen in the difference between wages and capital expenses) has such great productive potential that it allows for the self-expansion of surplus value, as profits are reinvested in new and better firms, technology, all of which increase productivity and, over time, profitability.

different things to very different people. For example, many Socialists are not Marxists; many Marxists deplore the Soviet-Union and/or the Chinese brand of communism; and many Western European Communists are viewed as "reformists" by other Marxists. While this topic will not be focused on in as much detail here as are the other elements of Marxist thought, the examples in this paragraph are meant to suggest that its complexity and importance are equal to the others.

Marxism's Materialist Approach to History: Implications for Professionalism

> In the social production of their existence, people inevitably enter into definite relations, which are independent of them, namely, relations of production appropriate to a given stage in the development of their material forces of production. The totality of these relations of production constitutes the economic structure of society, the real foundation, on which arises a legal and political superstructure and to which correspond definite forms of social consciousness. The mode of production of material life conditions the general process of social, political, and intellectual life. It is not the consciousness of people that determines their existence, but their social existence that determines consciousness.[5]

This famous passage from Marx has served as the guiding principle for countless other Marxists in their approach to the study of history. For us, the key elements here are the "forces of production," the social "relations of production," and the "superstructure." Briefly put, people in a society, at any given time in history, have a certain level of productive ability—for example, there is more productive ability under capitalism than under feudalism. The productive forces are people's knowledge and skills, then technology, and the geographic environment. Over time, in the process of developing their productive forces, people develop new economic capabilities *and* new personal desires to change their world even more. This purposive activity, as Gurley emphasized,[6] led to new changes and developments in economic life *and* social life.

For example, under feudalism, people's ideas, values, and aspirations were quite different from those held by people under capitalism, with its higher mode of production. Lords of the manor cared about military conquest and spiritual salvation; they were skilled fighters and often barely literate. Capitalists cared about the profitability of their firms and commerce; literacy and business acumen, not military strategy, were of greater importance. Such changes occurred not simply because technology improved. They occurred because people changed their own values, skills, and objectives in the process of developing that new technology.

So a materialist analysis begins with the perception that the forces of production create the social relations of production, which are the institutions and practices associated with *the way* goals and services are produced, exchanged, and delivered; that is, property relations, the recruitment and development of labor, the methods utilized for extracting and dispensing the surplus product, most often profit, but also benefits and other community needs.[7] In other words, the social relations of production are the class relations revealed through the work process.

As productive forces are always changing, eventually their new forms come into conflict with the prevailing class relations. This growing incompatibility makes conflict between old and new dominant social groupings (baron and capitalist) and between those who work within the emerging productive forms (capitalist and industrial worker) one of inevitable conflict and struggle, as each group fights to hold on to or to enhance its claim over the forces of production. Although only occasionally breaking out into social revolution, this struggle will always be part of economic and social life.

The struggle between class forces that occurs in the ongoing development of the mode of production is a fixture in the materialist conception of history; Marx considered it his most original insight.[8] It sees people as active agents in the making of social change, while rooting their efforts within the particular circumstances afforded by the forces of production at that time. Likewise, Marxists see the superstructure of a society as greatly determined by those forces. The superstructure is made up of a society's institutions (schools, churches, courts), which are seen as a reflection of the prevailing class relations. If the economic mode is transformed, so will be the institutions that support them. For example, the church is much less powerful under capitalism than under feudalism, while schools are more important under capitalism. This reflects the tremendous changes in both classes and ideas; under feudalism, such close church-state relations reinforced fealty to a land-based aristocracy; under capitalism, schools are expected to produce an adequately large labor supply with varying skills for its far more productive, larger workplaces.

The Primacy of Economic Forces in the Process of Social Change

For a Marxist, then, history is not the study of either great ideas or great men, but primarily of the development of productive economic forces. The formation of ideas can be explained greatly by those material changes. It is here that Marxism has much to contribute to social work's own understanding of itself, especially as a profession, for professionalization assumes a distinctive set of ideas, behaviors, and values that distinguish one craft from another.[9] I will return in later sections to the issue of craft, but here wish to concentrate on the *idea* of social work "from charitable impulse to professional clinician." Most histories of social work begin by tracing society's Poor Laws from the early 1600s up to the present day. This approach is the essence of what Marxism calls *idealism*, the presentation of people's actions as flowing primarily from subjectivity. Sometimes note is made of how communities in the North American Colonial period "cared" for their own poor, implying how ironic it was that such genuine concern was in the economically more barren past while today's richer society shows so much indifference. Regardless of twists and turns in the historical presentation, however, the progression is almost exclusively on the basis of increasing initiatives by the community, not on transformations in the mode of production and the ensuing shifts between class forces that necessitated entirely new methods of community (and, eventually, state) intervention.

A return to Joan Price in the 1930s can make this a little clearer. Her job began after the tremendous crisis of capitalism known as the Great Depression remained unresolved without state intervention. The crisis in the mode of production that left rates of profit falling and huge numbers of workers unemployed caused a shift in class relations between ruling and working classes unlike any before it. Class antagonism, apparently so muted in the 1920s, increased as militant working-class trade union and community organizing occurred across North America. The state intervention that ensued (signaling alterations needed in the superstructure) created public sector social work jobs that had never existed before. The huge numbers of previously unemployed college graduates swelled the ranks of social work, thus increasing pressure on defining how social work was to function. Joan Price and her colleagues, working under conditions quite distinct from those in far more comfortable private agencies, thus found the idea of unionization appealing in ways previous social workers had not.

The value in this example is on the perspective on what is fundamental in the process of change and what is, while not trivial, secondary. Likewise, this places the advance of social work as a profession in a different light. Social work could only develop under the conditions bred by the development of advanced capitalism. It was no more possible to have had "social work" as we know it today before the mid-twentieth century, when the newly advanced mode of industrial capitalism uprooted tens of thousands of workers for its manufacturing requirements and which now had the social surplus to perform certain community-wide charitable functions, than it is today possible to return to agrarian values common to feudal life. The social work field is a product of these conditions, rather than standing outside of them on its own.

Social Work as a Part of Capitalism: Implications for Professionalism

The perspective initially may appear disconcerting: Does this mean social work is capitalist? A tool of capitalism? What about the countless books and articles on ethics, values, and professions that suggest something quite different? Are they seen by Marxists as simply misguided? The answers to all these questions is an unequivocal "yes" as well as "no," though not in the ambivalent sense of hedging answers, but in the materialist, dialectical reality of simultaneous contradictions existing together and changing over time. "Yes," social work, as it is rooted on top of the mode of capitalism, is part of capitalism and cannot stand outside of its epoch. Joan Price could not have found a social work job if that crisis had not occurred under the condition of mid-twentieth-century capitalism. Social work is thus expected to perform tasks of social control. "No," in that social workers, while not independent of larger class forces, are capable of choosing to work in a manner and form that can allow for self-respect, self-determination, and helpful services. Price still had enough job autonomy to work in the field twenty hours a week, using her discretionary skill as she saw fit.

Individuals still choose, but the limits on the field are decided by larger productive forces. For the professional social worker, this frees one to be as actively engaged as possible. People don't have to feel guilty for not accomplishing work that no other grouping in society is attaining at that time. For the Marxist, it is no more possible for the individual social worker to end poverty than for the lone steelworker to stop plant closings. This placement of the social worker's class position on a material rather than an ethical basis ironically gives the individual more freedom to act in a principled fashion than if one were weighed down with the ethical dilemmas that come with primary responsibility for ending homelessness, child abuse, or hunger. It is not a social worker's fault that shelters are no answer to housing for the poor, but that doesn't free one to be indifferent to the quality of care she is able to provide.[10] Marxism's materialist approach provides a social worker with less guilt but more responsibility—an irony borne by the class position in which the worker is placed and through the choices provided within that position.[11]

We will go into craft issues later on, the point here is that social workers are seen as particular intellectual workers who have their own material interests concerning wage advances and better working conditions. Like other workers, these class interests necessitate organized, collective activity if they are to be met. This class analysis (endemic to materialism) also means that different social workers within the welfare state have different class interests; the line professional in a large H.R.A., working under increased productivity demands and with a declining real income, is in a far different class relationship than is the top-line M.S.W. administrator in charge of increasing that productivity. This differentiation leads Marxists to find similarities in class alignment between many social work clients (especially the working class and working poor) and the line social workers themselves.

Historical materialism explains why there is no reason for guilt in social workers seeking to improve working conditions or wages. It helps clarify why so many social workers seek private practice; not simply as an ethical cop-out, but as an individualized yet powerful vehicle to achieve some sense of control over working conditions and standards of living. (Private practice will be discussed in more detail later.) At the same time, a materialist analysis, in its emphasis on economics, necessarily views professionalization as a reified form of bourgeois class relations, not as an autonomous class grouping capable of sustaining its distinctiveness through its ethical values and skill base alone. If they were, then such behaviors and judgments should be demonstrated consistently across interorganizational lines, just as one can demonstrate that steelworkers (or steel owners) perform highly similar tasks wherever steel plants are found. In fact, as Kayla Conrad and Irwin Epstein found in a thorough examination of the literature, no such consistency on any measure of performance has been maintained.[12]

Instead, consistent with the process of reification—a process that falsely elevates superstructural elements to a position equal in power to economic forces—they found a series of rituals and formalized professional group actions that take on the appearance of real autonomy (holding conferences, licensing, professional group sanctions, etc.). This reified appearance masks the actual class distinctions within the profession itself—that is, while the field is overwhelmingly nonexecutive and female, the professional leadership is overwhelmingly executive and male.[13]

Those using a historical materialist analysis tend to increase their attention to the needs of social workers as workers while downplaying the interests of the profession. At the same time, too much emphasis on economics and a strict interpretation of class relations alone, as tended to occur within the 1930s Rank and File club movement in the United States, would ignore the very real power that professional ideas, craft concerns with clinical intervention, etc., have on individual workers.[14] Too many Marxists have denied the value in discussing ideas, concerns of status, and career advancement that exist within the field and have the power to activate people throughout social work.

They would ignore both Joan Price's and her granddaughter's interest in self-actualization through the work experience: "subjective conditions" with real power. The push toward private practice is an outgrowth of the desire to do meaningful work while facing productivity requirements that lessen job autonomy and trivialize skill in ways Jean Price never faced. The reification of professionalization, which implicitly suggests a profession that is powerful enough as a craft to withstand outside pressures from the larger political economy, unfortunately disguises this interest in job autonomy and creativity as simply "new interventions in practice." The dynamic found in the exploration between altered working conditions, which would be a threat to a significant layer of professional leaders, and the ongoing needs of social workers as skilled workers is too often ignored by the left. Instead, private practice is dismissed as "selling out," which immediately and personally threatens practitioners who otherwise might be open to a more progressive analysis of changing working conditions within the field. This entire topic needs greater exploration, of course, and would necessarily include such issues as ideological hegemony, social reproduction, and legitimation (briefly touched on later). But it must be acknowledged that Marxists and other radical critics of social work have ignored such topics in the past as so much "reformist diversion." Hopefully, the future will find social workers of many ideological stripes arguing over these issues so that human services can and do improve.

Marxism and the Critique of Capitalism

Everyone knows that Marx was a profoundly astute critic of capitalism. Fewer may realize that his condemnation grew out of a powerful *psychological* insight into the social relations between people that had been created under capitalism. Writing in the first (and most difficult) section of *Capital* (Vol. 1), Marx explored the development of what capitalism produces in such great abundance: the commodity. He explored the commodity's development in order to get beneath its surface appearance as "a thing" and reveal the relationship between people imbedded within it. That relationship, which he called the *fetishism of commodities*, became under capitalism the [definite social relation between men themselves (which) assumes . . . the fantastic form of a relationship between things.][15] As Heilbroner wrote:

> There are few insights in all of Marx's writings as striking as the "fetishism of commodities"—indeed, few in all of social science. The perception that commodities possess the property of exchange value because they are the repository of an abstract form of labor; that this abstract labor testifies to the social and technical relationships of a specific mode of production; *and that a commodity is therefore the carrier and encapsulator of the social history of Capitalism*—all this comes as a stunning realization. [Emphasis added.][16]

There are enough issues here to devote a few lifetimes of work (some have), but any person who has tried to end a depressing workweek through the purchase of a new hat or a pair of gloves can begin to get a glimmer of what Marx was driving at. Under feudalism, people rarely got depressed in their direct relations between work, themselves, family, and kin. They lived at a level of subsistence so meager that new hats and gloves weren't available, let alone purchased. If hats were needed, rudimentary ones were made and worn, not bought: their use value and exchange value, like the labor used to make it, were the same. Social relations and economic relations were very closely integrated yet unproductive: the relationship between producer, the labor process, and the commodity was clear-cut.

Under capitalism the difference between surface level and deeper level social relations grows wider and harder to fathom. So many more commodities are produced, not for immediate use but for market exchange. The social relations necessary for such large-scale production are so much more disparate and nonfamily based that social relations (between people) are turned into material ones and material relations between things are turned into social relations. People no longer interact except when they exchange their commodities, including the commodity of their own labor. Individuals exist for one another only insofar as their commodities exist.[17]

Perhaps most important, human labor, because it is creative and imaginative, has the flexibility to do what no other labor power can: be abstracted, quantified, and refined in ways that produce more and more. In its abstraction, labor itself becomes a commodity that is exchanged for subsistence wages within the mode of capitalist production. In essence, labor power (the actual expenditure of physical and mental energy to produce commodities) is transformed into a particular exchange value (wages) by capital, which is represented not as a "thing" but in the personification of the capitalist. The human relationship of work and production is now abstracted into a battle over wages, prices, and profit.

This struggle, however, lies beneath the apparent equanimity in the capitalist's right, based on his ownership of both private property and technology, to demand a certain rate of return on his "investment" by keeping labor costs as low as possible. The reification of capitalists' rights obscures the telling Marxian observation that capital—technology, instruments, etc.—is not prima facie the capitalist's but is *"dead labor"*—instruments of production made by the labor power of past workers.[18] In turn, these past workers had been paid at an exchange value low enough to allow for greater surplus value, investment in and maintenance of capital, and the purchasing of more property. Such rights assured even more explosive productive capacity as well as further uprooting of older forms of social relationships in community after community.[19]

Without question this process enhanced the material life of capitalist and wage earner alike, although in hardly an equivalent fashion. If that were all there was to this economic scenario, Marx's critique would have been little more than phenomenal carping about too much of a good thing, and social work would have been superfluous before it started. But mystification, if it keeps one from full awareness of the actual relationship one is experiencing, breeds alienation. Likewise, the further extraction of labor power—called "exploitation"[20]—breeds physical and mental exhaustion, family uprooting, and other problems (e.g., pollution) that create greater and greater disharmony. The growth in our material life, Marx observed, correspondingly decreases spiritual life.

The Dynamics of Capitalism and the Rise of the Welfare State

This unending antagonism between a decline in human relationships in the midst of increasing economic wealth is the yeast to all class struggle, and is what has made the growth of the welfare state inevitable. For as Marx predicted, capitalism, in order to expand its wealth, would become more and more concentrated and centralized, thus uprooting more and more workers, making their social plight even worse.[21] This is what happened during Joan Price's lifetime. At times, this meant that class struggle would grow from individual, atomized sparks of daily resistance to outright rebellion and, eventually, social revolution. Under capitalism, this meant that workers' struggles would be more protracted, wider ranging, and more threatening than they were under feudalism.[22] Likewise, the now-reified needs of capital for mobility and expanded market exchange would require some protection as well.

Marx, not unlike a good social worker, was always aware of the psychological and social dynamics imbedded in economic relations. Writing at a time of both great revolutionary fervor (1848 and 1871) and tremendous economic expansion, Marx's chosen emphasis was on the economic sphere he viewed as primary. His observations about the commodity help us understand the economic and social reasons why the modern state and, within it, the welfare state had to evolve. Since then, however, there have been innumerable arguments about the role of the state, primarily centering on the degree of autonomy held by the state from the ruling class.[23] I agree with Jan Gough, who wrote:

> What distinguishes Marxist theory is not the view that a particular class dominates the institutions of the state (though that is a normal enough state of affairs), but that *whoever occupies those positions is constrained by the imperative of the capital accumulation process.* But at the same time the separation and relative autonomy of the state permits numerous reforms to be won, and in no way acts as the passive tool of one class. We reject here both the pluralist view of the state, that it is a neutral arbiter between competing groups in society, and the crude econometric view, that it is but the instrument of the dominant class in society. [Emphasis added.][24]

This perspective, quite distinct from the 1960s radicals who saw the state as an agent of social control, has important implications for how the welfare state actually functions. Furthermore, it deepens our understanding of the roles social workers can play within the welfare state.[25] Drawing on the work of James O'Connor and Gough, the welfare state is neither the pluralist repository of good intentions and good works nor the economist view of a cabal-like setting filled with agents of social control. They instead argue that, given the ongoing dynamics of capital mobility and accumulation, labor exploitation, and class struggle, the state must perform a set of two contradictory functions, accumulation and legitimation, both of which aid the process of greater capital formation and, under appropriate conditions, reflect significant gains for workers' benefits, subsistence wages, and community services (hereafter called "social wages").

As O'Connor writes, "The state must try to create or maintain the conditions in which profitable capital accumulation is possible. However, the state must also try to create or maintain the conditions for social harmony."[26] All state functions, including those of the welfare state, will have elements of both functions. However, such functions create either social capital (either by increasing the productivity of labor or by lowering the reproduction costs of labor power) or social expenses (which maintain social harmony). Social capital expenditures are indirectly productive for capital; other things being equal, they augment the rate of profit and accumulation in society.[27] Social expenses, on the other hand, are not even indirectly productive for capital. They are a necessary but unproductive expense. Most areas of social welfare state activity, as O'Connor and Gough point out, will contain elements of both legitimation and accumulation (or, if you wish, social capital and social expenses).

For example, some educational spending increases social investment by raising skill levels that improve productivity; some of it serves the reproductive/consumption processes by socializing and integrating the young; some of it serves the legitimation functions by keeping otherwise hostile young people off the streets. *The conflicts in social policy over which element is given greater emphasis (production, consumption, or harmony) is greatly a reflection of the strength and direction of class struggle in society.* While there will be inevitable limits because of capital's preeminent need for greater and greater accumulation, there can be no static definition imposed on social wages wrought by workers and their allies through that class struggle. *Therefore, to struggle for reforms in the welfare state, in terms of policy and practice, as long as they are placed within a broader program for change that clearly addresses the limits of state intervention under capitalism, is to engage in highly progressive work of great meaning to social service workers.*

Marxism helps social workers understand that social welfare (and the social welfare state itself), rather than standing outside of existing class and social forces, is an active part of them. Workers have the potential to function not as simple agents of social control but as individuals utilizing the contradictory functions of the state to open up avenues of potential gain for workers and their families.

It needs reiteration here, however, that until the influence of O'Connor and Gough, many Marxist and radical social workers continued to view the welfare state as solely a repressive apparatus operating at the whim of capitalists. Certain perspectives on the state continue to take that view, although for new, sophisticated reasons.[28] Social workers, however, can find much theoretical insight and practice flexibility in understanding the dual, contradictory functions analyzed by O'Connor and Gough.

Dialectics and the Development of Critically Conscious Practice

Historical materialism helps root the actual class relations of social workers as workers. The Marxian analysis of capitalism reveals both the economic exploitation and psychological alienation endemic to the shifting relations of massive commodity production. It helps explain how the ensuing development of the modern welfare state contains both inevitable limits on change and very real opportunity. The use of Marxian dialectics, which has been implicitly integrated in the previous sections, will reveal how the use of contradiction can more fully engage practitioners in their work.

First, dialectics has nothing to do with such static formulations as "thesis-antithesis-synthesis," a concept of dialectics far too linear to make sense.[29] Left in such abstract forms, it is stripped of its material core that is fundamental to Marxism. What Marxian dialectics is concerned with, as Marx reiterated in his afterword to *Capital*, are the underlying, social relations between different forms of development, analyzing these relations as they changed over time. Thus, Marx studied the commodity in terms of the relationship between the mode of production and the relations of production, noting how changes in a particular form of commodity production (feudalism to capitalism) necessarily created changes in social relations (serf-lord, working class-capitalist). In turn, changes wrought over time between these classes influenced the manner, pace, and direction of future capitalist development.[30] For Marxists, contradiction is not simply "negation of a negation," but a tool for understanding the workings of social organisms as they change over time. By searching for the opposing elements linked to fundamental processes, the "diagnosis" one brings to society is richer and clearer. O'Connor's examination of the legitimation and accumulation functions of the state is a modern political economic example.

Of course, there are many who have called themselves Marxists who use the term "contradiction" with the turgid repetition of an obscure mantra. (I myself have been reduced to a stupor in various coalitions where everything seemed to be a contradiction!) This unfortunate tendency comes about not only from a confusion about the dialectical method. It also flows out of many speakers' desires to see those "contradictions" resolved by the emergence of a higher form of class struggle, preferably with the workers and other oppressed peoples winning. Marx and Engels fervently wanted workers to emancipate themselves, but their dialectical method has nothing to do with prescribing actual future events. They did predict a furthering and intensifying of crisis under capitalism because of the contradictions between the drive for profit and the drive of workers for higher subsistence wages, but such a prediction has not been proven incorrect empirically. What has been incorrect is the pacing and political expectation of events, not the dynamics.

Dialectics and Implications for Practice: Community Organization

In social work, community organizers have perhaps most often used a dialectical method in their approach to their work.[31] Given Marx's emphasis on broad economic and social issues and the fact that the social/historical forces he was writing about were analyzed most often on class-wide or national terms, it was inevitable that applications were most often on an equivalent scale. The political organizations that utilized much of his method were only interested in broad-scale organizing, not clinical issues. This is still true today.

For example, the dialectical method helps strategists see the limitations in Ronald Reagan's cuts in housing subsidies by noting the rise in homelessness and the inadequacy of shelters as providing a strategic cutting edge for future mobilization. As one recent Marxist analysis of homelessness analyzed these dynamics, Reagan's support for greater accumulation undercuts the state's legitimate functions drastically, as the funds for shelters prove inadequate to the spiraling need.[32] The push for greater profit through a reduction in *private costs* is pulled against the skyrocketing *social costs* created by the lack of inadequate housing and services for the larger and larger pool of homeless, unemployed people. The strategies flowing out of this dialectical analysis work to "heighten the contradictions" by forcing more "pull" in the direction of the poor—a pull that over time would undermine the accumulation "push." Furthermore, such a contradictory analysis exposes the limitations of the more dominant social grouping at that one moment in time, thus educating and preparing activists for long-time work. Without denying the present dominance of the ruling class in present social relations, a dialectical approach to strategy never succumbs to fatalism. By illuminating the innerconnected dynamics within the social problem, opportunities for change remain alive. Dialectical inquiry helps root community-based organizing strategies in even the most conservative of times.

Group Work

Dialectical inquiry has also been explored recently through group work processes. Well-known writers such as William Schwartz have consciously invoked a "dialectic" in their group work formulations, but have rooted their dynamics between "agency" and the "worker" and her group.[33] While capturing the dynamic tension of dialectics through this approach, the work resists a materialist interpretation by substituting the superstructural element of "agency" into a reified, more permanent position than it deserves. It ignores the larger-scale, "plane of production" issues occuring within the political economy that often affect agencies *and* group life.

A more materialist approach to a dialectical group practice has been identified as an *interventionist model of group practice*.[34] Drawing upon the lessons from the women's movement's use of consciousness-raising groups, here one roots the ongoing dynamics of a group's existence within the larger society's history, noting how such conditions alter group membership functioning. To be brief, in times when there are wide-scale progressive social forces, social work groups will often be more collective in task functioning and find support through task-oriented activity. In keeping with a dialectical tension, the social worker's intervention will here necessarily increase his focus on members' personal and emotional needs. In a conservative period, the dynamics of the group and the focus of practice intervention will shift. Here, where people's needs are greater and task-oriented projects less likely to succeed, members will be more individually and personally focused. The practitioner's focus will shift to increase the awareness of the political and social factors embedded within every individual member's personal problems. Such dialectical inquiry keeps the practitioner and clients alive to both the possible change in *any* one period while locating where there are inevitable limits to any practice solution. Such ongoing awareness holds out the promise of consistently engaged activism that neither fosters illusions nor undercuts client self-actualization—goals consistent with a Marxist framework for long-term social change.

Casework: New Developments in Marxist Inquiry

That said, if that were all Marxism had to offer social work in terms of practice, it would not be enough. Most social workers in North America have worked and will continue to work with individuals, often in clinical settings. There is no question that the least developed area of Marxist inquiry relates to the study and treatment of the individual. Some of this is because Marx and Engels emphasized political economy to the near exclusion of personal relations, with the oft-quoted pamphlet by Engels, *The Origins of the Family*, the most notable exception.[35] Some of this problem occurred because many Marxists and Socialists believed that the emergence of socialism would clear up individual problems; this is why North American and Western European psychoanalytic movements are still so poorly received in the U.S.S.R. And some of the problem has existed because many individual Marxist thinkers and activists have been afraid or unwilling to explore clinical issues, either because of their own personal problems or because they mistook individually based clinical intervention as necessarily dichotomized from and antagonistic to struggles occurring within the larger political economy.[36]

Marxist writers such as Herbert Marcuse[37] and the early Wilhelm Reich[38] did creative and original work in exploring the dynamics of capitalism, individual emotional development, and the response of a Marxian psychoanalysis. However, there is little question that the most important breakthroughs in exploring individual psychological and emotional life and social relations came less from Marxists than from feminists.[39] While it is impossible here to give justice to the debate that has ensued between feminists and Marxists, the tremendous vitality to this discussion has led to an emerging synthesis that continues to utilize the Marxian dialectic surrounding the contradictions between productive and social relations while expanding the framework to include a more central role to sex in the generation and reproduction of social relations.

Briefly, what theorists concerned with a "Socialist-feminist" linkage have concentrated on that is of value for social workers is their analysis of the family and personal life. For example, all of these writers, with varying emphases, analyzed the complex, interrelated structures that defined women's condition: sexuality, reproduction (functions primarily in the family); socialization (functions primarily in society); and production (functions primarily economic in nature). By tracing the historical developments from feudalism to capitalism and examining the rise of both a nuclear family removed from economic production and the intensification of sexism, these authors and others began to explain how and why "personal life," with all the attention to individual sexuality, highly defined women's roles, distinctive individual behaviors, and individually focused therapeutic interventions, came to dominate modalities of thought and action in the West.

They have attempted to do this without sacrificing the importance of the economic sphere. At the same time, this work has been developing a deeper appreciation for a theoretical construct of great value to social workers concerned with clinical and group practices: the role of the *process of social reproduction* that is imbedded in all spheres of economic and personal life. As Andre Gorz wrote some years ago:

> Capitalism, as a complex social formation, does not exist in its present form in some massive and static reality, *but is in the constant process of renewing conditions for its continued existence through all aspects of life.* The concept of social reproduction explains that not only do workers have to be fed, sheltered, and kept healthy if they are to return each day to the factory or work place . . . but [they need] their "own" ideas and attitudes, those which ultimately maintain them within the social hierarchy and which keep them subservient to the routines of daily life under the domination of capitalism. [Emphasis added.][40]

In other words, capitalism doesn't simply "tell" workers to be subservient while at work. The institutions under capitalism—the family, schools, religious bodies, *and* service organizations—develop their own particular processes (in terms of values, standards of behavior, sanctions, etc.) that reinforce ideas about "how the world is." This is in part why so many Marxists rejected clinical approaches to treatment. Its individual-to-individual *form* of interaction, when coupled with its necessary emphasis on emotional dynamics, suggested to them strategic conclusions that were equally individualized and thus reformist. Their error was in mistaking the form for the potential essence within that relationship; with the right content and conscious utilization of process, it is quite possible to undermine the dominant processes of social reproduction and to replace them with a far more liberating process.[41]

Some social workers have begun to utilize their awareness of the contradictions between economic and social relations and the processes of social reproduction within those relations to develop a socially charged practice. This has been especially evident in feminist practice perspectives,[42] but the same issues seem legitimate for racial nationalities and other class and social groupings as well.

By reexamining practice in part by being conscious of the power of social reproduction, such authors as Christopher Lasch, Scott Jacoby, and others have reexplored the history of psychoanalysis.[43] Perhaps surprisingly, their neo-Marxist work sees far more compatibility with the early Freud and later work by such Marxist Freudians as Marcuse and, to a lesser degree, the early Reich and the Frankfurt school. They are far more hostile to the less radicalizing, more benign work of the ego psychologists—such as Heinz Hartmann, Erik Erikson, and Erich Fromm—seeing their work as vitiating the radicalizing dynamics between individual and the inevitable repression demanded from the larger society. Jacoby argues that the contradictory dynamics between the striving individual and the repressive society that give rise to unconscious processes has been baldly replaced by the ego-striving, falsely labeled "strengths" of individuals. Such individuals' particular limitations are thus less a problem of society than within one's self—or, at the very most, that the strengths of individuals makes it possible for one in clinical treatment to eventually work out any individual issues. These neo-Freudian/Marxists see this latter ego psychological perspective as robbing the individual of the insight into the limitations imposed by the larger social order that would necessitate more collective approaches to mental health.

Through their analysis, we can see that an ego psychology based primarily on the strengths of the individual socially reproduces ideas about failure and reform that are individually focused and thus less threatening to society. The Neo-Freudian/Marxists argue for a more dialectical model that includes within its practice framework the assumption that capitalism will foster repression of some individual drives (especially sexual and social) that will necessarily undercut human growth and development in ways no one individual alone can overcome.* Such an approach continues to use clinical interventions with the individual but undermines dominant assumptions of social reproduction that are fraught with political significance for the client and worker alike.

The Dynamics of Social Reproduction as Applied in Casework

For the client, this Neo-Freudian/Marxist dialectic frees him from total responsibility over his own condition. While particular individual dynamics will demand immense personal effort for change, this materialist approach

*This dynamic would occur under any society, only would do so in different ways. This is why the Soviet Union continues to be hostile to Freudianism. Hopefully, in the future, other less repressive societies would undercut some of the more damaging forms in which this process now occurs.

will also ferret out some of the client's problems within the larger society that demand collective, societal change. For example, anorexia and bulimia may be primarily "female" problems that each woman must work on with tremendous emotional effort, but these problems exist in large part because of the particular forms of sexism fostered under late twentieth-century capitalism that reinforce images of women as thin yet consuming, sexually powerful but economically and socially impotent. To focus only on the eating disorder and the client's inherent "ego adaptability" to overcome such a problem vitiates the critical consciousness imbedded in the more dialectical approach that can note individual strength but also societally determined limitations. Women as a *social grouping* will continue to have these problems, both from generation-to-generation and developmentally throughout their lives in some form, if the sexism of our society is not confronted in more collective ways that forces alterations in our institutions and the ideas they socially reproduce. This combination of joining individual concerns with collectives ones is very freeing for the client as he learns to own his responsibility for emotional growth and where he must begin placing demands on the larger society for other forms of change. While neo-Freudian and other, materialist approaches need to deepen their own examinations into practice methodology, the effort holds out much promise for the future.

The practitioner is freed also from total responsibility over a client. A lot of mental health derives from full employment, job satisfaction, and an end to racism, sexism, and ageism as well. By willingly exploring these dynamics with clients, one reinforces within *oneself* a deeper recognition of how powerful and pervasive are the processes of social reproduction—even on practitioners. Your supervisor finds your attention to racism a "distraction"? Your agency only values clinical expertise that ignores or minimizes social issues? Such emphases within agencies and among departmental hierarchies can be expected for, as Antonio Gramsci noted, the (superstructural) institutions of a society are the vehicles by which the ruling class socially reproduces its ideas about "how the world is."[44] A large social welfare institution, dependent on foundation grants and state financing (both complete with oversight responsibilities) is no more likely to stand outside of that social reproduction process than is any other organization. *That is why, if you attempt to foster client self-determination by engaging in exploration of societally induced constraints on human growth and development (as well as individual strengths), you are engaging in a highly political form of practice.*

Thus, for the caseworker who grapples with the contradictory dynamics between production and social reproduction, there is the opportunity to politicize daily practice without succumbing to empty political phrase-making or to emotional subjectivisim. Such engagement in one's clinical work undoubtedly carries over into a practitioner's perceptions about her work life as well. As Thomas Keefe describes a more materialist form of empathy, we can see benefits for the social worker as well as the client:

Empathy (based on identification of economic constraints for client and worker) is a facilitator of growth. When a worker's empathy is effectively communicated to a client, he or she may be helped to give vent to despair and to work for the constructive expression of rage. The capacity to sense the frustrations and the anger of a client is enhanced by an understanding of the economic realities confronted by both client and worker. The worker's roles of broker, mediator, and advocate . . . demand an emphathic skill sensitive to clients and the infrastructural sources of their problem.[45]

To examine this on the worker's own productive dimension increases the likelihood that the social worker will see increased productivity demands as part of the larger society's demands for a more proletarianized work experience. Such proletarianization, when understood as occurring throughout the mode of production, opens the social worker to possible collective solutions at the workplace. On the dimension of social reproduction, the worker engaged in clinical practice would know that the loss of his own work autonomy and creativity would lead to a more intensified process of social reproduction designed to further alienate and demoralize clients. For example, short-term treatment plans, if developed as the primary practice model in an agency, would rob the client of the opportunity to explore longer-term, social and personal problems that defy quick treatment. Clients would be expected to "reform" more quickly than many people can; failure to do so would be perceived as their fault. Noting these practice shifts, the social worker knows that the changes in the mode of production that are stratifying the labor force create these practice demands to replicate types of behavior that make the new labor pool more compatible with this intensified stratification—more deference, fatalism, and a "willingness to accept less" would be some of the behaviors developed through the above.

Equally important, it is just these practice forms, when coupled with the increasing productivity demands in agencies, that are increasing the drives toward private practice. Private practice isn't simply a way to "cop out"— Joan Price's granddaughter no longer has the worker autonomy and job satisfaction of her grandmother, who worked in a nearby community on her own twenty hours a week. At the same time, the contradictions imbedded in private practice—more job autonomy but less community involvement, increased job creativity but heightened atomization, better pay but more vulnerability to long-term market forces—are the very issues that threaten the core legitimacy of social work as a craft.[46] For left unchecked, the surge in private practice creates tensions within the major sources of finance for this field—the insurance companies and banks whose profitability depend on high enough rates of return through maintenance of costs, costs that are skyrocketing as more and more people, unable to find clinic services, seek private treatment.

For the caseworker concerned about both these issues and those related to the process of social reproduction, an awareness of the Marxian dialectic can only enrich one's practice. Working against the tide of privatization and diminished worker autonomy in the workplace, politically and personally, works in favor of the social worker's own material self-interest in ways that speak to broader, collective actions. And there is much one can do on the plane of social reproduction through individual clinical work as well. One can note and then resist certain types of behaviors in her practice; these include the above-mentioned deference and self-blame, which intensify attitudes helpful for accepting the lowest paid positions in all workplaces (held disproportionately by racial minorities, women, and older people); assumptions of class prerogative, which include ideas about professional elitism and the need for centralization of power in all decision-making; and diminished expectations, where people at various levels of income learn to "accept less" given the desperate conditions faced by those in even worse economic straits. *If social workers practice in ways that consciously undermine such ideas, they are engaging in forms of empowerment and self-determination through a highly politicized form of practice.* While one recognizes that such individual approaches cannot in themselves be enough to affect the larger political economy, one's utilization of dialectics makes it possible to engage in a process that does help people become more able to directly confront the political economy at a later time.

Future Implications for Social Work Practice

Marx always stated that socialism could occur only after capitalism and its tremendous capacity (as well as more sophisticated social relations) were in place. Otherwise, planning could only be based on rationing, not distribution of adequate surpluses. The first Socialist revolution (in Russia), which served as a model for all others, was launched with the idea of it spreading to more industrialized countries, for example, Germany. Without that, Lenin knew,[47] they would be faced with economic and social problems that would undermine democratic principles.

Second, each Socialist revolution has been met with hostile political and economic forces that necessitated a more militaristic and stringently ordered social response that further eroded political freedom and more productive economic development. (We see these problems confronting Nicaragua today in the mid-eighties.) In short, neither the economic nor international political conditions have been available to create the elements of socialism as Marx foresaw (and as people in industrialized countries had come to expect). Faced with colonialism and imperialism from the United States and Western Europe, the people of these countries still fought for something they hoped would be better than the misery of the past; in some places with mixed success, in other places with little at all. The political mistakes—ranging from elitist "vanguardism" to racism and sexism—have been magnified by the economic marginality faced by each.

Economic preconditions for socialism do exist in North America: an advanced industrial mode of production; technology that can be utilized throughout any community; high levels of communication and transportation. It is objectively feasible to have planning that is far more orderly and without the degree of economic and political rationing in precapitalist societies.

But political feasibility is another matter. Marx never proposed that socialism *would* emerge out of capitalism; he predicted only an intensification of alienation and exploitation as the contradictions of capitalism remained unresolved. Such intensification would then lead workers, in alliance with other political cadre, to fight for socialism because they *had to*, not because they *wanted to*.[48] Socialism speaks to collective decision-making, democratic organization, and planning because individualized solutions alone cannot occur for everyone under capitalism. For the working class, their solutions to housing shortages, underemployment, etc., to Marxists, had to lead in the direction of socialism. The alternatives, as was said in an oft-quoted phrase, were "socialism or barbarism."

Such stark alternatives captured the boldest choices Marx saw confronting workers under the evolving character of capitalism. There is nothing intrinsically wrong with stating political directions so clearly, except for two not-so-minor problems. First, workers in industrial capitalist countries have not maintained long-term, political opposition to capitalism. There are many reasons for this, ranging from state repression of working-class and Socialist groups to racism within the class.[49] They need further exploration than can be given here. But it cannot be ignored that workers in general have maintained sufficient allegiance to capitalism to not align with political activists seeking its eventual overthrow.

The second problem is one less related to the working class than to the various elites who have lead the fight for socialism. Robert Michel's *Iron Law of Oligarchy*[50] is unduly pessimistic and ignores elements of state repression toward Socialist groups at the turn of the century, but his description of self-perpetuating elites continues to haunt progressive groups throughout the twentieth century. Regardless of particular commonly held beliefs about mass self-determination, groups ranging from the German Social Democratic Party in the 1900s to today's social workers, the modern welfare state professionals have all sacrificed collective goals in order to maintain their own positions of power.[51]

Marxists don't lack for reasons to explain these problems—usually centering on some inherent *political* inadequacy. They claim that if the political line or program were changed, the elitism would disappear. However, some of this situation—which today relates to such disparate groups as European social democracy, Third World socialism, and North American liberalism—is in part social psychological. The human needs for self-actualization and a less alienated life, when blocked by the limitations found in any society, as social workers know, will be psychologically displaced elsewhere, either personally or organizationally, if they are not understood and responded to in some consistent fashion.

This awareness of the drive to self-actualization and the ways it can be displaced is a fundamental part of social work professionalism as well. However, social work skills in individual and group dynamics, when placed within a Marxian framework that utilizes a dialectical, historical materialism to center one's practice, has much to contribute here. Without denying the contradictions faced by social work under capitalism, social workers' skills take on an even greater importance than in the past. For social work today is at a crossroads: either greater privatization and individualization (processes congruent with the needs of capitalism today); or, given the increasingly collective, material needs of social workers throughout the welfare state, a more mobilized and socially conscious field of professonals choosing to affect their own history. Either choice, of course, exposes just how political the field of social work really is. Viewing the simultaneous pauperization in communities alongside their own diminished resources at work, social workers may find that choosing between "socialism or barbarism" is perhaps not as unreal as may have once been thought.

Notes

1. Marx's reply to Ed.Bd.Sachs, *Marx-Engels Works*, Vol. 22 (New York: International Publishers, 1969), p. 69.

2. Robert Heilbroner, in *Marxism: For and Against* (New York: Norton, 1980), discusses this same controversy. He ends with a quotation from Eugene Kamenka that "the only serious way to analyze Marxist or socialist thinking may well be to give up the notion that there is a coherent doctrine called Marxism. . . . " Quoted by Daniel Bell, "The Once and Future Marx," *American Journal of Sociology*, Vol. 9 (July 1977), p. 196. Such a quotation seems unduly harsh, as few would say, for example, that there was a coherent doctrine of behaviorist positivism either.

3. Heilbroner, op. cit., p. 17. See also Hal Draper, *Karl Marx's Theory of Revolution, Vol. 1, The State and Bureaucracy; Vol. II, The Politics of Social Classes* (New York: Monthly Review Press, 1977, 1978).

4. On the welfare state, see James J. O'Connor, *The Fiscal Crisis of the State* (New York: St. Martin's Press, 1974); Ian Gough, *The Political Economy of Social Welfare* (London: Macmillan, 1981); on a history of social welfare policy in the United States, see Frances Fox Piven and Richard Cloward, *Regulating the Poor* (New York: Pantheon, 1971); on feminism, socialism, and issues of clinical and political life, see Nancy Chodorow, *The Reproduction of Mothering: Psychoanalysis and the Sociology of Gender* (Berkeley: University of California Press, 1978); Sheila Rowbotham, *Women's Consciousness, Man's World* (Baltimore: Penguin Books, 1973); Eli Zaretsky, *Capitalism, the Family and Personal Life*, (New York: Harper Colophon, 1976).

5. Karl Marx, *Capital*, Vol. 1, quoted by John Gurley in *Challengers to Capitalism: Marx, Lenin, and Mao* (San Francisco: San Francisco Book Co.), Chapter 2.

6. See Gurley, "The Materialist Conception of History," in Richard Edwards, Michael Reich, and Thomas Weisskopf (eds.), *The Capitalist System* (Englewood Cliffs, N.J.: Prentice-Hall, 1978), p. 45.

7. See Draper, op. cit., *Vol. II*, for a brilliant discussion of class relations.

8. Robert C. Tucker, *The Marx-Engels Reader* (New York: Hawthorne Press, 1978), p. 220.

9. Ernest Greenwood, "Attributes of a Profession," *Social Work*, Vol. 2, No. 3, (Summer 1957), pp. 45–55; Henry Meyer, "The Profession of Social Work: Contemporary Characteristics," in *Encyclopedia of Social Work* (New York: NASW, 1971), pp. 959–972.

10. *The Urban and Social Change Review*, Vol. 17, No. 1 (Winter 1984), explored these dynamics in great detail regarding the homeless. While all the articles were not Marxist in orientation, they lay out progressive approaches to this work.

11. An important debate within Marxist and social democratic circles is over the possible emergence of a professional-managerial class that under late capitalism may (or may not) have the equivalent social weight of the ruling and working classes. See Pat Walker (ed.), *Between Labor and Capital* (Boston: South Bend Press, 1981) for an overview of this debate.

12. Irwin Epstein and Kayla Conrad, "Limits of Social Work Professionalizaton," in Rosemary C. Sarri and Zeke Hasenfeld (eds.), *The Management of Human Services*, (New York: Columbia University Press, 1977), pp. 163–172.

13. Ruth Brandwein, "Descriptive Attributes of Social Work Agency Management and the Continuation of Sexism," *Social Work*, Vol. 14, No. 3 (June 1981).

14. See Rick Spano, *The Rank and File Movement* (New York: University Press, 1983) for an interesting discussion on the effect of such disinterest on the Rank and File Movement's mobilization efforts. For a thorough examination of the alterations of craft in the twentieth century, see Harry Braverman's *Labor and Monopoly Capital* (New York: Monthly Review Press, 1978).

15. Marx, *Capital, Vol. 1*, p. 165.

16. Heilbroner, op. cit., p. 103.

17. Marx, *Vol. I*, p. 167.

18. Ibid., p. 176.

19. The latter sections of *Capital, Vol. I*, graphically describe the shifting nature of productive and class relations in the seventeenth to nineteenth centuries. For a far more modest analysis of these dynamics in a modern form related to community organization, see Steve Burghardt, "The Strategic Crisis of Grass Roots Organizing," in Steve Burghardt, *Against the Current*, Vol. IV, No. 4.

20. Exploitation is an economic term, one loaded with social significance. In its most general sense it means the extraction of labor by one class over another through the productive process. Under capitalism, exploitation occurs after one produces commodities for which she receives no return in wages or benefits. It is *the* economic basis of class struggle under capitalism. As Engels wrote in *Origin of Family, Private Property, and the State*, "Since the exploitation of one class by another is the basis of civilization, its whole development moves in a continual contra-

diction. Every advance in production is at the same time a retrogression in the condition of the oppressed class, that is, the great majority. What is a boon for one is necessarily a bane for the other," quoted in *Karl Marx and Frederick Engels' Collected Works* (New York: New World Paperbacks, 1968), pp. 591.

21. There are innumerable eloquent examples by Marx on this phenomenon. For example, in a letter criticizing Proudhon, he wrote, "M Proudhon mixes up ideas and things. Men never relinquish what they have won, but this does not mean that they never relinquish the social form in which they have acquired certain productive forces. On the contrary, in order that they may not be deprived of the result attained and forfeit the fruits of civilization, they are obliged from the moment when their mode of carrying on commerce no longer corresponds to the productive forces acquired, to change all their traditional social forms. . . . For example, the privileges, the institutions of the guilds and corporations, the regulatory regime of the Middle Ages, were social relations that alone corresponded to the acquired productive forces and to the social conditions which had previously existed and from which these institutions had arisen. Under the protection of the regime of corporations and regulations, capital was accumulated, overseas trade developed, colonies were founded. But the fruits of these men would have been forfeited if they had tried to retain the forms under whose shelter these fruits had ripened. Hence burst two thunderclaps—the Revolutions of 1640 and 1688. All the old economic forms, the social relations corresponding to them, the political conditions which were the official expression of the old civil society, were destroyed in England. Thus the economic forms in which men produce, consume, and exchange, are *transitory* and *historical*. With the acquisition of new productive facilities, men change their mode of production and with the mode of production all the economic relations which are merely the necessary relations of this particular mode of production." *Karl Marx and Frederick Engels' Collected Works*, op. cit., pp. 670–671. This contradictory dynamic shows the direction of O'Connor's and Gough's works in explaining legitimation and accumulation functions of the state as well.

22. Draper's presentation of Marx's and Engels's ideas on the development of the working class and the reasons for its progression toward increasingly class-conscious levels of militant, collective activity is a brilliant synthesis. See especially Part One of his second volume: "The Proletariat and Proletarian Revolution," in Draper, op. cit., *Vol. II*, pp. 17–168.

23. Gough, op cit., p. 186.

24. Ibid., pp. 43–44.

25. I attempt to develop these dynamics within a new dialectical framework for practitioners in *The Other Side of Organizing* (Cambridge, Mass.: Schenkman, 1982).

26. O'Connor, op. cit., p. 7.

27. Gough, op. cit., Chapter 3 examines these dynamics with great thoroughness.

28. See, for example, N. Poulantzas, *Political Power and Social Classes* (London: New Left Books, 1973); R. Milliband, *The State in Capitalist Society* (London: Weidenfeld and Nicholson, 1969). For a recent critique of O'Connor, see Jared Epstein, "The Fiscal Crisis of the State Revisited," in *Against the Current, Vol. 4, No. 2.*

29. As Heilbroner pointed out, we owe this catchy little phrase to Johann Fichte, op. cit., p. 42.

30. See note 21.

31. See Michael Fabricant, "The Political Economy of Homelessness," in *Socialist Review*, forthcoming; Spano, op. cit., on rank and file movement strategy, especially Chapters 2–3; Steve Burghardt, op. cit., especially Chapters 1–2; and my *Organizing for Community Action* (Beverly Hills, Calif.: 1982). At the same time, very influential community organization strategists such as Saul Alinsky were quite anti-Marxist, see his *Rules for Radicals* (Boston: Beacon Press, 1969).

32. Michael Fabricant, "The Industrialization of Social Work Practice," *Social Work*, forthcoming, 1985. See Harvey Brenner, *Unemployment and Mental Illness* (Cambridge, Mass.: Harvard University Press, 1976), which explores these dynamics in terms of private costs versus social costs.

33. William Schwartz, "Social Group Work: The Interaction Approach," in *Encyclopedia of Social Work*, Vol. 2 (New York: National Association of Social Welfare, 1971), pp. 1257–1262.

34. Burghardt, *The Other Side of Organizing*, especially Chapters 7 and 8.

35. Engels, *Origin of the Family*.

36. I am not, however, stating that Marxists and other leftists have *more* personal problems than do other groups of people. I believe that the neurotic stances of people on the left tend to be less introspective personally than others, just as I have found clinicians' neurotic styles to be overly introspective. This issue is explored in greater detail in my *The Other Side of Organizing*. Furthermore, some clinical interventions *do* counterpose emotional growth and political activity; some give it short shrift. That dominant clinical methods do so does not mean that individual work *must* be so.

37. Herbert Marcuse, *Eros and Civilization* (Boston: Beacon Press, 1968), is an especially important contribution.

38. See *Sex-Pol, The Writings of Wilhelm Reich*, edited by Bertell Ollman (New York: Dell Books, 1971).

39. There are many important works here. Besides the works referred to in note 4, see Susan Schechter's *Women and Male Violence* (Boston: South End Press, 1982) for both its own analysis of these issues and for a very timely bibliography.

40. Andrew Gorz, *Strategy for Labor* (Boston: Beacon Press, 1967), p. 108. Of course, Marx discussed this in *Capital* one hundred years ago, but with much less emphasis than Marxists, Socialists, and feminists are giving it today. See *Capital, Vol. I*, p. 577.

41. Paulo Freire, *Pedagogy of the Oppressed* (New York: Seabury Press, 1972), is a brilliant examination of these dynamics in terms of methodology.

42. See especially Chodorow, op. cit.

43. Christopher Lasch, *Haven in a Heartless World* (New York: Praeger, 1981); Scott Jacoby, *Social Amnesia* (New York: Dalton, 1981).

44. Antonio Gramsci develops these and similar ideas around the concept of "ideological hegemony," a brilliant formulation concerning how the ruling class continues to rule through means other than military or economic force. See Antonio Gramsci, *Prison Notebooks* (New York: International Publishers, 1977).

45. Thomas Keefe, "Empathy Skills and Critical Consciousness," *Social Casework*, Vol. 61, No. 7 (September 1980), pp. 307–313; Peter Leonard, "Toward a Paradigm for Radical Practice," in Ray Bailey and Mike Brake (eds.), *Radical Social Work* (New York: Pantheon, 1975), pp. 46–61.

46. Fabricant, "The Industrialization of Social Work Practice," op. cit.

47. Tony Cliff, *Lenin, Vols. I–IV* (London: Pluto Press, 1976, 1977, 1979, 1980); Michel Liebman, *Leninism Under Lenin* (London: Macmillan, 1975).

48. Draper, op. cit., especially Vol. 2.

49. The most thorough example of this in U.S. labor history is Philip Foner's *The History of the Labor Movement in the United States, Vols. I–IV* (New York: International Press, 1947–1980). Equally important in the U.S. is his most recent volume, *The Black Working Class and the U.S. Labor Movement* (Philadelphia: Temple University Press, 1982).

50. Robert Michels, *Political Parties* (New York: Collier Books, 1962).

51. See Piven and Cloward, op. cit., and their *The New Class War* (New York: Pantheon, 1983).

Annotated Listing of Key References

BAILEY, RAY, and MIKE BRAKE (eds.). *Radical Social Work.* New York: Pantheon, 1975.

A collection of articles that examines the contradictions inherent in current social work goals and actual impact.

BURGHARDT, STEVE. "The Strategic Crises of Grass Roots Organizing," in Steve Burghardt, *Against the Current,* Vol. 4, No. 4.

A contemporary analysis of the dynamics of productive and class relations and their implication for community organization.

BURGHARDT, STEVE. *The Other Side of Organizing.* Cambridge, Mass.: Schenkman, 1982.

A helpful presentation of the utility of using a dialectical approach to the analysis of societal events and conditions.

FABRICANT, MICHAEL. "The Industrialization of Social Work Practice," *Social Work* (forthcoming, 1985).

A discussion of some current trends in practice from a perspective of economic forces.

Karl Marx and Frederick Engels' Collected Works. New York: New World Paperbacks, 1968.

A useful and important introduction to the key writings of these two leading thinkers.

KEEFE, THOMAS. "Empathy Skills and Critical Consciousness," *Social Casework,* Vol. 61, No. 7 (September 1980), pp. 307–313.

This article emphasizes the need to understand the client's reality within the economic situation of both client and worker and the need to put our professional efforts on changing both society and clients.

CHAPTER 23

The Life Model Approach to Social Work Practice Revisited

Carel B. Germain
and
Alex Gitterman

In our profession, the relationship between people and their environments has occasionally been dichotomized into two mutually exclusive foci. It is a dichotomy that had its roots in the late nineteenth century. Two streams of thought, derived from the settlement and charity organization movements, gave rise to an emphasis on environmental reform and action on one hand and on individual change and methods to achieve it on the other.

To the founders of the settlement movement, the sources of most urban misery lay in the environment. To live among the poor, sharing their joys and sorrows, their struggles and toil, was to be a good neighbor. For the "settlers" their work was not charity, but good neighboring. They became intensely aware of tenement conditions, lack of sanitation, poor schools, inadequate play space, long hours in factories and sweatshops, child labor, and the many obstacles faced by immigrant·populations in their attempts to adapt to a new environment.

For the founders of the charity organization society movement, people's problems were "social diseases" to be cured by "social physicians" prescribing remedies on the basis of a social "diagnosis" of individual need. By 1917 the principles of scientific philanthropy had been codified and organized into what was called the casework method. The medical metaphor was gradually institutionalized, and it reinforced a preoccupation with internal processes:

diagnosis and treatment focused primarily upon personality processes; the environment, seemingly fixed and intractible, received only scant and passing notice.

With the development of the three methods—casework, group work, and community organization—the tendency to dichotomize people and environments was improved. Needs or problems were often defined by the modality of service. Casework agencies and caseworkers developed casework services; group work agencies and group workers developed group work services; community organization agencies and community organizers developed community services. People's needs were fitted to the restrictive self-definitions of the service agency and the worker's method. In education, method specialization created dysfunctional curriculum accommodations, prevented an examination of the commonalities across methods, and inhibited the development of a distinctive, integrated social work method of practice.[1]

In response to the historical dialectic and to advance method integration, the Life Model approach attempts to develop (1) a conceptual framework (an ecological perspective) that provides a simultaneous focus on people and environments; and (2) a method of practice that integrates practice principles and skills for work with individuals, families, and groups within an organizational, community, and cultural context.

The Ecological Perspective

Ecology is a particularly useful practice metaphor as it seeks to understand the complex reciprocal relationships between people and environments; that is, how each acts and influences the other. The ecological perspective and its evolutionary, adaptive view of people and their environments lead quite naturally to an emerging approach to practice, now being referred to in the literature as the Life Model of Practice.[2] Before examining the dimensions of the Life Model, however, we will present the particular ecological concepts, that are pertinent to social work's function in society and underlie the Life Model approach.

Adaptation-Stress-Coping

Ecology is the science concerned with the relations between living organisms—in this case, human beings—and all elements of their environments. It examines how organisms and environments achieve a goodness-of-fit or *adaptive balance* and, equally important, how and why they sometimes fail to do so.

All forms of life strive toward a goodness-of-fit with their environments—over evolutionary times in case of the species, and over the developmental life span in the case of the individual. All living forms need to receive from the environment the stimuli and resources necessary for development and survival. Reciprocally, the environment becomes more and more differentiated through the actions of its life forms and thus capable of supporting more and increasingly diverse forms of life. At times, however, the fit may be achieved at the expense of other organisms, thus reflecting the issues of differential power and conflict. Or the fit may be poor, so that development or functioning may be impeded.

The physical environment constantly changes, not only because of the activities of living organisms, but because of weather, erosion, natural disasters, and the like. Living forms change the physical environment to make it conform to their needs as in the nest-building of birds or the dwellings, settlements, and technologies of humans, and must adapt to these changes as well. If organisms damage the environment too severely, it may no longer be able to support them or other life forms. Reciprocally, if the environment fails to provide what the organisms or species requires, it may damage or threaten the survival of the organism of these species.

In human beings, the adaptive processes are psychological, social, cultural as well as biological. Through language, knowledge, technology, and belief systems, human beings have changed both themselves and their environments and then have had to further adapt to those changes. In fact, modern urbanized and industrialized societies pose adaptive, biological, social, and cultural demands that often exceed the limits of many or most people.

Transactional upsets in the usual or desired person and environmental fit often generate life *stress*. When an imbalance exists between a perceived demand and a perceived capability to meet the demand through the use of available internal and external resources, people experience stress. As an inevitable life process, stress is not necessarily problematic. One person's challenge is another person's stress. While possibly stressful, challenge is associated with positive feelings of zest, anticipated mastery, and optimal self-esteem. Life stress is associated with negative feelings of low self-esteem, anxiety, guilt, anger, despair, and the like. Individual perceptions of challenge and stress are mediated by biopsychosocial functioning, age, sex, culture, and the nature of the perceived environment. As an external demand and emotional and physiological response, stress expresses a particular person-environment relationship and hence is transactive in nature. The social worker must therefore attend to both internal and external and to the relationship.[3]

Coping efforts are the special adaptations evoked by the experience of stress; that is, adaptation under relatively difficult circumstances and conditions. Coping requires both internal and external resources, and therefore expresses a person-environment relationship. For example, personality resources include motivation, a favorable level of self-esteem and psychic comfort, problem-solving skills, and the autonomy to make decisions and take effective action. Motivation, however, depends upon the incentives and rewards provided by the environment. Self-esteem and management of anxiety, depression, or other immobilizing feelings, so that problem-solving can proceed, depend upon social supports and emotional sustainment provided by the environment.[4] Problem-solving abilities depend upon adequate training by the family, school, and other institutions in the social environment. Adequate time and space, literally and figuratively, for the exercise of autonomous action must be provided by the physical and social environments. Viewed as the expression of a person-environment relationship, coping requires the social worker to embrace both personal and environmental resources.

Human Relatedness, Identity/Self-Esteem, and Competence

Human relatedness is a biological and social imperative for the human being over the life span. Without relationships, the human infant cannot survive, and without relatedness to others, the human being cannot learn to be human.[5] While the infant comes into the world preadapted for survival through innate equipment connecting her to the environment provided by evolution, she requires care-giving and a long, complex period of learning and socialization into her society and particular cultural group. Such learning and socialization can take place only within the context of human relationships, first within the family and later among peers, and in the social world of school, recreation, religious, health, work, and other institutional systems.

The young child, who is deprived, for whatever reason, of a continuing primary relationship with a consistent care-giver, may remain unrelated, trusting neither himself nor others. The infant without love, without attachment, however hygienic his care, fails to thrive. The loss of a loved person, either in childhood or adulthood, is perhaps the most difficult experience for a human being to undergo, and particularly excruciating in the case of a primary attachment such as parent, child, or spouse. These deeply painful experiences of emotional isolation, derived from loss and separation, are distinguishable from the pain of social isolation felt by the person who lacks a network of human relationships, such as the newcomer or migrant, and the person who has learned to fear relationships because of their potential for loss and pain.[6] Often the aged person—and, indeed, other individuals as well—suffers a double burden of both emotional and social isolation when, having lost a spouse, he is also without a network of caring others. To care and be cared for are among the most treasured of human experiences, and such experiences underscore the connection between dependence and independence. The appropriateness of each, in the varying circumstances of life, may best be expressed as interdependence, which is maintained across the life span by reciprocal processes of respect and caring in mutually valued relationships. Relatedness expresses people-environment relationships and helps the social worker maintain a dual focus on both.

Identity and *self-esteem* arise from relations with other human beings, beginning in the intimacy of the first relationship and later attachments within the family, and then moving outward in ever-widening circles of social experience. The infant has innate, genetically programmed capacities that assure her connectedness to the environment, including sucking, clinging, and rooting reflexes. But, in addition, the infant's appearance, her postural responses to being held, her spontaneous crying, her ability to soothe herself, and sensitivity to sensory stimuli evoke particular responses in the mother, to which the infant then responds. Mother also brings her own qualities and experiences to the interaction that improve the input. In these interactions the baby's image of herself develops and her early store of self-esteem is laid down.

As the child grows, social experiences continue to shape the sense of identity, self-image, and self-esteem. The perceptions and evaluations made by others of herself and of her family will have a profound impact, particularly as gender, race, and social class factors are incorporated into her identity. For Erik Erikson, the achievement of identity is the major task of adolescence in which past experiences, present realities, and future aspirations must coalesce into a sense of self that meshes well with the perceptions of significant others and the role definitions of the culture. Nevertheless, identity remains an issue across the life span, worked and reworked many times over through interactions with the social and physical environments and in the course of life events.[7] The sense of identity and self-esteem are significant outcomes of people-environment exchanges and require the attention of the social worker to both.

Competence is tied to the sense of identity, self-direction, and relatedness. In Robert White's view, it is the sum of the person's successful experiences in the environment.[8] As an innate motivation, it is gratified when the baby experiences his effects on the environment. If he has the opportunity to learn that his cries bring food or soothing or comfort in response to his signals, or that his smile and gaze bring interesting and pleasurable social interaction with mother and other care-givers, then he experiences a sense of competence. Curiosity, explorative behavior, and learning are related to competence motivation. Subsequent experiences of having an effect on the social and physical environments, of influencing them to meet one's need and to stimulate one, can contribute to or stifle the sense of competence in childhood and adulthood. For Erikson, industry (competence) is the major task of the school child.[9] But the family, school, and community must provide the conditions that will maintain curiosity and exploration and be responsive to the individual needs of the child for successful learning experiences within his unique capacities, interests, and life-style.[10] Further, the outer world must provide the resources necessary for the school to be a place where teachers are free to teach and children are free to learn. Competence is actually a lifelong issue, with opportunities for successful action in the environment strengthening the sense of competence so that future action is also likely to be successful. People who have had little or no opportunities for taking successful action, who have been deprived of social respect and power, are caught too often in cycles of failure that dampen or obscure the motivation for competence.[11] Like adaptiveness, stress and coping, relatedness, identity/self-esteem, and competence are expressions of people-environment relationships. They therefore help the social worker focus on both person and environment while seeking to enhance these qualities.

The Environment: Layers and Textures

The environment consists of layers and textures—layers being the social and physical environment, while textures are time and space. The social environment is the human environment of other people at many levels of relationships, ranging from social networks to social institutions. The physical environment is comprised of the built world constructed by human beings and the natural world inherited by human beings. The social and physical environments interact in complex ways, each shaping the other, influencing and influenced by culture.

The scientific and technological development (culture) of oral contraception, for example, influenced social behavior in the realm of sexuality by changing the norms for that behavior. It contributed to changes in the traditional roles of men and women and to the emergence of new family forms, and created new social structures within the health care system. These effects, in turn, have had a profound and unanticipated influence in other realms of life. Similarly, cultural values and social forces influence the construction, location, and design of public mental hospitals, housing projects, and welfare offices, which then have an impact on the self-image and sense of identity of those dependent upon their services, shaping the nature of their social intervention. One need only view the exterior and interior differences between a welfare office and a private family agency, between a ghetto school and a suburban school, or between a state hospital and a private psychiatric facility to see the interdependence of culture, the social environment, and the physical environment; and their cumulative impact upon people's daily lives and self-perceptions.

Bureaucratic organizations, a salient feature of the social environment, are established in response to a social need after being brought to public attention by social reformers of vision and zeal. In order to carry out its social assignment, an organization evolves certain structures (that is, chains of command, divisions of labor, policies, and procedures) that are essential to the provision of services.[12] But although they are essential, these same structures create numerous tensions and obstacles for professionals and clients.

Organizations, for example, require divisions of labor that allocate and specify work roles and tasks that purport to make services more effective. The organization must also develop procedures for maintaining accountability, integrating complex job requirements, distinguishing among specialized role tasks and skills, and minimizing duplication. Although the need for division of labor is widely accepted as a sine qua non, it also creates strain, red tape, and organizational nonsense. Differential role assignments may lead to preoccupation with particular roles and functions without regard to the total enterprise. One's turf takes on increasing personal importance; protecting that turf becomes a major concern. A consequence of this "protectionism" is that client needs are held hostage to turf interests. Organizational needs and professional interests may displace the original goals so that services and people's needs for services become secondary concerns. Hospital procedures, for example, may serve the convenience of the medical or nursing staff rather than the comfort and dignity of the patient. Long waiting lists or the lack of evening hours in a social work agency may serve the professional and personal preferences of staff, rather than the needs or life-styles of potential clients.

In addition, the organization's responsibility for services does not always prevent staff from defining some groups as "unmotivated" and "resistant." These service barriers function to maintain a pool of potential clients who are able to wait, whose lives are not in crisis, or whose employment and child care provisions create an implicit, reliable standard for the "preferred" client. The "unpreferred" becomes "inaccessible" and "resistant." Such labels are self-fulfilling diagnoses and provide a rationale for administrators and professionals for evading external and internal examination of organizational and professional failures. Thus it is that hospitals sometimes make people sicker, welfare organizations sometimes create generational cycles of poverty, schools may fail to teach children how to learn, and social agencies may fail to respond appropriately to human need. The social worker's concern with the nature of person-environment fit requires continuing attention to the impact of agency policies and procedures on those being served. Where it is negative, the social worker's responsibility involves efforts to influence change through internal advocacy and/or program innovation.[13]

Social networks, as salient features of the social environment, represent systems of relationships in which the linkages between and among members are influential in behavior.[14] Networks may be natural, occurring within the life space of the person or family or community as a result of real-life relationships and interests, and so, they may be composed of kin, friends, neighbors, workmates, and others.[15] Related to the concept of networks are the concepts of natural helpers—to whom others in the ecological context turn for help, guidance, and support—and self-help groups.[16] Natural helpers may be found in neighborhoods or in certain occupations or in certain statuses in ethnic groups (e.g., Puerto Rican spiritualists). Self-help groups may form out of a shared problem, need, or goal, with or without the assistance of a professional.

In general, social networks serve instrumental and affective functions. They are mutual aid systems for the exchange of resources, the provision of information, and the teaching of coping skills.[17] Affectively, they can provide emotional sustenance, contribute to self-esteem and feelings of worth, and provide experience in mutual caring. Social networks, when they fulfill these functions, may be described as nutritive environments for the nourishment of identity, self-direction, competence, and human relatedness. However, some networks may be nonnutritive, such as some adolescent peer networks, particularly within the drug culture, and an occasional kin, neighbor, or workmate network. They may undermine self-esteem, withhold resources, demand unreasoned conformity, exploit one member or scapegoat another, exert unrealistic or nonsocial expectations, and interfere with members' growth and development. As an environmental instrument of great power, social networks are an important means available to client and social worker for the development of relatedness, competence, and self-esteem.[18]

The *physical environment* provides the context for all human interaction. Part of the adaptive achievements in the human attribute of relatedness includes attachments to treasured objects and to the sense of kinship with the world of nature. Trust is based upon security; security requires stable physical arrangements as well as social arrangements. Socialization is as much the personal pronoun—my toys, my room, my clothes, my furniture, my apartment, my playground—as it is my parents, my siblings, my friends. The sense of identity is tied not only to primary and other human relationships, but is also associated with a sense of place—a country, a region, a town—the place of one's origin. A move away from one's roots and from a place to which one is attached can be painful. The loss of one's home, or any treasured possessions, may also be stressful, for such objects often represent attachments that have become incorporated as part of one's identity.

Rene Dubos, a biologist, and Harold Searles, a psychiatrist, have each written eloquently of the need of human beings for a sense of kinship with nature, arising out of their evolutionary heritage.[19] The joy in pets, plants, and gardening and the pleasures of experiences in parks, countryside, and seashore attest to this kinship. Adults and children who are imprisoned in urban slum environments are deprived of natural resources for psychological well-being, spiritual refreshment, and an enriched sense of identity, competence, and relatedness. Searles takes the position that childhood is spent in differentiating oneself not only from the human environment, but from the "nonhuman" environment as well, and the rest of life is struggling to become reintegrated into both. To the degree that the individual succeeds in differentiation and reintegration, she develops increasingly meaningful relatedness with other human beings and with the natural world.[20] Thus the natural world provides the social worker with an additional dimension to strengthening people-environment relationships where it is appropriate.[21]

Texture of space and people's spatial behaviors are mediated by age, sex, culture, experience, and physical condition. Space and spatial behavior can be understood by examining the concepts of personal, semi-fixed, and fixed space. *Personal space* refers to the desired amount of social interaction and distance. Each person carries a portable, invisible boundary that serves as a protective zone. We actively maintain a "spatial bubble" around ourselves into which others cannot penetrate without creating a reaction. Since the boundary is invisible, one is often unaware of its existence until after intrusion. Some react with subtle physical gestures, others with more apparent withdrawal, and still others with aggressive responses.[22]

In human behavior, what is a comfortable distance has to be negotiated and established between people and mutually experienced as neither intrusive to privacy nor disengaged. If more distance is achieved than is desired, there is too much space between self and others, and the person experiences an unpleasant state of disengagement. If the distance achieved is less than what is desired so that one's need for space exceeds the supply, then the person experiences an unpleasant state of *crowding*.[23] Since the amount of desired space is influenced by culture, sex, age, physical, emotional, and cognitive states, it carries the potential for distorted communications and relationships. Schizophrenic patients have a large personal distance and often react with flight if approached too closely, even by eye contact. Violent prisoners have also been found to have large personal distances, and misperceive intrusion into personal space as hostile.[24] Aged persons, because of declining activity in sense perception, often have very small personal distances, seeking to maintain physical nearness to people and objects. Similarly, Arabs, Latins, Hispanics, and Mediterraneans prefer close contact, while English and some north Europeans are more comfortable with greater distance.[25] Like the other ecological concepts, personal space is, therefore, a transactional phenomenon open to distorted or conflicted interpersonal perceptions and patterns needing the attention of the social worker.

Semi-fixed space refers to movable objects and their arrangement in space. These objects—furniture items, curtains, decorative figurines, paintings, plants, color, light, carpeting, etc.—clarify spatial boundaries and provide spatial meanings and cues. In dwellings and offices, people use signs, screens, locks, fences, verbal and nonverbal communication, and even weapons to mark control over space. Such props and *territorial* behaviors serve the functions of protection, distance regulation, and clarification of role relationships. In family life, children must learn early which objects and spaces are open to them and which objects and spaces are accessible only to their parents. Closed doors, locked doors, and spaces designated as shared or private are used to regulate interaction in family life.[26] Territorial behaviors are also observed in institutional life as newcomers seek to establish a niche, and others cling to "their" chairs.[27]

The actual physical space available, how it is designed, and the ways in which objects are arranged within it affect interpersonal interaction. Chairs placed side by side along walls of a common room in an institutional setting, for example, discourage interaction, whereas seating arrangements around small tables encourage interaction. Similarly, side-by-side seating arrangements at a table were found to be least conducive to social interaction, while right-angle, corner positions were associated with a high degree of interaction.[28] One of us working with a female adolescent group assumed that chairs arranged in a circle would create an intimate atmosphere and facilitate interaction. The adolescents, however, experienced self-consciousness about what to do with their hands and legs (protruding from their miniskirts). The small circle demanded too much physical and emotional intimacy with a professional stranger.

The actual physical space in relation to the number of people using it, *density,* also has a powerful impact upon people's daily lives. In institutional settings, a strong mandate for supervision and surveillance often results in a concentrated use of limited portion of available space (high density). A dependence upon routine and unchanging spatial arrangements limits residents' opportunities for privacy and spatial identity. In families where a large number of people share a limited amount of space, the degree of interpersonal coordination required is often stressful. The high density limits available space for physical movement, places demands for behavioral coordination, and increases the number of people with whom coordination is necessary. The close proximity, social overload, and spatial constraints create interpersonal vulnerability. Sharing a television, a dresser, a bathroom demands ongoing coordination and serves as a potential source for interpersonal conflict. Beyond task coordination, people living in high-density situations also confront difficulties in acquiring satisfactory levels of *privacy.* Every person needs some time to be alone with one's thoughts and feelings and to be safe from unwanted intrusion. Personal autonomy is dependent upon privacy: without privacy there can be no individuality. For an adolescent, for example, this represents a critical developmental need: the opportunity to be free from observation. Physical and emotional health depend upon periods of privacy for purposes of emotional release—the space to escape and be relieved from one's public and familial roles—a time just to be oneself. In highly dense situations, forms of privacy are difficult to achieve.

Fixed space refers to immovable objects and their arrangement in space. These objects' size, shape, location, and arrangement have a profound impact upon the quality of life. Tenants living in high rise public housing, for example, experienced their space as undefensible and unpredictable. With limited control over such public areas as hallways, lobbies, and elevators, these spaces represented dangerous threats to survival. Tenants perceptions were associated with feelings of withdrawal, alienation, and dissatisfaction. Similarly, students living in high-density college dorms were found to be more withdrawn, less friendly, less cooperative, and less socially responsible. These environmental forces have a powerful impact upon people's lives, creating a sense of functional apathy and learned helplessness.[29] These aspects of physical and social space may require social work intervention and enhance the person-environment fit.

The Life Model Approach to Practice

For the Life Model, the ecological perspective represents a philosophical conception of human beings as active, purposeful, and having potential for growth, development, and learning throughout life. It offers a view of human beings in constant exchange with their environments, each acting and reacting on and to the other through continuous adaptations. The Life Model proposes a framework for understanding and helping people with these complex transactions. People's needs and problems are viewed as outcomes of stressful person-environment relationships. Intervention is directed to changing those relationships so that people's potentialities for growth, health, and adaptive social functioning are released and environments are made more responsive to their needs, rights, goals, and capacities.

Problems in Living

In person-environment transactions, disturbances often occur between individual needs and capacities, and environmental demands and qualities. These transactional disturbances create problems in living generated by stress arising from three areas of the life space: life transitions; environmental pressures; and maladaptive interpersonal processes.

LIFE TRANSITIONS. Life transitions include developmental changes across the life span, changes in status that present new or conflicting role demands, and crisis events—all with reciprocal tasks for the individual, family, group or community, and the environment. Erikson, for example, suggests that the life cycle can be viewed as a series of stages marked by a biologically based push toward growth and development.[30] This maturational impetus interacts with expectations and requirements exerted by the society and the culture. The interaction results in phase-specific tasks for the developing individual, and reciprocal tasks for the social and physical environments according to the given culture and historical era. The successful resolution of these reciprocal tasks depends, in part, on what the individual brings to them by virtue of his physical, mental, emotional, and social capacities as these emerged from earlier task resolutions. It also depends, in part, on the qualities of the social and physical environments. When all goes well, innate adaptive potentialities such as cognition, sensory perception, motor abilities, and language structures are released, acquired adaptive capacities are developed through learning and other exchanges with the environment, and societal benefits accrue.

Families, as families, also go through developmental stages with associated adaptive tasks that may or may not mesh with the developmental tasks of the individual members. Family stages refer to the changes in family life that occur as the composition of the family, the ages of its members, and the nature of its interactions with its environment change over time and space.[31] The family faces different sets of adaptive tasks related to internal and external demands at each stage. Groups also go through developmental stages with associated tasks, although of a somewhat different character from those of individuals and families.[32] An "ostomy" group, for example, must not only deal with common life tasks connected to the disability, its members must also resolve group tasks as they proceed through stages of approach and avoidance, power and control, intimacy, differentiation, and separation. Should they be unable to handle a stage and its tasks successfully, they may not be able to achieve a mutual support system through which they help one another cope with shared concerns about their physical condition, social relationships, self-image, etc.

Various changes in status occur across the life cycle, resulting in new and sometimes conflicting role demands. These life transitions may or may not coincide with developmental stages. Occasionally they may even upset or distort a developmental stage, as in teenage motherhood. Certain statuses in our society carry particularly difficult role demands, including the statuses of mental patient, foster child, and AFDC mother.

As a life transition, crisis differs from other kinds of stress in its suddenness, its time-limited character, and the enormity of its impact on the individual, family, or group. Natural disasters, bereavement and other losses, grave illness, or injury are among the expectable and unexpectable events in life that are experienced by most people as crises. Their successful resolution often leads to growth, while unsuccessful resolution may lead to prolonged stress and maladaptive functioning. Like other life transitions, crisis states pose adaptive tasks for both person(s) and environment. For many different reasons, all life transitions can be stressful, and people seek help with them or are referred for help.

ENVIRONMENTAL PRESSURES. While the environment can support or interfere with life transitions, it can itself be a significant source of troubles and distress. For some, organizational and social network resources are available, but they are unable to use them. For others, the organizational and network structures and functions are unresponsive to their styles and needs. And for still others, essential organizational and network resources are unavailable and their essential needs remain unmet. Similarly, people may experience problems in dealing with their physical environment. In highly dense living situations, for example, task coordination and privacy are difficult to achieve. In these situations, people experience a "social overload" and the unpleasant state of crowding.

MALADAPTIVE INTERPERSONAL PROCESSES. In adapting and coping with life transitional and environmental issues, families and groups are powerful mediating forces. They may, however, encounter obstacles created by their own patterns of communication and relationships. Such maladaptive patterns generate tensions in the system, hinder the mutual-aid processes, and are expressed in such behaviors as withdrawal, dysfunctional alliance, and scapegoating.[33] While maladaptive for most members, such behaviors serve the latent good of maintaining the collectivity's functioning or even, perhaps, its continued existence. Thus, scapegoating may stave off disorganization in the family or group while promoting it in the scapegoated member. After a while these patterns become fixed and potential change resisted. At the same time, the status quo makes all members vulnerable. Similar maladaptive patterns can arise between worker and clients in the form of inappropriate perceptions, expectations, and responses.[34]

Social Work Purpose, Function, and Roles

Helping people with problems in living provides social work with a clear and distinctive social purpose, namely, to improve the transactions between people and their environments and to facilitate a better match—that is, a "goodness-of-fit"—between human needs and environmental resources. This conception of professional practice includes: helping people who are struggling with life stress, and designing services and environmental resources to promote growth, health, and adaptive functioning, preventing breakdown.

Life transitions are highly amenable to social work interventions. Helping individuals, families, and groups meet the particular life tasks associated with developmental stages, status changes, and crisis events includes preventive services as well as clinical interventions. Professional purpose is operationalized by the conception of professional roles: enabler, teacher, and facilitator. In the role of enabler, the social workers carry out the tasks of mobilizing or strengthening motivation to deal with the stress of life transitions and helping to manage the disabling feelings and maintain self-esteem. In the role of teacher, the social worker teaches or guides the problem-solving aspects of coping. In the role of facilitator, the social worker encourages people to make decisions and take action in their own behalf.

Some roles also require work with the environment. Here the purpose is to help people use available organizational and network resources and to influence these environmental forces to be responsive.

STRENGTHENING THE FIT BETWEEN PEOPLE AND THEIR ENVIRONMENTS PROVIDES SOCIAL WORK WITH A CORE FUNCTION. When organizational and network resources are available, but clients are unable or unwilling to use them, the previously discussed roles of facilitator, teacher, and enabler are utilized. An elderly client, for example, refused to apply for much-needed food stamps. In this situation the worker explored the reluctance to seek and use an available resource. To help this elderly man with his struggle to retain dignity, the worker explored the concerns, reached for ambivalence, provided hope, etc. A simple referral would have represented a paper service rather than an effective intervention.

In other instances, however, the problem is not located in the person's inability to use available resources. Five roles are particularly relevant in helping with environmental difficulties: coordinator, mediator, advocate, organizer, and innovator. In the role of coordinator, the worker links the client to available resources. When the problem lies in distorted transactions, the worker assumes the role of mediator to help the client and the organization and social network to connect with each other in a more effective manner. If the mediating efforts fail, the worker may assume the role of advocate to bring about a more effective person-environment fit. In the role of organizer, the social worker mobilizes informal networks, self-help or task groups to combat social and emotional isolation. In the role of innovator, the worker may need to work toward filling gaps in services, programs, and resources.

Helping families and groups deal with maladaptive relational and communication processes is a critical arena for preventive and restorative interventions. A family experiencing the birth of a handicapped infant is vulnerable to overwhelming stress in all areas of the life span. This life event may generate parental tensions, parent-sibling tensions, sibling tensions, family and extended family tensions, and, in general, create severe disruption in family life. It may also have a negative impact on the life transitions of all members and on such environmental processes as work, school, and the like so that the stress spreads to all areas of the life span. To help this family, the worker might connect the members to a parent education group, a support group, or a problem-solving group. The worker also might help family members to communicate more openly, to work on their common concerns, and to challenge interpersonal obstacles. To this end, the worker draws on the skills of the roles previously described. The worker also calls on the mediator role to focus on the family's maladaptive communication patterns.

Client and Worker Roles

Contracting with respect to problem definition, objectives, planning, and action sustains mutuality in the relationship. It also engages the client's decision-making and cognition, enhancing the sense of self-direction, self-esteem, and competence. Here we must give attention to the ways in which people take on the client role.[35] It is usually at the point where stress becomes problematic or unmanageable that people are propelled into social work service—either out of their own quest for help in managing the stress or out of concern by persons or organizations in their environment for or in reaction to the person's need, problem, or behavior. Another group of potential social work clients are those to whom the agency proffers a service that these clients may either accept or decline. Such offers are often made by social workers in hospitals, housing projects, or whenever a social work department or agency seeks to reach out to people in at-risk situations or to persons viewed as in need even though they may not themselves recognize the need or the agency as a source of help.

Engaging clients in a relationship and in contracting is a very different process across these groups.[36] With the person who defines her needs and objectives, the worker's responsibility is to find the common ground where client definition and professional definition and agency definition meet. With clients for whom services are mandated and who often disclaim the need for help, the worker must locate areas of personal discomfort that may or may not coincide with the definition of the referrer. The initial responses of such clients are usually defined as resistance and lack of motivation. But with patience, empathy, and skill the worker may find what it is the client would like to see changed, usually located in the environment. By conveying realistic hope that together they can change it, the worker may succeed in engaging the client in a relationship and in the contracting process.

In proffering a service, the worker's task is to establish an ethical balance between persistence and respect for a person's right to refuse a service. There are value dilemmas and knowledge issues involved, particularly as the profession seeks to move toward primary prevention programs, but discussion of them is beyond the scope of this chapter.[37]

Mutuality and authenticity characterize the relationship of worker and client to promote the client's competence and reduce social distance and power differentials. The worker is responsible, however, for protecting the vulnerability of the person being helped, and for assuring that the client's needs (and not the worker's needs) are the basis of their work together. What is being described is not an egalitarian relationship, although ideally characterized by openness and mutuality. The worker brings professional knowledge and skill to the encounter, while the client brings experiential knowledge of his situation or predicament and what might be helpful, and his own skills and capacities. The two sets of knowledge and skill are of differing orders. Eliot Studt has suggested that the client has primary responsibility for work toward his goals, while the worker has secondary responsibility for providing the conditions that will help assure the success of the client's work on his goals and tasks.[38]

The Helping Process

In the Life Model approach, activity is conceived as taking place in the initial phase of engagement, exploration, and contracting; the ongoing phase; and the ending phase of termination, which also includes evaluation in order to understand what was helpful and not helpful, and why.[39] As in any systematic approach to practice, intervention in the Life Model is continually guided by assessment of the interplay of dynamic forces within the life space, including the influence of the agency as a presence in the client's ecological context. Together, worker and client seek to understand the meaning and impact of the pertinent forces on the person and the problem/need in order to set objectives and to devise action that will engage positive forces in the person and in the environment, remove environmental obstacles, and change negative transactions. Assessment, as a habit of mind throughout the contact, focuses on the manifest and latent functions of what is going on rather than searching for linear chains of cause and effect.

The problems in living formulation, which covers the almost limitless variety of human needs and plights, provides a schema for designing services to promote adaptive functioning and preventing breakdown. It is also an assessment tool that lends greater focus and direction to clinical interventions. To illustrate the latter intent, a worker was assigned to a young couple who recently gave birth to a handicapped infant. In the fourth session, the parents were agitated and complained about their sense of isolation. At this particular moment: Were they asking for help with the life transition, that is, with exploring their grief and helping them through their mourning states? Or were they at this particular moment asking for help with their sense of environmental isolation and loneliness, that is, with getting more effectively connected to their natural support systems or requesting construction of new ones? Or, were they at this particular moment indirectly complaining that the worker was being unhelpful and requesting attention to their interpersonal issues, that is, in dealing with their struggles about each spouse's availability to the other or the worker's competence? Over time, after each session and at each moment, the worker has to consider when clients are asking for help with life transitional, environmental, and/or interpersonal issues.

In the area of techniques or helping procedures, the Life Model is not prescriptive since most practice skills are common to most models. What may be different are the ends toward which the procedures are directed, as well as the areas of the ecological context where action takes place. By education and experience, social workers are highly skilled in helping people deal with life stress. In their services to individuals, groups, and families, social workers help build self-esteem and strengthen defenses against disabling anxiety and depression so that coping can proceed, while gradually encouraging the more accurate perception of reality so that coping can continue. Social workers mobilize and support motivation through skilled use of incentives, rewards, and the balancing of hope and discomfort.[40] They provide needed information and teach problem-solving skills on which cognitive mastery of the stress often depends. They mobilize and strengthen social supports through the client's real-life relationships and her linkages to social networks. If the client is without a network, she and the worker may consider joining an existing, or establishing a new, self-help group. Role rehearsal, games, puzzles, and simulations such as family sculpting, genograms, and ecomaps are often used for cognitive, perceptual, and emotional mastery of what might otherwise be a hopelessly chaotic situation.[41]

Help directed to the person is coupled with providing opportunities for action and mastery in the life space, through the use of tasks, "homework," and action that the client herself can take in her own life space.[42] Action by client and worker can be directed to the physical environment, in reorganizing the use of space and time and in providing options for interactions and privacy in family life or in institutional life. It may involve the provision of more or less sensory stimuli, or of opportunities for exploration of the urban or natural environment or the care of a pet or a plant. Introducing such environmental props as calendars, clocks, signs, and labels can strengthen the orientation to space and time among institutional residents.

Action directed toward increasing the responsiveness of an organization, especially one's own agency, requires the use of practice skills that are different from but supplement those utilized with the users of the service. It hinges on the differences between helping and influencing, and requires skills of a political nature.[43] These include the use of knowledge and skill in locating organizational barriers to service, identifying the forces likely to support or to resist change in policy or procedure, developing bases of support and devising means for neutralizing opposition in both the formal and informal systems. Knowledge and skill are required, also, for analyzing the power and decision-making structures and devising strategies for introducing, implementing, and institutionalizing the proposed change.[44]

Professional Influence

Many social workers are skilled in individual case advocacy, with their own or another agency; securing entitlements for a particular individual, family, or group; or obtaining an exception to a policy or procedure. This very important activity must continue, of course, but an additional responsibility is suggested by the dual focus on person and environment, in the Life Model approach. This is the responsibility to maintain vigilance regarding the impact of agency policies, personnel, and practices on all those whom the organization serves or is expected to serve; and, where needed, to take well-planned, knowledgeable, and skilled action in feasible efforts to influence the organization to change those structures and practices that have an adverse effect or fail to meet a need.

The practitioner who is highly regarded for her competence, knowledge, and practice skill is in a position to propose needed innovations in services and programs, such as introducing group services to replace long waiting lists, proposing arrangements for helping people before stress arises or becomes problematic, developing team models of service, or assisting in designing organizational roles for service users, perhaps even as team members. If clients are to achieve a strengthened sense of relatedness, self-esteem, identity, and competence they must be regarded as users of services who have the right to participate in shaping the services that shape their own destinies. If services are to be more responsive to needs and life-styles, basic research is needed in such environmental areas as social networks, impact of physical environments on adaptation, coping styles of various population groups, and differential responses to particular kinds of stress.[45] There are also gaps in our knowledge about the connections between interventions and outcomes—of what works when, with whom, and in what situations, with what kinds of needs, and under what kinds of organizational arrangements.

In any field of social work practice, the ecological perspective suggests that the social worker's professional competence must go beyond the level of technical knowledge and skill in the service context. It must also encompass a breadth of knowledge about the interacting forces impinging on that field of practice, including fiscal and political forces, demographic trends, issues of social policy, changing needs, research findings and technological developments, and changing cultural values, all of which affect the nature of practice in that field. Obviously, the demands of ecologically oriented practice require not only a high level of professional competence, but a strong sense of professional identity and self-direction as well. Such practice also requires an agency that is willing to commit its resources to meeting client need according to how and where it is experienced, and to grant its staff the degree of professional autonomy needed to carry out the commitment. Social workers will then be professionally accountable not only to the agency and its funding sources, but also to the users of its services. While all of this may sound like a large order, it may also represent the minima by which the social work practitioner may become a proactive force in social change. It may also distinguish the graduate social worker from other practitioner levels.

Practice Illustration

Mrs. Smith (white) was referred to the family agency after she called a hotline because Jane and Linda, aged fifteen and thirteen, had stopped going to school. The agency's clientele is comprised of low-income families who face a variety of predicaments. Because Mrs. Smith was unable to come into the office, home visits were arranged. In the initial contact, the worker was struck by the physical appearance of the small apartment, which reflected a sense of isolation. Even the curtains were drawn shut as though the family felt itself under siege.

In this and subsequent sessions, the worker learned that Mrs. Smith blamed the children's school problems on her husband's drinking. She said Mr. Smith had been an alcoholic, in and out of treatment programs for years. He was a poor provider, and Mrs. Smith had recently asked him to leave because his drinking was disrupting the family. He continued to visit daily, which was all right with Mrs. Smith. About a month after service began, Mr. Smith was hospitalized with a serious ulcer condition, and this was a crisis for the family.

In addition to Jane and Linda, there was a son, Tim, age sixteen, who had not attended school in two years and was heavily involved with drugs. Jane told the worker she had stopped going to school because the kids teased her about an abortion she had had. Linda said she quit too because she wanted nothing to do with high school kids, lipstick, smoking, drinking, and boys, and she criticized Jane for her interest in these things.

Mrs. Smith said the family was supported by public assistance. She does all the household chores by herself, she has no relatives or friends, and has had no skills training. She explained there was no household routine because no one had to be anywhere at any particular time. Family members did not retire or arise at the same time. They did not eat meals together or share activities, except for constant quarreling over T.V. programs. The T.V. set was the focal point in the family and was apparently the major contact with the outside world. On the one hand, the family's use of time served to keep them apart. Yet on the other, their space was so cramped that when they did interact it was almost always in very angry ways, as though to maintain some sense of spatial distance or separateness. Helpless and hopeless feelings seemed to pervade the family, and they were especially marked in Mrs. Smith.

The family's lack of connectedness with environmental institutions such as school, the world of work, and supportive social networks, plus their poor housing, insufficient income, and the devalued statuses related to welfare, alcoholism, and drugs had made family and individual life tasks exceedingly difficult. Clearly, the problems and needs in living experienced by the Smiths went far beyond the school problems of Jane and Linda.

Based on her assessment, the worker offered extensive outreach including home visits, telephone contacts, transportation, and help with environmental pressures and inadequacies. Once some of the environmentally induced stress was relieved, it became possible to engage the family in weekly family sessions on interpersonal discomforts identified by the family, individual sessions with the girls on the mutually defined goal of returning to school, and help to the family in negotiating welfare, health, and school systems on a more sustained basis. It was not possible to engage Tim, although he did attend some family sessions.

ENVIRONMENTAL STRESS AND INTERVENTION. As might be expected, massive intervention in the environment was required from the outset with the whole family as well as in individual sessions. The severe winter presented a series of emergencies, and the worker used her skill as advocate and her professional contacts to help Mrs. Smith contest fuel bills and to secure special oil allowances and other entitlements for the family. Increasingly, Mrs. Smith was able to do some of this by herself, especially with arranging for better housing. Work was also done with the school in order to stave off legal action and its threat of foster placement for Jane and Linda. This included a tutoring program to capitalize on their own concern about falling behind, and helping them negotiate "individualized" programs to help ease the transition back to school. The worker also helped to expand the girls' social world. She took them on museum and library visits and shopping trips, and to recreational facilities, attempting to fit some of the activities to the girls' fantasies about wanting to act, travel, and do things they had never done before.

STRESSES IN LIFE TRANSITIONS AND INTERVENTIONS. In the individual sessions with the girls, the worker purposefully used herself as a role model. They had no alternative models in addition to their mother, and the worker made use of every life space event that occurred to aid in the process of identity formation. Jeering comments by boys on the street, an unpleasant gynecological examination experienced by Jane, and some episodes from family sessions were used to help the girls move toward greater acceptance of their approaching womanhood, more positive attitudes toward ethnic groups different from their own, more tolerance of their mother's passivity and of their own need to be both dependent and independent. These efforts were successful with Jane but less so with Linda, not only because of Linda's age, but because she was quite fragile, untrusting, negativistic, and unhappy. The worker supported Jane's attempts to achieve appropriate autonomy and distance from her mother. At the same time, family sessions were used to support Mrs. Smith's parental role and to help her see that Jane's need to grow up was not a rejection of herself.

INTERPERSONAL STRESSES AND INTERVENTION. The family sessions were directed to various issues, including individual differences, weekly reports on respective worker and client tasks in getting members moving again, and working on communication and relationship patterns. In one early session, for example, the worker helped Mr. and Mrs. Smith see their roles as parents and what this meant for them individually and as partners as well as family members:

> I pointed out how Mrs. Smith was seen as the "good" parent because of her oversensitivity to the children's feeling (e.g., how hard it is to go back to school), and how Mr. Smith was seen as the "bad" parent because of his strong need for rules and discipline in the family. Mrs. Smith said she didn't see herself as trying to be the good parent, instead she saw herself as weak because she didn't discipline the children. She always felt sorry for them, having an alcoholic father. Mr. Smith said his wife cares too much about every little thing about her kids, which drives him crazy. As the tension rose between them, Jane, who had been mumbling under her breath, announced that she wanted to be somewhere else—a foster home. She hated this house—it was no fun. Her anger and unhappiness triggered a burst of tears from Mrs. Smith and many words of hopelessness and guilt. I commented on how alone Mr. and Mrs. Smith felt in their respective persons and roles within the family. They expressed anxiety about whether they were still a couple. They talked of how they hadn't lived as man and wife during many of Mr. Smith's drinking years, how the kids seemed to try to divide the parents, and how Mr. Smith felt he was in competition with them for his wife. They looked at options, whether to come back together or stay separated temporarily or permanently. When we ended, I said that Mrs. Smith had cried a lot that day and wondered, if she cried during the coming week, could Mr. Smith help her with whatever was bothering her? He thought he could do this.

Many family sessions centered on communication patterns. For example:

> There was some silence, and then Jane said she wished Tim were here today because he would talk and could speak for everyone. I commented that happens a lot in this family: people talk for other people, which makes it easy for people never to have to say how they feel because someone else will do it for them. The rest of the session dealt with how people can talk about problems and issues without falling apart, so that feelings can be dealt with and issues can get resolved.

Frequently there were recriminations and name calling, and the worker tried to move the family members away from blaming the T.V. for their fights to looking at the hurt and anger they felt for each other, especially from the name-calling.

Six months after service began, Mrs. Smith entered the hospital for some needed surgery, and Mr. Smith moved into the home to look after the family. For Mrs. Smith's return home a week later the worker, Jane, and Linda planned a special dinner that involved all the family members in its preparation. This was in line with the worker's aim to make use of natural life situations to the greatest extent possible. Although earlier efforts to engage the Smiths in family activities had not been successful, this plan worked. Mrs.

Smith's temporary inability to perform her usual chores seemed to provide the lever for real change.

> After her return, Mrs. Smith said that if it weren't for their conflict over the children, she and her husband could be happy together, especially since her husband had been on the wagon since his illness. They have now asked to be seen alone for marital counseling. A new phase of the work is about to begin.

SUMMARY. At the time of the initial contact, this family seemed to be on the verge of entropy as a result of lack of interchange with their environment and disorganized relations within. All members were suffering stress associated with life transitions, interpersonal discomforts, and a harsh environment. The familial tasks did not mesh well with individual tasks, partly because earlier developmental stages of the family had not been successfully handled, and partly because of a nonnutritive environment. Out of their early and current deprivations, neither parent had achieved a sense of identity as a worthwhile person, or a sense of competence arising from successful actions in the environment. They had little autonomy or self-regulation, as Mrs. Smith was essentially passive, allowing the events of life to wash over her. Mr. Smith, enslaved by his impulses, was even less able than his wife to assume control of his life and guide his family. Mr. Smith's years of alcoholism, while probably fulfilling functions for the marriage, and perhaps even for the family, had also contributed to Mrs. Smith's overinvestment in her children, and her inability to view their "growing up" and their struggles with separation as positive. Mutuality, respect, and caring within the family, and between the family and others, had never been established. Indeed, the family had had a "bad name" in the neighborhood, which caused them to isolate themselves and withdraw even more.

Family interpersonal stress and apparent inability to locate supports in school and with peers meant that all three children found it hard to achieve a sense of identity, to exert effects upon their environment that would contribute to their own growth, development, and learning. Thus they were unable to reach an age-appropriate balance between dependence and independence, and, above all, they lacked the nourishment of human relatedness inside and outside the family.

The worker, by conveying hope, respect, and concern for concrete needs, was able to reinstate competence and motivation. Self-esteem was partially restored in the parents through providing opportunities for successful action in the environment. All members were helped to reach toward some separateness and intimacy, toward some interdependence and reciprocity. The likely outcomes are still uncertain. Whether Jane and Linda can tolerate remaining in school and whether Mrs. Smith can tolerate their being there remains to be seen. Whether Mr. and Mrs. Smith can rebuild their marriage so their children will be free to move outward and whether Mr. Smith can abstain from alcohol and regain his health and his role as provider is not yet known. The worker herself points out, "The multiplicity of needs and problems, the myriad of possible intervention points, and the well-established patterns make for slow progress and frustration at times—for the Smiths and for me."

But a successful beginning has been made.

Notes

1. For a historical perspective, see Carel B. Germain, and Alex Gitterman, *The Life Model of Social Work Practice* (New York: Columbia University Press, 1980), pp. 343–368; Carel B. Germain, "Casework and Science: A Historical Encounter," in Robert W. Roberts and Robert H. Nee (eds.), *Theories of Social Casework* (Chicago: University of Chicago Press, 1970), pp. 3–32; William Schwartz, "Group Work and the Social Scene," in Alfred J. Kahn (ed.), *Issues in American Social Work* (New York: Columbia University Press, 1959).

2. See, for example, Bernard Bandler, "The Concept of Ego-Supportive Psychotherapy," in Howard Parad and Roger Miller (eds.), *Ego-Oriented Casework* (New York: Family Service Association of America, 1963), pp. 27–44. To the best of our knowledge, the first use of the concept of a life model appeared in Dr. Bandler's article. See also Genevieve Oxley, "A Life-Model Approach to Change," *Social Casework*, Vol. 52 (1971), pp. 627–633; Herbert S. Strean, "Application of the 'Life Model' to Casework," *Social Work*, Vol. 17 (1972), pp. 46–53; Carel B. Germain and Alex Gitterman, op. cit.; Carel B. Germain, *Social Work Practice in Health Care* (New York: Free Press, 1984); Alex Gitterman and Carel B. Germain, "Social Work Practice: A Life Model," *Social Service Review*, Vol. 50 (1976), pp. 601–610. Alex Gitterman, "Uses of Resistance: A Transactional View," *Social Work*, Vol. 28 (1983), pp. 127–131; Judith A. B. Lee and Carol R. Swenson, "Theory in Action: A Community Social Service Agency," *Social Casework*, Vol. 59 (1978), pp. 359–370; K. J. Peterson, "Assessment in the Life Model: A Historical Perspective," *Social Casework*, Vol. 60 (1979), pp. 586–596; Lawrence Shulman and Alex Gitterman, "The Life Model, Mutual Aid and the Mediating Function," in Alex Gitterman and Lawrence Shulman (eds.), *Mutual Aid Groups and the Life Cycle* (Itasca, Ill.: Peacock Press, 1985).

3. R. S. Lazarus and R. Launier, "Stress-Related Transactions Between Person and Environment," in L. A. Pervin and M. Lewis (eds.), *Perspectives in Interactional Psychology* (New York: Plenum Press, 1978), pp. 287–327.

4. David Mechanic, "Social Structure and Personal Adaptation: Some Neglected Dimensions," in George V. Coelho, David A. Hamburg, and John E. Adams (eds.), *Coping and Adaptation* (New York: Basic Books, 1974), pp. 32–44.

5. See, for example, Otto Will, "Human Relatedness and the Schizophrenic Reaction," *Psychiatry*, Vol. 22, No. 3 (1959).

6. This is a useful distinction made by Robert Weiss in *Loneliness, The Experience of Emotional and Social Isolation* (Cambridge, Mass.: MIT Press, 1973).

7. Erik Erikson, "Growth and Crises of the Healthy Personality," in Erik Erikson

(ed.), "Identity and the Life Cycle," *Psychological Issues*, Vol. 1, No. 1 (1959), pp. 50–100.

8. Robert White, "Strategies of Adaptation: An Attempt at Systematic Description" in Coelho, et al., op. cit., pp. 47–68; Robert White, "Motivation Reconsidered: The Concept of Competence," *Psychological Review*, Vol. 66 (1959), pp. 297–333.

9. Erik Erikson, op. cit.

10. For discussion and illustration of social work intervention in these fields of forces, see Alex Gitterman, "Social Work in the Public Schools," *Social Casework*, Vol. 58 (1977), pp. 111–118; Alex Gitterman, "Group Work in the Public Schools," in William Schwartz and S. Zalba (eds.), *The Practice of Group Work* (New York: Columbia University Press, 1971), pp. 45–72.

11. M. Brewster Smith, "Competency and Socialization," in John A. Clausen (ed.), *Socialization and Society* (Boston: Little, Brown, 1968), pp. 270–320.

12. Porter Lee, "Social Work Cause and Function," *Proceedings*, National Conference Social Welfare, 1929, pp. 3–20.

13. Germain and Gitterman, op. cit., pp. 155–173.

14. Carol Swenson, "Social Networks, Mutual Aid, and the Life Model of Practice," in Carel B. Germain (ed.), *Social Work Practice: People and Environments* (New York: Columbia University Press, 1979), pp. 213–238.

15. Eugene Litwak and Ivan Szelenyi identify differential functions for these groups; see their "Primary Group Structures and Their Functions: Kin, Neighbors, and Friends," *American Sociological Review*, Vol. 34 (1969), pp. 465–481.

16. See, for example, Alfred H. Katz and Eugene I. Bender, *The Strength Within Us: Self-Help Groups in the Modern World* (New York: New Viewpoints, A Division of Franklin Watts, 1976); Alice H. Collins and Diane L. Pancoast, *Natural Helping Networks* (Washington, D.C.: National Association of Social Workers, 1976).

17. For one such example, see Carol B. Stack, *All Our Kin: Strategies for Survival in a Black Community* (New York: Harper Colophon Books, 1974).

18. Germain and Gitterman, op. cit., pp. 174–183.

19. Rene Dubos, *A God Within* (New York: Scribner's, 1972); Harold F. Searles, *The Nonhuman Environment* (New York: International Universities Press, 1960).

20. Searles, ibid., p. 30.

21. Germain and Gitterman, op. cit., pp. 183–196.

22. These ideas have been developed by Edward T. Hall; see his *The Hidden Dimension* (New York: Doubleday, 1966).

23. A social-psychological framework for understanding people's spatial behaviors, organized around concepts of privacy, personal distance, territoriality, and crowding have been developed by Irwin Altman; see *The Environment and Social Behavior* (Monterey, Calif.: Brooks/Cole Publishing Co., 1975).

24. Augustus Kinzel, "Body-Buffer Zone in Violent Prisoners," *American Journal of Psychiatry*, Vol. 127 (1970), pp. 59–64; A. Hildreth, "Body-Buffer Zone and Violence: Reassessment and Confirmation," *American Journal of Psychiatry*, Vol. 127 (1971), pp. 1641–1645.

25. Hall, op. cit.

26. David Kantor and William Lehr, *Inside the Family* (San Francisco: Jossey-Bass, 1975).

27. For studies of territorial relations among disturbed boys, see Aristide H. Esser, "Cottage Fourteen: Dominance and Territoriality in a Group of Institutionalized Boys," *Small Group Behavior*, Vol. 4 (1973), pp. 131–146.

28. Robert Sommer, *Personal Space* (Englewood Cliffs, N.J.: Prentice-Hall, 1969).

29. Oscar Newman, *Defensible Space* (New York: Collier Books, 1973).

30. Erikson, op. cit.

31. See, for example, Sonya Rhodes, "A Developmental Approach to the Life Cycle of the Family," *Social Casework*, Vol. 58 (1977), pp. 301–311.

32. James A. Garland, Hubert E. Jones, and Ralph L. Kolodny, "A Model for Stages of Development in Social Work Groups," in Saul Bernstein (ed.), *Explorations in Group Work* (Boston University School of Social Work, 1968), pp. 12–58; W. Bennis and H. Sheppard, "A Theory of Group Development," *Human Relations*, Vol. 9 (1956), pp. 415–537.

33. See, for example, Lynn Hoffman, "Breaking the Homeostatic Cycle," in Philip J. Guerin, Jr. (ed.), *Family Therapy, Theory and Practice* (New York: Gardner Press, 1975), pp. 501–519; Harry Aponte, "The Family-School Interview: An Eco-Structural Approach," *Family Process*, Vol. 15 (1976), pp. 303–312; and Lawrence Shulman, "Scapegoats, Group Workers, and Preemptive Intervention," *Social Work*, Vol. 12 (1967), pp. 37–43.

34. Gitterman, "Resistance: A Transactional View," op. cit.; Alex Gitterman and Alice Schaeffer, "The White Professional and the Black Client," *Social Casework*, Vol. 53 (1972), pp. 280–291.

35. Abraham Alcabes and James Jones, "Structural Determinants of Clienthood," *Social Work*, Vol. 52 (April 1971), pp. 223–233; Helen Harris Perlman, "Intake and Some Role Considerations," *Social Casework*, Vol. 41 (April 1960), pp. 171–176.

36. Anthony Maluccio and Wilma Marlow, "The Case for the Contract," *Social Work*, Vol. 19 (January 1974), pp. 28–36; Brett Seabury, "Uses and Abuses of Contract," *Social Work*, Vol. 21 (January 1976), pp. 16–26.

37. We are indebted to Professor Irving Miller for this distinction between imposed and proffered services.

38. Eliot Studt, "Social Work Theory and Implications for the Practice of Methods," *Social Work Education Reporter*, Vol. 16 (1968), pp. 22–24 and 42–46.

39. Germain and Gitterman, op. cit.

40. Lillian Ripple and Ernestina Alexander, *Motivation, Capacity and Opportunity* (Chicago: University of Chicago Press, 1964).

41. On the use of genograms, see Ann Hartman, "The Extended Family as a Resource for Change," in C. B. Germain (ed.), *Social Work Practice: People and Environments* (New York: Columbia University Press, 1979), pp. 239–266. On the use of network maps, see Carolyn Attneave, "Social Networks as the Unit of Intervention," in Guerin, op. cit., pp. 220–231. On the use of family sculpting, see Peggy Papp, "Family Choreography," in Guerin, op. cit., pp. 465–479; Frederick Duhl, Bunny Duhl, and David Kantor, "Learning, Space and Action in Family Therapy: A Primer of Sculpture," in Donald Bloch (ed.), *Techniques of Family*

Psychotherapy (New York: Grune and Stratton, 1974). On the use of puzzles and other activities, see Evelyn Lance, "Intensive Work with a Deprived Family," *Social Casework*, Vol. 50 (1969), pp. 454–460.

42. Anthony N. Maluccio, "Action as a Tool in Casework Practice," *Social Casework*, Vol. 55 (1974), pp. 30–35.

43. George Brager, "Helping vs. Influencing: Some Political Elements of Organizational Change." Paper presented at the National Conference on Social Welfare, San Francisco, May 1975 (mimeographed).

44. See, for example, George Brager and Stephen Holloway, *Changing Human Organizations: Politics and Practice* (New York: Free Press, 1978); Gitterman and Germain, *The Life Model of Social Work Practice*.

45. See Claudia J. Coulton, "Developing an Instrument to Measure Person-Environment Fit," *Journal of Social Service Research*, Vol. 3 (Winter 1979), pp. 159–173; Anthony Maluccio, *Learning from Clients: Interpersonal Helping as Viewed by Clients and Social Workers* (New York: Free Press, 1979); Shirley L. Patterson, "Matching Helping Roles Within the Characteristics of Older Natural Helpers," *Journal of Gerontological Social Work*, Vol. 5 (1983), pp. 55–66.

Annotated Listing of Key References

BRAGER, GEORGE, and STEPHEN HOLLOWAY. *Changing Human Organizations: Politics and Practice.* New York: Free Press, 1978.
The authors present the theory base and the specialized practice skills necessary for understanding how organizations work and for making them work better for clients. The book is particularly helpful for social workers at lower levels in the organization's hierarchy who may feel they lack the power to effect change.

COELHO, GEORGE V., DAVID A. HAMBURG, and JOHN E. ADAMS (eds.). *Coping and Adaptation.* New York: Basic Books, 1974.
Thirteen articles examine theoretical, practical, and research issues in coping and adaptation, with the emphasis on biological and social frames of reference. Each author is a highly regarded behavioral scientist.

DUBOS, RENE. *So Human an Animal.* New York: Scribner's, 1968.
Written by a microbiologist, who is also a humanist, this book presents an evolutionary perspective on human beings, and discusses the impact of modern physical and social environments on the development of human potentialities. The author suggests some components of the "good" environment.

GITTERMAN, ALEX, and CAREL B. GERMAIN. *The Life Model of Social Work Practice.* New York: Columbia University Press, 1980.
Designed as a textbook, this volume presents the theories, values, and practice skills incorporated within the Life Model. Illustrations are presented of services to families, groups, and individuals in which the worker focuses on the transactions between people and environments, in a dual effort to release adaptive potential and improve environments.

GORDON, WILLIAM E. "Basic Constructs for an Integrative and Generative Conception of Social Work," in Gordon Hearn (ed.), *The General Systems Approach: Contributions Toward an Holistic Conception of Social Work.* New York: Council on Social Work Education, 1969.
The author connects the two historical traditions of social work—a concern for people and a concern for environments that will promote the well-being of people—by drawing upon the constructs of general systems theory. The article represents the culmination of many years' effort to develop a working definition of practice, undertaken by the author and Harriett Bartlett on behalf of NASW.

MINUCHIN, SALVADOR. *Families and Family Therapy.* Cambridge, Mass.: Harvard University Press, 1974.
The literature on family therapy is prodigious, and the schools of thought diverse. We have found the writings of Minuchin and his colleagues, including the social workers Harry Aponte and Lynn Hoffman, congenial. Minuchin's ecostructural approach views the family as facing adaptive challenges in response to the stress of internal and external changes. He presents strategies for entering the family structure and influencing its internal and external relations.

CHAPTER 24

A Multitheory Perspective for Practice

Francis J. Turner

One of the most pressing questions that must emerge for the reader who has examined the rich range of perspectives presented thus far in this book is what do I as practitioner do with all of this material? How can I assimilate it in some useful way into my practice? A similar question arises for teachers and students from the viewpoint of teaching and learning.

One of the objectives of the first edition of this volume was to see if a comparison of the various systems along similar variables would begin to clarify the differential implications of each system for practice. Although some progress has been made in this direction, we still have far to go. The various systems are at different stages of development, and each addresses a somewhat different aspect of the human situation. Thus, comparison along similar variables by separate authors is extremely difficult, but it is evident that there is much more interest in doing so and more awareness of the potential of an interlocking perspective.

As was noted in the second edition, different as are the various theories one from the other, there are also similarities. Each attempts to address some aspect of the person-in-situation, that is considered essential in social work practice, and, importantly, there is much in common about the perspective of social work practice as it currently exists. A critical question that still remains unanswered is the one raised in the first chapter: What observable differences are there in the practice of persons based on a difference in theoretical perspective? That is, are there then twenty-two or more styles of practice reflecting the twenty-two or more thought systems currently identifiable?

Certainly there is much less fadism about new theories. We are more accepting of the fact that the possibility of major theoretical breakthroughs is remote. A great unifying theoretical panacea is not going to emerge. This reality has made us more cautious, humble, critical, and inquiring in our approach to theory building and utilization. More efforts are being made to examine theory and its relevance for practice. More people are involved in the process. The expanded bibliographies in the chapters are one indication of this. Some new perspectives of practice are resulting in the development of new theory as manifested in feminist theory, and some older existing theory is being applied to practice as with Marxist thinking. We are thus trying to make better use of what we have, as well as being ready to look at new ideas and perspectives.

We are much more comfortable with the prospect of being multitheoretical in our practice. There is an increasing awareness that each system need not stand alone but can be enriched by seeking and permitting areas of connection with other systems. This, either as cause or effect, has resulted in a diminution of intensity of some of our holy wars. We are more prepared to accept that each system does have something to offer and that it is possible to practice from a pluralistic theory base. Concomitant with these perceptual shifts is a growing perception, excitement, and appreciation of the need for stronger theory as a basis for practice. This is especially important as the pressure for evaluation of practice continues.

Related to these are two further themes: first, the awareness of the complexity of the task of developing and testing theory in an evaluative mode; second, an understanding of the possibility, desirability, and, indeed, necessity of developing a perspective to research that which is broader than the classical experimental design. Increased understanding of and sophistication with the single subject research has expanded our repertoire of techniques and helped us to become more specific about what we are doing (3, 9, 14), as well, the potential of phenomenological research is being better appreciated.

One of the inherent risks in pursuing the concept of interrelatedness and interlocking concepts is that similarities will be magnified and differences minimized. As we seek the implications of diversity it is just as important to see where and how a thought system differs from other systems as it is to see how it is similar. But in looking for differences we must be sure they are real. In the second edition the role of strawmen was discussed; that is, enduring themes that were used to underscore alleged differences between systems. There seems to be much less of this now. Increased acceptance of a pluralistic approach to practice seems to have lessened the need to create distorted perspectives of some aspects of some theories to strengthen the presumed importance of a particular theory.

Certainly one area of continuing interest where there are differences of emphasis between the systems is the importance of unconscious material in social work treatment. Even with the range of differences about the relative importance of the unconscious, there is recognition that the focus of treatment should be on the client and/or clients and their psychosocial situation and not exclusively on inner-functioning. This is not to say that a client's instinctual and inner life is ignored, but to recognize that this component is only one part of our reality—thus the necessity for understanding and assessing the current situation and all of its relevant aspects rather than focusing solely on a detailed understanding of the past. The latter is not excluded from our purview, only that it is not stressed as much as some critics have suggested.

There are some emerging themes that are influencing our perspective of necessary knowledge. One is the growing awareness of the effects of our biological reality on our functioning. Gestalt and its awareness of the way our body and its functioning can convey messages about our psychological status and Meditations' interest in body and mind connections have helped bring into clearer focus the importance of this material.

Throughout, there is an emphasis on the client's current reality: the inherent thrust to growth, health, and strength; ability to reason, to take responsibility, to change both self and situation, to adjust; to plan reflectively both our present and future life and to be accountable. This theme is not a naive one that holds a client can change all aspects of his reality, but one that is less pessimistic about the extent to which change can take place. Undoubtedly there are differences in the weighting of various components of reality and of the potential for change, but again there is more consensus than disagreement on the importance on the components of the significant environments and their intermixture.

There is some beginning awareness that technology is an emerging societal variable that we need to begin to incorporate into our theoretical perspective of practice. Clients are being influenced by technology in their day-to-day lives, and this influence, certainly not always negative, needs to be assessed. As well, we need to examine the extent to which technology can be used as a variable of intervention.

More attention is beginning to be paid to efforts to understand the extent to which the potential climate in which service is being provided influences the theoretical orientation of practitioners. In times of economic restraint and negative reaction to social programs are theories that hold clients more accountable than others, more prevalent than in other political periods? From a less cynical perspective it may be that some thought systems have more potential for clients in different political situations. This is an area where considerable careful thought is needed to help clarify the impact of this variable.

A further question about the effect of the societal climate in practice relates to accountability. The fact that the health and social services are under heavy pressure to demonstrate the effectiveness of their interventions is well known. One question that has not been considered is the extent to which this demand for accountability influences the types of theories that emerge or gain prevalence in practice. For example, an interesting question might be whether systems such as task-centered and behavioral will be more popular and have a higher profile because of their potential for being evaluated than systems more speculative in nature where the variables of intervention are less concrete.

The question of why some theories are more popular in some parts of the profession, and in some times in our history, is an interesting one. Why is it that some systems have become mainstream and others remain only on the fringe of practice? If we had data supporting the concept that this was related to specific utility, this question would not be important. Such data do not exist and it appears the critical variables have not yet been identified. This is an important question for it may well mean that we are failing to make the resources of theory available to some clients for extraneous reasons. Bill Rowe speculates on this from the perspective of Rogerian theory in his chapter.

Earlier it was mentioned that among these systems there is consensus that social work practice must continue to be what it always has been: a commitment to person-in-situation. In spite of this we continue to focus more attention on direct work with clients, rather than work in their significant environments. We are not ignoring the social reality of our clients, but we are still in a society where matters related to direct work with a person's psychological reality is more highly valued than work in the environment. It appears we are continuing to both underestimate the importance as well as the knowledge and skills required to work effectively in this "indirect work" to use Richmond's terminology. It is interesting that conceptually we have still not given this material the emphasis it demands; this to the detriment of our conceptual base and ultimately to our clients and communities. Clearly, psychosocial therapy, systems theory, task-centered, problem-solving, and ecological theory stress the importance of the clients external reality. No one theory in fact ignores it completely. But more still needs to be done.

Related to the focus on the interpersonal component of practice, among these chapters there is a continuing theme that emphasizes one-to-one intervention over work with groups and communities. Families appear to be in a somewhat different category; that is, we seem to take as given that regardless of theoretical orientation we can work with families and individuals but less so with groups. It is interesting to point out that although the book contains a chapter on family theory it does not yet have one on group theory.

But in the world of practice many clinicians do make use of a cluster of methodologies in their practice. It is hoped that these practitioners will report their perspectives of the advantages of this multimethod form of practice in the professional literature. We are not suggesting a unitary practice method, nor do we mean to imply that we are approaching a point where we will have a general theoretical system as a basis for practice. What is urged is the need to be open to influence from all responsible thought systems and the methods and techniques that flow from them so that, in time, individual practitioners will be comfortable with a multimethod, multitheory, multi-technique armamentarium.

In 1964, Charlotte Towle wrote, "Certainly a profession does not come of age until it develops its own theory" (23, p. vii). With the marked dissolution of professional boundaries and areas of responsibility that has taken place during the years that have passed since Towle wrote the above, the criticism of cross-fertilization is not as valid; nevertheless, the need for careful and conscious assimilation of material is still as important.

Although a tendency for enthusiasm about the content of each particular theory can be noted and fully understood, it is of particular importance also to note how each author has sought to consider the implications of his theory for practice. I think we are well beyond the point of easily adopting a body of thought in an unquestioning way, or applying it in the cliché-ridden style about which Dr. Towle warns us. Each author struggles with the strengths and limitations, the uses and gaps in her system. Most identify the process of search, the concept of incompleteness, the necessity of seeing the theory in transition rather than as a final word, and are far from the point where they could be seen as "theory imperialists."

Each author subscribes to the necessity of each individual practitioner having his own theoretical base, as well as the necessity of continued search for linkages between theories and new theories. There are suggestions about connections between theories and the utility of theories serving as bases on which other theories can be developed or integrated. There is general consensus on the function of theory and on the utility of theory in giving direction and understanding to responsible practice.

In evaluating these theoretical systems from the practitioner's perspective, a key question is one of utility. "What intervention, conducted by what therapist, with what client to resolve what psychosocial dysfunctions, produces what effects" (12, p. 434). We are far from being able to answer this question precisely. Few of our current theories give specific direction to the practitioner in particular instances; i.e., they are not practice theories in the precise use of that term, although some, such as behavior modification, task-centered, crisis theory, and, to some extent, Transactional Analysis do this. As our research becomes more specific and our precision more exact, we will make further progress.

Most of our systems at this point conceptualize practice at a middle-range level or beyond. Most are seen by their promoting authors as being in development. Some are seen to be derivatives from earlier theories and others' efforts to translate material from other fields into concepts relevant for our practice. Thus, cognitive theory is presented as a development from earlier functional thinking, and systems concepts have been brought to our profession from other disciplines. As the content of each chapter is considered, we can see how early differences between theories disappear and new differences emerge as progress is made; that is, the multiplicity of thought systems in social work practice is seen as an enriching phenomenon, given the present state of practice and the demands on it.

It isn't that the existence of a multifaceted conceptual base is a desirable thing any more than is the existence of a unitary base. What is important is that there exists a multiple-theory-based practice that is not isolated. Thus one of the exciting observations that can be made on examining the various chapters is the lack of isolation in each approach to practice. It is intriguing to see to what extent each writer indicated how her approach is compatible with, developed from, or influenced by other systems presented in this book. No one presented her theory in an exclusive approach independent of the others. Most indicated the areas where their approach was compatible or identified linkages between other theories. Both the chapter on functional theory and that on cognitive theory mention how the ego psychological development in the psychodynamic tradition aided in bringing the thought systems closer to the dynamic tradition. An interlocking process is also taking place between cognitive and behavioral thinking, between existential and Gestalt, as well as existential and client-centered, systems theory and the life model, task-centered and problem-solving, systems and psychosocial to identify some of the more obvious. Others are beginning to emerge.

As we have continued to struggle with ways of examining and comparing this range of theories, it has become apparent that each system as a base for therapy is attempting to find ways to help individuals, families, groups, and systems become more fulfilled and more able to achieve their potential as humans. In so doing, each has to address a series of similar issues. Differences emerge according to the perception each system has about each issue and the importance it gives that issue in the total scheme. To date there appears to be six clusters of factors that need to be addressed to compare systems in a way that could be useful for practitioners. These are:

1. Each thought system has to be assessed from the viewpoint of its historical origins, the nature of its specificity, and the extent of its empirical base.
2. Each system has to address the nature of the individual, value assumptions about the individual, the nature of personality, and the nature and predominance of rationality.
3. Each system has to develop a position about the nature of behavior, the determinants of personality and the differential weight of external influences, the causes of problem functioning, and the nature of personality change.
4. Each thought system must also identify the characteristics of the therapeutic process and the kind and nature of change agents.
5. Each system needs to specify the required knowledge and skills of the therapist.
6. Each thought system needs to identify the spectrum of its applicability.

This approach has proven useful, and specific subtopics for each of these six major points have been developed with the assistance of several graduate students. As a part of the process of preparing this book, each author was asked to complete each item under the six major headings. These are now being assembled into a composite chart which will permit comparison between various systems on a range of variables. It is hoped that such a chart will be of considerable assistance to practitioners interested in a differential use of theory.

Presuming that there is a higher degree of consensus among different thought systems than is usually considered, important questions to be faced are: What are the implications for practice of this multifaceted, interlocking conceptual base? To what extent can and should a practitioner be knowledgeable about and comfortable with the range of systems here presented, as well as others not considered or still to emerge? In the first chapter it was pointed out that we do not really know at this point how extensive is the influence of this spectrum on practice. It was clearly advocated that responsible practice should be theory based, but it was also acknowledged that we did not know if it is or not. It would be cynical in the extreme to speculate that these theories have no influence on practice, but I think it would be equally naive to imply that practitioners consciously, deliberately, and consistently formulate their interventive strategies from a specific conceptual base.

This project began from a conviction that all of the various thought systems influencing current practice were important and that it was our responsibility to be aware of each, to strive to understand it, and deliberately try to put some of the concepts of each system into practice. In approaching the project's conclusion, I am even more convinced of the soundness, yet the challenge, of this approach to practice. Too long have we labored under the impression that adherence to one approach to practice by definition excluded others; that there was some component of disloyalty or some quality of Machiavellian manipulation to attempt to move from one approach of practice to another, depending on the situation, the setting, the resources, the persons, or the request. Probably this would be truer if one held that the various approaches were mutually exclusive and contradictory, but clearly less true if one is convinced of a large element of interconnectedness and interinfluence.

One of the areas in which each author was asked to comment, if it seemed appropriate, was the kind of clients, situations, or setting in which his system seemed most relevant or most appropriate.

In general, the authors tended to indicate a broad base of applicability rather than a specific one and preferred not to have the applications of a particular viewpoint seen in too restricted a way.

Nevertheless, I think it appropriate to speculate briefly on some of the particular applications that one could make in using the various approaches. The implication of this discussion is that one of the components of the differential diagnostic component of practice is to speculate on which of the various approaches, or which combination of approaches, appears most relevant to a presenting situation. Practice from this viewpoint would suggest a more conceptually open approach than is the case where one has a more strongly fixed theoretical base. In no way am I suggesting support for a non-theory approach to practice, nor even for a theoretically neutral approach, but rather for an open approach in a period in our history when we are still very much in transition. As mentioned in the preface, it is necessary for a person to develop as firm a theoretical base as is possible; however, in this process it is necessary to keep all options and all alternatives open. If this was a more prevalent approach to practice there would be a richer opportunity to develop linkages and integrative structures between the various theories that are already emerging. Such an approach would also provide richer opportunities for our clients.

In considering the possibility of a clearer awareness of the differential utility of each system, it is important not to forget the concept of equifinality from general systems theory. This concept emphasizes that there are frequently many ways of achieving similar goals; that is, it may well be that many of the therapeutic systems under consideration, different though they may be, are capable of achieving the same outcomes. Nevertheless, this does not rule out the possibility of specific use for each approach.

In looking at the various theories it is possible to identify situations where each system can be seen as having a specific utility. Most have important implications for large segments of practice.

The following paragraphs contain brief comments concerning the apparent specific utility of each system as a first step in moving toward a differential use of each system.

PSYOCHOANALYTIC THEORY.   This theory is probably the most influential yet most criticized theory in social work practice. Its influence has been pervasive, universal, and continuing. The real-life problems created by transference, developmental fixations, and regressions are a frequent reality in current practice and many can only be addressed from this theoretical perspective. Although many systems stress a more present-focused orientation, large numbers of clients, in seeking a more comfortable and less alienated self-concept, want to understand their emotional and developmental history from this perspective.

FUNCTIONAL THEORY.   This theory, once considered passé, continues to influence current practice. It focuses on the client's internal resources and the healthy and functioning components of personality. It is important to keep in focus the fact that the setting in which treatment is provided is a particular aspect of the client's significant environment and how the use of structure, time, and available resources can be helpful. This approach to practice has been and continues to be particularly helpful in situations where authority is a predominant aspect of the presenting situation or setting.

GESTALT THEORY.   In addition to being a therapeutic system, Gestalt is also a popular movement. It is an approach to therapy that urges therapists to be free to be themselves, to be innovative, creative, and imaginative in working with clients. It is an approach that is very well suited to clients interested in a total and integrated sense of self and use of self. It aims at helping clients achieve close conscious contact with self and life.

COGNITIVE THEORY.   This cluster of theories is strongly influencing practice in an overall fashion by giving more importance to our rational abilities. In a specific way these theories are useful in those situations where our objective is to help people think about and plan appropriate solutions. In these situations the focus is on responsibility, ability, and effective use of one's executive capacities to deal with the present and to function better in the future.

BEHAVIOR MODIFICATION.   These theories of learning and the extensive range of related behavioral techniques have provided practitioners with a wide range of resources for achieving specific changes in clients. In addition to an increased understanding of the processes involved in the acquiring and modification of general behavioral traits, learning theory has particular relevance for helping clients alter specific problem areas of functioning without having to understand the origins or interconnections between behaviors. In this way a man who can alter his eating habits to improve his health and thus continue working can be significantly better off without his having to understand why he was overeating.

MEDITATION.   This is probably the approach to practice that has been given the least attention by the field in general. It has much to offer many clients in both a general and a specific way. It is useful for those essentially intact individuals experiencing confusion about themselves, their contact with their external world, and their place in the universe. In this way it is similar to existentialism. Further, it is quite useful for persons who very much want to achieve a greater sense of self-mastery and a more disciplined approach to life.

EXISTENTIAL.   This is not a system of therapy as such but rather a basis for understanding oneself, others, and the human condition, and some derived implications that follow for the therapeutic process. Probably all of us as members of the helping professions are partially influenced by existential thinking and these influences carry over into our practice. In addition there are specific practice situations where an existential perspective helps us to understand clients and to develop a helping perspective. There appears to be an increasing number of persons whose problems revolve around questions of their own identity and sense of alienation. For these an existential perspective is indeed helpful.

COMMUNICATION THEORY.   This cluster of theories, concerned with the way in which humans transmit and receive information, is an essential general knowledge base for social workers in all areas of practice. Too, these concepts can be of particular assistance in keeping the therapeutic process open and effective. These concepts have had considerable impact on the treatment of marital pairs and families.

PROBLEM-SOLVING.   Like task-centered, this long-standing theory emphasizes the use of our own problem-solving processes in seeking to understand the client and the reality in which he or she functions and to partialize the situation into manageable goals related to the nature of the setting involved. It is a particularly useful framework to help avoid diffuse and unfocused intervention goals.

TASK-CENTERED.   This system, like crisis intervention, focuses on brief, time-limited intervention. It is particularly useful in situations when a parsimonious use of resources is essential. It is also useful in cases where the goal is to maximize the client's involvement in the therapeutic process, and to enhance their autonomy. It requires both practitioners and clients to focus on the setting of clear, identified, and attainable goals. This latter quality can be of particular importance to some clients as an additional learning experience beyond the original problem.

CRISIS THEORY.   This theory provides a useful framework in which to understand the dynamics and expected behavior of persons experiencing various life traumas. It provides a basis for swift assessment of clients and the setting of discrete objectives and procedures for diagnosed crises. It is both an orientation to the dynamics of crises as well as a well-tested set of strategies to reduce the impact of the crises and return the client to at least the same level or an even higher level of psychosocial functioning.

NEUROLINGUISTICS.   This is probably the least well known of the systems. It represents a unique approach to social work practice that directly takes into account neurological aspects of communications and uses these both diagnostically and therapeutically. It is a positive approach to practice that stresses a wish to help persons enhance their practice not to supplement one approach with another. It appears to be most useful with intact clients capable of introspection and ready use of their inner images.

EGO PSYCHOLOGY.   In ego psychology the therapeutic focus is on both the conscious and unconscious components of the personality as well as on the client's external reality. It is particularly useful in situations where growth and movement for the client require an understanding of self, patterns of behavior, and their derivatives. Many clients both want and need to be understood in developmental terms and can be greatly helped by a sensitive understanding of their personality and its developmental history.

CLIENT-CENTERED TREATMENT. Although this system was for a long time scarcely acknowledged in social work literature, it is useful, like others in this group, in situations where the goal is to help clients regroup their own personality resources, and to accept and come to terms with themselves in a positive way to more effectively pursue established life goals satisfactorily.

FAMILY THEORY. In addition to providing a theoretical and therapeutic base for dealing with family-related situations, family theory has also been useful in understanding and managing individual problems in clarifying the extent to which such problems are related to family issues. Family treatment is in great demand in all areas of practice to respond to the complex and prevalent problems in current family life.

TRANSACTIONAL ANALYSIS. Like Gestalt theory, Transactional Analysis is a popular movement. It appeals and is useful to persons who do not see themselves or want to be seen as needful of or recipients of traditional psychotherapy. It is health-oriented and emphasizes the positive. The system stresses the responsibility to decide on the kind of person the client wants to be and on the kind of relationships he or she wishes to have with others. It places great importance on working with groups, a modality that is attractive to many clients.

PSYCHOSOCIAL. This system has a broad spectrum of applicability in that it focuses on the critical relationships between persons and their significant environment and the interaction between the two. It is most useful in cases where the goal is to help the client both to understand issues of personality and how these effects are effected by societal realities, and to seek solutions in both the person and the environment.

SYSTEM. Social work practitioners have long sought a theory such as systems that would provide a framework, so critical to social work practice, for understanding and ordering the multifaceted milieux in which our clients function. In particular, it is useful in those multiproblem situations involving a complex interaction of stress-producing significant environments.

ROLE THEORY. We meet many clients in our caseloads whose problems are stress-related to an inability to cope with complex role sets or because they cannot deal appropriately with role transitions in their lives, such as being newly married or separated, ill, or retired. Role theory has proven highly useful in helping people sort out role-related situations, understand them, and better order their life priorities.

FEMINISM THEORY.   As our society has become more conscious of the complex and frequently unfair and unjust ways that we respond to women, and the effects this has on self-image and functioning, a growing body of relevant therapeutic theory is emerging. This theory is useful in situations when women are seeking to get a better understanding of themselves and their potential, and to find strategies to help set and achieve appropriate life, personal, and career goals.

MARXIST THEORY.   As with systems theory, Marxist thinking gives an orientation to broader society, its operation, and its impact on individuals, families, and groups. As such it is not yet a system of therapy but a perspective from which therapy can begin. It provides some parameters within which treatment objectives can be developed. Its basic premises would not be acceptable to many clients and this could be counterproductive in such situations.

LIFE MODEL.   Sometimes called an ecological perspective, this system provides a basis for helping the client understand and make use of the potential for growth in themselves and their broad environment. It is particularly useful in those cases met so frequently where the problems are heavily influenced by issues arising from interfacing systems and subsystems.

As is evident from the above overview of the twenty-two systems discussed in this book, many, indeed most, have a broad scope. It is probably true that a practitioner could practice in a responsible and effective manner based on a thorough understanding and utilization of any one of these broadbased approaches. But it is certain that as practitioners we are more effective, imaginative, sensitive, economical, and responsible to the extent that we strive to understand and incorporate into practice an interlocking approach that seeks to build connections between theories.

But more is needed than exhortation. What is needed is an acceptance that this goal is possible and desirable, and a demonstration in concrete ways that it does improve our practice. Much carefully focused research is required to examine the impact of theory on practice and further the differential impact of theory on practice. Although progress will be slow we need not be discouraged. There is a new spirit of scholarly commitment and practice responsiblity evident. It is also apparent that there is indeed a considerable rippling effect among the various theories. Even the most declared unitheory practitioners appear to be multitheory influenced. Over the past decade we have all become more behaviorally oriented, more cognitive in our practice, more existential in our perceptions, more conscious of and attentive to systems, roles, families, specific tasks, and evaluation of therapy itself. Other examples could be given where we are finding ways of connecting with aspects of virtually all the systems currently influencing practice. Our practice is very much in the here and now, it probably always was, yet few have put aside completely psychodynamic theory and a developmentally based approach to treatment.

Conclusion

Clinical social work practice remains an essential part of the profession's practice endeavors. The wave of sweeping criticism and challenges of direct practice has passed. There is accumulating evidence that our interventions are effective. But we are daily reminded that practice that seeks to understand and dares to intervene in the process of human growth and psychosocial development is indeed an overwhelmingly difficult task, replete with risks and uncertainties. But it is equally enriched with satisfactions and achievements. There is not to date, nor indeed will there be, a single theory of social work practice. There are, and will continue to be, a range of understandings and tested findings about effective and planned change. Such findings will in some instances complement each other and strengthen the interconnection between systems; others will contradict, necessitating additional conceptualization and testing. Throughout, the practice of social work treatment will be from a base of interlocking theoretical approaches.

References

1. Baldwin, Alfred S. *Theories of Child Development*. New York: Wiley, 1968.
2. Bartlett, Harriett. *The Common Base of Social Work Practice*. New York: National Association of Social Workers, 1970.
3. Berlin, Sharon B. "Single Case Evaluation: Another Version," *Social Work Research and Abstracts*, Vol. 19, No. 1 (1983), pp. 3–11.
4. Biestek, Felix. *The Casework Relationship*. Chicago: Loyola University Press, 1957.
5. Carew, R. "The Place of Knowledge in Social Work Activity," *British Journal of Social Work*, Vol. 9 (1979), pp. 349–364.
6. Carkhuff, Robert R., and Bernard G. Berenson. *Beyond Counseling and Therapy*. New York: Holt, Rinehart and Winston, 1967.
7. Caroff, Phyllis (ed.). *Treatment Formulations and Clinical Social Work*. Washington, D.C.: NASW, 1982.
8. Curnock, K., and P. Hardicker. *Towards Practice Theory*. London: Routledge and Kegan Paul, 1979.
9. Fischer, Joel. *Effective Casework Practice: An Eclectic Approach*. New York: McGraw-Hill, 1978.
10. Hall, Calvin S., and Gardiner Lindsay. *Theories of Personality*, 2nd edition. New York: Wiley, 1970.
11. Hollis, Florence. "Letter to the Editor," *Social Casework*, Vol. 52 (December 1971), pp. 652–653.

12. Kendall, Phillip C., and James N. Butcher (eds.). *Handbook of Research Methods in Clinical Psychology.* New York: Wiley, 1982.
13. Murray, Henry A., and Clyde Kluckhohn. "Outline of a Conception of Personality," in Clyde Kluckhohn, Henry Murray (eds.), *Personality in Nature and Society,* 2nd edition. New York: Knopf, 1953.
14. Nelsen, Judith C. "Issues in Single-Subject Research for Nonbehaviorists," *Social Work Research and Abstracts,* Vol. 17, No. 2 (1981), pp. 31–37.
15. Patterson, C. H. *Theories of Counseling and Psychotherapy.* New York: Harper and Row, 1966.
16. Reid, William J. "Treatment of Choice or Choice of Treatments: An Essay Review," *Social Work Research and Abstracts,* Vol. 20, No. 3 (1984), pp. 33–38.
17. ———, and P. Hanrahan. "Recent Evaluations of Social Work: Grounds for Optimism," *Social Work,* Vol. 27, No. 4 (1982), pp. 328–340.
18. Roberts, Robert W., and Robert H. Nee (eds.). *Theories of Social Casework.* Chicago: University of Chicago Press, 1970.
19. Segalman, Ralph. *Theories of Personality: A comparative schematic chart.* El Paso, Texas, 1964.
20. Simon, Bernice K. "Relationship Between Theory and Practice in Social Casework, Social Work Practice in Medical Care and Rehabilitation Settings," Monograph 4. New York: National Association of Social Workers, 1960.
21. Stanton, John Ormond. "A Social Work Model for Developing and Empirically Testing Practice Principles in Marital Counseling." Unpublished doctoral dissertation. University of Toronto, Faculty of Social Work, 1972.
22. Stevenson, Olive. "Problems in the Use of Theory in Social Work Education," *British Journal of Psychiatric Social Work,* Vol. 9, No. 1 (1967), pp. 27–29.
23. Towle, Charlotte. "Preface," in Florence Hollis (ed.), *Casework: A Psychosocial Therapy.* New York: Random House, 1964, pp. v–xiv.

Index

I would like to acknowledge the assistance of Shannon Biggs, Elaine Tanner, and Anne-Marie
Turner in the preparation of this index—F. J. T.